ATHENAEUS

V

274

AMPHORA

Museum of Fine Arts, Boston

ATHENAEUS

THE DEIPNOSOPHISTS

WITH AN ENGLISH TRANSLATION BY

CHARLES BURTON GULICK, Ph.D.

ELIOT PROFESSOR OF GREEK LITERATURE EMERITUS,
HARVARD UNIVERSITY

IN SEVEN VOLUMES

V

CAMBRIDGE, MASSACHUSETTS
HARVARD UNIVERSITY PRESS
LONDON
WILLIAM HEINEMANN LTD
MCMLXXX

American
ISBN 0-674-99302-0

British
ISBN 0 434 99274 7

First printed 1933
Reprinted 1943, 1955, 1963, 1980

Printed in Great Britain

CONTENTS OF VOLUME V

PREFATORY NOTE

In the summer of 1931 I was able to make a fresh study of the Codex Marcianus (A) at Venice, confining myself, in the limited time at my disposal, to Books XI-XV. For the courteous treatment accorded to me by the authorities of the Biblioteca Marciana I offer sincere thanks. The notation " *sic* " in the critical apparatus indicates where my report of readings differs from that of Kaibel.

I have also studied carefully the readings in the Paris Excerpts (C), with the result that I have gained increased respect for that codex.

As for attempting to identify all the names of pottery catalogued in Book XI. with extant vases, I have been obliged to conclude, with many others who are wiser than I, that the game is not worth the candle.

C. B. G.

Cambridge, Massachusetts,
December 1933.

ABBREVIATIONS

Allinson = *Menander*, in Loeb Classical Library.
Aristoph. = Aristophanes.
Aristot. = Aristotle.
Athen. = Athenaeus.
Brandt = *Parodorum Epicorum Graecorum Reliquiae*, ed. P. Brandt, 1888.
Diehl = *Anthologia Lyrica*, ed. E. Diehl, 1922-1924.
Diels = *Poetarum Philosophorum Fragmenta*, ed. Hermann Diels, 1901.
Diels[3] = *Vorsokratiker*, 3rd edition.
Edmonds = *Elegy and Iambus*, in Loeb Classical Library.
= *Lyra Graeca*, in Loeb Classical Library.
F.H.G. = *Fragmenta Historicorum Graecorum*, ed. C. Müller.
Frag. ep. = *Epicorum Graecorum Fragmenta*, ed. G. Kinkel.
G. and H. = Grenfell and Hunt, *Hellenica Oxyrhynchia*.
H.S.C.P. = *Harvard Studies in Classical Philology*.
Hort = *Theophrastus*, in Loeb Classical Library.
I.G. = *Inscriptiones Graecae*.
J. = Jacoby, *Fragmente der griechischen Historiker*.
Kaibel = *Comicorum Graecorum Fragmenta*, ed. G. Kaibel (for Epicharmus, Sophron, Sopater).
Kock = *Comicorum Atticorum Fragmenta*, ed. Th. Kock.
P.L.G.[4] = Bergk, *Poetae Lyrici Graeci*, 4th edition.
P.L.G.[5] = 5th edition of the preceding work, Vol. i. (Pindar), by Schroeder, 1900, reprinted with a new appendix (*P.L.G.[6]*), 1923. Vols. ii. and iii. reprinted with indices by Rubenbauer, 1914.
Powell = *Collectanea Alexandrina*, ed. J. U. Powell, Oxford, 1925.

ABBREVIATIONS

P.-W.   = Pauly-Wissowa, *Real-Encyclopädie.*
Script. Al. M. = *Scriptores Historiarum Alexandri Magni.*
T.G.F.²   = *Tragicorum Graecorum Fragmenta*, ed. A.
                 Nauck, 2nd edition.

The references are to pages, unless otherwise indicated.

In the case of an ancient author whose work is known only through quotations, a proper name following a reference indicates the modern editor or compiler of the quoted fragments. Thus, " Frag. 200 Rose " means the edition of Aristotle's *Fragmenta* by Valentin Rose; " Frag. 72 Gaede," Gaede's edition of the *Fragmenta* of Demetrius of Scepsis, etc.

PERSONS OF THE DIALOGUE

AEMILIANUS MAURUS, grammarian.
ALCEIDES OF ALEXANDRIA, musician.
AMOEBEUS, harp-player and singer.
ARRIAN, grammarian.
ATHENAEUS OF NAUCRATIS, the author.
CYNULCUS, nickname of a Cynic philosopher, Theodorus.
DAPHNUS OF EPHESUS, physician.
DEMOCRITUS OF NICOMEDIA, philosopher.
DIONYSOCLES, physician.
GALEN OF PERGAMUM, physician.
LARENSIS (P. Livius Larensis), Roman official, *pontifex minor*, *procurator patrimonii*.
LEONIDAS OF ELIS, grammarian.
MAGNUS, probably a Roman.
MASURIUS, jurist, poet, musician.
MYRTILUS OF THESSALY, grammarian.
PALAMEDES THE ELEATIC, lexicographer.
PHILADELPHUS PTOLEMAEENSIS, philosopher.
PLUTARCH OF ALEXANDRIA, grammarian.
PONTIANUS OF NICOMEDIA, philosopher.
RUFINUS OF NICAEA, physician.
TIMOCRATES, to whom Athenaeus relates the story of the banquet.
ULPIAN OF TYRE, Roman jurist and official.
VARUS, grammarian.
ZOÏLUS, grammarian.

ATHENAEUS

ΑΘΗΝΑΙΟΥ ΝΑΥΚΡΑΤΙΤΟΥ ΔΕΙΠΝΟΣΟΦΙΣΤΩΝ

ΙΑ

459   ῎Αγε δή, τίς ἀρχὴ τῶν λόγων γενήσεται
κατὰ τὸν κωμῳδιοποιὸν Κηφισόδωρον, ἑταῖρε
Τιμόκρατες; συναχθέντων γὰρ ἡμῶν καθ' ὥραν
μετὰ σπουδῆς διὰ τὰ ἐκπώματα ὁ Οὐλπιανός, ἔτι
καθημένων ἁπάντων, πρὶν καί τι διαλεχθῆναι[1] ἔφη·
" παρὰ μὲν τῷ ᾿Αδράστῳ, ἄνδρες φίλοι, καθίσαντες
οἱ ἀριστεῖς δειπνοῦσιν, ὁ δὲ Πολύιδος ἱερὰ θύων
ἐν ὁδῷ παραπορευόμενον τὸν Πετεὼ κατέσχεν καὶ
κατακλίνας ἐν τῇ πόᾳ θαλλίαν τε καᾳτακλάσας ἀντὶ
460 τραπέζης παρέθηκε τῶν τυθέντων. καὶ τῷ Αὐτο-
λύκῳ ἐλθόντι ' ᾿Ιθάκης ἐς πίονα δῆμον ' ἡ τροφὸς
καθημένῳ δηλονότι—οὕτως γὰρ ἐδείπνουν οἱ τότε
—τὸν ᾿Οδυσσέα, φησὶν ὁ ποιητής,

παῖδα νέον γεγαῶτα κιχήσατο θυγατέρος ἧς,
τόν ῥά οἱ Εὐρύκλεια φίλοις ἐπὶ γούνασι θῆκε
παυομένῳ δόρποιο·[2]

---

[1] καί τι διαλεχθῆναι Kaibel: καί τινα λεχθῆναι Α.
[2] These verses deleted by Meineke, but they must have
stood in the fuller text. I have added " served him " in the
translation.

2

THE DEIPNOSOPHISTS OF ATHENAEUS OF NAUCRATIS

BOOK XI

"Come now, what shall be the beginning of our recital" as the comic poet Cephisodorus[a] puts it, friend Timocrates? For we had gathered early, spurred to eagerness for the cups[b]; and while all the guests were still seated,[c] and before conversation had begun, Ulpian said : "At the table of Adrastus, my friends, the nobles dine seated[d]; but Polyidus, when offering sacrifices on a highway, made Peteôs, who was walking by, stop and recline in the grass ; he then broke up some green twigs to serve as a table and placed before Peteôs some of the sacrificial meat. Again, Autolycus once went 'to the rich land of Ithaca,' and the nurse (served him) while he was seated, of course, for that is the way in which the men of that time dined[e]; and, says the poet,[f] 'He found his daughter's son Odysseus a child new-born, and when he was making an end of supper, then Eurycleia placed the child on his knees'; she seated him, I

---

[a] Kock i. 802.
[b] Meaning both the prospect of drinking and also the discussion of drinking-cups promised in the preceding book (448 b).   [c] Not reclining on couches.   [d] *Cf.* 11 f.
[e] See **11 e, 17 f** (vol. i. pp. 50, 78).   [f] *Od.* xix. 400.

ἐκάθισεν ἐπὶ τῶν γονάτων καὶ οὐχὶ παρὰ τοῖς
γόνασιν ἔστησεν. ἡμεῖς δ'[1] οὖν μὴ διατρίβωμεν,
ἀλλ' ἤδη κατακλινώμεθα, ἵν' ἡμῖν ὁ Πλούταρχος
b περὶ ὧν ἐπαγγέλλεται ποτηρίων ἀποδοὺς τὸν λόγον
καὶ τὰς κύλικας πλήρεις ἅπασι προπίῃ.

"Ποτήρια δὲ πρῶτον οἶδα ὀνομάσαντα τὸν
Ἀμόργιον ποιητὴν Σιμωνίδην ἐν Ἰάμβοις οὕτως·

ἀπὸ τράπεζαν εἶλεν ᾗ[2] ποτήρια . . .

καὶ ὁ τὴν Ἀλκμαιωνίδα δὲ ποιήσας φησίν·

νέκυς δὲ χαμαιστρώτου ἐπὶ τείνας[3]
εὐρείης στιβάδος παρέθηκ'[4] αὐτοῖσι θάλειαν
δαῖτα[5] ποτήριά τε, στεφάνους δ'[6] ἐπὶ κρασὶν
ἔθηκεν.

ἅπερ ὠνομάσθη ἀπὸ τῆς πόσεως, ὡς τὸ ἔκπωμα
c οἱ Ἀττικοί, ἐπεὶ ὑδροποτεῖν καὶ οἰνοποτεῖν
λέγουσιν. Ἀριστοφάνης ἐν Ἱππεῦσιν·

γαμφηλαῖσι δράκοντα κοάλεμον[7] αἱματοπώτην.

κἂν τῷ αὐτῷ δὲ ἔφη·

πολλῷ γ' ὁ Βάκις διεχρῆτο τῷ ποτηρίῳ.

καὶ Φερεκράτης ἐν Τυραννίδι·

ἡ δὲ[8] κρείττων ἡ[8] μί' ἐστὶ χιλίων ποτηρίων.

ὁ δὲ Ἀνακρέων ἔφη·

---

[1] δ' added by Meineke; but more has been lost.
[2] εἶλεν ᾗ Wilamowitz: εἰλέ νιν A.
[3] χαμαιστρώτου ἐπὶ τείνας Welcker: χαμαιστρώτους ἐπί τινας A.
[4] Meineke: προέθηκ' A.   [5] Fiorillo: δὲ τὰ A.
[6] Kaibel: τ' A.   [7] Aristoph.: κόλλαιμον A.
[8] ἡ δὲ and ἡ added from 481 d.

4

say, *on* his knees and did not stand him *beside* his knees.[a] However that may be, let *us* not dally, but recline forthwith, for I want Plutarch to render to us the account of cups as he has promised, and drink the health of all in the cups filled to the brim.

" The first mention of the word *poteria* (cups) that I know of occurs in the poet of Amorgos, Semonides; he says, in his *Iambic Verses* [b] : ' He took away the table, whither the cups . . .' And the author of the *Alcmaeonis* also says [c] : ' He laid out the dead bodies on a broad pallet strewn on the ground, and set before them a bountiful feast and cups as well, and placed crowns on their heads.' These cups (*poteria*) got their name from the word for drinking (*posis*), like the word *ekpôma* (cup) used by Attic writers; for they speak of water-drinking (*hydropotein*) and wine-drinking (*oinopotein*). Aristophanes in *The Knights* [d] : ' In its bill the blood-drinking (*haimatopotên*) booby-dragon.' And in the same play he has said [e] : ' Bacis certainly used the cup over much.' So Pherecrates in *Tyranny* [f] : ' But this single cup is mightier than a thousand.' And Anacreon has said [g] :

[a] When an Athenian dined *en famille*, he reclined on a couch while his children stood beside him.

[b] *P.L.G.*[4] frag. 26, Diehl frag. 23, Edmonds frag. 26.

[c] *Frag. ep.* 76.

[d] vs. 198; a mock oracle satirizing Cleon the tanner and beginning, " When the tanner-eagle with hooked claws shall seize . . ."

[e] vs. 124, meaning that Bacis, reputed author of many prophecies, overworked both the word " cup " and its contents.

[f] Kock i. 187; for the context see Athen. 481 b-c (below, p. 133).

[g] *P.L.G.*[4] frag. 97, Diehl frag. 99, Edmonds frag. 119.

οἰνοπότης δὲ πεποίημαι.

ἔστι δὲ τὸ ῥῆμα καὶ παρὰ τῷ ποιητῇ· οἰνοποτάζων
d γὰρ εἴρηκε. καὶ Σαπφὼ δ' ἐν τῷ β' ἔφη·

> πολλὰ δ' ἀνάριθμα ποτήρια
> κἀλέφαις.[1]

καὶ Ἀλκαῖος·

> ἐκ δὲ ποτήριον[2] πώνης Διννομένῃ[3] παρίσδων.

τιμᾶται δὲ καὶ ἐν Ἀχαίᾳ Δημήτηρ ποτηριοφόρος
κατὰ τὴν Ἀνθέων χώραν, ὡς Αὐτοκράτης ἱστορεῖ
ἐν β' Ἀχαϊκῶν. ἄξιον δὲ εἶναι νομίζω ζητῆσαι
ὑμᾶς πρὸ τοῦ καταλόγου τῶν ποτηρίων, ὧν πλῆρές
ἐστι τὸ κυλικεῖον τοδί—εἴρηται γὰρ οὕτως ἡ τῶν
ποτηρίων σκευοθήκη παρ' Ἀριστοφάνει μὲν ἐν
Γεωργοῖς·

e   ὥσπερ κυλικείου τουθόνιον προπέπταται.

ἔστι καὶ παρὰ Ἀναξανδρίδῃ ἐν Μελιλώτῳ.
Εὔβουλος δ' ἐν Λήδᾳ·

> ὥσπερεὶ[4] σπονδὴν διδοὺς
> ἐν τῷ κυλικείῳ συντέτριφε τὰ ποτήρια.

κἀν Ψαλτρίᾳ δ' ἔφη·

> τὰ κυλικεῖα δὲ
> ἐξεῦρεν ἡμῖν.

ἐν δὲ Σεμέλῃ ἢ Διονύσῳ·

> Ἑρμῆς ὁ Μαίας λίθινος, ὃν προσεύγμασιν
> ἐν τῷ κυλικείῳ λαμπρὸν ἐκτετριμμένον . . .

---

[1] κἀλέφαις *Ox. Papyri*, x. no. 1232 : καλαιφις A.
[2] Bergk : ποτηρίων A.   [3] Ahrens : διννομενη A.
[4] Schweighäuser : ὥσπερ A.

'I have been made a wine-drinker' (*oinopotês*). This
expression also occurs in the Poet; for he says,[a]
'When wine-drinking' (*oinopotazôn*). So Sappho,
in the second book, said[b]: 'Many cups without
number, and ivory too.' And Alcaeus[c]: 'Thou
drinkest out the cup, seated by Deinomenes' side.'
There is also a 'cup-bearing' Demeter, worshipped
in Achaea in the neighbourhood of Antheia, as
Autocrates records in the second book of his *Achaean
History*.[d] But there is another problem which I
think worth your consideration before we have the
catalogue of drinking-cups, of which the sideboard
here (*kylikeion*) is full; for this is the name given to
the piece of furniture[e] in which cups (*kylikes*) are
kept, by Aristophanes in *The Farmers*[f]: 'Covered
like a sideboard in front of which the linen curtain
is drawn.' It occurs also in Anaxandrides' *Melilot*.[g]
Eubulus has it in *Leda*[h]: 'Like one who, about to
pour a libation, has smashed the cups in the sideboard.' And in *The Harp-girl* he said[i]: 'He has
also invented the sideboards for us.' So in *Semelê* or
Dionysus[j]: 'Hermes, Maia's son in stone,[k] whom
(we approach) with offerings as he stands in the sideboard, scoured to brightness.' Cratinus the Younger

---

[a] *Il.* xx. 84; Apollo taunts Aeneas. The same participle
is used by Anacreon, 463 a (below, p. 18).
[b] *P.L.G.*[4] frag. 67, Diehl frag. 55 a, Edmonds 66, vs. 10.
[c] *P.L.G.*[4] frag. 52, Diehl frag. 34, Edmonds 59.
[d] *F.H.G.* iv. 346.
[e] Lit. utensil-receptacle, aumbry.   [f] Kock i. 418.
[g] Kock ii. 145.   [h] *Ibid.* 185.
[i] *Ibid.* 206.   [j] *Ibid.* 197.
[k] A small image of Hermes seems to have been kept in the
cupboard.

7

f Κρατῖνος δ' ὁ νεώτερος ἐν Χείρωνι·

πολλοστῷ δ' ἔτει[1]
ἐκ τῶν πολεμίων οἴκαδ' ἥκω, συγγενεῖς
καὶ φράτερας καὶ δημότας εὑρὼν μόλις
εἰς τὸ κυλικεῖον ἐνεγράφην[2]· Ζεὺς ἔστι μοι
ἑρκεῖος, ἔστι φρατέριος,[3] τὰ τέλη τελῶ.

"Ἄξιον δ' ἐστὶ ζητῆσαι εἰ οἱ ἀρχαῖοι μεγάλοις
ἔπινον ποτηρίοις. Δικαίαρχος μὲν γὰρ ὁ Μεσ-
461 σήνιος, ὁ Ἀριστοτέλους μαθητής, ἐν τῷ περὶ
Ἀλκαίου μικροῖς φησιν αὐτοὺς ἐκπώμασι κεχρῆ-
σθαι καὶ ὑδαρέστερον πεπωκέναι. Χαμαιλέων δ'
ὁ Ἡρακλεώτης ἐν τῷ περὶ Μέθης, εἴ γε τῆς φωνῆς
μνημονεύω, φησίν· ' εἰ δὲ οἱ ταῖς ἐξουσίαις χρώμενοι καὶ τῷ πλουτεῖν προτιμῶσι τὴν μέθην
ταύτην,[4] οὐδὲν θαυμαστόν.[5] οὐκ ἔχοντες γὰρ
ἑτέραν ἡδονὴν ταύτης καλλίω οὐδὲ μᾶλλον εὐχερῆ
b καταφεύγουσιν εἰκότως ἐπὶ τὸν οἶνον. ὅθεν δὴ
καὶ τὰ μεγάλα τῶν ἐκπωμάτων ἐπιχώρια γέγονε
τοῖς δυνάσταις. οὐ[6] γὰρ παλαιὸν οὐδὲ τοῦτό γέ
ἐστι παρὰ τοῖς Ἕλλησιν, ἀλλὰ νεωστὶ εὑρέθη,
πεμφθὲν ἐκ τῶν βαρβάρων. ἐκεῖνοι γὰρ ἀπεστε-
ρημένοι τῆς παιδείας ὁρμῶσιν ἐπὶ τὸν πολὺν οἶνον
καὶ πορίζονται τροφὰς περιέργους καὶ παντοίας.
ἐν δὲ τοῖς περὶ τὴν Ἑλλάδα τόποις οὔτ' ἐν γραφαῖς
οὔτ' . . .[7] ἐπὶ τῶν πρότερον εὑρήσομεν ποτήριον

---

[1] Musurus: ἔτι A.
[2] Eustath. 1271. 31: ἐγράφην AC.
[3] Bergk: φρατόριος ACE.
ταύτην om. E. [5] θαυμαστόν A: καινόν CE.
[6] οὐ Kaibel: οὐδὲ ACE.
[7] Lacuna marked by Schweighäuser.

---

[a] Kock ii. 291.

in *Cheiron* [a] : ' After many a year I have come home
out of the land of the enemy, and since I had difficulty
in finding the members of my family, brotherhood,
and deme, I have had myself enrolled in the—sideboard.[b] *That* is my Zeus of the enclosure and of the
brotherhood, and I pay my dues to it.' [c]

" I say then,[d] it is worth considering whether the
men of old drank from large cups. For Dicaearchus
of Messenê, the pupil of Aristotle, says [e] in his book
On Alcaeus that they used small cups and drank wine
mixed with too much water. Chamaeleon of Heracleia, also, in the work *On Drunkenness*, says, if I
remember his words [f] : ' If those who enjoy power
and wealth esteem this devotion to drunkenness
above everything else, it is not to be wondered at.
For having no other pleasure better than this, or
more easily indulged, they naturally find refuge in
wine. This is why the larger forms of drinking-cups
grew to be the fashion among persons in power. But
this is, in fact, not at all an ancient custom among
the Greeks, but is a recent invention, imported from
the barbarians. For they, being lost to all culture,
betake themselves to quantities of wine and procure
for themselves superfluous foods of all sorts. But in
the regions of Greece we shall not find a cup that
has been wrought to very great size either represented in art or . . .[g] in earlier times, except those in

[b] By surprise for the ληξιαρχικὸν γραμματεῖον, the register
of a deme.
[c] An altar of Zeus Herkeios, protector of the house, stood
in the court; the hiccupping drunkard leans against it for
support.
[d] Resuming the sentence broken off at d, above.
[e] *F.H.G.* ii. 247.   [f] Frag. 32 Koepke.
[g] See critical note **7**. Something like " in poems written "
may be supplied.

9

εὐμέγεθες εἰργασμένον πλὴν τῶν ἐπὶ τοῖς ἡρωικοῖς. τὸ γὰρ ῥυτὸν ὀνομαζόμενον μόνοις τοῖς ἥρωσιν ἀπεδίδοσαν.   ὃ καὶ δόξει τισὶν ἔχειν ἀπορίαν, εἰ
c μή τις ἄρα φήσειε διὰ τὴν ὀξύτητα τῆς ἐπιφανείας τῶν δαιμόνων καταδειχθῆναι τοῦτο. χαλεποὺς γὰρ καὶ πλήκτας τοὺς ἥρωας νομίζουσι καὶ μᾶλλον νύκτωρ ἢ μεθ' ἡμέραν. ὅπως οὖν μὴ διὰ τὸν τρόπον, ἀλλὰ διὰ τὴν μέθην φαίνωνται[1] τοιοῦτοι, δημιουργοῦσιν αὐτοὺς πίνοντας ἐκπώμασι μεγάλοις. καί μοι δοκοῦσι λέγειν οὐ κακῶς οἱ φάσκοντες τὸ μέγα ποτήριον φρέαρ ἀργυροῦν εἶναι.' ἐν τούτοις ἀγνοεῖν ἔοικεν ὁ Χαμαιλέων ὅτι οὔκ ἐστι μικρὸν
d τὸ παρ' Ὁμήρῳ διδόμενον τῷ Κύκλωπι ὑπ' Ὀδυσσέως κισσύβιον. οὐ γὰρ ἂν τρὶς πιὼν οὕτως κατηνέχθη ὑπὸ μέθης τηλικοῦτος ὤν. ἦν οὖν καὶ τότε μεγάλα ποτήρια, εἰ μὴ αἰτιάσεταί τις τὴν δύναμιν τοῦ οἴνου, ἣν αὐτὸς Ὅμηρος ἐξηγήσατο, ἢ τὸ ἄηθες τῆς πόσεως τοῦ Κύκλωπος, ἐπεὶ τὰ πολλὰ ἐγαλακτοπότει.[2] ἢ τάχα καὶ βαρβαρικὸν ἦν τὸ ἔκπωμα, εἴπερ μέγα ἦν, ἐκ τῆς τῶν[3] Κικόνων εἰλημμένον λείας. τί οὖν ἔχομεν λέγειν περὶ τοῦ Νέστορος ποτηρίου, ὃ μόλις ἂν νέος βαστάσαι ἴσχυσεν, ' Νέστωρ δ' ὁ γέρων ἀμογητὶ ἄειρε ';
e περὶ οὗ καὶ αὐτοῦ διδάξει τι ἡμᾶς ὁ Πλούταρχος. ὥρα οὖν κατακλίνεσθαι.''

---

[1] CE: φαίνονται A.
[2] CE: ἐγαλακτοπώτει A.   [3] τῶν CE: om. A.

[a] A large drinking horn ; this remark goes back to Theophrastus, Athen. 497 e (p. 220 and note b).
[b] Aristoph. Birds 1490: " If any mortal met the hero Orestes [here a footpad] by night, he was stripped and smitten by him on all his right side." The angry heroes sent apoplexy ; Roscher, Lex. Myth. s. Heros 2470, 2478.

10

honour of heroic beings. For they assigned the cup called rhyton [a] only to the heroes. This will seem puzzling to some, unless one explained, perhaps, that this custom was introduced because the demigods are so quick to show wrath when they appear. For people regard the heroes as harsh and ready to deal blows, and by night more than by day.[b] In order, then, that the heroes may appear to be cruel, not because of their inborn character, but because they are drunk, the artists represent them as drinking from large cups. And for my part I think that they are quite right who say that the large cup is a " silver well." ' [c] In all this it is plain that Chamaeleon ignores the fact that the bowl given to the Cyclops by Odysseus, in Homer,[d] cannot be small. Otherwise the Cyclops, who was so huge, would not have been so completely overcome with intoxication after only three drinks. Hence cups must have been large even in those days, unless one is to put the blame on the potency of the wine, as to which Homer himself was explicit [e]; or on the unaccustomed nature of the drink taken by the Cyclops, since in most cases he was a milk-drinker. Or perhaps the cup, if it really was large, was of barbarian origin, taken from the spoil of the Ciconians. What, then, can we say about Nestor's cup, which a young man would scarcely have had the strength to lift, ' but Nestor, that old man, raised it easily ' [f] ? Concerning this also Plutarch will give us some information. It is time, therefore, to take our places on the couches."

[c] See vol. ii. p. 368.   [d] *Od.* ix. 346 ; below, 481 e (p. 134).
[e] *Od.* ix. 209 ; twenty parts of water were mixed with one of wine.   [f] *Il.* xi. 637.

Καὶ κατακλιθέντων " ἀλλὰ μήν," ὁ Πλούταρχος ἔφη, " κατὰ τὸν Φλιάσιον ποιητὴν Πρατίναν,

οὐ γᾶν αὐλακισμέναν ἀρῶν,[1] ἀλλ' ἄσκαφον[2] ματεύων,

κυλικηγορήσων ἔρχομαι, οὐ τῶν Κυλικράνων εἷς ὑπάρχων, οὓς χλευάζων Ἕρμιππος ὁ κωμῳδιοποιὸς ἐν τοῖς Ἰάμβοις φησίν·

εἰς τὸ Κυλικράνων βαδίζων σπληνόπεδον[3] ἀφικόμην·

εἶδον οὖν τὴν Ἡράκλειαν καὶ μάλ'[4] ὡραίαν πόλιν.

Ἡρακλεῶται δ' εἰσὶν οὗτοι οἱ ὑπὸ τῇ Οἴτῃ κατοικοῦντες, ὥς φησι Νίκανδρος ὁ Θυατειρηνός, ὀνομασθῆναι φάσκων αὐτοὺς ἀπό τινος Κύλικος γένος Λυδοῦ, ἑνὸς τῶν Ἡρακλεῖ συστρατευσαμένων. μνημονεύει δ' αὐτῶν καὶ Σκυθῖνος ὁ Τήιος ἐν τῇ ἐπιγραφομένῃ Ἱστορίῃ λέγων οὕτως· ' Ἡρακλῆς λαβὼν Εὔρυτον καὶ τὸν υἱὸν ἔκτεινε φόρους 462 πρήσσοντας παρ' Εὐβοέων. καὶ[5] Κυλικρῆνας[6] ἐξεπόρθησε ληζομένους καὶ αὐτόθι πόλιν ἐδείματο Ἡράκλειαν τὴν Τρηχινίαν[7] καλεομένην.' Πολέμων δ' ἐν τῷ πρώτῳ τῶν πρὸς Ἀδαῖον καὶ Ἀντίγονόν φησιν οὕτως· ' τῆς δ' Ἡρακλείας τῆς ὑπὸ τὴν Οἴτην καὶ Τραχῖνος[8] τῶν οἰκητόρων μεθ' Ἡρακλέους τινὲς ἀφικόμενοι ἐκ Λυδίας Κυλικρᾶνες, οἱ δ' Ἀθαμᾶνες, ἀφ' ὧν οἱ τόποι δια-

---

[1] ἀρῶν " vir magnus " (Scaliger ?) cited by Casaubon: δρῶν A, om. CE.

[2] ἀλλ' ἄσκαφον Bergk: ἀλλὰ σκάφον A (σκύφον CE).

[3] σκληρόπεδον " hard-soiled " Schweighäuser.

[4] μάλ' CE: μᾶλλ' A.   [5] καὶ added by Kaibel.

[6] Meineke: κυλικρινας A, κυλικρᾶνας CE.

When we had lain down, Plutarch said : " Well, as the poet Pratinas of Phlius says,[a] ' Not ploughing land already furrowed, but exploring a field undigged,' I am going to give a cup-talk [b] although I am not one of the inhabitants of Cup-ville,[c] of whom the comic poet Hermippus in his *Iambic Verses* mockingly says [d] : ' Proceeding on my way I came to the spongy soil of Cup-ville. I saw, therefore, Heracleia, and a very fine city it was.' Now the Heracleots here meant are those who live at the foot of Oeta, according to Nicander of Thyateira ; he asserts that they got their name from Cylix,[e] a native of Lydia, one of those who accompanied Heracles in his expedition. They are mentioned also by Scythinus of Teos in the work entitled *History*,[f] who says : ' Heracles captured and put to death Eurytus and his son when they exacted tribute from the Euboeans. He also pillaged the Cylicranians, who lived by plunder, and built in that place Heracleia, which is called the Trachinian.' Polemon in the first book of his *Address to Adaeus and Antigonus* says [g] : ' As for the Heracleia at the foot of Oeta and Trachis, some of their inhabitants, the Cylicranians, arrived with Heracles from Lydia, while others were Athamanians ; the

---

[a] *P.L.G.*[4] and Diehl frag. 3.
[b] On κυλικηγορεῖν cf. below, 480 b (p. 126).
[c] Cylicranians, who lived at the foot of Mt. Oeta.
[d] Kock i. 246.
[e] Also the name of a drinking-cup, below 480 b-481 d (pp. 126, 128).
[f] Or *Inquiry*, *F.H.G.* iv. 491, Diels, *Poet. Phil.* iii. 1. 168, J. 1. 176. The passage is quoted in its original Ionic.
[g] Frag. 56 Preller.

---

[7] CE : τρηχηνίαν A.   [8] Wilamowitz : τραχῖνα A.

μένουσιν[1]· οἷς οὐδὲ τῆς πολιτείας μετέδοσαν οἱ
Ἡρακλεῶται συνοικοῦσιν,[2] ἀλλοφύλους ὑπολα-
βόντες. Κυλικρᾶνες δὲ λέγονται ὅτι τοὺς ὤμους
κεχαραγμένοι[3] κύλικας ἦσαν.'

"Οἶδα δὲ καὶ Ἑλλάνικον ἐν Ἐθνῶν Ὀνομασίαις
b λέγοντα ὅτι Λιβύων τῶν Νομάδων τινὲς οὐδὲν
ἄλλο κέκτηνται ἢ κύλικα καὶ μάχαιραν καὶ ὑδρίαν,
καὶ ὅτι οἰκίας ἔχουσιν ἐξ ἀνθερίκου πεποιημένας
μικρὰς ὅσον σκιᾶς ἕνεκα, ἃς καὶ περιφέρουσιν ὅπου
ἂν πορεύωνται. πολλοῖς δὲ καὶ ὁ ἐν Ἰλλυριοῖς
τόπος[4] διαβόητός ἐστιν ὁ καλούμενος Κύλικες, παρ'
ᾧ ἐστι τὸ Κάδμου καὶ Ἁρμονίας μνημεῖον, ὡς
ἱστορεῖ Φύλαρχος ἐν τῇ δευτέρᾳ καὶ εἰκοστῇ τῶν
Ἱστοριῶν. καὶ Πολέμων δ' ἐν τῷ περὶ τοῦ
Μορύχου ἐν Συρακούσαις φησὶν ἐπ' ἄκρᾳ τῇ νήσῳ
πρὸς[5] τῷ Γῆς[5] Ὀλυμπίας ἱερῷ ἐκτὸς τοῦ τείχους
c ἐσχάραν τινὰ εἶναι, ἀφ' ἧς, φησί, τὴν κύλικα
ναυστολοῦσιν ἀναπλέοντες μέχρι τοῦ γενέσθαι τὴν
ἐπὶ τοῦ νεὼ τῆς Ἀθηνᾶς ἀόρατον ἀσπίδα· καὶ
οὕτως ἀφιᾶσιν εἰς τὴν θάλασσαν κεραμέαν κύλικα,
καθέντες[6] εἰς αὐτὴν ἄνθεα καὶ κηρία καὶ λιβανωτὸν
ἄτμητον καὶ ἄλλα ἄττα μετὰ τούτων ἀρώματα.

"Ὁρῶν οὖν ὑμῶν καὶ αὐτὸς τὸ συμπόσιον
κατὰ τὸν Κολοφώνιον Ξενοφάνη πλῆρες ὂν πάσης
θυμηδίας·

---

[1] ὠνομασμένοι added by Kaibel.
[2] Kaibel: συνοίκους A.
[3] Schweighäuser (cf. Hesych. s.v. Κυλικράνων): κεχραι-
μένοι A.
[4] CE: τόποις A.
[5] Γῆς Kaibel: τῆς A.
[6] καταθέντες (?) Kaibel.

[a] See critical note 1.
[b] F.H.G. i. 57, J. 1. 124.
[c] F.H.G. i. 345, J. 2 A 172.

regions continue (to be named [a]) from both ; but the Heracleots, regarding them as of alien stock, allowed no share in the citizenship to them, though they dwelt with them. They are called Cylicranians because their shoulders have cups (*cylices*) tattooed on them.'

" I am also aware that Hellanicus, in his *Tribal Names*, says [b] that some of the Numidians, in Libya, own nothing else but a cup (*cylix*), a knife, and a water - jar, and that they have houses made of asphodel, quite small, just big enough to afford shade, which they carry about wherever they go. To many persons, also, the place in Illyria is well known which is called Cups, and near which is the tomb of Cadmus and Harmonia, as Phylarchus records in the twenty-second book of his *Histories*.[c] Polemon, too, in his book *On Morychus*, says [d] that at Syracuse there is an altar [e] at the extreme end of the island near the shrine of Olympian Earth, and outside the wall, from which they take on shipboard the cup when they put out to sea, and carry it until the shield on the temple of Athena becomes invisible ; they then drop into the sea an earthenware cup,[f] having put into it flowers, honeycomb, frankincense in lumps, and some other spices with them.

" Since I see [g] then, myself also, that your symposium, like that described by Xenophanes of Colophon, is full of every delight [h] : ' Now, at last, the

[d] Frag. 75 Preller ; *cf.* Athen. 109 a (vol. ii. p. 12).

[e] Lit. " brazier," for burnt offerings.

[f] Apparently a different cup from that in the Temple of Gê ; the quotation from Polemon is incomplete.

[g] The sentence is never concluded, but resumed in a different shape at 463 c, p. 18.

[h] *P.L.G.*⁴, Edmonds, and Diehl frag. 1, Diels, *Vorsokrat.* i. 44, *Poet. Phil.* iii. 1. 35.

νῦν γὰρ δὴ ζάπεδον καθαρὸν καὶ χεῖρες ἁπάντων
d   καὶ κύλικες· πλεκτοὺς δ' ἀμφιτιθεῖ[1] στεφάνους,
ἄλλος δ' εὐῶδες μύρον ἐν φιάλῃ παρατείνει·
κρατὴρ δ' ἔστηκεν μεστὸς εὐφροσύνης·
ἄλλος δ' οἶνος ἕτοιμος,[2] ὃς οὔποτέ φησι προ-
    δώσειν,
μείλιχος ἐν κεράμοις, ἄνθεος ὀζόμενος·
ἐν δὲ μέσοις ἁγνὴν ὀδμὴν λιβανωτὸς ἵησι·
ψυχρὸν δ' ἐστὶν ὕδωρ καὶ γλυκὺ καὶ καθαρόν.
e πάρκεινται δ' ἄρτοι ξανθοὶ γεραρή τε τράπεζα
τυροῦ καὶ μέλιτος πίονος ἀχθομένη·
βωμὸς δ' ἄνθεσιν ἂν τὸ[3] μέσον πάντῃ πεπύκασται,
μολπὴ δ' ἀμφὶς ἔχει δώματα καὶ θαλίη.
χρὴ δὲ πρῶτον μὲν θεὸν ὑμνεῖν[4] εὔφρονας ἄνδρας
εὐφήμοις μύθοις καὶ καθαροῖσι λόγοις·
σπείσαντάς τε[5] καὶ εὐξαμένους τὰ δίκαια δύνασθαι
f   πρήσσειν (ταῦτα γὰρ ὦν[6] ἐστι προχειρότερον)·
οὐχ ὕβρις[7] πίνειν δ'[8] ὁπόσον κεν ἔχων ἀφίκοιο
οἴκαδ' ἄνευ προπόλου, μὴ πάνυ γηραλέος.
ἀνδρῶν δ' αἰνεῖν τοῦτον ὃς ἐσθλὰ πιὼν[9] ἀναφαίνη[10]
ὡς οἱ[11] μνημοσύνη, καὶ τόνος[12] ἀμφ' ἀρετῆς.
οὔτι μάχας διέπειν[13] Τιτήνων οὐδὲ Γιγάντων
οὐδέ τι[14] Κενταύρων, πλάσματα τῶν[15] προτέρων,
ἢ στάσιας σφεδανάς,[16] τοῖς οὐδὲν χρηστὸν ἔνεστι,
463   θεῶν δὲ[17] προμηθείην αἰὲν ἔχειν ἀγαθόν.[18]

καὶ ὁ χαρίεις δ' Ἀνακρέων φησίν·

[1] Dindorf: ἀμφιτιθεὶς A.
[2] ἄλλος δ' οἶνος ἕτοιμος Musurus: οἶνος ἐστὶν ἕτοιμος ACE.
[3] ἂν τὸ CE: ἀντο A.   [4] CE: ὑμνὲν A.   [5] ACE: δὲ Bergk.
[6] ὦν A.   [7] Musurus: ὕβρεις A.   [8] δ' ACE: del. Bergk.
[9] CE: πιω A.   [10] Hermann: ἀναφαίνει ACE.
[11] ὡς οἱ Schneidewin: ωση A, ὡς ἡ CE.

16

floor is swept, and clean are the hands of all the
guests, and their cups as well; one slave puts plaited
wreaths on their heads, another offers sweet-smelling
perfume in a saucer; the mixing-bowl stands full
of good cheer; and other wine is ready, which promises never to give out—mellow wine in jars, redo-
lent of its bouquet; and in the midst the frankincense
sends forth its sacred fragrance; and there is water,
cool and fresh and pure. The yellow loaves lie ready
at hand, and a lordly table groans with the weight of
cheese and luscious honey; an altar in the middle is
banked all round with flowers, and singing and dancing
and bounty pervade the house. But men of good cheer
should first of all praise the god with pious stories and
pure words; they should pour libations and pray for
power to do the right (for that is the duty closer to
hand); 'tis no sin to drink as much as you can hold
and still get home without an attendant, unless you
be very old. Praise that man who even in his cups
can show forth goodly thoughts, according as memory
serves him and his zeal for virtue is at full stretch.[a]
In no wise is it good to relate the fights of Titans and
Giants nor of Centaurs, the fictions of men aforetime,
or their violent factions, in which there is nought
that is wholesome; but it is good ever to have regard
for the gods.' And the graceful Anacreon says[b]:

[a] For τόνος (see critical note 12) cf. Pind. *Pyth.* xi. 54 ξυναῖσι
δ' ἀμφ' ἀρεταῖς τέταμαι, "for excellences within the reach of
all I am at full stretch."

[b] *P.L.G.*[4] frag. 94, Diehl frag. 96, Edmonds 116.

---

[12] τόνος Diels: τὸν δς ACE.   [13] A: διέπει CE.
[14] τι added by Meineke (κε Kalinka).
[15] πλάσματα τῶν Schweighäuser: πλασμάτων ACE.
[16] Osann: φενδόνας A.
[17] δὲ added by Scaliger.   [18] Hermann: ἀγαθήν A.

οὐ φιλέω ὅς[1] κρητῆρι παρὰ πλέω οἰνοποτάζων
   νείκεα καὶ πόλεμον δακρυόεντα λέγει,
ἀλλ' ὅστις Μουσέων τε καὶ ἀγλαὰ δῶρ' Ἀφροδίτης
συμμίσγων ἐρατῆς μνήσκεται[2] εὐφροσύνης.

καὶ Ἴων δὲ ὁ Χῖός φησιν·

b χαιρέτω ἡμέτερος βασιλεύς, σωτήρ τε πατήρ τε·
   ἡμῖν δὲ κρητῆρ' οἰνοχόοι θέραπες
κιρνάντων προχύταισιν ἐν ἀργυρέοις,[3] ὁ δὲ
   χρυσοῦ
δεῖνον[4] ἔχων χειροῖν ἱζέτω[5] εἰς ἔδαφος.
σπένδοντες δ' ἁγνῶς Ἡρακλέι τ' Ἀλκμήνη τε,
   Προκλέι Περσείδαις τ', ἐκ Διὸς ἀρχόμενοι,
c πίνωμεν, παίζωμεν, ἴτω διὰ νυκτὸς ἀοιδή,
   ὀρχείσθω τις, ἑκὼν δ' ἄρχε φιλοφροσύνης.
ὅντινα δ' εὐειδὴς μίμνει θήλεια πάρευνος,
   κεῖνος τῶν ἄλλων κυδρότερον πίεται.

ἐποιοῦντο δὲ καὶ οἱ ἑπτὰ καλούμενοι σοφοὶ συμ-
ποτικὰς ὁμιλίας. ' παραμυθεῖται γὰρ ὁ οἶνος καὶ
τὴν τοῦ γήρως δυσθυμίαν ' φησὶ Θεόφραστος ἐν
τῷ περὶ Μέθης.

"Διόπερ συνιοῦσι καὶ ἡμῖν ἐπὶ τὰς Διονυσιακὰς
ταύτας λαλιὰς οὐδεὶς ἂν εὐλόγως φθονήσαι νοῦν
ἔχων, κατὰ τοὺς Ἀλέξιδος Ταραντίνους,

---

[1] φιλέω ὅς CE: φιλεος A.
[2] μνήσκεται ACE (cf. I.G. xii. 3. 1065, Et. M. 452. 34):
μνῆεται Franke, Kaibel.
[3] 496 c: προχοαῖσιν ἐν ἀργυρεαις A (om. CE). See Fraenkel,
Nomina Agentis 242.
[4] χρυσοῦ δεῖνον (δῖνον) Hiller: χρυσὸς οἶνον A.
[5] χειροῖν ἱζέτω Bentley: χειρῶν νιζέτω A.

18

' I love him not who, when drinking his wine beside
the brimming bowl, speaks of strifes and tearful
battle, but rather him who, mingling the bright gifts
of the Muses and of Aphrodite together, is ever
mindful of welcome good cheer.' And Ion of Chios
says [a] : ' Long live our king, saviour and father !
For us let the wine-pouring henchmen mix the bowl
from silver pitchers,[b] while another, with a golden jar [c]
in his hands, sets it on its base. Let us reverently
pour libations to Heracles and Alcmena, to Procles
and the Perseidae, beginning with Zeus, and let us
drink, let us play, let our song go through the night ;
let everyone dance and gladly lead in the way of
friendliness. And he for whom a fair female bed-
fellow waits shall drink more lustily than the others.'
The so-called Seven Wise Men, also, composed for
themselves dinner-conversations. ' Verily wine con-
soles even the despondency of old age,' says Theophrastus in the treatise *On Drunkenness.*[d]

" For this reason, when we also come together for
these Dionysiac talks, nobody with any sense can find
plausible excuse for blaming us, ' who,' in the words
of *The Tarentines* of Alexis,[e] ' are doing none of our

[a] *P.L.G.*[4] and Edmonds frag. 2, *cf.* Athen. 496 c (p. 212).
[b] *i.e.* fill the mixing-bowl from silver pitchers, containing
wine and water. Eur. *I.A.* 955 πικροὺς δὲ προχύτας χέρνιβάς
τ᾽ ἐνάρξεται, and below 496 c (p. 212).
[c] The *deinos* was a large bowl (not goblet, as L. & S. say)
used for cooling wine; below, 467 d (p. 60). But the text is
uncertain. [d] Frag. 120 Wimmer.
[e] Kock ii. 377 ; the words of Alexis began with οὐδὲ εἷς ἂν
εὐλόγως | ἡμῖν φθονῆσαι νοῦν ἔχων, οἳ τῶν πέλας, incorporated
by the writer in his prose introduction.

οἳ τῶν πέλας

d οὐδέν' ἀδικοῦμεν οὐδέν.[1] ἆρ' οὐκ[2] οἶσθ' ὅτι
τὸ καλούμενον ζῆν τοῦτο διατριβῆς χάριν
ὄνομ'[3] ἐστίν, ὑποκόρισμα τῆς ἀνθρωπίνης
μοίρας; ἐγὼ γάρ, εἰ μὲν εὖ τις ἢ κακῶς
φήσει[4] με κρίνειν, οὐκ ἔχοιμ' ἄν σοι[5] φράσαι·
ἔγνωκα δ' οὖν[6] οὕτως ἐπισκοπούμενος
εἶναι μανιώδη πάντα τἀνθρώπων ὅλως,
ἀποδημίας δὲ τυγχάνειν ἡμᾶς ἀεὶ[7]
τοὺς ζῶντας, ὥσπερ εἰς πανήγυρίν τινα
ἀφειμένους ἐκ τοῦ θανάτου καὶ τοῦ σκότους
εἰς τὴν διατριβὴν εἰς τὸ φῶς τε τοῦθ' ὃ δὴ
e ὁρῶμεν. ὃς δ' ἂν πλεῖστα γελάσῃ καὶ πίῃ
καὶ τῆς Ἀφροδίτης ἀντιλάβηται τὸν χρόνον
τοῦτον ὃν ἀφεῖται, καὶ[8] Τύχης[9] ἐράνου τινός,
πανηγυρίσας ἥδιστ' ἀπῆλθεν οἴκαδε.

καὶ κατὰ τὴν καλὴν οὖν Σαπφώ·

ἐλθέ, Κύπρι,
χρυσίαισιν[10] ἐν κυλίκεσσιν ἁβρῶς[11]
συμμεμιγμένον θαλίαισι νέκταρ
οἰνοχοοῦσα

τούτοις[12] τοῖς ἑταίροις ἐμοῖς τε[13] καὶ σοῖς.

"Πρὸς οὓς λεκτέον ὅτι τρόποι εἰσὶ πόσεων κατὰ
πόλεις ἴδιοι, ὡς Κριτίας παρίστησιν ἐν τῇ Λακεδαι-

---

[1] οὐδέν' . . . οὐδέν Kock : οὐδὲν ἀδικοῦμεν οὐδένα ACE.
[2] οὐκ added by Dobree.
[3] ὄνομ' ACE : μόνον Madvig, Kaibel.
: Dobree : φήσειε ACE.   [5] σοι added by Dindorf.
[6] C : γοῦν A.   [7] ἀεὶ AC.
[8] καὶ A (om. CE) : κἂν Meineke.
[9] Τύχης Lumb : τύχηι τ' AC (γ' Musurus).
[10] Neue : χρυσείαισιν A.

neighbours any harm. Don't you know that what, to amuse ourselves, we call "life" is but a name, a coaxing flattery of our human lot? Whether anybody will say that my judgement is good or bad I cannot tell you ; but this, at least, I have made up my mind to on careful study : that all the doings of men are out-and-out crazy, and that we who for the time being are alive are only getting an outing, as though let loose [a] from death and darkness to keep holiday, to amuse ourselves and to enjoy this light which we can see. And the man who laughs and drinks the most, and holds fast to Aphrodite, during the time he is set free, and to such gifts as Fortune offers, after he has had a most pleasant holiday can depart for home.' Therefore, as the fair Sappho also says [b] : ' Come, goddess of Love, and daintily, from golden cups, pour out mingled nectar for our merry-making,' for these boon-companions, mine and thine.[c]

" In answer to those [d] persons it should be said that there are special modes of drinking in different cities, as Critias explains in these words in his *Con-*

---

[a] *i.e.* set free to enjoy a vacation ; ἀποδημίας and πανήγυριν suggest the practice of going abroad to attend a great national festival. What Fortune offers is a contribution to the picnic (ἔρανος).

[b] *P.L.G.*⁴ frag. 5 Diehl, Edmonds frag. 6. "Aeolic" forms, of course, once stood here as elsewhere in the text of Sappho and Alcaeus. Athenaeus and his immediate predecessors usually quote in a "modernized" version.

[c] These last words are adapted from Sappho by the speaker, Plutarch; *cf.* 571 d.

[d] *i.e.* those who would find fault with us, above 463 c.

---

[11] Bergk (ἄβρως, the correct Lesbian form): ἀβρῶς A.
[12] τούτοισι A.   [13] Schweighäuser: γε A.

μονίων Πολιτεία διὰ τούτων· ' ὁ μὲν Χῖος καὶ
f Θάσιος ἐκ μεγάλων κυλίκων ἐπιδέξια, ὁ δ' Ἀττι-
κὸς ἐκ μικρῶν ἐπιδέξια, ὁ δὲ Θετταλικὸς ἐκπώματα προπίνει ὅτῳ ἂν βούλωνται¹ μεγάλα. Λακεδαιμόνιοι δὲ τὴν παρ' αὑτῷ ἕκαστος πίνει, ὁ δὲ
παῖς ὁ οἰνοχόος ὅσον ἂν ἀποπίῃ.²' τοῦ δ' ἐπιδέξια
πίνειν μνημονεύει καὶ Ἀναξανδρίδης ἐν Ἀγροίκοις
οὕτως·

464 τίνα δὴ παρεσκευασμένοι
πίνειν τρόπον ἐστὲ νυνί, λέγεθ'. Β. ὅντινα³ τρόπον
ἡμεῖς⁴; τοιοῦτον οἷον ἂν καὶ σοὶ δοκῇ.
Α. βούλεσθε δήπου τὸν ἐπιδέξι', ὦ πάτερ,
λέγειν ἐπὶ τῷ πίνοντι. Β. τὸν ἐπιδέξια
λέγειν; "Ἀπολλον, ὡσπερεὶ⁵ τεθνηκότι.

'' Παραιτητέον δ' ἡμῖν τὰ κεράμεα ποτήρια. καὶ
γὰρ Κτησίας ' παρὰ Πέρσαις,' φησίν, ' ὃν ἂν
βασιλεὺς ἀτιμάσῃ, κεραμέοις ποτηρίοις⁶ χρῆται.'
Χοιρίλος δ' ὁ ἐποποιός φησι·

χερσὶν ἔχω κολοβὸν⁷ κύλικος τρύφος ἀμφὶς ἐαγός,
b ἀνδρῶν δαιτυμόνων ναυάγιον, οἷά τε πολλὰ
πνεῦμα Διωνύσοιο⁸ πρὸς Ὕβριος⁹ ἔκβαλεν ἀκτάς.¹⁰
ἐγὼ δὲ εὖ οἶδα ὅτι ἥδιστα πολλάκις ἐστὶ τὰ κεράμεα

ὧν
¹ AC: βούληται E. ² ἐπιχεῖ added by Meineke.
³ λέγεθ' ὅντινα Madvig: λέγετε τίνα A.
⁴ πίνειν repeated before ἡμεῖς in A, deleted by Dobree.
⁵ ὥσπερ ἐπὶ Schweighäuser.
⁶ ποτηρίοις C: om. A.
⁷ ἔχω κολοβὸν Valckenaer: ὄλβον ἔχω AC, ὀλίζον (" small ")
ἔχω Morel. ⁸ διωνύσοιο AE.
⁹ ὕβρεως AE. ¹⁰ Canter: ἔκβαλ' ἄνακτος AE.

ᵃ F.H.G. ii. 68, Diels 623.
ᵇ Athen. 152 d and note a (vol. ii. p. 194), 600 e.

stitution of the Lacedaemonians [a] : ' The Chian and the
Thasian drink a health out of large cups from left to
right,[b] the Athenian from small cups from left to
right, while the Thessalian pledges in large cups to
whomsoever he wishes.[c] But the Lacedaemonians
drink each his own cup separately,[d] and the slave who
pours the wine (fills up again) with the quantity he
has drunk off.' The custom of drinking from left to
right is mentioned by Anaxandrides in *The Farmers*
thus [e] : ' A. In what way, then, are you prepared to
drink on this occasion ? Tell me ! B. In what way,
you ask ? We ? In any way you please. A. Of
course, then, my father, you mean to say the
" left-to-right manner " when a man drinks. B. Say
the " left-to-right manner " ? Apollo save us ! As
though for a dead man [f] ! '

" We must beg to be excused from earthenware
cups. For Ctesias says [g] that ' among the Persians
any man who falls under the king's displeasure uses
earthenware drinking-cups.' And the epic poet
Choerilus says [h] : ' I hold in my hands the chipped
sherd of a cup, broken on all sides, the shipwrecked
remnant of feasters, such as a gale from Dionysus
often casts forth upon the shores of Wantonness.'
And yet I am well aware that earthenware drinking-

---

[c] *i.e.* in any order desired.
[d] Not passing it round. [e] Kock ii. 135.
[f] To what this alludes I do not know, unless the responses in
a dirge were taken up by the singers from left to right. Statius,
Theb. vi. 215 " lustrantque, ex more, sinistro orbe rogum,"
on which the Schol. says: " quia nihil dextrum mortuis con-
venit, ut funeribus absolvant dextro orbe redeunt." But the
left-to-right motion is ingrained in Indo-European habit,
e.g. dealing at cards, passing the bottle at table, motion of
the hands of a clock, etc.
[g] *Frag.* 51 Müller. [h] *Frag. ep.* 9.

ἐκπώματα, ὡς καὶ τὰ παρ' ἡμῖν ἐκ τῆς Κόπτου
καταγόμενα· μετὰ γὰρ ἀρωμάτων συμφυραθείσης
c τῆς γῆς ὀπτᾶται. καὶ Ἀριστοτέλης δὲ ἐν τῷ περὶ
Μέθης ' αἱ Ῥοδιακαί,' φησί, ' προσαγορευόμεναι
χυτρίδες διά τε τὴν ἡδονὴν εἰς τὰς μέθας παρ-
εισφέρονται καὶ διὰ τὸ θερμαινομένας τὸν οἶνον
ἧττον ποιεῖν μεθύσκειν. σμύρνης γὰρ καὶ σχοίνου
καὶ τῶν τοιούτων ἑτέρων εἰς ὕδωρ ἐμβληθέντων
ἕψονται καὶ παραχεόντων εἰς τὸν οἶνον ἧττον
μεθύσκουσιν.' κἂν ἄλλῳ δὲ μέρει φησίν· ' αἱ
Ῥοδιακαὶ χυτρίδες γίνονται σμύρνης, σχοίνου,
ἀνήθου,[1] κρόκου, βαλσάμου, ἀμώμου, κινναμώμου
d συνεψηθέντων· ἀφ' ὧν τὸ γινόμενον[2] τῷ οἴνῳ παρα-
χυθὲν οὕτω μέθας ἵστησιν ὥστε καὶ τῶν ἀφροδισίων
παραλύειν τὰ πνεύματα πέττον.' οὐ δεῖ οὖν ἡμᾶς
ἐκμανῶς πίνειν ἀποβλέποντας εἰς τὸ πλῆθος τῶν
καλῶν τούτων καὶ παντοδαπῶν κατὰ τὰς τέχνας
ἐκπωμάτων. τὴν δὲ μανίαν τοὺς πολλούς φησιν ὁ
Χρύσιππος ἐν τῇ Εἰσαγωγῇ, τῇ[3] περὶ ἀγαθῶν καὶ
κακῶν πραγματείᾳ, τοῖς πλείστοις προσάπτειν.[4]
καλεῖσθαι γοῦν τὴν μὲν γυναικομανίαν, τὴν δ'
ὀρτυγομανίαν. ' τινὲς δὲ καὶ δοξομανεῖς καλοῦσι
e τοὺς φιλοδόξους, καθάπερ τοὺς φιλογύνας γυναικο-
μανεῖς καὶ τοὺς φιλόρνιθας ὀρνιθομανεῖς, τὸ αὐτὸ
σημαινόντων τῶν ὀνομάτων τούτων. ὥστε καὶ τὰ

---

[1] Wilamowitz: ἄνθους ACE.
[2] Meineke: πινόμενον ACE.
[3] εἰσαγωγῇ τῇ A: but cf. 159 d (Εἰσαγωγικῇ περὶ ἀ. κ. κ.
Πραγματείᾳ Kaibel).
[4] Meineke: τοῖς πλείστοις προσάπτεσθαι AE, πολλαχοῦ
προσάπτεσθαι (om. τοὺς πολλούς) C.

---

[a] The speaker, Plutarch, lived in Alexandria.
[b] Frag. 96 Rose.   [c] Frag. 97 Rose.

vessels are often very pleasant, like those we use, brought down the river from Coptos[a]; for the clay of which they are made is mingled and baked with spices. Aristotle, too, in his work *On Drunkenness*, says[b]: 'The pots called Rhodian are used in drinking-bouts because of their pleasant taste and also because, when heated, they cause the wine to be less intoxicating. For myrrh and aromatic rush and other similar spices are placed in water and the pots are set to boil; when this liquid is added to the wine, it causes less drunkenness.' And in another part of his work he says[c]: 'The Rhodian pots are prepared by steeping myrrh, aromatic rush, anise, saffron, costmary,[d] cardamom, and cinnamon together; the liquor resulting from this, when added to the wine, arrests intoxication to such an extent that it even dispels erotic desires by softening the spirits.'[e] We, therefore, must not drink too madly as we gaze upon the large number of these beautiful cups, wrought with every variety of art. That word 'madness,' as Chrysippus says in his *Introduction*, the treatise *On Good and Evil*, is applied by the vulgar to the greatest number of things.[f] There is, for example, the term 'woman-madness,' and the term 'quail-madness.'[g] 'Some people even call fame-lovers "fame-mad," just as they call lovers of women "women-mad," and lovers of birds "bird-mad," since these words signify the same thing.[h]

[d] *Cf.* Gerarde: "Costmarie is put in ale to steep."
[e] For the three kinds of "spirits" in the body, natural, vital, and animal, see Brock's Galen (L.C.L.) p. xxxv.
[f] Or "in many ways." See critical note 4.
[g] *i.e.* a mad devotion to quail-fights.
[h] *i.e.* they all emphasize madness. *Cf.* Aristoph. *Av.* 1284, Plat. *Rep.* 475 A–C. See 599 e (vol. vi. p. 231).

λοιπὰ μὴ ἀλλοτρίως[1] καλεῖσθαι τὸν τρόπον τοῦτον. καὶ γὰρ ὁ φίλοψος καὶ ὁ ὀψοφάγος οἷον ὀψομανής ἐστι καὶ ὁ φίλοινος οἰνομανὴς καὶ ὡσαύτως ἐπὶ τῶν ὁμοίων, οὐκ ἀλλοτρίως τῆς μανίας κειμένης ἐπ'[2] αὐτοῖς ὡς ἁμαρτάνουσι μανικῶς καὶ τῆς ἀληθείας ἐπὶ πλεῖον[3] ἀπαρτωμένοις.[4]' ἡμεῖς οὖν, ὡς καὶ παρ' Ἀθηναίοις ἐγίνετο, ἅμα ἀκροώμενοι τῶν γελωτοποιῶν τούτων καὶ μίμων, ἔτι δὲ τῶν f ἄλλων τεχνιτῶν ὑποπίνωμεν. λέγει δὲ περὶ τούτων ὁ Φιλόχορος οὑτωσί· ' Ἀθηναῖοι τοῖς Διονυσιακοῖς ἀγῶσι τὸ μὲν πρῶτον ἠριστηκότες καὶ πεπωκότες ἐβάδιζον ἐπὶ τὴν θέαν καὶ ἐστεφανωμένοι ἐθεώρουν, παρὰ δὲ τὸν ἀγῶνα πάντα οἶνος αὐτοῖς ᾠνοχοεῖτο[5] καὶ τραγήματα παρεφέρετο, καὶ τοῖς χοροῖς εἰσ-ιοῦσιν ἐνέχεον πίνειν καὶ διηγωνισμένοις ὅτ' ἐξ-επορεύοντο ἐνέχεον πάλιν· μαρτυρεῖν δὲ τούτοις καὶ Φερεκράτη τὸν κωμικόν, ὅτι μέχρι τῆς καθ' ἑαυτὸν ἡλικίας οὐκ ἀσίτους εἶναι τοὺς θεωροῦντας.'

465 Φανόδημος δὲ πρὸς τῷ ἱερῷ φησι τοῦ ἐν Λίμναις Διονύσου τὸ γλεῦκος φέροντας τοὺς Ἀθηναίους ἐκ τῶν πίθων τῷ θεῷ κιρνάναι, εἶτ' αὐτοὺς[6] προσ-φέρεσθαι· ὅθεν καὶ Λιμναῖον κληθῆναι τὸν Διό-νυσον, ὅτι μιχθὲν τὸ γλεῦκος τῷ ὕδατι τότε πρῶτον ἐπόθη κεκραμένον. διόπερ ὀνομασθῆναι τὰς[7] Νύμφας καὶ τιθήνας τοῦ Διονύσου, ὅτι τὸν

---

[1] ἀλόγως CE. [2] ἐπ' Kaibel: ἐν ACE.
[3] πλεῖστον Kaibel. [4] Casaubon: ἀπαρτώμενοι A.
[5] CE: οἰνοχοεῖτο A.
[6] Schweighäuser: αὐτοῖς A, αὐτοὶ C (in paraphrase) E.
[7] The gloss πηγάς, "springs," after τὰς deleted by Kaibel.

---

[a] F.H.G. i. 411.
[b] τραγήματα are nuts, raisins, figs, dried beans, etc., making a dessert after dinner. Aristotle, Nic. Eth. 1175 b ἐν τοῖς

Hence it is not strange that other terms should be given in the same way. For the lover of fish and the fish-eater are in a way fish-mad, the lover of wine is wine-mad, and so on in similar cases ; it is not strange that the word "madness" is applied to them, since they err madly, and are too far removed from the truth.' As for ourselves, therefore, let us, as they used to do in Athens, sip our wine, while listening to the clowns and the mimes here, and all the other artists as well. Of the Athenian custom Philochorus speaks as follows *a* : ' At the Dionysiac festivals the Athenians, after they had finished their luncheon and their drinking, would go to the spectacle and gaze at it with garlands on their heads, and throughout the entire festival wine was served to them and sweet-meats *b* were passed among them ; when the choruses marched in they poured out drinks for them, and when they were marching out after the contest they poured again ; this is attested by the comic poet Pherecrates, who says *c* that up to his time the spectators were not left unfed.' Phanodemus says *d* that at the temple of Dionysus in the Marshes the Athenians mix the must which they bring from their casks in honour of the god, and then drink it themselves ; hence Dionysus was called god of the marsh, because the must was mixed and drunk with water on that occasion for the first time. Hence, too, the Nymphs *e* were called nurses of Dionysus,

θεάτροις οἱ τραγηματίζοντες, ὅταν φαῦλοι οἱ ἀγωνιζόμενοι, τότε μάλιστ' αὐτὸ δρῶντες, "people chewing sweetmeats in the theatre do it most when the actors are bad."

c Kock i. 202, *cf.* Athen. 485 d (p. 156).

d F.H.G. i. 368.

e See critical note 7, and *cf.* Athen. 38 d (vol. i. p. 166), 693 e.

οἶνον αὐξάνει τὸ ὕδωρ κιρνάμενον. ἡσθέντες οὖν
τῇ κράσει ἐν ᾠδαῖς ἔμελπον τὸν Διόνυσον, χορεύον-
τες καὶ ἀνακαλοῦντες Εὐανθῆ[1] καὶ Διθύραμβον καὶ
b Βακχευτὰν καὶ Βρόμιον. καὶ Θεόφραστος δ᾽ ἐν
τῷ περὶ Μέθης φησὶν ὅτι ᾽τοῦ Διονύσου τροφοὶ
αἱ Νύμφαι κατ᾽ ἀλήθειαν. αἱ γὰρ ἄμπελοι πλεῖστον ὑγρὸν χέουσι τεμνόμεναι καὶ κατὰ φύσιν
δακρύουσι.᾽ διόπερ καὶ Εὐριπίδης ἕνα τῶν τοῦ
Ἡλίου ἵππων φησὶν εἶναι

Βακχίου φιλανθέος[2]
Αἴθοπα[3] πεπαίνοντ᾽ ὀρχάτους[4] ὀπωρινούς·
ἐξ οὗ βροτοὶ καλοῦσιν οἶνον αἴθοπα.

καὶ Ὀδυσσεὺς ὤπασεν[5]

μελιηδέα οἶνον ἐρυθρόν,

c ἓν δέπας ἐμπλήσας, ὕδατος δ᾽ ἀνὰ εἴκοσι μέτρα
χεῦ[6]· ὀδμὴ δ᾽ ἡδεῖα ἀπὸ κρητῆρος ὀδώδει.

Τιμόθεος δ᾽ ἐν Κύκλωπι·

ἔγχευε[7] δ᾽ ἐν μὲν δέπας κίσσινον μελαίνας
σταγόνος ἀμβρότας ἀφρῷ βρυάζον·
εἴκοσιν δὲ μέτρ᾽ ἐνέχευ᾽,[8] ἀνέμισγε δ᾽
αἷμα[9] Βακχίου[10] νεορρύτοισι[11] δακρύοισι[12] Νυμφᾶν.[13]

---

[1] εὐάνθη A: Εὔαν τε Schweighäuser (though Kaibel claimed it as his own emendation).

[2] CE: φιλανθέου A, φιλανθέμου Schweighäuser, Nauck, Kaibel.

[3] C (αἴθωπα E): αἰθίοπα A.

[4] CE: πεπαίνοντοαρχατους A.

[5] C, which introduces this quotation after the one from Timotheus, more correctly has ἔστι δὲ παρὰ τὸ ὁμηρικόν.

[6] χεῦεν ACE.   [7] Bergk: ἔχευεν A.

[8] Kaibel: ἀνέχευαν A, ἀνέχευεν C, ἐνέχευεν E.

[9] ἀνέμισγε δ᾽ αἷμα Grotefend: ἀνέμισγε δ᾽ ἅμα CE, ἔμισγε διαμα A.   [10] βακχεῖα CE.

because water increases the wine [a] when mixed with it. Delighted, then, with the mixture, men celebrated Dionysus in song, dancing, and calling upon him with the names Flowery, Dithyrambus, Reveller, and Bromius. Theophrastus, also, in the treatise *On Drunkenness*, says [b] that 'the Nymphs are in very truth nurses of Dionysus. For the vines when pruned pour forth a great deal of moisture, and weep according to their nature.' Hence Euripides says [c] that one of the horses of the Sun is ' Fiery, ripening the autumn vine-rows of the Bacchic god, who loves flowers ; because of this mortals call wine fiery.' [d] And Odysseus gave ' honey-sweet red wine, filling one cup, and poured into it twenty measures of water ; and a sweet smell breathed from the mixing-bowl.' [e] Timotheüs in *Cyclops* [f] : ' Into it he poured one ivy-wood cup of red drops ambrosial, bubbling with foam ; then he poured in twenty measures,[g] and mingled together the blood of the Bacchic god with fresh-flowing tears of the Nymphs.'

[a] As nurses help the growth of their children.
[b] Frag. 121 Wimmer.
[c] *T.G.F.*[2] 647 ; this quotation is added to illustrate the epithet Εὐανθῆ, " Flowery."
[d] Or " sparkling."
[e] *Od.* ix. 208. The writer mistakenly thinks of the gift of Odysseus to Cyclops, but the passage is taken from the description by Odysseus of the gift he had received from Maron, priest of Apollo ; see critical note 5, and *cf.* Athen. 26 b, 28 e (vol. i. pp. 112, 124).
[f] *P.L.G.*[4] frag. 5, Diehl frag. 2, Edmonds 12.
[g] *sc.* of water.

---

[11] Wilamowitz : νεορρύτοις CE, νεωρυτως A.
[12] C : δακρύουσι AE.
[13] A : πηγᾶν CE, *cf.* 465 a and Soph. *El.* 894 νεορρύτους πηγὰς γάλακτος.

" Οἶδα δέ τινας, ἄνδρες θιασῶται, καὶ μέγα φρο-
νήσαντας οὐχ οὕτως ἐπὶ πλούτῳ ὡς ἐπὶ τῷ
κεκτῆσθαι πολλὰ ἐκπώματα ἀργυρᾶ τε καὶ χρυσᾶ.[1]
d ὧν εἷς ἐστι καὶ Πυθέας ὁ 'Αρκὰς ἐκ Φιγαλείας,[2]
ὃς καὶ ἀποθνῄσκων οὐκ ὤκνησεν ὑποθέσθαι[3] τοῖς
οἰκείοις ἐπιγράψαι αὐτοῦ τῷ μνήματι τάδε·

Πυθέα μνῆμα τόδ' ἔστ', ἀγαθοῦ καὶ σώφρονος
    ἀνδρός,
  ὃς κυλίκων ἔσχεν πλῆθος ἀπειρέσιον
ἀργυρέων χρυσοῦ τε καὶ ἠλέκτροιο φαεινοῦ,
  τῶν προτέρων πάντων πλείονα πασάμενος.[4]

τοῦτο δ' ἱστορεῖ 'Αρμόδιος ὁ Λεπρεάτης ἐν τῷ
e περὶ τῶν κατὰ Φιγάλειαν[5] Νομίμων. Ξενοφῶν δ'
ἐν ὀγδόῳ Παιδείας περὶ Περσῶν λέγων γράφει
καὶ ταῦτα· ' καὶ μὴν ἐκπώματα ἦν μὲν ὡς πλεῖστα
ἔχωσιν, τούτῳ καλλωπίζονται· ἦν δ' ἐξ ἀδίκων[6]
φανερῶς ᾖ μεμηχανημένα, οὐδὲν τούτῳ[7] αἰσχύνον-
ται. πολὺ γὰρ ηὔξηται ἐν αὐτοῖς ἡ ἀδικία τε καὶ
αἰσχροκέρδεια.' ὁ δὲ Οἰδίπους δι' ἐκπώματα τοῖς
υἱοῖς κατηράσατο, ὡς ὁ τὴν κυκλικὴν Θηβαΐδα
πεποιηκώς φησιν, ὅτι αὐτῷ παρέθηκαν ἔκπωμα ὃ
ἀπηγόρευκε, λέγων οὕτως·

f   αὐτὰρ ὁ διογενὴς ἥρως ξανθὸς Πολυνείκης
  πρῶτα μὲν Οἰδιπόδῃ καλὴν παρέθηκε τράπεζαν
  ἀργυρέην Κάδμοιο θεόφρονος· αὐτὰρ ἔπειτα
  χρύσεον ἔμπλησεν καλὸν δέπας ἡδέος οἴνου.
  αὐτὰρ ὅ γ' ὡς φράσθη παρακείμενα πατρὸς ἑοῖο

---

[1] ἐκπώματος ἀργυροῦ καὶ χρυσοῦ C.
[2] φιαλίας A, cf. Steph. Byz. 664.
[3] CE: ἐπιθέσθαι A.
[4] Casaubon: πασσάμενος A, ἀσπασάμενος (om. πλείονα) CE.
30

" I know of some persons, fellow-members of our company, who took great pride not so much in their money as in the possession of many cups of silver and gold. One of these is Pytheas, the Arcadian from Phigaleia, who, even when he was dying, did not hesitate to admonish his relatives to write this epigram on his tomb[a]: ' This is the tomb of Pytheas, a good and sober man, who acquired a boundless number of cups of silver, gold, and shining electrum, and came to own more than all others before him.' This is recorded by Harmodius of Lepreum in his book on the *Customs of Phigaleia*.[b] Xenophon, speaking of the Persians in the eighth book of *Cyropaedeia*, writes this[c] : ' And what is more, if they own the greatest possible number of cups, they pride themselves on that ; and if they have openly contrived to get them by dishonest methods, they feel no shame at that. For dishonesty and avarice have grown to great proportions among them.' And it was on account of cups that Oedipus cursed his sons, according to the author of the Cyclic poem *Thebaïs*, because they had set before him a cup which he had forbidden ; the author says[d] : ' But the divine hero, yellow-haired Polyneices, first set the beautiful silver table of godly Cadmus before Oedipus ; and then he filled a fair golden cup with sweet wine. But when Oedipus recognized the precious possessions of his

[a] See Cahen, *Callimaque*, p. 218.
[b] *F.H.G.* iv. 411.
[c] *Cyrop.* viii. 8. 18, describing the Persians of his own time.
[d] *Frag. ep.* 2, Welcker, *Ep. Cycl.* ii. 549 f., Bethe, *Theban. Heldenlieder* 102 ff. The sons, in using the heirlooms of Cadmus, violate a family taboo.

[5] φιγαλίαν A.   [6] ἀδίκου Xenophon.
[7] Kaibel : τῶι A (om. CE).

τιμήεντα γέρα, μέγα οἱ κακὸν ἔμπεσε θυμῷ,
466   αἶψα δὲ παισὶν ἑοῖσι μετ' ἀμφοτέροισιν[1] ἐπαρὰς
ἀργαλέας ἠρᾶτο (θεῶν[2] δ' οὐ λάνθαν' Ἐρινύν),
ὡς οὔ οἱ πατρώι' ἐνηέι ἐν φιλότητι[3]
δάσσαιντ',[4] ἀμφοτέροισι·δ' αἰεὶ πόλεμοί τε μάχαι
τε. . . .

"Καικίλιος δὲ ὁ ῥήτωρ ὁ ἀπὸ Καλῆς ἀκτῆς ἐν
τῷ περὶ Ἱστορίας Ἀγαθοκλέα φησὶ τὸν τύραννον
ἐκπώματα χρυσᾶ ἐπιδεικνύντα τοῖς ἑταίροις φά-
σκειν, ἐξ ὧν ἐκεράμευσε κατεσκευακέναι ταῦτα.
b ὁ δὲ παρὰ Σοφοκλεῖ ἐν τοῖς Λαρισαίοις Ἀκρίσιος
καὶ αὐτὸς ἐκπώματα ὅσα πλεῖστα εἶχεν, ὥς φησιν
ὁ τραγικός·

πολὺν δ' ἀγῶνα πάγξενον[5] κηρύσσεται,
χαλκηλάτους λέβητας ἐκτιθεὶς φέρειν
καὶ κοῖλα χρυσόκολλα καὶ πανάργυρα
ἐκπώματ', εἰς ἀριθμὸν ἐξήκοντα δίς.

Ποσειδώνιος δ' ἐν ιϛ'[6] τῶν Ἱστοριῶν Λυσίμαχόν
φησι τὸν Βαβυλώνιον, καλέσαντα ἐπὶ δεῖπνον
Ἱμερον τὸν τυραννήσαντα οὐ μόνον Βαβυλωνίων
ἀλλὰ καὶ Σελευκέων μετὰ τριακοσίων, μετὰ τὸ
c τὰς τραπέζας ἀρθῆναι τετράμνουν ἑκάστῳ τῶν
τριακοσίων ἔκπωμα δοῦναι ἀργυροῦν, καὶ σπον-
δοποιησάμενον προπιεῖν ἅμα πᾶσιν· καὶ ἀπο-
φέρεσθαι ἔδωκε τὰ ποτήρια. Ἀντικλείδης δ' ὁ
Ἀθηναῖος ἐν τῷ ϛ'[7] Νόστων περὶ Γρᾶ διηγού-

---

[1] μεταμφοτέροισιν Meineke.   [2] Meineke: θεὸν ACE.
[3] πατρώι' ἐνηέι ἐν φιλότητι Hermann, W. Ribbeck : πατρωιαν
εἴη φιλότητι A (om. C).
[4] δάσσαιντ' Hermann: δάσαντο A; but the negative οὐ
instead of μή is strange.
[5] W. Schneider: πανξενα A (om. C).

32

own father set before him, mighty woe fell upon his spirit, and swiftly he called down harsh curses upon both his sons—and it escaped not the avenging fury of the gods—that they should never divide his father's goods in lovingkindness, but that wars and fights should ever be upon them both. . . .'

" Caecilius, the orator from Calacte, says[a] in his book *On History* that the tyrant Agathocles, while showing golden cups to his companions, remarked that he had made them by *pottering* in state affairs.[b] Acrisius also, mentioned by Sophocles in *The Men of Larisa*, had a prodigious number of cups, as the tragic poet says[c]: ' A mighty contest for all strangers he proclaimed, setting out as prizes to win cauldrons of beaten copper, and hollow cups inlaid with gold and all of silver, to the number of twice threescore.' And Poseidonius, in the sixteenth book of his *Histories*, says[d] that Lysimachus of Babylon invited to dinner Himerus, who had been made ruler not only of the Babylonians but of the people of Seleuceia as well, in company with three hundred men ; after the tables had been removed he gave a silver cup weighing four pounds to every one of the three hundred, and after the libation he drank all their healths together ; and he gave the cups to be carried home.   Anticleides of Athens, in the sixth book of his *Returns*, relates[e] the

[a] Ofenloch 3, J. 2 B 911.
[b] Schol. Aristoph. *Eccl.* 253 ἔλεγον κεραμεύειν καὶ τὸ κακῶς ποιεῖν τὰ κοινά, " they used to say ' pottering ' for ' causing trouble to the commonwealth.' "
[c] *T.G.F.*[2] 214.
[d] *F.H.G.* iii. 259, J. 2 A 228.
[e] *Script. Alex. Mag.* p. 148, J. 2 B 800, P.W. i. 2425.

[6] ιϛ΄ Müller : κϛ΄ A.
[7] ϛ΄ Wilamowitz : ιϛ΄ A.

μενος τοῦ τὴν ἀποικίαν εἰς Λέσβον στείλαντος σὺν
ἄλλοις βασιλεῦσι, καὶ ὅτι χρησμὸς ἦν αὐτοῖς
δηλώσας καθεῖναι[1] διαπλέοντας τῷ Ποσειδῶνι εἰς
τὸ πέλαγος παρθένον, γράφει καὶ ταῦτα· 'μυθο-
λογοῦσι δὲ[2] τῶν ἐν Μηθύμνῃ τινὲς περὶ τῆς
ἀφεθείσης εἰς τὴν θάλασσαν παρθένου καὶ φασὶν
d ἐρασθέντα αὐτῆς τῶν ἡγεμόνων τινά, ᾧ ἦν τοὔνομα
Ἔναλος, ἐκκολυμβῆσαι βουλόμενον ἀνασῶσαι τὴν
παιδίσκην. τότε μὲν οὖν ὑπὸ κύματος αὐτοὺς
ἀμφοτέρους κρυφθέντας ἀφανεῖς γενέσθαι, χρόνῳ
δ' ὕστερον ἤδη τῆς Μηθύμνης οἰκουμένης παρα-
γενέσθαι τὸν Ἔναλον καὶ διηγεῖσθαι τὸν τρόπον,[3]
καὶ ὅτι ἡ μὲν παρθένος παρὰ ταῖς Νηρῇσι διέτριβεν,
αὐτὸς δὲ τὰς τοῦ Ποσειδῶνος ἔβοσκεν ἵππους· καὶ
781 ποτε κύματος[4] ἐπιφερομένου μεγάλου συγκολυμ-
c βήσαντα αὐτὸν ἐκβῆναι ἔχοντα κύπελλον χρυσοῦ
οὕτω θαυμασίου ὡς τὸν παρ' αὐτοῖς[5] αὐτῷ παρα-
βαλλόμενον οὐδὲν διάφορον εἶναι χαλκοῦ.'''

Τιμιώτατον δ' ἦν πάλαι τὸ τῶν ἐκπωμάτων
κτῆμα. Ἀχιλλεὺς οὖν ὡς ἐξαίρετόν τι εἶχεν ἀνάθημα δέπας, '' οὐδέ τις ἄλλος οὔτ' ἀνδρῶν[6] πίνεσκεν
ἀπ' αὐτοῦ οὔτε τεῳ σπένδεσκε θεῶν,[7] ὅτε μὴ Δίί.''
καὶ ὁ Πρίαμος δὲ τὸν υἱὸν λυτρούμενος τοῖς ἐπι-
σημοτάτοις κειμηλίοις καὶ δέπας δίδωσι περικαλλές. αὐτός γε μὴν ὁ Ζεὺς τῆς Ἡρακλέους

---

[1] Coraes: καταθεῖναι ACE.
[2] περὶ after δὲ deleted by Meineke.
[3] τὸν τρόπον om. C; quo pacto evaserat Dalechamp.
[4] ποτε κύματος CE: ποτε καὶ κύματος A.

At this point several leaves have been torn from A. The
epitome in CE, here inserted by Schweighäuser from the last
part of Casaubon's *Animadversiones* (pp. 781 ff.), extends to
466 e (στρογγύλον, p. 56).

[5] ἀνθρώποις Herwerden.　　　　[6] θεῶν CE.

story of Gras, who led the colony to Lesbos with other chieftains, and says that an oracle told them to let down into the sea as they sailed across a maiden as offering to Poseidon ; he writes also the following : ' Some of the people in Methymna tell the story of the maiden who was dropped into the sea, and they declare that one of the leaders, whose name was Enalus, had fallen in love with her and dived off the ship to save the girl. At that moment they were both hidden by a wave and disappeared from sight, but some time after, when Methymna was already settled, Enalus appeared and related the manner of life he had led,[a] and he said that the girl was staying with the Nereids, while he himself had fed the horses of Poseidon ; and finally, when a great wave came sweeping on he plunged along with it and emerged with a cup made of gold so marvellous that the gold they[b] had, when compared with it, was no better than copper.' "

The possession of drinking-cups was held in very high esteem in ancient times. Achilles, therefore, kept his cup as a special treasure, " and neither did any other man drink out of it, nor did he pour libation from it to any god excepting Zeus." [c] And when Priam wanted to ransom his son with his most notable heirlooms, he offered also " a very beautiful cup." [d] In fact, even Zeus himself thought that an adequate reward for bringing forth Heracles

[a] Something has been lost after τὸν τρόπον ; see critical note 3. Plut. *Conv.* 163 D tells the story differently.

[b] *i.e.* the people to whom he related the adventure ; see crit. note 5.

[c] *Il.* xvi. 225 ; below, 783 b (p. 46).   [d] *Il.* xxiv. 234.

---

[7] θεῶν added from Homer.

γενέσεως ἄξιον ἡγεῖται δῶρον Ἀλκμήνῃ δοθῆναι
ποτήριον, ὅπερ Ἀμφιτρύωνι εἰκασθεὶς δίδωσιν,

d   ἁ δ' ὑποδεξαμένα θαήσατο χρύσεον αἶψα

ποτήριον. τὸν δὲ Ἥλιον ὁ Στησίχορος ποτηρίῳ
διαπλεῖν φησι τὸν Ὠκεανόν, ᾧ καὶ τὸν Ἡρακλέα
περαιωθῆναι ἐπὶ τὰς Γηρυόνου βόας ὁρμῶντα.
οἴδαμεν δὲ καὶ τὸ Βαθυκλέους τοῦ Ἀρκάδος
ποτήριον, ὃ σοφίας ἆθλον ὁ Βαθυκλῆς τῷ κριθέντι
ἀρίστῳ τῶν καλουμένων ζ'[1] σοφῶν ἀπέλιπε. τὸ
δὲ Νέστορος ποτήριον πολλοὶ κεραμεύουσι· πλεῖστοι
γὰρ περὶ αὐτοῦ συνεγράψαντο. καὶ θεοφιλὲς δὲ
τὸ ποτήριον· "χρυσέοις" γοῦν "δεπάεσσιν ἀλλήλους" δεξιοῦνται. ἐλευθέριον δέ, φησί, καὶ ἐμμελῶς ἐν οἴνῳ διάγειν, μὴ κωθωνιζόμενον μηδὲ
Θρακίῳ νόμῳ ἄμυστιν οἰνοποτεῖν, ἀλλὰ τῷ πόματι
φάρμακον ὑγείας ἐγκιρνάναι τὸν λόγον.

e   Ὅτι διὰ σπουδῆς εἶχον οἱ ἀρχαῖοι ἐγκόλαπτον[2]
ἱστορίαν ἔχειν ἐν ἐκπώμασιν. ἐν ταύτῃ δὲ τῇ τέχνῃ
εὐδοκίμησαν Κίμων καὶ Ἀθηνοκλῆς. ἐχρῶντο δὲ
καὶ λιθοκολλήτοις ἐκπώμασι. Μένανδρος δέ πού
φησι καὶ ποτήριον τορνευτὸν καὶ τορευτά. Ἀντι-
φάνης·

   ἄλλοι δὲ καὶ δὴ βακχίου[3] παλαιγενοῦς
   ἀφρῷ σκιασθὲν[4] χρυσοκόλλητον δέπας

---

[1] ζ' added by Meineke.
[2] Schweighäuser: ἀκόλαστον CE.
[3] βακχείου CE.
[4] σκιασθὲν Valckenaer: σκια· καὶ CE.

---

[a] Cf. below, 474 f (p. 96).
[b] An hexameter from some Alexandrian poet (Rhianus ?).

36

was to give Alcmena a cup,[a] which, putting on the likeness of Amphitryon, he gave to her, " and she received it straightway and marvelled at the golden " cup.[b] Stesichorus says [c] that the Sun voyages over Oceanus in a cup, by means of which Heracles also made his way over when he set out to get the cattle of Geryonês. We know also of the cup of the Arcadian Bathycles, which he left behind as a prize for wisdom to him who was adjudged the best among the Seven Wise Men, as they are called. As for Nestor's cup, many potter with that ; I mean that very many have written about it.[d] The cup is a thing even loved by the gods ; at any rate, they welcome " one another with golden cups." [e] It is even gentlemanly, Athenaeus says, to pass the time with wine, provided that one does it reasonably, not drinking too deeply, and not gulping it down in a single breath, Thracian fashion, but mingling discourse with the potion as a medicine for health.

The ancients[f] were very fond of having stories embossed on their cups. Cimon and Athenocles achieved fame in this art. People also made use of cups inlaid with precious stones. Menander speaks somewhere [g] of " a cup turned on the lathe," and of " cups ornamented in relief." Antiphanes[h] : " Others also drain, with jaws which never cease draining, a gold-inlaid cup filled with wine of ancient

---

[c] *P.L.G.*[4] frag. 8, Edmonds frag. 8 ; below, 469 e (p. 70).
[d] *Cf.* above, 461 d (p. 10).   [e] *Il.* iv. 3.
[f] For ὅτι, beginning this excerpt, see vol. i. p. 15, note *a*. The reading ἐγκόλαπτον, here rendered by " embossed," is not wholly certain, but is the best that has been suggested. For toreutic works see below, 782 b (p. 40), where one of the favourite " stories " is seen to be the sack of Troy.
[g] Kock iii. 249.   [h] Kock ii. 115.

μεστὸν κύκλῳ τορευτὸν[1] ἕλκουσι γνάθοις
ὁλκῆς[2] ἀπαύστοις, παντελῶς ἐστραμμένον
f τἄνω κάτω δεικνύντες.

φησὶ πρός τινα Νικόμαχος·

ὦ χαῖρε,[3] χρυσόκλυστα[4] καὶ χρυσοῦς ἐμῶν . . .

Φιλιππίδης·

τὰ ποτήρι᾽ ἂν ἴδῃς τὰ παρεσκευασμένα,
ἅπαντα χρυσᾶ, Τρόφιμε, νὴ τὸν Οὐρανόν,
ὑπερήφαν᾽ ἔργ᾽.[5] ἐγὼ μὲν[6] ἐξέστην ἰδών.
κρατῆρες ἀργυροῖ, κάδοι[7] μείζους ἐμοῦ . . .

Ὅτι Παρμενίων συγκεφαλαιούμενος ἐν ταῖς πρὸς
Ἀλέξανδρον Ἐπιστολαῖς τὰ Περσικὰ λάφυρα
782 "ποτηρίων," φησί, "χρυσῶν σταθμὸς τάλαντα Βαβυλώνια ογ΄, μναῖ νβ΄. ποτηρίων λιθοκολλήτων
σταθμὸς τάλαντα Βαβυλώνια νϛ΄, μναῖ λδ΄."
Ἔθος δ᾽ ἦν πρότερον ἐν τῷ ποτηρίῳ ὕδωρ ἐμ-
βάλλεσθαι, μεθ᾽ ὃ τὸν οἶνον. Ξενοφάνης·

οὐδέ κεν ἐν κύλικι πρότερον κεράσειέ τις οἶνον
ἐγχέας, ἀλλ᾽ ὕδωρ καὶ καθύπερθε μέθυ.

Ἀνακρέων·

φέρ᾽ ὕδωρ, φέρ᾽ οἶνον, ὦ παῖ, φέρε δ᾽[8] ἀνθε-
    μεῦντας[9] ἡμῖν
στεφάνους ἔνεικον, ὡς δὴ[10] πρὸς Ἔρωτα[11] πυκ-
    ταλίζω.

---

[1] τορευτὸν Kock: χορεῦον CE.
[2] ὁλκῆς Wilamowitz: ὁλκοῖς CE.
[3] χαῖρε added by Meineke.
[4] Letronne: χρυσοκλαύστα CE.
[5] ὑπερήφαν ἔργ᾽ Kaibel: οὐ περήφανα C, ὑπερήφανα E.
[6] γὰρ after μὲν deleted by Wilamowitz.

38

vintage, covered with foam—a cup skilfully turned on the lathe ; and the drinkers, when they twist it completely round, show the top at the bottom."[a] Nicomachus says to someone[b]: " O hail, you that vomit forth gold-washed cups and golden . . ." Philippides[c]: " If you will glance at the cups set forth in readiness, they are all of gold, Trophimus, so help me Heaven, magnificent works of art ! I was in ecstasy when I saw them, mixing-bowls of silver, jars bigger than myself. . . ."

Parmenion, summing up the booty taken from the Persians, in his *Letters to Alexander*, says : " Gold cups, weight seventy-three Babylonian talents, fifty-two minae[d] ; cups inlaid with precious stones, weight fifty-six Babylonian talents, thirty-four minae."

It was the custom to put water in the cup first, after that the wine. Thus Xenophanes[e]: " And no one would mix wine by pouring it in first, but the water first, and on top of it wine." Anacreon[f]: " Bring water, slave, bring wine, and bring me flowery wreaths, for I want to box with Eros." And long

---

[a] Apparently a reference to "bottoms up " ; but the text is very obscure.

[b] Kock iii. 389 ; perhaps addressed to some rich man.

[c] Kock iii. 309; perhaps from the play, *The Abolition of Money* (Schweighäuser), *cf.* Athen. 230 a (vol. iii. p. 34).

[d] If the Babylonian gold talent is meant, the total weight of the gold cups was considerably over four tons.

[e] *P.L.G.*⁴, Edmonds, and Diehl frag. 4, Diels, *Vorsokr.* 47, *Poet. Phil.* iii. 1. 37. Cratinus, a heavy drinker, objected to this method of mixing ; below, p. 42.

[f] *P.L.G.*⁴ frag. 62, Diehl frag. 27, Edmonds 75.

---

⁷ καὶ after κάδοι deleted by Schweighäuser.
⁸ δ' C: om. E.   ⁹ ἀνθεμβέντας Bergk.
¹⁰ δὴ Orion 62. 31, ἤδη *Et. Mag.*: μὴ CE, Eustath.
¹¹ ἔρωτα Orion: τὸν ἔρωτα CE.

πρὸ δὲ τούτων Ἡσίοδος·

κρήνης τ᾽ ἀενάου[1] καὶ ἀπορρύτου, ἥτ᾽ ἀθόλωτος,
τρὶς ὕδατος προχέειν, τὸ δὲ τέτρατον[2] ἱέμεν οἴνου.

Θεόφραστος· " ἐπεὶ καὶ τὰ περὶ τὴν κρᾶσιν ἐναν-
b τίως εἶχε τὸ παλαιὸν τῷ νῦν παρ᾽ Ἕλλησιν ὑπ-
άρχοντι. οὐ γὰρ τὸ ὕδωρ ἐπὶ τὸν οἶνον ἐπέχεον,
ἀλλ᾽ ἐπὶ τὸ ὕδωρ τὸν οἶνον, ὅπως ἐν τῷ πίνειν
ὑδαρεστέρῳ[3] χρῶντο[4] τῷ ποτῷ καὶ τούτου ποιησάμενοι τὴν ἀπόλαυσιν ἧττον ὀρέγοιντο τοῦ λοιποῦ.
καὶ τὸ πλεῖστον δὲ εἰς τοὺς κοττάβους κατ-
ανήλισκον."

Ἔνδοξοι δὲ τορευταὶ Ἀθηνοκλῆς, Κράτης, Στρα-
τόνικος, Μυρμηκίδης ὁ Μιλήσιος, Καλλικράτης ὁ
Λάκων καὶ Μῦς, οὗ εἴδομεν σκύφον Ἡρακλεωτικὸν
τεχνικῶς ἔχοντα Ἰλίου ἐντετορευμένην πόρθησιν,
ἔχοντα ἐπίγραμμα τόδε·

γράμμα[5] Παρρασίοιο,[6] τέχνα Μυός. ἐμμὶ δὲ
ἔργον[7]
Ἰλίου αἰπεινᾶς, ἂν ἕλον Αἰακίδαι.

c Ὅτι κλεινοὶ λέγονται παρὰ Κρησὶν οἱ ἐρώμενοι.
σπουδὴ δὲ αὐτοῖς παῖδας ἁρπάζειν· καὶ τοῖς καλοῖς
παρ᾽ αὐτοῖς ἄδοξόν ἐστιν ἐραστοῦ μὴ τυχεῖν.
καλοῦνται δὲ οἱ ἁρπασθέντες παρασταθέντες.
διδόασι δὲ τῷ ἁρπασθέντι στολὴν καὶ βοῦν καὶ

---

[1] ἀεννάου CE.   [2] C: τέταρτον E.
[3] Kaibel: ὑδαρέστερον CE.
[4] Schweighäuser: χρῶνται CE.

[5] γράμμα Meineke: γράμ̆μ C.
[6] Jacobs (cf. Paus. i. 28. 2): πηρασίοιο CE.
[7] εἰκὼν Meineke; but ἔργον often means " work of art."

before them Hesiod wrote [a] : " And toward a spring
ever-gushing and flowing and untroubled, and pour
forth three parts of water, then put in the fourth part,
of wine." Theophrastus [b] : " For as regards the
practices pertaining to the mixture of wine, antiquity
was opposed to present-day usage among the Greeks
They did not pour the water on the wine, but rather
the wine on the water, in order that they might use
a drink that was more diluted, and that, having
obtained satisfaction with this, they might have less
appetite for more. And besides, they used up most
of the wine in playing cottabus-games." [c]

Famous workers in relief were Athenocles, Crates,
Stratonicus, Myrmecides of Miletus, Callicrates of
Laconia, and Mys, whose Heracleot bowl we have
seen ; it has an artistic relief representing the sack
of Troy, and bears the following inscription : " The
design is by Parrhasius, the work by Mys. I am
the representation of lofty Ilios, which the Aeacidae
captured."

Favourite boys among the Cretans are called
" illustrious." Eager zeal possessed them to carry
off boys ; and so, in the eyes of the fair among them,
it is a disgrace not to get a lover. Those who have
been carried off are said to be " won over." [d] They
give to the boy thus carried off a cloak, an ox, and

[a] *Opp.* 593 ; the poet has just said, " In summer . . .
drink wine seated in the shade . . . turning thy face toward
the brisk West Wind, and toward," etc.

[b] Probably from the treatise Περὶ Μέθης ; om. Wimmer.

[c] See 665 e-668 f, 427 d.

[d] A euphemistic term, like " illustrious " (κλεινοί) just
mentioned ; Strabo 483, 484. *Cf.* παραστάται 395 f (vol. iv.
p. 290).

ποτήριον· ἦν καὶ πρεσβύτεροι γενόμενοι φέρουσιν,
ἵνα δῆλοι ὦσι κλεινοὶ γενόμενοι.

'Ορᾷς δ', ὅταν πίνωσιν ἄνθρωποι, τότε
πλουτοῦσι, διαπράττουσι, νικῶσιν δίκας,
εὐδαιμονοῦσιν, ὠφελοῦσι τοὺς φίλους.

d αὔξει γὰρ καὶ τρέφει μεγαλύνει τε τὴν ψυχὴν ἡ
ἐν τοῖς πότοις διατριβή, ἀναζωπυροῦσα καὶ ἀν-
εγείρουσα μετὰ φρονήσεως τὸν ἑκάστου νοῦν, ὥς
φησιν ὁ Πίνδαρος·

ἁνίκ' ἀνθρώπων καματώδεες οἴχονται μέριμναι
στηθέων ἔξω, πελάγει δ' ἐν πολυχρύσοιο[1]
πλούτου
πάντες ἴσᾳ[2] νέομεν ψευδῆ πρὸς ἀκτάν·
ὃς μὲν ἀχρήμων, ἀφνεὸς[3] τότε, τοὶ δ' αὖ πλου-
τέϲντες . . .

εἶτ' ἐπάγει·

ἀέξονται φρένας ἀμπελίνοις[4] τόξοις δαμέντες.

ΑΓΚΤΛΗ ποτήριον πρὸς τὴν τῶν κοττάβων παι-
διὰν χρήσιμον. Κρατῖνος·

πιεῖν δὲ θάνατος οἶνον ἂν ὕδωρ ἐπῇ.[5]
ἀλλ' ἴσον ἴσῳ μάλιστ' ἀκράτου δύο χόας[6]

---

[1] ἔξω . . . πολυχρύσοιο Mitscherlich: ἔξωθεν . . . πολυ-
χρύσου CE.
[2] ἴσᾳ Hermann (ἴσον Schroeder): ἴσα C.
[3] Hermann: ἀφνειὸς CE.
[4] C: ομπελίτοις E.
[5] ῥέπῃ "weighs too much" (or more than the wine)
Kaibel.   [6] Pierson: χοέας CE.

---

[a] Cf. below, 502 b (p. 248). These three gifts were
required by law, but many others were bestowed.

a cup [a]; they wear the cloak even when they have grown older, to show that they were once "illustrious."

"But you can see that when men drink, then are they rich, they succeed, they win law-suits, they are happy, they help their friends." [b] And it is a fact that the time passed in drinking-parties expands, nourishes, and enlarges the soul; it rekindles and awakens, with the exercise of wisdom, every man's senses, as Pindar says [c]: "When the wearisome cares of men have vanished from their bosoms, and as on a sea of golden wealth, we all swim together to the shore of illusion [d]; he that hath no wealth is then rich, while they that are wealthy . . ." He then continues: "Expand their hearts, overmastered by the arrows of the vine."

Ankylê [e] is a cup used in the game of cottabus. Cratinus [f]: " It's death to drink wine if the water be on top. [g] No, she drinks by preference two pitchers of strong wine, mixed half-and-half, and as

[b] Aristoph. *Eq.* 92.

[c] *P.L.G.*[5] 439, Sandys (L.C.L.) 586 ; from an encomium addressed to Thrasybulus of Agrigentum, *cf.* below, 480 c (p. 126).

[d] *Cf.* 464 b (p. 22) πρὸς Ὕβριος . . . ἀκτάς.

[e] Lit. "bend" of the arm, is here explained as the cup used in tossing wine at the figure (*manês*) poised on a lampstand, 667 c, 487 d. In this famous alphabetical catalogue words are sometimes included which are associated in some way with drinking, but have no reference to material or shape. Nor, in the case of many terms, is it possible to fit them to the vases in our museums. See Pfuhl, *Malerei*, i. § 43.

[f] Kock i. 93, *cf.* Sophilus at 431 a (vol. iv. p. 452).

[g] See critical note 5, and above, 782 a with note [e] (p. 39).

43

πίνουσ' ἀπ' ἀγκύλης ἐπονομάζουσ' ἅμα[1]
e ἵησι λάταγας τῷ Κορινθίῳ πέει.

καὶ Βακχυλίδης·

εὖτε τὴν ἀπ' ἀγκύλης ἵησι τοῖς νεανίαις,[2]
λευκὸν ἀντείνασα[3] πῆχυν.

ἐντεῦθεν ἐννοοῦμεν[4] τοὺς παρ' Αἰσχύλῳ ἀγκυλητοὺς
κοττάβους. λέγονται δὲ καὶ δόρατα ἀγκυλητὰ καὶ
μεσάγκυλα· ἀλλ' ἀπὸ ἀγκύλης ἤτοι τῆς δεξιᾶς
χειρός. καὶ ἡ κύλιξ δὲ ἡ ἀγκύλη[5] διὰ τὸ ἐπαγκυ-
λοῦν[6] τὴν δεξιὰν χεῖρα ἐν τῇ προέσει. ἦν γὰρ τοῖς
παλαιοῖς πεφροντισμένον καλῶς καὶ εὐσχημόνως
κότταβον προίεσθαι. καὶ οἱ πολλοὶ ἐπὶ τούτῳ
μᾶλλον ἐφρόνουν μέγα ἢ ἐπὶ τῷ εὖ ἀκοντίζειν.
ὠνομάσθη οὖν ἀπὸ τοῦ τῆς χειρὸς σχηματισμοῦ,
ὃν ποιούμενοι εὐρύθμως ἐρρίπτουν εἰς τὸ κοττάβιον.
f καὶ οἴκους δὲ ἐπιτηδείους κατεσκεύαζον εἰς ταύτην
τὴν παιδιάν.

Ὅτι παρὰ Τιμαχίδα ΑΙΑΚΙΣ[7] ἡ κύλιξ καλεῖται.
ΑΚΑΤΟΣ ποτήριον ἐοικὸς πλοίῳ. Ἐπικράτης·

κατάβαλλε τἀκάτια, τὰ[8] κυμβία[9]
αἴρου τὰ μείζω, κεὐθὺ τοῦ καρχησίου
ἄνελκε τὴν γραῦν, τὴν νέαν δ'[10] ἐπουρίσας

---

[1] ἅμα added by Meineke.   [2] τοῖσδε τοῖς νεανίαις 667 c.
[3] ἀντείνασα A at 667 c: ἐντείνουσα CE, perhaps rightly,
"with all the force of her white arm."
[4] Kaibel: νοοῦμεν CE.
[5] ἡ ἀγκύλη deleted by Kaibel (cf. Bekk. An. 338. 3).
[6] Schol. Aristoph. Pac. 1243: ἀπαγκυλοῦν CE.
[7] αἰακίξ Suidas, Hesychius.
[8] τὰ added by Kaibel.   [9] Meineke: κυλίκια CE.
[10] δ' Casaubon: τ CE.

she calls out his name she tosses the drops with a bend of the arm (*ankylê*) at the Corinthian—member.[a] " And Bacchylides [b] : " When, raising high her white arm, she makes the ' bend-toss ' for the young chaps." Hence we can form a notion of what Aeschylus means [c] by his " bended cottabi." But spears also are spoken of as " bent-arm " spears—or " mid-arm " spears ; but they are so called from the " bend," that is, the right arm.[d] And so the cup, the *ankylê*, is so called because the right arm is bent in the toss. For the ancients were very careful to toss the cottabus nicely and in good form. In fact the vulgar were apt to take more pride in that than in the skilful throwing of the javelin. Hence the name " bent " arose from the proper position of the arm which they observed when they tossed wine in due form at the prize. What is more, they built rooms specially adapted for this game.

The cylix is called *Aiakis* in Timachidas.

Akatos is a cup shaped like a boat. Epicrates [e] : " Cast off the pinnaces, raise up the larger skiffs, drag the old lady straight to the schooner, man the

[a] *Sens. obs.* ; a parody of Euripides, *Stheneboea*, τῷ Κορινθίῳ ξένῳ, Athen. 427 e (vol. iv. p. 436).

[b] *P.L.G.*⁴ frag. 24, Edmonds frag. 68, from the Ἐρωτικά ; see Athen. 667 c.

[c] *T.G.F.*² 58.

[d] Rather, they are so called because a cord (ἀγκύλη), one end of which was held in the thrower's hand, was bound tightly round the shaft and caused it to spin like a rifle-bullet, Athen. 667 c, *cf.* 534 e (p. 414).

[e] Kock ii. 286 ; a ludicrous mixture of nautical terms which were also names of cups ; obscene meanings intended throughout.

ATHENAEUS

πλήρωσον, εὐτρεπῆ τε τὸν κοντὸν ποοῦ
καὶ τοὺς κάλως[1] ἔκλυε καὶ χάλα πόδα.

ΑΩΤΟΝ παρὰ Κυπρίοις τὸ ἔκπωμα, ὡς Πάμφιλος
Φιλίτας δὲ ποτήριον οὓς οὐκ ἔχον.

ΑΡΟΚΛΟΝ[2] ἡ φιάλη παρὰ τῷ Κολοφωνίῳ Νικ-
άνδρῳ.

ΑΛΕΙΣΟΝ καὶ ΔΕΠΑΣ τὸ αὐτό. Ὅμηρος ἐν Ὀδυσσείᾳ περὶ Πεισιστράτου· '' ἐν δ' οἶνον ἔχευε χρυσείῳ
δέπαι.'' εἶτα παρακατιὼν τὸ αὐτό· '' τούνεκα σοὶ
δώσω χρύσειον ἄλεισον.'' καὶ ἑξῆς τὸ αὐτὸ πάλιν·
'' δῶκε δὲ Τηλεμάχῳ καλὸν δέπας ἀμφικύπελλον.[3] ''
φησὶν οὖν Ἀσκληπιάδης ὁ Μυρλεανός· '' δοκεῖ μοι
φιαλῶδες εἶναι τὸ δέπας· σπένδουσι γὰρ ἐν αὐτῷ.
b λέγει γοῦν Ὅμηρος δέπας, δι' οὗ Διὶ μόνῳ σπέν-
δεσκεν Ἀχιλλεύς. καλεῖται δὲ δέπας ἤτοι ὅτι δίδο-
ται πᾶσι τοῖς σπένδειν βουλομένοις εἴτε καὶ τοῖς
πίνειν, ἢ ὅτι δύο ὦπας εἶχε· ταῦτα δὲ ἂν εἴη τὰ
ὦτα. τὸ δὲ ἄλεισον ἤτοι ἀπὸ τοῦ ἄγαν λεῖον εἶναι
ἢ ὅτι ἁλίζεται ἐν αὐτῷ τὸ ὑγρόν. ὅτι δὲ δύο ὦτα
εἶχε δῆλον·

ἤτοι ὃ καλὸν ἄλεισον ἀναιρήσεσθαι ἔμελλε
χρύσεον ἄμφωτον.

---

[1] Valckenaer: κάλους CE.
[2] Thought to be corrupt. If Nicander could have used a
Latin word, possibly it represents *arcula*, a small ointment
box or salver. For the meanings of *phialê* see Athen. 501 a.
[3] ἀμφικύπελλον added from Homer.

---

[a] For the double meaning in πούς *cf.* the oracle given to
Aegeus, Eur. *Med.* 679 and Schol.
[b] Frag. 39 Bach, om. Powell.
[c] Lit. " ear," etymologizing ἄ-ωτον.
[d] Frag. 129 Schneider. See critical note 2.

young one and let the breezes blow, get the pole ready, let out the halyards and loosen the sheet." [a]

Aoton among the Cyprians means drinking-cup, according to Pamphilus. Philitas says [b] that it is a cup without a handle. [c]

Aroklon means the *phialê* in Nicander of Colophon. [d]

Aleison and *Depas* are identical. Homer in the *Odyssey* says of Peisistratus [e] : " He poured wine into a golden cup (*depas*)." Then, proceeding a little further, he says of the same [f] : " Therefore I will give thee [g] the golden cup (*aleison*)." Still further on he again says of the same [h] : " And she [i] gave to Telemachus the beautiful double cup (*depas*)." Consequently Asclepiades of Myrlea says : " I think that the *depas* is a cup shaped like a *phialê*; for they pour libations with it. Homer, at any rate, speaks [j] of the *depas* with which Achilles was wont to pour a libation to Zeus alone. And it is called *depas* either because it is given to all (*didotai pâsi*) who wish to make libation or who wish to drink, or else because it had two faces (*dyo ôpas*) ; these must be the handles. But the word *aleison* comes either from its being very smooth (*agan leion*) or because the liquid is contained (*alizetai*) in it. [k] And that it had two handles is plain [l] : ' Now he was just on the point of raising a fair two-handled cup (*aleison*) of gold.' In calling it ' double '

---

[e] *Od.* iii. 40. [f] *Ibid.* 50.
[g] Mentor. [h] *Od.* iii. 63. [i] Athena.
[j] *Il.* xvi. 225; above, 781 c (p. 34).
[k] The first derivation is ascribed to Apollonius, son of Archibius, *Etym. Magn.* 61. 32; see also *Etym. Magn.* 90. 43, where Aristarchus is cited on the word ἀμφικύπελλον. Below, 482 e, f (p. 140).
[l] *Od.* xxii. 9; of Antinoüs, before Odysseus shot his arrow at him.

ἀμφικύπελλον δὲ λέγων αὐτὸ οὐδὲν ἄλλο σημαίνει
ἢ ὅτι ἦν ἀμφίκυρτον." Σιληνὸς δὲ ἀμφικύπελλόν
φησι τὸ μὴ ἔχον ὦτα. ἄλλοι δὲ τὴν ἀμφὶ ἀντὶ
τῆς περὶ εἶναι, ἵν' ᾖ περίποτον, τὸ πανταχόθεν
πίνειν ἐπιτήδειον. Παρθένιος δὲ διὰ τὸ περι-
κεκυρτῶσθαι τὰ ὠτάρια· κυφὸν γὰρ εἶναι τὸ κυρ-
c τόν. Ἀνίκητος[1] δὲ τὸ μὲν κύπελλόν φησι φιάλην
εἶναι, τὸ δ' ἀμφικύπελλον ὑπερφίαλον, τὸ ὑπερ-
ήφανον καὶ καλόν. εἰ μὴ ἄρα τὸ ποικίλον τῇ κατασκευῇ ἄλεισον θέλει τις ἀκούειν, ἔξω λειότητος ὄν.
Πείσανδρος δέ φησιν Ἡρακλέα Τελαμῶνι τῆς ἐπὶ
Ἴλιον στρατείας ἀριστεῖον ἄλεισον δοῦναι.

Ὅτι ἐστὶ ποτήριον ΑΜΑΛΘΕΙΑΣ ΚΕΡΑΣ καὶ ΕΝΙΑΥΤΟΣ
καλούμενον.

d ΑΜΦΩΞΙΣ[2] ξύλινον ποτήριον ᾧ χρῆσθαι τοὺς ἀγροίκους Φιλίτας φησι, ἀμέλγοντας[3] εἰς αὐτὸ καὶ
οὕτως πίνοντας.

ΑΜΥΣΤΙΣ. καλεῖται μὲν οὕτω πόσις τις, ἣν ἔστιν
ἀπνευστὶ πίνειν μὴ μύσαντα. καλοῦσι δ' οὕτω καὶ
τὰ ποτήρια ἀφ' ὧν ἔστι πιεῖν εὐμαρῶς. καὶ τὸ
ῥῆμα δὲ ἐξημύστισε[4] φασί, τὸ ὑφ' ἕν[5] πνεῦμα πιεῖν,
ὡς ὁ κωμικὸς Πλάτων·

[1] Ἀνίκητος is unknown. We should expect the name of a comic poet.
[2] Hesychius, Etym. Magn. 94. 7 : ἄμφωτις CE.
[3] τοὺς before ἀμέλγοντας deleted by Kaibel.
[4] Schweighäuser: ἐξεμύστισε CE. So below.
[5] ὑφ' ἕν Charitonides: ἐφ' ἕν CE.

---

[a] i.e. hollow at top and bottom ; against Aristarchus.
[b] i.e. being hollow top and bottom, it could be turned upside down, and still have the same shape and use.
[c] His etymology is a pun ; hyperphialon is related to Lat. superbus, but here it means a super-phialè.

he means nothing else than that it was doubly-convex.[a] " Silenus, too, says that a "double" cup was one that had no handles. Others declare that the preposition *amphi* (on both sides) is used for *peri* (round about) so as to be drunk from on both sides, or convenient for drinking in any way.[b] But Parthenius says the name *amphikypellon* arises from the handles being formed in a convex shape; for convexity is a curving round. Anicetus says that the *kypellon* is a shallow cup (*phialê*), whereas the *amphikypellon* is *hyperphialon*, that is, proud [c] and beautiful. To be sure, one may understand by *aleison* whatever is ornamental in its design,[d] being a departure from utter smoothness (*leiotês*). Peisander says [e] that Heracles gave an *aleison* to Telamon as a prize of valour in the expedition against Ilios.

Note that there is a cup called Amaltheia's Horn [f] and The Year.

Amphoxis is a wooden cup which Philitas says [g] is used by rustics, who do their milking into it and so drink.

Amystis. This, to be sure, is the name given to a sort of drinking which is to be accomplished without taking breath or closing the mouth. But the name is also given to those cups which may be drunk out with dexterity. And the verb used for this is *examystizein*, which means drinking in one breath, as the comic poet Plato shows [h]: " He broke open an

---

[d] Probably referring to external ornaments in relief.

[e] Not in *Frag. ep.*

[f] Horn of Plenty; Roscher, *Lexikon Myth. s.v.* Amaltheia. For " The year" *cf.* Athen. 198 a (vol. ii. p. 396).

[g] Frag. 35 Bach: *cf.* ανφοξυν, *Jh. öst. Inst.* iii., 1900, 133.

[h] Kock i. 654.

49

λύσας διαρκῆ[1] στάμνον εὐώδους ποτοῦ
ἵησιν εὐθὺς κύλικος εἰς κοῖλον κύτος·
c ἔπειτ’ ἄκρατον κοὐ τεταργανωμένον[b]
ἔπινε κἀξημύστισεν.[a]

ἔπινον δὲ τὴν ἄμυστιν μετὰ μέλους, μεμετρημένου
πρὸς ὠκύτητα χρόνου. ὡς Ἀμειψίας·

αὔλει μοι μέλος·
σὺ δ’ ᾆδε πρὸς τήνδ’, ἐκπίομαι δ’ ἐγὼ τέως.
αὔλει σύ, καὶ σὺ[2] τὴν ἄμυστιν λάμβανε.
Β. οὐ χρὴ πόλλ’ ἔχειν θνητὸν ἄνθρωπον,
ἀλλ’ ἐρᾶν καὶ κατεσθίειν· σὺ δὲ κάρτα φείδῃ.

ΑΝΤΙΓΟΝΙΣ ἔκπωμα ἀπὸ τοῦ βασιλέως Ἀντιγόνου,
ὡς ἀπὸ Σελεύκου ΣΕΛΕΥΚΙΣ καὶ ἀπὸ Προυσίου[3]
ΠΡΟΥΣΙΑΣ.[4]

f ΑΝΑΦΑΙΑ ἡ θερμοποτὶς παρὰ Κρησίν.

ΑΡΥΒΑΛΛΟΣ ποτήριον κάτωθεν εὐρύτερον, ἄνω δὲ
συνηγμένον, ὡς τὰ συσπαστὰ βαλάντια, ἃ καὶ αὐτὰ
διὰ τὴν ὁμοιότητα ἀρυβάλλους τινὲς καλοῦσιν.
Ἀριστοφάνης Ἱππεῦσι·

κατασπένδειν κατὰ τῆς κεφαλῆς ἀρυβάλλῳ
ἀμβροσίαν.

οὐ πόρρω δέ ἐστι τοῦ ἀρυστίχου ὁ ἀρύβαλλος, ἀπὸ

---

[1] Jacobs: δὲ ἀργὴν CE.
[2] σὺ added by Jacobs.   [3] C: προυσεου E.
[4] Schweighäuser (cf. 475 f): προυσίς CE.

---

[a] Without waiting to mingle it with water.
[b] The participle refers to wine that has spoiled or turned to vinegar by long standing.
[c] Kock i. 676.

ample jar of fragrant liquor and straightway tossed [a]
it into the hollow inside of the cup ; then, when it
was all unmixed and unspoiled [b] he began to drink,
and quaffed it at a single draught." And they used
to drink this " breathless " cup to the accompaniment
of music, measured at a tempo that conduced to
speed. So Ameipsias [c] : " A. Play me a tune on
the pipes ; (to another girl) and you, sing to her music,
and I will drink out a cup the while. Play now, you,
and do you (to a companion) take the ' breathless '
cup. B. (singing) Mortal man needs not much [d]
but to love and eat heartily ; but you are much too
sparing."

Antigonis is a cup named after King Antigonus, just
as the *seleukis* [e] was named after Seleucus, and the
prusias after Prusias.

Anaphaia is the name of the cup used for hot
drinks among the Cretans.

Aryballos is a cup that is wider at bottom, but
contracted at the top, like those purses which can be
drawn together (at the top), and which some persons
actually call *aryballi* on account of their likeness in
shape. Aristophanes in *The Knights* [f] : " To pour
over the head an *aryballos* of ambrosia." The
aryballos is not much different from the *arystichos*,[g]

[d] " Man wants but little here below." But Kaibel thought
that the verb depending on χρή has been lost, and that the
sense was " Be not sparing when you have much." The
verses of the singer are in Aeolic rhythm.

[e] Below, 488 e (p. 172), 497 f (p. 220).

[f] vs. 1094. It is clear from this and other examples to
come that Athenaeus uses the word ποτήριον, not merely in
the special sense of cup for drinking, but in the general sense
of pottery, vessels of any kind. " Pottery " in English has
much the same history.

[g] Athen. 424 c (vol. iv. p. 420).

τοῦ ἀρύτειν καὶ βάλλειν. λέγουσι δὲ καὶ πρόχουν ἄρυστιν. Σοφοκλῆς·

> κακὴ¹ κακῶς σὺ πρὸς θεῶν ὀλουμένη,
> 784 ἢ τὰς ἀρύστεις ὧδ' ἔχουσ' ἐκώμασας.

ἐστὶ δὲ καὶ πόλις² Ἰώνων Ἄρυστις.

ΑΡΓΥΡΙΣ εἶδος ποτηρίου, οὐ μόνον ἐξ ἀργύρου. Ἀναξίλας·

> καὶ πίνειν ἐξ ἀργυρίδων χρυσῶν.

ΒΑΤΙΑΚΙΟΝ, λαβρώνιος, τραγέλαφος, πρίστις, ποτηρίων ὀνόματα. Περσικὴ δὲ φιάλη ἡ βατιάκη. Ἀλεξάνδρου δὲ τοῦ βασιλέως ἐν ταῖς Ἐπιστολαῖς ταῖς πρὸς τοὺς ἐν τῇ Ἀσίᾳ σατράπας φέρεταί τις ἐπιστολὴ ἐν ᾗ ταῦτα γέγραπται· " βατιάκαι ἀργυραῖ κατάχρυσοι τρεῖς. κόνδυα ἀργυρᾶ ρος'· τούτων b ἐπίχρυσα λγ'. τισιγίτης ἀργυροῦς εἷς. μύστροι ἀργυροῖ κατάχρυσοι λβ'. λαγυνοθήκη³ ἀργυρᾶ μία. οἰνοφόρον βαρβαρικὸν ἀργυροῦν ποικίλον ἕν. ἄλλα ποτήρια παντοδαπὰ μικρὰ κθ', ῥυτὰ⁴ καὶ βατιάκαι Λυκιουργεῖς⁵ ἐπίχρυσοι καὶ θυμιατήρια καὶ τρύβλια."

ΒΗΣΣΑ⁶ ποτήριον παρ' Ἀλεξανδρεῦσι πλατύτερον ἐκ τῶν κάτω μερῶν, ἐστενωμένον ἄνωθεν.

---

¹ κακὴ added by Meineke. ² πόσις "drink" Kaibel.
³ Kaibel: λαχανοθήκη CE.
⁴ ἄλλα ποτήρια μικρά repeated before ῥυτά deleted by Wilamowitz. ⁵ Schweighäuser: λυκοεργοὶ C.
⁶ βῆσσα CE: βῆσα Eustath. 1405. 15, βησίον Hesych.

ᵃ T.G.F.² 296.

its name being derived from *arytein* (draw) and *ballein* (pour). They also speak of a pitcher as *arystis*. Sophocles [a] : " Miserable woman, miserably shall you perish at the hands of the gods for revelling in such a condition with the pitchers." There is also a city [b] in Ionia named Arystis.

Argyris is a kind of cup, not always made of silver (*argyros*). Anaxilas [c] : " And to drink from golden *argyrides*."

Batiakion, *labronios*, *tragelaphos*, and *pristis* are names of cups.[d] The *batiakê* is a Persian saucer. In the collection of *Letters* of King Alexander [e] addressed to the satraps in Asia there is contained a letter in which the following is written : " Three silver *batiakai*, gilded. Silver *kondya* 176 ; of these thirty-three are gilded. One silver *tisigitês*. Silver spoons,[f] gilded, thirty-two. One silver flask-castor. One ornamented [g] silver wine-container of native manufacture. Other small cups of every variety, twenty-nine ; drinking-horns, gilded *batiakai* made in Lycia, censers, and bowls."

Bêssa, name of a cup among the Alexandrians ; [h] it is broader at the lower parts, narrowed above.

[b] See critical note 2; Ἄρυστις may be due to some confusion with Ἀρουσία or Ἀριουσία, both famous for wine.
[c] Kock ii. 275.
[d] See 480 a, 484 e, 496 b, 497 f. The *batiakion* or *batiakê* is often mentioned in inscriptions from Delos.
[e] Not all written by him ; the quotation is from an inventory reported by a provincial governor to him ; Athen. 393 c (vol. iv. p. 278). [f] Athen. 126 e (vol. ii. p. 284).
[g] Probably in relief, *cf*. above, 783 c (p. 48). Since the word for " wine-container " (οἰνοφόρον) is the only Greek word in the list, this entire item may be a definition of the *tisigites* which has become dislocated.
[h] *Cf*. the name Besas, 497 d.

ΒΑΥΚΑΛΙΣ. ἐν Ἀλεξανδρείᾳ καὶ αὕτη, ὡς Σώ-
πατρος ὁ παρῳδός·

> βαυκαλὶς ἡ τετρακότυλος.[1]

καὶ πάλιν·

> νᾶμα μελισσῶν ἡδὺ μὲν ὄρθρου
> καταβαυκαλίσαι τοῖς ὑπὸ πολλῆς
> κραιπαλοβόσκου δίψης κατόχοις.

c κατασκευάζουσι δέ, φησίν, οἱ ἐν Ἀλεξανδρείᾳ τὴν
ὕαλον μεταρρυθμίζοντες πολλαῖς καὶ ποικίλαις[2]
ἰδέαις ποτηρίων, παντὸς τοῦ πανταχόθεν κατα-
κομιζομένου κεράμου τὴν ἰδέαν μιμούμενοι.
Λύσιππον τὸν ἀνδριαντοποιὸν φασι Κασάνδρῳ
χαριζόμενον, ὅτε συνῴκισε τὴν Κασάνδρειαν, φιλο-
δοξοῦντι καὶ βουλομένῳ ἴδιόν τινα εὑρέσθαι κέραμον διὰ τὸ πολὺν ἐξάγεσθαι τὸν Μενδαῖον οἶνον
ἐκ τῆς πόλεως, φιλοτιμηθῆναι καὶ πολλὰ καὶ παντοδαπὰ γένη παραθέμενον κεραμίων ἐξ ἑκάστου
ἀποπλασάμενον ἴδιον[3] ποιῆσαι πλάσμα.

d ΒΙΚΟΣ. Ξενοφῶν Ἀναβάσεως πρώτῳ· “ Κῦρος
ἔπεμπε βίκους οἴνου ἡμιδεεῖς.” ἐστὶ δὲ φιαλῶδες
ποτήριον κατὰ τὸν Παριανὸν Πολυδεύκην.

ΒΟΜΒΥΛΙΟΣ, θηρίκλειον Ῥοδιακόν, οὗ περὶ τῆς
ἰδέας Σωκράτης φησίν· “οἱ μὲν ἐκ φιάλης πίνοντες
ὅσον θέλουσι τάχιστ᾽ ἀπαλλαγήσονται, οἱ δ᾽ ἐκ

---

[1] τετρακότυλος Meineke: τετράκυκλος CE.
[2] πολλαῖς καὶ ποικίλαις Nauck: πολλάκις πολλαῖς CE.
[3] ἴδια superscr. ον CE.

Baukalis. This vessel also is so named in Alexandria, as Sopater the parodist says [a] : " A *baukalis* is the cup containing four half-pints "; and again [b] : " Pleasant it is, for those in the grip of a mighty thirst that is fed by the morning-headache, to drink down (*katabaukalisai*) at dawn the flood that gushes from the bees." Athenaeus further says that the men of Alexandria make glass, working it into many varied shapes of cups, and copying the shape of every kind of pottery that is imported among them from everywhere. They say that in order to gratify Cassander at the time when he founded the metropolis of Cassandreia, he being fond of glory and desirous of appropriating to himself a special kind of vessel because Mendaean wine was exported from his city in large quantities, the sculptor Lysippus exerted his best efforts and, after comparing many pieces of earthenware of every description, copied something from each and so invented a special model.

Bikos. Xenophon in the first book of his *Anabasis* [c] : " Cyrus used to send half-filled jars of wine." But according to Polydeuces of Parium the *bikos* is a cup shaped like a *phialê.*

Bombylios, a Rhodian cup made by Thericles,[d] concerning the shape of which Socrates [e] says : " Those who drink all they want from a *phialê* will quit soonest, whereas those who drink from a *bomby-*

---

[a] Kaibel 197. [b] *Ibid.*

[c] Chap. 9. 25 ; βῖκος is probably Semitic.

[d] So Luc. *Lexiph.* 7 ; see below, 470 f (p. 76).

[e] The philosopher, in Antisthenes' *Protrepticus* ; *cf.* Pollux x. 68 ; so Heitz.

βομβυλιοῦ κατὰ μικρὸν στάζοντος[1] . . ." ἐστὶ δὲ καὶ ζῷόν τι.

ΒΡΟΜΙΑΔΕΣ, ἔκπωμα ὅμοιον τοῖς μακροτέροις τῶν σκύφων.

ΓΡΑΜΜΑΤΙΚΟΝ ΕΚΠΩΜΑ τὸ γράμματα ἔχον ἐγκεχαραγμένα. Ἄλεξις·

τὴν ὄψιν εἴπω τοῦ ποτηρίου γέ σοι[2]
466 πρώτιστον. ἦν γὰρ στρογγύλον,[3] μικρὸν πάνυ,
e παλαιόν, ὦτα συντεθλασμένον σφόδρα,
ἔχον κύκλῳ τε γράμματ'. Β. ἆρά γ' ἔνδεκα
χρυσᾶ "Διὸς σωτῆρος"; Α. οὐκ ἄλλου μὲν οὖν.

τοιοῦτον εἴδομεν ποτήριον γραμματικὸν ἀνακείμενον ἐν Καπύῃ τῆς Καμπανίας τῇ Ἀρτέμιδι, ἀργυροῦν, ἐκ τῶν Ὁμηρικῶν ἐπῶν κατεσκευασμένον, καὶ ἐντετυπωμένα[4] ἔχον τὰ ἔπη χρυσοῖς γράμμασιν, ὡς τὸ Νέστορος ὄν. Ἀχαιὸς δ' ὁ τραγικὸς ἐν Ὀμφάλῃ καὶ αὐτὸς περὶ γραμματικοῦ ποτηρίου ποιεῖ τοὺς σατύρους τάδε λέγοντας·

f ὁ δὲ σκύφος με τοῦ θεοῦ καλεῖ πάλαι
τὸ γράμμα φαίνων,[5] δέλτ', ἰῶτα καὶ τρίτον
οὗ,[6] νῦ τό τ' ὗ[7] πάρεστι, κοὐκ ἀπουσίαν
ἐκ τοὐπέκεινα σὰν τό τ' οὗ κηρύσσετον.

ἐν τούτοις λείπει τὸ ὗ στοιχεῖον, ἐπεὶ πάντες οἱ ἀρχαῖοι τῷ[8] οὗ ἀπεχρῶντο[9] οὐ μόνον ἐφ' ἧς νῦν

---

[1] Koppiers, cf. Hesych. s.v. βομβυλιός: στάζοντες CE.
[2] Schweighäuser: σου CE.
[3] At this word the text in A is continued and Casaubon's original pagination is resumed. See p. 34, crit. note 4.
[4] Musurus: ἐντετυπωμένον A.
[5] Toup: φαῖνον A.
[6] Porson: ὦ A.
[7] τό τ' ὗ Toup: του ὗ A.
[8] τῷ CE: τὸ A.
[9] προσεχρῶντο C.

56

lios, which drips little by little [a] . . ." The *bombylios* is also a kind of animal.[b]

Bromiades, a drinking-cup similar to the larger sorts of bowl.

A *Lettered* cup is that which has letters inscribed on it. Alexis [c] : " a. Let me tell you first of all the shape of the cup. It was round, very small, old, its handles terribly chipped, and it had letters all about it. b. There were eleven, weren't there, in gold, dedicating it to *Saviour Zeus* ? a. To no other, be sure." A lettered cup of that sort we have seen, dedicated to Diana in Capua, in Campania ; it was made of silver according to the pattern described in the Homeric poems, and had the verses stamped on it in letters of gold, and was said to be the cup which belonged to Nestor.[d] The tragic poet Achaeus, in *Omphalê,* also mentions a lettered cup and represents the satyrs saying this about it [e] : " The cup of the god has long been inviting me, showing plainly its inscription— *d, i,* and third *o ; n* and *y* are also there ; and after that *san* (*s*) and *o* (= *ou*) proclaim their presence." In this last syllable the letter *u* is wanting, because all the ancients not only used [f] the letter *o* with the value

---

[a] Whence the name Βομβυλιός, " Gurgler " ; Athen. 262 b (vol. iii. p. 178).

[b] A gnat or mosquito according to Hesychius ; but in Aristoph. *Vesp.* 107 it is the bumble-bee ; also the cocoon of a silkworm.

[c] Kock ii. 397 ; *cf.* below, 481 f (p. 136), and Aristoph. fr. 623 (Kock i. 547) γίγνωσκε τὸν ἄλεισόν τε καὶ τὰ γράμματα.

[d] Below, 489 c (p. 176), where the text is quite different.

[e] *T.G.F.*² 754, Athen. 498 d. On the names (*ou, ei*) and the sounds of Greek *o* and ε see 453 d (vol. iv. p. 555 note *h*); the inscription read ΔΙΟΝΤϹΟ.

[f] The word almost means " misused."

467 τάττεται δυνάμεως, ἀλλὰ καὶ ὅτε τὴν δίφθογγον
διασημαίνει διὰ τοῦ οὗ μόνου γράφουσι. παραπλησίως δὲ καὶ τὸ εῖ γράφουσιν καὶ ὅταν[1] καθ'
αὑτὸ μόνον ἐκφωνῆται καὶ ὅταν συζευγνυμένου
τοῦ ἰῶτα. κἂν τοῖς προκειμένοις οὖν οἱ σάτυροι
τοῦ Διονύσου τὴν τελευταίαν συλλαβὴν διὰ τοῦ οὗ[2]
μόνου ὡς βραχέος ἐγκεχαραγμένου ἐδήλωσαν ὅτι
συννυπακούεσθαι δεῖ καὶ τὸ ὔ, ἵν' ᾖ Διονύσου. τὸ
δὲ σὰν ἀντὶ τοῦ σίγμα Δωρικῶς εἰρήκασιν. οἱ
γὰρ μουσικοί, καθάπερ πολλάκις Ἀριστόξενός
φησι, τὸ σίγμα λέγειν παρῃτοῦντο διὰ τὸ σκληρό-
b στομον εἶναι καὶ ἀνεπιτήδειον αὐλῷ· τὸ δὲ ρ̄[3] διὰ
τὸ εὔκολον πολλάκις[4] παραλαμβάνουσι. καὶ τοὺς
ἵππους τοὺς τὸ C̄ ἐγκεχαραγμένον ἔχοντας σαμ-
φόρας καλοῦσιν. Ἀριστοφάνης Νεφέλαις· .

> οὔτ' αὐτὸς οὔθ' ὁ ζύγιος οὔθ' ὁ σαμφόρας.

καὶ Πίνδαρος δέ φησι·

> πρὶν μὲν ἧρπε σχοινοτένειά τ' ἀοιδὰ
> καὶ τὸ σὰν κίβδηλον ἀπὸ στομάτων.

μνημονεύει δὲ τοῦ γραμματικοῦ ἐκπώματος ὡς
οὕτως καλουμένου Εὔβουλος ἐν Νεοττίδι οὕτως·

c > μισῶ κάκιστον γραμματικὸν ἔκπωμ' ἀεί.
> ἀτὰρ ὡς ὅμοιον οὑμὸς υἱὸς ᾤχετο

---

[1] καὶ ὅταν Kaibel: ὅταν καὶ A.
[2] Kaibel: ō A.
[3] ρ̄ AC: ρ̄ω E, Kaibel.
[4] εὔκολον πολλάκις A: εὔκολον πολλοὶ C; the latter may be
right, εὔκολπον referring to the rolling or unfolding of r̄ on
the tip of the tongue (Dionys. *De comp. verb.* 79).

---

[a] *i.e.* ε represented *e* and *ei*.
[b] The name, as usual in such cases, was in the genitive.

now attached to it, but even when it denotes the diphthong (*ou*) they wrote *o* simply. In similar fashion, also, they wrote the letter *e* both when it was pronounced by itself alone and when *i* was combined with it.[a] And so in the lines above quoted the satyrs have made it plain that the final syllable of the word *Dionysou*,[b] since only the *o* was incised upon it, as though it were a short syllable, must have the *u* understood therein. As for the letter *san*, they constantly use that Doric name instead of *sigma*. Musicians, indeed, as Aristoxenus often says, advised against the use of *s* because it is harsh-sounding[c] and unfitted to the flute ; but they often adopt the sound *r* because of its nimble quality.[d] Horses which had the letter *san* branded on them were called " *san*-bearers." Aristophanes in *The Clouds*[e] : "Neither yourself nor your cart-horse nor your *san*-bearer (racer)." Pindar says[f] : "Erstwhile there came the long-drawn-out lay, and *san* (*s*), which has a false ring on the lips of men." The lettered drinking-cup is mentioned under this name by Eubulus in *The Chick* thus[g] : " A. I've always hated worst of all a lettered cup. And yet how like this one is the

---

[c] See Dionys. Hal. *De comp. verb.*, Roberts p. 148, Athen. 455 c (vol. iv. p. 565 note *d*).

[d] It was pronounced "trippingly on the tongue." Dionysius, *op. cit.* 79. As for sigma, see Roberts, p. 147 : " *s* is [a] . . . disagreeable letter, positively offensive when used to excess." See crit. note 4.   [e] vs. 122.

[f] *P.L.G.*⁴ frag. 79 ; see Athen. 455 c (vol. iv. p. 564) ; Sandys, *Pindar* (L.C.L.) 559 ; Schroeder³ 299, 346. The meaning : Along with the new dithyrambic song there came also an excess of sibilant sounds.

[g] Kock ii. 188 ; the title is a woman's name.

ἔχων φιάλιον τῷδε. Β. πολλὰ γίνεται
ὅμοια.

ΓΥΑΛΑΣ.[1] Φιλίτας ἐν Ἀτάκτοις Μεγαρέας οὕτω
φησὶ καλεῖν τὰ ποτήρια, γυάλας. Παρθένιος δ'
ὁ τοῦ Διονυσίου ἐν α' περὶ τῶν παρὰ τοῖς ἱστορικοῖς Λέξεων ζητουμένων φησί· '' γυάλας ποτηρίου εἶδος, ὡς Μαρσύας γράφει ὁ ἱερεὺς τοῦ
Ἡρακλέους οὕτως· ' ὅταν εἰσίῃ ὁ βασιλεὺς εἰς τὴν
πόλιν, συναντᾶν[2] οἴνου πλήρη γυάλαν[3] ἔχοντά τινα,
τὸν δὲ λαβόντα σπένδειν.' ''

d   ΔΕΙΝΟΣ. Ὅτι καὶ τοῦτο ποτηρίου ὄνομα[4] Διονύσιος ὁ Σινωπεὺς ἐν Σωζούσῃ καταλέγων ὀνόματα ποτηρίων μνημονεύει καὶ τούτου λέγων
οὕτως·

ὅσα δ' ἐστὶν εἴδη Θηρικλείων τῶν καλῶν,
γύναι,[5] δικότυλοι, τρικότυλοι, δεῖνος μέγας
χωρῶν μετρητήν, κυμβίον, σκύφοι, ῥυτά.
Β. ποτήρι' ἡ γραῦς, ἄλλο δ' οὐδὲ ἓν βλέπει.

Κλεάνθης δ' ὁ φιλόσοφος ἐν τῷ περὶ Μεταλήψεως
e ἀπὸ τῶν κατασκευασάντων φησὶν ὀνομασθῆναι τήν
τε Θηρίκλειον κύλικα καὶ τὴν Δεινιάδα. Σέλευκος
δ' εἰπὼν ἐκπώματος εἶναι γένος τὸν δεῖνον παρατίθεται Στράττιδος ἐκ Μηδείας·

οἶσθ' ᾧ προσέοικεν, ὦ Κρέων, τὸ βρέγμα σου;
ἐγᾦδα· δείνῳ περὶ κάτω τετραμμένῳ.[6]

---

[1] Schweighäuser: γύαλα A, γνάλα CE, γυλλάς Hesych.
[2] ὑπαντᾶν Kaibel.   [3] γυάλοις C.
[4] ὅτι . . . ὄνομα deleted by Dindorf.
[5] κοτύλαι Meineke.
[6] περικατω τετραμμεινω A.

little *phialê* which my son took with him when he disappeared. B. But a lot of things look alike."

Gyalas. Philitas in *Irregular Words*[a] says that the Megarians give this term to cups, *gyalai*. But Parthenius, the disciple of Dionysius, in the first book *On Words found in the Historians*, says : " The *gyalas* is a kind of cup, as Marsyas, the priest of Heracles, writes[b] : ' Whenever the king[c] enters the capital, he is met by someone with a *gyalas* full of wine ; taking it, he pours a libation (from it).' "

Deinos. This also is the name of a cup. Dionysius of Sinope, when giving a list of names for cups in *The Woman who Saved*, mentions this also, and says[d] : " A. And every sort of lovely Thericleian vessels, my lady ; double cups,[e] triple cups, a large *deinos* holding ten gallons, a little sauce-boat, bowls, and drinking-horns. B. The old woman has an eye for cups, but for nothing else whatsoever." Now the philosopher Cleanthes, in his book *On Substitution of Terms*, says that the Thericleian cylix and the Deinias were named from their respective makers.[f] Seleucus, after saying that the *deinos* is a kind of cup, quotes from the *Medea* of Strattis[g] : " Do you know, Creon, what your head looks like ? I know myself ; a *deinos* turned upside down." And Archedicus, in *The*

[a] A glossary of Alexandrian and other terms ; Frag. 41 Bach.
[b] *Scrip. Alex. Magn.* 45, J. 2 B 741.
[c] Of Macedonia.
[d] Kock ii. 427. Stobaeus 125. 8 gives the title as Σώτειρα, which would point to a goddess, *e.g.* Demeter, Aristoph. *Ran.* 378.
[e] The " cup " as a measure contained about a half-pint.
[f] But see below, 471 b (end).   [g] Kock i. 720.

Ἀρχέδικος δ' ἐν Διαμαρτάνοντι παράγων οἰκέτην τινὰ περὶ ἑταιρίδων διαλεγόμενόν φησι·

Νικοστράτην τιν' ἤγαγον πρῴην σφόδρα
γρυπήν, Σκοτοδίνην[1] ἐπικαλουμένην ὅτι
f δεινόν ποτ' ἦρεν ἀργυροῦν ἐν τῷ σκότῳ.
Β. δεινὸν καὶ δεινόν,[2] ὦ θεοί.

ἐστὶ καὶ γένος ὀρχήσεως, ὡς Ἀπολλοφάνης ἐν Δαλίδι παρίστησιν·

οὑτοσὶ δεῖνος τι δεινὸς[3] καὶ καλαθίσκος οὑτοσί.

Τελέσιλλα[4] δὲ ἡ Ἀργεία καὶ τὴν ἅλω καλεῖ δῖνον.[5] Κυρηναῖοι[6] δὲ τὸν ποδονιπτῆρα δεῖνον ὀνομάζουσιν, ὡς Φιλίτας φησὶν ἐν Ἀτάκτοις.[7]

468 ΔΕΠΑΣΤΡΟΝ. Σιληνὸς καὶ Κλείταρχος ἐν Γλώσσαις παρὰ Κλειτορίοις τὰ ποτήρια καλεῖσθαι. Ἀντίμαχος δ' ὁ Κολοφώνιος ἐν πέμπτῳ Θηβαΐδος φησί·

πάντα μάλ' ὅσσ' Ἄδρηστος ἐποιχομένους ἐκέλευσε
ῥεξέμεν· ἐν μὲν ὕδωρ, ἐν δ' ἀσκηθὲς μέλι χεῦαν[8]
ἀργυρέῳ κρητῆρι, περιφραδέως κερόωντες·
νώμησαν δὲ δέπαστρα θοῶς βασιλεῦσιν Ἀχαιῶν

---

[1] σκοτοδίνην CE superscr. ει: σκοτοιδεινην A.
[2] δεῖνον; (a question): δεινὸν C.
[3] τι δεινος A. Dindorf thought that these words, which are wrong as they stand, have dropped from their place after ὀρχήσεως (accenting δεῖνος).
[4] τελεσίλλα C.   [5] δῖνον superscr. ει CE: δεῖνον A.
[6] E: κυριναῖοι AC.   [7] Schweighäuser: ἀττικοῖς A.
[8] χεῦαν Schellenberg: χεῦε A.

Man who went Wrong, bringing on a slave who is
talking about some joy-girls, says[a] : " A. The other
night I brought a girl Nicostratê, with a terribly
hooked nose, who was nicknamed Vertigo (*Skotodinê* [b])
because she had once lifted a silver *deinos* in the
darkness (*skotos*). B. Vertigo converting a vase, ye
gods ! " [c] The *deinos* is also a kind of dance, as
Apollophanes shows in *The Bride* [d] : " This here is a
wonderful *deinos* (whirl), and the other here is the
basket-dance." [e] But the Argive poetess Telesilla
calls [f] even the threshing-floor a *dinos* (whirl). The
people of Cyrene give the name of *deinos* to the foot-
basin, as Philitas says in *Irregular Words*.[g]

Depastron. Silenus and Cleitarchus in their *Glos-
saries* say that this is a general term for drinking-
cups among the people of Cleitoria.[h] Antimachus of
Colophon says, in the fifth book of the *Thebaïs* [i] :
" Verily all things, whatsoever Adrastus bade them
do, they did with busy motion ; water they poured,
and virgin honey, into a silver mixing-bowl, mixing
them very carefully ; then they quickly dispensed the
cups (*depastra*) to the princes of the Achaeans as they

[a] Kock iii. 276.
[b] Literally " whirling in darkness." Aristoph. *Acharn.*
1219 makes the verbs σκοτοδινιῶ and εἱλιγγιῶ synonymous.
[c] The pun in δεῖνος (jar) and δεινός (skilful) hangs on
the accent, like δῆμος (people) and δημός (fat) in Aristoph.
Vesp. 40, 41. " Skilful with the skillet " is the nearest
English equivalent. δεῖνος is more properly spelt δῖνος,
which also means " whirl " or " eddy." Throughout this
passage the wits ring the changes on this meaning as well as
on that of δεινός " skilful."
[d] Kock i. 797 ; see critical note 3.
[e] This term recurs in a list of dances 630 a.
[f] *P.L.G.*[4] and Edmonds frag. 7.   [g] Frag. 42 Bach.
[h] In Arcadia.   [i] *Frag. ep.* 16.

ἐνσχερὼ[1] ἑστηῶσι,[2] καὶ ἐς λοιβὴν χέον εἶθαρ
χρυσείη προχόῳ.

b καὶ πάλιν·

ἄλλοι[3] δὲ κρητῆρα πανάργυρον ἠδὲ δέπαστρα
οἰσόντων χρύσεια, τά τ᾿ ἐν μεγάροισιν ἐμοῖσι
κεῖαται.

κἂν τοῖς ἑξῆς δέ φησι·

καὶ χρύσεια δέπαστρα καὶ ἀσκηθέος[4] κελέβειον
ἔμπλειον μέλιτος, τό ῥά οἱ προφερέστερον εἴη.

c ΔΑΚΤΥΛΩΤΟΝ ἔκπωμα οὕτως καλούμενον παρὰ
Ἴωνι ἐν Ἀγαμέμνονι·

οἴσῃ[5] δὲ δῶρον ἄξιον δραμήματος
ἔκπωμα δακτυλωτόν, ἄχραντον πυρί,
Πελίου μὲν[6] ἆθλον, Κάστορος δ᾿ ἔργον ποδῶν.

Ἐπιγένης[7] μὲν οὖν ἀκούει τὸ ἄμφωτον ποτήριον,
εἰς ὃ οἷόν τε τοὺς δακτύλους διείρειν ἑκατέρωθεν·
ἄλλοι δὲ τὸ ἐν κύκλῳ τύπους ἔχον οἷον δακτύλους,
ἢ τὸ ἔχον ἐξοχὰς οἷα τὰ Σιδώνια[8] ποτήρια, ἢ τὸ
λεῖον. ἄχραντον δὲ πυρὶ παρὰ τὸ Ὁμηρικὸν
d "ἄπυρον κατέθηκε λέβητα," τὸ[9] ἐπιτήδειον εἰς
ψυχρῶν ὑδάτων ὑποδοχὴν ἢ τὸ πρὸς ψυχροποσίαν
εὔθετον. τινὲς δὲ τὸ κέρας. περὶ δὲ τὴν Μολοσ-
σίδα οἱ βόες ὑπερφυῆ ἱστοροῦνται κέρατα ἔχειν·
περὶ ὧν τῆς κατασκευῆς Θεόπομπος ἱστορεῖ. ἐξ

---

[1] Jacobs: ἐνχερως A.   [2] Hermann: ἑστιῶσι A.
[3] Schellenberg: ἄλλος A.   [4] Kaibel: ἀσκηθὲς A.
[5] οἴσει Musurus: οἶσι A.   [6] μὲν Osann: μέγ᾿ ACE.
[7] ἐπιγένης E in corr.: ἐπιμένης AE (κατ᾿ ἐπιμένην C struct.
mut.).

stood in a row, and for the libation they straightway poured (wine) from a silver pitcher." And again [a]: " Let others, too, fetch the mixing bowl all of silver, and the golden cups (*depastra*) which are stored in my chambers." And in the succeeding verses Antimachus says [b] : " Golden cups, too, and a jar full of virgin honey, whatever may be his more precious sort."

Daktyloton is a cup called by this name in Ion's *Agamemnon* [c] : " And you shall win a gift worthy of your speed in running, a *dactylote* cup, unsullied by the fire, the prize that Pelias cherished, the work of art won by Castor's feet." Now Epigenes understands here the cup with two handles (*amphoton*), into which it is possible to insert the fingers (*dactyloi*) on both sides ; but others interpret as the cup which has figures like fingers all round it, or which has projections like those on the Sidonian cups ; others define as " smooth " (to the touch). The phrase " unsullied by fire " imitates the Homeric " he offered as prize a cauldron untouched by fire," [d] that is, one adapted to the receiving of cold water, or convenient for cold drinks. But some say it is the drinking-horn. Now in the Molossian country it is recorded that the cattle have extraordinarily large horns ; Theopompus gives an account of their con-

---

[a] *Frag. ep.* 15. [b] *Ibid.* 17.

[c] *T.G.F.*² 732. All the interpretations of the adjective δακτυλωτόν here given were rejected by Toup, who explained it as meaning a cup not turned on the potter's wheel, but moulded entirely by the hand and fingers. It may, however, refer to some pattern in *buccero* ware.

[d] *Il.* xxiii. 267, referring simply to a brand-new pot.

[8] Kaibel (Σιδόνια Musurus): σιδενια A.

[9] τὸ Schweighäuser: τὸν ACE.

ὧν πιθανὸν καὶ αὐτὸν[1] ἐσχηκέναι. πλησίον δὲ τῆς
Μολοσσίας ἡ Ἰωλκός, ἐν ᾗ ὁ ἐπὶ Πελίᾳ ἀγὼν
ἐτέθη. " βέλτιον δὲ λέγειν," φησὶν ὁ Δίδυμος ἐν
τῷ τοῦ δράματος ἐξηγητικῷ, " ὅτι παρήκουσεν
Ἴων[2] Ὁμήρου λέγοντος·

πέμπτῳ δ᾽ ἀμφίθετον φιάλην ἀπύρωτον ἔθηκεν.

e ἔδοξε γὰρ ἔκπωμα εἶναι· ἐστὶ δὲ χαλκίον[3] ἐκπέταλον
λεβητῶδες, ἐπιτηδείως ἔχον πρὸς ὑδάτων ψυχρῶν
ὑποδοχάς. δακτυλωτὸν δ᾽ οἷον κύκλῳ τὴν φιάλην
κοιλότητας[4] ἔχουσαν ἔνδοθεν οἷον δακτύλων, ἢ
ἐπεὶ[5] περιείληπται τοῖς τῶν πινόντων δακτύλοις.
τινὲς δὲ ἀπύρωτον φιάλην τὸ κέρας· οὐ γὰρ γίνεται
διὰ πυρός. λέγοι δ᾽ ἂν ἴσως κατὰ μεταφορὰν
f ἔκπωμα τὴν φιάλην." Φιλήμων δ᾽ ἐν τοῖς Ἀττικοῖς Ὀνόμασιν ἢ Γλώτταις προθεὶς καλπίς φησι·
" δακτυλωτὸν ἔκπωμα καὶ τὸ ἄμφωτον, εἰς ὃ
ἐστιν οἷόν τε τοὺς δακτύλους ἑκατέρωθεν διείρειν.[6]
οἱ δὲ τὸ ἔχον κύκλῳ δακτυλοειδεῖς τύπους τινάς."

ΕΛΕΦΑΣ. οὕτως ἐκαλεῖτο ποτήριόν τι, ὡς Δαμό-
ξενός φησιν ἐν Αὑτὸν πενθοῦντι·

εἰ δ᾽ οὐχ ἱκανόν σοι, τὸν ἐλέφανθ᾽ ἥκει φέρων
ὁ παῖς. Β. τί δ᾽ ἐστὶ τοῦτο, πρὸς θεῶν; Α. ῥυτὸν

---

[1] Ἄκαστον Wilamowitz. But in C the clause ἐξ ὧν . . .
ἐσχηκέναι follows ἐτέθη, thus expressly referring αὐτόν to
Pelias.　　　　　　　　　　　　　　[2] Ἴων C: om. AE.
[3] Meineke: χαλκεῖον ACE.
[4] Eustath. 1300. 7: κοιλότητα ACE.
[5] CE: ἐπὶ A.　　　　　　　　[6] Casaubon: διαιρεῖν A.

[a] *i.e.* of the drinking-horn from the horns of oxen; *F.H.G.*
i. 285, J. 2 B 597.

[b] Acastus founded the games in honour of his father Pelias,
whose home was in Iolcus, Thessaly, and whose cup was the
prize, *cf.* Paus. iii. 18. 16. Molossis was 100 miles to the east.

struction.*a* From these it is probable that Pelias*b* also had obtained his. For Iolcus is near the Molossian country, and there the games were established in honour of Pelias. " It is better to say," Didymus declares*c* in his *Commentary* on this play, " that Ion misunderstood Homer when he said*d* : ' And for the fifth (in the contest) he set up a two-handled *phialê* untouched by the fire.' For Ion thought that the *phialê* was a drinking-cup ; but in Homer it is a spreading*e* cauldron-like vessel of bronze, adapted for the receiving of cold water. And the *phialê* is called *daktyloton* because it has hollows round it on the inside, as though made by fingers, or because it is grasped by the fingers of the drinkers. Yet some understand ' *phialê* untouched by fire ' as meaning the drinking-horn ; for that is not made by firing. However, Ion might perhaps call the *phialê* a drinking-cup by a trope." Philemon in *Attic Words or Glosses*, under the heading *kalpis,f* says : " A *dactylote* cup also is the one with two handles, into which is it possible to insert the fingers on both sides. But others say that it is one which has certain figures all about it, shaped like fingers."

Elephas.g This was the name given to a kind of drinking-cup, as Damoxenus says in *Mourning his own Demise h* : " A. If that isn't enough for you, the slave has come with the elephant. B. In the gods' name, what is that ? A. A drinking-horn with two spouts,

c Schmidt p. 89.
d *Il.* xxiii. 270.
e For ἐκπέταλον, " outspread," *cf.* 485 e.
f *Kalpis* has a wide range of meaning ; in Pindar, *Ol.* vi. 40, it is a pitcher, at 553 d a box, here a cup.
g " Elephant."
h Kock iii. 348. See Index, *s.* Adaeus, and 532 e.

469 δίκρουνον ἡλίκον τι τρεῖς χωρεῖν[1] χοᾶς,
"Αλκωνος ἔργον. προὔπιεν δέ μοί ποτε
ἐν Κυψέλοις 'Αδαῖος.

μνημονεύει τοῦ ποτηρίου τούτου καὶ 'Επίνικος ἐν
'Υποβαλλομέναις, οὗ τὸ μαρτύριον παρέξομαι ἐν
τῷ περὶ τοῦ ῥυτοῦ λόγῳ.

ΕΦΗΒΟΣ. τὸ καλούμενον ποτήριον ἐμβασικοίταν
οὕτως φησὶ καλεῖσθαι Φιλήμων ὁ 'Αθηναῖος ἐν τῷ
περὶ 'Αττικῶν 'Ονομάτων ἢ Γλωσσῶν. Στέφανος
δ' ὁ κωμικὸς ἐν Φιλολάκωνί φησι·

b τούτῳ προέπιεν ὁ βασιλεὺς κώμην τινά.
Β. καινόν τι[2] τοῦτο γέγονε νῦν ποτήριον;
Σ. κώμη μὲν οὖν τίς ἐστι περὶ τὴν Θουρίαν.
Β. εἰς τὰς 'Ροδιακὰς[3] ὅλος ἀπηνέχθην ἐγὼ
καὶ τοὺς ἐφήβους, Σωσία, τοὺς δυσχερεῖς.

ΗΔΥΠΟΤΙΔΕΣ. ταύτας φησὶν ὁ Σάμιος Λυγκεὺς
'Ροδίους ἀντιδημιουργήσασθαι πρὸς τὰς 'Αθήνησι
Θηρικλείους, 'Αθηναίων μὲν αὐτὰς τοῖς πλουσίοις[4]
διὰ τὰ βάρη χαλκευσαμένων τὸν ῥυθμὸν τοῦτον,
'Ροδίων δὲ διὰ τὴν ἐλαφρότητα τῶν ποτηρίων καὶ
τοῖς πένησι τοῦ καλλωπισμοῦ τούτου μεταδιδόντων.
c μνημονεύει δ' αὐτῶν καὶ 'Επιγένης ἐν 'Ηρωίνῃ διὰ
τούτων·

---

[1] χωρεῖν Corais: χωροῦν ACE.
[2] νῦν after τι in A deleted by Jacobs.
[3] Adam: ὁ' οδιακος A.
[4] αὐτὰς τοῖς πλουσίοις Musurus: αὐτοῖς πλουσίως A.

---

a i.e. wives who foist a supposititious child upon their
husbands. Cf. Aristoph. Thesm. 407 γυνή τις ὑποβαλέσθαι
βούλεται | ἀποροῦσα παιδῶν, "a wife, despairing of having
children, wishes to substitute one."

big enough to hold six quarts, and made by Alcon. Adaeus once toasted me with it in Cypsela." This cup is mentioned also by Epinicus in *Child-foisting Wives*,[a] whose testimony I will cite in the account of the drinking-horn.[b]

Ephebus.[c] The cup called *embasicoetas* is also named *ephebus* according to Philemon of Athens in his work *On Attic Words or Glosses*. And the comic poet Stephanus says, in *The Pro-Laconian*[d] : " SOSIAS. To him the king pledged a village. B. Is that some new kind of cup that is now the fashion ? s. No, it is a real village in the territory of Thurii. B. I was entirely carried away for the moment, Sosias, into thinking of those Rhodian vessels and those *ephebi* which are so hard to manage."

Hedypotides.[e] Lynceus of Samos says that the Rhodians manufactured these in competition with the " Thericleians " made at Athens ; that whereas the Athenians could make this style only for the rich, on account of the weight of metal contained in them, the Rhodians enabled even the poor to share in this beautiful luxury, because of the lightness of the cups. They are mentioned by Epigenes in these lines from

[b] Below, 497 a, Kock iii. 331.

[c] *Adulescens*, 424 c. The term *embasicoetas* is used of a cinaedus, Petronius, *Sat.* 24 (L.C.L. 34) ; κοίτη was used sometimes to indicate any receptacle for food and drink (Pollux x. 91), hence the " cup " here mentioned is thought to have been a kind of dipper or ladle (Daremberg et Saglio *s. Arystichos*). Why it was called *ephebus* or why it was hard to manage is not known.

[d] Kock iii. 360. The title apparently refers to one of the Laconomaniacs satirized by Aristophanes, *Av.* 1281, *cf.* Plato, *Protag.* 342 B, Plut. *Phoc.* 10. The king mentioned is Pyrrhus (Kock).

[e] Lit. " sweet-draughts," or " draught-sweeteners."

ψυκτῆρα,[1] κύαθον, κυμβία, ῥυτὰ τέτταρα,
ἡδυποτίδας τρεῖς, ἠθμὸν ἀργυροῦν.

Σῆμος δ᾽ ἐν πέμπτῃ Δηλιάδος ἀνακεῖσθαί φησιν
ἐν Δήλῳ χρυσῆν ἡδυποτίδα Ἐχενίκης ἐπιχωρίας
γυναικός, ἧς μνημονεύει καὶ ἐν τῇ η΄. Κρατῖνος
δ᾽ ὁ νεώτερός φησι·

παρ᾽ Ἀρχεφῶντος ἡδυποτίδας[2] δώδεκα.

ΗΡΑΚΛΕΙΟΝ. Πείσανδρος ἐν δευτέρῳ Ἡρακλείας
d τὸ δέπας ἐν ᾧ διέπλευσεν ὁ Ἡρακλῆς τὸν Ὠκεανὸν εἶναι μέν φησιν Ἡλίου, λαβεῖν δ᾽ αὐτὸ παρ᾽
Ὠκεανοῦ[3] τὸν[4] Ἡρακλέα. μήποτε δὲ ἐπεὶ μεγάλοις ἔχαιρε ποτηρίοις ὁ ἥρως, διὰ τὸ μέγεθος
παίζοντες οἱ ποιηταὶ καὶ συγγραφεῖς πλεῖν αὐτὸν
ἐν ποτηρίῳ ἐμυθολόγησαν. Πανύασις δ᾽ ἐν πρώτῳ[5]
Ἡρακλείας παρὰ Νηρέως φησὶ τὴν τοῦ Ἡλίου
φιάλην κομίσασθαι τὸν Ἡρακλέα καὶ διαπλεῦσαι
εἰς Ἐρύθειαν. ὅτι δὲ εἷς ἦν ὁ Ἡρακλῆς τῶν
e πλεῖστον πινόντων προείπομεν. ὅτι δὲ καὶ ὁ
Ἥλιος ἐπὶ ποτηρίου διεκομίζετο ἐπὶ τὴν δύσιν
Στησίχορος μὲν οὕτως φησίν·

Ἀέλιος[6] δ᾽ Ὑπεριονίδας δέπας ἐσκατέβαινε
χρύσεον, ὄφρα δι᾽ Ὠκεανοῖο περάσας
ἀφίκοιθ᾽[7] ἱερᾶς ποτὶ βένθεα νυκτὸς ἐρεμνᾶς

---

[1] 502 e: ψυκτήρια A.
[2] ἡδυποτίδας or ἡδυποτίδες Musurus: ἡδυπότια A.
[3] Musurus: ὠκεανὸν A.   [4] τὸν added by Kaibel.
[5] ἐν τετάρτῳ Dübner.
[6] Schweighäuser: ἄλιος A, ἆμος Kaibel.
[7] Blomfield: ἀφίκηθ᾽ A.

---

[a] Kock ii. 417; below, 502 e.
[b] F.H.G. iv. 494. The official record of this gift is still
extant, Ditt. Syll.² 588. 7.

The Glorified Woman [a] : " A cooler, a ladle, sauce-boats, four drinking-horns, three draught-sweeteners, a silver strainer." Semus, in the fifth book of his *History of Delos*, says [b] that in Delos there is a votive offering of a gold draught-sweetener dedicated by a native woman named Echenicê; this he mentions again in the eighth book. And Cratinus the Younger says [c] : " From Archephon, a dozen draught-sweeteners."

Heracleion. Peisander, in the second book of his *Epic of Heracles*, says [d] that the cup in which Heracles traversed Oceanus belonged to the Sun, but that Heracles received it from Oceanus. Perhaps it was so called because the hero delighted in large cups, and on account of its size poets and writers in prose have invented in jest the story of his voyage in a cup (instead of a ship). [e] But Panyassis, in the first book of his *Epic of Heracles*, declares [f] that Heracles carried off the cup, which belonged to the Sun, from Nereus, and in it sailed across to Erytheia. That Heracles was one of those who drank great quantities we have stated already. [g] And that the Sun also was conveyed to the west in a cup is told by Stesichorus in the following [h] : " Now the Sun, begotten of Hyperion, was descending into his golden cup, that he might traverse Oceanus and come to the depths of dark and

[c] Kock ii. 293. On Archephon see Athen. vol. iii. p. 98.
[d] *Frag. ep.* 5.
[e] In the expedition against Geryonês. See Ps.-Apollodorus, *Bibl.* ii. 5. 10 (L.C.L. i. 210), and the Attic black-figured lekythos in Roscher, *Lexikon d. griech. u. röm. Mythologie*, i. 2204.
[f] *Frag. ep.* 7.
[g] *Cf.* the story in 441 a (vol. iv. p. 496). On his gluttony *cf.* 411 a.
[h] *P.L.G.*[4] and Edmonds fr. 8; above, 781 d (p. 36).

ποτὶ ματέρα κουριδίαν τ’ ἄλοχον πάιδάς[1] τε
    φίλους.

f ὁ δ’ ἐς ἄλσος ἔβα δάφναισι κατάσκιον
ποσὶν πάις[2] Διός.

καὶ Ἀντίμαχος δ’ οὑτωσὶ λέγει·

          τότε δὴ χρυσέῳ ἐν δέπαϊ
Ἥλιον πόμπευεν[3] ἀγακλυμένη Ἐρύθεια.

καὶ Αἰσχύλος ἐν Ἡλιάσιν·

ἔνθ’ ἐπὶ δυσμαῖς τεοῦ[4]
πατρὸς Ἡφαιστοτευχὲς
δέπας, ἐν τῷ διαβάλλει
πολὺν οἰδματόεντα περίδρομον πόρον συθείς,[5]
μελανίππου προφυγὼν
ἱερᾶς νυκτὸς ἀμολγόν.

A70 Μίμνερμος δὲ Ναννοῖ[6] ἐν εὐνῇ φησι χρυσῇ
κατεσκευασμένῃ πρὸς τὴν χρείαν ταύτην ὑπὸ
Ἡφαίστου τὸν Ἥλιον καθεύδοντα περαιοῦσθαι
πρὸς τὰς ἀνατολάς, αἰνισσόμενος τὸ κοῖλον τοῦ
ποτηρίου. λέγει δ’ οὕτως·

Ἥλιος μὲν γὰρ πόνον ἔλλαχεν[7] ἤματα πάντα,
οὐδέ ποτ’ ἄμπαυσις γίγνεται οὐδεμία
ἵπποισίν τε καὶ αὐτῷ, ἐπὴν ῥοδοδάκτυλος Ἠὼς
Ὠκεανὸν προλιποῦσ’ οὐρανὸν εἰσαναβῇ·
b τὸν μὲν γὰρ διὰ κῦμα φέρει πολυήρατος εὐνή,
κοίλη[8] Ἡφαίστου χερσὶν ἐληλαμένη
χρυσοῦ τιμήεντος, ὑπόπτερος,[9] ἄκρον ἐφ’ ὕδωρ
εὕδονθ’[10] ἁρπαλέως χώρου ἀφ’ Ἑσπερίδων
γαῖαν ἐς Αἰθιόπων, ἵνα δὴ θοὸν[11] ἅρμα καὶ ἵπποι

---

[1] Holsten : πάιδάς A.   [2] Blomfield : παῖς A.
[3] Schweighäuser : πόμπει A.   [4] τεοῦ Hermann : ισου A.
72

awful night, even to his mother and wedded wife and
beloved children. Meanwhile he, the son of Zeus,[a]
strode into the grove o'ershadowed with bay-trees."
Antimachus, too, has this to say [b] : " So then, in the
golden cup Erytheia of glorious fame was conducting
the Sun-god." And Aeschylus, in *Daughters of the
Sun* [c] : " There, at the place of thy Sire's setting,
was the cup wrought by Hephaestus, wherein he
crosses the mighty circling path of the billows as he
speeds forth, flying into the dead of sacred night,
driver of black steeds."

Mimnermus, in *Nanno,* says that it is in a couch of
gold constructed for this purpose by Hephaestus that
the Sun is conveyed, while he sleeps, toward the place
of his rising ; thus the poet hints at the hollow shape
of the cup. He says [d] : " Yea, even the Sun-god hath
received the lot of toil all his days, nor ever cometh
any surcease for his horses or for himself, when rosy-
fingered Dawn hath left Oceanus and mounted the
sky ; for a lovely winged hollow couch of precious gold,
made by the hands of Hephaestus, bears him lightly
across the billow, on the top of the wave, while he
sleeps ; it carries him from the land of the Hesperides
even to the country of the Aethiopians,[e] where his

[a] Heracles.   [b] *P.L.G.*[4], Edmonds, and Diehl frag. 4.
[c] *T.G.F.*[2] 23.   The sisters of Phaëthon deplore his rash-
ness (Hermann).
[d] *P.L.G.*[4] fr. 12, Diehl frag. 10, Edmonds frag. 8.
[e] *i.e.* from the West to the East ; we are not told how his
chariot gets back (see crit. note 11).

---

[5] περίδρομον . . συθείς M. Schmidt: φέρει δρόμου . . οὐθεις A.
[6] δὲ Ναννοῖ Meineke : δ' ἐναννοι A.
[7] πόνον ἔλλαχεν Hermann: ἔλαχεν πόνον A.
[8] κοιίλη Meineke: κοίλη ACE.   [9] Heyne: ὑπόπτερον A.
[10] Musurus: εὔδονθ' ὁθ' A.
[11] ἵνα δὴ θοὸν Meineke: ἵν' ἀληθοον A.

ἑστᾶσ' ὄφρ' Ἠὼς ἠριγένεια μόλη.
ἔνθ' ἐπεβήσεθ' ἑῶν[1] ὀχέων Ὑπερίονος υἱός.

Θεόλυτος δ' ἐν δευτέρῳ Ὥρων ἐπὶ λέβητός φησιν
c αὐτὸν διαπλεῦσαι, τοῦτο πρώτου εἰπόντος τοῦ τὴν
Τιτανομαχίαν ποιήσαντος. Φερεκύδης δ' ἐν τῇ
τρίτῃ τῶν Ἱστοριῶν προειπὼν περὶ τοῦ Ὠκεανοῦ
ἐπιφέρει· " ὁ δ' Ἡρακλῆς ἕλκεται ἐπ' αὐτὸν τὸ
τόξον ὡς βαλῶν,[2] καὶ ὁ Ἥλιος παύσασθαι κελεύει,
ὁ δὲ δείσας παύεται. Ἥλιος δὲ ἀντὶ τούτου
δίδωσιν αὐτῷ τὸ δέπας τὸ χρύσεον ὃ αὐτὸν ἐφόρει
σὺν ταῖς ἵπποις, ἐπὴν δύῃ, διὰ τοῦ Ὠκεανοῦ
τὴν νύκτα πρὸς ἑῴην ἵν'[3] ἀνίσχει ὁ ἥλιος. ἔπειτα
d πορεύεται Ἡρακλῆς ἐν τῷ δέπαι τούτῳ ἐς τὴν
Ἐρύθειαν. καὶ ὅτε δὲ ἦν ἐν τῷ πελάγει, Ὠκεανὸς
πειρώμενος αὐτοῦ κυμαίνει τὸ δέπας φανταζόμενος.
ὁ δὲ τοξεύειν αὐτὸν μέλλει, καὶ αὐτὸν δείσας
Ὠκεανὸς παύσασθαι κελεύει."[4]

ΗΘΑΝΙΟΝ. Ἑλλάνικος ἐν Αἰγυπτιακοῖς οὕτως
γράφει· " Αἰγυπτίων ἐν τοῖς οἴκοις κεῖται φιάλη
χαλκέη[5] καὶ κύαθος χάλκεος[5] καὶ ἠθάνιον χάλκεον."

ΗΜΙΤΟΜΟΣ ἔκπωμά τι παρ' Ἀττικοῖς ἀπὸ τοῦ
σχήματος οὕτως[6] ὀνομασθέν, φησὶν Πάμφιλος ἐν
Γλώσσαις.

e ΘΗΡΙΚΛΕΙΟΣ. ἡ κύλιξ αὕτη ἐγκάθηται περὶ τὰς
λαγόνας ἱκανῶς βαθυνομένη ὦτά τε ἔχει βραχέα
ὡς ἂν κύλιξ οὖσα. καὶ μήποτε Ἄλεξις ἐν Ἡσιόνῃ

[1] ἐπεβήσεθ' ἑῶν Schneidewin: ἐπέβη ἑτέρων A.
[2] Casaubon: βαλὸν A.
[3] ἑῴην ἵν' Kaibel: ἕω ἢ νῦν A.
[4] The reading in C is quite divergent: κυμαίνοντα τὸν
Ὠκεανόν, ὅτε εἰς Ἐρύθειαν διέπλει Ἡρακλῆς, μικροῦ κατετόξευσεν
Ἡρακλῆς, εἰ μὴ δείσας ἐπαύσατο.
[5] χαλκῇ and χαλκοῦς A.　　　　[6] οὕτως add. C.

swift chariot and steeds stand waiting until early-born Dawn shall come. Then the son of Hyperion mounts his car." But Theolytus, in the second book of his *Chronicles*, says [a] that the Sun voyages in a cauldron, the first to describe it thus being the poet who wrote *The Battle with the Titans*.[b] Pherecydes, in the third book of the *Histories*, speaks first of Oceanus and then proceeds [c]: "Now Heracles was drawing his bow against him with the intention of shooting him, when the Sun bade him stop, and he in fear desisted. In return for this the Sun gave him the golden cup which was wont to carry him, when he sets, with his horses at night over Oceanus to the eastern land where the Sun rises. Thereupon Heracles journeyed in this cup to Erytheia, and when he was on the high seas, Oceanus made trial of him by appearing in a vision and rocking the cup. Heracles was just on the point of shooting him when Oceanus in fear bade him stop."

Ethanion (strainer). Hellanicus in his *History of Egypt* writes as follows [d]: "In the houses of Egyptians are kept a bronze *phialê*, a bronze ladle, and a bronze strainer."

Hemitomos (half-cut [e]) is a kind of cup among the Athenians, so named from its shape, according to Pamphilus in his *Glossary*.

Therikleios. This is a cylix which is sunk in at the sides [f]; it is hollowed rather deeply, and has short handles like any cylix. And perhaps it is from a

[a] *F.H.G.* iv. 515.　　　　[b] *Frag. ep.* p. 312, Powell 9.
[c] *F.H.G.* i. 80, J. 1. 66.
[d] *F.H.G.* i. 66, J. 1. 121.
[e] The epithet is used of the half-moon, Moschus ii. 88.
[f] Apparently meaning with concave, not convex, sides. On Thericleian ware see Pfuhl, *Malerei* i. 46; above, 469 b (p. 68).

θηρικλείῳ ποιεῖ τὸν Ἡρακλέα πίνοντα, ὅταν οὑτωσὶ λέγῃ·

> γενόμενος δ' ἔννους μόλις
> ᾔτησε κύλικα[1] καὶ λαβὼν ἑξῆς πυκνὰς
> ἕλκει, καταντλεῖ, κατά τε τὴν παροιμίαν
> αἰεί ποτ' εὖ μὲν ἀσκός, εὖ δὲ θύλακος
> ἄνθρωπός[2] ἐστιν.

ὅτι δὲ κύλιξ ἐστὶν ἡ Θηρίκλειος σαφῶς παρίστησιν
f Θεόφραστος ἐν τῇ περὶ Φυτῶν Ἱστορίᾳ. διηγούμενος γὰρ περὶ τῆς τερμίνθου φησί· "τορνεύεσθαι
δὲ ἐξ αὐτῆς καὶ κύλικας Θηρικλείους, ὥστε μηδένα
ἂν[3] διαγνῶναι πρὸς τὰς κεραμέας." κατασκευάσαι
δὲ λέγεται τὴν κύλικα ταύτην Θηρικλῆς ὁ Κορίνθιος
κεραμεύς, ἀφ' οὗ καὶ τοὔνομα ἔσχε,[4] γεγονὼς τοῖς
χρόνοις κατὰ τὸν κωμικὸν Ἀριστοφάνη. μνημονεύει δὲ τῆς κύλικος Θεόπομπος μὲν ἐν Νεμέᾳ
οὕτως·

> ΣΠΙ. χώρει σὺ δεῦρο, Θηρικλέους πιστὸν τέκνον,
> γενναῖον εἶδος, ὄνομά σοι τί θώμεθα[5];
471 ἆρ' εἰ[6] κάτοπτρον φύσεος[7]; ἢν πλῆρες δοθῇς,
> οὐδέν ποτ' ἄλλο. δεῦρο δή, γεμίσω σ' ἐγώ.
> γραῦ Θεολύτη, γραῦ. ΘΕΟΛ. τί με καλεῖς σύ,
> φίλτατε[8];
> ΣΠΙ. ἵν'[9] ἀσπάσωμαι· δεῦρο παρ' ἐμέ, Θεολύτη,
> παρὰ τὸν νέον ξύνδουλον. οὑτωσὶ καλῶς.
> ΘΕΟΛ. Σπινθὴρ τάλας, πειρᾷς με. ΣΠΙ. ναί,[10]
> τοιοῦτό τι·

[1] CE: κύλην A. C gives this quotation just before Ἴσθμιον (472 e).
[2] Meineke: ἄνθρωπος ACE.   [3] ἂν added by Wimmer.
[4] ἔσχε CE: ἔχει A.   [5] τί θώμεθα Casaubon: τοθωμεθα A.
[6] ἆρ' εἰ Coraes: ἀρει A.   [7] Dindorf: φύσεως A.

76

Therikleios that Alexis, in *Hesionê*, represents Heracles as drinking, when he says *a* : " Recovering his senses at last, he demanded a cylix ; and when he had got it he pulled off and swilled down many draughts in quick succession; and so, as the proverb says, the fellow is ever at one time a very pretty wine-skin, at another a very pretty mealsack." *b* That the *Therikleios* is a cylix Theophrastus clearly shows in his *Inquiry into Plants*. In his account of the terebinth-tree he says *c* : " From it, too, Therikleian cylices can be turned on the lathe, such that no one could tell them from those made of clay." This cylix is said to have been made by Thericles of Corinth, a potter, from whom it got its name ; he lived about the same time as the comic poet Aristophanes. And Theopompus mentions the cylix thus in *Nemea d* : " SPINTHER : Come this way, trusty child of Thericles ; noble form, what name are we to give you? You're the mirror of a man's features, aren't you ? *e* Ay ! If you are full when offered, you are nothing else in the world. This way, then, I am going to fill you up. Theolytê ! old woman, I say, old woman ! THEOLYTÊ : Why do you call me, dearest one ? SPINTH. : I want to kiss you ; this way, Theolytê, into my arms, to the arms of your new companion in slavery. That's nice. THEOL. : Naughty Spinther, you're hurting me *f* ! SPINTH. : Yes, something like that. But I am

---

a Kock ii. 324.
b *i.e.* he is both thirsty and voracious; on ἀσκός see 552 f.
c v. 3. 2 (L.C.L. i. p. 432). *d* Kock i. 741.
e Thericleian ware must have been noted for its lustre.
f For the euphemistic πειρᾷς see Aristoph. *Eq.* 517, *Plut.* 1067.

---

8 Porson: φιλτάτη A. *9* Porson: τίν' A.
10 τάλας . . . ναί Adam: ταλα σπειραις μεναι A.

φιλοτησίαν δὲ τήνδε[1] σοι προπίομαι.[2]
δέξαι· πιοῦσα δ' ὁπόσον ἄν σοι θυμὸς ᾖ,
παράδος τὸ περιόν.[3]

b Κλεάνθης δ' ἐν τῷ περὶ Μεταλήψεως συγγράμματί
φησι· " τὰ τούτων[4] εὑρήματα καὶ ὅσα τοιαῦτα
εὐκατάληπτα[5] ἐστιν, οἷον Θηρίκλειος, Δεινιάς,[6]
'Ιφικρατίς[7]· ταῦτα γὰρ πρότερον συνιστορεῖν τοὺς
εὑρόντας, φαίνεται δ' ἔτι καὶ νῦν· εἰ δὲ μὴ ποιεῖ
τοῦτο, μεταβεβληκὸς ἂν εἴη μικρὸν τοὔνομα. ἀλλά,
καθάπερ εἴρηται, οὐκ ἔστιν πιστεῦσαι τῷ τυχόντι."
ἄλλοι δ' ἱστοροῦσι θηρίκλειον ὀνομασθῆναι τὸ
ποτήριον διὰ τὸ δορὰς θηρίων αὐτῷ ἐντετυπῶσθαι.

c Πάμφιλος δ' ὁ 'Αλεξανδρεὺς ἀπὸ τοῦ τὸν Διόνυσον
τοὺς θῆρας κλονεῖν σπένδοντα ταῖς κύλιξι ταύταις
κατ' αὐτῶν. μνημονεύει τοῦ ἐκπώματος καὶ 'Αντιφάνης ἐν 'Ομοίοις οὕτως·

ὡς δ' ἐδείπνησαν (συνάψαι βούλομαι γὰρ τἀν[8]
μέσῳ)
καὶ Διὸς σωτῆρος ἦλθε Θηρίκλειον ὄργανον,
τῆς τρυφερᾶς ἀπὸ Λέσβου σεμνοπόνου[9] σταγόνος
πλῆρες, ἀφρίζον, ἕκαστος δεξιτερᾷ δ' ἔλαβεν ...

καὶ Εὔβουλος ἐν μὲν Δόλωνι·

διένιψα δ' οὐδὲν σκεῦος οὐδεπώποτε·
d καθαρώτερον γὰρ τὸν κέραμον εἰργαζόμην
ἢ Θηρικλῆς τὰς κύλικας, ἡνίκ' ἦν νέος.

---

[1] τήνδε added by Meineke.   [2] Musurus: προσπίομαι A.
[3] τὸ περιόν Kock: τὸ πρῶτον A.
[4] Wilamowitz: τοίνυν A.
[5] εὐκατάληπτά Wilamowitz: ἔτι καὶ τὰ λοιπά A.
[6] δεινίας A.   [7] Leopardi: ἰφικράτης A.
[8] Koppiers: τὰ A.
[9] σεμνοπόνου AC: σεμνοπότου Casaubon, σεμνογόνου Kaibel.

78

going to pledge you this loving-cup. Take it ; and after you have drunk all that your heart desires, hand me what's left over." Now Cleanthes, in his treatise *On Substitution of Terms*, says.[a] : " The inventions of these men, and all of a similar character, have names easily understood, like *Therikleios, Deinias,*[a] *Iphi-kratis*[b] ; for such names at once indicated in earlier times their inventors, and make them plain even to this day ; if this is not so, the name must have been changed slightly. However, as has already been said, in such matters one is not to take the word of every casual person." But others record that the cup was named *therikleios* because it had the skins of wild animals (*theria*) figured on it. On the other hand, Pamphilus of Alexandria derives it from the circumstance that Dionysus drove away the wild beasts in confusion when he poured libations over them from these cylices. The cup is mentioned also by Antiphanes in *Just Alike*, in these words[c] : " When they had finished their dinner (for I want to cut short what they did in the interval), and there entered the therikleios, instrument of Zeus the Saviour, brimful and bubbling with the voluptuous drops from Lesbos made with reverent pains,[d] and each guest [in turn] had seized it with right hand. . . ." So Eubulus in *Dolon*[e] : " I have never yet washed a single dish ; for I could make the crockery cleaner than Thericles could make his cylices when I was a youngster."

[a] *Cf.* above, 467 d-e (p. 60).
[b] Name of a military boot, not a cup.
[c] Kock ii. 82, Athen. 642 a. In libations Zeus the Saviour was honoured first.
[d] See critical note 9.
[e] Kock ii. 175. The slave who speaks omits to tell how he cleaned the dishes—of course by licking them.

ἐν δὲ Κυβευταῖς·

ἄρτι μὲν μάλ' ἀνδρικὴν[1]
τῶν θηρικλείων ὑπεραφρίζουσαν σορόν,[2]
κωθωνόχειλον,[3] ψηφοπεριβομβήτριαν,
μέλαιναν, εὐκύκλωτον, ὀξυπύνδακα,[4]
στίλβουσαν, ἀνταυγοῦσαν, ἐκνενιμμένην,
κισσῷ κάρα βρύουσαν,[5] ἐπικαλούμενοι[6]
e   εἷλκον Διὸς σωτῆρος.

Ἀραρὼς δ' ἢ Εὔβουλος ἐν Καμπυλίωνι·

ὦ γαῖα κεραμί, τίς σε[7] Θηρικλῆς ποτε
ἔτευξε κοίλης λαγόνος εὐρύνας βάθος;
ἦ που κατειδὼς τὴν γυναικείαν φύσιν
ὡς οὐχὶ μικροῖς ἥδεται ποτηρίοις.

Ἄλεξις δ' ἐν Ἱππεῖ·

καὶ θηρίκλειός τις κύλιξ, στέφανον κύκλῳ
ἔχουσα[8] χρυσοῦν· οὐ γὰρ ἐπίτηκτόν[9] τινα.

καὶ ἐν Ἱππίσκῳ[10]·

μεστὴν ἀκράτου θηρίκλειον ἔσπασε
f   κοίλην ὑπερθύουσαν . . .

Τίμαιος δ' ἐν τῇ ὀγδόῃ καὶ εἰκοστῇ τῶν Ἱστοριῶν
θηρικλείαν καλεῖ τὴν κύλικα γράφων οὕτως·
"Πολύξενός τις τῶν ἐκ Ταυρομενίου μεθεστηκότων
ταχθεὶς ἐπὶ τὴν πρεσβείαν ἕτερά τε δῶρα παρὰ
τοῦ Νικοδήμου καὶ κύλικα θηρικλείαν[11] λαβὼν
ἐπανῆκεν." Ἀδαῖος δ' ἐν τοῖς περὶ Διαθέσεως τὸ
αὐτὸ ὑπολαμβάνει θηρίκλειον εἶναι καὶ καρχήσιον.

---

[1] μάλ' ἀνδρικὴν CE : μαλαν αν δρικην A.
[2] σορόν Capps : παρα ACE.
[3] Ahlwardt : -χειρον ACE.
[4] Schweighäuser : ὀξυπίνδακα ACE.

And in *The Dicers* [a] : "Only just now they were draining a big lusty vessel—a thericleian—bubbling over the brim, lipped like a Spartan flask, shaped like a buzzing ballot-box, dark, beautifully rounded, with pointed bottom, glistening, reflecting the rays of light, nicely washed, its head wreathed with teeming ivy-leaves; and as they swigged they named the draught in honour of Saviour Zeus." Again, Araros or Eubulus in *The Hunchback* [b] : "O potter's Earth, what Thericles, I wonder, hath fashioned thee and broadened the depth of thy hollow flanks? Verily it was one who knew well the nature of woman, that she delights not in little cups." Alexis in *The Horseman* [c] : "And a kind of thericleian cylix, with a wreath of gold about it; for it wasn't a gilded thing." Also in *The Scarf* [d] : "He drained a deep thericleian chock-full and foaming over with unmixed wine." But Timaeus, in the twenty-eighth book of his *Histories*, calls the cylix *thericleian*. He writes as follows [e] : "Polyxenus, one of those who had gone over from Tauromenium, was assigned to the embassy and returned with gifts from Nicodemus, including a thericleian cylix." Adaeus in his chapters *On the Use of Words* assumes that *therikleion* and *karchesion* are the same thing. But that they are

[a] Kock ii. 183. See critical note 2.
[b] Kock ii. 179. A bibulous woman invokes Mother Earth, then adds the epithet.
[c] Kock ii. 328; this and the two following quotations illustrate the varying inflexion of the adjective, either *therikleios* or *-kleiā*.
[d] *Ibid.* 299. [e] *F.H.G.* i. 226.

[5] Porson: καταβρύουσαν ACE. [6] A: ἐπικαλούμενος CE.
[7] Porson: κεραμῖτι· σὲ CE, κεραμιτιοσε A.
[8] Musurus: ἔχουσαν A.
[9] Porson: ἐπίκτητον A. [10] Casaubon: ηπακωι A.
[11] Schweighäuser: θηρίκλειον A.

472 ὅτι δὲ διαφέρει σαφῶς παρίστησι Καλλίξεινος ἐν
τοῖς περὶ Ἀλεξανδρείας φάσκων τινὰς ἔχοντας
θηρικλείους πομπεύειν, τοὺς δὲ καρχήσια. ὁποῖον
δ᾽ ἐστὶ τὸ καρχήσιον ἐν τοῖς ἑξῆς λεχθήσεται.
καλεῖται δέ τις καὶ θηρίκλειος κρατήρ, οὗ μνημονεύει Ἄλεξις ἐν Κύκνῳ·

> φαιδρὸς δὲ κρατὴρ θηρίκλειος ἐν μέσῳ
> ἕστηκε λευκοῦ νέκταρος παλαιγενοῦς
> πλήρης, ἀφρίζων· ὃν λαβὼν ἐγὼ κενὸν
> τρίψας, ποήσας λαμπρόν, ἀσφαλῆ βάσιν
> στήσας, συνάψας καρπίμοις κισσοῦ κλάδοις
> b ἔστεψα.

θηλυκῶς δὲ τὴν θηρίκλειον εἶπε Μένανδρος[1] ἐν
Θεοφορουμένῃ·

> μέσως μεθύων τὴν[2] θηρίκλειον ἔσπασε.

καὶ ἐν Μηναγύρτῃ·

> προπίνων θηρίκλειον[3] τρικότυλον μίαν[4].

καὶ Διώξιππος ἐν Φιλαργύρῳ·

> τῆς θηρικλείου τῆς μεγάλης χρεία ἐστί μοι.
> ΑΙΣΧ. εὖ οἶδα. Α. καὶ τῶν Ῥοδιακῶν. ἥδιστα
>   γὰρ
> ἐκ τῶν τοιούτων, Αἰσχρέα,[5] ποτηρίων
> εἴωθα πίνειν.

Πολέμων δ᾽ ἐν πρώτῳ περὶ τῆς Ἀθήνησιν
c Ἀκροπόλεως οὐδετέρως ὠνόμασεν εἰπών· "τὰ
χρυσᾶ θηρίκλεια ὑπόξυλα Νεοπτόλεμος ἀνέθηκεν."

---

[1] λέγει δὲ καὶ θηλυκῶς Μένανδρος τὴν θηρίκλειον καὶ ἄλλοι C,
preceding the quotation from Alexis.
[2] τὴν added by Schweighäuser.
[3] θηρικλείαν Dindorf, Kock.

different is clearly shown by Callixeinus, who says, in his account of events in Alexandria,[a] that some persons in the procession carried *thericleia,* others *karchesia.* What the latter is will be explained in the following.[b] But there is also a mixing-bowl called *thericleios,* mentioned by Alexis in *The Swan*[c] : " There stands shining a thericleian mixing-bowl right in our midst, filled with white nectar of ancient vintage, all a-foam ; I had taken it empty and polished it up, making it bright ; I set it firmly on its base, and wreathed it with berry-laden sprigs of ivy which I had plaited together." Menander used the adjective *thericleios* as a feminine in *The Inspired Woman*[d] : " Half-way drunk already, he drained the (fem.) *thericleios.*" Also in *The Priest of Mênê*[e] : " Pledging one *thericleios* which held six gills." So Dioxippus in *The Miser*[f] : " A. I want that big (fem.) *thericleios.* AESCHREAS : I know that well ! A. And the Rhodian cups[g] as well. For that's my custom ; I like most, Aeschreas, to drink from cups like those." Polemon, however, in the first book of his work *On the Athenian Acropolis,* mentioned the cup in the neuter gender[h] : " The wooden (neut.) *thericleia,* coated with gold, were dedicated by Neoptolemus." Apollodorus

---

[a] See 199 b (vol. ii. p. 400).   [b] Below, 474 e.
[c] Kock. ii. 339, *cf.* Antiphanes 237 (above, 781 e (p. 36)). A slave had washed a mixing-bowl when it was empty and suddenly discovered it full.
[d] Kock iii. 65, Allinson 358.
[e] Kock iii. 93 ; the quotation must be supplemented by μίαν to prove the feminine gender (see critical note 3). Mênê was Cybelê, and a μηναγύρτης was her mendicant priest. See 553 c (p. 513 note *e*).   [f] Kock iii. 359.
[g] See above, 469 b (p. 68).   [h] Frag. 1 Preller.

---

[4] μίαν added by Capps.   [5] Meineke: αἴσχεα A.

Ἀπολλόδωρος δ᾽ ὁ Γελῷος ἐν Φιλαδέλφοις ἢ
Ἀποκαρτεροῦντί φησιν·

   ἐφεξῆς στρώματ᾽, ἀργυρώματα,
θηρίκλειοι καὶ τορευτὰ[1] πολυτελῆ ποτήρια
ἕτερα.

Ἀριστοφῶν δ᾽ ἐν Φιλωνίδη·

   τοιγαροῦν ἐμοὶ μὲν ἀρτίως ὁ δεσπότης
δι᾽ ἀρετὴν τῶν θηρικλείων εὐκύκλωτον ἀσπίδα,
ὑπεραφρίζουσαν, τρυφῶσαν, ἴσον ἴσῳ κεκραμένην,
d προσφέρων ἔδωκεν· οἶμαι, χρηστότητος οὕνεκα.
εἶτ᾽ ἐλευθέραν ἀφῆκε βαπτίσας ἐρρωμένως.

Θεόφιλος δ᾽ ἐν Βοιωτίᾳ[2]·

  τετρακότυλον δὲ κύλικα κεραμέαν τινὰ
τῶν θηρικλείων (πῶς δοκεῖς[3]) κεραννύει
καλῶς, ἀφρῷ ζέουσαν. οὐδ᾽ ἂν Αὐτοκλῆς
οὕτως μὰ τὴν Γῆν[4] εὐρύθμως τῇ δεξιᾷ
ἄρας ἐνώμα.[5]

e ἐν δὲ Προιτίσι·

  καὶ κύλικ᾽ ἀκράτου[6] θηρίκλειον εἰσφέρει
πλέον ἢ κοτύλας χωροῦσαν ἕπτ᾽ Ἀγαθῆς Τύχης.

ΙΣΘΜΙΟΝ. Πάμφιλος ἐν τοῖς περὶ Ὀνομάτων
Κυπρίους τὸ ποτήριον οὕτως καλεῖν.

ΚΑΔΟΣ. Σιμμίας ποτήριον, παρατιθέμενος Ἀνα-
κρέοντος·

---

[1] καὶ τορευτὰ Schweighäuser: τορευταὶ (om. καὶ) A.
[2] Βοιωτίδι Kock, Βοιωτίῳ Kaibel.
[3] δοκεῖς Musurus: δοκεῖ A.
[4] Γῆν Schweighäuser: την A.

of Gela says, in *Brothers in Love with Sisters*, or *Starving to Death* [a] : "One after the other—rugs for the couches, silver vessels, *thericleioi*, and expensive embossed cups besides." Aristophon in *Philonides* [b] : "For that reason, just lately, my master gave me as a reward of merit the well-rounded bowl [c] of thericleians ; he brought it to me foaming over the brim, daintily alluring, mixed half-and-half ; I suppose it was because I am so good. He then let me go free, after he had soused me lustily." Theophilus in *The Boeotian Woman* [d] : "He mixes a two-quart cylix, one of those thericleians made of pottery, you can't think how nicely ; it boils over with foam. Not even Autocles,[e] Earth is my witness, could pick it up and manage it with his right hand so tidily." And in *The Daughters of Proetus* [f] : "He brought in a thericleian cylix of unmixed wine, containing more than seven half-pints, in honour of Good Luck."

Isthmion. Pamphilus, in his work *On Names*, (says that) the Cyprians call the drinking-cup by this name.

Kados. Simmias says this is a cup, citing the lines

---

[a] Kock iii. 279 ; the adjective *thericleios* is here masculine, not neuter.

[b] Kock ii. 281.

[c] Lit. "shield": the expression is parodic, *cf.* Aesch. *Sept.* 489, 540.

[d] Kock ii. 473.

[e] If this is the Athenian general accused of high treason for ill-success in a diplomatic mission to Thrace (361 B.C., Demosth. xxiii. 104, xxxvi. 53, l. 12, Hypereides xi. frag. 55 ff.), the comparison is highly ironical.

[f] Kock ii. 476.

---

⁵ ἄρας ἐνώμα Jacobs. Porson : ἀιρασαν ὦμον A.

⁶ ἀκράτου added by Kock : κύλικα A.

ἠρίστησα μὲν ἰτρίου λεπτοῦ μικρὸν[1] ἀποκλάς,
οἴνου δ' ἐξέπιον κάδον.

'Επιγένης δ' ἐν Μνηματίῳ φησίν·

κρατῆϝες, κάδοι,
f ὁλκεῖα, κρουνεῖ'. Β. ἔστι γὰρ κρουνεῖα; Α. ναί·[2]
λουτήρι'[3]—ἀλλὰ τί καθ' ἕκαστον δεῖ λέγειν;
ὄψει γὰρ αὐτός. Β. βασιλέως υἱὸν λέγεις
Καρῶν[4] ἀφῖχθαι; Α. δηλαδή, Πιξώδαρον.

'Ηδύλος 'Επιγράμμασι·

473 πίνωμεν· καὶ γάρ τι νέον, καὶ γάρ τι παρ' οἶνον
εὕροιμ' ἂν[5] λεπτὸν καί τι μελιχρὸν ἔπος.
ἀλλὰ κάδοις Χίου με κατάβρεχε καὶ λέγε " παῖζε,
'Ηδύλε." μισῶ ζῆν[6] ἐς κενόν, οὐ μεθύων.

καὶ ἐν ἄλλῳ·

ἐξ ἠοῦς εἰς νύκτα καὶ ἐκ νυκτῶν πάλι Σωκλῆς[7]
εἰς ἠοῦν πίνει τετραχόοισι κάδοις,
εἶτ' ἐξαίφνης που τυχὸν οἴχεται. ἀλλὰ παρ'
οἶνον
Σικελίδεω[8] παίζει πουλὺ[9] μελιχρότερον,
b ἐστὶ δὲ καὶ[10] πολὺ δὴ[11] στιβαρώτερος. ὡς δ'
ἐπιλάμπει
ἡ χάρις. ὥστε φίλος[12] καὶ γράφε καὶ μέθυε.

Κλείταρχος δ' ἐν ταῖς Γλώσσαις τὸ κεράμιόν φησιν

---

[1] λεπτοῦ μικρὸν Hephaestion: λεπτὸν (om. μικρὸν) A.
[2] 480 a: ἔστι δὲ κρουνιαναι A.
[3] λουτήρι' added from 486 b.
[4] Καρῶν added by Bergk.
[5] Jacobs: εὕροιμεν A.   [6] Jacobs: ἡδύλεμε σωζην A.
[7] Bergk: πασισωκλης A.
[8] Wilamowitz: σικελίδου A.

of Anacreon[a]: "I have lunched on a small bit of cake which I had broken off, but I drank up a *kados* of wine." Epigenes says, in *The Souvenir*[b]: " A. There'll be mixing-bowls, jars (*kadoi*), basins, and jugs. B. What! there are jugs? A. Yes; wash-basins—but why need I tell you in detail? You shall see for yourself. B. Do you mean that the son of the Carian king has arrived? A. Sure as can be— Pixodarus." Hedylus in his *Epigrams*: " Let us drink; for it is true, ay, it is true, that in my cups I shall find a theme that's new, something subtle and sweet. So then, soak me in jars (*kadoi*) of Chian and say 'Write thy playful verse, Hedylus.' I hate living for nothing and not being drunk." And in another epigram : " From daybreak till nightfall and again from the night-watches until dawn, Soclês drinks out of twelve-quart jars (*kadoi*). Then, all of a sudden, as chance will have it, he is gone! Yet in his cups he can write his playful verse much more sweetly than Sicelidas,[c] and he is also, as you know, much stronger.[d] How his charm shines upon us! Wherefore, dear friend, keep on writing and getting drunk." Cleitarchus, however, says in his *Glossary*

[a] *P.L.G.*[4] frag. 17, Diehl frag. 69, Edmonds frag. 18, Athen. 646 d, Hephaestion 10. 4, p. 335 c. The κάδος was a jar of various sizes, not properly a cup (Plat. *Rep.* 616 D), but the quotations here given imply bigness.
[b] Kock ii. 418, Athen. 480 a, 486 b (p. 161 note *f*). Pixodarus, youngest son of Hecatomnus, ejected his sister Ada from the throne of Caria and became king 341/0 B.C.
[c] Asclepiades. See Theocr. vii. 40, Wilamowitz, *Hellenistische Dichtung*, i. 145 : for the thought *cf.* Hor. *Ep.* i. 19. 4.
[d] *i.e.* he can " carry his liquor better."

[9] πουλὺ Musurus : πολὺ A.
[11] δὴ added by Kaibel.
[10] Wilamowitz : δὴ A.
[12] Wilamowitz : φίλε A.

Ἴωνας κάδον[1] καλεῖν. Ἡρόδοτος δ' ἐν τῇ τρίτῃ " φοινικηίου,[2]" φησίν, " οἴνου κάδον."

ΚΑΔΙΣΚΟΣ. Φιλήμων ἐν τῷ προειρημένῳ συγγράμματι ποτηρίου εἶδος. ἀγγεῖον δ' ἐστὶν ἐν ᾧ τοὺς κτησίους Δίας ἐγκαθιδρύουσιν, ὡς Αὐτοκλείδης[3]

c φησὶν ἐν τῷ Ἐξηγητικῷ γράφων οὕτως· " Διὸς κτησίου σημεῖα[4] ἱδρύεσθαι χρὴ ὧδε· καδίσκον καινὸν δίωτον ἐπίθημα ἔχοντα[5] στέψαι τὰ[6] ὦτα ἐρίῳ λευκῷ καὶ ἐκ τοῦ ὤμου τοῦ δεξιοῦ καὶ ἐκ τοῦ μετώπου . . . τοῦ κροκίου, καὶ ἐσθεῖναι ὅ τι ἂν εὕρῃς καὶ εἰσχέαι[7] ἀμβροσίαν. ἡ δ' ἀμβροσία ὕδωρ ἀκραιφνές, ἔλαιον, παγκαρπία· ἅπερ ἔμβαλε." μνημονεύει τοῦ καδίσκου καὶ Στράττις[8] ὁ κωμικὸς ἐν Λημνομέδᾳ λέγων οὕτως·

Ἑρμῆς, ὃν ἕλκουσ' οἱ μὲν ἐκ προχοιδίου,
οἱ δ' ἐκ καδίσκου σ'[9] ἴσον ἴσῳ κεκραμένον.

d ΚΑΝΘΑΡΟΣ. ὅτι μὲν πλοίου ὄνομα κοινόν, ὅτι δὲ καὶ ποτήριόν τι οὕτω καλεῖται Ἀμειψίας ἐν Ἀποκοτταβίζουσί φησι·

[1] lemma: καλὸν A.
[2] A and Herodotus: φοινικήου Kaibel.
[3] Αὐτοκλείδης Plut. Nic. 23, Harpocr.: Ἀντικλείδης A.
[4] σιπύας Hesychius s. καδίσκοι.
[5] ἐπίθημα ἔχοντα Müller: ἐπιθηματοῦντα A.
[6] στέψαι τὰ Jacobs: στέψαντα A.
[7] εἰσχέαι CE, ἴσχεαι A.   [8] Casaubon: στράτων A.
[9] σ' added by Porson (γ' Fritzsche).

---

[a] A large jar used for storing wine—the more usual application of the term; above, 472 e (p. 87 note a). Bekker, Anec. 268. 18 κάδοι: ὑπὸ Σολίων κάδοι (πίθοι?), ὑπὸ Ἰώνων κεραμια.
[b] Chap. 20.   [c] Attic Words or Glosses, 469 a.
[d] Frag. 13 Müller, J. 2 B 803. The work dealt with ritual practice; cf. the term ἐξηγητής, of an instructor in religion, Plat. Euthyphro 9 A.

that "the Ionians call the earthenware jar[a] a *kados*. So Herodotus in the third book[b] has 'a jar of date wine.'"

Kadiskos. Philemon, in the treatise before-mentioned,[c] defines the *kadiskos* as a kind of drinking-cup. It is also a vessel in which they set up the images of Zeus, god of property, as Autocleides says in his *Expositor*, writing thus[d] : "The figures[e] of Zeus, god of property, are to be consecrated in the following manner : a new, two-handled *kadiskos*, furnished with a lid, should have its handles wreathed with white[f] wool, while from the right shoulder and the forehead . . . the fillet, and into the vessel you place whatever you find, and pour in ambrosia. This 'ambrosia' consists of pure water, olive-oil, and all kinds of fruit ; these things put in." The *kadiskos* is mentioned by the comic poet Strattis in *Lemnomeda* in these words[g] : "The Hermes-potion, which they drain, some from a jug, others from a *kadiskos*, mixing thee half-and-half."

Kantharos. That this is the name of a boat is well known, but that a kind of cup is also called by this name Ameipsias makes clear in *Playing at Cottabus*[h] :

---

[e] Lit. "tokens"; but possibly "meal-jars" should be read; see critical note 4.

[f] A white ox is sacrificed to Ζεὺς Κτήσιος, Demosth. xxi. 53. The sense of the following clause may have been: Let the fillet (always worn by one performing an act of consecration) descend from his forehead and right shoulder.

[g] Kock i. 717, Athen. 32 b (vol. i. p. 140).

[h] Kock i. 670, Athen. 667 f. So γαυλός meant both pail and boat, below, 500 f (p. 238 note *b*). See also "trireme," 497 b (p. 216) and 500 f (p. 238). On the kantharos and its significance in Dionysiac worship see Elderkin, *Kantharos*, Princeton, 1924.

ἡ Μανία,[1] φέρ' ὀξύβαφα καὶ κανθάρους.

Ἄλεξις δ' ἐν Κρατείᾳ[2] (ὁ δὲ λόγος περί τινος ἐν
καπηλείῳ πίνοντος)·

εἶθ' ὁρῶ τὸν Ἑρμαϊσκον τῶν ἀδρῶν[3] τούτων τινὰ
κάνθαρον[4] καταστρέφοντα, πλησίον δὲ κείμενον
στρωματέα τε[5] καὶ γύλιον αὐτοῦ.

e Εὔβουλος δ' ἐν Παμφίλῳ πολλάκις μεμνημένος τοῦ
ὀνόματός φησιν·

ἐγὼ δὲ (καὶ γὰρ ἔτυχεν ὃν καταντικρὺ
τῆς οἰκίας καινὸν καπηλεῖον μέγα)
ἐνταῦθ' ἐπετήρουν τὴν τροφὸν τῆς παρθένου,
κεράσαι κελεύσας τὸν κάπηλόν μοι χόα
ὀβολοῦ παραθεῖναί θ' ὡς μέγιστον κάνθαρον.

καὶ πάλιν·

ὁ δὲ κάνθαρος πάλαι κενὸς ξηραίνεται.[6]

f καὶ ἔτι·

ἅμα δὲ λαβοῦσ' ἠφάνικε πηλίκον τινὰ
οἴεσθε μέγεθος ἐγκρυφίαν[7] μέγαν πάνυ,
καὶ ξηρὸν ἐπόησ' εὐθέως τὸν κάνθαρον.

Ξέναρχος δ' ἐν Πριάπῳ φησὶ τάδε·

σὺ δὲ μηκέτ' ἔγχει, παιδάριον, εἰς ἀργυροῦν,
εἰς τὸ βαθὺ δ' ἐπανάγωμεν·[8] εἰς τὸν κάνθαρον,
474 παιδάριον, ἔγχει, νὴ Δί' εἰς[9] τὸν κάνθαρον.

Ἐπιγένης Ἡρωίνῃ·

ἀλλ' οὐδὲ κεραμεύουσι νῦν τοὺς κανθάρους,

---

[1] ἡ Μανία 677 f : ημαμαι A. [2] κρατίαι A.
[3] Hermann : ἀνδρῶν A.
[4] κανθάρων (?) Kaibel, cf. 474 a.

" You, Mania, hand me vinegar-cruets and *kantharoi*."
So Alexis in *Crateias* (the talk is about a man drinking
in a wineshop) [a] : " Thereupon I saw Hermaïscus
drinking bottoms-up [b] one of those fat *kantharoi*, and
lying near him were his blanket and knapsack."
Eubulus often mentions the word in *Pamphilus*, and
says [c] : " As for myself (there happened to be a large
new wineshop across the street from the house) I
was keeping an eye out there on the young girl's
nurse, for I had ordered the bar-keeper to mix me
up a quart for a penny, and to set beside us the largest
kantharos he had." And again [d] : " But the *kantharos* has long since been emptied dry." Then
further : " With that she seized and made away
with a very large loaf baked in the ashes [e]—you
can't think how big it was in size—and straightway
drained that *kantharos* dry." Xenarchus, in *Priapus*,
has these lines [f] : " You there, boy, stop pouring
out wine into a silver cup, and let's put off into the
deep : yes, by Zeus, pour it into the *kantharos*, boy,
into the *kantharos* ! " Epigenes in *The Glorified
Woman* [g] : " But the potters don't even make those

---

[a] Kock ii. 338.
[b] For κατατρέφοντα *cf.* Sophron below, 479 b : Hor.
Sat. ii. 8. 39, " invertunt." [c] Kock ii. 192.
[d] *Ibid.* The nurse complains that " it is a long time
between drinks." See critical note 6. Her satisfaction is recorded in the next quotation.
[e] See critical note 7, and Athen. 110 a (vol. ii. p. 16).
[f] Kock ii. 472. A silver cup would presumably be smaller
than an earthenware *kantharos*. [g] Kock ii. 417.

---

[5] τε deleted by Dindorf, on account of στρωματέᾰ.
[6] Schweighäuser, Musurus : πάλαι δὴ καινὸς ὡς ξηραίνεται A.
[7] Gulick : ἀρεσιαν A, ἀθαρίαν (?) Kaibel.
[8] δ᾽ ἐπανάγωμεν Meineke : δὲ πάλιν ἄγωμεν A.
[9] Meineke : νὴ A.

91

ὦ τάλαν, ἐκείνους τοὺς ἁδρούς, ταπεινὰ δὲ
καὶ γλαφυρὰ πάντες . . . ὡσπερεὶ
αὐτὰ τὰ ποτήρι’, οὐ τὸν οἶνον πιόμενοι.

Σωσικράτης δὲ Φιλαδέλφοις ἐπὶ πλοίου[1]·

λεπτὴ δὲ κυρτοῖς ἐγγελῶσα κύμασιν
αὔρα, κόρη Σκίρωνος,[2] ἡσύχῳ ποδὶ
b   προσῆγε πρᾴως καὶ καλῶς τὸν κάνθαρον.

Φρύνιχος Κωμασταῖς·

εἶτα κεραμεύων ἂν οἴκοι[3] σωφρόνως Χαιρέ-
στρατος
ἑκατὸν ἂν[4] τῆς ἡμέρας ἔκλαιεν[5] οἴνου κανθάρους.

Νικόστρατος Διαβόλῳ·

ἡ ναῦς δὲ πότερον εἰκόσορός ἐστ’ ἢ[6] κύκνος
ἢ κάνθαρος; τουτὶ γὰρ ἂν[7] πύθωμ’ ἔτι,[8]
αὐτὸς περανῶ[9] τὰ πάντ’. Β. ἀμέλει κυκνοκάν-
θαρος.

(ἐξ ἀμφοτέρων τούτων κεκεραμευμένος.)[10] Μένανδρος
δὲ Ναυκλήρῳ·

ἥκει λιπὼν Αἰγαῖον ἁλμυρὸν βάθος
c   Θεόφιλος ἡμῖν, ὦ Στράτων. ὡς ἐς καλὸν

---

         [1] δὲ and ἐπὶ πλοίου C: om. A.
  [2] Σκείρωνος AC.   [3] Letronne: οἴκω A.
        [4] ἂν added by Erfurdt.
  [5] ἔκαεν Letronne, ἔπλαττεν Cobet, ἔλαπτεν Kock.
  [6] ἐστ’ ἢ Stephanus: εστιν ἢ A.   [7] ἐὰν A.
  [8] Jacobs: ὅτι A.   [9] Jacobs: περιανω A.
  [10] This remark of some commentator, bracketed by Dindorf.

---

    [a] Kock iii. 391. The north-west wind was called Sciron,
as coming from the Scironian Rocks on the Corinthian Gulf,
Strabo 28.
    [b] ἡσύχῳ ποδί, "with quiet foot," seems to be borrowed

kantharoi to-day, you poor fool, those fat ones; they all make things that are shallow and dainty, just as if it were the cups themselves we were going to drink, not the wine." Sosicrates, on the other hand, uses the word of a boat in *Brothers in Love with Sisters*[a]: " A light breeze, daughter of Sciron, laughing among the swelling billows, gently and nicely brought up the *kantharos* without a ripple." [b] Phrynichus in *The Revellers*[c]: " Then Chaerestratus, soberly working on his pots in the house, would weep daily a hundred *kantharoi* of wine." [d] Nicostratus in *The Slanderer*[e]: " A. This ship—is it twenty-oared, or a ' swan,' or a *kantharos* ? For if I learn that further, I shall be able to infer all the rest myself. B. Of course, it's a swan-*kantharos*." (This is a word plastered together from both of them.) Menander in *The Skipper*[f]: " A. From the salt depths of the Aegean[g] has Theophilus come for our joy, Straton. How happily it turns out that I am the

---

from Eur. *Orestes* 136, *cf. Bacchae* 647. There is a play on the nautical sense of πόδι, " sheet "; the sheets were neither flapping idly nor whistling in a gale. Kantharos, as the name of both cup and ship, is comparable to the American " schooner " (of lager beer).

[c] Kock i. 374.

[d] If the text is right and the quotation is not misplaced, the meaning must be that his tears would fill a hundred sloops that ordinarily carried wine. Kock's ἔλαπτεν would mean " he lapped up a hundred goblets of wine in sober fashion " (σωφρόνως ironical). In that case the citation is out of place.

[e] Kock ii. 222. Apparently some types of boat were called swans (κύκνοι), as others were called beetles (κάνθαροι). For the quaint alternative *cf.* Aristoph. *Av.* 1203 (addressed to Iris), " Are you a boat or a head-dress ? " L.C.L. ii. p. 244 note *d*.   [f] Kock iii. 101, Allinson 414.

[g] Eur. *Troad.* 1, Athen. 4 a (vol. i. p. 14), *cf.* 551 b (p. 500).

τὸν υἱὸν εὐτυχοῦντα καὶ σεσωσμένον
πρῶτος λέγω σοι τόν τε χρυσοῦν κάνθαρον.
ΣΤΡ. ποῖον; τὸ πλοῖον; Α. οὐδὲν οἶσθας, ἄθλιε.[1]

καὶ μετ' ὀλίγα·

ΣΤΡ. τὴν ναῦν σεσῶσθαί μοι λέγεις; Α. ἔγωγε μὴν
τὴν ναῦν ἐκείνην ἣν ἐπόησε Καλλικλῆς[2]
ὁ Καλύμνιος,[3] Εὐφράνωρ δ' ἐκυβέρνα[4] Θούριος.

Πολέμων δ' ἐν τοῖς πρὸς Ἀντίγονον περὶ Ζωγράφων
φησίν· "᾽Αθήνησιν ἐν τῷ τοῦ Πειρίθου γάμῳ
πεποίηκεν Ἱππεὺς[5] τὴν μὲν οἰνοχόην καὶ τὸ κύπελλον
λίθινα, χρυσῷ τὰ[6] χείλη περιτεραμνίσας, τὰς
d δὲ κλισίας ἐλατίνας χαμᾶζε ποικίλοις στρώμασι
κεκοσμημένας, ἐκπώματα δὲ κεραμέους κανθάρους,
καὶ τὸν λύχνον ὁμοίως τὸν[7] ἐκ τῆς ὀροφῆς ἐξηρτη-
μένον, ἀνακεχυμένας ἔχοντα τὰς φλόγας." ὅτι δὲ
καὶ ἀπὸ Κανθάρου κεραμέως ὠνομάσθη τὸ ἔκπωμα
Φιλέταιρός φησιν ἐν Ἀχιλλεῖ·

Πηλεύς· ὁ Πηλεὺς δ' ἐστὶν ὄνομα κεραμέως,
ξηροῦ λυχνοποιοῦ, Κανθάρου, πενιχροῦ πάνυ,
ἀλλ' οὐ τυράννου, νὴ Δί'.

ὅτι δὲ καὶ γυναικεῖον κοσμάριόν ἐστι κάνθαρος
Ἀντιφάνης εἴρηκεν ἐν Βοιωτίδι.[8]

ΚΑΡΧΗΣΙΟΝ. Καλλίξεινος ὁ Ῥόδιος ἐν τοῖς περὶ
Ἀλεξανδρείας φησὶν ὅτι ποτήριόν ἐστιν ἐπίμηκες,

---

[1] οὐδὲν . . . ἄθλιε added from Macrob. v. 21. 15.
[2] τὴν ναῦν . . . ἐπόησε Καλλικλῆς Grotius: ἐκείνην ναῦν . . .
Καλλικλῆς ἐπόησε A.
[3] ὁ Καλύμνιος Heringa: τὸν καλούμενον A.
[4] εὐφράνωρ δ' ἐκυβέρνα Grotius: ευφρανορ εκυβέρνα A.
[5] ACE: Ἵππυς Schweighäuser (cf. Pliny xxxv. 141).
[6] χρυσῷ τὰ Musurus: χρυσωτὰ ACE.
[7] τὸν added by Kaibel.

first to tell you that your son is successful, that he is safe and sound, and your golden *kantharos* as well. STRATON. *Kantharos* indeed! You mean the boat? A. You poor fool, you don't know anything." A little later he says: " STRATON. You mean my ship is safe and sound? A. Indeed I do, that ship which was built by Callicles of Calymna and piloted by Euphranor of Thurii.[a] " Polemon, in the chapters *On Painters* addressed to Antigonus, says [b] : " In the Marriage of Peirithoüs, at Athens, Hippeus represents the wine-pitcher and the goblet as bejewelled, with the rims covered over with gilt; the couches are fir-boughs laid on the ground, decorated with rugs in many designs, the drinking-cups are *kantharoi* of pottery, as is likewise the lamp which is suspended from the ceiling, with wide-spreading jets of flame." That the cup got its designation from a potter named Kantharus is stated by Philetaerus in *Achilles* [c] : " Ay, Peleus ; for Peleus is a potter's surname—a lean lampmaker he is, Kantharus by name, miserably poor, no lordly person, I swear by Zeus." That *kantharos* is also a brooch worn by women is asserted by Antiphanes in *The Boeotian Woman.*[d]

Karchesion. Callixeinus of Rhodes in his books *On Alexandria* says [e] this is a tall drinking-cup, moder-

---

[a] Possibly a word-play on θούριος " impetuous "?
[b] Frag. 63 Preller.
[c] Kock ii. 231. For the scene *cf.* Eur. *Iph. Aul.* 700:
ΚΛΤΤΑΙΜΝΗΣΤΡΑ. τοῦ δ' Αἰακοῦ παῖς τίς κατέσχε δώματα;
ΑΓΑΜΕΜΝΩΝ. Πηλεύς· ὁ Πηλεὺς δ' ἔσχε Νηρέως κόρην.
The name Πηλεύς is here connected with πηλός "clay." See vol. iv. p. 233, vol. vii. p. 247. [d] Kock ii. 36.
[e] *F.H.G.* iii. 65; this doubtless formed part of the description given at 199 d (vol. ii. pp. 402 ff.).

---

[8] Βοιωτίδι Kock : βοιωτιαι A, Βοιωτίῳ Kaibel, *cf.* 367 f, 650 e.

συνηγμένον εἰς μέσον ἐπιεικῶς, ὦτα ἔχον μέχρι
τοῦ πυθμένος καθήκοντα. ἐστὶ δὲ ἱκανῶς ἐπί-
f μηκες τὸ ποτήριον τὸ καρχήσιον,[1] καὶ τάχα διὰ
τὸ ἀνατετάσθαι οὕτως ὠνόμασται. ἀρχαιότατον δ᾽
ἐστὶ ποτήριον τὸ καρχήσιον, εἴ γε ὁ Ζεὺς ὁμιλήσας
Ἀλκμήνῃ ἔδωκε[2] δῶρον αὐτὸ τῆς μίξεως, ὡς
Φερεκύδης ἐν τῇ δευτέρᾳ ἱστορεῖ καὶ Ἡρόδωρος ὁ
Ἡρακλεώτης. Ἀσκληπιάδης δ᾽ ὁ Μυρλεανὸς κε-
κλῆσθαί φησιν αὐτὸ ἀπό τινος τῶν ἐν τῇ νηὶ κατα-
σκευασμάτων. "τοῦ γὰρ ἱστοῦ τὸ μὲν κατωτάτω
πτέρνα καλεῖται, ἣ[3] ἐμπίπτει εἰς τὴν ληνόν, τὸ δ᾽
οἷον εἰς μέσον τράχηλος, τὸ δὲ πρὸς τῷ τέλει
475 καρχήσιον. ἔχει δὲ τοῦτο κεραίας ἄνωθεν νευούσας[4] ἐφ᾽ ἑκάτερα τὰ μέρη, καὶ ἐπίκειται τὸ λεγόμενον αὐτῷ θωράκιον, τετράγωνον πάντη πλὴν
τῆς βάσεως καὶ τῆς κορυφῆς· αὗται δὲ προὔχουσι
μικρὸν ἐπ᾽ εὐθείας ἐξωτέρω. ἐπὶ δὲ τοῦ θωρακίου[5]
εἰς ὕψος ἀνήκουσα καὶ ὀξεῖα γιγνομένη ἐστὶν ἡ
λεγομένη ἠλακάτη." μνημονεύει δὲ τῶν καρχησίων
καὶ Σαπφὼ ἐν τούτοις·

κῆνοι δ᾽ ἄρα πάντες καρχήσιά τ᾽ ἦχον[6]
κἄλειβον· ἀράσαντο δὲ πάμπαν ἐσλὰ
τῷ γαμβρῷ.[7]

[1] This awkward repetition (ἐστὶ δὲ . . . καρχήσιον) is
omitted in C, which has καθήκοντα· καὶ τάχα κτλ.
[2] δέδωκε CE.   [3] ἣ ACE: ἦ Coraes, Kaibel.
[4] ἄνωθεν νευούσας Dobree: ἄνω συννευούσας ACE.
[5] θωρακίου εἰς A: θωρακίου ἡ εἰς C.
[6] καρχήσιά τ᾽ ἦχον Bergk: καρχῆσι᾽ ἔχον A, καρχήσια ἔσχον
Macrobius, καρχάσι᾽ ὄνηχον (=ἀνεῖχον) Hoffmann.
[7] Lesbian accentuation, ἔσλα τῷ γάμβρῳ.

[a] See critical note 1.
[b] καρχήσιον also meant a masthead, cf. below, and Schol.
Pind. Nem. v. 94.

ately contracted in the middle ; it has handles which
extend down to the base. The cup known as the
karchesion is rather tall [a] and perhaps has been thus
named because it extends so high.[b] Moreover, the
karchesion is a very old type of cup, seeing that Zeus,
when he consorted with Alcmena, gave it as a reward
for lying with her ; this is recorded by Pherecydes in
the second book,[c] and by Herodorus of Heracleia.[d]
Asclepiades of Myrlea says that its name is derived
from one of the arrangements in a ship. " The
lowest part of the mast is called the heel, which
drops into the socket ; the part approximately in
the middle is the neck, and that at the top is the
karchesion. This part has yards sloping downward
on both sides, and upon it is fixed the so-called
thorakion (crow's-nest),[e] which is everywhere rect-
angular except at the base and the top ; these extend
a little farther out in a straight line.[f] Above the
crow's-nest, reaching aloft and tapering to a point, is
the so-called distaff." Sappho mentions the *karchesia*
(as cups) in these lines [g] : " And so they all, with
karchesia in hand, began to pour libations ; and they
fervently wished all good things for the bridegroom."

[c] *F.H.G.* i. 77, J. 1. 63.
[d] *F.H.G.* ii. 29, J. 1. 219.
[e] Lit. " breast-work." See 208 e (vol. ii. p. 442).
[f] The meaning is uncertain. The *karchesion* shown on
monuments was usually a bell-shaped extension of the mast,
in which the halyards played, and corresponding to the main-
top. Here it seems to have been considerably enlarged in
the form of a cube (to serve as a crow's-nest), except that the
floor and the roof extended beyond the line of the walls or
sides. See Jal, *Archéologie navale*, i. 163 ; Köster, *Das antike
Seewesen*, pp. 32, 89. The distaff was the peak, capable of
revolving.
[g] *P.L.G.*[4] frag. 51, Diehl 136, Edmonds 146, Athen. 425 c.

Κρατῖνος ἐν Διονυσαλεξάνδρῳ·

στολὴν δὲ δὴ τίν' εἶχεν; τοῦτό μοι φράσον.
Β. θύρσον, κροκωτόν, ποικίλον, καρχήσιον.[1]

Σοφοκλῆς Τυροῖ·

προσπτῆναι μέσην[2]
τράπεζαν ἀμφὶ σῖτα[3] καὶ καρχήσια,

b πρὸς τὴν τράπεζαν φάσκων προσεληλυθέναι τοὺς
δράκοντας καὶ γενέσθαι περὶ τὰ σιτία καὶ τὰ
καρχήσια. ἔθος γὰρ ἦν τοῖς ἀρχαίοις ἐπὶ τῶν
τραπεζῶν κεκραμένα τιθέναι ποτήρια, καθὰ καὶ
Ὅμηρος ποιεῖ. ὠνομάσθη δὲ τὸ καρχήσιον διὰ
τὸ τραχύσματα ἔχειν κερχνοειδῆ,[4] καὶ εἴρηται κατὰ
ἐναλλαγὴν τοῦ εἶ[5] πρὸς τὸ ᾱ ἀντὶ τοῦ κερχήσιον·
διὸ καὶ Ὅμηρος τοὺς ὑπὸ δίψους κρατουμένους
καρχαλέους εἶπεν. Χάρων δ' ὁ Λαμψακηνὸς ἐν
c τοῖς Ὥροις[6] παρὰ Λακεδαιμονίοις φησὶν ἔτι καὶ
εἰς αὐτὸν δείκνυσθαι τὸ δέπας τὸ δοθὲν Ἀλκμήνῃ
ὑπὸ Διός, ὅτε Ἀμφιτρύωνι εἰκάσθη.

ΚΑΛΠΙΟΝ. ποτηρίου τι γένος[7] Ἐρυθραίου, ὥς φησι
Πάμφιλος. εἶναι[8] δ' αὐτὸ οἷόν ἐστι τὸ σκαφίον.

ΚΕΛΕΒΗ. τούτου τοῦ ἐκπώματος Ἀνακρέων μνη-
μονεύει·

ἄγε δή, φέρ' ἡμίν,[9] ὦ παῖ,
κελέβην, ὅκως[10] ἄμυστιν

---

[1] Κρατῖνος . . . καρχήσιον added by Kaibel from Macrobius.
[2] προσπτῆναι μέσην Bergk (cf. Aristoph. Av. 1287):
προσπτῆναι μέσην A, πρὸς γηνδειμι Macrobius, πρὸς τήνδε μοι
Jan.   [3] σῖτα Macrobius: σιτία τὰ A.
[4] Kaibel: κεγχροειδῆ AC.   [5] ε̄ C.
[6] Schweighäuser: ὅροις A.
[7] εἶδος CE.   [8] Kaibel: οἶμαι A.
[9] ἡμίν ACE.   [10] ὅκως 427 a: ὅπως ACE.

98

Cratinus in *Dionysalexander*[a]: " A. What outfit did
he have then ? Tell me that. B. He had a Bacchic
wand, a saffron-coloured tunic,[b] an embroidered coat,
a *karchesion*." Sophocles in *Tyro*[c]: " Flew to the
midmost table among the foods and the *karchesia*,"
by which he means that the serpents came up to the
table and were found among the foods and the cups.
For it was a custom among the people of old to place
cups with wine already mixed upon the tables, even
as Homer represents them. Now the *karchesion* got
its name from the circumstance that it had bead-
like (*kerchnoeidê*) roughnesses, and the word is formed
by change of *e* to *a*, making *karchesion* instead of
kerchesion ; hence also Homer calls[d] men who are
overcome with thirst *karchaleoi* (having rough throats).
Charon of Lampsacus in his *Annals* says[e] that even
to his day there was shown at Sparta the cup which
was given to Alcmena by Zeus when he disguised
himself as Amphitryon.

Kalpion. A class of cup from Erythrae, as Pamphilus says. It is like the *skaphion.*[f]

Kelebê. This drinking-cup[g] is mentioned by
Anacreon[h]: " Up then, my boy, and hand us a cup
(*kelebê*), that I may pledge a deep draught, pouring in

---

[a] Kock i. 24 ; see critical note 1.

[b] Such as Dionysus wore, reaching to the feet.

[c] *T.G.F.*[2] 275.

[d] *Il.* xxi. 541 δίψῃ καρχαλέοι, "asper siti " Verg. *Georg.* iii.
434. But καρφαλέοι " dry " is also read.

[e] *F.H.G.* i. 35.

[f] A small bowl, shaped like a boat ; Athen. 142 d (vol. ii.
p. 150).

[g] The example immediately quoted, and the subsequent
discussion, point rather to a jar of some size.

[h] *P.L.G.*[4] frag. 63, Diehl 43, Edmonds 76, Athen. 427 **a**
(vol. iv. p. 432).

προπίω, τὰ μὲν δέκ' ἐγχέας
ὕδατος, τὰ πέντε δ' οἴνου
κυάθους.

ἄδηλον δὲ πότερον[1] εἶδός ἐστι ποτηρίου ἢ πᾶν[2]
d ποτήριον κελέβη καλεῖται ἀπὸ τοῦ χέειν εἰς αὐτὸ
τὴν λοιβὴν ἤτοι[3] λείβειν· τοῦτο δὲ ἐπὶ τοῦ ὑγροῦ
συνήθως ἔταττον, ἀφ' οὗ λέγεται καὶ ὁ λέβης.
Σιληνὸς δὲ καὶ Κλείταρχος τοὺς Αἰολεῖς φασιν
οὕτω καλεῖν τὸ ποτήριον. Πάμφιλος δὲ μόνην
τὴν θερμοποτίδα καλουμένην[4] τὴν κελέβην εἶναι.
Νίκανδρος δ' ὁ Κολοφώνιος ἐν ταῖς Γλώσσαις
ποιμενικὸν ἀγγεῖον μελιτηρὸν τὴν κελέβην εἶναι·
καὶ γὰρ Ἀντίμαχος ὁ Κολοφώνιος ἐν πέμπτῳ
Θηβαΐδος φησί·

κήρυκάς θ' ἅμα τοῖσι[5] φέρειν μέλανος οἴνοιο
ἀσκὸν ἐνίπλειον κελέβειόν θ'[6] ὅττι φέριστον
e οἷσιν ἐνὶ μεγάροις κεῖτο[7] μέλιτος πεπληθός.

καὶ πάλιν·

ἀτὰρ ἀμφίθετον κελέβειον ἑλόντες
ἔμπλειον μέλιτος, τό ῥά οἱ προφερέστερον[8] ἦεν.

ἀλλαχοῦ δέ φησιν·

καὶ χρύσεια δέπαστρα καὶ ἀσκηθέος[9] κελέβειον
ἔμπλειον μέλιτος, τό ῥά οἱ προφερέστερον[10] εἴη.

[1] Kaibel: ποῖον A.
[2] C, after the lemma κελέβη, has ἴσως πᾶν ποτήριον, ἀπὸ τοῦ
χέειν . . . ἢ τὸ λείβειν, ἀφ' οὗ καὶ λέβης.
[3] ἤτοι Meineke: ἢ τὸ ACE.
[4] Πάμφιλος δὲ μόνην τὴν θ. καλουμένην CE (om. τὴν κελέβην
εἶναι): Π. δὲ τὸ ποτήριον θ. κ. τὴν κελέβην εἶναι A.
[5] κήρυκάς θ' ἅμα τοῖσι Stoll: κήρυκας ἀθανάτοισι A (ῠ unex-
ampled, except in κηρύκιον Anth. P. xi. 124).
[6] θ' added by Schweighäuser.

100

ten cups [a] of water and five of wine." It is uncertain
whether the *kelebê* is a special kind of cup or any cup
whatever, since it is so called from the act of pouring
(*cheein*) the libation (*loibên*) into it, that is, making a
libation [b]; and they habitually applied this word
(*leibein*) in the case of any liquid, hence the word *lebês*
(kettle) arose. Silenus and Cleitarchus say the
Aeolians call a drinking-cup by this name.[c] But
Pamphilus says that only the so-called *thermopotis* [d]
is (properly) the *kelebê*. Further, Nicander of
Colophon in his *Glossary* says [e] the *kelebê* is a shepherd's bowl used for honey; and this is borne out
by Antimachus of Colophon, who says in the fifth
book of his *Thebaïs* [f]: " And (he commanded) that
the heralds with them should bring a skin full of
red wine, and the best *kelebeion* [g] that lay in his
halls, filled with honey." And again [h]: "Then,
grasping a *kelebeion* set with two handles [i] and
full of honey, the bowl which was his better one."
In still another place he says [j]: " And golden
drinking-cups, and a *kelebeion* full of pure honey, the
bowl which was his better one." Indeed he has in

[a] The κύαθος was a cup with a large handle like that of a
ladle, holding about $\frac{1}{12}$ of a pint: this κελέβη, therefore,
contained at least 1 pint, 1 gill. But see below, 475 f.

[b] This impossible etymology assumes that κελέβη is for
χελείβη. It is perhaps a Semitic word, Levy, *Semit. Fremd-
wörter*, p. 104.　　　　[c] κελέβη.

[d] Cup for hot drinks, Hesychius *s.* κελέβη and σκαμβίς;
see ἀναφαία, 783 f (p. 51).

[e] Frag. 138 Schneider.　　　　[f] *Frag. ep.* 19.

[g] A diminutive in form, though not in meaning.

[h] *Frag. ep.* 18.　　　　[i] *Cf.* below, 500 f–501 a (p. 238).

[j] *Frag. ep.* 17.

---

[7] Bergk: ἐνὶμμεγάροις κεῖται A.　　　　[8] προφερέστατον Stoll.
[9] Kaibel: ἀσκηθές A.　　　　[10] προφερέστατον Stoll.

σαφῶς γὰρ νῦν κελέβειον ἀντὶ ἀγγείου τινὸς
τέθεικε, προειπὼν ποτήρια δέπαστρα. Θεόκριτος
δ᾽ ὁ Συρακόσιος ἐν ταῖς Φαρμακευτρίαις φησίν·

στέψον τὰν κελέβαν φοινικέῳ οἰὸς ἀώτῳ·

f καὶ Εὐφορίων·

ἠέ ποθεν ποταμῶν κελέβη ἀποήφυσας ὕδωρ.

Ἀνακρέων·

ᾠνοχόει δ᾽ ἀμφίπολος μελιχρὸν
οἶνον τρικύαθον κελέβην ἔχουσα.

Διονύσιος δ᾽ ὁ Λεπτὸς ἐξηγούμενος Θεοδωρίδα τὸ
εἰς τὸν Ἔρωτα μέλος τὴν κελέβην φησὶ τίθεσθαι
ἐπὶ τοῦ ὀρθοῦ ποτηρίου οἷον Προυσιάδος καὶ
Θηρικλείου.

476 ΚΕΡΑΣ.   τοὺς πρώτους[1] λέγεται τοῖς κέρασι τῶν
βοῶν πίνειν· ἀφ᾽ οὗ τὸν Διόνυσον[2] κερατοφυῆ
πλάττεσθαι ἔτι τε ταῦρον καλεῖσθαι ὑπὸ πολλῶν
ποιητῶν. ἐν δὲ Κυζίκῳ καὶ ταυρόμορφος ἵδρυται.
ὅτι δὲ τοῖς κέρασιν ἔπινον δῆλον ἐκ τοῦ καὶ μέχρι
νῦν λέγεσθαι, ὅταν συμμίσγωσι τῷ οἴνῳ τὸ ὕδωρ,
κεράσαι φάσκοντες.[3]   καὶ τὸ ἀγγεῖον δ᾽ ἐν ᾧ
κιρνᾶται[4] ὁ οἶνος κρατὴρ ἀπὸ τοῦ συγκιρνᾶσθαι ἐν
αὐτῷ τὸ ὕδωρ, ἀπὸ[5] τοῦ κέρατος, οἱονεὶ[6] κερατήρ,

---

[1] τοὺς πρώτους ἀνθρώπους Dobree (Athen. 12 d).
[2] CE: διονύσιον A.
[3] C, more lucidly, reads: καὶ μέχρι δὲ νῦν τὴν τοῦ οἴνου μίξιν
τῷ ὕδατι κεράσαι φαμέν.
[4] CE: κερνᾶται A.
[5] ἢ before ἀπὸ added by Kaibel; but a comparison with C
shows that the repetitious passage is a conflation of text and
glosses.
[6] οἱονεὶ CE: οἷον A.

this example definitely used the word *kelebeion* for any bowl, since he has first mentioned drinking-cups in the word *depastra*. So Theocritus of Syracuse says in *Girls practising Witchcraft*[a]: "Wreath the bowl (*kelebên*) with crimson tufts from the sheep." And Euphorion[b]: "Or else from some rivers thou hast drawn off water in a *kelebê*." Anacreon[c]: "Then the handmaid, holding a *kelebê* containing a gill, poured out honey-sweet wine." But Dionysius the "Lanky,"[d] in his exposition of Theodoridas's song *To Eros*, says that the word *kelebê* is used of the tall drinking-cup such as the Prusian and the Therikleian.[e]

The Horn. It is said that primitive men drank from the horns of oxen; hence Dionysus is represented as growing horns, and he is still called a bull by many poets.[f] So in Cyzicus there is set up a bull-shaped statue of him. That they used to drink from horns (*kerata*) is evident from the word employed even to-day when they mix together water with wine, for they say that they have "horned" (*kerasai*) it.[g] And the vessel in which the wine is mixed is a *krater*,[h] from the water being mixed together (with the wine) in it, being from *keras*, as though it were

---

[a] ii. 2 ; Simaetha gives directions to her maid Thestylis, who holds some red wool in her hands.

[b] Frag. 72 Meineke, Powell 52.

[c] *P.L.G.*⁴ frag. 32, Diehl 58, Edmonds 33. See p. 101 note *a*.

[d] See *Etym. Mag.* 278. 1. He was the teacher of Fronto, "meus magister Dionysius Tenuior," Naber 154, Haines ii. 83.

[e] See 496 d, 470 e.

[f] Cf. *P.L.G.*⁴ iii. 656, Diehl, *Carm. pop.* 46.

[g] κέρας, it need scarcely be said, is related to Eng. "hart," "horn"; with κεράννυμι "mingle" it has nothing to do, etymologically or semantically. See crit. note 3.

[h] Athen. 123 a (vol. ii. p. 70).

b ἀπὸ τοῦ εἰς κέρας[1] ἐγχεῖσθαι τὸ πόμα. διαμένει δὲ
ἔτι καὶ νῦν ἡ τῶν κεράτων κατασκευή. καλοῦσι
γοῦν ἔνιοι ταῦτα ῥυτά.[2] καὶ τῶν ποιητῶν δὲ
πολλοὶ παράγουσι πίνοντας τοὺς ἀρχαίους κέρασι.
Πίνδαρος μὲν ἐπὶ τῶν Κενταύρων λέγων·

    ἀνδροδάμαντα[3] δ' ἐπεὶ Φῆρες δάεν ῥιπὰν
       μελιαδέος[4] οἴνου,
    ἐσσυμένως ἀπὸ μὲν λευκὸν γάλα χερσὶ τραπεζᾶν[5]
       ὤθεον, αὐτόματοι δ' ἐξ ἀργυρέων κεράτων πί-
       νοντες ἐπλάζοντο.

καὶ Ξενοφῶν δ' ἐν τῇ ζ' τῆς Ἀναβάσεως διηγούμενος τὸ παρὰ τῷ Θρακὶ Σεύθῃ συμπόσιον γράφει
c οὕτως· "ἐπεὶ δὲ Ξενοφῶν σὺν τοῖς μετ' αὐτοῦ
εἰσῆλθε πρὸς τὸν Σεύθην, ἠσπάζοντο μὲν πρῶτον
ἀλλήλους καὶ κατὰ τὸν Θράκιον νόμον κέρατα
οἴνου προὔτεινον.[6]" ἐν δὲ τῇ ἕκτῃ περὶ Παφλα-
γόνων διηγούμενός φησι· "κατακείμενοι δ' ἐν
στιβάσιν[7] ἐδείπνουν καὶ ἔπινον κερατίνοις ποτηρίοις[7]." Αἰσχύλος δ' ἐν Περραιβίσι τοὺς Περραιβοὺς[8] παρίστησιν ἀντὶ ποτηρίων τοῖς κέρασι χρω-
μένους διὰ τούτων·

            ἀργυρηλάτοις
    κέρασι χρυσᾶ στόμια προσβεβλημένοις.[9]

καὶ Σοφοκλῆς Πανδώρᾳ·

    [1] εἰς κέρας CE: εἰς τὸ κέρας A.
    [2] διαμένει . . . ἡ τῶν κ. κατασκευὴ καὶ καλοῦνται ῥυτὰ C.
    [3] Casaubon, Boeckh: οδαμαν A.
    [4] Boeckh: μελιηδέος AC.   [5] CE: τράπεζαν A.
    [6] σκίμποσιν Xenophon.
    [7] προὔπινον and ἐκ κερατίνων ποτηρίων the better MSS. of
Xen.

kerater, because the potion is poured into a *keras* from it. The manufacture of drinking-horns continues even to the present time. They are at any rate called *rhyta* by some people. So also many poets represent the men of old as drinking from horns. Pindar, for example, says of the Centaurs[a] : " And when the Pheres perceived the man-subduing smell wafted from the honey-sweet wine, furiously they thrust with their hands the white milk from the tables, and drinking unbidden out of silver horns, they began to reel." Xenophon also, in the seventh book of *The Anabasis*, writes as follows when describing the symposium held in the house of the Thracian Seuthes[b] : " When Xenophon and his companions had entered and come before Seuthes, they first saluted one another and in accordance with the Thracian custom tendered[c] horns of wine." Again, in the sixth book, when he describes the Paphlagonians he says[d] : " They lay down on pallets and dined and wined from horn cups." Aeschylus in *Women of Perrhaebia* represents the Perrhaebians as using horns instead of cups, in these words[e] : " With silver-mounted drinking-horns fitted with golden mouthpieces." And Sophocles in *Pandora*[f]: " And

---

[a] *P.L.G.*[5] i. 455, Sandys (L.C.L.) 602. The Φῆρες, or Centaurs, were fighting against the Lapithae at the wedding of Peirithoüs, king of the Lapithae.
[b] *Anab.* vii. 2. 23 ; the first clause is a paraphrase.
[c] " Clinked glasses " ? See critical note 6.
[d] vi. 1. 4 ; again a paraphrase.
[e] *T.G.F.*[2] 61, L.C.L. Aeschylus ii. p. 444.
[f] *T.G.F.*[2] 237 ; text and meaning are uncertain.

---

[8] ἐν Περραιβίσι and Περραιβοὺς Dindorf: ἐν περρεβοις and περρεβους A.
[9] A : προβεβλημένοις CE, περιβεβλημένοις Blomfield.

καὶ πλῆρες ἐκπιόντι χρύσεον κέρας
d   τρίψει γέμοντα[1] μαλθακῆς ὑπ' ὠλένης.[2]

Ἕρμιππος Μοίραις[3]·

οἶσθά νυν ὅ μοι ποίησον; τήνδε νῦν μή μοι
   δίδου,
ἐκ δὲ τοῦ κέρατος αὖ μοι δὸς πιεῖν ἅπαξ μόνον.

Λυκοῦργος δ' ὁ ῥήτωρ ἐν τῷ κατὰ Δημάδου
Φίλιππόν φησι τὸν βασιλέα προπίνειν κέρατι τούτοις[4] οἷς ἐφιλοφρονεῖτο. τοὺς δὲ Παιόνων βασιλεῖς
φησι Θεόπομπος ἐν δευτέρᾳ Φιλιππικῶν, τῶν
βοῶν τῶν παρ' αὐτοῖς γινομένων μεγάλα κέρατα
φυόντων, ὡς χωρεῖν τρεῖς καὶ τέτταρας χόας, ἐκ-
e πώματα ποιεῖν ἐξ αὐτῶν, τὰ χείλη περιαργυροῦν-
τας καὶ χρυσοῦντας· καὶ Φιλόξενος δ' ὁ Κυθήριος
ἐν τῷ ἐπιγραφομένῳ Δείπνῳ φησίν·

πίνετο[5] νεκτάρεον πόμ'[6] ἐν χρυσέαις[7] προτομαῖς
   ταύρων[8] κεραστῶν,[9]
ἐβρέχοντο[10] δὲ κατὰ μικρόν.

Ἀθηναῖοι δὲ καὶ ἀργυρᾶ ποιοῦντες κέρατα ἔπινον
ἐξ αὐτῶν. ἔστι γοῦν τοῦτο εὑρεῖν ἐν τοῖς δημιο-
πράτοις ἀναγεγραμμένον οὕτως . . .[11] ἐκ στήλης
ἀνακειμένης ἐν ἀκροπόλει ᾗ τὰ ἀναθήματα περιέχει·

---

[1] γέροντα Adam.   [2] Musurus: ὑπολαινης A.
[3] Casaubon: μυραις A.   [4] τούτοις om. C.
[5] Meineke: ἐπίνετο A.   [6] πόμα A : πῶμ' Fiorillo.
[7] Meineke: χρυσαῖς A.   [8] Wilamowitz: τε ἄλλων A.
[9] Kaibel: κεράτων A.   [10] ἐβρέχοντο Bergk: ἔβρεχον A.
[11] Lacuna marked by Kaibel, following Köhler (Hermes
xxiii. 399), who thinks the δημιόπρατα are the goods confiscated from the Hermocopidae, whereas the στήλη next
mentioned contained an inventory of treasures delivered over
by the State curator to his successor.

106

when one has tossed off his brimming golden horn, and he is full to repletion, she will hug him in her soft arms." Hermippus in *The Fates* [a] : " Do you know, then, what I want you to do ? Don't offer me that little cup,[b] but just give me instead one drink out of the horn." The orator Lycurgus, in the speech *Against Demades*, says [c] that Philip always pledged with a horn those toward whom he felt friendly. And Theopompus, in the second book of his *History of Philip*, says [d] that the kings of Paeonia, in which country the cattle grew horns so large that they hold three or four *choes*,[e] made drinking-cups of them, overlaying the rims with silver or gold.[f] Philoxenus of Cythera, also, in the poem entitled *The Banquet*, says [g] : " The draught of nectar was drunk in the gilded faces of horned bulls,[h] and little by little they drenched themselves." The Athenians also manufactured horns of silver and drank out of them. At least one may find the following record inscribed in the list of confiscated goods . . . on a stele set up on the Acropolis, which contains votive

---

[a] Kock i. 236.

[b] So Dalechamp, understanding τήνδε to mean a small cylix. The scene may have been like that in Aristoph. *Acharn.* 178-200.   [c] B. and S. ii. 262.

[d] *F.H.G.* i. 285, J. 2 B 543, G. and H. 40.

[e] The *chous* nearly = 3 quarts.

[f] For the omission of περι- in χρυσοῦντες *cf.* 214 b προβασανίσας καὶ στρεβλώσας, with which Kaibel compares Soph. *Trach.* 89 προταρβεῖν καὶ δειμαίνειν.

[g] *P.L.G.*⁴ frag. 5, Diehl (Philoxenus Leucadius, *cf.* Athen. 146 f, 409 e) frag. d, Edmonds iii. 360.

[h] Referring to the *rhyta*, of which many specimens are extant, shaped like the heads of bulls, horses, etc.

" κέρας ἔκπωμα ἀργυροῦν, καὶ περισκελὶς[1] πρόσεστι ἀργυρᾶ.[2] "

ΚΕΡΝΟΣ ἀγγεῖον κεραμεοῦν, ἔχον ἐν αὐτῷ πολλοὺς κοτυλίσκους[3] κεκολλημένους, ἐν οἷς, φησίν,[4] μήκωνες λευκοί, πυροί,[5] κριθαί, πισοί, λάθυροι, ὦχροι, φακοί.[6] ὁ δὲ βαστάσας αὐτὸ οἷον λικνοφορήσας τούτων γεύεται, ὡς ἱστορεῖ Ἀμμώνιος ἐν γ´ περὶ Βωμῶν καὶ Θυσιῶν.

ΚΙΣΣΥΒΙΟΝ τὸ μόνωτον ποτήριον Φιλήμων. Νεοπτόλεμος δ᾽ ὁ Παριανὸς ἐν τρίτῳ Γλωσσῶν τὸ κίσσινον ποτήριον σημαίνειν παρ᾽ Εὐριπίδῃ ἐν Ἀνδρομέδᾳ·

477

πᾶς δὲ ποιμένων ἔρρει λεώς,[7]
ὁ μὲν γάλακτος κίσσινον φέρων σκύφος
πόνων ἀναψυκτῆρ᾽,[8] ὁ δ᾽ ἀμπέλων γάνος.

τὸ γὰρ κισσύβιον, φησί, λέγεται ἐπὶ συνόδου ἀγροικικῆς, ἔνθα προσήκει μάλιστα τὸ ξύλινον ποτήριον. Κλείταρχος δέ φησιν Αἰολεῖς τὸν σκύφον κισσύβιον καλεῖν· Μαρσύας δὲ κύπελλον καὶ τὸ ξύλινον ποτήριον. Εὔμολπος δὲ γένος τι ποτηρίου,

---

[1] Schweighäuser: περισκελεις A.
[2] ἀργυρᾶ added by Kaibel from inscriptions; why not also σταθμὸν ΗΗΔ ?
[3] 478 d: κοτυλισμοὺς ACE.   [4] εἰσὶ CE.
[5] λευκοί, πυροί om. C.
[6] C adds κύαμοί, ζειαί, βρόμος, παλάθιον, μέλι, ἔλαιον, οἶνος.
[7] λαός C.   [8] A: πίνων ἀνὰ ψυκτῆρα CE.

---

[a] *I.G.* ii. 665. 8, 667. 38. See p. 106 crit. note 11. The inscription adds the weight, 210 drams. Its date is 385/4 B.C. Polemon wrote a work on such treasures, Athen. 472 b, Strabo 396. See Boeckh, *Staatshaushaltung*[3] i. 251.

[b] More fully explained below, 478 d; the *kernos* or *kerchnos* was a sort of tray or caster borne in the procession

articles[a]: " A horn drinking-cup of silver, and attached to it is a silver support."

Kernos.[b] An earthenware vessel, holding within it a large number of small cups cemented together. " In these," Polemon says, " are white poppy-heads, grains of wheat and barley, peas, vetches, okra-seeds, and lentils.[c] The man who carries it, resembling the bearer of the sacred winnowing-fan, tastes these articles, as Ammonius records in the third book *On Altars and Sacrifices.*"

Kissybion. The cup with one handle, according to Philemon. But Neoptolemus of Parium in the third book of his *Glossary* says that it signifies the cup made of ivy-wood (*kissos*) in Euripides, *Andromeda*[d]: " All the shepherd folk rushed together, one man bringing an ivy bowl[e] of milk, that gives refreshment after toil, another the joyous fruit of the vine." For the *kissybion,*[f] he says, is always spoken of when rustics get together, since there the wooden cup is especially appropriate. Cleitarchus, however, says that the Aeolians call the *skyphos* a *kissybion*; but Marsyas calls the wooden cup also a *kypellon.*[g] Eumolpus says that it is a variety of cup, perhaps

of the Mysteries, Pollux iv. 103, *Ath. Mitt.* xxiii. Plate xiii. A fine specimen has been found by Dr. Shear in the Agora at Athens. A large bowl, set on a stem, contains eight small bowls. The surface is covered with a polished black glaze.

[c] C adds: beans, rice-wheat, oats, compressed fruit, honey, oil, wine.

[d] *T.G.F.*[2] 402, *cf.* Macrobius v. 21. 13. But Pollux vi. 97 says its name is derived from the ivy-wreaths with which it was decorated.

[e] *Skyphos*, below, 498 a-500 c.

[f] Used by the swineherd Eumaeus, *Od.* xiv. 78, *cf.* below, 477 b (Odysseus and Cyclops), Theocritus i. 27.

[g] Below, 482 e, J. 2 B 741.

ἴσως, φησίν, κατ' ἀρχὰς ἐκ κισσίνου κατασκευασθὲν
b ξύλου. Νίκανδρος δὲ ὁ Κολοφώνιος ἐν τῷ πρώτῳ
τῶν Αἰτωλικῶν γράφει· " ἐν τῇ ἱεροποιίῃ[1] τοῦ
Διδυμαίου Διὸς κισσοῦ[2] σπονδοποιέονται πετά-
λοισιν, ὅθεν τὰ ἀρχαῖα ἐκπώματα κισσύβια
φωνέεται." Ὅμηρος·

κισσύβιον μετὰ χερσὶν ἔχων μέλανος οἴνοιο.

Ἀσκληπιάδης δ' ὁ Μυρλεανὸς[3] ἐν τῷ περὶ τῆς
Νεστορίδος " σκύφει," φησί, " καὶ κισσυβίῳ τῶν
μὲν ἐν ἄστει καὶ μετρίων οὐδεὶς ἐχρῆτο, συβῶται
c δὲ καὶ νομεῖς καὶ οἱ ἐν ἀγρῷ· Πολύφημος μὲν τῷ
κισσυβίῳ, θατέρῳ δὲ Εὔμαιος." Καλλίμαχος δ'
ἔοικε διαμαρτάνειν ἐν τῇ συγχρήσει τῶν ὀνομάτων,
λέγων ἐπὶ τοῦ Ἰκίου[4] ξένου τοῦ παρὰ τῷ Ἀθηναίῳ
Πόλλιδι συνεστιασθέντος[5] αὐτῷ·

καὶ γὰρ ὁ Θρηικίην μὲν ἀπέστυγε[6] χανδὸν ἄμυστιν
ζωροποτεῖν,[7] ὀλίγῳ δ' ἥδετο κισσυβίῳ.
τῷ μὲν ἐγὼ τόδ' ἔλεξα περιστείχοντος ἀλείσου
τὸ τρίτον . . .

ὁ γὰρ λέγων ἄλεισον τὸ αὐτὸ καὶ κισσύβιον τὴν
d ἀκριβῆ θέσιν τῶν ὀνομάτων οὐ διαφυλάττει. εἰ-
κάσειε δ' ἄν τις τὸ κισσύβιον τὸ πρῶτον ὑπὸ ποιμένων ἐργασθῆναι ἐκ κισσίνου ξύλου. ἄλλοι δὲ ἐτυμο-
λογοῦσιν αὐτὸ ἀπὸ τοῦ χεῖσθαι, ὅ ἐστι[8] χωρεῖν·

[1] Musurus: ἱεροποιηΐῃ A. [2] CE: κισσοὺς A.
[3] μυραλεανὸς A.
[4] Ox. Pap. 1362: οἰκείου A. [5] συνεστιαθέντος Meineke.
[6] Athen. 442 f, Pap.: ἀπήνατο A, ἀνήνατο Macrobius.
[7] A: οἰνοποτεῖν 442 f, 781 d, Pap.
[8] ὅ ἐστι CE Etym. Magn. 809. 52: τὸ δ' ἐστι A.

[a] Frag. 1 Schneider, Macrobius v. 21. 12, Trans. Am. Phil.
Assoc. lxiii., 1932, 253. [b] Od. ix. 346; Odysseus speaks.

so called, he says, because in the beginning it was
made out of ivy wood.   Nicander of Colophon, in the
first book of his *Aetolian History*, says[a] : " In the
ritual of the Zeus of Didyma they offer libations with
leaves of ivy (*kissos*), whence the ancient drinking-
cups are called *kissybia*." Homer[b] : " Holding in
my hands a bowl (*kissybion*) of dark wine."   Now
Asclepiades of Myrlea, in his treatise *On Nestor's
Cup*,[c] says : " No dweller in a city, even in moderate
circumstances, ever used a *skyphos* or a *kissybion* ; it
is only swineherds, shepherds, and country-people
who do ; thus Polyphemus drinks from the *kissybion*,
but Eumaeus drinks from the other vessel.[d] " So it
appears that Callimachus is in error in using the
terms synonymously ; he says of the Ician stranger
who was entertained with him at the house of
the Athenian Pollis[e] : " For verily he loathed
swilling in greedy fashion a Thracian magnum of
strong wine,[f] and was content with a small bowl
(*kissybion*).   To him, then, I said, while the bowl
(*aleison*) was going round for the third time . . ."
Anyone, that is, who says that *aleison*[g] and *kissybion*
are the same fails to observe the exact use of the
terms.   One may conjecture that the *kissybion* was
made in the beginning by shepherds from ivy wood.
Others, however, derive the word from *cheisthai*, and

---

[c] Athen. 487 f, *cf.* 433 b-d (vol. iv. p. 462), 498 f.

[d] The σκύφος, mentioned later (*Od.* xiv. 78, quoted below,
498 f).

[e] Frag. 109 Schneider, *cf.* Athen. 442 f (vol. iv. p. 506),
Macrobius v. 21. 12, and E. Cahen in Dr. Loeb's translation
of Couat, *Alexandrian Poetry*, p. 554.   Icos is an island in
the north Aegean east of Peparethos.

[f] For ζωροποτεῖν see 423 d (vol. iv. p. 416).

[g] At 783 a (p. 47) the *aleison* is identified with the *depas*
" cup."

οὐδὸς δ' ἀμφοτέρους ὅδε χείσεται.[1]

καὶ ἡ τοῦ ὄφεως κατάδυσις χειή, ἡ καταδεχο-
μένη τὸ ζῷον. καὶ κήθιον[2] τὸ χήτιον τὸ χωροῦν
τοὺς ἀστραγάλους. Διονύσιος δ' ὁ Σάμιος ἐν τοῖς
e περὶ τοῦ Κύκλου τὸ Ὁμηρικὸν κισσύβιον κυμβίον
ἔφη γράφων οὕτως· " καὶ αὐτὸν Ὀδυσσεὺς ὁρῶν
ταῦτα ποιοῦντα πληρώσας τοῦ οἴνου κυμβίον
δίδωσι πιεῖν."

ΚΙΒΩΡΙΟΝ. Ἡγήσανδρος ὁ Δελφὸς Εὐφορίωνά
φησι τὸν ποιητὴν παρὰ Πρυτάνιδι δειπνοῦντα καὶ
ἐπιδεικνυμένου τοῦ Πρυτάνιδος κιβώριά τινα
δοκοῦντα πεποιῆσθαι πολυτελῶς, τοῦ κώθωνος εὖ
μάλα προβεβηκότος, λαβὼν ἓν τῶν κιβωρίων ὡς
ἐξοινῶν[3] ἐνεούρησε. Δίδυμος δέ φησι ποτηρίου
f εἶδος εἶναι, καὶ τάχ' ἂν εἴη τὰ λεγόμενα σκυφία
διὰ τὸ κάτωθεν εἰς στενὸν συνῆχθαι ὡς τὰ Αἰγύπτια
κιβώρια.

ΚΟΝΔΥ ποτήριον Ἀσιατικόν. Μένανδρος Κόλακι·

κοτύλας χωροῦν δέκα[4]
ἐν Καππαδοκίᾳ κόνδυ χρυσοῦν, Στρουθία.[5]

Ἵππαρχος Ἀνασῳζομένοις·

---

[1] χήσεται Nauck (from χανδάνω).
[2] κήθιον CE: τὸ κήτιον A.
[3] ὡς ἔξοινον καὶ μεθύοντα CE (in a different construction):
ὡς ἔοινος ὢν Casaubon; καὶ μεθύων after ἐξοινῶν bracketed by
Herwerden. Cf. Poll. vi. 21. [4] δέκα 434 c: δέκα καὶ A.
[5] 434 c: στρουθίον A. C has ποτήριον ἀσιατικὸν· στρουθίον
περσικὸν ποτήριον.

---

[a] Od. xviii. 17; Odysseus, standing at his own door
answers the beggar Arnaeus.

that means " to hold " ; thus,[a] " this threshold will hold us both." So also the snake's hiding-place is a *cheiê*,[b] that which shelters the creature. Again, there is *kethion*, the box which holds dice.[c] Finally, Dionysius of Samos, in his work on *The Cycle*,[d] has called the Homeric *kissybion* a *kymbion*. He writes thus : "When Odysseus saw him[e] doing that, he filled a *kymbion* with the wine and gave it to him to drink."

Kiborion.[f] Hegesander of Delphi says[g] that the poet Euphorion was dining at the house of Prytanis when the latter displayed some *kiboria* of evidently expensive manufacture ; and as the drinking had advanced to a very high point, Euphorion seized one of the *kiboria*, being tipsy, and made water in it. Didymus says[h] it is a kind of drinking-cup, and perhaps the so-called *skyphia* are the same, because they are contracted to a narrow point at the bottom, like Egyptian beans (*kiboria*).

Kondy, an Asiatic drinking-cup. Menander in *The Flatterer*[i] : " In Cappadocia, Struthias, (I drank up) a golden beaker (*kondy*) holding ten half-pints." Hipparchus in *Safe Home*[j] : " A. Do you pay any

---

[b] *Il.* xxii. 93, 95 ; Pindar, *Isthm.* viii. 70 (metaph.).

[c] Various forms occur : κηθάριον Aristoph. *Vesp.* 674, κείτιον, Ion. κείθιον Eustath. 1259. 36.

[d] *F.H.G.* ii. 10, J. 1. 179. The full title was κύκλος ἱστορικός Suid. *s.v.* Διονύσιος Μιλήσιος), a mythological romance based on the old poets ; *cf.* below, 481 d.

[e] Polyphemus preparing his cannibal meal, *Od.* ix. 346 ; *f.* Macrobius v. 21. 11.

[f] See 72 a (vol. i. p. 314).   [g] *F.H.G.* iv. 417.

[h] Schmidt 75.

[i] Kock iii. 83, Allinson 394, *cf.* Athen. 434 b-c.

[j] Kock iii. 272 ; a brothel-keeper warns one of his girls against an impecunious soldier.

προσέχεις τι τούτῳ τῷ στρατιώτῃ; Β. τῷδ';
ἔχει[1]
ἀργύριον οὗτος. Α. οὐδαμόθεν, εὖ οἶδ' ἐγώ,
ἀλλ' ἢ δαπίδιον ἓν ἀγαπητὸν ποικίλον,
τέρα τ'[2] ἔχον καὶ γρῦπας ἐξώλεις τινὰς
478 τῶν Περσικῶν— Β. εἰς κόρακας, ὦ μαστιγία.
Α. καὶ κόνδυ καὶ ψυκτῆρα καί τι[3] κυμβίον.

Νικόμαχος δ' ἐν πρώτῳ περὶ Ἑορτῶν Αἰγυπτίων
φησί· "τὸ δὲ κόνδυ ἐστὶ μὲν Περσικόν, τὴν δὲ
ἀρχὴν ἣν Ἕρμιππος ἀστρολογικὸς ὡς ὁ κόσμος
ἐξ οὗ τῶν θεῶν τὰ θαύματα καὶ τὰ καρπώσιμα
γίνεσθαι ἐπὶ γῆς· διὸ ἐκ τούτου σπένδεσθαι.
Παγκράτης δ' ἐν πρώτῳ Βοκχορηΐδος·

αὐτὰρ ὅ γε σπείσας ἐκ κόνδυος ἀργυφέοιο
b   νέκταρ ἐπ' ἀλλοδαπὴν οἶμον ἔβαινε πόδα."

ΚΟΝΩΝΕΙΟΣ.[4] Ἴστρος ὁ Καλλιμάχειος[5] ἐν πρώτῳ
Πτολεμαΐδος[6] τῆς ἐν Αἰγύπτῳ πόλεως γράφει
οὕτως· "κυλίκων Κονωνείων ζεῦγος καὶ Θηρικλείων χρυσοκλύστων ζεῦγος."

ΚΟΤΤΛΟΣ. τὰ μόνωτα ποτήρια κότυλοι, ὧν καὶ
Ἀλκαῖος μνημονεύει. Διόδωρος δ' ἐν τῷ πρὸς
Λυκόφρονα παρὰ Σικυωνίοις καὶ Ταραντίνοις ἐπι-
πολάζειν φησὶ τὸ ἔκπωμα, εἶναι δ' αὐτὸ λουτρίῳ
ἐοικὸς βαθεῖ. ἔχει δὲ καὶ οὖς ἐνιαχῇ. μνημονεύει

[1] τῷδ'; ἔχει Capps (πολύ γ' ἔχει Wilamowitz): τοῦ δ
δειου Α.
[2] τέρα τ' Kock: πέρσας Α.   [3] τι added by Kaibel
[4] κονώνιος AC.
[5] Musurus (Καλλιμάχιος): καλλίμαχος Α.
[6] περὶ Πτολεμαΐδος Meineke.
114

attention to that trooper ? B. This one here ? He has a lot of money ! A. Nowhere ! Of that I'm sure ; except perhaps one embroidered rug that he loves dearly, with figures of monsters on it and some damned griffins in Persian style.[a] B. To the devil with you, you jail-bird ! A. Or perhaps a beaker (*kondy*) or cooler or sauce-boat." Nicomachus in the first book of his work *On Egyptian Festivals* says : " The *kondy* is a Persian drinking-cup ; but in the beginning it was what the astrologer Hermippus (describes)[b] as the globe from which magic wonders and profitable signs sent by the gods appear upon the earth ; hence libations were poured from it. So Pancrates in the first book of his *Bocchoreïs* : ' Then he, after pouring a libation of nectar from the silvery *kondy*, set forth on a journey to foreign parts.' "

Kononeios. Istrus, the disciple of Callimachus, writes in the first book of his *Ptolemaïs*, the city in Egypt, as follows[c] : " A pair of Kononeian cylices, and a pair of gold-washed Thericleians."

Kotylos. The drinking-cups with one handle are *kotyloi* ; they are mentioned by Alcaeus[d] as well as others. Diodorus in his *Answer to Lycophron* says[e] this cup is common among the Sicyonians and the Tarentines, and that it is like a deep wash-bowl. It sometimes has a handle. Ion of Chios

[a] *Cf.* Aristoph. *Ran.* 937, " no horse-cocks, let me tell you, nor goat-stags, such as they represent on Persian tapestry."

[b] *F.H.G.* iii. 54 ; the text is corrupt, nor is it known what Hermippus is meant (Pauly-Wissowa viii. 853, *cf.* 846). The translation suggests that the *kondy* was a globe used in magic, a horoscope; *cf.* Plat. *Tim.* 40 D. See Reitzenstein, *Naasenerpredigt* (1916), p. 109. [c] *F.H.G.* i. 423, *cf.* below, 486 c.

[d] *P.L.G.*⁴ frag. 139, also Kock i. 764. On the poets named Alcaeus see Capps, *Class. Rev.* 1899, 384 ff.

[e] *Cf.* Lycophr. frag. 76 Streck.

δὲ αὐτοῦ καὶ Ἴων ὁ Χῖος " κότυλον οἴνου πλέων[1]"
c λέγων. Ἕρμιππος δὲ ἐν Θεοῖς·

τόν τε κότυλον πρῶτον ἤνεγκ' ἐνέχυρον τῶν
γειτόνων.

καὶ Πλάτων ἐν Διὶ κακουμένῳ " τὸν κότυλον
φέρει[2]" φησί, καὶ Ἀριστοφάνης ἐν Βαβυλωνίοις.
Εὔβουλος δ' ἐν Ὀδυσσεῖ ἢ Πανόπταις·

ὁ δ' ἱερεὺς Εὐήγορος[3]
ἐν μέσοις αὐτοῖσιν ἑστὼς τὴν καλὴν σκευὴν ἔχων
οἶνον ἐξέσπενδε κοτύλῳ.

Πάμφιλος δὲ ποτηρίου φησὶν εἶναι γένος, ἴδιον δ'
εἶναι Διονύσου. Πολέμων δ' ἐν τῷ περὶ τοῦ Δίου
Κωδίου φησί· " μετὰ δὲ ταῦτα τὴν τελετὴν ποιεῖ
d καὶ αἱρεῖ τὰ ἐκ τῆς θαλάμης καὶ νέμει ὅσοι ἂν ὦσι[4]
τὸ κέρνος περιενηνοχότες. τοῦτο δ' ἐστὶν ἀγγεῖον
κεραμεοῦν ἔχον ἐν αὑτῷ πολλοὺς κοτυλίσκους
κεκολλημένους· ἔνεισι[5] δ' ἐν αὐτοῖς ὅρμινοι, μήκωνες
λευκοί, πυροί, κριθαί, πισοί, λάθυροι, ὦχροι, φακοί,
κύαμοι, ζειαί, βρόμος, παλάθιον, μέλι, ἔλαιον,
οἶνος, γάλα, ὄιον[6] ἔριον[7] ἄπλυτον. ὁ δὲ[8] τοῦτο
βαστάσας οἷον λικνοφορήσας τούτων γεύεται."

ΚΟΤΥΛΗ. Ἀριστοφάνης Κωκάλῳ·

ἄλλαι δ'[9] ὑποπρεσβύτεραι γρᾶες[10] Θασίου μέλανος
μεστὸν

---

[1] Dindorf: πλέον A.
[2] φέρε "give me as a pledge" Schweighäuser (Pollux
x. 85).
[3] Εὐήγορος Wilamowitz, Kaibel (cf. the law quoted in Dem.
Meid. 10): εὐήγορος as adj. or εὐηγορῶν early edd.
[4] ἂν ὦσι Casaubon: ἄνω A.
[5] Kaibel: ἔνιοι A.   [6] ᾠόν "egg" Meineke.
[7] Wilamowitz χόριον "fetal membrane."   [8] δὲ 476 f : δὴ A.

mentions it, saying,[a] " a cup (*kotylos*) full of wine."
So Hermippus in *The Gods* [b] : " And first he brought
the *kotylos* as security for the neighbours." Plato
also, in *Zeus Outraged*, says [c] "he brings the *kotylos* " ;
so Aristophanes in *The Babylonians*.[d] Eubulus in
Odysseus or *The All-seeing Ones* [e] : " Then the priest
Euegorus, standing in the midst of them in all his
fair vestments, poured forth a libation of wine from
a *kotylos*." Pamphilus says that it is a variety of
cup and the peculiar attribute of Dionysus. Moreover Polemon, in the treatise *On the Sacred Fleece*,
says [f] : " After these preliminaries (the priest)
proceeds to the celebration of the mystic rites ; he
takes out the contents of the shrine and distributes
them to all who have brought round their tray. The
latter is an earthenware vessel, holding within it a
large number of small cups cemented together ; and
in them are sage, white poppy-seeds, grains of wheat
and barley, peas, vetches, okra-seeds, lentils, beans,
rice-wheat, oats, compressed fruit, honey, oil, wine,
milk, and sheep's wool unwashed.[g] The man who
carries it, resembling the bearer of the sacred winnowing-fan, tastes these articles."

Kotylê. Aristophanes in *Cocalus* [h] : ".But other
rather oldish women with large earthen-made cups

---

[a] *T.G.F.*[2] 742.   [b] Kock i. 232.   [c] *Ibid.* 613.
[d] *Ibid.* 410, Pollux x. 85.   [e] Kock ii. 189.
[f] Frag. 88 Preller. This quotation is designed to illustrate
the use of the diminutive *kotyliskos*; on the κέρνος *cf.* above,
476 e-f, and p. 108 note *b*, also von Prott, *Fasti Sacri*, p. 10.
[g] See critical note 6.
[h] Kock i. 484; the quotation, originally in anapaestic tetra-
meters, is badly garbled.

---

9 δ' added by Madvig.
10 γρᾶες deleted as a gloss by Madvig.

κεραμευομέναις[1] κοτύλαις μεγάλαις ἔγχεον ἐς[2]
σφέτερον δέμας[3] οὐδένα κόσμον,[4]
ἔρωτι βιαζόμεναι μέλανος οἴνου ἀκράτου.

e Σιληνὸς[5] καὶ Κλείταρχος ἔτι τε Ζηνόδοτος τὴν
κύλικα·

πάντη δ᾽ ἀμφὶ νέκυν κοτυλήρυτον ἔρρεεν αἷμα.

καί·

πολλὰ μεταξὺ πέλει κοτύλης καὶ χείλεος ἄκρου.

Σιμάριστος δὲ τὸ λεπτὸν ποτήριον οὕτως καλεῖσθαι.
Διόδωρος δὲ τὸν παρά τισι κότυλον κοτύλην ὠνομακέναι τὸν ποιητήν "πύρνον καὶ κοτύλην." ὃν
κύλικα μὲν οὐκ εἶναι, οὐ γὰρ ἔχειν δύο[6] ὦτα,
παραπλήσιον δ᾽ ὑπάρχειν λουτηρίῳ βαθεῖ, ποτηρίου
f δὲ εἶδος εἶναι. δύνασθαι δὲ καὶ τὸν παρὰ τοῖς
Αἰτωλοῖς[7] καί τισι τῶν Ἰώνων λεγόμενον κότυλον,
ὃν ὅμοιον ὄντα τῷ προειρημένῳ[8] ἓν οὖς ἔχειν.
μνημονεύει δ᾽ αὐτοῦ Κράτης ἐν Παιδιαῖς[9] καὶ
Ἕρμιππος ἐν Θεοῖς. Ἀθηναῖοι δὲ μέτρον τι
καλοῦσι κοτύλην. Θουκυδίδης· "ἐδίδοσαν μὲν αὐτῶν ἑκάστῳ ἐπὶ ὀκτὼ μῆνας κοτύλην ὕδατος καὶ
δύο κοτύλας σίτου." Ἀριστοφάνης Προαγῶνι[10]·

---

[1] κέραμον θέμεναι Madvig.   [2] ἐς deleted by Madvig.
[3] δέπας Blaydes.   [4] Toup: οὐδὲν ἀ οσμον A.
[5] σειληνος A.   [6] δύο added by Strecker.
[7] Αἰολεῦσι Kaibel.   [8] Madvig: τῶν προειρημένων A.
[9] Casaubon: παιδείαις A.   [10] προαγῶνι later hand in A.

---

[a] Il. xxiii. 34.

(*kotylai*) poured their bodies full, in no decorous fashion,
of red Thasian, overcome as they were by a passion
for the red, unmixed wine." Silenus, Cleitarchus,
and Zenodotus besides define it as a cylix [a] : " And
on all sides round the corpse blood was flowing in
cupfuls." Also [b] : " Many things there are between
the cup and the edge of the lip." Simaristus says
that a little cup is called by this name. [c] Diodorus
says that the Poet has used the name *kotylê* for the
kotylos of some authors, " wheat-bread and a cup
(*kotylê*)" [d]; this certainly is not a cylix, because it has
not two handles, but it is like (in shape) a deep wash-
bowl, though it is a variety of drinking-cup. It is
also equivalent to the cup, called *kotylos* among the
Aetolians [e] and some Ionians, which, like it, [f] has
only one handle. It is mentioned by Crates in
Games of Childhood [g] and by Hermippus in *The Gods*. [h]
The Athenians, moreover, call a certain measure a
kotylê. Thus Thucydides [i] : " They doled out to
each of them, for a period of eight months, a half-pint
of water and two half-pints of grain." Aristophanes

[b] Zenobius v. 71 ; see Bartlett's *Familiar Quotations*[10],
p. 190.
[c] *Kotylê* ; as a measure it held nearly half a pint, or six
kyathoi, p. 101 note *a*.
[d] *Od.* xv. 312 αἴ κέν τις κοτύλην καὶ πύρνον ὀρέξῃ. κότυλος
does not occur in *Il.* or *Od.*; κοτύλη is used thrice in *Il.*,
twice in *Od.*   [e] Aeolians ?
[f] Lit. " the before-mentioned cup," *i.e. kotylê*; but Madvig
understood it of the λουτήριον.
[g] Kock i. 138 ; the play dealt with almost all the games
played by children, Pollux ix. 114.
[h] Kock i. 232 ; above, 478 c.
[i] vii. 87. 2, the daily ration of Athenian prisoners in the
quarries of Syracuse, only half the amount usually given
to slaves ; *cf.* Plut. *Nic.* 29, and Browning, *Balaustion's
Adventure*.

119

ὁ δ' ἀλφίτων μοι[1] πριάμενος τρεῖς χοίνικας
κοτύλης δεούσας εἴκοσ'[2] ἀπολογίζεται.

479 Ἀπολλόδωρος δὲ ποτηρίου τι γένος ὑψηλὸν καὶ
ἔγκοιλον.[3] πᾶν δὲ τὸ κοῖλον κοτύλην, φησίν,
ἐκάλουν οἱ παλαιοί, ὡς καὶ τὸ τῶν χειρῶν κοῖλον·
ὅθεν καὶ κοτυλήρυτον αἷμα τὸ ἀμφοτέραις ταῖς
χερσὶν ἀρυσθῆναι δυνάμενον. καὶ ἐγκοτύλη[4] δέ[5]
τις παιδιὰ καλεῖται, ἐν ᾗ κοιλάναντες τὰς χεῖρας
δέχονται τὰ γόνατα τῶν νενικηκότων οἱ νενι-
κημένοι καὶ βαστάζουσιν αὐτούς. Διόδωρος δ' ἐν
Ἰταλικαῖς Γλώσσαις καὶ Ἡράκλειτος,[6] ὥς φησι
Πάμφιλος, τὴν κοτύλην καλεῖσθαι καὶ ἡμίναν,
παρατιθέμενος Ἐπιχάρμου·

b καὶ πιεῖν ὕδωρ διπλάσιον χλιαρόν, ἡμίνας δύο.

καὶ Σώφρων·

κατάστρεψον, τέκνον, τὰν ἡμίναν.

κοτυλίσκην δ' εἴρηκε Φερεκράτης ἐν Κοριαννοῖ·

τὴν κοτυλίσκην, μηδαμῶς.

Ἀριστοφάνης ἐν Ἀχαρνεῦσι·

κοτυλίσκιον τὸ χεῖλος ἀποκεκρουμένον.

---

[1] μοι added by Kock.
[2] εἴκοσ' Casaubon " ex membranis Italicis ": οἴκαδ' A.
[3] εὔκοιλον C.
[4] ἐγκοτύλη ACE: ἐν κοτύλῃ Kaibel (Pollux ix. 122).
[5] δέ om. C.   [6] Ἡρακλείδης Wilamowitz.

---

[a] Kock i. 511. The *choenix* = 4 *kotylai*, hence the rascally slave cheated his master out of nine *kotylai*.
[b] J. 2 B 1112.
[c] *Cf.* Pollux ix. 122, Pausanias grammaticus fr. 143

in *The Rehearsal* [a] : " But he, when he bought for me three *choenices* of barley meal lacking a *kotylê*, charged me with the price of twenty *kotylai*." Apollodorus [b] describes it as a kind of cup, tall and deeply hollowed. Moreover he says that the ancients called anything that is hollow a *kotylê*, as, for example, the hollow of the hand ; whence also the expression " blood flowing in cupfuls " means what can be scooped up in both hands. There is also a game called " in-the-cup," wherein the boys who lose hollow their hands to receive the knees of the boys who win, and so carry them about.[c] Diodorus in *Italic Glosses*, also Heracleitus,[d] according to Pamphilus, say that the *kotylê* is called also *hemina* ; Diodorus cites the verse of Epicharmus [e] : " And to drink twice as much warm water, two *heminai*.[f]" Also Sophron [g] : " Toss off the *hemina*, son, bottoms up ! " Pherecrates in *Corianno* has the (diminutive) form *kotyliskê* [h] : " That tiny half-pint ? Never ! " Aristophanes has another diminutive *kotyliskion* in *The Acharnians* [i] : " A poor little half-pint cup with its brim nicked off." And

Schwabe; Robert, *Arch. Zeitung* xxxvii. Plate 5. It seems to have differed from the pick-a-back game known as ἐφεδρισμός, Poll. ix. 118.

[d] Perhaps a mistake for Heracleides, celebrated physician of Tarentum (*ca.* 75 B.C.), who is cited not as a grammarian, but as one who used the word ἡμίνα in his professional books. But it is found also in the East, *e.g.* Leg. Gortyn ii. 49. E. Schwabe (Ael. Dionys. p. 66) follows Valckenaer in reading Ἡρακλέων. See Pauly-Wissowa viii. 515.

[e] Kaibel 144, Athen. 648 d, Diels i. 88, 99.

[f] A pint.

[g] Kaibel 171 ; for κατάστρεψον *cf.* above, 473 d.

[h] Kock i. 164 ; below, 481 a-b.

[i] *Acharn.* 459, one of the theatrical properties which Dicaeopolis solicits from the poet of stark realism, Euripides. But the mss. of Aristoph. have κυλίσκιον.

κοτύλη δὲ καλεῖται καὶ ἡ τοῦ ἰσχίου κοιλότης,
καὶ αἱ τοῦ πολύποδος ἐν ταῖς πλεκτάναις ἐπι-
φύσεις παραγώγως κοτυληδόνες. καὶ τὰ κύμβαλα
δ' Αἰσχύλος ἐν Ἠδωνοῖς κοτύλας εἴρηκεν·

ὁ δὲ χαλκοδέτοις κοτύλαις ὀτοβεῖ.

c Μαρσύας δέ φησι τὸ ἐν τῷ ἰσχίῳ ὀστοῦν καλεῖσθαι
ἄλεισον καὶ κύλικα.[1] κοτυλίσκος δὲ καλεῖται ὁ
ἱερὸς τοῦ Διονύσου κρατηρίσκος ᾧ[2] χρῶνται[3] οἱ
μύσται, ὡς Νίκανδρός φησιν ὁ Θυατειρηνὸς παρατιθέμενος τὸ ἐκ Νεφελῶν Ἀριστοφάνους·

μηδὲ στέψω κοτυλίσκον.

Σιμμίας δὲ ἀποδίδωσι τὴν κοτύλην ἄλεισον.

ΚΟΤΤΑΒΙΣ. Ἁρμόδιος ὁ Λεπρεάτης ἐν τῷ περὶ
τῶν κατὰ Φιγάλειαν[4] Νομίμων διεξιὼν περὶ τῶν
ἐπιχωρίων δείπνων γράφει καὶ ταῦτα· " καθαγι-
σάντων ταῦτα ἐν κεραμέᾳ κοτταβίδι πιεῖν ἑκάστῳ
μικρόν, καὶ ὁ προσφέρων ἂν εἴπεν[5] 'εὐδειπνίας.[6]'"
d Ἡγήσανδρος δ' ὁ Δελφὸς ἐν Ὑπομνήμασιν, ὧν
ἀρχὴ " ἐν τῇ ἀρίστῃ πολιτείᾳ," φησίν· " ὁ καλούμενος κότταβος παρῆλθεν εἰς τὰ συμπόσια τῶν
περὶ Σικελίαν, ὥς φησι Δικαίαρχος, πρῶτον
εἰσαγαγόντων. τοσαύτη δὲ ἐγένετο σπουδὴ περὶ
τὸ ἐπιτήδευμα ὥστε εἰς τὰ συμπόσια παρεισφέρειν

---

[1] Something is lost here (cf. 480 f). Kaibel, after
καλεῖσθαι, proposed κοτύλην, Ἑρμῶναξ δὲ συνώνυμα ἀναγράφει
κοτύλην καὶ ἄλεισον, etc.
[2] ᾧ Kaibel, cf. 496 a, Hesychius s.v. κοτυλίσκος: καὶ οἷς A.
[3] Casaubon: χέονται A. [4] φιγάλιαν A.
[5] 149 b: ἀνεῖπεν A. [6] Dobree: ευδειπνειας A.

[a] Il. v. 305. Aeneas is hit κατ' ἰσχίον, ἔνθα τε μηρὸς | ἰσχίῳ
ἐνστρέφεται, κοτύλην δέ τέ μιν καλέουσιν, a passage which must

kotylê is also the name given to the hollow part of the hip-joint [a]; and the growths on the arms of the polyp are called by the derived term *kotyledons*. Further, Aeschylus in *The Edonians* even calls cymbals *kotylai* [b]: "And another crashes loudly with the brazen *kotylai*." Marsyas says that the bone in the hip-joint is called *aleison*,[c] also *cylix*. *Kotyliskos* is the name given to the sacred basin of Dionysus used by the initiates at the Mysteries, according to Nicander of Thyateira, who cites the verse in *The Clouds* of Aristophanes [d]: "Nor shall I wreath a *kotyliskos*." Simmias, too, renders the word *kotylê* by *aleison*.[e]

Kottabis. Harmodius of Lepreum in his work *On the Customs of Phigaleia*, describing the dinners of that place, writes the following [f]: "Having consecrated this food, each man was permitted to drink a little from an earthenware basin (*kottabis*), and the one offering it would say 'Good dinner to you!'" Hegesander of Delphi in his *Commentaries*, which begin with the phrase, "In the best form of government," says [g]: "The game called *kottabos* was introduced into their symposia, the inhabitants of Sicily, according to Dicaearchus,[h] being the first to bring it in. So great an interest was aroused in the pastime that prizes, called *kottabeia*, were also intro-

have been quoted in the original work of Athenaeus or in his sources.
   [b] *T.G.F.*[2] 20 (frag. 57 vs. 6), of the orgiastic rites of Cotyto.
   [c] "Cup" or "socket," *cf.* above, 783 a (p. 46), and below, 480 f, *Etym. Mag.* 478. 57. Marsyas is quoted above, 477 a, for the meaning of *kissybion*; see Suidas *s.v.* Μαρσύας Πελλαῖος, J. 2 B 741.
   [d] Kock i. 491, from the earlier edition of the play.
   [e] Powell 120.
   [f] *F.H.G.* iv. 411, Athen. 149 b (vol. ii. p. 180).
   [g] *F.H.G.* iv. 419.   [h] *F.H.G.* ii. 247.

ἆθλα κοτταβεῖα καλούμενα. εἶτα κύλικες αἱ πρὸς
τὸ πρᾶγμα χρήσιμαι μάλιστ' εἶναι δοκοῦσαι κατεσκευάζοντο, καλούμεναι κοτταβίδες. πρὸς δὲ
τούτοις οἶκοι κατεσκευάζοντο κυκλοτερεῖς, ἵνα
e πάντες εἰς τὸ μέσον τοῦ κοττάβου τεθέντος ἐξ
ἀποστήματος ἴσου καὶ τόπων[1] ὁμοίων ἀγωνίζοιντο
περὶ τῆς νίκης. οὐ γὰρ μόνον ἐφιλοτιμοῦντο βάλλειν ἐπὶ τὸν σκοπόν, ἀλλὰ καὶ καλῶς ἕκαστα
ἀνύτειν.[2] ἔδει γὰρ εἰς τὸν ἀριστερὸν ἀγκῶνα ἐρεί-
σαντα καὶ τῇ δεξιᾷ κυκλώσαντα[3] ὑγρῶς[4] ἀφεῖναι
τὴν λάταγα· οὕτω γὰρ ἐκάλουν τὸ πῖπτον[5] ἐκ τῆς
κύλικος ὑγρόν· ὥστε ἔνιοι μεῖζον ἐφρόνουν ἐπὶ τῷ
καλῶς κοτταβίζειν τῶν ἐπὶ τῷ ἀκοντίζειν μέγα
φρονούντων."

f KPATANION. Μήποτε τὸ νῦν καλούμενον κρανίον[6]
ἔκπωμα οὕτως ὠνόμαζον οἱ ἀρχαῖοι. Πολέμων
γοῦν ἢ ὅστις ἐστὶν ὁ ποιήσας τὸν ἐπιγραφόμενον
Ἑλλαδικὸν περὶ τοῦ ἐν Ὀλυμπίᾳ λέγων Μετα-
ποντίνων ναοῦ γράφει καὶ ταῦτα· "ναὸς Μετα-
ποντίνων, ἐν ᾧ φιάλαι ἀργυραῖ ρλβ', οἰνοχόαι
ἀργυραῖ β', ἀποθυστάνιον[7] ἀργυροῦν, φιάλαι γ'
480 ἐπίχρυσοι. ναὸς Βυζαντίων, ἐν ᾧ Τρίτων κυπαρίσ-
σινος ἔχων κρατάνιον ἀργυροῦν, Σειρὴν ἀργυρᾶ,
καρχήσια β' ἀργυρᾶ, κύλιξ ἀργυρᾶ, οἰνοχόη χρυσῆ,

---

[1] ἐπὶ τῶν Kaibel (?).
[2] ἀνύτειν Gulick (ἀνύειν Lumb): αὐτῶν A.
[3] τῆι δεξιᾶι κυκλώσαντα ACE: τὴν δεξιὰν ἀγκυλώσαντα Kaibel (cf. 427 d, 667 b).
[4] εὐρύθμως Kaibel (?); but why not εὐσχημόνως (782 e)?
[5] πῖπτον AC: πίπτειν E.
[6] κρανίον (κράνιον) E: κρανεῖον A, κράνειον C.
[7] ἀποθυστάνιον A (but -θυστάνιον below).

duced into the symposia.[a] Thereupon cups (cylices) which were thought to be especially adapted to the purpose were manufactured, and they were called *kottabides*. In addition to this, circular rooms were constructed in order that when the *kottabos*[b] was set up in the centre, all might compete for the victory at an equal distance and from similar positions.[c] For they made it a point not merely to hit the mark, but also to carry through each motion in the correct form. For the player, leaning on his left elbow,[d] was obliged to swing his right arm with supple motion and so toss the *latax*; for that is what they called the liquid which fell from the cup; consequently some persons took greater pride in playing *kottabos* well than do persons who pride themselves on hurling the javelin."

Kratanion. Perhaps the cup which is now called *kranion* (skull) was thus named by the men of old. Polemon at any rate, or whoever is the author of the book entitled *Of Hellas*, when discussing the temple of the Metapontines at Olympia writes as follows[e] : " The temple of the Metapontines, in which are 132 silver saucers, two silver wine-jugs, a silver vessel for sacrifice, three gilded saucers. The temple of the Byzantians, in which are a Triton in cypress-wood holding a silver *kratanion*, a silver Siren, two silver *karchesia*,[f] a silver cylix, a golden wine-jug, two

---

[a] The game is discussed again at 665 a, see 427 d note *b* (vol. iv. p. 437), 782 e (above, p. 44). Smith's *Dict. Antiq.* i. 559.

[b] An ordinary lampstand, so called when used for this purpose.

[c] Or " with like conditions for all " (crit. note 1).

[d] As he lay on a couch or on the floor.

[e] Frag. 22 Preller. The ἀποθυστάνιον mentioned in the list may have been a kind of censer, not a drinking-vessel.

[f] Above, 474 e.

κέρατα δύο. ἐν δὲ τῷ ναῷ τῆς Ἥρας τῷ παλαιῷ φιάλαι ἀργυραῖ λ', κρατάνια ἀργυρᾶ β', χύτρος ἀργυροῦς, ἀποθυστάνιον χρυσοῦν, κρατὴρ χρυσοῦς, Κυρηναίων ἀνάθημα, βατιάκιον ἀργυροῦν.''

ΚΡΟΥΝΕΙΑ. Ἐπιγένης Μνηματίῳ·

κρατῆρες, κάδοι,
ὁλκεῖα, κρουνεῖ'. Β. ἔστι γὰρ κρουνεῖα; Α. ναί.

b ΚΥΑΘΙΣ, κοτυλῶδες ἀγγεῖον. Σώφρων ἐν τῷ ἐπιγραφομένῳ μίμῳ Γυναῖκες αἳ τὰν θεὸν φαντὶ ἐξελᾶν[1]· '' ὑποκατώρυκται δὲ ἐν κυαθίδι τρικτὺς[2] ἀλεξιφαρμάκων.''

ΚΥΛΙΞ. Φερεκράτης Δουλοδιδασκάλῳ·

νυνὶ δ' ἀπόνιζε[3] τὴν κύλικα δώσων πιεῖν,
ἔγχει τ' ἐπιθεὶς τὸν ἠθμόν.[4]

ταῦτα δ' ἐστὶ κεράμεα ποτήρια καὶ λέγεται ἀπὸ τοῦ κυλίεσθαι τῷ τροχῷ· ἀφ' ὧν καλεῖται τό τε κυλικεῖον, ἐν ᾧ τίθεται τόπῳ τὰ ποτήρια κἂν ἀργυρᾶ τυγχάνῃ ὄντα, καὶ τὸ κυλικηγορεῖν, ὅταν c ἐπὶ τῇ κύλικί τις ἀγορεύῃ. Ἀθηναῖοι δὲ καὶ τὴν ἰατρικὴν πυξίδα καλοῦσι κυλιχνίδα[5] διὰ τὸ τῷ τόρνῳ κεκυλίσθαι. ἐγένοντο δ' ἐπίσημοι κύλικες αἵ τε Ἀργεῖαι καὶ αἱ Ἀττικαί. καὶ τῶν μὲν Ἀττικῶν μνημονεύει Πίνδαρος ἐν τοῖσδε·

ὦ Θρασύβουλ', ἐρατᾶν ὄχημ' ἀοιδᾶν
τοῦτό τοι[6] πέμπω μεταδόρπιον. ἐν ξυνῷ κεν εἴη

---

[1] ἐξελᾶν Apollon. de Adv. 592. 14 Bekk.: ἔλεξαν A.
[2] κυαθίδι τρικτὺς Schweighäuser: κυαθίδι τρικτοι A.
[3] Kaibel: ἀπονίζειν A.   [4] ἠθμόν A.
[5] Kaibel, cf. below, 480 f, Pollux vi. 98, Hesychius and Photius s.v.: κυλικίδα ACE.   [6] τοι added by Boeckh.

---

[a] Above, 476 a-e.   [b] Above, 784 a (p. 52).

horns.[a] In the old temple of Hera there are thirty silver saucers, two silver *kratania*, a silver pot, a gold vessel for sacrifice, a golden mixing-bowl—a votive offering of the Cyrenaeans—a silver saucer." [b]

Krouneia. Epigenes in *The Souvenir* [c] : " A. There'll be mixing-bowls, jars, basins, and jugs (*krouneia*). B. What ! there are jugs ? A. Yes."

Kyathis, a vessel shaped like a *kotylos.*[d] Sophron, in the mime entitled *Women who say they will expel the Goddess* [e] : " Buried deep down in a cup (*kyathis*) is a triad [f] of magic spells."

Kylix. Pherecrates in *Slave-teacher* [g] : " And now rinse out the cylix and give me a drink, putting the strainer over it before you pour in the wine." These are earthenware drinking-cups, and the name is derived from their being rolled (*kyliesthai*) on the wheel ; from them also comes the term *kylikeion*, the place [h] in which the cups are kept if they happen to be of silver, and the verb *kylikegorein*,[i] said when one talks over one's cups. The Athenians also call the physician's box a *kylichnis*, because it has been turned (*kekylisthai*) on the lathe. Celebrated cups of the cylix-type were those of Argos and of Attica. The Attic cylices are mentioned by Pindar in these verses [j] : " I send thee, Thrasybulus, this chariot of lovely songs to follow the banquet. To thy com-

[c] Kock ii. 418, Athen. 472 e, 486 b. C, after the lemma κρουνεῖον, has εἶδος ποτηρίου. But the κρουνεῖον seems to have had a spout.

[d] Above, 478 b.   [e] Kaibel 154.

[f] A τρικτύς (cf. Hesych. *s.v.* τρικτεῖρα) or τριττύς was a sacrifice of three victims, Eustath. 1676. 38. *Cf.* the Roman *suovetaurilia.*   [g] Kock i. 156.

[h] *i.e.* cupboard, above, 460 d.   [i] Cf. above, 461 e.

[j] *P.L.G.*⁵ 438, Sandys 586 ; continued in Athen. 782 d (above, p. 42).

127

συμπόταισίν τε γλυκερὸν καὶ Διωνύσοιο[1] καρπῷ
καὶ κυλίκεσσιν Ἀθηναίαισι[2] κέντρον.

αἱ δ' Ἀργεῖαι δοκοῦσι καὶ τὸν τύπον ἔχειν διάφορον
d πρὸς τὰς Ἀττικάς. φοξαὶ γοῦν ἦσαν τὸ χεῖλος,
ὡς Σιμωνίδης φησὶν ὁ Ἀμόργιος·

αὕτη[3] δὲ φοξὴ χεῖλος[4] Ἀργείη κύλιξ,[5]

ἡ εἰς ὀξὺ ἀνηγμένη, οἷοί εἰσιν οἱ ἄμβικες καλούμενοι. τὸ γὰρ φοξὸν ἐπὶ τούτου τάττουσι, καθότι
Ὅμηρος ἐπὶ τοῦ Θερσίτου·

φοξὸς ἔην κεφαλήν.

καὶ ἔστιν οἷον φαοξός, ὁ πρὸς τὰ φάη ὀξὺς
ὁρώμενος. διάφοροι δὲ κύλικες γίνονται[6] καὶ ἐν
τῇ τοῦ συσσίτου ἡμῶν Ἀθηναίου πατρίδι Ναυ-
e κράτει. εἰσὶν γὰρ φιαλώδεις μέν, οὐ κατὰ τόρνον,
ἀλλ' ὥσπερ δακτύλῳ πεποιημέναι, καὶ ἔχουσιν ὦτα
τέσσαρα, πυθμένα εἰς πλάτος ἐκτεταμένον (πολλοὶ
δ' ἐν τῇ Ναυκράτει κεραμεῖς· ἀφ' ὧν καὶ ἡ πλησίον
τῶν κεραμείων πύλη Κεραμικὴ καλεῖται) καὶ
βάπτονται εἰς τὸ δοκεῖν εἶναι ἀργυραῖ. ἐπαινοῦνται
δὲ καὶ αἱ Χῖαι κύλικες, ὧν μνημονεύει Ἕρμιππος
ἐν Στρατιώταις·

Χία δὲ κύλιξ ὑψοῦ κρέμαται
περὶ πασσαλόφιν.

f Γλαύκων δ' ἐν ταῖς Γλώσσαις Κυπρίους φησὶ τὴν
κοτύλην κύλικα καλεῖν. Ἑρμῶναξ[7] δ' ἐν Συν-

---

[1] διονύσοιο A.   [2] Schneider: ἀθηναιεσι A.
[3] αὕτη Schol. Il. ii. 219, Etym. Mag. 798. 21: αὐτὴ AC.
[4] φοξὴ χεῖλος Bergk: φοξίχειλος AC, φοξίχηλος (from χηλή,
not χεῖλος) "taper-footed" Edmonds.
[5] Ἀργείη κύλιξ Etym. Mag.: om. AC.
[6] Basle ed.: πίνονται A.   [7] Dobree: ἱππώναξ A.

panions gathered at the feast, to the fruit which Dionysus grants, and to the cups from Athens, they shall be a sweet goad." But the Argive cylices seem to have had a shape different from those of Attica. At any rate they were pointed (*phoxai*) at the brim, as Semonides of Amorgos says [a] : " This is an Argive cylix with pointed brim," that is, one that is raised to a point, like the spouted cups called *ambikes*. For they use the adjective *phoxos* of this, as Homer does in the case of Thersites [b] : " His head was pointed at the top." The word, therefore, is for *phaoxos*, that which looks pointed at the place where the eyes are. Excellent cylices are also made in Naucratis, the native city of our boon-companion Athenaeus. They are like *phialai*,[c] made not as on a lathe but as if fashioned by the finger ; moreover they have four handles and a broadly extended base (there are, by the way, many potters in Naucratis ; from them also the gate which is near the potters' workshops is called the Ceramic Gate) ; and these cups are dyed to look as if they were of silver. In high esteem also are the cylices of Chios ; they are mentioned by Hermippus in *Soldiers* [d] : " And the Chian cylix is now being hung high on its peg." Glaucon in his *Glossary* says that the Cyprians call the *kotylê* [e] a cylix. Hermonax, in *Synonyms*, writes

[a] *P.L.G.*⁴ ii. 457, Diehl frag. 24, Edmonds frag. 27.

[b] *Il.* ii. 219 and Schol., who, however, defines φοξός as " tapered (twisted to a point) in the firing." I have followed L. & S. in rendering ἄμβικες " spouted cup," but may it not mean " cups with offset rim " ? *Cf.* ἄμβη, " raised edge." Many cylices have large eyes painted on the outside of the bowl. See critical note 4.

[c] *i.e.* shallow and saucer-like.

[d] Kock i. 240, describing preparations for war.

[e] Above, 478 d.

ωνύμοις οὗτως γράφει· " ἄλεισον ποτήριον,[1] κύπελλον, ἄμφωτις, σκύφος, κύλιξ, κώθων, καρχήσιον,
φιάλη." Ἀχαιὸς δὲ ὁ Ἐρετριεὺς ἐν Ἀλκμαίωνι
ἀντὶ τοῦ κύλικες παραγώγως κυλιχνίδας εἴρηκε διὰ
τούτων·

> ἀλλ' ὡς τάχιστα μέλανα δεῦρ' ἀμνὸν[2] φέρειν
> κοινόν τε χρὴ κρατῆρα καὶ κυλιχνίδας.

καὶ Ἀλκαῖος κυλίχνας[3] ἐν τῷ . . .[4]

481 > πίνωμεν· τί τὰ λύχν'[5] ὀμμένομεν[6]; δάκτυλος
> ἀμέρα.[7]
> κὰδ δ' ἄειρε[8] κυλίχναις μεγάλαις, ἄιτα, ποι-
> κίλαις.[9]
> οἶνον γὰρ Σεμέλας καὶ Διὸς υἱὸς λαθικαδέα[10]
> ἀνθρώποισιν ἔδωκ'.[11] ἔγχεε κέρναις[12] ἕνα καὶ δύο[13]
> πλέαις[14] κὰκ κεφαλᾶς.[15]

καὶ ἐν τῷ δεκάτῳ·

> λάταγες ποτέονται[16] κυλιχνᾶν ἀπὸ Τηιᾶν,[17]

ὡς διαφόρων γινομένων καὶ ἐν Τέῳ κυλίκων.
Φερεκράτης Κοριαννοῖ·

> ἐκ τοῦ βαλανείου γὰρ δίεφθος[18] ἔρχομαι,
> ξηρὰν ἔχουσα τὴν φάρυγα.[19] Β. δώσω πιεῖν

---

[1] ποτήριον to be deleted (Kaibel)?
[2] δεῦρ' ἀμνὸν Nauck: δευραμονον A.
[3] κυλίχνας add. C: om. A.
[4] ἐν τῷ . . . added by Meineke.
[5] Porson: τὸν λύχνον A. [6] Ahrens: ἀμμένομεν A.
[7] ἀμέρα edd. Other cases of " Aeolic " psilosis, as well as
of barytonesis, undoubtedly correct for the time of Alcaeus,
are not here noted.
[8] ἄερρε edd. [9] ἄιτα, ποικίλαις Hiller: αιταποικιλλις A.
[10] υἱὸς added from 430 d; λαθικηδέα A. [11] ἔδωκεν A.
[12] ἔγχεε κέρναις cf. 430 d: ἐγχεαι κερνα A.

130

thus[a] : "The *aleison* is a drinking-cup, so also *kypellon*, *amphotis*, *skyphos*, *kylix*, *kothon*, *karchesion*, and *phialê*." Achaeus of Eretria, in *Alcmeon*, uses the derived form *kylichnides* in place of *kylikes* in these lines[b] : " Up then ! With all speed you must fetch here a black lamb, a mixing-bowl for all, and some cups (*kylichnidas*)." And Alcaeus has *kylichnai* in one place[c] : " Let us drink ! Why wait we for the lamps ? Daylight hath but a finger's breadth. Boy, take down the large painted cups (*kylichnai*) ; for the son of Semelê and Zeus gave wine to men to banish care. Pour it out, mixing it one and two, full to the brim." And in the tenth book Alcaeus has,[d] " The winedrops fly from the Teian cups (*kylichnai*)," showing that in Teos also the cylices were very fine.

Pherecrates in *Corianno* (has the form *kyliskê*[e]) : " A. I've come from the bath completely boiled, with a throat all dry. B. I'll give you a drink. A. Yes,

[a] This can be understood only as a list of cups, not as a list of synonyms. The ἄλεισον had other uses (479 c).

[b] *T.G.F.*[2] 749 ; from a satyric play (vol. ii. p. 286). A black lamb was sacrificed to avert a storm, Aristoph. *Ran.* 847.

[c] *P.L.G.*[4] frag. 41, Diehl 96, Edmonds 163, Athen. 430 d (vol. iv. p. 450).

[d] *P.L.G.*[4] frag. 43, Diehl 24, Edmonds 172. For λάταγες, of the wine flung in the game of kottabos, see above, 479 e.

[e] Kock i. 164 ; a woman speaks. *Cf.* above, 479 b, where the reading is κοτυλίσκην, not κυλίσκην. But the latter form is well attested. It would seem that the text of Pherecrates was corrupted at an early period, hence the grammarian has cited it for both forms ; κοτυλίσκην, probably, is what Pherecrates wrote originally.

[13] δύο added from 430 d.   [14] 430 d : πλείους A.
[15] κὰκ κεφαλᾶς added from 430 d.   [16] πότηνται edd.
[17] Casaubon : κυλίχναν ἀπὸ (edd. ἀπὺ) τηίαν A.
[18] Casaubon : διεφθορὸς A.   [19] φάρυγγα A.

Α. γλίσχρον γέ μουστὶ τὸ¹ σίαλον νὴ τὼ θεώ.

b Β. τί² λάβω; κεράσω σοι³ τὴν κυλίσκην; Α.
μηδαμῶς
μικράν γε. κινεῖται γὰρ εὐθύς μοι χολή,
ἐξ οὗπερ ἔπιον ἐκ τοιαύτης φάρμακον.
εἰς τὴν ἐμὴν νῦν ἔγχεον τὴν μείζονα.

ὅτι δὲ μεγάλοις ποτηρίοις αἱ γυναῖκες ἐχρῶντο ὁ
αὐτὸς εἴρηκε Φερεκράτης ἐν Τυραννίδι διὰ τούτων·

εἶτ' ἐκεραμεύσαντο⁴ τοῖς μὲν⁵ ἀνδράσιν ποτήρια
πλατέα, τοίχους οὐκ ἔχοντ', ἀλλ' αὐτὸ τοὔδαφος
μόνον,

c κοὐχὶ χωροῦντ'⁶ οὐδὲ κόγχην, ἐμφερῆ γευστη-
ρίοις·
σφίσι δέ γ'⁷ αὐταῖσιν βαθείας κύλικας ὥσπερ
ὁλκάδας
οἰναγωγούς, περιφερεῖς, λεπτάς, μέσας⁸ γαστροι-
ίδας,⁹
οὐκ ἀβούλως, ἀλλὰ πόρρωθεν κατεσκευασμέναι
αὔθ' ὅπως ἀνεκλογίστως πλεῖστος οἶνος ἐκποθῇ.

d εἶθ' ὅταν τὸν οἶνον αὐτὰς αἰτιώμεθ' ἐκπιεῖν,
λοιδοροῦνται κὠμνύουσι¹⁰ μὴ πιεῖν¹¹ ἀλλ' ἢ μίαν.
ἡ δὲ κρείττων ἡ μί' ἐστὶ χιλίων ποτηρίων.

ΚΥΜΒΙΑ τὰ ποτήρια καὶ πλοῖα μικρὰ¹² Σιμάριστος.
Δωρόθεος δέ· " γένος ποτηρίων βαθέων τὰ κυμβία

---

¹ Dobree: τέ μου τὸ Α. ² τί Jacobs: εἰ Α.
³ κεράσω σοι Toup: κυρισοι Α.
⁴ Bergk: εἶτα κεραμεύσαντα Α. ⁵ μὲν CE: om. A.
⁶ Casaubon: δωροῦντ' Α.
⁷ σφίσι δέ γ' Bergk (ταῖς δὲ γυναιξὶ in paraphr. C): φασὶ
δ' Α.
⁸ Α: μεστὰς CE. ⁹ γαστρώνιδας Kock.

132

my spit is sticky, by the two goddesses.[a] B. What shall I get ? Shall I mix you up a little cup (*kyliskê*) ? A. No, by no means a little one. For the bile gets stirred up in me at once, ever since I drank medicine [b] from that kind of cup. Pour it now into this bigger cup that I have." That women liked to use big cups is attested by Pherecrates again in these verses from *Tyranny* [c] : "Thereupon, for the men, they caused to be made flat drinking-cups which had no sides, only just a bottom holding not even so much as a thimbleful, like little ' tasters '[d] ; but for themselves alone they had cups (cylices) manu- factured as deep as wine-transporting merchantmen, well rounded, delicately fashioned, yet bellying out in the middle ; the women had had them made not without shrewd planning, and long before, for they wanted to be able to drink up the greatest possible quantity of wine without being called to account. And then, when we men accuse them of drinking up all the wine, they scold us and swear they haven't taken more than a single cup. But this single cup is mightier than a thousand ! ''

Kymbia are cups, and also small boats, according to Simaristus. Dorotheus says : " The *kymbia* are a

---

[a] Demeter and Korê, often in Athenian women's oaths.
[b] In this case the " medicine " is wine.
[c] Kock i. 187, above, 460 c. The title apparently referred to a gynaecocracy, as in Aristoph. *Ecclesiazusae.* Women were often derided in comedy for bibulousness.
[d] Very small cups used by wine tasters ; *cf.* Athen. 380 f (vol. iv. p. 222).

---

[10] C : κὸμνύουσι A.   [11] πιεῖν CE : κπιεῖν A.
[12] τὰ ποτήρια καὶ πλοῖα μικρὰ Kaibel : τὰ κοῖλα ποτήρια καὶ μικρὰ A.

καὶ ὀρθῶν,[1] πυθμένα μὴ ἐχόντων μηδὲ ὦτα."
Πτολεμαῖος δὲ ὁ τοῦ Ἀριστονίκου τὰ κυφά.
Νίκανδρος δ᾽ ὁ Θυατειρηνὸς τὸ χωρὶς ὠτίων
ποτήριον ὠνομακέναι Θεόπομπον ἐν Μήδῳ. Φιλήμων Φάσματι·

                          ἔπιεν[2] ἡ Ῥόδη
e   κυμβίον ἀκράτου· κατασέσειχ᾽ ὑμᾶς[3] ἄφνω.[4]

Διονύσιος δ᾽ ὁ Σάμιος ἐν ἕκτῳ περὶ τοῦ Κύκλου
τὸ αὐτὸ οἴεται εἶναι κισσύβιον καὶ κυμβίον. φησὶ
γὰρ ὡς Ὀδυσσεὺς πληρώσας κυμβίον ἀκράτου
ὤρεξε τῷ Κύκλωπι. οὐκ ἔστι δὲ μικρὸν τὸ διδόμενον αὐτῷ κισσύβιον παρ᾽ Ὁμήρῳ· οὐ γὰρ ἂν
τρὶς πιὼν μέγιστος ὢν τὸ σῶμα ταχέως ἂν ὑπὸ
τῆς μέθης κατηνέχθη. τοῦ κυμβίου μνημονεύει
καὶ Δημοσθένης ἐν τῷ κατὰ Μειδίου ἀκολουθεῖν
αὐτῷ φάσκων ῥυτὰ καὶ κυμβία. καὶ[5] πάλιν ἐν τῷ
αὐτῷ· " ἐπ᾽ ἀστράβης δὲ ὀχούμενος ἐξ Ἀργούρας
τῆς Εὐβοίας,[6] χλανίδας δ᾽ ἐπ᾽ ὄχου[7] καὶ κυμβία
καὶ κάδους[8] ἔχων, ὧν ἐπελαμβάνοντο οἱ πεντη-
f κοστολόγοι." καὶ ἐν τῷ κατὰ Εὐέργου καὶ Μνησι-

---

[1] C (e corr.) E : ὀρθὸν A.
[2] ἔπιεν Macrobius v. 21. 7 : ἐπεὶ δ᾽ A.
[3] ἡμᾶς Meineke.   [4] ἄφνω Kock : ἄνω A.
[5] καὶ . . . οἱ πεντηκοστολόγοι added by Kaibel (Macrob. v. 21. 8).
[6] ἀστράβης ἀργυρᾶς τῆς ἐξ Εὐβοίας Demosth. Cod. Σ and Schol.
[7] δ᾽ ἐπ᾽ ὄχου Schneidewin : δε οχο cod. Macrob., om. Dem.
[8] καὶ κάδους added by Schneidewin from Dem.: οσι Macrob.

---

[a] Cf. Macrobius v. 21. 9 : " haec cymbia, pocula procera
ac navibus similia." This explains the "curving brim" (lit.
" hunched brim ") in the following, rising high like the prow
and stern of a Greek ship.   [b] Kock i. 741.

variety of cups, deep and high,[a] having no stem and
no handles." But Ptolemy the son of Aristonicus
says they are the kind with curving brim. Nicander
of Thyateira says that Theopompus, in *The Mede*,[b] so
named the cup which has no handles. Philemon in
The Ghost[c] : " Rosa drank a *kymbion* of unmixed
wine ; she soon had you all under the table."
Dionysius of Samos, in the sixth book of his work
On the Cycle, expresses the belief that *kymbion* and
kissybion are the same thing.[d] For he says that
Odysseus filled a *kymbion* with unmixed wine and
handed it to the Cyclops. Certainly the *kissybion*
given to him in Homer[e] cannot be small ; otherwise
he, so huge of body, would not have been quickly
overcome with intoxication after only three drinks.
The *kymbion* is mentioned by Demosthenes, also, in
the speech *Against Meidias*, in which he says[f] that
Meidias was accompanied by drinking-horns and
kymbia. And in the same speech again[g] : " He
rode on a pillion[h] from Argura in Euboea, with fine
robes and *kymbia* and jars in a cart, which were
seized by the customs-officers.[i] " The word occurs
also in the speech *Against Euergus and Mnesibulus*.[j]

---

[c] Kock ii. 502. For κατασείω, " drink under the table,"
cf. 431 b (vol. iv. p. 454).
[d] *F.H.G.* ii. 10, J. 1. 179, above, 477 d-e.
[e] *Od.* ix. 346 ; cf. 461 d (p. 10).
[f] § 158 : " With three or four attendants he swaggers
through the market-place, calling out loudly the names of
his horns and *kymbia* and saucers to make the passers-by
hear."
[g] § 133, or " a pillion with silver trappings which came
from Euboea "; critical note 6.
[h] The use of a pillion by men was condemned as effeminate.
[i] Lit. " collectors of one-fiftieth, or two per cent "; cf.
εἰκοστολόγος, Aristoph. *Ran.* 363.   [j] [Dem.] *Or.* xlvii. 58.

βούλου. φησὶ δὲ Δίδυμος ὁ γραμματικὸς ἐπίμηκες εἶναι τὸ ποτήριον καὶ στενὸν τῷ σχήματι, παρόμοιον πλοίῳ ὃ καλεῖται κύμβη.[1] καὶ Ἀναξανδρίδης ἐν Ἀγροίκοις·

μεγάλ' ἴσως ποτήρια[2]
προπινόμενα καὶ μέστ' ἀκράτου κυμβία
ἐκάρωσεν[3] ὑμᾶς. Β. ἀνακεχαίτικεν[4] μὲν οὖν.

Ἄλεξις Ἱππεῖ·

τά τε κυμβία
482 ἆρ'[5] ἦν πρόσωπ' ἔχοντα χρυσᾶ παρθένων;
Β. νὴ τὸν Δί', ἦν γάρ. Α. ὦ τάλαιν' ἐγώ[6] κακῶν.

Ἐρατοσθένης δ' ἐν τῇ πρὸς Ἀγήτορα τὸν Λάκωνα Ἐπιστολῇ ὡς κυαθῶδες ἀγγεῖον τὸ κυμβίον παραδίδωσι γράφων οὕτως· "θαυμάζουσι δὲ οἱ αὐτοὶ καὶ πῶς κύαθον μὴ κεκτημένος, ἀλλὰ κυμβίον μόνον, φιάλην[7] προσεκέκτητο. δοκεῖ δή μοι τὸ μὲν τῆς τῶν ἀνθρώπων χρείας ἕνεκα, τὸ δὲ τῆς τῶν θεῶν τιμῆς εἰς τὴν κτῆσιν παρειληφέναι. κυάθῳ μὲν οὖν οὐδὲν ἐχρῶντο τότε οὐδὲ κοτύλῃ.
b κρατῆρα γὰρ ἵστασαν[8] τοῖς θεοῖς, οὐκ ἀργυροῦν οὐδὲ λιθοκόλλητον, ἀλλὰ γῆς Κωλιάδος.[9] τούτου δ' ὁσάκις ἐπιπληρώσαιεν,[10] ἀποσπείσαντες τοῖς θεοῖς ἐκ τῆς φιάλης ᾠνοχόουν ἐφεξῆς, τὸν νεοκρατα

---

[1] δ . . . κύμβη added by Egenolff (Bekker, Anec. 274. 29, cf. Etym. Mag. 545. 31).
[2] ποτήρια deleted by Kaibel (cf. Macrob. v. 21. 8).
[3] ἐκάκωσεν Macrob.   [4] ἀνακεχέτικεν Α.
[5] ἆρ' added by Dobree.   [6] Dindorf: ἔγωγε Α.
[7] Casaubon: κυμβίον· μόνην φιάλην Α.
[8] ἔστησαν Macrob.
[9] γῆς Κωλιάδος H. Sauppe: τῆς κωλιάδος γῆς Α (ΤΗΟ ΚΩΛΙΑΔΟϹ Macrob.).

Didymus the grammarian says [a] that the cup is long and narrow in shape, similar to a boat which is called *kymbê*.[b] So Anaxandrides in *The Farmers* [c]: " A. Perhaps the big cups with which we were challenged and the *kymbia* full of unmixed wine have stupefied us. B. Stupefied! They've upset us completely!" Alexis in *The Horseman* [d]: " A. And how about the *kymbia*? Did they have faces of girls in gold? B. Yes, by Zeus, they did indeed. A. Alas, what bad luck is mine!" Eratosthenes, on the other hand, in the *Letter to Agetor of Lacedaemon*, represents the *kymbion* as shaped like a *kyathos*. He writes as follows [e]: " The same persons wonder how it was that if he had no *kyathos*, but only a *kymbion*, he also owned a *phialê*. It seems to me, then, that the first was for the use of men, whereas he had acquired possession of the second in order to honour the gods.[f] In those days they made no use of a *kyathos*, nor again of a *kotylê*. For they used to set up a mixing-bowl in honour of the gods, one not made of silver, nor set with precious stones, but made of clay from Cape Colias.[g] Every time that they filled up this bowl they would make a libation to the gods from the *phialê*, and then have the wine poured for themselves in due order, dipping up the fresh mixture

[a] Schmidt 75.
[b] *Cf.* below, 482 d. So Hor. *Odes* ii. 3. 28 uses *cumba* of Charon's boat.　　　　　　　　　[c] Kock ii. 136.
[d] *Ibid.* 328 ; *cf.* above, 784 d-466 (p. 56). Apparently an hetaera has suffered the loss of valuable cups by theft.
[e] Bernhardy 201, Macrobius v. 21. 10.
[f] Since the *phialê* was very often used in libations, as explained below.　　　　　[g] A fine quality of white clay.

---

[10] ἐπιπληρώσαιεν Schweighäuser (so apparently Macrob.): ἐπί τι πληρώσαιεν A.

βάπτοντες τῷ κυμβίῳ, καθὰ καὶ νῦν παρ' ὑμῖν
ποιοῦσιν ἐν τοῖς φιδιτίοις.[1] εἰ δέ ποτε πλεῖον πιεῖν
βουληθεῖεν, προσπαρετίθεσαν τοὺς καλουμένους
κοτύλους, κάλλιστα καὶ εὐποτώτατα ἐκπωμάτων.
ἦσαν δὲ καὶ οὗτοι τῆς αὐτῆς κεραμείας." ὅταν δ'
Ἔφιππος ἐν Ἐφήβοις λέγῃ·

c ⟨οὐ⟩ κύλικας ἐπὶ τὰ δεῖπνα Χαιρήμων φέρει,
οὐ κυμβίοισι πεπολέμηκ' Εὐριπίδης;

οὐ τὸν τραγικὸν λέγει ποιητήν, ἀλλά τινα ὁμώνυμον
αὐτῷ, ἤτοι φίλοινόν τινα ἢ αἰτίαν ἔχοντα οὐ χρηστήν,
ὥς φησιν Ἀντίοχος ὁ Ἀλεξανδρεὺς ἐν τῷ περὶ
τῶν ἐν τῇ μέσῃ κωμῳδίᾳ κωμῳδουμένων Ποιητῶν.
τὸ γὰρ ἐπάγεσθαι κατὰ τὰς ἑστιάσεις κυμβία καὶ
δοκεῖν τούτοις διαμάχεσθαι εἰς ἑκάτερα τείνει.
μνημονεύει δ' αὐτοῦ καὶ Ἀναξανδρίδης ἐν Νηρηΐσιν·

d
δὸς δὴ τὸν χόα
αὐτῷ σύ, Κῶμε,[2] καὶ τὸ κυμβίον φέρων·
Εὐριπίδης τις σήμερον γενήσεται.

καὶ Ἔφιππος ἐν Ὁμοίοις ἢ Ὀβελιαφόροις·
Διονυσίου δὲ δράματ' ἐκμαθεῖν δέοι
καὶ Δημοφῶντος ἅττ' ἐποίησεν[3] εἰς Κότυν,[4]
ῥήσεις τε κατὰ δεῖπνον[5] Θεόδωρός μοι λέγοι,
Λάχητί τ'[6] οἰκήσαιμι τὴν ἑξῆς θύραν,
κυμβία τε παρέχοιμ' ἑστιῶν Εὐριπίδῃ.[7]

---

[1] φιδιτείοις A.   [2] σύ, Κῶμε Meineke: σύγκωμε A.
[3] Petit: ατεποιησεν A.   [4] Casaubon: κοτύλην A.
[5] Porson: κατὰ τὸ δεῖπνον A.   [6] Porson: ληγιτ A.
[7] Dobree: εὐριπίδης A.

---

[a] In Athens the ladle-like κύαθος was used for this purpose.
[b] Kock ii. 255. Ephippus, as Athenaeus sees, is satirizing
men of his own time (fourth century B.C.).
[c] i.e. to the charge of drinking too much and of having
a disreputable character in general.

with the *kymbion*,[a] just as people do to-day in your
messes at Sparta.   But if they ever wanted to drink
more, they used also to set before them the so-called
kotyloi, best and easiest of all cups to drink from.
These also were of the same clay workmanship."
Again, when Ephippus in *The Recruits* says,[b] " Does
not Chaeremon always bring cylices to dinners,
hasn't Euripides fought with *kymbia*? " he does not
mean the tragic poet but someone with the same
name, a wine-bibber, that is, or one having a bad
reputation, as Antiochus of Alexandria avers in his
work *On the Poets ridiculed in the Middle Comedy*.
For to bring along *kymbia* to an entertainment and
to have the reputation of fighting with them points
in each direction.[c]   This Euripides is mentioned also
by Anaxandrides in *The Nereids*[d] : " You there,
Comus, fetch the *kymbion* and give the pitcher to
him.   He will turn into a Euripides to-day."   And
Ephippus in *Just Alike* or *The Obeliaphoroi*[e] : " Yes,
and may I have to learn by heart some plays of
Dionysius,[f] or Demophon's lines against Cotys;
and may I have to listen to Theodorus reciting
pieces at dinner, and live next door to Laches,
and supply the *kymbia* when I entertain Euripides."

[a] Kock ii. 146.
[e] *Ibid.* 259 ; for the title see Athen. 111 b, 359 a (vol. ii.
p. 23, vol. iv. p. 125). The scene is perhaps like that in Aristoph.
Ran. 146 ff., esp. 151 ἢ Μορσίμου τις ῥῆσιν ἐξεγράψατο, involving a comic imprecation ; *cf.* also *Lysistr.* 233 ff., and
the whimsical curse, *Acharn.* 1150 ff.
[f] Dionysius the Elder affected tragedy, Aelian, *V.H.*
xiii. 18.   Cotys (see Athen. 131 a), King of Thrace, at first
an ally of Athens, became her enemy *ca.* 365 B.C.   Theodorus
was celebrated for his acting in the character of Antigone,
Demosth. xix. 246 ; *cf.* Diog. L. ii. 102.

ὅτι δὲ καὶ πλοῖον ἡ κύμβη Σοφοκλῆς ἐν Ἀνδρομέδᾳ φησίν[1]·

e   ἵπποισιν ἢ κύμβαισι ναυστολεῖς χθόνα;

κύββα[2] ποτήριον Ἀπολλόδωρος Παφίους.[3]

ΚΥΠΕΛΛΟΝ. τοῦτο πότερόν ἐστιν ταὐτὸν τῷ ἀλείσῳ καὶ τῷ δέπαι καὶ μόνον[4] ὀνόματι διαλλάσσει—

    τοὺς μὲν ἄρα χρυσέοισι κυπέλλοις υἷες Ἀχαιῶν
    δειδέχατ' ἄλλοθεν ἄλλος ἀνασταδόν—

ἢ διάφορος ἦν ὁ τύπος καὶ οὐχ ὥσπερ τὸ δέπας καὶ τὸ ἄλεισον ἀμφικύπελλον, οὕτω καὶ[5] τοῦτο, κυφὸν δὲ μόνον; ἀπὸ γὰρ τῆς κυφότητος τὸ

f κύπελλον, ὥσπερ καὶ τὸ ἀμφικύπελλον· ἢ ὅτι παραπλήσιον ἦν ταῖς πέλλαις, συνηγμένον μᾶλλον εἰς τὴν κυφότητα· ἢ ἀμφικύπελλα οἷον ἀμφίκυρτα ἀπὸ τῶν ὤτων, διὰ τὸ τοιαῦτα εἶναι τῇ κατασκευῇ. φησὶ γὰρ καὶ ὁ ποιητής·

    ἦ τοι ὁ καλὸν ἄλεισον ἀναιρήσεσθαι ἔμελλεν[6]
    χρύσεον ἄμφωτον.

Ἀντίμαχος δ' ἐν ε' Θηβαΐδος·

    πᾶσιν δ' ἡγεμόνεσσιν ἐποιχόμενοι κήρυκες
    χρύσεα καλὰ κύπελλα τετυγμένα νωμήσαντο.

---

[1] παρίστησιν Kaibel, and so translated.
[2] κύββα A, Hesychius *s.v.*, κύμβα C.
[3] π φιους A.   [4] καὶ μόνον Casaubon, Kaibel: ἢ A.
[5] οὕτω καὶ Kaibel: οὕτω δὲ καὶ A.
[6] ἦ τοι . . . ἔμελλεν added from 783 b, *Etym. Mag.* 90. 46.

---

[a] *T.G.F.*[2] 158. This remark belongs more properly at 481 f after the citation from Didymus, and is so placed in C, which, however, omits the remainder of 481 f and all of 482 a-d.

[b] J. 2 B 1108.   [c] Above, 783 a (p. 46).

That the *kymbê* is also a boat Sophocles shows in *Andromeda*[a] : " With horses or in boats (*kymbai*) dost thou travel over the earth ? " *Kybba* is a cup, Apollodorus says,[b] in Paphos.

Kypellon. Is this the same cup as the *aleison*[c] and the *depas*, differing only in name—" So then the sons of the Achaeans, standing upon this side and on that, pledged them in cups (*kypella*) of gold "[d]—or can it be that the *kypellon* had a different shape, and was not a double-cup (*amphikypellon*), as the *depas* and the *aleison* were, but simply had a curving brim ? For the word *kypellon* is derived from the word meaning rotundity (*kyphotês*),[e] just as the word *amphikypellon* is ; or perhaps it is called *kypellon* because it resembles the *pellai*,[f] though with a more contracted curve ; or else *amphikypella* may be as it were *amphikyrta* or doubly convex, said of the handles, since they are like that in construction.[g] For the Poet says[h] : " Now he was just on the point of raising a fair golden, two-handled cup (*aleison*)." So Antimachus in the fifth book of the *Thebaïs*[i] : " And the heralds, going to them in turn, dispensed to all the leaders fair cups (*kypella*) wrought in gold." But

[d] *Il.* ix. 670 ; a δέπας ἀμφικύπελλον had been used for a libation (656). Doubtless other quotations once stood here, to prove the identity in Homer of the three terms.

[e] Lit. "curvingness." The root of the word, referring to any hollow place or thing, is widely extended throughout the Indo-European languages, and is still seen in Eng. "cup." See *Glotta* 16, 1928, 88.

[f] Bowls, often used as milk-pails ; below, 495 c.

[g] So Aristarchus, *Etym. Mag.* 90. 46.

[h] *Od.* xxii. 9, above, 783 a (p. 46). The quotation merely proves that the *aleison* (= *amphikypellon*) had two handles. It proves nothing as to the etymology.

[i] *Frag. ep.* 281.

141

Σιληνὸς δέ φησι· " κύπελλα ἐκπώματα σκύφοις
ὅμοια, ὡς καὶ Νίκανδρος ὁ Κολοφώνιος . . .
483 ' κύπελλα δ' ἔνειμε συβώτης.' " Εὔμολπος δὲ
ποτηρίου γένος, ἀπὸ τοῦ κυφὸν εἶναι. Σιμάριστος
δὲ τὸ δίωτον ποτήριον Κυπρίους, τὸ δὲ δίωτον
καὶ τετράωτον Κρῆτας. Φιλίτας δὲ Συρακοσίους
κύπελλα καλεῖν τὰ τῆς μάζης καὶ τῶν ἄρτων ἐπὶ
τῆς τραπέζης καταλείμματα.

κυμβη. Φιλήμων ἐν ταῖς Ἀττικαῖς Φωναῖς κύλικος εἶδος. Ἀπολλόδωρος δ' ἐν τῷ περὶ Ἐτυμο-
λογιῶν Παφίους τὸ ποτήριον καλεῖν κύββα.[1]

b κωθων Λακωνικὸν ποτήριον, οὗ μνημονεύει
Ξενοφῶν ἐν α΄ Κύρου Παιδείας. Κριτίας δ' ἐν
Λακεδαιμονίων Πολιτείᾳ γράφει οὕτως· " χωρὶς
δὲ τούτων τὰ σμικρότατα ἐς τὴν δίαιταν· ὑποδήματα ἄριστα Λακωνικά· ἱμάτια φορεῖν ἥδιστα
καὶ χρησιμώτατα· κώθων[2] Λακωνικός, ἔκπωμα
ἐπιτηδειότατον εἰς στρατείαν καὶ εὐφορώτατον ἐν
γυλιῷ. οὗ δὲ[3] ἕνεκα στρατιωτικόν, πολλάκις
ἀνάγκη ὕδωρ πίνειν οὐ καθαρόν. πρῶτον μὲν οὖν

---

[1] κύββα Kaibel (cf. 482 e): κύμβα A, κύμβαν CE.
[2] κώθων Casaubon: καθ' ὦν A.
[3] οὗ δὲ Casaubon: οὐδὲ A.

---

[a] That is, they were like bowls without handles ; Silenus
held, against Aristarchus, that the *amphikypellon* had no
handles (783 b).

[b] Frag. 140 Schneider ; the quotation is lost.

Silenus says : " *Kypella* are drinking-cups similar to *skyphoi*,[a] as Nicander of Colophon shows . . .[b] 'The swineherd distributed *kypella*.' "[c] Eumolpus says that it is a kind of cup, derived from the word *kyphos* (curved). Simaristus, however, defines it as the two-handled cup among the Cyprians, whereas in Crete it is the two-handled and four-handled cup. Again, Philitas says [d] that the people of Syracuse call the crumbs of barley-cake and wheat loaves left on the table *kypella*.

Kymbê.[e] Philemon in his *Attic Words* says that this is a kind of cylix. Apollodorus in his work *On Etymologies* says that the inhabitants of Paphos call this cup *kybba*.[f]

Kothon. A Lacedaemonian cup which Xenophon mentions in the first book of *Cyropaedeia*.[g] And Critias in *The Constitution of the Lacedaemonians* writes as follows [h] : " Apart from those things, the smallest details of their daily life (are commendable) : Lacedaemonian shoes are the best ; their cloaks are the pleasantest and most convenient to wear ; the Lacedaemonian *kothon* is a drinking-vessel most suitable for military service and most easily carried in a knapsack. It is adapted to military purposes for the reason that it is often necessary to drink water that is not pure. In the first place it was useful in that the water drunk could not be too

[c] *Od.* xx. 253 ; here *kypella* seems to be generic for " cups," though a *depas* is mentioned presently (261).
[d] Om. Powell, Kaibel 201.
[e] This lemma and definition originally stood at 482 e (p. 140).   [f] J. 2 B 1108.
[g] Chap. 2. 8, of the cup carried by every Persian boy to school.
[h] *F.H.G.* ii. 68, Diels 623 : *cf.* Plut. *Lycurg.* 9.

τὸ μὴ λίαν κατάδηλον[1] εἶναι τὸ πόμα· εἶτα ἄμβωνας
ὁ κώθων ἔχων ὑπολείπει[2] τὸ οὐ καθαρὸν ἐν αὐτῷ."
c καὶ Πολέμων δ' ἐν τῇ . . .[3] τῶν πρὸς 'Αδαῖον καὶ
'Αντίγονον, ὅτι κεραμέοις ἀγγείοις ἐχρῶντο οἱ
Λακεδαιμόνιοι γράφει οὕτως· " ἀλλὰ μὴν ὅτι
ἀρχαϊκὸν ἦν τὸ τοιόνδε[4] τῆς ἀγωγῆς γένος . . . δ
καὶ νῦν ὁρᾶται[5] παρά τισι τῶν Ἑλλήνων· ἐν "Αργει
μὲν ἐν ταῖς δημοσίαις θοίναις, ἐν Λακεδαίμονι δὲ
κατὰ τὰς ἑορτάς, ἔν τε τοῖς ἐπινικίοις καὶ τοῖς
γάμοις τῶν παρθένων, πίνουσιν ἐκ κεραμέων ποτη-
ρίων· ἐν δὲ τοῖς ἄλλοις συμποσίοις καὶ φιδιτίοις
d ἐν πιθάκναις . . .'' μνημονεύει αὐτοῦ καὶ 'Αρχί-
λοχος ἐν Ἐλεγείοις ὡς ποτηρίου οὕτως·

ἀλλ' ἄγε[6] σὺν κώθωνι θοῆς διὰ σέλματα νηὸς
φοίτα καὶ κοίλων πώματ' ἄφελκε κάδων,
ἄγρει δ' οἶνον ἐρυθρὸν ἀπὸ τρυγός· οὐδὲ γὰρ ἡμεῖς
νήφειν ἐν[7] φυλακῇ τῇδε δυνησόμεθα,

ὡς τῆς κύλικος λεγομένης κώθονος. 'Αριστοφάνης
Ἱππεῦσιν·

εἰς τὰς ἱππαγωγοὺς εἰσεπήδων ἀνδρικῶς
πριάμενοι κώθωνας, οἱ δὲ σκόροδα καὶ[8] κρόμμυα.

e Ἡνίοχος Γοργόσι·

[1] Basle ed.: κατάδολον A.
[2] H. Stephanus: ὑπολείπειν A.
[3] ἐν τῇ πέμπτῃ Schweighäuser, assuming that the quotation
from Polemon 484 c also came here. That now given in A
has no pertinence here.   [4] τοιόνδε Kaibel: τοιοῦτον δὲ A.
[5] ὁρᾶται Wilamowitz: δρᾶται A.   [6] Musurus: ἀλλά τε A.
[7] ἐν (ἐσ Papyrus) Musurus: μὲν A.
[8] οἱ δὲ καὶ σκόροδα καὶ Aristoph. Aldine edition; οἱ δὲ σκόροδα
(Aristoph. codd., Athen. A σκόροδα) ἐλάας κρόμμυα Bergk.

[a] Plutarch, loc. cit., says that the colour of the κώθων disguised the muddy water !   Aristoph. Pac. 1094 (in a parody)

clearly seen [a] ; and in the second place, since the
kothon had inward-curving edges, it retained a residue
of the impurities inside it." Polemon, also, in the
. . . book of his *Address to Adaeus and Antigonus*, after
saying that the Lacedaemonians used vessels of
earthenware, writes as follows [b] : "But certainly, that
this sort of discipline was ancient . . . (It is a custom)
which may be seen even to-day among some of the
Greek peoples : in Argos at the public banquets, in
Lacedaemon during their festivals and on the occasion of dinners celebrating victory or the marriage
of their maidens, they drink from earthenware cups ;
but in the case of the symposia and at the public
ness (the wine is mingled) in casks . . ." Archi-
ochus mentions the *kothon* as a drinking-cup in his
Elegiac Verses thus [c] : "Up then, and with your
wine-bottle pace up and down by the rowing-benches
of the swift ship, and pull off the lids from the hollow
ars ; take the red wine from the very lees ; for even
we shall not be able to keep sober on such a watch
as this." Evidently the *kothon* here is what is ordinarily called a cylix.[d] Aristophanes in *The Knights* [e] :
'They leaped aboard the cavalry-transports like
men, after purchasing wine-bottles (*kothones*), or
garlic and onions." Heniochus in *Gorgons* [f] : "Here,

---

ays it was shiny, φαεινός. The vessel, like the canteen or
water-bottle, was an essential item in the soldier's kit. The
word φλασκίον superseded κώθων later; see the Emperor
Maurice's *Strategikon*, vii. 11.
  [b] Frag. 61 Preller ; see critical note 3.
  [c] *P.L.G.*[4] ii. 384, Diehl frag. 5 a, Edmonds frag. 4, *Ox.
Pap.* vi. 149.   [d] Wine-cup in a general sense.
  [e] vs. 599, from the first parabasis.
  [f] Kock ii. 431. The text is uncertain ; the metre may be
lochmiac (Wilamowitz), appropriate to this turgid parody.

πιεῖν πιεῖν τις ἐγχείτω λαβὼν
πυριγενῆ κυκλοτερῆ βραχύωτον παχύστομον
κώθωνα, παῖδα φάρυγος.[1]

Θεόπομπος Στρατιώτισιν·

ἐγὼ γὰρ ἂν[2] κώθωνος ἐκ στρεψαύχενος
πίοιμι τὸν[3] τράχηλον ἀνακεκλασμένη;

Ἄλεξις Ἐρίθοις·

εἶτα[4] τετρακότυλον ἐπεσόβει κώθωνά μοι,
παλαιὸν[5] οἴκων κτῆμα.

ἀπὸ δὲ τοῦ ποτηρίου τούτου καὶ ἀκρατοκώθωνας
καλοῦσι τοὺς πλέονα[6] ἄκρατον σπῶντας, ὡς
Ὑπερείδης ἐν τῷ κατὰ Δημοσθένους. Καλλίξεινος
f δ᾽ ἐν τετάρτῳ περὶ Ἀλεξανδρείας ἀναγράφων τὴν
τοῦ Φιλαδέλφου πομπὴν καὶ καταλέγων πολλὰ
ἐκπώματα γράφει καὶ τάδε· " κώθωνες διμέτρητοι
β᾽." περὶ δὲ τοῦ κωθωνίζεσθαι καὶ ὅτι χρήσιμός
ἐστι διὰ χρόνου ὁ κωθωνισμὸς Μνησίθεος
Ἀθηναῖος ἰατρὸς ἐν τῇ περὶ Κωθωνισμοῦ ἐπιστολῇ
φησιν οὕτως· " συμβαίνει τοὺς μὲν πολὺν ἄκρατον
ἐν ταῖς συνουσίαις πίνοντας μεγάλα βλάπτεσθαι
484 καὶ τὸ σῶμα καὶ τὴν ψυχήν. τὸ μέντοι κωθωνίζεσθαι διά τινων ἡμερῶν δοκεῖ μοι ποιεῖν τινα κα
τοῦ σώματος κάθαρσιν καὶ τῆς ψυχῆς ἄνεσιν·
γίγνονται γάρ τινες ἡμῖν ἐκ τῶν καθ᾽ ἡμέρας

---

[1] φάρυγγος ACE.
[2] ἂν added by Liebel from vs. 2.
[3] πίοιμι τὸν Schweighäuser: ποιμαντὸν A, πιόμιαν τὸν CE.
[4] Porson: εἶτ᾽ ἐν A; Kaibel proposed the Ionic form εἶτε (with τρικότυλον), condemned by Phrynichus 101.
[5] Porson: πλέον A.
[6] Kaibel: πλέον A, πολὺν CE.
[7] Athen. 199 f: διάμετροι A.

146

somebody! Seize the fire-born, round, small-eared, thick-lipped wine-bottle (*kothon*), minister to our throats, and pour out a drink, a drink!" Theopompus in *Militant Females*[a]: "What, am I to bend my throat away back and drink from a neck-twisting canteen (*kothon*)?" Alexis in *Toilers*[b]: "Thereupon he socked me with a quart canteen—O ancient chattel of our house!" It is from this kind of cup that those who take too large a pull at unmixed wine are called "neat-wine-canteeners," as Hypereides says in the *Speech against Demosthenes*.[c] And Callixeinus, describing in the fourth book of his work *On Alexandria* the procession of Philadelphus, in which he enumerates many drinking-cups, writes also,[d] "Two canteens holding twenty gallons." Now with regard to drinking from these large cups, and demonstrating that such hard drinking, at intervals of time, is beneficial, Mnesitheus, the Athenian physician, says in his letter *On Hard Drinking* this: "The result of people drinking large quantities of unmixed wine at social gatherings is considerable injury done to body and to mind. And yet hard drinking after several days' interval[e] seems to me to produce a kind of purgation of the body and a relaxation of the mind. For certain superficial manifestations of acidity are caused in our systems by daily attendance at symposia;

[a] Kock i. 747. The play represented women assuming military duties.
[b] Kock ii. 363; the second vs. is taken from Eur. *Medea* 49.
[c] Blass, p. 23; Sir F. G. Kenyon, in his edition, quotes Priscian xviii. 235 ἀλλὰ τοὺς νεωτέρους ἐπὶ βοήθειαν καλεῖς, οὓς ὕβριζες καὶ ἐλοιδοροῦ ἀκρατοκώθωνας ἀποκαλῶν. *Cf.* Athen. 246 a (vol. iii. p. 106).
[d] *F.H.G.* iii. 58 ff., Athen. 196 a (vol. ii. pp. 386-418).
[e] *Sc.* following the last spree.

συμποσίων ἐπιπόλαιοι¹ δριμύτητες· ταύταις οὖν
ἔστι τῶν μὲν πόρων οἰκειότατος ὁ διὰ τῆς οὐρή-
σεως, τῶν δὲ καθάρσεων ἥ² διὰ τῶν κωθωνισμῶν
πρέπει μάλιστα. κατανίζεται γὰρ τὸ σῶμα τοῖς
οἴνοις· ὑγρὸν γὰρ καὶ θερμὸν ὁ οἶνος· τὸ δὲ ἀφ'
ἡμῶν διηθούμενον οὖρόν ἐστιν δριμύ. τὰ γοῦν
ἱμάτια τούτῳ χρώμενοι ῥύμματι πλύνουσιν οἱ
b γναφεῖς.³ τρία δὲ παραφύλαττε ὅταν κωθωνίζῃ·
μὴ πονηρὸν οἶνον πίνειν μηδὲ ἄκρατον μηδὲ τραγη-
ματίζεσθαι ἐν τοῖς κωθωνισμοῖς. ὅταν δ' ἱκανῶς
ἔχῃς ἤδη, μὴ κοιμῶ πρὶν ἂν ἐμέσῃς πλέον ἢ
ἔλαττον. εἶτα ἐὰν μὲν ἐμέσῃς ἱκανῶς, ἀναπαύου
μικρὸν⁴ περιχεάμενος· ἐὰν δὲ μὴ δυνηθῇς ἱκανῶς
κενῶσαι σαυτόν, πλείονι χρῆσαι τῷ λουτρῷ κα
εἰς τὴν πύελον κατακλίθητι⁵ σφόδρα εἰς θερμὸ
ὕδωρ." Πολέμων δ' ἐν πέμπτῳ τῶν πρὸς Ἀδαῖο
c καὶ Ἀντίγονόν φησι· " Διόνυσος τέλειος καθήμενος ἐπὶ πέτρας· ἐξ εὐωνύμων δ' αὐτοῦ σάτυρος
φαλακρός, ἐν τῇ δεξιᾷ κώθωνα μόνωτον ῥαβδω-
τὸν κρατῶν."

ΛΑΒΡΩΝΙΑ ἐκπώματος Περσικοῦ εἶδος ἀπὸ τῆς ἐ
τῷ πίνειν λαβρότητος ὠνομασμένον. πλατὺ δ'
ἐστὶ τῇ κατασκευῇ καὶ μέγα· ἔχει δὲ καὶ ὦτα

¹ CE: ἐπιπόλεοι A. ² ἡ BP: ὁ ACE.
³ βαφεῖς "dyers" C.
⁴ μικρὸν C, μικρὸν superscr. ὡς E: μικρῶς A, μετρίω
Casaubon.
⁵ κατακλιθέντι C. ⁶ πλατὺ μεγάλως C.

ᵃ The Greeks had no soap, in the modern sense. Various
substances (Κιμωλία γῆ, Aristoph. Ran. 711), potash or lye
nitrum (cf. χαλεστραῖον, Plat. Rep. 430 a), and ammonia
(said to have been first obtained from camels' dung near the
temple of Ammon) were used instead in fulling and dyeing

148

now the most appropriate outlet for them is by means
of urination, while among the purgative processes
that which is brought about by hard drinking is the
most natural. For the body is thoroughly washed
out by wine, since wine is both liquid and warm ;
the urine which is filtered out of us is acrid. At any
rate the fullers cleanse garments by the use of it as
a washing agent.[a] Observe three points when you
indulge in hard drinking. First, do not drink poor
wine or neat wine, or chew nuts and raisins while
drinking. Secondly, when you have had enough of
it, do not lie down until you have vomited more or
less. Thirdly, when you have vomited sufficiently,
go to bed after a light shower-bath ; but if you
have not been able to empty yourself sufficiently, take
a more extended bath, lying in a tub of very warm
water." Polemon in the fifth book of his *Address to
Adaeus and Antigonus* says [b] : " Dionysus Perfecter.
He is seated on a rock ; on his left is a bald-headed
satyr, holding in the right hand a canteen with one
handle and fluted sides."

Labronia are a kind of Persian cup, so named from
the violence (*labrotês*)[c] which arises in drinking. In
design it is flat and large ; it also has large handles ;

---

[a] All were disagreeably harsh in their action, as Dicaeopolis
complains in Aristoph. *Ach.* 18 οὕτως ἐδήχθην ὑπὸ κονίας.
See Athen. 409 c (vol. iv. p. 352).

[b] Frag. 60 Preller ; see 483 c, where perhaps this quotation
originally stood. It describes a painting or relief in catalogue
fashion. The epithet Teleios, often given to gods, means
" bringing to fulfilment," " granting perfection " (*e.g.*
through the Mysteries). It is omitted in Bruchmann,
Epitheta Deorum, who cites, however, τελεσσίγαμος from
Nonnus.

[c] The same etymology is given to explain the name of the
sea-bass, *labrax*, Athen. 310 f (vol. iii. p. 396).

μεγάλα· εἴρηται δὲ καὶ ἀρσενικῶς ὁ λαβρώνιος[1]
Μένανδρος Ἁλιεῖ·

εὐποροῦμεν,[2] οὐδὲ μετρίως· ἐκ Κυίνδων[3] χρυσίον
d   Περσικαὶ στολαὶ δὲ κεῖνται[4] πορφυραῖ, τορεύ
    ματα[5]
ἔνδον ἔστ᾽, ἄνδρες, ποτήρι᾽ ἄλλα τ᾽ ἀργυρώματα,
κἀκτυπωμάτων πρόσωπα, τραγέλαφοι, λαβρώ
νιοι.[7]

ἐν δὲ Φιλαδέλφοις·

ἤδη δ᾽ ἐπιχύσεις[8] διάλιθοι, λαβρώνιοι,
Πέρσαι δ᾽ ἔχοντες μυιοσόβας[9] ἑστήκεσαν.

Ἵππαρχος δ᾽ ἐν Θαΐδι·

ὁ λαβρώνιος δ᾽ ἔσθ᾽[10] οὗτος ὄρνις; Β. Ἡράκλεις
e   ποτήριον χρυσοῦς διακοσίους ἄγον.
    Α. ὦ περιβοήτου, φιλτάτη, λαβρωνίου.

Δίφιλος Τιθραύστῃ[11] καὶ ἄλλα γένη καταλέγω
ποτηρίων φησί·

πρίστις, τραγέλαφος,[12] βατιάκη, λαβρώνιος.
ἀνδραπόδι᾽ ἤδη[13] ταῦθ᾽, ὁρᾷς, ἥκιστά γε,
ἐκπωμάτων δ᾽ ὀνόματα. Β. πρὸς τῆς Ἑστίας.
Α. ὁ λαβρώνιος χρυσῶν δέ, παῖδες, εἴκοσι.

---

[1] εἴρηται . . . λαβρώνιος CE: om. A.
[2] Bentley: εὐπόρου μὲν A.   [3] Meineke: ἐκ κυλινδων A.
[4] δὲ κεῖνται Heindorf: δ᾽ ἐκεῖναι A.
[5] πορφυραῖ, τορεύματα Kock: πορφυραῖ τορεύματ᾽ A.
[6] ποτήρι . . . ἀργυρώματα Kock: ποτηρίδια τορεύματα A.
[7] Gulick (cf. 500 e): λαβρώνια A.
[8] Ritschl: ἐπίχυσις A.
[9] μυιοσοβας A, but cf. Pollux x. 94.
[10] ἔστιν A.   [11] Casaubon: πιθραυστηι A.
[12] Jacobs: τραγέλαφος πρίστις A.
[13] ἀνδραπόδι᾽ ἤδη Dobree: ἀνδραπόδιον δὴ A.

nd it occurs, too, in the masculine form *labronios*; Menander in *The Fisherman*[a] : " We're living high, and I don't mean moderately ; we have gold from Cyinda ; purple robes from Persia lie in piles ; we have in our house, gentlemen, embossed vessels, drinking-cups, and other silver ware, and masks in high relief, goat-stag drinking-horns, and *labronioi*." And in *Brothers in Love with Sisters*[b] : " By this time beakers set with gems and *labronioi* (were brought in), and Persians stood there holding fly-flaps." Hipparchus in *Thaïs*[c] : " A. This *labronios* that you speak of, is it a bird ? B. Heracles, no ! It's a cup, and it weighs four pounds.[d] A. Oh, what a famous *labronios*, dearie ! " Diphilus, giving a list of other kinds of cups in *Tithraustes*, says[e] : " A. The whale,[f] goat-stag, Persian saucer, *labronios*. You must see by this time that these are by no means poor little slaves, but the names of drinking-cups.[g] B. Now by the Hearth-goddess ! A. Yes, and this *labronios*, boys,[h] cost twenty gold staters." Didymus, more-

[a] Kock iii. 10, Allinson 316 ; the title is sometimes in the plural, ‘Αλιεῖς. A *miles gloriosus* boasts of his loot; the treasury at Cyinda was seized in 318 B.C. by Eumenes to carry on operations against Antigonus in the interest of Polyperchon and Olympias, Diod. xviii. 57, 58, Strab. 672.

[b] Kock iii. 145, Allinson 456.

[c] Kock iii. 273 ; someone is putting a derisive question to a woman, perhaps Thaïs herself.

[d] Lit. " 200 golden (staters)."

[e] Kock ii. 568 ; Tithraustes was a Persian proper name. On the first verse see 784 a (p. 52).

[f] A cup the shape of which recalled the fish named πρίστις πρῆστις ?), Athen. 333 f (vol. iv. p. 14).

[g] Apparently the unfamiliar terms had suggested to the other speaker the outlandish names of foreign-born slaves.

[h] *i.e.* slaves, as often. The gold stater (as a coin) was worth more than a guinea, or about $5.40.

f Δίδυμος δ' ὅμοιον εἶναί φησιν αὐτὸ βομβυλιῷ
βατιακίῳ.

ΛΑΚΑΙΝΑΙ κυλίκων¹ εἶδος οὕτως λεγόμενον ἢ ἀπ
τοῦ κεράμου, ὡς τὰ ᾿Αττικὰ σκεύη, ἢ ἀπὸ το
σχήματος ἐπιχωριάσαντος² ἐκεῖ, ὥσπερ . . . α
Θηρίκλειαι λέγονται. ᾿Αριστοφάνης Δαιταλεῦσι·

Συβαρίτιδάς τ' εὐωχίας, καὶ Χῖον ἐκ Λακαινᾶν
κυλίκων μεθ' ἡδέων σπάσαι φίλων.³

ΛΕΠΑΣΤΗ. οἱ μὲν ὀξύνουσι τὴν τελευταίαν, ὦ
485 καλή, οἱ δὲ παροξύνουσιν, ὡς μεγάλη. τοῦτο δ
τὸ ποτήριον ὠνομάσθη ἀπὸ τῶν εἰς τὰς μέθας κα
τὰς ἀσωτίας πολλὰ ἀναλισκόντων, οὓς λαφύκτα
καλοῦμεν. κύλικες δ' ἦσαν μεγάλαι. ᾿Αριστο
φάνης Εἰρήνῃ·

τί δῆτ' ἂν εἰ πίοις⁴ οἴνου κύλικα λεπαστήν;

ἀφ' ἧς ἐστι λάψαι, τουτέστιν ἀθρόως πιεῖν, κατ
εναντίον τῷ λεγομένῳ βομβυλιῷ. φησὶν γάρ που
αὐτός·

¹ κυλικίων C.   ² CE : ἐπιχωριάσαντες A
³ μεθ' . . . φίλων Kaibel : μέθυ ἡδέως καὶ φίλος A.
⁴ τί . . . πίοις Dindorf: τί δῆται νηπίοις A, τί δῆται πίο
E, πίοις alone C : φήσεις ἐπειδὰν ἐκπίῃς οἴνου νέου λεπαστή
Aristoph.

ᵃ Schmidt, p. 75.
ᵇ It is difficult to see how this can be true, since th
labronios and *batiakion* were shallow, like a saucer, wherea
the *bombylios*, or *alabastron*, had a neck with a small orific
(above, 784 a and d).   ᶜ *i.e.* Laconian (fem.).
ᵈ We may, with Kaibel, supply "Corinthian jars ar
named from the shape that was popular in Corinth; o

ver, says [a] that it was similar to the *bombylios* or the *atiakion*.[b]

Lakainai,[c] a kind of cylix, so called either from the lay, as the Attic ware (is named from Attic clay), or rom their shape, as being the customary one in ᴸaconia, just as . . .[d] the Thericleian cylices are so alled. Aristophanes in *Men of Dinnerville* [e] : " And easts such as the Sybarites have, and to take a swig ᴼf ' Chian from Laconian' cups amid jolly boon-ᴼmpanions."[f]

Lepastê. Some authorities put the acute accent ᴼn the last syllable, as in *kalé* (beautiful), others on he next to the last, as in *megálê* (great). This cup ᵍot its name from men who squander large sums on ᴅrunken parties and acts of prodigality, men whom ᵛe call *laphyktai*.[g] They were large cylices.[h] Aristo-ᴼhanes in *The Peace* [i] : " What, then, if you should ᴅrink a *lepastê*-cup of wine ? " From this word ᴼomes *lapsai*, that is, to drink at a gulp, opposed to he gurgling drink called *bombylios*. For Aristophanes ᴵso says somewhere [j] : " But you have gulped down

inally, they may be so called after their first manufacturer, ᴸs the Ther. cylices are named after Thericles " (above, ᴸ67 e, p. 60, 470 f, p. 76).

   [e] Kock i. 446, Athen. 527 c; and for the luxury of the ᴵites mentioned *cf.* 25 e (vol. i. p. 112), Plat. *Rep.* 404 ᴅ.

   [f] See critical note 3; the Doric gen. Λακαινᾶν should be ᴸoted.

   [g] Gourmands, Lat. *liguritores*, Aristot. *Eth. Eudem.* iii. ᴸ. 7. But the name is derived from λέπας, "limpet," *patella vulgata*.

   [h] So Aristophanes of Byzantium and Apollodorus, below, ᴸ85 d (p. 156).

   [i] In Aristoph. *Pac.* 914 the chorus say to Trygaeus: " You have become the saviour of all mankind." To which ᵀrygaeus replies : " You will say so when you have drunk ᵘut a *lepastê* of new wine."   [j] Kock i. 544.

τὸ δ᾽ αἷμα[1] λέλαφας τοὐμόν, ὦναξ δέσποτα,

οἷον ἄθρουν μ᾽ ἐξέπιες. ἐν δὲ Γηρυτάδῃ·

ἦν δὲ

b τὸ πρᾶγμ᾽ ἑορτή. περιέφερε δὲ κύκλῳ[2] λεπα
στὴν
ἡμῖν ταχὺ προσφέρων παῖς οἰνοχόος[3] σφόδρ
κυανοβενθῆ,

τὸ βάθος παρίστησιν ὁ κωμικὸς τοῦ ποτηρίου
Ἀντιφάνης δὲ ἐν Ἀσκληπιῷ·

τὴν δὲ[4] γραῦν τὴν ἀσθενοῦσαν πάνυ πάλαι, τὴ
βρυτικήν,
ῥίζιον τρίψας τι μικρὸν δελεάσας τε γεννικῇ[5]
τὸ μέγεθος κοίλῃ λεπαστῇ, τοῦτ᾽ ἐποίησε
ἐκπιεῖν.

Φιλύλλιος Αὔγῃ·

πάντα γὰρ ἦν
μέστ᾽[6] ἀνδρῶν καὶ[7] μειρακίων
πινόντων· ὁμοῦ δ᾽ ἄλλων[8]
γρᾴδι᾽ ἦν μεγάλαισιν οἴ-
νου χαίροντα λεπασταῖς.

Θεόπομπος Παμφίλῃ·

c σπόγγος, λεκάνη, πτερόν, λεπαστὴ πάνυ πυκνὴ
ἦν[9] ἐκπιοῦσ᾽ ἄκρατον Ἀγαθοῦ Δαίμονος
τέττιξ κελαδεῖ.

καὶ ἐν Μήδῳ·

[1] A: τὸ δέμα E, τὸ δέμας C, τὸ δέπας Eustath. 1246. 38.
[2] δὲ κύκλῳ Pollux: δ᾽ ἐν κύκλῳ A.

my blood, lord master," that is, you have drunk me
up at a gulp. In *Gerytades*, when he says,[a] " The
occasion was a holiday. And a wine-pouring slave
was swiftly carrying round and offering to us a
lepastê of very dark depths," our comic poet indicates that the cup was deep.[b] So Antiphanes in
Asclepius[c] : " The doctor pounded a little rootlet,
and enticing her with the bait of a deep[d] and
generous-sized *lepastê*, he made that old hag, the one
who has been sick so very long, the one soaked with
beer, drink it all up." Philyllius in *Augê*[e] : " Every
place was crowded with men and lads drinking ; and
near the others[f] were some old crones enjoying large
lepastai of wine." Theopompus in *Pamphila*[g] : " A
sponge, a pan, a feather, a very stout *lepastê* ; from
this she drank up neat wine with a ' Here's to Good
Luck,' and now gabbles like a cicada." Also in *The*

---

[a] Kock i. 432 ; the text is somewhat uncertain, the same
corruption appearing also in Pollux.

[b] Pollux x. 75, on the other hand, infers that the *lepastê* was
a pitcher. So Amerias below, 485 d (p. 156).

[c] Kock ii. 28 ; as physician, possibly Asclepius himself
is the subject. For βρυτικήν (for which Kock reads Βρυττικήν,
Bruttian) *cf.* 447 b-c (vol. iv. p. 526).

[d] Lit. "hollow" ; for γεννικῇ "generous," of size, *cf.* Plat.
Rep. 372 в μάξας γενναίας. [e] Kock i. 783.

[f] Or, reading Ἄλεῳ, " along with Aleôs " (father of Augê).

[g] Kock i. 744, *cf.* below in e.

---

³ ἡμῖν . . . οἰνοχόος Capps: ἡμῖν . . . ὁ παῖς ἐνέχει τε A,
Pollux.

⁴ Schweighäuser: δὴ A.   ⁵ Casaubon: γεννητικηι A.

⁶ Jacobs: μετ᾽ A.   ⁷ καὶ added by Jacobs.

⁸ ὁμοῦ δ᾽ Ἄλεῳ Wilamowitz. ὁμοῦ with gen. is rare and
doubtful; yet see Jebb's note on Soph. *Philoct.* 1218 and
App. p. 251.

⁹ πυκνή, ἣν Schweighäuser: πυκνὴν A.

ὡς ποτ᾽ ἐκήλησεν Καλλίστρατος υἷας Ἀχαιῶν,
κέρμα φίλον διαδοὺς[1] ὅτε συμμαχίαν ἐρέεινεν·
οἷον δ᾽ οὐ κήλησε δέμας λεπτὸν Ῥαδάμανθυν
Λύσανδρον κώθωνι, πρὶν αὐτῷ δῶκε λεπαστήν.

d Ἀμερίας δέ φησι τὴν οἰνοχόην λεπαστὴν καλεῖσθαι. Ἀριστοφάνης δὲ καὶ Ἀπολλόδωρος γένος εἶναι κύλικος. Φερεκράτης Κραπατάλλοις·

> τῶν θεατῶν δ᾽ ὅστις ἂν[2] δι-
> ψῇ, λεπαστὴν ἐγχεάμενον
> ἔστιν[3] ἐκχαρυβδίσαι.

Νίκανδρος δ᾽ ὁ Κολοφώνιός φησιν Δόλοπας οὕτω καλεῖν τὴν κύλικα. Λυκόφρων δ᾽ ἐν τῷ θ᾽ περὶ Κωμῳδίας παραθέμενος τὰ Φερεκράτους καὶ αὐτὸς e εἶναί φησι γένος κύλικος τὴν λεπαστήν. Μόσχος δ᾽ ἐν ἐξηγήσει Ῥοδιακῶν Λέξεων κεραμεοῦν ἀγγεῖόν φησιν αὐτὸ εἶναι, ἐοικὸς ταῖς λεγομέναις πτωματίσιν,[4] ἐκπεταλώτερον δέ. Ἀρτεμίδωρος δ᾽ ὁ Ἀριστοφάνειος ποτήριον ποιόν. Ἀπολλοφάνης δὲ Κρησί·

> καὶ λεπαστά μ᾽ ἀδύοινος εὐφρανεῖ[5] δι᾽ ἀμέρας.

---

[1] Dindorf: διδοὺς A.   [2] ἂν added by Toup.
[3] δι|ψῇ . . . ἐγχεάμενον | ἔστιν Kaibel: | διψῇ . . . λαψάμενος μεστὴν A.
[4] πωματίσιν (?) Casaubon, στοματίσιν (?) Kaibel.
[5] Porson: λεπαστὰν ἀδύοινον (with η written above α) εὐφραίνει A.

---

[a] Kock i. 740.   The hexameters are a mocking comment on the dissensions among the Greeks after the Peloponnesian War, of which the Persians were quick to take advantage.   Callistratus of Aphidnae, the Athenian leader mentioned also at 44 a, 166 e, 449 f, urged the Arcadians to side with Athens, C. Nepos, *Epam.* 6.

Mede [a] : " Thus did Callistratus once beguile the sons of the Achaeans, distributing welcome coin among them when he asked for an alliance ; but one alone he could not beguile, Lysander, light of frame but a veritable Rhadamanthys—at least not with a canteen—before he had given him a *lepasté*." [b] Amerias, however, says that the wine-jug was called a *lepasté*.[c] But Aristophanes says [d] it was a kind of cylix, and so does Apollodorus. Pherecrates in *Good-for-Nothings* [e] : " And whoever in the audience is thirsty may have a *lepasté* filled, and swill it like Charybdis.[f] " Nicander of Colophon says [g] that the Dolopes give this name to the cylix. Lycophron, too, in the ninth book of his work *On Comedy*, also cites [h] the lines from Pherecrates and explains that the *lepasté* is a kind of cylix. Moschus, in his interpretation of *Rhodian Diction*, says that it is an earthenware vessel, like the so-called *ptomatides*,[i] but more outspread. Artemidorus, disciple of Aristophanes, says it is a kind of cup. Apollophanes in *The Cretans* [j] : " And a *lepasté* of sweet wine will cheer

[b] Apparently Lysander remained as inexorable as Rhadamanthys, the judge in the lower world, to the offer of a canteen, but was finally won by a larger offering.

[c] *Cf.* above, p. 153, note *h*.

[d] Nauck p. 220, J. 2 B 1113.

[e] Kock i. 171, who attempts to restore the verses as Eupolidean. *Cf.* above, 464 f (p. 26) ; as the parabasis of Aristoph. *Av.* (*cf.* 723 ff.) promises good things to the audience in the bird kingdom, so here the good things of the lower world are set forth.

[f] *Cf.* Aristoph. *Eq.* 248 (of Cleon) Χάρυβδιν ἁρπαγῆς, " a regular Charybdis for plunder " ; Cicero, *Phil.* ii. 27 " quae Charybdis tam vorax ? "

[g] Frag. 142 Schneider.   [h] Frag. 85 Strecker.

[i] Lit. " tumblers," but the word *lepasté* would suggest a cylix without a stem.   [j] Kock i. 799 ; in Doric.

Θεόπομπος Παμφίλη·

λεπαστὴ μάλα συχνή,

f   ἣν ἐκπιοῦσ' ἄκρατον 'Αγαθοῦ Δαίμονος
περίστατον[1] βοῶσα τὴν κώμην ποεῖ.

Νίκανδρος δ' ὁ Θυατειρηνὸς " κύλιξ," φησί, " μείζων," παρατιθέμενος Τηλεκλείδου ἐκ Πρυτάνεων·

καὶ μελιχρὸν οἶνον ἕλκειν
ἐξ ἡδύπνου[2] λεπαστῆς.

486 "Ερμιππος Μοίραις·

ἂν[3] ἐγὼ πάθω τι τήνδε τὴν λεπαστὴν ἐκπιών,
τῷ Διονύσῳ πάντα τἀμαυτοῦ δίδωμι χρήματα.

ΛΟΙΒΑΣΙΟΝ κύλιξ, ὥς φησι Κλείταρχος καὶ Νίκανδρος ὁ Θυατειρηνός . . .[4] ᾧ τὸ ἔλαιον ἐπι-
σπένδουσι τοῖς ἱεροῖς, σπονδεῖον δὲ ᾧ τὸν οἶνον,
καλεῖσθαι λέγων λοιβίδας καὶ τὰ σπονδεῖα ὑπὸ
'Αντιμάχου τοῦ Κολοφωνίου.

ΛΕΣΒΙΟΝ ὅτι ποτηρίου εἶδος, 'Ηδύλος παρίστησιν
ἐν 'Επιγράμμασιν οὑτωσὶ λέγων·

b   ἡ διαπινομένη Καλλίστιον[5] ἀνδράσι, θαῦμα
κοὐ ψεῦδες, νῆστις τρεῖς χόας ἐξέπιεν·
ἧς τόδε σοί, Παφίη, ζωραῖς μύρρῃσι[6] θυωθὲν
κεῖται πορφυρέης λέσβιον ἐξ ὑέλου.

---

[1] περιστατὸν A.   [2] Elmsley: ἡδυπνόου A.
[3] ἂν CE: ἐὰν A.
[4] Kaibel proposed ὁ δεῖνα δὲ λοιβάσιον ἢ λοιβεῖον.
[5] Musurus: κάλλιστον A.
[6] Kaibel: ζωρεσμιτρησι A.

158

ne through the day." Theopompus in *Pamphila*[a] :
'A very large *lepastê*; from this she drinks up unmixed wine to Good Luck, and with her bawling
makes all the village stand agape." Nicander of
Thyateira defines it as a rather large cylix, quoting
from *The Prytanes* of Telecleides[b] : " And take a
pull of honey-sweet wine from a fragrant *lepastê*."
Hermippus in *The Fates*[c] : " If anything happen to
me after I have drunk out this *lepastê*, I give and
bequeath all my goods to Dionysus."

Loibasion, a cylix, as Cleitarchus and Nicander of
Thyateira declare. . . . With it they pour oil as a
libation over the sacrifice, whereas a *spondeion* is
that with which they pour wine, although he[d] says
that even the *spondeia* are called *loibides* by Antimachus of Colophon.[e]

Lesbion. That this is a kind of cup is indicated by
Hedylus in his *Epigrams*, as follows : " Callistion, she
who could hold her own in the drinking contest with
men—no sham miracle either—drank up six quarts
on an empty stomach ; it is her *lesbion*,[f] filled with the
sweet smell of pure balsam, and made of lustrous
glass, that is here dedicated to thee, Paphian

---

[a] Kock i. 744, *cf.* above in c.
[b] *Ibid.* 215 ; for the title see vol. ii. p. 275 note *a.*
[c] Kock i. 236 ; *cf.* a similar bequest 341 c (vol. iv. p. 46).
[d] A third authority must have been quoted in the gap.
Cf. Pollux x. 65.   [e] Om. Kinkel.
[f] Not a cup, as Athenaeus says, but a vessel filled with
ointment, the prize of her victory, as θυωθέν shows (Kaibel).

ἦν σὺ[1] σάου πάντως, ὡς καὶ πάλι τῶν[2] ἀπ'
  ἐκείνης
σοὶ τοῖχοι γλυκερῶν σῦλα φέρωσι πόθων.

ΛΟΥΤΗΡΙΟΝ. Ἐπιγένης Μνηματίῳ ἐν τῷ τῶν ποτηρίων καταλόγῳ φησί·

            κρατῆρες, κάδοι,
c ὁλκεῖα, κρουνεῖ'. Β. ἔστι γὰρ κρουνεῖα[4]; Α. ναί
λουτῆρι'—ἀλλὰ τί καθ' ἕκαστα δεῖ λέγειν;
ὄψει γὰρ αὐτός.

ΛΥΚΙΟΥΡΓΕΙΣ.[5] φιάλαι τινὲς οὕτως καλοῦνται ἀπὸ
Λύκωνος τοῦ κατασκευασαμένου,[6] ὡς καὶ Κονώ-
νειοι[7] αἱ ὑπὸ Κόνωνος ποιηθεῖσαι. μνημονεύει τοῦ
Λύκωνος Δημοσθένης ἐν τῷ περὶ τοῦ στεφάνου
κἀν τῷ πρὸς Τιμόθεον ὑπὲρ χρέως[8] λέγων οὕτως·
" φιάλας Λυκιουργεῖς δύο." ἐν δὲ τῷ πρὸς Τιμό-
d θεον γράφει· "δίδωσιν ἀποθεῖναι τῷ Φορμίων'
μετὰ τῶν χρημάτων καὶ ἄλλας φιάλας[9] Λυκιουργεῖς
δύο." Ἡρόδοτος δ' ἐν ζ' " προβόλους δύο
Λυκιουργίδας[10] ἢ λυκοεργέας,[11]" ὅτι ἀκόντιά ἐστι
πρὸς λύκων θήραν ἐπιτήδεια ἢ[12] ἐν Λυκίᾳ εἰργα-

---

[1] σὺ added by Dindorf.   [2] πάλι τῶν Kaibel: πάντων A.
[3] ἀπ' Musurus: ἐπ' A.   [4] Cf. 472 f: ὁλκεῖα κρουνιαναι A
[5] περὶ λυκιουργίδων φιαλῶν lemma in A, λυκιουργεῖς φιάλαι C
[6] κατασκευασαμένου C: κατεσκευασμένου A.
[7] κονώνιοι ACE.
[8] ὑπὲρ χρέως (χρέους) Casaubon: ὕβρεως A.
[9] μετ' ἄλλων χρημάτων καὶ φιάλας Demosth.
[10] λυκοεργέας or λυκεργέας Herod. codd.
[11] ἢ λυκοεργέας Schweighäuser (deleting the entire passage
which originally stood below in e): ἡμιεργέας A.
[12] ἢ added by Kaibel (after Schweighäuser).

---

[a] Aphrodite; for such offerings brought by courtesans
cf. the mirror of Laïs, Plato, Epigr. 4, Diehl 15, Edmonds 11
[b] Of the temple.   [c] i.e. reward, lit. reprisals.

goddess.[a] Do thou by all means preserve her, that once again thy walls [b] may carry the booty [c] of sweet desires inspired by her." [d]

Louterion.[e] Epigenes in *The Souvenir*, including this in the list of cups, says [f]: " A. There'll be mixing-bowls, jars, basins, and jugs. B. What, there are jugs ? A. Yes, and wash-basins—but why need I tell you in detail ? You shall see for yourself."

Lykiourgeis. Certain *phialai* [g] have this name from their manufacturer Lycon, just as *Kononeioi* [h] are those made by Conon. Demosthenes mentions Lycon in the oration *On the Crown* and in the speech *Against Timotheus concerning Debt* as follows [i] : " Two *phialai* of Lycian workmanship." And in the speech *Against Timotheus* he writes : " He gave to Phormion to keep for him, among other possessions, two *phialai* of Lycian workmanship besides." Herodotus in the seventh book has [j] : " Two hunting-spears, *Lyki-ourgides* or *lykoergeis*," (so called) because they are javelins adapted to hunting wolves (*lykoi*), or because they were made in Lycia. In explaining this

[d] Love was an emanation from the loved one, Soph. *Ant.* 783, Eur. *Hipp.* 525, Athen. 604 a.
[e] Really a wash-bowl ; it is included here because of the wild party predicted in the quotation following.
[f] Kock ii. 418, Athen. 472 e, 480 a. *Cf.* the promise of abundant entertainment in Aristoph. *Ran.* 503 ff.
[g] Saucer-shaped cups.
[h] Above, 478 b, where the *kononeios* is called a cylix. Correct etymology derives λυκιουργεῖς from Lycia, as in section d below.
[i] [Dem.] *Or.* xlix. 31. Lycon is not mentioned in either speech, nor is this ware mentioned in the oration *On the Crown.* Preller bracketed the offending words.
[j] Chap. 76. There is a gap in the text of Herodotus, so that the subject is unknown ; see How and Wells, *ad loc.* The remarks about javelins seem irrelevant, but are quoted to illustrate the two etymologies of λυκιουργεῖς. See below.

σμένα. ὅπερ ἐξηγούμενος Δίδυμος ὁ γραμματικὸς
τὰς ὑπὸ Λυκίου φησὶ κατεσκευασμένας. ἦν δὲ
οὗτος τὸ γένος Βοιώτιος ἐξ Ἐλευθερῶν,[1] υἱὸς
Μύρωνος τοῦ ἀνδριαντοποιοῦ, ὡς Πολέμων φησὶν
ἐν α΄ περὶ Ἀκροπόλεως. ἀγνοεῖ δ᾽ ὁ γραμματικὸς
ὅτι τὸν τοιοῦτον σχηματισμὸν[2] ἀπὸ κυρίων ὀνομάτων οὐκ ἄν τις εὕροι γινόμενον, ἀλλ᾽ ἀπὸ πόλεων
e ἢ[3] ἐθνῶν. Ἀριστοφάνης τε γὰρ ἐν Εἰρήνῃ φησί·
    τὸ δὲ πλοῖον ἔσται Ναξιουργὴς κάνθαρος.

Κριτίας τε[4] ἐν τῇ Λακεδαιμονίων Πολιτείᾳ
" κλίνη Μιλησιουργὴς καὶ δίφρος Μιλησιουργής,
κλίνη Χιουργὴς[6] καὶ κρούπεζα ῾Ρηναιουργής."
῾Ηρόδοτός τε ἐν τῇ ἑβδόμῃ φησί· " προβόλους δύο
Λυκοεργέας." μήποτ᾽ οὖν καὶ παρὰ τῷ ῾Ηροδότῳ
ὡς καὶ παρὰ[8] τῷ Δημοσθένει γραπτέον Λυκιο-
εργέας, ἵν᾽ ἀκούηται[9] τὰ ἐν Λυκίᾳ εἰργασμένα.

ΜΕΛΗ. οὕτω καλεῖταί τινα ποτήρια ὧν μνημονεύει Ἀνάξιππος ἐν Φρέατι λέγων οὕτως·

f   σὺ δὲ τὴν μέλην, Συρίσκε, ταυτηνὶ λαβὼν
    ἔνεγκον[10] ἐπὶ τὸ μνῆμ᾽ ἐκείνῃ, μανθάνεις;
    καὶ κατάχεον.

[1] Casaubon: ἐλευθέρων A.   [2] μετὰ σχηματισμὸν C.
[3] ἢ AC, Eust.: καὶ Harpocration.   [4] Meineke: δὲ A.
[5] Θεσσαλουργὸς Kaibel (cf. Athen. 28 b).
[6] κλίνη μιλησιουργὴς κτλ. A and Harpocr. s. Λυκιουργεῖς :
κλίνη μολοσσιουργὴς καὶ κλίνη χιουργὴς (om. δίφρος Μιλησιουργὴς)
CE, κρήνη Μολοσσιουργὴς Eust. 907. 25.
[7] κρούπεζα ῾Ρηναιουργὴς Kaibel: τράπεζα ῥηνιουργὴς A (cf. Poll.
vii. 93).   [8] τῷ ῾Η. . . . παρὰ added by Schweighäuser.
[9] Schweighäuser: καίηται A, ὀνομάζηται Harpocr., καλῆται
(?) Kaibel.   Lumb's κέηται is tempting, but κεῖται seems not
to be used by the Grammarians in exactly this sense.
[10] Porson: ἔνεγκ᾽ A.

[a] i.e. Λυκιουργεῖς in Demosthenes.

word [a] the grammarian Didymus says [b] they are the cups manufactured by Lycius. Now he was from Eleutherae, a Boeotian by birth, son of Myron the sculptor, according to Polemon in the first book of his work *On the Acropolis*.[c] But the grammarian fails to see that you cannot find a form like this made from personal names ; they are made only from names of cities or nations. And so, in fact, Aristophanes says in *The Peace* [d] : " My boat will be a Naxian-made schooner." Also Critias in his *Constitution of the Lacedaemonians* [e] : " A Milesian-made couch and Milesian-made stool, a Chian-made couch and Rhenaean-made clogs." And Herodotus says in the seventh book [f] : " Two hunting-spears Lycus-made." Perhaps, therefore, both in Herodotus and in Demosthenes we should write Lycian-made (*Lykiourgeas*),[g] so as to understand it of things made in Lycia.

Melê. This is a name given to certain cups which are mentioned by Anaxippus in *The Well.* He says [h] : " You, Syriscus,[i] take this *melê* and carry it to her tomb, do you understand ? Then pour over it (the libation)."

[b] Schmidt, p. 314.　　　　　　[c] Frag. 2 Preller.
[d] vs. 143. Trygaeus, the speaker, is mounting his beetle, the name of which (κάνθαρος, above, p. 93 note *e*) signifies also boat and cup.
[e] *F.H.G.* ii. 69. For the wares for which different cities were famous see Critias *ap.* Athen. 28 b (vol. i. p. 122). Milesian beds were especially noted for their luxurious coverings, Aristoph. *Ran.* 542 στρώμασιν Μιλησίοις.
[f] Chap. 76 ; see above, d, and critical note 11 (p. 160).
[g] This emendation is accepted by edd. of Herodotus.
[h] Kock iii. 301. The word was apparently understood as a plural (from μέλος), defined as σκεύη by Hesychius. But C has θηλϊκῶς (*i.e.* θηλυκῶς) ποτήριον τί, which is supported by the quotation, if the text is right.
[i] *i.e.* " little Syrian " (slave).

163

ΜΕΤΑΝΙΠΤΡΟΝ ἡ μετὰ τὸ δεῖπνον[1] ἐπὴν[2] ἀπονίψων-
ται διδομένη κύλιξ. Ἀντιφάνης Λαμπάδι·

Δαίμονος
Ἀγαθοῦ μετάνιπτρον, ἐντραγεῖν, σπονδή, κρότος.

487 Δίφιλος Σαπφοῖ·

Ἀρχίλοχε, δέξαι τήνδε τὴν μετανιπτρίδα
μεστὴν Διὸς σωτῆρος, Ἀγαθοῦ Δαίμονος . . .

ἔνιοι δὲ τὴν μετὰ τὸ νίψασθαι πόσιν, ὡς Σέλευκος
ἐν Γλώσσαις. Καλλίας δ' ἐν Κύκλωπι·

καὶ δέξαι τηνδὶ μετανιπτρίδα τῆς Ὑγιείας.

Φιλέταιρος Ἀσκληπιῷ·

ἐνέσεισε μεστὴν ἴσον ἴσῳ μετανιπτρίδα
μεγάλην, ἐπειπὼν[3] τῆς Ὑγιείας τοὔνομα.

Φιλόξενος δ' ὁ διθυραμβοποιὸς ἐν τῷ ἐπιγραφομένῳ Δείπνῳ μετὰ τὸ ἀπονίψασθαι τὰς χεῖρας
προπίνων τινί φησι·

b   σὺ δὲ τάνδε Βακχίαν[4]
εὔδροσον πλήρη μετανιπτρίδα δέξαι.
πραῢ τί τοι Βρόμιος γάνος τόδε δοὺς ἐπὶ τέρψιν
πάντας[5] ἄγει.

Ἀντιφάνης Λαμπάδι·

τράπεζα φυστημινεις, ἅμα δ' ἦν[6] Δαίμονος
Ἀγαθοῦ μετάνιπτρον.

νίπτρον C.   [2] ἐπὰν CE.
[3] Schweighäuser: ὑπειπὼν A.
[4] Meineke: τάνδ' ἐκβακχια A, τάνδ' ἀβακχίωτον Edmonds.
[5] Meineke: ἄπαντας A.
[6] ἅμα δ' ἦν Kaibel: ἀλλὰ μὴν A.

---

[a] For ἀπονίψασθαι see 409 a (vol. iv. p. 350).

164

Metaniptron. The cup which is offered after dinner, when they have finished the hand-washing.[a] Antiphanes in *The Torch*[b]: " An after-dinner cup to Good Luck, a bit of dessert to nibble, a libation, and clapping of hands." Diphilus in *Sappho*[c]: " Archilochus, accept this brimming after-dinner cup in honour of Saviour Zeus, and to Good Luck. . ." But some, like Seleucus in his *Glossary*, explain it as the *drink* after the hand-washing. Callias in *The Cyclopes*[d]: " And accept this after-dinner drink to Hygieia."[e] Philetaerus in *Asclepius*[f]: " He brandished a huge, brimming, after-dinner drink, mixed half and half, pronouncing over it the name of Hygieia." And the dithyrambic poet Philoxenus, pledging someone in his poem entitled *The Banquet*, after the washing of the hands, says[g] : " Accept thou this after-dinner cup full of the refreshing dew of Bacchus. Verily the Bromian god, with this soothing joy that he hath given, invites all to take their delight." Antiphanes in *The Torch*[h]: " The table (was then removed), and at once came an after-dinner cup to Good Luck." Nicostratus in

[b] Kock ii. 68, below, 487 b. On ἐντραγεῖν *cf.* 74 a (vol. i. p. 318).
[c] Kock ii. 564. Six comedies, by different writers, bore this title. Schol. Aristoph. *Eq.* 85 explains that the first cup drunk after dinner was of unmixed wine, to Good Luck. Three bowls of mixed wine followed, the last to Zeus the Saviour.
[d] Kock i. 695.
[e] The cult of Hygieia in Athens was earlier than that of Asclepius. The quotations are interesting as showing the antiquity of the invocation, " Your health ! " [f] Kock ii. 230.
[g] *P.L.G.*⁴ iii. 608, Diehl (Philoxenus Leucadius), p. 318, Edmonds iii. p. 362 ; here the hand-washing occurs after the meal.
[h] Kock ii. 68, above, 486 f. What followed τράπεζα remains in doubt.

165

Νικόστρατος 'Αντερώσῃ·

μετανιπτρίδ' αὐτῷ τῆς Ὑγιείας ἔγχεον.

ΜΑΣΤΟΣ. Ἀπολλόδωρος ὁ Κυρηναῖος, ὡς Πάμφιλός φησι, Παφίους τὸ ποτήριον οὕτως καλεῖν.

c ΜΑΘΑΛΙΔΑΣ Βλαῖσος ἐν Σατούρνῳ φησίν·

ἑπτὰ μαθαλίδας
ἐπίχεον ἁμὶν[1] τῷ γλυκυτάτῳ.[2]

Πάμφιλος δέ φησι· " μήποτε ἐκπώματός ἐστιν εἶδος, ἢ μέτρον οἷον κύαθος." Διόδωρος δὲ κύλικα ἀποδίδωσι.

ΜΑΝΗΣ ποτηρίου εἶδος. Νίκων Κιθαρῳδῷ·

καὶ πάνυ τις εὐκαίρως "προπίνω," φησί, "σοί,[3]
πατριῶτα." μάνην δ' ἔλαβε[4] κεραμεοῦν ἁδρόν,
χωροῦντα κοτύλας πέντ' ἴσως. ἐδεξάμην.

παρέθετο τὰ ἰαμβεῖα καὶ Δίδυμος καὶ Πάμφιλος.
d καλεῖται δὲ μάνης καὶ τὸ ἐπὶ τοῦ κοττάβου ἐφεστηκός, ἐφ'[5] οὗ τὰς λάταγας ἐν παιδιᾷ ἔπεμπον·
ὅπερ ὁ Σοφοκλῆς ἐν Σαλμωνεῖ[6] χάλκειον[7] ἔφη κάρα,
λέγων οὕτως·

τάδ' ἐστὶ κνισμὸς καὶ φιλημάτων ψόφος·
τῷ καλλικοτταβοῦντι νικητήρια
τίθημι καὶ βαλόντι χάλκειον[7] κάρα.

---

[1] ἐπίχεον ἁμὶν Meineke: ἐπίχεε ἡμῖν A.
[2] Casaubon: τῶι γλυκυτάτωι A.
[3] Heringa: προπίνων φησὶ πατριῶτα A.
[4] Kaibel (cf. Pollux vi. 99): δ' εἶχε A.
[5] Bentley: ἀφ' A.
[6] Musurus: σάλμωνι A.
[7] χαλκεῖον A.

Rival in Love [a] : " Pour him out an after-dinner cup to Hygieia."

Mastos. [b] Apollodorus of Cyrene, quoted by Pamphilus, says that the Paphians call the drinking-cup by this name.

Mathalidas is (an accusative form) used by Blaesus in *Saturnus* [c] : " Pour out for us seven *mathalidae* of your sweetest wine." And Pamphilus says : " Perhaps this is a kind of drinking-cup, or a measure of capacity, like the *kyathos.* [d] " But Diodorus renders it by *cylix.*

Manês is a kind of cup. Nicon in *The Harp-singer* [e] : " And one said, right in the nick of time, ' I pledge you a cup, my countryman.' Then he took a stout *manês* of earthenware, holding perhaps five *kotylai.* [f] I accepted it." These verses in iambic metre were cited by Didymus [g] and by Pamphilus. The name *manês* is given also to the figure surmounting the kottabos, at which they used to aim the wine-drops in the game ; this is what Sophocles in *Salmoneus* called " the bronze head," as follows [h] : " Here are ticklings and the smack of kisses ; for the one who best shoots the kottabos and hits the bronze head I set up prizes for victory." Antiphanes in *Birth*

---

[a] Kock ii. 220. The title refers to a woman, but the same verse is cited at 693 a from *Pandrosus*, which Kock preferred to read here. [b] Lit. "breast."
[c] Kaibel 191. *Cf.* Hesych. *s.v.* This is the only quotation from Blaesus consisting of more than a single word (Pauly-Wissowa iii. 556). C has the form μασθαλίς, influenced by μαστός. [d] See p. 101 note *a*.
[e] Kock iii. 389 ; nine comedies of this title were known in antiquity. This is the only quotation from Nicon.
[f] Nearly three quarts. [g] Schmidt, p. 73.
[h] *T.G.F.*[2] 250 ; the prizes, eggs, cakes, etc., are mentioned by Athen. 667 d.

'Αντιφάνης 'Αφροδίτης Γοναῖς·

  ἐγὼ 'πιδείξω[1] καθ' ἕν· ὃς[2] ἂν τὸν κότταβον
  ἀφεὶς[3] ἐπὶ τὴν πλάστιγγα ποιήσῃ πεσεῖν—
  B. πλάστιγγα;[4] ποίαν;[5] τοῦτο τοὐπικείμενον[6]

e ἄνω τὸ μικρόν, τὸ πινακίσκιον λέγεις;
  A. τοῦτ' ἐστὶ πλάστιγξ—οὗτος[7] ὁ κρατῶν γίνεται.
  B. πῶς δ' εἴσεταί τις τοῦτ'; A. ἐὰν τύχῃ[8] μόνον
  αὐτῆς, ἐπὶ τὸν μάνην πεσεῖται καὶ ψόφος
  ἔσται πάνυ πολύς. B. πρὸς θεῶν, τῷ κοττάβῳ
  πρόσεστι καὶ Μάνης τις ὥσπερ οἰκέτης;

Ἕρμιππος Μοίραις·

  ῥάβδον δ' ὄψει (φησί) τὴν κοτταβικὴν
  ἐν τοῖς ἀχύροισι κυλινδομένην,
  μάνης δ' οὐδὲν λατάγων ἀίει·
  τὴν δὲ τάλαιναν πλάστιγγ' ἂν ἴδοις

f παρὰ τὸν στροφέα τῆς κηπαίας
  ἐν τοῖσι κορήμασιν οὖσαν.

ΝΕΣΤΟΡΙΣ. περὶ τῆς ἰδέας τοῦ Νέστορος ποτηρίου
φησὶν ὁ ποιητής·

  πὰρ δὲ[9] δέπας περικαλλές, ὃ οἴκοθεν ἦγ' ὁ
    γεραιός,
  χρυσείοις ἥλοισι πεπαρμένον· οὔατα δ' αὐτοῦ
  τέσσαρ' ἔσαν, δοιαὶ δὲ πελειάδες[10] ἀμφὶς ἕκαστον
  χρύσειαι νεμέθοντο· δύω[11] δ' ὑπὸ πυθμένες ἦσαν.

488 ἄλλος μὲν μογέων ἀποκινήσασκε τραπέζης
  πλεῖον ἐόν· Νέστωρ δ' ὁ γέρων ἀμογητὶ ἄειρεν.

---

[1] διδάξω 666 f.
[2] καθ' ἕν· ὃς Kaibel (καθ' ὃν· ὃς Schweighäuser): καθόσον A.
[3] ἀφῇς A.
[4] ποιήσῃ . . . πλάστιγγα added with emendation by Toup
from Schol. Lucian Lexiph. 3.   [5] ποίαν 666 f: ποῖον ἂν A.
[6] 666: τὸ ὑποκείμενον A.   [7] 667: ἵν' οὗτος Λ.

of Aphrodite[a] : " A. I will show you step by step ;
whoever when he shoots at the pan causes the
kottabos to fall— B. The pan ? What pan ? Do
you mean that little thing that lies up there on top,
the tiny platter ? A. Yes, that's the pan—he becomes the winner. B. How is one going to know
that ? A. Why, if he just hits it, it will fall on the
manês, and there will be a very loud clatter. B. In
the gods' name, tell me, has the kottabos got a
manês,[b] attending it like any slave ? " Hermippus
in *The Fates* says[c] : " You will see the shaft of the
kottabos rolling neglected in the husks, and *manês*
pays no attention to wine-drops tossed at him ; as
for the unhappy pan, you may see that resting beside
the socket[d] of the back door in a pile of sweepings."

Nestoris. With regard to the appearance of Nestor's
cup the Poet says[e] : " And beside these viands a
cup of exceeding beauty which the aged man had
brought from home, pierced with golden studs ; and
there were four handles to it, and two doves of gold
were feeding round each ; and there were two stems
below the cup. Another man had scarcely moved
it from the table when it was full, yet Nestor, that
old man, raised it easily." With regard to these

---

[a] Kock ii. 33, Athen. 666 f.

[b] *Manês* was also a name commonly given to slaves. *Cf.*
Tzetzes, *Chiliad.* vi. 886 αἱ λεκανίσκαι μέσον δὲ εἶχον ἀνδριαν-
τίσκους (little figures of men) οὓς μανᾶς ἐκάλουν οἱ τότε.

[c] Kock i. 237, Athen. 668 a ; a description of the effect of
war on the ordinary utensils and amusements of life.

[d] The Greek door turned on pivots set in sockets in the
lintel and the threshold.

[e] *Il.* xi. 632-637, below, 492 e-f.

---

8 θίγῃ Jacobs.   9 δὲ CE : om. A.
10 CE : πελιάδες A.   11 δύο ACE ; so at 488 f, 489 f.

ἐν τούτοις ζητεῖται πρῶτον μὲν τί ποτ' ἐστὶ τὸ
χρυσείοις ἥλοισι πεπαρμένον, ἔπειτα τί τὸ οὔατα
δ' αὐτοῦ τέσσαρ' ἔσαν. τὰ γὰρ ἄλλα ποτήριά
φησιν ὁ Μυρλεανὸς Ἀσκληπιάδης ἐν τῷ περὶ τῆς
Νεστορίδος δύο ὦτα ἔχειν. πελειάδας[1] δὲ πῶς ἂν
τις ὑπόθοιτο νεμομένας περὶ ἕκαστον τῶν ὤτων;
πῶς δὲ καὶ λέγει δύο πυθμένας εἶναι τοῦ ποτηρίου;
b ἰδίως δὲ καὶ τοῦτο λέγεται ὅτι οἱ μὲν ἄλλοι μογοῦν-
τες ἐβάσταζον τὸ ποτήριον, Νέστωρ δ' ὁ γέρων
ἀμογητὶ ἄειρεν. ταῦτα προθέμενος ὁ Ἀσκληπιάδης
ζητεῖ περὶ τῶν ἥλων, πῶς πεπαρμένους αὐτοὺς δεῖ
δέχεσθαι.   οἱ μὲν οὖν λέγουσιν ἔξωθεν δεῖν ἐμ-
πείρεσθαι τοὺς χρυσοῦς ἥλους τῷ ἀργυρῷ ἐκ-
πώματι κατὰ τὸν τῆς ἐμπαιστικῆς τέχνης λόγον,
ὡς καὶ ἐπὶ τοῦ Ἀχιλλέως σκήπτρου·

ὣς φάτο χωόμενος, ποτὶ δὲ σκῆπτρον βάλε γαίῃ
χρυσείοις ἥλοισι πεπαρμένον.

ἐμφαίνεται γὰρ ὡς τῶν ἥλων ἐμπεπερονημένων
c καθάπερ ἐπὶ τῶν ῥοπάλων. καὶ ἐπὶ τοῦ ξίφους
τοῦ Ἀγαμέμνονος·

ἀμφὶ δ' ἄρ' ὤμοισιν βάλετο ξίφος· ἐν δέ οἱ ἥλοι
χρύσειοι[2] πάμφαινον· ἀτὰρ περὶ κουλεὸν ἦεν
ἀργύρεον.

Ἀπελλῆς μὲν οὖν ὁ τορευτὴς ἐπεδείκνυεν, φησίν,
ἡμῖν ἔν τισι Κορινθιακοῖς ἔργοις τὴν τῶν ἥλων
θέσιν. ἐξοχὴ δ' ἦν ὀλίγη τοῖς κολαπτῆρσιν ἐπ-

---

[1] CE: πελιάδες A.   [2] χρύσεοι A.

[a] Quoted on the same subject above, 477 b (p. 110).   On
this curious passage, wherein philology distorted by allegory
and astrology is seen at its worst, see Lehrs, *Aristarch. Stud.
Hom.*[3] 196, B. A. Müller, *De Asclepiade Myrleano*, Leipzig,

verses the first question is, what is the meaning of " pierced with golden studs "; secondly, what means the phrase, " there were four handles to it." For in the case of all other cups Asclepiades [a] of Myrlea, in his treatise *On Nestor's Cup*, says that they had only two handles. And how can one imagine doves feeding round each one of the handles ? What does he mean in saying there were " two stems " to the cup ? Peculiar, too, is the statement that whereas others lifted the cup with difficulty, " Nestor, that old man, raised it easily." Having posed these questions, Asclepiades asks about the studs, in what way they should be taken as " piercing." Some authorities, to be sure, assert that the golden studs must be affixed to the silver cup from the outside, in the method required by the art of embossing, illustrating this from the case of Achilles' staff [b] : " So he spake in his wrath, and hurled to earth the staff pierced with golden studs." Here, indeed, it is manifest that they are driven into the staff as nails are on clubs. Again, in the case of Agamemnon's sword [c] : " Then round his shoulders he cast his sword ; and on it studs of gold glistened ; but the scabbard about it was silver." Now Apelles, the metal-worker, showed us, he says,[d] the method of setting the studs in some Corinthian works of art. There was a small promi-

1903, 18 ff., and the cup found by Schliemann at Mycenae, reproduced in Leaf's edition², i. 599, also 600; also Helbig, *Hom. Epos²*, 272, 371, *J.H.S.* 1925, 73. The word here rendered " stems " (Leaf " supports") refers to the two strips of gold binding the bowl to the base in addition to the central stem.

[b] *Il.* i. 245. The subject of φάτο is Achilles.

[c] *Il.* xi. 29.

[d] Asclepiades. But C has κατὰ δέ τινας, as if another explanation were offered (*cf.* οἱ μὲν οὖν above, 488 b).

171

ηρμένη καὶ οἱονεὶ κεφαλίδας ἥλων ἀποτελοῦσα.
πεπάρθαι δὲ λέγεται τοὺς ἥλους ὑπὸ τοῦ ποιητοῦ
οὐχ ὅτι ἔξωθεν πρόσκεινται καὶ πεπαρμένοι εἰσίν,
d ἀλλ' ὅτι ἐμπεπαρμένοις ἐοίκασιν ἔξω τε ὀλίγῳ
προὔχουσι, μετέωροι τῆς ἄλλης ἐπιφανείας ὄντες.
καὶ περὶ τῶν ὤτων οὕτως διορίζονται, ὅτι εἶχε
μὲν δύο ὦτα ἄνω καθότι καὶ τἆλλα ποτήρια, ἄλλα
δὲ δύο κατὰ τὸ κύρτωμα μέσον ἐξ ἀμφοῖν τοῖ
μεροῖν μικρά, παρόμοια ταῖς Κορινθιακαῖς ὑδρίαις.
ὁ δὲ 'Απελλῆς[1] ἐντέχνως ἄγαν ὑπέδειξε τὴν τῶν
τεσσάρων ὤτων σχέσιν ἔχουσαν ὧδε. ἐκ μιᾶς
οἱονεὶ ῥίζης, ἥτις τῷ πυθμένι προσκυρεῖ,[2] καθ'
ἑκάτερον τὸ οὖς διασχιδεῖς εἰσι ῥάβδοι ἐπ' ἀμφοῖν,
e οὐ πολὺ ἀπ'[3] ἀλλήλων διεστῶσαι διάστημα.
αὗται μέχρι τοῦ χείλους διήκουσαι τοῦ ποτηρίου
καὶ μικρὸν ἔτι μετεωριζόμεναι κατὰ μὲν τὴν ἀπό-
στασιν τοῦ ἀγγείου φυλάττουσι τὴν διάσχισιν, κατὰ
δὲ τὸ ἀπολῆγον πρὸς τὴν τοῦ χείλους ἔρεισιν πάλιν
συμφυεῖς εἰσιν.[4] καὶ γίνεται τὸν τρόπον τοῦτον
τέτταρα ὦτα. τοῦτο δὲ οὐκ ἐπὶ πάντων, ἀλλ' ἐπ'
ἐνίων ποτηρίων τὸ εἶδος τῆς κατασκευῆς θεωρεῖται
μάλιστα[5] δὲ τῶν λεγομένων Σελευκίδων. [6]τὸ δ'
f ἐπὶ τῶν δυεῖν πυθμένων ζητούμενον, πῶς λέγεται
τὸ δύο δ' ὑπὸ πυθμένες ἦσαν, διαλύουσιν οὕτως
τινές. τῶν ποτηρίων τινὰ μὲν ἕνα πυθμένα ἔχειν[7]

---

[1] οἱ δὲ C.   [2] CE: προσκυρρει A.   [3] ἀπ' A: om. CE.
[4] εἰσιν added by Wilamowitz (cf. 491 f): συμφύονται CE.
[5] AC: ἥκιστα E.
[6] τὸ δὲ περὶ τῶν δύο πυθμένων λύουσιν οὕτω C.
[7] Schweighäuser: ἔχει ACE.

nence raised above the surface by the artist's punch, giving as it were the effect of nail-heads. Hence the studs are said by the poet to be " pierced," not because they are attached and inserted by piercing from the outside, but because they look as if they had been inserted and were projecting a little outward, though being in reality merely elevations [a] above the rest of the surface. And with regard to the handles they make this explanation, that whereas it had two handles at the brim as other cups have, it also had two other small handles at the middle of the curving bowl on both sides, resembling the handles on Corinthian water-jars. But Apelles further indicated by a very skilful drawing that the position of the four handles was as follows. Branching from a single root, as it were, which is attached to the base of the cup, are bands at the side of each handle, on both alike, at a small distance from each other. These bands extend as far as the brim of the cup and project also a little above the brim ; they maintain the branching (most) where the distance from the bowl is greatest,[b] but where their extremities are joined to the brim, the bands come together again. In this manner four handles are formed. This pattern is observed on only a few cups, not on all ; it is especially characteristic of those called *Seleukides*.[c] As for the question raised concerning the two " stems " and what is meant by " and there were two stems below," some authorities settle it in this wise : some cups have

[a] Lit. " elevated," or in relief, as in embossed ware. No actual rivets were used, according to this interpretation.
[b] Lit. " according to the distance from the bowl."
[c] Mentioned above, 783 e (p. 50), and below, 497 f (p. 220).

τὸν φυσικὸν καὶ συγκεχαλκευμένον τῷ ὅλῳ ποτηρίῳ,
καθότι τὰ λεγόμενα κυμβία καὶ τὰς φιάλας καὶ εἴ
τι φιαλῶδές ἐστι τὴν ἰδέαν· τινὰ δὲ δύο, ὥσπερ τὰ
ᾠοσκύφια καὶ τὰ κανθάρια καὶ τὰς Σελευκίδας
καὶ τὰ¹ καρχήσια καὶ τὰ τούτοις ὅμοια· ἕνα μὲν
γὰρ εἶναι πυθμένα τὸν κατὰ τὸ κύτος συγκεχαλκευ-
μένον² ὅλῳ τῷ ἀγγείῳ, ἕτερον δὲ τὸν προσθετόν,
ἀπὸ ὀξέος ἀρχόμενον, καταλήγοντα δ' εἰς πλατύ-
489 τερον, ἐφ' οὗ ἵσταται τὸ ποτήριον. καὶ τὸ τοῦ
Νέστορος οὖν δέπας φασὶν εἶναι τοιοῦτον. δύναται
δὲ καὶ δύο πυθμένας ὑποτίθεσθαι, τὸν μὲν οἷον τοῦ
ποτηρίου φέροντα τὸν ὅλον ὄγκον καὶ κατὰ μείζονα
κυκλοειδῆ περιγραφὴν ἔξαρσιν ἔχοντα τοῦ ὕψους
σύμμετρον, τὸν δὲ κατ' ἐλάττω κύκλον συνεχό-
μενον ἐν τῷ μείζονι,³ καθ' ὅσον συννεύειν συμ-
βέβηκεν εἰς ὀξὺ τὸν φυσικὸν τοῦ ποτηρίου πυθμένα,
ὥστε ὑπὸ δυοῖν πυθμένοιν φέρεσθαι τὸ ἔκπωμα.
Διονύσιος δὲ ὁ Θρᾷξ ἐν Ῥόδῳ λέγεται τὴν Νεσ-
τορίδα κατασκευάσαι τῶν μαθητῶν αὐτῷ συν-
b ενεγκάντων τἀργύριον· ὅπερ Προμαθίδας ὁ Ἡρακλεώτης ἐξηγούμενος τὴν κατὰ τὸν Διονύσιον
διάταξίν φησιν σκύφον εἶναι παρακειμένως ἔχοντα
τὰ ὦτα, καθάπερ αἱ δίπρωροι τῶν νεῶν, περὶ δὲ
τὰ ὦτα τὰς περιστεράς· ὡσπερεὶ δέ τινα ῥοπάλια

---

¹ CE: om. A.　　　² CE: συγχαλκευόμενον A.
³ ἐν τῷ μείζονι Kaibel: ἐν κύκλῳ μείζονι ACE.

ᵃ i.e. it is virtually a part of the bowl, or body of the vessel,
and is scarcely discernible, as in a modern saucer. The
other kind is a stem and base combined, such as may be seen
in the modern goblet and the ancient cylix (with stem).
ᵇ Below, 503 e.

one base, the natural one which is welded together with the cup as a whole[a]—such as the so-called *kymbia* (sauce-boats), the *phialai*, and any other vessel shaped to look like a *phialê*; some, again, have two bases, like the egg-shaped *skyphoi*,[b] the *kantharoi*, the *Seleukides*, the *karchesia*, and the cups similar to these; one base, that is, is that which is fashioned at the rounded body along with the cup as a whole, whereas the other is that which is attached separately, beginning in a narrow stem, and ending in one that is broader, being the support on which the cup stands. And so they assert that Nestor's cup (*depas*) was of this latter sort. But it is also possible that Homer suggests two stems, the one as it were supporting the entire weight of the cup and having a vertical height proportional to its larger circumference, whereas the other, describing a smaller circle, is contained within the larger, where the natural bottom of the cup converges to narrow dimensions, so that the cup is really supported by two stems.[c] It is said that Dionysius of Thrace constructed Nestor's cup at Rhodes with silver contributed by his pupils; Promathidas of Heracleia, then, in expounding the design made by Dionysius, says that the cup is a *skyphos* with handles in juxtaposition,[d] like ships with double prows, and on the handles were the pigeons; as though two bars,[e] placed transversely

[c] This means, apparently, that one stem of slighter circumference is superimposed, in the same axis, upon the other, which is larger and affords a firmer base.

[d] This is better expressed by Schol. *Il.* xi. 632 (Aristarchus), who says that there were two handles on each side of the bowl, so arranged as not to interfere with the lips in drinking, therefore below the brim.

[e] Lit. "staves." This sentence has become displaced, giving as it does a new explanation of the stem and handles.

δύο ὑποκεῖσθαι τῷ ποτηρίῳ πλάγια διὰ μήκους·
ταῦτα δ' εἶναι τοὺς δύο πυθμένας. ὁποῖόν τι καὶ νῦν
ἔστιν ἰδεῖν[1] ἐν Καπύῃ πόλει τῆς Καμπανίας ἀνακεί-
c μενον τῇ Ἀρτέμιδι ποτήριον, ὅπερ λέγουσιν ἐκεῖνοι
Νέστορος γεγονέναι· ἐστὶ δὲ ἀργύρεον, χρυσοῖς
γράμμασιν ἐντετυπωμένα ἔχον τὰ Ὁμηρικὰ ἔπη.
" 'Εγὼ δέ,'' φησὶν ὁ Μυρλεανός, " τάδε λέγω περὶ
τοῦ ποτηρίου. οἱ παλαιοὶ καὶ τὰ περὶ τὴν ἥμερον
τροφὴν πρῶτοι διαταξάμενοι τοῖς ἀνθρώποις, πειθό-
μενοι τὸν κόσμον εἶναι σφαιροειδῆ, λαμβάνοντες ἔκ
τε τοῦ ἡλίου καὶ τῆς σελήνης σχήματος ἐναργεῖς[2]
τὰς φαντασίας,[3] καὶ τὰ[4] περὶ τὴν ἰδίαν[5] τροφὴν[6]
τῷ περιέχοντι κατὰ τὴν ἰδέαν τοῦ σχήματος ἀφ-
ομοιοῦν εἶναι δίκαιον ἐνόμιζον. διὸ τὴν τράπεζαν
κυκλοειδῆ κατεσκευάσαντο καὶ τοὺς τρίποδας τοὺς
d τοῖς θεοῖς καθαγιζομένους κυκλοτερεῖς καὶ ἀστέρας
ἔχοντας,[7] καὶ φθόεις, οὓς καὶ καλοῦσι σελήνας.
καὶ τὸν ἄρτον δ' ἐκάλεσαν ὅτι τῶν σχημάτων ὁ
κύκλος ἀπήρτισται καὶ ἔστι τέλειος. καὶ τὸ ποτήριον οὖν τὸ δεχόμενον τὴν ὑγρὰν τροφὴν κυκλοτερὲς
ἐποίησαν κατὰ μίμημα τοῦ κόσμου. τὸ δὲ τοῦ
Νέστορος καὶ ἰδιαίτερόν ἐστιν. ἔχει γὰρ καὶ ἀστέρας, οὓς ἥλοις ὁ ποιητὴς ἀπεικάζει διὰ τὸ τοὺς

---

[1] ὁποῖόν τι ἦν C.   [2] CE: ἐνεργεῖς A.
[3] καὶ before τὰς φαντασίας (A) deleted by Casaubon:
φαντασίας simply CE.
[4] τὰ LP: τὰς A. Wilamowitz reads τῆς σελήνης τοῦ σχήματος, but τοῦ is unnecessary, see Harv. Studies xii. 137.
[5] ἰδίαν Schweighäuser: ἀίδιον A.
[6] Casaubon: στροφὴν A.
[7] C, omitting all mention of φθόεις: τοὺς τοῖς θεοῖς καθ.
φθόεις κυκλ. καὶ ἀστέρας ἔχοντας A. I have transposed φθόεις,
adding καί. Kaibel: τοὺς τρίποδας ἀστέρας ἔχοντας καὶ τοὺς τ.
θ. καθ. φθόεις κυκλοτερεῖς κτλ.

and lengthwise to the cup, acted as its supports;
these, then, were the two "stems." What it was like
it is still possible to see to-day in the city of Capua,
in Campania,—a cup dedicated to Diana, which the
people there say belonged to Nestor; it is of silver,
and has the Homeric verses embossed upon it in
letters of gold.

"I, then," says our authority of Myrlea, "have the
following comments to add concerning the cup. The
ancients, who were the first to ordain for men the
things pertaining to civilized life, being convinced
that the universe is spherical in shape, and deriving
distinct mental images from the shape of the sun and
moon, thought it was only right to make the things
pertaining to their own food like the element which
encompasses the earth, according to the shape it
seemed to have.[a] Hence they made a table round;
also the tripods consecrated to the gods they made
circular and covered with stars, and (round) cakes also
which they call 'moons.'[b] So also they called a loaf
artos, because, among geometrical shapes, the circle
is perfectly even[c] and complete. Hence, too, the
cup, which contains liquid food, they made circular in
imitation of the universe. But Nestor's cup is even
more characteristic. For it has stars also,[d] which
the Poet likens to studs, because stars are round

---

[a] Only a literal translation can reproduce the awkward
prolixity of the original.
[b] For the φθόϊς see Athen. 647 d, *cf.* Hesych. *s.v.* σελήνας.
For the tripods with stars see a coin of Cyzicus, W. Wroth,
Cat. xiv. Pl. ix. 15.
[c] ἄρτος is here connected with ἀπαρτίζω, "make even."
[d] In addition to being circular.

ἀστέρας περιφερεῖς εἶναι τοῖς ἥλοις ὁμοίως καὶ
ἐμπεπηγέναι[1] τῷ οὐρανῷ, καθὼς καὶ Ἄρατός φησιν
ἐπ᾿ αὐτῶν·

e   οὐρανῷ αἰὲν ἄρηρεν[2] ἀγάλματα νυκτὸς ἰούσης.

περιττῶς δὲ καὶ τοῦτ᾿ ἔφρασεν ὁ ποιητής, τοὺς χρυσοῦς ἥλους παρατιθεὶς τῇ τοῦ ἀργύρου ἐκπώματος
φύσει, τὴν τῶν ἀστέρων καὶ τοῦ οὐρανοῦ ἐκτυπῶν
κατὰ τὴν ἰδέαν τῆς χρόας οὐσίαν. ὁ μὲν γὰρ
οὐρανὸς ἀργύρῳ προσέοικεν, οἱ δὲ ἀστέρες χρυσῷ
διὰ τὸ πυρῶδες.

    " Ὑποθέμενος οὖν κατηστερισμένον[3] τὸ τοῦ
Νέστορος ποτήριον μεταβαίνει καὶ ἐπὶ τὰ κράτιστα
τῶν ἀπλανῶν ἀστέρων, οἷς δὴ τεκμαίρονται τὰ
περὶ τὴν ζωὴν οἱ[4] ἄνθρωποι· λέγω δὲ τὰς πελειά-
f δας.[5] ὅταν γὰρ εἴπῃ·

        δύω[6] δὲ πελειάδες ἀμφὶς ἕκαστον
    χρύσειαι νεμέθοντο,

πελειάδας οὐ σημαίνει τὰς ὄρνιθας, ἅς[7] τινες
ὑπονοοῦσι περιστερὰς εἶναι, ἁμαρτάνοντες. ἕτερον
γὰρ εἶναί φησιν Ἀριστοτέλης πελειάδα καὶ ἕτερον
περιστεράν. πελειάδας δ᾿ ὁ ποιητὴς καλεῖ νῦν τὰς
Πλειάδας, πρὸς ἃς σπόρος τε καὶ ἀμητός,[8] καὶ
τῶν καρπῶν ἀρχὴ γενέσεως καὶ συναιρέσεως,[9]
καθά φησι καὶ Ἡσίοδος·

---

    [1] καὶ ἐμπεπηγέναι CE: καὶ ὡς ἐμπεπηγέναι A (ὥσπερ
Wilamowitz).
    [2] εὖ ἐνάρηρεν Arat. The reading in A is a reminiscence of
Phaen. 22.   [3] CE: κατεστηρισμένον A.
    [4] οἱ CE: om. A.   [5] CE: πελιάδας A.
    [6] δύο ACE. Cf. 487   [7] Kaibel: ὡς ACE.

just as nails are, and are fastened to the sky, as
Aratus says of them [a] : 'They are ever fixed in the
sky as the ornaments of the passing night.' In
striking fashion the Poet has made this also plain,
in that, by setting the golden studs side by side with
the silver substance of the cup, he has brought out
by contrast the true character of the stars and the
sky in accordance with the outward appearance
of their colours. For the sky is like unto silver,
whereas the stars resemble gold in their fiery nature.

"Imagining, therefore, Nestor's cup as entirely
covered with stars, the Poet passes on next to the
most important of the constellations,[b] those, namely,
by the help of which men determine the acts of their
daily lives;[c] I mean the Doves.[d] For when he
says, 'And two doves of gold were feeding round
each,' he does not mean by 'doves' the birds, which
certain persons erroneously understand here as
pigeons. No, for Aristotle says [e] that the dove is
one thing, the pigeon another. On the contrary, the
Poet in this instance uses 'doves' for 'Pleiades,' and
it is with reference to them that men sow and reap ;
they mark the beginning of the birth of the crops
and of their harvesting, as Hesiod says [f] : 'Begin

[a] *Phaenom.* 453, G. R. Mair (L.C.L.) p. 416. See critical
note 2. *Cf.* Plat. *Tim.* 40.
[b] Lit. "the non-wandering stars."
[c] The rising or setting of the constellations leads to in-
ferences about the seasons, the weather, etc. *Cf.* the movement of flocks and herds as determined by Arcturus, Soph.
Oed. Tyr. 1137, and Jebb's note in the App. p. 230.
[d] *i.e.* Pleiades. [e] *Hist. An.* 544 b 2 (v. 13. 3).
[f] *Opp.* 383.

---

[8] The comma is better placed here than after τῶν καρπῶν
(γίνεται τῶν καρπῶν Kaibel): C does not punctuate here.
[9] συναιρέσεως Kaibel: συναίρεσις ACE.

179

Πληιάδων Ἀτλαγενέων[1] ἐπιτελλομενάων
490 ἄρχεσθ᾽[2] ἀμητοῖ᾽,[3] ἀρότοιο δὲ δυσομενάων.

καὶ Ἄρατος·

αἱ μὲν ὁμῶς ὀλίγαι καὶ ἀφεγγέες, ἀλλ᾽ ὀνομασταὶ
ἦρι καὶ ἑσπέριαι, Ζεὺς δ᾽ αἴτιος, εἱλίσσονται·
ὅς σφισι[4] καὶ θέρεος καὶ χείματος ἀρχομένοιο
σημαίνειν ἐπένευσεν ἐπερχομένου τ᾽ ἀρότοιο.

τὰς οὖν τῆς τῶν καρπῶν γενέσεως καὶ τελειώσεως
προσημαντικὰς Πλειάδας οἰκείως ἐνετόρευσε[5] τῷ
τοῦ σοφωτάτου Νέστορος ὁ ποιητὴς ποτηρίῳ· καὶ
γὰρ τοῦτο τῆς ἑτέρας[6] τροφῆς δεκτικὸν ἀγγεῖον.
b διὸ καὶ τῷ Διὶ τὴν ἀμβροσίαν τὰς Πελειάδας
φέρειν φησί[7]·

τῇ μέν τ᾽ οὐδὲ ποτητὰ[8] παρέρχεται οὐδὲ Πέλειαι
τρήρωνες, ταί τ᾽[9] ἀμβροσίην Διὶ πατρὶ φέρουσι.

οὐ γὰρ τὰς πελειάδας τὰς ὄρνεις φέρειν νομιστέον
τῷ Διὶ τὴν ἀμβροσίαν, ὡς οἱ[10] πολλοὶ δοξάζουσιν
(ἄσεμνον γάρ), ἀλλὰ τὰς Πλειάδας. οἰκεῖον γὰρ
τὰς προσημαινούσας τῷ τῶν ἀνθρώπων γένει τὰς
ὥρας, ταύτας καὶ τῷ Διὶ φέρειν τὴν ἀμβροσίαν.
διόπερ ἀπὸ τῶν πτηνῶν αὐτὰς χωρίζει λέγων·

c τῇ μέν τ᾽ οὐδὲ ποτητὰ[8] παρέρχεται οὐδὲ Πέλειαι.

ὅτι δὲ τὰς Πλειάδας τὸ ἐνδοξότατον τῶν[11] ἀπλανῶν

---

[1] CE: πλειάδων ἀτλαιγενέων A.
[2] CE: ἄρχεσθαι A.   [3] ἀμητοῖο ASE.
[4] ὃς καὶ σφίσι C.
[5] Hemsterhuys: ἐνετόρνευσε ACE.
[6] ἑκατέρας (?) Schweighäuser, cf. 492 d.
[7] ἐν ὀδυσσείᾳ add. C.   [8] τοῦ δὲ ποτητα A.
[9] πέλεια τρήρων ἔσται τ᾽ A.
[10] οἱ added by Dobree.   [11] τῶν Kaibel: καὶ ACE.

ye the reaping when the Pleiades, daughters of Atlas, rise, and the ploughing, when they begin to set.' And Aratus[a] : ' These, to be sure, are alike small and dim, yet are they famous as they revolve—Zeus is the cause—in the morning and the evening. It is he who ordained that they should give the sign when summer and winter begin and the season of ploughing approaches.' So, then, the Poet has, through the embosser's art, quite properly represented the Pleiades as presaging the germination of the crops, and their coming to perfection, on the cup of the most sapient Nestor : for it is a vessel capable of receiving the other kind of food as well.[b] Hence also he declares that the Doves (*Peleiades*) bring the ambrosia for Zeus[c] : ' On this side even winged things cannot pass by, not even the timorous Doves (*Peleiai*), which bring ambrosia to Father Zeus.' It must not be thought that it is the *birds* called *peleiades* that bring ambrosia to Zeus, as the majority imagine (for that would be beneath his dignity), but rather the Pleiades. For it is the appropriate office of those Maidens who give sign of the seasons to the human race that they should also bring ambrosia to Zeus. Hence he really distinguishes them from fowls when he says : ' Even winged things cannot pass by, nor even the Peleiai.' Further, that he regards the Pleiades as the most notable of the constellations is

---

[a] *Phaen.* 264, Mair p. 400.

[b] *i.e.* dry food, which Toup read ($\xi\eta\rho\hat{\alpha}s$ for $\dot{\epsilon}\tau\dot{\epsilon}\rho\alpha s$).

[c] *Od.* xii. 62, of the Wandering Rocks (Planctae or Symplegades, 492 d).

ἄστρων ὑπείληφε, δῆλον ἐκ τοῦ προτάττειν αὐτὰς
κατὰ τὴν τῶν[1] ἄλλων συναρίθμησιν·

ἐν δὲ τὰ τείρεα πάντα τά τ᾽ οὐρανὸς ἐστεφάνωται,
Πληιάδας θ᾽ Ὑάδας τε τό τε σθένος Ὠρίωνος
Ἄρκτον θ᾽, ἣν καὶ Ἄμαξαν ἐπίκλησιν καλέουσιν.

d ἐπλανήθησαν δ᾽ οἱ πολλοὶ νομίζοντες τὰς πελειάδας[2]
ὄρνεις εἶναι πρῶτον μὲν ἐκ τοῦ ποιητικοῦ σχηματισμοῦ τοῦ κατὰ τὴν πρόσθεσιν τοῦ γράμματος·
ἔπειτα δ᾽ ὅτι τὸ τρήρωνες μόνον[3] ἐδέξαντο εἶναι
ἐπίθετον πελειάδων, ἐπεὶ διὰ τὴν ἀσθένειαν εὐλαβὴς
ἡ ὄρνις αὕτη· τρεῖν δ᾽ ἐστὶ τὸ εὐλαβεῖσθαι. πιθανὸν δ᾽ ἐστὶ τὸ ἐπίθετον καὶ ἐπὶ τῶν Πλειάδων
τιθέμενον· μυθεύονται γὰρ καὶ αὗται τὸν Ὠρίωνα
φεύγειν, διωκομένης τῆς μητρὸς αὐτῶν Πληιόνης
e ὑπὸ τοῦ Ὠρίωνος. ἡ δὲ τοῦ ὀνόματος ἐκτροπή,
καθ᾽ ἣν αἱ Πλειάδες λέγονται Πέλειαι καὶ Πελειάδες, παρὰ πολλοῖς ἐστι τῶν ποιητῶν. πρώτη δὲ
Μοιρὼ ἡ Βυζαντία[5] καλῶς ἐδέξατο τὸν νοῦν τῶν
Ὁμήρου ποιημάτων ἐν τῇ Μνημοσύνῃ ἐπιγραφομένῃ φάσκουσα τὴν ἀμβροσίαν τῷ Διὶ τὰς Πλειάδας
κομίζειν. Κράτης δ᾽ ὁ κριτικὸς σφετερισάμενος
αὐτῆς τὴν δόξαν ὡς ἴδιον ἐκφέρει τὸν λόγον. καὶ
Σιμωνίδης δὲ τὰς Πλειάδας Πελειάδας[6] εἴρηκεν ἐν
τούτοις·

f   δίδωτι δ᾽ εὖχος Ἑρμᾶς[7] ἐναγώνιος,
    Μαίας εὐπλοκάμοιο παῖς, ἔτικτε δ᾽ Ἄτλας

---

[1] τῶν CE: om. A. [2] Kaibel: πλειάδας ACE.
[3] μόνων C: μόνον A. [4] CE: πληιόμης A.
[5] πρώτη γοῦν ἡ βυζαντία μοιρὼ C.
[6] οὐρανίας add. C. [7] Jacobs: δευτεσερμας A.

---

[a] Il. xviii. 485, on the shield of Achilles.

manifest from the way in which he puts them first in his enumeration of them and the other stars [a] : 'And on it all the signs wherewith the sky is wreathed, Pleiades, and Hyades, and mighty Orion, and the Bear that men call also the Wain.' And so the majority have gone wrong in thinking that the *peleiades* are birds, first because of the poetic form which is made by adding the letter [b]; then secondly, because they took the word ' timorous ' to be an epithet only of doves, since this bird, on account of its lack of strength, is cautious ; for to be cautious is to be timorous. But the epithet is appropriate even when applied to the Pleiades ; for in mythology they too are said to fly from Orion when their mother Pleionê is pursued by Orion. And the collateral form of their name, by which the Pleiades may be called either Peleiai or Peleiades, is to be found among many of the poets. Moero of Byzantium was the first to understand correctly the sense of the Homeric verses, declaring, in the work entitled *Memory*, that the Pleiades carried ambrosia to Zeus. Then the philologist [c] Crates appropriated her idea as his own and published that interpretation.[d] Simonides also calls the Pleiades *Peleiades* in these lines [e] : ' Hermes, god of the games, grants renown, he the son of Maia with the fair tresses, and she loveliest in beauty

---

[b] The letter *e*, giving *peleiades* instead of *pleiades*, and so suggesting (of course rightly, despite our learned but misguided pleader) the meaning " doves."

[c] Crates of Mallos was the first to assume this title (κριτικός) instead of γραμματικός: Gudeman, *Geschichte d. class. Phil.* 3.

[d] Wachsmuth, p. 53.

[e] *P.L.G.*[4] iii. 394, Diehl frag. 30, Edmonds frag. 49, emended from Schol. Pind. *Nem.* ii. 16.

ἑπτὰ[1] ἰοπλοκάμων φιλᾶν θυγατρῶν[2] τάν γ’ ἔξοχο
εἶδος,
ταὶ καλέονται[3] Πελειάδες οὐράνιαι.

σαφῶς γὰρ τὰς Πλειάδας[4] οὔσας Ἄτλαντος θυγατέρας Πελειάδας καλεῖ, καθάπερ καὶ Πίνδαρος·

ἐστὶ δ’ ἐοικὸς
ὀρειᾶν γε[5] Πελειάδων
μὴ τηλόθεν Ὀαρίωνα νεῖσθαι.[6]

σύνεγγυς γάρ ἐστιν ὁ Ὠρίων τῇ ἀστροθεσίᾳ τῶ
Πλειάδων διὸ καὶ ὁ περὶ ταύτας μῦθος, ὅτ
φεύγουσι μετὰ τῆς μητρὸς τῆς Πληιόνης τὸ
Ὠρίωνα. ὀρείας[7] δὲ λέγει τὰς Πλειάδας ἐν ἴσῳ τῷ
οὐρείας[8] κατὰ παράλειψιν τοῦ ῡ, ἐπειδὴ[9] κεῖντα
491 ἐπὶ τῆς οὐρᾶς τοῦ Ταύρου. καὶ Αἰσχύλος δ’
ἐκφανέστερον προσπαίζων τῷ ὀνόματι κατὰ τὴ
ὁμοφωνίαν φησί[10]·

αἱ δ’ ἕπτ’ Ἄτλαντος παῖδες ὠνομασμέναι
πατρὸς μέγιστον ἆθλον οὐρανοστεγῆ
κλαίεσκον, ἔνθα νυκτέρων φαντασμάτων
ἔχουσι μορφὰς ἄπτεροι Πελειάδες.

ἀπτέρους γὰρ αὐτὰς εἴρηκε διὰ τὴν πρὸς τὰς ὄρνεις
ὁμωνυμίαν. ἡ δὲ Μοιρὼ καὶ αὐτὴ τὸν τρόπον τοῦ-
τόν φησι·

b Ζεὺς δ’ ἄρ’ ἐνὶ Κρήτῃ τρέφετο μέγας, οὐδ’ ἄρα
τίς νιν
ἠείδει μακάρων· ὁ δ’ ἀέξετο πᾶσι μέλεσσι.
τὸν μὲν ἄρα τρήρωνες ὑπὸ ζαθέῳ τράφον[11] ἄντρῳ

---

[1] Musurus: ἐπιτα A.
[2] Schneidewin: φιλαν θυγατερων A.
[3] Hartung: ἀγικαλέονται A.　　　　　　　[4] πελιάδας A.

184

among the seven dear daughters with violet tresses
born unto Atlas, who are called the Peleiades of the
heavens.' It is perfectly evident that he means the
Pleiades, who are daughters of Atlas, in calling them
Peleiades, as Pindar does [a] : ' And it is indeed seemly
that Orion should move not far from the mountain-
Peleiades.' As a matter of fact, Orion is very close
to the constellation of the Pleiades ; hence also the
story about them, that they fly from Orion with their
mother Pleionê. Further, he calls the Pleiades
reias (mountain), equivalent to *oureias* by omission
of the letter *u*, because they are situated at the tail
(*oura*) of the Bull. And Aeschylus, also, more plainly
punning on the name because of the similarity of
sound, says [b] : ' And they that are called the seven
daughters of Atlas bemoaned their father's mighty
task of bearing up the heavens, where in phantom
forms at night they have their station—the wingless
Peleiades.' [c] For he calls them wingless because their
name is similar to that of the doves. And Moero herself speaks in this wise [d] : ' So then Zeus was nourished
to full growth in Crete, nor did any of the Blessed have
knowledge of him ; anon he waxed strong in all his
limbs. Him the timorous ones nourished within the

---

[a] *Nem.* ii. 16, Sandys (L.C.L.) 328.
[b] *T.G.F.*[2] 97.
[c] Aeschylus, of course, understood Pleiades or Peleiades
to mean doves. For the oxymoron in " wingless " *cf.* Eur.
Iph. T. 1095 ἄπτερος ὄρνις.
[d] Powell 21.

---

[5] οριαν γε A, ὁρίαν om. γε CE.
[6] CE : ὁαρίων ἀνεισθαι A. See Schroeder *ad loc.*
[7] ὁρίας CE, οριας A.   [8] οὐρίας ACE.
[9] ἐπεὶ C.   [10] φησί add. C.
[11] Schweighäuser : τράφεν A, ἔτρεφον C in paraphr.

ἀμβροσίην φορέουσαι ἀπ' Ὠκεανοῖο ῥοάων·
νέκταρ δ' ἐκ πέτρης[1] μέγας αἰετὸς αἰὲν ἀφύσσω
γαμφηλῆς[2] φορέεσκε ποτὸν[3] Διὶ μητιόεντι.
τὸν καὶ νικήσας πατέρα Κρόνον εὐρύοπα Ζεὺς
ἀθάνατον ποίησε καὶ οὐρανῷ ἐγκατένασσεν.
ὡς δ' αὕτως τρήρωσι Πελειάσιν ὤπασε τιμήν,
c   αἳ δή τοι θέρεος καὶ χείματος ἄγγελοί εἰσι.

καὶ Σιμμίας δ' ἐν τῇ Γοργοῖ φησιν·

    αἰθέρος ὠκεῖαι[4] πρόπολοι πίλναντο Πέλειαι.

Ποσείδιππός[5] τ' ἐν τῇ Αἰσωπίᾳ[6]·

    οὐδέ τοι ἀκρόνυχοι ψυχραὶ δύνουσι Πέλειαι.

Λαμπροκλῆς δ' ὁ διθυραμβοποιὸς καὶ ῥητῶς αὐτὰ
εἶπεν ὁμωνυμεῖν ταῖς περιστεραῖς ἐν τούτοις·

                    αἵ τε ποταναῖς
    ὁμώνυμοι πελειάσιν αἰθέρι κεῖσθε.[7]

καὶ ὁ τὴν εἰς Ἡσίοδον δὲ ἀναφερομένην ποιήσας
Ἀστρονομίαν αἰεὶ Πελειάδας αὐτὰς λέγει·

d   τὰς δὲ[8] βροτοὶ καλέουσι Πελειάδας.

καὶ πάλιν·

    χειμέριαι δύνουσι Πελειάδες.

καὶ πάλιν·

    τῆμος ἀποκρύπτουσι Πελειάδες.

οὐδὲν οὖν ἄπιστον καὶ Ὅμηρον τὰς Πλειάδας κατὰ
ποιητικὸν νόμον Πελειάδας ὠνομακέναι.

---

[1] Πέτρης Ludwich (cf. Paus. ix. 34. 4, itself doubtful).
[2] γαμφηλῆς Eustath. 1484. 48: γαμφηλῆς CE, γαμφηλῇ A Ταλλαίης (?) Kaibel.   [3] Camerarius: πετὸν A
[4] αἱ θέρος ὠκεῖαι A: ὠκεῖαι θέρεος (?) Kaibel, as supporting
186

shelter of a sacred grotto, bearing ambrosia from the streams of Oceanus ; and a great eagle ever drew nectar from a rock, and in its beak brought it for Zeus the all-wise to drink. And when far-thundering Zeus had overcome his father Cronus, he made the eagle immortal and appointed him to dwell in Heaven. Likewise he bestowed honour upon the timorous Doves (Peleiades) which are the messengers of summer and of winter.' Simmias, on the other hand, says in Gorgo[a] : ' The Peleiai, swift ministers of the sky, were approaching.' And likewise Poseidippus in his *Epic of Aesopus*[b] : ' Nor, verily, do the cold Peleiai set at nightfall.' Lamprocles, the composer of dithyrambs, has said expressly that the Pleiades have the same name as the pigeons in these lines[c] : ' Ye that are of like name with the winged doves (*peleiades*) and are set in the sky.' And the author of the poem on *Astronomy* ascribed to Hesiod always speaks of them as Peleiades[d] : ' Which mortals call Peleiades.' And again[e] : ' The wintry Peleiades are sinking low.' Still again[f] : ' Then do the Peleiades hide their light.' It is, therefore, not at all improbable that Homer also, in accord with the poetic custom, has called the Pleiades ' Peleiades.'

---

[a] Powell 112 ; see critical note. This verse and the following are cited for the form *peleiai*, not *peleiades*.
[b] Wilamowitz, *Hellenistische Dichtung* i. 148 note 2.
[c] *P.L.G.* iii. 556, Diehl, Edmonds, frag. 2.
[d] *i.e.* not Pleiades ; Rzach frag. 9, Diels 499.
[e] Frag. 10.   [f] Frag. 11.

---

better the contention of Asclepiades that Peleiai meant not doves, but Pleiades.
[5] ποσίδιππος A.   [6] Αἰσωπίᾳ Schott : ἀσωπίαι A.
[7] κεῖνται C, Eustath. 1713. 5.
[8] Hermann : τάσδε A.

"'Αποδεδειγμένου οὖν τοῦ ὅτι Πλειάδες ἦσαν
ἐντετορευμέναι[1] τῷ ποτηρίῳ, καθ' ἕκαστον τῶν
ὤτων δύο ὑποθετέον εἴτε βούλεταί τις ὀρνιθοφυεῖς
κόρας εἴτ' αὖ καὶ ἀνθρωποειδεῖς, ἄστροις δὲ πεποι-
κιλμένας. τὸ μέντοι ' ἀμφὶς ἕκαστον χρύσειαι
c νεμέθοντο ' οὐχ ὡς περὶ ἓν ἕκαστον ἀκουστέον·
γενήσονται γὰρ οὕτως ηʹ τὸν ἀριθμόν· ἀλλ' ἐπείπερ
ἔσχισται μὲν ἑκάτερον τῶν ὤτων εἰς δύο σχίσεις,
τούτων δ' αὖ συνάφεια κατὰ τὴν τελευταίαν
ὑπόληξιν,[2] ἕκαστον μὲν ἂν λέγοιτο καθὸ τέτταρες
αἱ πᾶσαι σχίσεις τῶν ὤτων, ἑκάτερον δὲ καθὸ
συμφυῆ πάλιν ἐπὶ τέλει γίνεται τῆς ἀνατάσεως[3]
αὐτῶν. ὅταν οὖν εἴπῃ·

δοιαὶ δὲ πελειάδες ἀμφὶς ἕκαστον
χρύσειαι νεμέθοντο, δύω[4] δ' ὑπὸ πυθμένες ἦσαν,

f καθ' ἑκατέραν τὴν σχίσιν τῶν ὤτων ἀκουσόμεθα
μίαν πελειάδα· ἃς δοιὰς εἶπεν καθὸ συμφυεῖς εἰσιν
ἀλλήλαις καὶ συνεζευγμέναι. τὸ γὰρ δοιοὶ καὶ
δοιαί[5] σημαίνει καὶ τὸ κατ' ἀριθμὸν εἶδος, τὸ δύο,
οἷον·

δοιοὺς δὲ τρίποδας, δέκα δὲ χρυσοῖο τάλαντα.

καὶ ' δοιὼ[6] θεράποντε.' σημαίνει δὲ καὶ τὸ
συμφυὲς καὶ τὸ συνεζευγμένον κατ' ἀριθμόν, ὡς
ἐν τούτοις·

δοιοὺς[8] δ' ἄρ' ὑπήλυθε θάμνους
ἐξ ὁμόθεν πεφυῶτας, ὁ μὲν φυλίης, ὁ δ' ἐλαίης.

492 γενήσονται οὖν ἐπὶ τῶν ὤτων τέσσαρες πελειάδες.

---

[1] CE: -τορνευμέναι A.   [2] ἀπόληξιν Kaibel, cf. 488 e.
[3] ἀνατάσεως C: ἀναστάσεως A, ἀποστάσεως Kaibel.

" It has, then, been proved that the Pleiades were embossed on the cup, and one must assume two at each handle, whether one insists that they were bird-shaped maidens or again human-shaped, and spangled with stars. But the phrase ' round each, golden Peleiades were feeding ' must not be understood as meaning round every single handle ; for that will make the Pleiades eight in number ; on the contrary, since each pair of handles is separated into two divisions, and their joining again occurs almost at the point where the cup ends, the word ' each ' must have reference to the fact that all the divisions of the handles number four, while ' each pair ' refers to the fact that they grow together again at the point where their extension ceases. When, therefore, the Poet says, ' And two doves (*peleiades*) of gold were feeding round each, and there were two stems below the cup,' we shall understand that at each of the two points where the handles divide there was one dove ; these he calls ' two ' (*doiai*) because they grow into one another and are closely joined.[a] For the forms *doioi* and *doiai* signify the general idea of number, ' two,' as in [b] ' Two (*doioi*) tripods and ten talents of gold.' Also ' two (*doiô*) henchmen.' [c] But it signifies also the idea of grown together, and closely joined in pairs, as in these lines [d] : ' So then he crept beneath two bushes that grew from one stem, the one a mastic, the other an olive.' Thus there will be only four doves on the handles.

---

[a] *i.e.* twofold, or twin.   [b] *Od.* iv. 129.
[c] *Od.* xvi. 253, example of the dual.   [d] *Od.* v. 476.

---

[4] δύο CE.   [5] CE : αἱ δοιαί A.
[6] CE : δύο A.   [7] θεράποντες CE.
              [8] CE : δυοὺς A.

Ἔπειθ' ὅταν ἐπενέγκῃ τὸ

       δοιαὶ δὲ πελειάδες ἀμφὶς ἕκαστον
χρύσειαι νεμέθοντο, δύω δ' ὑπὸ πυθμένες ἦσαν,
ἀκουστέον οὐ πυθμένας δύο, ἀλλ' οὐδὲ κατὰ
διαίρεσιν ἀναγνωστέον, ὡς ὁ Θρᾷξ Διονύσιος, ἀλλὰ
κατὰ σύνθετον ὑποπύθμενες, ὅπως ἐπὶ τῶν πελειάδων ἀκούωμεν,[1] ὅτι τέσσαρες μὲν ἦσαν ἐπὶ τῶν
b ὤτων, δύο δὲ ὑποπύθμενες, τουτέστιν ὑπὸ τῷ
πυθμένι οἷον ὑποπυθμένιοι· ὥστε διακρατεῖσθαι τὸ
δέπας ὑπὸ δυεῖν Πελειάδων ὑποκειμένων τῷ πυθμένι, ἓξ δὲ τὰς πάσας γενέσθαι[2] Πλειάδας, ἐπείπερ
ὁρῶνται τοσαῦται, λέγονται δὲ ἑπτά, καθότι καὶ
Ἄρατός φησιν·

ἑπτάποροι δὴ ταί γε μετ' ἀνθρώποις καλέονται,
ἓξ οἷαί περ ἐοῦσαι ἐπόψιαι ὀφθαλμοῖσιν.
οὐ μέν πως ἀπόλωλεν ἀπευθὴς ἐκ Διὸς ἀστήρ,
ἐξ οὗ καὶ γενέηθεν ἀκούομεν· ἀλλὰ μάλ' αὕτως
εἴρεται,[3] ἑπτὰ δ' ἐκεῖναι ἐπιρρήδην καλέον-
    ται. . . .

c ἐξ οἷαί περ ἐοῦσαι ἐπόψιαι ὀφθαλμοῖσιν.[4] τὸ ὁρώ-
μενον οὖν ἐν τοῖς ἄστροις καὶ ἐν τῇ φαινομένῃ
κατασκευῇ προσηκόντως ἐτόρευσεν. τοῦτο μέντοι
καὶ ἐπὶ τοῦ Διὸς σημαίνειν πείθονται τὸν ποιητὴν
ὅταν λέγῃ·

τῇ μέν τ' οὐδὲ ποτητὰ[5] παρέρχεται οὐδὲ πέλειαι
τρήρωνες ταί τ'[6] ἀμβροσίην Διὶ πατρὶ φέρουσιν.

---

[1] ἀκούσωμεν CE.   [2] γίνεσθαι (?) Kaibel.
[3] Arat.: εἴρηται A.
[4] ἐξ . . . ὀφθαλμοῖσιν omitted in the later MSS. and bracketed
by Kaibel; but to prune the prolixity of this disquisition
would be a thankless task.

" Again, when he adds (after 'two doves of gold were feeding round each ') the phrase, ' and there were two stems below ' (*hypo pythmenes*),[a] we are not to understand two bases, nor are we to divide the words in reading, as Dionysius of Thrace does, but we should read the compound *hypopythmenes*, in order to construe it as an adjective modifying *peleiades*, because there were four on the handles, but two at the bottom of the cup ; that is, it means ' at the bottom,' like the epithet *hypopythmenioi*. Thus the cup was supported by two Peleiades set beneath the bottom, and the whole number of Pleiades (on the cup) amounted to six, since that is the number visible (in the sky), though they are spoken of as seven, as Aratus also says[b] : '" Moving in seven paths," then, men say of them, though only six are plain for the eyes to see. Not in any wise is a star lost beyond the ken of Zeus, whose offspring we also are said to be ;[c] yet is it said for all that,[d] and they are expressly called seven.' . . . "Only six are plain for the eyes to see." The artist, therefore, has fittingly depicted by embossed work, in the pattern that we see, what is actually observed in the constellation. Authorities believe, moreover, that the Poet indicates this also of Zeus when he says[e] : ' On this side even winged things cannot pass by, not even the timorous Doves which bring ambrosia to Father Zeus. But the

---

[a] At this point the writer interprets ὑποπύθμενες as one word, as shown in the following. Eustath. 869. 8.

[b] *Phaen.* 257, G. R. Mair (L.C.L.) p. 400.

[c] *Cf.* the famous vs. *Phaen.* 5 τοῦ γὰρ καὶ εἰμέν, *Act. Apostol.* xvii. 28.

[d] *Sc.* that they are seven in number, not six.

[e] *Od.* xii. 62, above, 490 b.

---

[5] CE: τοῦ δὲ ποτῆτα A.   [6] αἵ τ' ACE.

ἀλλά τε[1] καὶ τῶν αἰεὶ ἀφαιρεῖται λὶς[2] πέτρη.
ἀλλ' ἄλλην ἐνίησι[3] πατὴρ ἐναρίθμιον εἶναι

d ὑπὸ τῆς ὀξύτητος τῶν Πλαγκτῶν Πετρῶν καὶ τῆς
λειότητος ἀφαιρεῖσθαι λέγων μίαν τῶν Πλειάδων,
ἄλλην δὲ πρὸς τοῦ[4] Διὸς ἐνίεσθαι χάριν τοῦ σῴζειν
τὸν ἀριθμὸν αὐτῶν, ποιητικῶς αἰνιττόμενος ὅτι
τῶν Πλειάδων ἓξ ὁρωμένων ὅμως ὁ ἀριθμὸς αὐτῶν
οὐκ ἀπόλλυται, λέγονται δὲ καὶ τῷ ἀριθμῷ καὶ
τοῖς ὀνόμασιν ἑπτά.

"Πρὸς δὲ τοὺς λέγοντας οὐκ οἰκείως τῷ ποτηρίῳ
ἐντετυπῶσθαι τὰς Πλειάδας, ξηρῶν τροφῶν οὔσας
σημαντικάς, λεκτέον ὅτι τὸ δέπας ἀμφοτέρων τῶν
e τροφῶν ἐστιν δεκτικόν. κυκεὼν γὰρ ἐν αὐτῷ
γίνεται· τοῦτο δ' ἐστὶ πόσις ἐν τῷ κράματι τυρὸν
ἔχουσα καὶ ἄλφιτον· ἄμφω δὲ ταῦτα κυκώμενα
καὶ οὕτω πινόμενα λέγει ὁ ποιητής·

τοῖσι δὲ τεῦχε κυκεῶ[5] εὐπλόκαμος Ἑκαμήδη ...
ἣ σφῶιν πρῶτον[6] μὲν ἐπιπροίηλε τράπεζαν
καλὴν κυανόπεζαν[6] εὔξοον, αὐτὰρ[7] ἐπ' αὐτῆς
χάλκειον κάνεον· ἐπὶ δὲ κρόμυον ποτῷ ὄψον
ἠδὲ μέλι χλωρόν, παρὰ[8] δ' ἀλφίτου ἱεροῦ ἀκτήν,
f πὰρ δὲ δέπας περικαλλές, ὃ οἴκοθεν ἦγ'
γεραιός ...
ἐν τῷ ῥά σφι κύκησε γυνὴ εἰκυῖα θεῇσιν[9]
οἴνῳ Πραμνείῳ, ἐπὶ δ' αἴγειον κνῆ τυρὸν

<hr />

[1] τε om. C.   [2] CE: λεις A.
[3] CE: ἀνίησι A.   [4] CE: τοὺς A.
[5] This unmetrical form (for κυκειῶ or κυκηῶ) in ACE occurs
also in Cod. D (Laur.) of Homer; so also below in f (Athen.
Cod. A, Hom. Cod. Vind.).
[6] πρῶτον and καλὴν κυανόπεζαν supplied from Homer.
[7] αὐτασ' A.   [8] ἐπὶ A.   [9] θεοῖσιν A.

smooth rock ever steals one of them away. Yet the Father sends in another to make up the number,' meaning that one of the Pleiades is stolen away by the suddenness and slipperiness of the Wandering Rocks, although another dove is sent in by Zeus to maintain their full number; in poetic fashion he implies that though only six Pleiades can be seen, nevertheless their full number is never lost, and they are counted as seven in number as well as in name.

"And in answer to those who say that the embossing of the Pleiades on the cup is not appropriate, since they are harbingers of dry foods, we may say that the cup (*depas*) is capable of holding both kinds of food.[a] For a posset (*kykeôn*) is made in it, and this is a drink containing in its ingredients cheese and barley meal; both of these are mixed and drunk in this way, the Poet says[b]: 'For them Hecamedê of the beautiful tresses prepared a posset. . . . She it was that had first set in front of them a table fair, with black legs, well polished, and upon it had placed a bronze basket; then, as a relish for their drink, she had brought an onion, and yellow honey, and the fruit of sacred barley besides, and a cup of exceeding beauty which the aged man had brought from home. . . . In it, then, the woman fair as a goddess made a mixture for him with Pramnian wine,[c] and in it she grated goat's milk cheese with a bronze grater, and sprinkled

---

[a] Dry as well as liquid.
[b] *Il.* xi. 624, 628-632, 638-641.
[c] Athen. 30 c-31 e (vol. i. p. 132). See also 10 a (vol. i. p. 42).

κνήστι χαλκείῃ, ἐπὶ δ' ἄλφιτα λευκὰ πάλυνεν·
πινέμεναι δ' ἐκέλευεν, ἐπεί ῥ' ὥπλισσε κυκεῶ.[1]

" Τὸ δὲ

ἄλλος μὲν μογέων[2] ἀποκινήσασκε τραπέζης
493   πλεῖον ἐόν, Νέστωρ δ' ὁ γέρων ἀμογητὶ ἄειρεν

οὐκ ἀκουστέον ἐπὶ μόνων Μαχάονος καὶ Νέστορος,
ὡς οἴονταί τινες, τὸ ὃς ἀντὶ τοῦ ὃ λαμβάνοντες[3]
ἐπὶ τοῦ Μαχάονος·

ἀλλ' ὃς[4] μὲν μογέων ἀποκινήσασκε τραπέζης,

ἐκ τοῦ μογέων δηλοῦσθαι[5] νομίζοντες, ἐπειδὴ[6] τέτρωται. ὅτι δὲ[7] καθ' Ὅμηρον ὁ Μαχάων οὐ τέτρωται
ἐν ἄλλοις δειχθήσεται. ἀγνοοῦσιν δ' ὅτι τὸ ἄλλος
Ὅμηρος οὐκ ἐπὶ μόνων Μαχάονος καὶ Νέστορος
b ἔθηκε, δύο γὰρ οὗτοι πίνουσιν, ἀλλ' εἶπεν ἂν
ἕτερος. τοῦτο γὰρ ἐπὶ δύο τάσσεσθαι πέφυκεν,
ὡς καὶ ἐπὶ τούτων·

οἴσετε δ' ἄρν' ἕτερον[8] λευκόν, ἑτέρην δὲ μέλαιναν.

ἔπειτα δὲ τὸ ὃς ἀντὶ προτακτικοῦ τοῦ ὃ Ὅμηρος
οὐδέποτε τίθησι· τοὔμπαλιν δὲ ἀντὶ τοῦ ὃς ὑπο-
τακτικοῦ παραλαμβάνει τὸ προτακτικὸν[9] ὅ, οἷον·

---

[1] So A; cf. p. 192 note 5 above.   [2] κοτέων C.
[3] λέγοντες C.
[4] ἀλλ' ὃς CE: ἀλλ' ὃ A.   [5] ἡγεῖσθαι C.
[6] ἐπεὶ C.   [7] γὰρ C.
[8] ἕτερον CE: ἕτερον μὲν A.   [9] πρότερον C.

---

[a] Cf. above, 488 a.
[b] A promise fortunately not redeemed, at least by Athe
naeus. Machaon, grievously wounded in the right shoulder
by a triple-barbed arrow, was forced to leave the battle, Il
xi. 505 ff.   [c] Il. iii. 103.
[d] Il. vi. 153. It is true that ὅς is never used as a mere

white barley meal over it ; then she bade him drink, for that she had prepared the posset.'

"Now, when he says,[a] ' Another (ἄλλος) had with difficulty moved it from the table when it was full, but Nestor, that old man, easily raised it,' the verse is not to be understood of Machaon and Nestor alone, as some think. They (read ἀλλ ὅς for ἄλλος and) take ὅς (who) in the sense of ὅ (he), making it refer to Machaon *alone* : ' But he (ἀλλ᾿ ὅς) had with difficulty removed it from the table ' ; they think this clear from the expression ' with difficulty,' meaning that he has been wounded. But that Machaon, according to Homer, has not been wounded will be shown in another chapter.[b] And these interpreters are unaware that Homer did not apply the word ἄλλος (another) to Machaon and Nestor alone ; (he would not have used that form), since there are two persons here drinking, but he would have said ἕτερος (the other). For this is the word naturally used when two things are involved, as in the following case[c] : ' Bring two lambs, the one (ἕτερον) a white male, the other (ἑτέρην) a black female.' Furthermore, Homer never uses the form ὅς (who) in place of the prepositive article ὁ (the) ; conversely, however, he uses the prepositive ὅ in place of the relative ὅς, as for example[d] : ' Where also

article (*the*) ; but it often occurs as a demonstrative (*that, he*), which is the original function of ὁ (*that, the*) ; and when ὅ is used as a relative, as often happens, it is of course no longer prepositive or articular. Monro, *Hom. Gram.*[2] § 265. The correct reading ἄλλος is that of Aristarchus and Ptolemy of Ascalon, Schol. B, *Il.* xi. 636. It is noteworthy that however wrong the reasoning may be, the final conclusion is correct, viz. that the lines make Nestor the *only* one capable of raising the cup.

ἔνθα δὲ[1] Σίσυφος ἔσκεν, ὃ κέρδιστος γένετ᾽
ἀιδρῶν.

ἐλλείπει οὖν τὸ τις μόριον· τὸ γὰρ πλῆρές ἐστι
c ' ἄλλος μέν τις μογέων ἀποκινήσασκε τραπέζης
πλεῖον ἐόν, Νέστωρ δ᾽ ὁ γέρων ἀμογητὶ ἄειρεν,'
ὡς παντὸς ἀνθρώπου μόλις ἂν ἀποκινήσαντος[2] ἀπὸ
τῆς τραπέζης τὸ ποτήριον, τοῦ δὲ Νέστορος αὐτὸ
ῥᾳδίως βαστάζοντος δίχα πόνου καὶ κακοπαθείας.
τὸ γὰρ ποτήριον ὑφίσταται μέγα[3] κατὰ τὸ κύτος
καὶ βαρὺ τὴν ὁλκήν, ὅπερ φιλοπότης[4] ὢν ὁ Νέστωρ
ἐκ τῆς συνεχοῦς συνηθείας ῥᾳδίως βαστάζειν
ἔσθενε.

" Σωσίβιος δ᾽ ὁ λυτικὸς προθεὶς τὰ ἔπη·

ἄλλος μὲν μογέων ἀποκινήσασκε τραπέζης
d πλεῖον ἐόν, Νέστωρ δ᾽ ὁ γέρων ἀμογητὶ ἄειρεν,

γράφει κατὰ λέξιν· ' νῦν τὸ μὲν ἐπιτιμώμενόν ἐστι
τῷ ποιητῇ ὅτι τοὺς μὲν λοιποὺς εἶπε[5] μογέοντας
ἀείρειν τὸ δέπας, τὸν δὲ Νέστορα μόνον ἀμογητί.
ἄλογον δ᾽ ἐδόκει Διομήδους καὶ Αἴαντος, ἔτι δ᾽
Ἀχιλλέως παρόντων εἰσάγεσθαι τὸν Νέστορα γεν-
ναιότερον, τῇ ἡλικίᾳ προβεβηκότα. τούτων τοίνυν
οὕτως κατηγορουμένων τῇ ἀναστροφῇ χρησάμενοι
ἀπολύομεν τὸν ποιητήν. ἀπὸ γὰρ τούτου τοῦ
e ἑξαμέτρου " πλεῖον ἐόν, Νέστωρ δ᾽ ὁ γέρων ἀμογητὶ
ἄειρεν " ἀπὸ τοῦ μέσου ἐξελόντες τὸ γέρων τάξομεν
τοῦ πρώτου στίχου πρὸς τὴν ἀρχὴν ὑπὸ τὸ ἄλλος
μέν, εἶτα τὸ ἐξ ἀρχῆς συνεροῦμεν " ἄλλος μὲν γέρων
μογέων ἀποκινήσασκε τραπέζης πλεῖον ἐόν, ὃ δὲ

---

[1] ἐνθάδε A.   [2] Basle ed.: ἀποκινήσοντος A.
[3] μέγα C: μέγα καὶ A.   [4] CE: φιλοπώτης A.
[5] Madvig: ἔστι A.

dwelt Sisyphus, who (ὅ) was the craftiest of men.'
Hence the part of speech to be supplied is τις (any) ;
the complete line, in fact, is ' *Any* other had with
difficulty moved it from the table when it was full,
but Nestor, that old man, easily raised it,' meaning
that any other man would have found it hard to
budge the cup from the table, but Nestor lifted it
easily, without labour or trouble. For the cup is
large in bulk and heavy in weight—this cup which
Nestor, being a drink-lover, was strong enough to
raise easily through constant habit.

" Now Sosibius, who is clever at solving problems,
quotes the hexameters (as above): ' Another had
with difficulty moved the cup from the table when it
was full, but Nestor, that old man, raised it easily,'
and then writes, exactly in these words : ' To-day
the charge is brought against the Poet that, whereas
he said all others raised the cup with difficulty, Nestor
alone did it without difficulty. And it *did* seem
unreasonable that, in the presence of Diomedes and
Ajax, to say nothing of Achilles, Nestor should be
represented as more vigorous than they, though he
was more advanced in years. From these criticisms,
then, we can absolve the Poet by assuming the figure
called *anastrophe.*[a] That is, from this (second) hexameter, " when it was full, but Nestor, that old man,
raised it without difficulty," we shall remove the
word " old man " from the middle of the verse
and place it at the beginning of the first line after
" another," and construe the words at the beginning
thus : " Another old man had with difficulty moved
it from the table when it was full, but Nestor raised

---

[a] A change in the natural order of words, as conceived by
the later Greeks. See Sophocles' *Lexicon s.v.*

197

Νέστωρ ἀπονητὶ[1] ἄειρεν." νῦν οὖν οὕτω τεταγ
μένων ὁ Νέστωρ φαίνεται τῶν μὲν[2] λοιπῶν πρεσ
βυτῶν μόνος τὸ δέπας ἀμογητὶ ἀείρων.' ταῦτα
καὶ ὁ θαυμάσιος λυτικὸς Σωσίβιος, ὃν οὐκ ἀχαρίτως
διέπαιξε[3] διὰ τὰς πολυθρυλήτους ταύτας καὶ τὰς

f τοιαύτας λύσεις Πτολεμαῖος ὁ Φιλάδελφος βασιλεύς·
λαμβάνοντος γὰρ αὐτοῦ σύνταξιν βασιλικήν, μετα
πεμψάμενος τοὺς ταμίας ἐκέλευσεν, ἐὰν παρα
γένηται ὁ Σωσίβιος ἐπὶ τὴν ἀπαίτησιν τῆς συντά
ξεως, λέγειν αὐτῷ ὅτι ἀπείληφε. καὶ μετ' οὐ πολὺ
παραγενομένῳ καὶ αἰτοῦντι εἰπόντες δεδωκέναι
αὐτῷ τὰς ἡσυχίας εἶχον,[4] ὁ δὲ τῷ βασιλεῖ προσ
ελθὼν κατεμέμφετο τοὺς ταμίας. Πτολεμαῖος δὲ[5]

494 μεταπεμψάμενος αὐτοὺς καὶ ἥκειν κελεύσας μετὰ
τῶν βιβλίων, ἐν οἷς αἱ ἀναγραφαί εἰσι τῶν τὰς
συντάξεις λαμβανόντων,[6] λαβὼν ταύτας[7] εἰς χεῖρας
ὁ βασιλεὺς καὶ κατιδὼν ἔφη καὶ αὐτὸς εἰληφέναι
αὐτὸν οὕτως[8]· ἦν ὀνόματα ἐγγεγραμμένα ταῦτα,
Σωτῆρος Σωσιγένους Βίωνος Ἀπολλωνίου[9]· εἰς ἃ
ἀποβλέψας ὁ βασιλεὺς εἶπεν ' ὦ θαυμάσιε λυτικέ,
ἐὰν ἀφέλῃς τοῦ Σωτῆρος τὸ σω καὶ τοῦ Σωσιγένους
τὸ σι καὶ τοῦ Βίωνος τὴν πρώτην συλλαβὴν[10] καὶ
τὴν τελευταίαν τοῦ Ἀπολλωνίου,[11] εὑρήσεις σαυτὸν

b ἀπειληφότα κατὰ[12] τὰς σὰς ἐπινοίας. καὶ "ταῦτ'
οὐχ ὑπ' ἄλλων, ἀλλὰ τοῖς αὐτοῦ πτεροῖς " κατὰ τὸν

---

[1] ἀμογητὶ Schol. *Il.* xi. 636 (*cf.* below).
[2] μὲν om. CE.   [3] A (διέπαιξεν C): διέπαιξεν E.
[4] ἦγον CE; *cf.* 113 f τὰς ἡσυχίας οὐκ ἄγετε.
[5] δὲ added by Musurus; CE have it in a different structure.
[6] λαβόντων C.   [7] ταῦτα Meineke.
[8] οὕτως A: ταύτας οὕτως CE.
[9] Lehrs: ἀπόλλωνος ACE. Δίωνος after ἀπόλλωνος in A,
om. CE.   [10] βι after συλλαβὴν in A om. CE.
[11] Lehrs: ἀπόλλωνος AC.   [12] κατὰ om. C.

it without labour." With the words in this order, it is clear that Nestor is the only one of the *old* men, no matter who they were, who raised the cup without difficulty.' Thus the marvellous solver of problems, Sosibius! He is the man whom King Ptolemy Philadelphus not unwittily satirized for this famous solution and others like it. For while he was the recipient of a royal stipend, the king summoned his stewards and commanded them, whenever Sosibius came to ask for his stipend, to tell him that he had already received it. And in fact he did appear not long afterward and made his request; but they told him that they had given it to him, and would say no more; so he went to the king and complained of the stewards. Ptolemy summoned them and commanded them to fetch the rolls containing the accounts of those who received stipends; taking them in his hands the king examined them and affirmed, as the stewards had, that Sosibius had received his stipend, proving it in this way : there were the following names [a] recorded therein, Soteros, Sosigenous, Bionos, Apolloniou. Scanning them, the king said, ' Marvellous solver of problems, if you take the *so* from Soteros, the *si* from Sosigenous, the first syllable from Bionos, and the last from Apolloniou,[b] you will find that you yourself have received your due according to your own fantastic notions.[c] And thus, " not by others, but by thine own feathers art thou

[a] In the genitive case; the nominatives are Soter, Sosigenes, Bion, Apollonius. On these records see Harper, *Amer. Journ. Phil.* xlix. 1. 2.
[b] Making, of course, Sosibiou (gen.).
[c] Of interpreting Homer.

θαυμάσιον Αἰσχύλον ἀλίσκῃ, ἀπροσδιονύσους λύσεις
πραγματευόμενος.'"

ΟΛΜΟΣ ποτήριον κερατίου τρόπον εἰργασμένον.
Μενεσθένης ἐν δ' Πολιτικῶν γράφει οὕτως
" Ἀλβατάνης δὲ στρεπτὸν καὶ ὅλμον χρυσοῦν. ὁ
δὲ ὅλμος ἐστὶ ποτήριον κερατίου τρόπον εἰργασμένον, ὕψος ὡς πυγονιαῖον.[1]"

ΟΞΥΒΑΦΟΝ. ἡ μὲν κοινὴ συνήθεια οὕτως καλεῖ τὸ
ὄξους δεκτικὸν σκεῦος· ἐστὶ δὲ καὶ[2] ὄνομα ποτηρίου, οὗ μνημονεύει Κρατῖνος μὲν ἐν Πυτίνῃ οὕτως

c   πῶς τις αὐτόν, πῶς τις ἂν
ἀπὸ τοῦ πότου παύσειε, τοῦ λίαν πότου;
ἐγῷδα. συντρίψω γὰρ αὐτοῦ τοὺς χόας
καὶ τοὺς καδίσκους συγκεραυνώσω σποδῶν
καὶ τἄλλα πάντ' ἀγγεῖα τὰ περὶ τὸν πότον,
κοὐδ' ὀξύβαφον οἰνηρὸν ἔτι κεκτήσεται.

ὅτι δέ ἐστι τὸ ὀξύβαφον εἶδος κύλικος μικρᾶς
κεραμέας σαφῶς παρίστησιν Ἀντιφάνης ἐν Μύστιδι
διὰ τούτων· γραῦς ἐστι φίλοινος ἐπαινοῦσα κύλικα
d μεγάλην καὶ ἐξευτελίζουσα τὸ ὀξύβαφον[3] ὡς βραχύ.

---

[1] CE: πυγωνιαῖον A.   [2] καὶ CE, om. A.
[3] τὸ ὀξύβαφον Koppiers: τὴν κύλικα A, which has nevertheless βραχυ (no accent).

---

[a] T.G.F.[2] 45, from The Myrmidons. The eagle in the
fable (Halm, Aesop. Fab. 4, Chambry i. 44, La Fontaine,
Fables ii. 6) saw his own feathers in the arrow by which he
had been shot down. The line is quoted as a proverb by

caught," as the admirable Aeschylus says,[a] because you labour to invent irrelevant [b] solutions.' "

Holmos, a drinking-cup made in the style of a horn.[c] Menesthenes in the fourth book of his *Politics* writes as follows [d] : " From Albatanê, a collar and a golden *holmos*. The holmos is a cup made in the style of a horn, in height about fourteen inches."

Oxybaphon. Common usage gives this name to the vessel made to hold vinegar ; but it is also the name of a drinking-cup, which Cratinus mentions in *The Flask* thus [e] : " How, oh how can one stop him from his drinking, his excessive drinking ? I know a way. I'll smash his pitchers, I'll come down like a thunderbolt on his jugs and grind them to powder, as well as all the rest of the vessels he uses for drinking, and he won't own even so much as a vinegar-cruet of wine any more." Antiphanes, also, clearly shows in *Mystis* that the oxybaphon is a kind of small, earthenware cylix, in the following lines ; a bibulous old hag is singing the praises of a large cylix and rejecting with contempt the oxybaphon as being too

Aristoph. *Av.* 808, and in sense is equivalent to " hoist with his own petard."

[b] The adjective ἀπροσδιονύσους alludes to another proverb, " Nothing to do with Dionysus," the complaint of those who saw a play the plot of which seemed to have nothing in common with the Dionysiac tradition of the theatre. Plut. 615 A, Suidas *s.* Οὐδὲν πρὸς τὸν Διόνυσον, Haigh, *Tragic Drama*, pp. 33, 41.

[c] The word more commonly means a mortar ; originally a cylindrical stone, *Il.* xi. 147.

[d] *F.H.G.* iv. 451 ; the author's name, otherwise unknown, is suspected, nor is ἀλβατάνης known with certainty to be a proper name.

[e] Kock i. 70 ; the speaker, a friend of Cratinus, wishes to reform him and restore him to his art.

εἰπόντος οὖν τινος πρὸς αὐτήν, " σὺ δ' ἀλλὰ πῖθι,"[1]
λέγει·

> τοῦτο μέν σοι πείσομαι.
> καὶ γὰρ ἐπαγωγόν, ὦ θεοί, τὸ σχῆμά πως
> τῆς κύλικός ἐστιν ἄξιόν τε τοῦ κλέους
> τοῦ τῆς ἑορτῆς. οὗ μὲν ἦμεν ἄρτι γὰρ[2]
> ἐξ ὀξυβαφίων[3] κεραμεῶν ἐπίνομεν·
> τούτῳ δέ, τέκνον, πολλὰ κἀγάθ' οἱ θεοὶ
> τῷ δημιουργῷ δοῖεν ὃς ἐποίησέ σε,[4]
> τῆς συμμετρίας καὶ τῆς ἀφελείας[5] οὕνεκα.

κἂν τοῖς Βαβυλωνίοις οὖν τοῖς Ἀριστοφάνους
ἀκουσόμεθα[6] ποτήριον τὸ ὀξύβαφον, ὅταν ὁ Διό-
e νυσος λέγῃ περὶ τῶν Ἀθήνησι δημαγωγῶν ὡς
αὐτὸν ᾔτουν ἐπὶ τὴν δίκην ἀπελθόντα ὀξυβάφω
δύο. οὐ γὰρ ἄλλο τι ἡγητέον εἶναι ἢ ὅτι ἐκπώματα
ᾔτουν. καὶ τὸ τοῖς ἀποκοτταβίζουσι δὲ ὀξύβαφον
τιθέμενον εἰς ὃ τὰς λάταγας ἐγχέουσιν οὐκ ἄλλο
τι ἂν εἴη ἢ ἐκπέταλον ποτήριον. μνημονεύει δὲ
τοῦ ὀξυβάφου ὡς ποτηρίου καὶ Εὔβουλος ἐν
Μυλωθρίδι·[7]

> καὶ πιεῖν χωρὶς μετρῶ[8]
> ὀξύβαφον εἰς τὸ κοινόν· εἶθ' ὑπώμνυτο

---

[1] σὺ δ' . . . λέγει added by Schweighäuser (cf. 446 c).
[2] οὗ μὲν . . . γὰρ 446 c: οὐ μὲν οὐ μέν· ἀρτίως γὰρ A.
[3] ὀξυβάφων C.   [4] σε added from 446 c.
[5] 446 c: ἀσφαλείας A.   [6] Musurus: ἀκουσώμεθα A.
[7] Dalechamp: μυλωθρίδηι A.
[8] μετρῶ Schweighäuser (doubtfully): μέτρω A.

---

[a] Kock ii. 77, Athen. 446 b (vol. iv. p. 520). The title may
mean " the female initiate," fem. of μύστης (vol. iv. p. 499
note c).

mall. Someone, then, says to her [a] : " But do take
. drink." She replies : " I'll yield to you in this ;
or somehow the cylix has an alluring shape—O ye
;ods !—and is in keeping with the glory of the festival.
'or where we were a little while ago, we had to
lrink out of little earthenware cruets (*oxybaphia*).
As for this man, my child [b]—may the gods grant
nany blessings—to this artist who made you, such
re your beautiful proportions and your simplicity."
Again, in *The Babylonians* of Aristophanes we shall
understand the word oxybaphon as meaning a cup [c] ;
hat is when Dionysus says of the demagogues at
Athens that when he departed to face his trial they
lemanded of him two cruets. One cannot infer that
hese were anything else than drinking-cups. Also,
he " cruet " set up for persons playing at kottabos,
nto which they pour the drops of wine,[d] cannot be
nything else than a broad and shallow cup. The
xybaphon is mentioned as a cup by Eubulus also in
Maid of the Mill [e] : " I measured out separately a
lrink in a cruet, share and share alike. But then a
lemurrer was put in, the wine swearing that it was

[b] Here she addresses the cup, on which she reads the
naker's signature. The broken sentence imitates her hiccup-
·ing.
[c] Kock i. 410 ; Dionysus, brought to trial by the Athenian
lemagogues, is blackmailed by them.
[d] *Cf.* 667 e for a more detailed account.
[e] Kock ii. 186. The disjointed fragment apparently refers
o a kind of fable depicting the results of mixing wine and
·inegar, here personified. A case at law has arisen between
he two, the verb ὑπώμνυτο referring to the ὑπωμοσία, or
·lea made on oath for postponement of a trial. *Cf.* Eupolis
r. 326 (Kock i. 345): οἴνου παρόντος ὄξος ἠράσθη πιεῖν, " he
·earned to drink vinegar, though wine was to be had."

ὁ μὲν οἶνος ὄξος αὐτὸν[1] εἶναι γνήσιον,
τὸ δ' ὄξος οἶνον αὐτὸ[1] μᾶλλον θατέρου.

f ΟΙΝΙΣΤΗΡΙΑ. οἱ μέλλοντες ἀποκείρεσθαι[2] τὸν σκόλ-
λυν ἔφηβοι, φησὶ Πάμφιλος, εἰσφέρουσι τῷ Ἡρακλεῖ
μέγα ποτήριον πληρώσαντες οἴνου, ὃ καλοῦσιν οἰνι-
στηρίαν, καὶ σπείσαντες τοῖς συνελθοῦσι διδόασι πιεῖν.

ΟΛΛΙΞ. Πάμφιλος ἐν Ἀττικαῖς Λέξεσι τὸ ξύλινον
ποτήριον ἀποδίδωσι.

ΠΑΝΑΘΗΝΑΙΚΟΝ.[3] Ποσειδώνιος ὁ φιλόσοφος ἐν
ἕκτῃ καὶ τριακοστῇ τῶν Ἱστοριῶν ὡς οὕτω καλου-
495 μένων τινῶν ποτηρίων μέμνηται γράφων οὕτως·
" ἦσαν δὲ καὶ ὀνύχινοι σκύφοι καὶ συνδέσεις τούτων μέχρι δικοτύλων· καὶ Παναθηναϊκὰ μέγιστα,
τὰ μὲν δίχοα, τὰ δὲ καὶ μείζονα."

ΠΡΟΑΡΟΝ κρατὴρ ξύλινος, εἰς ὃν τὸν οἶνον κιρ-
νᾶσιν[4] οἱ Ἀττικοί.[5] " κοίλοις ἐν προάροις " φησὶ
Πάμφιλος.

ΠΕΛΙΚΑΙ. Καλλίστρατος ἐν Ὑπομνήμασι Θρατ-
τῶν Κρατίνου ἀποδίδωσι κύλικα. Κράτης δ' ἐν
δευτέρῳ Ἀττικῆς Διαλέκτου γράφει οὕτως· " οἱ
χόες πελίκαι, καθάπερ εἴπομεν, ὠνομάζοντο. ὁ δὲ

---

[1] αὐτὸν A.
[2] Kaibel (cf. Hesych. s. οἰνιστήρια): ἀποκείρειν A.
[3] ὄλλιξ: ξύλινον ποτήριον παναθηναϊκὸν C, omitting the rest.
[4] κερνᾶσιν A, κιρνῶσιν CE.
[5] οἱ ἀγροῖκοι Wilamowitz. C has ἀττικοὶ without οἱ.

---

[a] Boys who have just attained their majority (eighteen
years). The form οἰνιστηρία (fem.) is not recorded elsewhere.
Οἰνιστήρια (sc. ἱερά, neut. plur.) is the name of the ceremony.
Pollux vi. 22 gives ἡ οἰνίστρια, " a portion of wine." See
also Hesych. and Phot. s.v.
[b] i.e. their fathers or guardians, who presented them to
the members of their phratries.

now real vinegar, the vinegar, that it was better wine than the other."

Oinisteria. The ephebi,[a] when on the point of having their long hair cut off, says Pamphilus, offer to Heracles a large cup which they have filled with wine and which they call *oinisteria* ; after a libation from it they give it to their companions [b] assembled together to drink from.

Ollix. Pamphilus in his *Attic Diction* renders this word by " cup made of wood." [c]

Panathenaïkon. The philosopher Poseidonius, in the thirty-sixth book of his *Histories*, mentions certain cups as being so called, writing as follows [d] : " There were also bowls made of onyx, and combinations of these extending to bowls measuring three quarts [e] ; also very large *Panathenaïka*, some holding six quarts, and some even larger."

Proaron, a wooden mixing-bowl, in which the people of Attica [f] mingle their wine. " In hollow *proara* " is quoted by Pamphilus.[g]

Pelikai. Callistratus, in his *Commentary on the Women of Thrace*, by Cratinus,[h] interprets (the *pelikê*) as a cylix. But Crates, in the second book of his *Attic Dialect*, writes as follows[i] : " Pitchers, as we have said, used to be called *pelikai*. The form of the vessel was

---

[c] The word ὄλλιξ does not occur elsewhere. Possibly this and the next lemma formed a single paragraph headed by the word Ὄνυξ, not Ὄλλιξ, *cf.* below and the reading in C.

[d] *F.H.G.* iii. 264, J. 2 A 232.

[e] The meaning of συνδέσεις is very uncertain. Probably we have to do with different sizes neatly fitting together, καθάπερ οἱ κάδοι οἱ εἰς ἀλλήλους ἁρμόττοντες, Plat. *Rep.* 616 D. The κοτύλη, as a measure, nearly equalled a half-pint.

[f] Or simply " country people," crit. note 5.

[g] From some poet, as the order of words shows.

[h] Kock i. 38.   [i] Wachsmuth, p. 64.

b τύπος ἦν τοῦ ἀγγείου πρότερον μὲν τοῖς Παν-
αθηναϊκοῖς ἐοικώς, ἡνίκα ἐκαλεῖτο πελίκη, ὕστερον
δὲ ἔσχεν οἰνοχόης σχῆμα, οἷοί εἰσιν οἱ ἐν τῇ ἑορτῇ
παρατιθέμενοι, ὁποίους δή ποτε ὅλπας ἐκάλουν,
χρώμενοι πρὸς τὴν τοῦ οἴνου ἔγχυσιν, καθάπερ
Ἴων ὁ Χῖος ἐν Εὐρυτίδαις[1] φησίν·

 ἐκ ζαθέων πιθακνῶν ἀφύσσοντες ὅλπαις
 οἶνον ὑπερφίαλον κελαρύζετε.

νυνὶ δὲ τὸ μὲν τοιοῦτον ἀγγεῖον καθιερωμένον τινὰ
τρόπον ἐν τῇ ἑορτῇ παρατίθεται μόνον, τὸ δ' ἐς
c τὴν χρείαν[2] πῖπτον μετεσχημάτισται, ἀρυταίνῃ
μάλιστα ἐοικός, ὃ δὴ καλοῦμεν χόα." τὴν δὲ
ὅλπην[3] Κλείταρχος[4] Κορινθίους μέν φησι καὶ
Βυζαντίους καὶ Κυπρίους τὴν λήκυθον ἀποδιδόναι
Θεσσαλοὺς δὲ τὴν πρόχοον. Σέλευκος δὲ πελίχναι
Βοιωτοὺς μὲν τὴν κύλικα, Εὐφρόνιος δὲ ἐν Ὑπομνήμασι τοὺς χόας.

ΠΕΛΛΑ ἀγγεῖον σκυφοειδές, πυθμένα ἔχον πλατύτερον, εἰς ὃ ἤμελγον τὸ γάλα. Ὅμηρος·

 ὡς ὅτε μυῖαι
σταθμῷ ἐνιβρομέωσιν ἐυγλαγέας κατὰ πέλλας.

τοῦτο δὲ Ἱππῶναξ λέγει πελλίδα·

 ἐκ πελλίδος πίνοντες· οὐ γὰρ ἦν αὐτῇ[5]
d κύλιξ, ὁ παῖς γὰρ ἐμπεσὼν κατήραξε,

δῆλον, οἶμαι, ποιῶν ὅτι ποτήριον μὲν οὐκ ἦν, δι

---

[1] εὑριτίδαις A.   [2] χρεαν A.   [3] ὅλπην δὲ Kaibel
[4] Casaubon: καὶ τάριχος A.   [5] αὐτοῖς CE.

---

 [a] T.G.F.[2] 734. Eurytus of Oechalia, mighty archer, Od.
viii. 224, xxi. 32; above, 461 f.
 [b] Or " spilling over the brim."
 [c] Lit. "pourer," "pitcher."

originally similar to that of the Panathenaic jars, and then it was called *pelikê*; but later it took on the shape of a wine-jug, such as are set before drinkers at the holiday season, in fact the kind which they once called *olpai* and which they used for pouring the wine into cups, as Ion of Chios says in *The Sons of Eurytus* [a] : ' From sacred casks ladle out the potent [b] wine with your jugs (*olpai*), and make it gurgle loudly.' But to-day the vessel of that type is in a manner specially consecrated and set before the drinkers only at a festival, whereas the kind that occurs in daily use has undergone a change in form, being now most like a dipper, and we call it a *chous*.[c] "

As for the term *olpê*, Cleitarchus says that the Corinthians, Byzantians, and Cyprians use it for *lekythos*,[d] the Thessalians, on the other hand, for a wine-jug with spout. (Besides *pelikê*), there is a term *pelichna*, by which, Seleucus says, the Boeotians mean the cylix, but Euphronius in his *Commentaries* [e] explains it as a pitcher.

Pella, a vessel shaped like a *skyphos*,[f] with a rather wide bottom, into which they did their milking. Homer [g] : " As when flies in a stall buzz around the well-filled pails (*pellai*) of milk." But Hipponax calls this vessel a *pellis* [h] : " They were drinking from a pail (*pellis*), since she [i] had no cup ; for the slave-boy had fallen down and smashed it to bits " ; he thus makes it clear, I think, that the *pellis* was not a cup,

---

[d] The well-known oil-jug, tall, with one handle, and cup-shaped top.

  [e] Frag. 107 Strecker.   [f] Below, 498 a.
  [g] *Il.* xvi. 641.   [h] *P.L.G.*⁴ ii. 475, Diehl fr. 16.
  [i] Possibly the Arêtê of the next fragment. But see critical note 5.

ἀπορίαν δὲ κύλικος ἐχρῶντο τῇ πελλίδι. καὶ
πάλιν·

ἐκ δὲ τῆς πέλλης
ἔπινον, ἄλλοτ' αὐτός, ἄλλοτ' 'Αρήτη
προὔπινεν.

Φοῖνιξ δ' ὁ Κολοφώνιος ἐν τοῖς 'Ιάμβοις ἐπὶ
φιάλης τίθησι τὴν λέξιν λέγων οὕτως·

Θαλῆς γάρ, ὅστις ἀστέρων[1] ὀνήιστος
καὶ τῶν τότ', ὡς λέγουσι, πολλὸν[2] ἀνθρώπων
ἐών[1] ἄριστος, ἔλαβε πελλίδα[3] χρυσῆν.

e καὶ ἐν ἄλλῳ δὲ μέρει φησίν·

ἐκ πελλίδος δὲ[4] τάργανον κατηγυίης[5]
χωλοῖσι δακτύλοισι τητέρῃ σπένδει,
τρέμων οἷόνπερ ἐν βορηίῳ νωδός.[6]

Κλείταρχος δὲ ἐν ταῖς Γλώσσαις πελλητῆρα μὲν
καλεῖν Θεσσαλοὺς καὶ Αἰολεῖς τὸν ἀμολγέα, πέλ-
λαν δὲ τὸ ποτήριον. Φιλίτας δ' ἐν 'Ατάκτοις τὴν
κύλικα Βοιωτούς.

ΠΕΝΤΑΠΛΟΑ.[7] μνημονεύει αὐτῆς Φιλόχορος ἐν
f δευτέρᾳ 'Ατθίδος. 'Αριστόδημος δ' ἐν τρίτῳ περὶ

---

[1] ἴστωρ ἀστέρων Gerhard, ὅστις ἱστόρων Haupt. Meineke
assumed a lacuna after ὀνήιστος: otherwise ἐών must be
changed to ἔην.   [2] Toup: πολλῶν A.
[3] CE: πελλιάδα A.   [4] δὲ added by Schweighäuser.
[5] Porson: καὶ τηγυίης A.
[6] πῶλος Kaibel, λωτός Gerhard. Both equally futile; for
νωδός used substantively see Theocr. ix. 21.
[7] C wrongly joins this with the preceding.

---

a P.L.G.[4] ii. 475, Diehl fr. 17.
b Below, 500 f-502 b (pp. 238-246).
c Diehl fr. 5, Powell 234. Cf. Athen. 421 d, Powell and
Barber, New Chapters in Greek Literature, p. 14. Diog.
Laert. i. 28 says that Bathycles of Arcadia bequeathed a

but that they used it in default of a cup. And again [a] ᵢ
' They were drinking from the pail (*pella*) ; now he
himself, now Arêtê, proposed a toast." But Phoenix
of Colophon in his *Iambic Verses* uses the word of a
phialê,[b] speaking as follows [c] : " For Thales, who was
most useful in his knowledge of the stars, and of all
the men of his day, as they say, by far the best,
received a golden *pellis*.[d] " And in another part he
says [e] : " And from a broken *pellis*, with the rheu-
matic fingers of one hand, he pours a libation of sour
wine, shivering like a toothless old man in the north
wind." Cleitarchus, however, explains in his *Glossary*
that the Thessalians and Aeolians call the milk-pail a
pelleter, whereas they call the drinking-cup a *pella*.
And Philitas, in his *Irregular Words*, says [f] that the
Boeotians call the cylix a *pella*.

Pentaploa. Philochorus mentions it in the second
book of his *History of Attica*.[g] Now Aristodemus, in

phialê to be given τῶν σοφῶν ὀνήϊστῳ. It was accordingly
given to Thales. *Cf.* the story of his weather lore, by which
he was able to speculate in " futures " in the olive market,
told by Aristotle, *Pol.* 1259 a ; his star-gazing, Plat. *Theaet.*
174 A. On the cup see Callimachus, fr. 83 a, 89, 94 Schneider,
Ox. Pap. vii. 31, A. W. Mair (L.C.L.) 290 f.

[d] C, which quotes merely πελλίδα χρυσῆν, adds ἤτοι φιάλην,
that is, a *phialê* (for a libation).

[e] Powell 235, Diehl fr. 6.

[f] Powell om., Bach fr. 50. The Boeotians, speaking a
dialect related to the Thessalian and " Aeolic " (Lesbian),
might be supposed to use πέλλα in the same sense, *i.e.* of
drinking-cup.

[g] *F.H.G.* i. 391. The Skira (Festival of the White Parasol)
was held in honour of Athena in the month Pyanopsion
(autumn). It was different from the Skirophoria, a festival
of Athena celebrated at the end of the Attic year (end of
June), Paus. i. 1. 4, Schol. Aristoph. *Vesp.* 925, Mommsen,
Feste 282-283, Plut. *Theseus* 22 ; see p. 210, critical note 1.

Πινδάρου τοῖς Σκίροις φησὶν Ἀθήναζε[1] ἀγῶνα
ἐπιτελεῖσθαι τῶν ἐφήβων δρόμου· τρέχειν δ' αὐτοὺς
ἔχοντας ἀμπέλου κλάδον κατάκαρπον τὸν καλούμενον ὦσχον. τρέχουσι δ' ἐκ τοῦ ἱεροῦ τοῦ Διονύσου μέχρι τοῦ τῆς Σκιράδος Ἀθηνᾶς,[2] καὶ ὁ
νικήσας λαμβάνει κύλικα τὴν λεγομένην πεντα-
496 πλόαν καὶ κωμάζει μετὰ χοροῦ. πενταπλόα δ' ἡ
κύλιξ καλεῖται καθ' ὅσον οἶνον ἔχει καὶ μέλι καὶ
τυρόν καὶ ἀλφίτων[3] καὶ ἐλαίου βραχύ.

ΠΕΤΑΧΝΟΝ[4] ποτήριον ἐκπέταλον, οὗ μνημονεύει
Ἄλεξις ἐν Δρωπίδη· πρόκειται δὲ τὸ μαρτύριον.
μνημονεύει αὐτοῦ καὶ Ἀριστοφάνης ἐν Δράμασι
λέγων·

πάντες δ' ἔνδον πεταχνοῦνται.[5]

ΠΛΗΜΟΧΟΗ σκεῦος κεραμεοῦν βεμβικῶδες ἑδραῖον
ἡσυχῇ,[6] ὃ κοτυλίσκον ἔνιοι προσαγορεύουσιν, ὥς
φησι Πάμφιλος. χρῶνται δὲ αὐτῷ ἐν Ἐλευσῖνι τῇ
τελευταίᾳ τῶν μυστηρίων ἡμέρᾳ, ἣν καὶ ἀπ' αὐτοῦ
b προσαγορεύουσι Πλημοχόας· ἐν ᾗ δύο πλημοχόας
πληρώσαντες τὴν μὲν πρὸς ἀνατολάς,[7] τὴν δὲ πρὸς
δύσιν ἀνιστάμενοι ἀνατρέπουσιν,[8] ἐπιλέγοντες ῥῆσιν

---

[1] ACE: Ἀθήνησι Meineke. Ἀθήναζε cannot be right as the text now stands. Something may have been lost, describing the transfer *to* Athens of a ceremony originating in Phalerum. A. Mommsen proposed to read τῇ Σκιρράδι φησὶν Ἀθηνᾷ for τοῖς Σκίροις κτλ.

[2] ἱεροῦ after Ἀθηνᾶς (A) om. CE.

[3] Kaibel: ἄλφιτον A, ἄλφιτα CE.

[4] πένταχνον, *i.e.* πέδαχνον, CE, see Hesych. *s.v.* The spelling πεντ- was perhaps further caused by confusion with πεντέχουν, Poll. x. 74.

[5] Casaubon (*cf.* Photius *s.v.*): πενταχνευται (no accent A), -ται CE.   [6] ἑδραῖόν τε καὶ στάσιμον Poll. x. 74.

[7] ἀνατολὴν CE.   [8] ἀνατρέπουσιν, C: ἀνατρέπουσίν τε A

he third book of his work *On Pindar*, says that at
:he festival of the Skira at Athens there was held a
·unning-contest of the ephebi ; and as they ran they
:arried a wine-branch laden with grapes—the branch
:alled the *oschos*. The course extends from the
·emple of Dionysus to the temple of Athena Skiras,[a]
and the winner receives a cup, the so-called *pentaploa*,
and riots through the streets with a band of singers
and dancers. Now the cup is called *pentaploa*[b] for
·he reason that it contains wine, honey, and cheese,
and a little barley and oil.

Petachnon is a broad, shallow cup, mentioned by
Alexis in *Dropides* ; his testimony is set before you
above.[c] It is referred to by Aristophanes also in
Dramas, who says[d] : " They are all indoors, drinking
·rom broad cups."

Plemochoê is an earthen dish shaped like a top, but
:olerably firm on its base[e] ; some call it a *kotyliskos*,
according to Pamphilus. They use it at Eleusis on
:he last day of the Mysteries, a day which they call
·rom it *Plemochoai*[f] ; on that day they fill two *plemo-
·hoai*, and they invert them (standing up and facing
:he east in the one case, the west in the other),

---

[a] Plut. *Thes.* 17, Pausanias i. 36. 4, and Frazer's note.
[b] *Fivefold. Cf.* Eng. *punch*, Sanskrit *pañca*, "five," so
:alled from its five ingredients.
[c] Athen. 125 f (vol. ii. p. 82), Kock ii. 317.
[d] Kock i. 466. Apparently a slave's report of the drinking
·f the Centaurs. Photius *s.v.* πεταχνοῦνται seems to be the
·nly authority for the verb-form, *cf.* Hesych. *s.v.* πεταλοῦνται
.nd critical note 4.
[e] *i.e.* the base, though seemingly rounded, permits a
:ertain stability ; *cf.* Pollux x. 74, who says its base is not
·ointed. Some words may be lost, but ἡσυχῇ is not corrupt.
[f] Full-pitchers-day ; Pollux *loc. cit.* wrongly has the singu-
:ar, Πλημοχόην.

μυστικήν. μνημονεύει αὐτῶν καὶ ὁ τὸν Πειρίθουν
γράψας, εἴτε Κριτίας ἐστὶν ὁ τύραννος ἢ Εὐριπίδης
λέγων οὕτως·

ἵνα πλημοχόας τάσδ' εἰς χθόνιον
χάσμ' εὐφήμως προχέωμεν.[1]

ΠΡΙΣΤΙΣ ὅτι ποτηρίου εἶδος προείρηται ἐν τῷ περ
τοῦ βατιακίου λόγῳ.

c ΠΡΟΧΥΤΗΣ εἶδος ἐκπώματος, ὡς Σίμαριστος ἐ
τετάρτῳ Συνωνύμων. Ἴων δ' ὁ Χῖος ἐν Ἐλεγείοις

ἡμῖν δὲ κρητῆρ' οἰνοχόοι[2] θέραπες[3]
κιρνάντων προχύταισιν ἐν ἀργυρέοις.

Φιλίτας[4] δ' ἐν Ἀτάκτοις ἀγγεῖον ξύλινον, ἀφ' οἱ
τοὺς ἀγροίκους πίνειν. μνημονεύει αὐτοῦ κα
Ἀλέξανδρος ἐν Ἀντιγόνῃ.[5] Ξενοφῶν δ' ἐν ὀγδόῳ
Παιδείας προχοΐδας τινὰς λέγει,[6] γράφων ὧδε (ὁ δ
λόγος ἐστὶν αὐτῷ περὶ Περσῶν)· " ἦν δὲ αὐτοῖ
νόμιμον μὴ προχοΐδας εἰσφέρεσθαι εἰς τὰ συμπόσια
d δῆλον ὅτι νομίζοντες τὸ μὴ ὑπερπίνειν ἧττον ἂν κα
σώματα καὶ γνώμας σφάλλειν· νῦν δὲ τὸ μὲν μ
εἰσφέρεσθαι ἔτι αὖ καταμένει· τοσοῦτον δὲ πίνουσι
ὥστε ἀντὶ τοῦ εἰσφέρειν αὐτοὶ ἐκφέρονται, ἐπειδὰ
μηκέτι δύνωνται ὀρθούμενοι[7] ἐξιέναι."

ΠΡΟΥΣΙΑΣ. ὅτι τὸ ποτήριον τοῦτο ἔξορθόν[8] ἐστ

---

[1] Casaubon: προσχέωμεν Α.
[2] 463 b: κρητῆρι οἰνοχόοι CE, κρητῆρι οἰνοχόαι Α.
[3] θεράποντες C.   [4] Α (as usual): φιλήτας CE.
[5] Ἀντιγόνῃ Kaibel: τιγονι Α, Τιγονίῳ Meineke.
[6] τινὰς λέγει. CE: τινὰς λεγει· κύλικας Α.
[7] Xen., CE: ὀρχούμενοι Α.   [8] Α ἅπαξ εἰρημένον.

---

[a] Critias, Diels, Vorsokr. 618; Euripides, T.G.F.[2] 548
See Powell, New Chapters 148.
[b] Above, 784 a (p. 52). The word also meant "whale."

·eciting a mystical formula over them. They are nentioned by the author of *Peirithoüs*, whether that s Critias, one of the Thirty Tyrants, or Euripides ; ι̣e speaks as follows [a] : "That we may pour out ːhese *plemochoai* into earth's chasm in holy silence."

Pristis. That this is a kind of drinking-cup has ɔeen stated before in our account of the *batiakion*.[b]

Prochytês is a kind of cup, according to Simaristus ᵢn the fourth book of his *Synonyms*. But Ion of Ɔhios, in his *Elegiacs*, says [c] : " For us let the wine-ɔouring henchmen mix the bowl from silver pitchers '*prochytai*)." Philitas in *Irregular Words* says [d] it is a ᵥvooden vessel from which country-folk drink. Alex-ander [e] mentions it also in *Antigone*. But Xenophon, ᵢn the eighth book of his *Cyropaedeia*,[f] speaks of ɔertain *prochoïdes*, writing as follows (he is giving an ιccount of the Persians) : " It was their custom that ɔrochoïdes should not be carried to their symposia, ∋vidently because they thought that avoidance of ∋xcessive drinking would be less likely to injure body ιnd mind ; to-day, however, though the practice of ιot having them carried in still continues, on the ɔther hand they drink so much that instead of carry-ᵢng them in they are themselves carried out when ːhey can no longer stand up and walk out."

Prusias. That this cup stands up high has been

[c] *P.L.G.*⁴ ii. 252, Diehl i. 69, Edmonds fr. 2, above, 453 b ͅp. 19 note *a*). [d] Bach fr. 52, Powell om.
[e] Powell 129. Kock iii. 373, following Meineke (see ιote *a*), ascribes the fragment to Alexander, poet of the New Comedy, and gives the title of the play as Τιτιγόνιον (*Cricket*), ᵢf. Eustath. 229. 28, *Etym. Magn.* 396. 1, 760. 47. P.-W. ᵢ. 1446-1447.
[f] Chap. 8. 10. The προχοΐς served the same sanitary purpose as the ἀμίς ; *cf.* Athen. 17 c-e, and especially 150 a ͅvol. ii. p. 184), of Naucratis.

προείρηται. καὶ ὅτι τὴν προσηγορίαν ἔσχεν ἀπὸ
Προυσίου τοῦ Βιθυνίας βασιλεύσαντος καὶ ἐπὶ
e τρυφῇ καὶ μαλακίᾳ διαβοήτου γενομένου ἱστορεῖ
Νίκανδρος ὁ Καλχηδόνιος ἐν τετάρτῳ Προυσίου
Συμπτωμάτων.

ΡΕΟΝΤΑ. οὕτως ποτήριά τινα ἐκαλεῖτο. μνημονεύει δ' αὐτῶν 'Αστυδάμας ἐν Ἑρμῇ λέγων
οὕτως·

κρατῆρε μὲν πρώτιστον ἀργυρῶ δύο,
φιάλας δὲ πεντήκοντα, δέκα δὲ κυμβία,
ῥέοντα δώδεχ', ὧν τὰ μὲν δέκ' ἀργυρᾶ
ἦν, δύο δὲ χρυσᾶ, γρύψ,[1] τὸ δ' ἕτερον Πήγασος

ΡΥΣΙΣ. φιάλη χρυσῆ, Θεόδωρος. Κρατῖνος ἐν
Νόμοις·

ῥυσίδι σπένδων.

ΡΟΔΙΑΣ. Δίφιλος Αἱρησιτείχει (τὸ δὲ δρᾶμα
f τοῦτο Καλλίμαχος ἐπιγράφει Εὐνοῦχον)· λέγει δὲ
οὕτως·

πιεῖν δ' ἔτι[2]
ἁδρότερον[3] ἢ τῶν 'Ροδιάδων[4] ἢ τῶν ῥυτῶν;

μνημονεύει αὐτῶν καὶ Διώξιππος ἐν Φιλαργύρῳ
καὶ 'Αριστοτέλης ἐν τῷ περὶ Μέθης Λυγκεύς τε
ὁ Σάμιος ἐν ταῖς 'Επιστολαῖς.

---

[1] Casaubon: γρυψί ACE.
[2] δ' ἔτι Meineke: δὲ A, γέτι 497 a.
[3] 497 a: ἄνδρ' ἔτερον A.
[4] 'Ροδιάδων Schweighäuser, cf. lemma and Photius s.v.: ῥοδιακῶν A. The punctuation here and at 497 a is due to Capps.

entioned before.[a]   Also that it got its name from
rusias the king of Bithynia, who became notorious
or luxury and effeminacy, is recorded by Nicander
f Calchedon in the fourth book of his *Adventures of
rusias.*[b]

Rheonta.[c]   This was a name given to certain cups.
stydamas mentions them in *Hermes*, saying as
llows[d] : " First of all, two mixing-bowls of silver,
fty *phialai*, ten *kymbia*, a dozen *rheonta* ; of these ten
ere silver, two were of gold—a griffin the one, a
egasus the other."

Rhysis.   A golden *phialê*, according to Theodorus.
ratinus in *The Laws*[e] : " Pouring a libation from a
hysis."

Rhodias.[f]   Diphilus in *The Rampart-taker* (Calli-
achus gives this play the title of *Eunuch*[g]) ; Diphilus
ays[h] : " And drink still more copiously than from the
hodiades or from the drinking-horns ? "   They are
entioned also by Dioxippus[i] in *The Miser*, by
ristotle[j] in the treatise *On Drunkenness*, and by
ynceus[k] of Samos in his *Letters*.

[a] Above, 475 f (p. 102), where we have implication merely,
ot an express statement.
[b] *F.H.G.* iv. 462.
[c] Participle of ῥέω " flow " (*cf.* ῥυτόν and " flowing bowl ").
he description shows that they were not different from the
hyta (p. 216).   [d] *T.G.F.*[2] 778.
[e] Kock i. 52 : the fuller quotation below (502 b, p. 244)
hows that ῥυσίς is a mistake for χρυσίς ; so Hesych. *s.v.*
[f] C, dropping the catalogue form, has here τῶν ᾀδομένων
αἱ ἡ ῥοδιάς, " among the cups sung of (mentioned in poetry)
s the *Rhodias*."   [g] Frag. 100 d 4 Schneider.
[h] Kock ii. 542, repeated below. ῥοδιάς and ῥοδιακόν were
dentical, Photius, *s.v.*
[i] Above, 472 b (p. 82), Kock iii. 359.
[j] Frag. 96 Rose, Athen. 464 c (p. 24).
[k] 469 b (p. 68).

ΡΥΤΟΝ ἔχει τὸ ῦ βραχὺ καὶ ὀξύνεται. Δημοσθένη,
ἐν τῷ κατὰ Μειδίου " ῥυτὰ καὶ κυμβία," φησί, " κα
φιάλας." Δίφιλος δ' ἐν Εὐνούχῳ ἢ Στρατιώτ
(ἐστὶ δὲ τὸ δρᾶμα διασκευὴ τοῦ Αἱρησιτείχους)·

497   ἔσθ' ὑποχέασθαι πλείονας, πιεῖν δ' ἔτι[1]
       ἁδρότερον ἢ τῶν Ῥοδιάδων[2] ἢ τῶν ῥυτῶν;
'Επίνικος δ' ἐν Ὑποβαλλομέναις·

   A. καὶ τῶν ῥυτῶν τὰ μέγιστα τῶν ὄντων τρία
      πίνειν δεήσει τήμερον πρὸς κλεψύδραν
      κρουνιζόμενον. B. ἀμφότερα δ' οἰωνίζομαι.
   A. ἕν ἐστιν ἐλέφας[3]—B. ἀλλ'[4] ἐλέφαντας περιάγει[5]
   A. χωροῦν[6] δύο χόας.[7] B. οὐδ' ἂν ἐλέφας ἐκπίο
b A. ἐγὼ δὲ[8] τοῦτό γ' ἐκπέπωκα[9] πολλάκις.
   B. οὐδὲν ἐλέφαντος γὰρ διαφέρεις. A. οὐδὲ σύ
      ἕτερον τριήρης· τοῦτ' ἴσως[10] χωρεῖ χόα.
περὶ δὲ τοῦ τρίτου[11] λέγων φησίν·

   ὁ Βελλεροφόντης ἐστὶν ἀπὸ τοῦ Πηγάσου
   τὴν πύρπνοον Χίμαιραν εἰσηκοντικώς.
   εἶεν, δέχου καὶ τοῦτο.
ἐκαλεῖτο δὲ τὸ ῥυτὸν πρότερον κέρας. δοκεῖ δ

[1] Meineke: γέτι A.
[2] Ῥοδιάδων Schweighäuser, cf. lemma and Photius s.v.
ῥοδιακῶν A. See p. 214, note 4.
[3] οἰωνίζομαι Musurus, ἕν ἐστιν ἐλέφας Kaibel: οἰωνιζόμενα
ἔστιν δ' ἐλέφας A. The division of rôles is that of Capps.
[4] ἀλλ' added by Kaibel.
[5] ῥυτόν after περιάγει deleted by Dobree (cf. 468 f).
[6] Dobree: χωροῦντα ACE. Hence Eustath. 1286. 2
imagined a masculine form ῥυτός.
[7] ὃν after χόας deleted by Meineke.
[8] δὲ added by Casaubon.
[9] γ' ἐκπέπωκα Meineke, Dindorf: πέπωκα A.
[10] Schweighäuser: τουτις ὡς A.   [11] Dobree: ῥυτοῦ A

   [a] Chap. 158 ; above, 481 e (p. 134).

Rhyton. The word has a short *y* and is accented with an acute on the last syllable. Demosthenes in the speech *Against Meidias* has[a] " drinking-horns (*rhyta*), kymbia, and phialai." Diphilus in *The Eunuch* or *Trooper* (the play is a revised edition of *The Rampart-taker*)[b]: " May we not have more cups poured out, and drink still more copiously than from the *Rhodiades* or from the drinking-horns (*rhyta*)? " And Epinicus in *Child-foisting Wives*[c]: " A. And what is more, to-day he will be obliged to drink three of the biggest horns in existence, letting them squirt to the time of the water-clock.[d] B. Absit omen! I shudder at both.[e] A. One is an elephant[f]—B. Why, do you lead elephants about in your train? A.—holding six quarts. B. But an elephant, big as he is, couldn't drink up all that! A. Yes, he could; I my-self have done it often. B. Ay, for you are as big a brute as an elephant.[g] A. And so are you! The second cup is a trireme[h]; this holds possibly three quarts." And describing the third cup he says: " A. It is Bellerophon, on the back of Pegasus, having just hurled his javelin at the fire-breathing Chimaera. All right; take this too." Now the rhyton was earlier called a horn; and it appears to have been manu-

[b] Kock ii. 542. Yet in the Peiraeus inscription, *I.G.* i. 992, Λιρησιτείχης and Στρατιώτης are mentioned as separate plays.
[c] Kock iii. 331. For the title see above, 469 a (p. 68 note *a*).
[d] Speeches in the courts were timed by the water-clock. The slow drinking from the bottom of the horn will resemble the dribbling from the water-clock.
[e] *i.e.* at the suggestion of litigation in the water-clock and at the unpleasant squirting. For οἰωνίζομαι *cf.* Dem. *Against Aristogeiton* 794. [f] Above, 468 f.
[g] Diogenian. iv. 43 quotes this as a proverb, ἐπὶ τῶν ἀναισθήτων. [h] A cup; below, 500 f.

σκευοποιηθῆναι ὑπὸ[1] πρώτου τοῦ Φιλαδέλφου Πτο
λεμαίου βασιλέως φόρημα[2] γενέσθαι τῶν Ἀρσινόη
c εἰκόνων. τῇ γὰρ εὐωνύμῳ χειρὶ ἐκείνη[3] τοιοῦτο
φέρει δημιούργημα πάντων τῶν ὡραίων πλῆρες
ἐμφαινόντων τῶν δημιουργῶν ὡς καὶ τοῦ τῇ
Ἀμαλθείας ἐστὶν ὀλβιώτερον τὸ κέρας τοῦτο
μνημονεύει αὐτοῦ Θεοκλῆς ἐν Ἰθυφάλλοις οὕτως

> ἐθύσαμεν γὰρ σήμερον Σωτήρια
> πάντες οἱ τεχνῖται·
> μεθ᾽ ὧν πιὼν τὸ δίκερας[4] ὡς τὸν φίλτατον
> βασιλέα πάρειμι.

Διονύσιος δ᾽ ὁ Σινωπεὺς ἐν Σῳζούσῃ καταλέγων
τινὰ ποτήρια καὶ τοῦ ῥυτοῦ ἐμνήσθη, ὡς προεῖπον
d Ἡδύλος δ᾽ ἐν Ἐπιγράμμασι περὶ τοῦ κατασκευα
σθέντος ὑπὸ Κτησιβίου τοῦ μηχανοποιοῦ ῥυτοῦ μνη
μονεύων φησί·

> ζωροπόται, καὶ τοῦτο φιλοζεφύρου[5] κατὰ νηὸν
> τὸ ῥυτὸν εὐδίης[6] δεῦτ᾽ ἴδετ᾽ Ἀρσινόης,
> ὀρχηστὴν Βησᾶν[7] Αἰγύπτιον· ὃς λιγὺν ἦχον
> σαλπίζει κρουνοῦ πρὸς ῥύσιν οἰγομένου,[8]
> οὐ[9] πολέμου σύνθημα, διὰ χρυσέου δὲ γέγωνεν

---

[1] ἐπὶ "in the reign of" Meineke.
[2] φόρημα C: φορήματα A, φόρημά τι early edd.
[3] ἐκείνη CE: om. A.
[4] τοδὶ κέρας CE (δίκερας A at 202 b).
[5] Casaubon: φιλοζειφυρου A.
[6] Kaibel: εἰδείης A, αἰδοίης Jacobs.
[7] Kaibel: βησαν A.
[8] Salmasius: ἠγομένου A.
[9] οὐ Jacobs: καὶ A.

---

[a] Athen. 198 a (vol. ii. p. 396).
[b] Diehl vi. 251. The title denotes a festival of Dionysus
also the metre of odes sung thereat, especially the trochaic
tripody (− ᴗ − ᴗ − ᵜ) seen in vss. 2 and 4.

actured first under the orders of King Ptolemy
Philadelphus, that it might be used as an attribute
borne by the statues of Arsinoë. For in her left
hand the queen carries that sort of object filled with
all kinds of fruit, the artists thus indicating that this
horn is even richer in blessings than the horn of
Amaltheia.*a* Theocles mentions it in his *Ithyphallic
Verses* thus *b* : " All we artists have to-day celebrated
with sacrifice the festival of Salvation *c* ; in their
company I have drunk the double horn and am come
into the presence of our dearest king.*d* " Dionysius
of Sinope, when giving a list of some cups in *The
Woman who Saved*, mentioned also the rhyton, as I
have said before.*e* And Hedylus in his *Epigrams*, mentioning the rhyton made by the engineer Ctesibius,
says *f* : " Come hither, ye drinkers of strong wine,
look also at this rhyton in the temple of Arsinoë the
Gracious, lover of the West Wind *g* : it is in the form
of the Egyptian Besas,*h* the dancer, who trumpets
forth a shrill note when the spout is opened for the
flowing wine—no signal for battle is this, but through

c Xen. *Anab.* iii. 2. 9 εὔξασθαι τῷ θεῷ τούτῳ (*i.e.* τῷ Διὶ τῷ
Σωτῆρι) θύσειν Σωτήρια. But here the Saviour Gods are
Ptolemy I Soter and Berenice. (See Additional Note on
p. 522.) On the artists of Dionysus see Athen. 198 c and
note *c* (vol. ii. p. 397), 212 d (vol. ii. p. 460).

d Ptolemy Philadelphus. For coins showing Arsinoë and
the double horn see Svoronos iv. Pl. xv.

e 467 d (p. 61 and note *d*), Kock ii. 427.

f Wilamowitz, *Hellenist. Dichtung*, i. 145.

g *Cf.* her title Zephyritis, Lady of Zephyrium (a promon-
tory between Alexandria and the Canobic mouth of the Nile,
Strabo 800), in a similar epigram of Callimachus, Athen.
318 b, L.C.L. p. 141.

h Besas (Bes) was a grotesque, dwarf-like divinity of Arabian
origin ; the wine flowing from the horn produced a musical
tone. *Cf.* the cup *bessa*, 784 b (p. 52).

κώδωνος κώμου σύνθεμα[1] καὶ θαλίης,
Νεῖλος ὁκοῖον[2] ἄναξ μύσταις φίλον ἱεραγωγοῖς
εὗρε μέλος θείων πάτριον ἐξ ὑδάτων.
e ἀλλ᾽ εἰ[3] Κτησιβίου σοφὸν εὕρεμα τίετε τοῦτο,
δεῦτε, νέοι, νηῷ τῷδε παρ᾽ Ἀρσινόης.

Θεόφραστος δ᾽ ἐν τῷ περὶ Μέθης τὸ ῥυτὸν φησι
ὀνομαζόμενον ποτήριον τοῖς ἥρωσι μόνοις ἀπο-
δίδοσθαι. Δωρόθεος δ᾽ ὁ Σιδώνιός φησιν τὰ ῥυτὰ
κέρασιν ὅμοια εἶναι, διατετρημένα δ᾽ εἶναι, ἐξ ὧν
κρουνιζόντων λεπτῶς κάτωθεν πίνουσιν, ὠνομάσθαι
τε[4] ἀπὸ τῆς ῥύσεως.

ΣΑΝΝΑΚΡΑ.[5] Κράτης ἐν πέμπτῳ Ἀττικῆς Διαλέκτου ἔκπωμά φησιν εἶναι οὕτως καλούμενον·
f ἐστὶ δὲ Περσικόν. Φιλήμων δ᾽ ἐν τῇ Χήρᾳ
βατιακῶν μνησθεὶς καὶ τῇ γελοιότητι τοῦ ὀνόματος
προσπαίξας φησί·

σαννάκρα, ἱπποτραγέλαφοι, βατιάκια, σαννάκια.

ΣΕΛΕΥΚΙΣ. ὅτι ἀπὸ Σελεύκου τοῦ βασιλέως τὴν
προσηγορίαν ἔσχεν τὸ ἔκπωμα προείρηται, ἱστο-
ροῦντος τοῦτο καὶ Ἀπολλοδώρου τοῦ Ἀθηναίου.
Πολέμων δ᾽ ἐν πρώτῳ τῶν πρὸς Ἀδαῖον " ποτήρια,"
φησί, " παραπλήσια Σελευκίς, Ῥοδιάς,[6] Ἀντιγονίς."

---

[1] Musurus: σύνθεμα A.   [2] Schweighäuser: ὁκοῖος A.
[3] ἀλλ᾽ εἰ Meineke: ἀλλὰ A.   [4] τε A: δὲ CE.
[5] σαννάκρα ACE: σαννάκια Kaibel, bracketing σαννάκρα
below.   [6] δοριὰς C.

---

[a] For κώδων, " bell," see Athen. 185 a (vol. ii. p. 317).
[b] Frag. 122 Wimmer, above, 461 b (p. 10). The rhyton
often contained fruits (ὡραῖα above, 497 c), which were appropriate offerings to heroes, Plat. *Critias* 116 c. For the
gods other cups, especially the *phialê*, were used.
[c] At the pointed end. Dorotheus is usually spoken of as
a citizen of Ascalon.   [d] Above, 784 a (p. 52).

he golden mouthpiece [a] there rings the signal for
evelling and mirth ; it is like the ancestral melody
vhich the Lord Nile produced from the divine waters,
lear to the initiates who bring him their offerings.
Jay then, if ye will honour this clever device of
Ctesibius, come hither, young men, beside the
emple of Arsinoë here." Theophrastus in his
reatise *On Drunkenness* says [b] that the cup called the
hyton is rendered only to the Heroes.   Dorotheus
f Sidon says that the rhyta are like horns, but have a
tole bored in them,[c] and from them, as the liquid is
lischarged in a slender stream, people drink at the
ower end, and so they have got their name from this
lowing (*rhysis*).

Sannakra. Crates, in the fifth book of his work *On
he Attic Dialect*, says that there is a cup so called.
t is Persian.   Philemon, after mentioning *batiakai* [d]
n *The Widow* and joking at the ridiculous nature
f the word, says [e] : " *Sannakra*, horse-goat-stags,
atiakia, sannakia* ! "

Seleukis. That this cup got its designation from
King Seleucus has been stated before [f] ; the fact
s recorded also by Apollodorus of Athens.[g]   And
Polemon, in the first book of his *Addresses to Adaeus*,
mentions[h] as cups resembling each other the *Seleukis*,
Rhodias, and *Antigonis*.

[e] Kock ii. 503.   *Cf.* the puzzled question of Dionysus,
Aristoph. *Ran.* 931 νυκτὸς διηγρύπνησα τὸν ξουθὸν ἱππαλεκτρυόνα
ητῶν τίς ἐστιν ὄρνις, " I've been kept awake nights wondering
vhat bird the tawny horse-cock (griffin) is."   So also
Aeschines iii. 82 (quoted by Kaibel) mocks Demosthenes'
·lib use of outlandish names, Δορίσκον καὶ Ἐργίσκην καὶ
ιυρτίσκην.   Below, 500 d and p. 237 note *b*.
   [f] Above, 783 e (p. 50).   [g] J. 2 B 1114.
   [h] Frag. 57 Preller.   The resemblance apparently lay in
heir derivation from proper names.

498 ΣΚΑΛΛΙΟΝ[1] κυλίκιον μικρὸν ᾧ σπένδουσιν Αἰολεῖς, ὡς Φιλίτας φησὶν ἐν Ἀτάκτοις.

ΣΚΥΦΟΣ. τούτου τινὲς τὴν γενικὴν σὺν τῷ ō προφέρονται διὰ παντός, οὐκ εὖ· ὅτε γὰρ ἀρσενικόν ἐστιν ὁ σκύφος, ὡς λύχνος, ἄνευ τοῦ ō προοισόμεθα, ὅτε δὲ οὐδέτερον τὸ σκύφος, σὺν τῷ ō κλινοῦμεν σκύφος σκύφους, ὡς τεῖχος τείχους. οἱ δ᾽ Ἀττικοὶ τὴν εὐθεῖαν καὶ ἀρσενικῶς καὶ οὐδετέρως λέγουσιν. Ἡσίοδος δ᾽ ἐν τῷ δευτέρῳ Μελαμποδίας σὺν τῷ π̄[2] σκύπφον λέγει·

b τῷ δὲ Μάρις[3] θοὸς ἄγγελος ἦλθε δι᾽ οἴκου,
πλήσας δ᾽ ἀργύρεον σκύπφον φέρε, δῶκε δ᾽
ἄνακτι.

καὶ πάλιν·

καὶ τότε Μάντις[4] μὲν δεσμὸν βοὸς[5] αἴνυτο χερσίν,
Ἴφικλος δ᾽ ἐπὶ νῶτ᾽ ἐπεμαίετο. τῷ δ᾽ ἐπ᾽
ὄπισθεν[6]
σκύπφον ἔχων ἑτέρῃ, ἑτέρῃ δὲ σκῆπτρον ἀείρας
ἔστειχεν Φύλακος καὶ ἐνὶ δμώεσσιν ἔειπεν.

ὁμοίως δὲ καὶ Ἀναξίμανδρος ἐν τῇ Ἡρωολογίᾳ
c λέγων ὧδε· " Ἀμφιτρύων δὲ τὴν λείην δασάμενος τοῖς συμμάχοις καὶ τὸν σκύπον ἔχων ὃν εἴλετο αὑτῷ.[8]" καὶ πάλιν· " τὸν δὲ σκύπον Τηλεβόῃ δίδωσι Ποσειδῶν παιδὶ τῷ ἑαυτοῦ, Τηλεβόης δ᾽

---

[1] Casaubon: κάλλιον A. Hesych.: οἱ δὲ σκαλλόν.
[2] μετὰ τοῦ π̄ CE.
[3] Μάρις Wilamowitz (cf. Il. xvi. 319): τὸ δ᾽ εμαρης A, τῷ δ᾽ Μάρης Musurus.
[4] Μάντις (cf. Μάντιος Od. xv. 242, 249): μάντης A, μάντι Schweighäuser.   [5] Hemsterhuys: βιος A.
[6] τῷ δ᾽ ἐπόπισθεν Musurus: τὸ δ᾽ ἐποπισθεν A.
[7] ἠρωιολογίαι A.   [8] αὐτῶι A.

Skallion, a tiny cylix with which the Aeolians offer libations, according to Philitas in *Irregular Words*.[a]

Skyphos. Some authorities pronounce the genitive of this word with an *s*[b] under all circumstances, but wrongly; for when the word *skyphos* (ὁ σκύφος) is masculine, like *lychnos*,[c] we shall pronounce it (in the genitive) without the *s*, but when it is neuter (τὸ σκύφος) we shall decline it with the *s*, *skyphos, skyphous*, like *teichos, teichous*.[d] The Athenians give the nominative case sometimes as masculine (ὁ σκύφος), sometimes as neuter (τὸ σκύφος). Moreover Hesiod, in the second book of *The Epic of Melampus*, says *skypphos*, with *p* [e]: "To him came Maris, the nimble messenger, through the hall, and filling a silver cup (*skypphos*), brought it and gave it to his lord." And again Hesiod says [f] : "Thereupon Mantis grasped a thong of ox-hide in his hands, but Iphiclus laid hold of his back. Then up from behind him came Phylacus, holding a cup (*skypphos*) in one hand, with the other raising his staff, and spake amongst his henchmen." Likewise also Anaximander in his *Tale of Heroes*, speaking as follows [g] : "Amphitryon divided the booty among his allies and kept the cup (*skypphos*) which he had chosen for himself." And again: "Now Poseidon gave this cup (*skypphos*) to Teleboas, his own son, and Teleboas gave it to Pterelaüs; this he took when he

[a] Frag. 53 Bach, om. Powell.
[b] σκύφους, as of the third declension neuter, instead of κύφου, second declension masculine.
[c] λύχνος, "lamp" (masc.), was occasionally heteroclitic, *dur.* τὰ λύχνα as from τὸ λύχνον.
[d] τεῖχος, "wall," was consistently neuter, third declension.
[e] In addition to the digraph *ph*, to make the first syllable long: Frag. 193 Rzach.
[f] *Ibid.* 194.   [g] *F.H.G.* ii. 67, J. 1. 160.

Πτερέλεῳ· τοῦτον ἑλὼν ἀπέπλεεν." ὁμοίως εἴρηκ‹
καὶ Ἀνακρέων μετὰ τοῦ π̄[1]·

> ἐγὼ δ' ἔχων σκύπφον[2] Ἐρξίωνι
> τῷ λευκολόφῳ μεστὸν ἐξέπινον,

—ἀντὶ τοῦ προέπινον. κυρίως γὰρ ἐστι τοῦτ‹
προπίνειν, τὸ ἑτέρῳ πρὸ ἑαυτοῦ δοῦναι πιεῖν.[3] κα‹
ὁ Ὀδυσσεὺς δὲ παρὰ τῷ Ὁμήρῳ τῇ

d   Ἀρήτῃ δ' ἐν[4] χερσὶ τίθει δέπας ἀμφικύπελλον.

καὶ ἐν Ἰλιάδι Ὀδυσσεύς[5]·

> πλησάμενος δ' οἴνοιο δέπας δείδεκτ' Ἀχιλῆα.

πληροῦντες γὰρ προέπινον ἀλλήλοις μετὰ προσ‹
αγορεύσεως.
    Πανύασσις τρίτῳ Ἡρακλείας φησίν·

> τοῦ κεράσας κρητῆρα μέγαν χρυσοῖο φαεινὸν[6]
> σκύπφους αἰνύμενος[7] θαμέας[8] ποτὸν ἡδὺν ἔπινεν‹

Εὐριπίδης δ' ἐν Εὐρυσθεῖ[10] ἀρσενικῶς ἔφη·

> σκύφος τε μακρός.

καὶ Ἀχαιὸς δ' ἐν Ὀμφάλῃ·

e   ὁ δὲ σκύφος με τοῦ θεοῦ καλεῖ.[11]

Σιμωνίδης δὲ " οὐατόεντα σκύφον " ἔφη. Ἴων δ‹
ἐν Ὀμφάλῃ·

> οἶνος οὐκ ἔνι
> ἐν τῷ σκύφει,

τὸ[12] σκύφει ἰδίως ἀπὸ τοῦ σκύφος σχηματίσα‹

---

[1] μετὰ τοῦ π̄ added in C. [2] κύπφον A.
[3] διδόναι τινὶ C.

sailed away." Likewise Anacreon also has the word
with a *p* [a] : " And I, with a cup (*skypphos*) filled to
the brim, drank it out in honour of Erxion of the
white crest," where " drank it out " is for " pledged."
For, properly speaking, that is what pledging is, to
give another a drink before oneself. So Odysseus
also in Homer [b] : " Placed in Arêtê's hands the double
cup." And Odysseus in the *Iliad* [c] : " Filled the cup
with wine and greeted Achilles." For they filled
and pledged each other with a greeting.

Panyassis, in the third book of his *Epic of Heracles*,
says [d] : " With the wine he mixed a mighty, shining
mixing-bowl of gold, and taking frequent cups (*skyp-
phous*) he quaffed the pleasant drink." Euripides in
Eurystheus used the word *skyphos* as a masculine [e] :
" And a deep bowl." So too Achaeus in *Omphalê* [f] :
" The cup of the god invites me." And Simonides
said [g] : "The eared [h] bowl." Ion, also, in *Omphalê* [i] :
"There is no wine in the cup"; he has formed a peculiar
dative *skyphei* from the nominative *skyphos* and em-

[a] *P.L.G.*[4] iii. 277, Diehl frag. 75, Edmonds frag. 94.
[b] *Od.* xiii. 57.
[c] *Il.* ix. 224. The greeting was in the usual form (vs. 225),
χαῖρ', Ἀχιλλεῦ. [d] *Frag. ep.* 255.
[e] *T.G.F.*[2] 476; the adj. μακρός ("long," "large ") is masc.
[f] *Ibid.* 754, above, 466 f (p. 56). The article is masculine.
[g] *P.L.G.*[4] iii. 534, Edmonds frag. 103.
[h] *i.e.* furnished with a handle ; the adj. is masculine.
[i] *T.G.F.*[2] 737.

[4] τῇ . . . δ' ἐν Casaubon: τῆι ἀρήτηι· ἡ δ' ἐν A.
[5] ὀδυσσεὺς added in C.   [6] φαεινοῦ Kinkel.
[7] αἰνυμένους A.   [8] θαμεὰς A.
[9] ἔνειμεν Koechly.   [10] Casaubon: ευρυσθεῖαι A.
[11] 466 f: καλεῖς A.
[12] τὸ Wilamowitz: τῶι A. τῶι repeated after σκύφει deleted
by Musurus.

οὐδετέρως ἔφη.   ὁμοίως καὶ Ἐπίχαρμος ἐν Κύκλωπι·

> φέρ᾽ ἐγχέας εἰς τὸ σκύφος.

καὶ Ἄλεξις ἐν Λευκαδίᾳ·

> οἴνου γεραιοῖς χείλεσιν μέγα σκύφος.

καὶ Ἐπιγένης ἐν Βακχίδι[1]·

> τὸ σκύφος ἔχαιρον δεχόμενος.

Φαίδιμός τε ἐν πρώτῳ Ἡρακλείας·

> δουράτεον σκύφος εὐρὺ μελιζώροιο ποτοῖο.

f καὶ παρ᾽ Ὁμήρῳ δ᾽ Ἀριστοφάνης[2] ὁ Βυζάντιος γράφει·

> πλησάμενος δ᾽ ἄρα οἱ δῶκε σκύφος ᾧπερ[3] ἔπινεν

Ἀρίσταρχος δέ·

> πλησάμενος δ᾽ ἄρα οἱ δῶκε σκύφον ᾧπερ ἔπινεν

Ἀσκληπιάδης δ᾽ ὁ Μυρλεανὸς ἐν τῷ περὶ τῆς Νεστορίδος φησὶν ὅτι τῷ σκύφει καὶ τῷ κισσυβίῳ τῶν μὲν ἐν ἄστει καὶ μετρίων οὐδεὶς ἐχρῆτο συβῶται δὲ καὶ νομεῖς καὶ οἱ ἐν ἀγρῷ, ὡς ὁ Εὔμαιος

> πλησάμενος δῶκε σκύφος ᾧπερ ἔπινεν,
> οἴνου ἐνίπλειον.

καὶ Ἀλκμὰν δέ φησι·

499
> πολλάκι δ᾽ ἐν κορυφαῖς ὀρέων, ὄκα
> θεοῖσιν[4] ἄδη πολύφανος ἑορτά,

---

[1] Kock: βακχίαι A.
[2] τὸ δὲ παρ᾽ ὁμήρῳ ἀριστοφάνης μὲν C.   [3] CE: ὦνπερ A.
[4] Hermann: θεοῖς A, θεοῖσι Fάδη Crusius.

---

[a] *i.e.* σκύφει as from τὸ σκύφος, instead of σκύφῳ from ὁ σκύφος; *cf.* above, p. 222.
[b] Kaibel 105 ; Polyphemus addresses Odysseus.

ployed it as a neuter word.[a] Similarly (in the neuter gender) Epicharmus in *The Cyclops* [b] : "Come, pour it into the cup." And Alexis in *Leucadia* [c] : " A mighty cup of wine, with venerable brim." Epigenes, too, in *The Bacchant* [d] : " I was glad to accept the cup." And so Phaedimus in the first book of his *Epic of Heracles* [e] : " A broad, wooden cup of strong honeyed wine." And in Homer Aristophanes of Byzantium also writes [f] : " So then, filling the cup (*skyphos*) from which he was wont himself to drink, he gave it to him." But Aristarchus writes : " So then, filling the cup (*skyphon*) from which he was wont himself to drink, he gave it to him." Asclepiades of Myrlea, in his treatise *On Nestor's Cup*, says [g] : " No dweller in a city, even in moderate circumstances, ever used a *skyphos* or a *kissybion* ; it is only swine-herds, shepherds, and country people who do, like Eumaeus [h] : ' Filling the cup (*skyphos*) from which he was wont himself to drink, he gave it to him filled with wine.' " And Alcman also says [i] : " Oft-times on the peaks of the mountains, whensoe'er the festival with many torches [j] delights the gods, thou

---

[c] Kock ii. 344 ; the construction cannot be determined with certainty.

[d] *Ibid.* 417. The title of the play is given variously, Athen. 75 c, 384 a.

[e] *Frag. ep.* 214 ; the adjectives modifying " cup " are in the neuter gender.

[f] *Od.* xiv. 112 (Eumaeus and Odysseus), Nauck, *Ar. Byz.* 42 f note *n*. The mss. of Homer read : καί οἱ πλησάμενος δῶκε σκύφον (masc.) ὧπερ ἔπινεν. This is the only occurrence of the word σκύφος in Homer.

[g] Above, 477 b (p. 110). [h] *Od.* xiv. 112.

[i] *P.L.G.*[4] iii. 49, Diehl frag. 37, Edmonds frag. 47. The subject is a Bacchant.

[j] On the φανός see Athen. 699 d.

χρύσεον[1] ἄγγος ἔχοισα μέγαν σκύφον,
οἷά τε ποιμένες ἄνδρες ἔχουσιν,
χερσὶ λεόντεον ἐγ γάλα θεῖσα[2]
τυρὸν ἐτύρησας μέγαν ἄτρυφον ἀργιφόνταν.[3]

Αἰσχύλος δ' ἐν Περραιβίσι φησί·

πῶ μοι τὰ πολλὰ δῶρα κἀκροθίνια;
πῶ χρυσότευκτα κἀργυρᾶ σκυφώματα;

Στησίχορος δὲ τὸ παρὰ Φόλῳ τῷ Κενταύρῳ ποτήριον σκύφιον δέπας καλεῖ ἐν ἴσῳ τῷ σκυφοειδές·
λέγει δ' ἐπὶ τοῦ Ἡρακλέους·

b   σκύφιον[4] δὲ λαβὼν δέπας ἔμμετρον ὡς τριλάγυνον
πί[5] ἐπισχόμενος, τό ῥά οἱ παρέθηκε Φόλος[6] κεράσας.

καὶ Ἄρχιππος δὲ ἐν Ἀμφιτρύωνι οὐδετέρως
εἴρηκε.

Λάγυνον δὲ μέτρου λέγουσιν εἶναι ὄνομα παρὰ
τοῖς Ἕλλησιν, ὡς χοὸς καὶ κοτύλης. χωρεῖν δ'
αὐτὸ κοτύλας Ἀττικὰς δώδεκα. καὶ ἐν Πάτραις
δέ φασι[7] τοῦτ' εἶναι τὸ μέτρον τὴν λάγυνον. ἀρσενικῶς δὲ εἴρηκε τὸν λάγυνον Νικόστρατος μὲν ἐν
Ἑκάτῃ·

c   τῶν κατεσταμνισμένων
ἡμῖν λαγύνων πηλίκοι τινές;[8] Β. τρίχους.

καὶ πάλιν·

τὸν μεστὸν ἡμῖν φέρε λάγυνον.

---

[1] χρύσιον Bergk.
[2] ἐγ γάλα θεῖσα Hermann: ἐπαλαθεισα A.
[3] Welcker: ἀργειοφόνται A, ἀργιφόεντα Edmonds.
[4] σκύπφειον Casaubon.   [5] πί' CE: πι' A.
[6] λόφος C.   [7] Casaubon: φησι A.
[8] πηλίκοι τινές; Schweighäuser   πηλίκοι· ἀρσενικῶς δὲ εἴρηκε
τὸν λάγυνον τινές A.

carriest a golden vessel, a mighty cup (*skyphon*) like those that shepherds have, and with thy hands pouring into it the milk of a lioness, thou didst mould a large solid cheese glistening white." Aeschylus, further, (has the term *skyphoma*) in *Women of Perrhaebia* [a]: "Where are my many rewards and choicest prizes? Where my cups (*skyphomata*) wrought in gold and silver?" And Stesichorus calls the cup used in the cave of the Centaur Pholus a *skyphion depas*, equivalent to " skyphos-like "; of Heracles he says [b]: " And taking the skyphos-like cup, measuring as much as three flagons, he put it to his lips and drank it [c]— that cup which Pholus had mingled and set before him." Archippus, also, used the word *skyphos* as a neuter in *Amphitryo*.[d]

Now they say that the flagon (*lagynos*) is the name of a measure among the Greeks,[e] as are the *chous* and the *kotylê*. It contains twelve Attic *kotylai*. Moreover in Patrae they say there is this measure, the *lagynos*.[f] Nicostratus uses the word as a masculine in *Hecate* [g]: " A. How large are our flagons of wine racked off from the casks? B. They hold three *choes* each.[h] " Again he says: " Hand us that brimming flagon." And in the play entitled *The*

---

[a] *T.G.F.*[2] 61.

[b] *P.L.G.*[4] iii. 208, Diehl frag. 5, Edmonds frag. 7; *cf.* below, 499 e, where the title of the poem is given.

[c] So of Socrates drinking the hemlock, Plat. *Phaedo* 117 c ἐπισχόμενος ἐξέπιε.

[d] Kock i. 680.

[e] *i.e.* other Greeks than the Athenians. But since the word is found in Attic writers quoted here, and the lagynos is further said to contain only the same number of kotylai (about 12 half-pints) as the chous, Kaibel bracketed χωρεῖν δ' . . . δώδεκα.   [f] Feminine.

[g] Kock ii. 223.   [h] Eighteen quarts.

καὶ ἐν τῇ ἐπιγραφομένῃ Κλίνῃ·

καὶ δυσχερὴς λάγυνος οὗτος πλησίον
ὄξους.

καὶ[1] Δίφιλος ἐν Ἀνασῳζομένοις·

λάγυνον ἔχω κενόν, ὦ γραῦ, θύλακον δὲ μεστόν.

Λυγκεὺς δ' ὁ Σάμιος ἐν τῇ πρὸς Διαγόραν Ἐπιστολῇ γράφει· "καθ' ὃν χρόνον ἐπεδήμησας ἐν[2]
Σάμῳ, Διαγόρα, πολλάκις οἶδά σε παραγινόμενον
εἰς τοὺς παρ' ἐμοὶ πότους, ἐν οἷς λάγυνος κατ'
ἄνδρα κείμενος οἰνοχοεῖτο, πρὸς ἡδονὴν διδοὺς[3]
d ἑκάστῳ ποτήριον." Ἀριστοτέλης δ' ἐν τῇ Θετταλῶν
Πολιτείᾳ θηλυκῶς λέγεσθαί φησιν ὑπὸ Θετταλῶν
τὴν λάγυνον. καὶ Ῥιανὸς ὁ ἐποποιὸς ἐν Ἐπι-
γράμμασιν·

ἥμισυ μὲν πίσσης κωνίτιδος,[4] ἥμισυ δ' οἴνου,
Ἀρχῖν', ἀτρεκέως ἥδε λάγυνος ἔχει.
λεπτοτέρης δ' οὐκ οἶδ' ἐρίφου κρέα[5]· πλὴν ὅ γε
πέμψας
αἰνεῖσθαι πάντων ἄξιος Ἱπποκράτης.

οὐδετέρως δὲ Δίφιλος[6] ἐν Ἀδελφοῖς εἴρηκεν·

e
ὦ τοιχωρύχων[7]
ἐκεῖνο καὶ τῶν δυνομένων[8] λαγύνιον·
ἔχον βαδίζειν εἰς τὰ γεύμαθ' ὑπὸ μάλης,
καὶ τοῦτο πωλεῖν, μέχρι ἂν ὥσπερ ἐν ἐράνῳ

---

[1] καὶ added in C.   [2] ἐν added by Musurus.
[3] διδοὺς A : δ' ἰδίως Lumb. But several words have been lost.
[4] Toup: κωπίτιδος A.   [5] Meineke: κρέας A.
[6] ἀλλαχοῦ δὲ Δίφιλος C.
[7] τοιχωρύχων Kaibel, τοιχωρύχον Musurus: τυχωρυχον A.
[8] δυνομένων Schweighäuser: δυναμένων A.

Couch [a] : " Nauseating, too, is this flagon that comes next; it's full of vinegar." So Diphilus in *Safe Home* [b] : " The flagon that I have, aged crone, is empty, but my meal sack is chock full." Now Lynceus of Samos in the *Letter to Diagoras* writes : " At the time you stayed in Samos, Diagoras, I remember that you often attended the drinking-parties at my house ; at these a flagon [c] of wine, set at each man's place, was kept filled, thus allowing each to have a cup at his pleasure. [d] " But Aristotle in *The Constitution of Thessaly* [e] asserts that *lagynos* is used in the feminine gender by the Thessalians. So, too, the epic poet Rhianus in his *Epigrams* [f] : " This flagon, Archinus, contains exactly one-half resin from pine cones, one-half wine. And I know not the flesh of a leaner kid than this ; yet Hippocrates who sent them is worthy to be praised on all accounts." On the other hand, Diphilus has it in the neuter in *Brothers* [g] : " Oh, that little flagon (*lagynion*) of burglars and sneaks, which is able to make its way into the sample-rooms [h] under an arm-pit, and to sell the stuff until,

---

[a] Kock ii. 224; on δυσχερής see p. 69 note *c*.   [b] *Ibid.* 544.
[c] Masculine, like the examples just given.
[d] Meaning that a whole flagon was set before each guest to empty at will, without waiting for the attendant (οἰνοχόος) to fill the cups.
[e] Frag. 499 Rose.   [f] Powell 21.
[g] Kock ii. 541 ; the form cited (λαγύνιον) is a diminutive, and of course neuter. The meaning of the verses is hard to see.—Alexis, Philemon, Apollodorus, Hegesippus, Euphron, and Menander also wrote plays entitled *Brothers*. The pro-logue of Terence's *Adelphoe* ascribes it largely to Menander, not Diphilus ; yet the latter's *Dying Together* (Συναποθνή-σκοντες) also furnished material for Terence.
[h] For γεύματα, the booths where one might " taste " wines, *cf.* Ephippus, Athen. 380 f (vol. iv. p. 222).

εἷς λοιπὸς ᾖ, κάπηλος ἠδικημένος
ὑπ᾽ οἰνοπώλου.

τὸ δ᾽ ἐν Γηρυονηίδι[1] Στησιχόρου[2] " ἔμμετρον ὡς
τριλάγυνον " τὴν τῶν τριῶν γενῶν ἀμφιβολίαν
ἔχει. Ἐρατοσθένης δέ φησι λέγεσθαι τὴν πέτασον[3]
καὶ τὴν στάμνον ὑπό τινων.

Τὸ δὲ σκύφος ὠνομάσθη ἀπὸ τῆς σκαφίδος. καὶ
τοῦτο δ᾽ ἐστὶν ὁμοίως ἀγγεῖον ξύλινον στρογγύλον
γάλα καὶ ὀρὸν[4] δεχόμενον, ὡς καὶ παρ᾽ Ὁμήρῳ
f λέγεται·

ναῖον[5] δ᾽ ὀρῷ ἄγγεα πάντα
γαυλοί τε σκαφίδες τε τετυγμένα τοῖς ἐνάμελγεν.

εἰ μὴ σκύφος οἷον σκύθος τις διὰ τὸ τοὺς Σκύθας
περαιτέρω τοῦ δέοντος μεθύσκεσθαι. Ἱερώνυμος
δ᾽ ὁ Ῥόδιος ἐν τῷ περὶ Μέθης καὶ τὸ μεθύσαι
σκυθίσαι φησί· συγγενὲς γὰρ εἶναι τὸ φ τῷ θ.
500 ὕστερον δὲ κατὰ μίμησιν εἰργάσαντο κεραμέους τε
καὶ ἀργυροῦς σκύφους. ὧν πρῶτοι μὲν ἐγένοντο
καὶ κλέος ἔλαβον οἱ Βοιώτιοι λεγόμενοι, χρησα-
μένου κατὰ[6] τὰς στρατείας πρώτου Ἡρακλέους τῷ
γένει· διὸ καὶ Ἡρακλεωτικοὶ πρός τινων καλοῦν-

---

[1] Heringa: γηρυονίδηι A.
[2] Casaubon: λαγύνοις στησιχόρου A, τὸ δὲ παρὰ στησιχόρῳ CE.
[3] πέταχνον (?) Strecker.   [4] ὁρρὸν CE.
[5] ναῖον Aristarchus and a few mss. of Homer: νέον A, νᾶον
or νάον Hom., ἔναον Herwerden.
[6] κατὰ Meineke: διὰ ACE.

---

[a] On the ἔρανος see Athen. 362 e (vol. iv. p. 140); but
what the allusion is here I know not. One may surmise that
the bar-keeper (or peddler) mentioned is a bootlegger who
has bought wine, much diluted, from thieves who carry it out

as at a contribution-dinner,[a] only one man is left, a bar-keeper cheated by a wine-seller." Now the phrase in Stesichorus's *Tale of Geryonês*,[b] "measuring as much as three flagons," contains an ambiguity as regards the three genders.[c] And Eratosthenes declares[d] that *petasos* (hat) and *stamnos* (wine-jar) are used as feminines by some writers.

As to the *skyphos*, that was named from the word *skaphis*.[e] This latter is likewise a round wooden vessel used as a receptacle for milk and whey, as it is told in Homer[f] : " And all the vessels swam with whey—the pails and the bowls—the well-wrought vessels into which he milked." But the word *skyphos* may be as it were for *skythos*, since the Scythians are in the habit of drinking to great excess. And Hieronymus of Rhodes, in his work *On Drunkenness*, even says[g] that " to get drunk is to behave like a Scythian; for the sound of *ph* (as in *skyphos*) is related to the sound of *th*." In later times, by way of imitation,[h] they manufactured *skyphoi* of clay and of silver. Of these the first to be made and to acquire repute were the so-called Boeotian *skyphoi*, and Heracles while on his campaigns was the first to make use of the style ; hence they are also called

---

[a] surreptitiously from the sample-rooms (γεύματα). The bar-keeper is left, cheated out of his legitimate profits, as one drinker may be left at the close of a dinner-party. *Cf.* Socrates in Plat. *Symp.*

[b] Above, 499 b (p. 228).

[c] One cannot decide whether he meant ὁ λάγυνος, ἡ λάγυνος or τὸ λάγυνον.

[d] Frag. 82 Strecker. Ordinarily ὁ πέτασος and ὁ στάμνος, not ἡ, *i.e.* masc. not fem.

[e] Also meaning cup, bowl, basin.　　　　　　　　　[f] *Od.* ix. 222.

[g] Frag. 2 Hiller ; *cf.* Athen. 424 f (vol. iv. p. 424).

[h] *i.e.* imitating the shape of the earlier wooden *skyphoi*.

ται. ἔχουσι μέντοι πρὸς τοὺς ἄλλους διαφοράν·
ἔπεστι γὰρ ἐπὶ τῶν ὤτων αὐτοῖς ὁ λεγόμενος
Ἡράκλειος δεσμός. μνημονεύει δὲ τῶν Βοιωτίων
σκύφων Βακχυλίδης ἐν τούτοις ποιούμενος τὸν
b λόγον πρὸς τοὺς Διοσκόρους, καλῶν αὐτοὺς ἐπὶ
ξένια·

> οὐ βοῶν πάρεστι σώματ' οὔτε χρυσὸς οὔτε πορ-
> φύρεοι τάπητες, ἀλλὰ θυμὸς εὐμενὴς
> Μοῦσά τε γλυκεῖα καὶ Βοιωτίοισιν ἐν σκύφοισιν
> οἶνος ἡδύς.

διήνεγκαν δὲ μετὰ τοὺς Βοιωτίους οἱ Ῥοδιακοὶ
λεγόμενοι Δαμοκράτους δημιουργήσαντος. τρίτοι
δ' εἰσὶν οἱ Συρακόσιοι. καλεῖται δ' ὁ σκύφος ὑπὸ
Ἠπειρωτῶν, ὥς φησι Σέλευκος, γυρτός,[1] ὑπὸ δὲ
Μηθυμναίων, ὡς Παρμένων[3] φησὶν ἐν τῷ περὶ
c Διαλέκτου, σκύθος. ἐκαλεῖτο δὲ καὶ Δερκυλίδας[4]
ὁ Λακεδαιμόνιος Σκύφος,[5] ὥς φησιν Ἔφορος ἐν
τῇ ὀκτωκαιδεκάτῃ λέγων οὕτως· " Λακεδαιμόνιοι
ἀντὶ Θίμβρωνος Δερκυλίδαν[4] ἔπεμψαν εἰς τὴν
Ἀσίαν, ἀκούοντες ὅτι πάντα πράττειν εἰώθασιν οἱ
περὶ τὴν Ἀσίαν βάρβαροι μετὰ ἀπάτης καὶ δόλου.
διόπερ Δερκυλίδαν ἔπεμψαν ἥκιστα νομίζοντες
ἐξαπατηθήσεσθαι· ἦν γὰρ οὐδὲν ἐν τῷ τρόπῳ
Λακωνικὸν οὐδ' ἁπλοῦν ἔχων, ἀλλὰ πολὺ τὸ

---

[1] Kaibel: βοιωτικῶν A.
[2] Kaibel (?) cf. Hesychius s. γυρτόν: λυρτὸς AC.
[3] Παρμενίων ? cf. Schol. Il. i. 591.
[4] δερκυλλίδας, δερκυλλίδαν AC.
[5] Σίσυφος Xen. Hellen. iii. 1. 8, σκύθος C.

---

^a For the adjective " Heracleotic," apparently used of

" Heracleotic[a] bowls " by some. Nevertheless when compared with other *skyphoi* they show a difference ; for upon their handles there is the so-called Heraclean chain. The Boeotian *skyphoi* are mentioned by Bacchylides in the following lines, in which he addresses the Dioscuri and invites them to a feast[b] : " No carcasses of oxen are there, nor gold, nor purple carpets, but a kindly heart, and a sweet Muse, and pleasant wine in Boeotian cups (*skyphoi*)." Next after the Boeotian, the Rhodian cups, so-called, were celebrated ; Damocrates was the artist who made them. Third come the Syracusan. The *skyphos* is called by the people of Epeirus *gyrtos*, according to Seleucus ; but by the people of Methymna, as Parmenon says in his book *On Dialect*, it is called *skythos*.[c] Further, the Spartan Dercylidas was called Skyphos,[d] according to Ephorus in the eighteenth book, speaking as follows[e] : " The Lacedaemonians sent Dercylidas into Asia to replace Thimbron,[f] hearing that the barbarians of Asia are accustomed to transact all business with deceit and cunning. Hence they sent Dercylidas, because they thought that he was least likely to be hoodwinked ; for he was a man that had nothing in his character either Laconian or forthright, but on the contrary

anything very large, *cf.* Athen. 153 c (vol. ii. p. 196) παρα-σκευὴ Ἡρακλεωτική.

[b] *P.L.G.*⁴ iii. 579, Jebb, *Bacchylides* 216, Edmonds frag. 6. For the feasts to the gods called Θεοξένια *cf.* Athen. 82 e, 137 e, 237 e, 252 b, 372 a.

[c] *Cf.* above, 499 f.

[d] This is a very old mistake for " Sisyphus." Xenophon, *Hell.* iii. 1. 8 Δερκυλίδας . . . ἀνὴρ δοκῶν εἶναι μάλα μηχανη-τικός (resourceful)· καὶ ἐπεκαλεῖτο δὲ Σίσυφος. On the ingenious Sisyphus *cf.* the proverbial μηχανὰς τὰς Σισύφου, Aristoph. *Acharn.* 391.

[e] *F.H.G.* i. 271, J. 2 A 63.   [f] More correctly Thibron.

πανοῦργον καὶ τὸ θηριῶδες. διὸ καὶ Σκύφον[1]
αὐτὸν οἱ Λακεδαιμόνιοι προσηγόρευον.''

d ΤΑΒΑΙΤΗ.[2] Ἀμύντας ἐν τῷ πρώτῳ τῶν τῆς Ἀσίας
Σταθμῶν περὶ τοῦ ἀερομέλιτος καλουμένου δια-
λεγόμενος γράφει οὕτως· '' σὺν τοῖς φύλλοις δρέ-
ποντες συντιθέασιν εἰς παλάθης Συριακῆς τρόπον
πλάττοντες, οἱ δὲ σφαίρας ποιοῦντες. καὶ ἐπειδὰν
μέλλωσι προσφέρεσθαι, ἀποκλάσαντες ἀπ' αὐτῶν
ἐν τοῖς ξυλίνοις ποτηρίοις οὓς καλοῦσι ταβαίτας,
προβρέχουσι καὶ διηθήσαντες πίνουσι. καὶ ἔστιν
ὅμοιον ὡς ἂν εἴ[3] τις μέλι πίνοι διείς, τούτου[4] δὲ
καὶ πολὺ ἥδιον.''

ΤΡΑΓΕΛΑΦΟΣ. οὕτω τινὰ καλεῖται ποτήρια ὧν
e μνημονεύει Ἄλεξις μὲν ἐν Κονιατῇ[5]·

κυμβία,
φιάλαι, τραγέλαφοι, κύλικες.

Εὔβουλος δ' ἐν Κατακολλωμένῳ[6]·

ἀλλ' εἰσὶ φιάλαι πέντε, τραγέλαφοι δύο.

Μένανδρος δ' ἐν Ἁλιεῖ φησι·

τραγέλαφοι, λαβρώνιοι.

Ἀντιφάνης Χρυσίδι·

. . σαπροπλούτῳ[7] δ', ὡς λέγουσι, νυμφίῳ,
κεκτημένῳ τάλαντα, παῖδας, ἐπιτρόπους,
ζεύγη, καμήλους, στρώματ', ἀργυρώματα,
φιάλας, τριήρεις, τραγελάφους, καρχήσια,

---

[1] σκύφον AC.
[2] ταβαίτη CE: ταβαίτας after erasure A.
[3] εἴ added by Kaibel.   [4] Meineke: τοῦτο A.
[5] κονιάτηι A.
[6] Schweighäuser: μετακολλωμένωι A.
[7] σαπροπλούτωι A: τῷ σατραποπλούτῳ Dobree.

236

much that was rascally and brutal. Hence, also, the Lacedaemonians called him Skyphos."

Tabaitê. Amyntas in the first book of his *Itinerary in Asia,* discoursing on the so-called oak-manna, writes as follows [a] : " They gather it, leaves and all, and press it in a mass, moulding it like a Syrian cake of fruit, or in some cases making balls of it. And when they are about to eat it, they break off portions from the mass into wooden cups which they call *tabaitai,* and after first soaking it and straining it off they drink (the syrup). And it is as if one soaked honey (in wine) and drank it, but very much pleasanter than that."

Tragelaphos.[b] Thus are called certain cups which Alexis mentions in *The Plasterer*[c] : " Sauce-boats, saucers, *tragelaphoi,* cylices." And Eubulus in *Glued Together*[d] : " But we've got five saucers, two *tragelaphoi.*" And Menander says in *The Fisherman*[e] : ' Goat-stags (*tragelaphoi*) and *labronioi.*" Antiphanes in *Chrysis*[f] : " A. The bridegroom, stinking-rich as the saying is, has money by the ton, slaves, stewards, teams, camels, rugs, silver ware, saucers, triremes,[g]

---

[a] Müller p. 135, J. 2 B 627 ; *cf.* Athen. 442 b (vol. iv. p. 502). Oak-manna is a sweet substance (honey-dew) which exudes from the leaves of certain oaks. Galen vi. 739 (Kühn) gives also the name δροσόμελι.
[b] " Goat-stag," a word often used of fantastic animals in art, Aristoph. *Ran.* 937, Plat. *Rep.* 488 A, above, 497 f (p. 221 and note *e*).
[c] Kock ii. 333. [d] *Ibid.* 180.
[e] Kock iii. 10, Allinson 316, Athen. 484 d (p. 151 and note *a*).
[f] Kock ii. 110 ; for the title see Athen. 172 c (vol. ii. p. 283 note *b*).
[g] *i.e.* cups, p. 238.

f γαυλοὺς ὁλοχρύσους. Β. πλοῖα; Α. τοὺς κάδους
    μὲν οὖν

καλοῦσι γαυλοὺς πάντες οἱ[1] προγάστορες.

ΤΡΙΗΡΗΣ. ὅτι καὶ τριήρης εἶδος ἐκπώματος Ἐπί-
νικος[2] ἐν Ὑποβαλλομέναις δεδήλωκε. προείρηται
δὲ τὸ μαρτύριον.

ΥΣΤΙΑΚΟΝ.[3] ποτήριον ποιόν, Ῥίνθων ἐν Ἡρακλεῖ·

ἐν ὑστιακῷ τε καθαρὸν ἐλατῆρα σὺ[4]
καθαρῶν τ' ἀλήτων κἀλφίτων ἀπερρόφεις.

ΦΙΑΛΗ. Ὅμηρος μὲν ὅταν λέγῃ·

ἀμφίθετον φιάλην ἀπύρωτον ἔθηκε

501 καὶ " χρυσῆν φιάλην καὶ διπλάκα δημόν," οὐ τὸ
ποτήριον λέγει, ἀλλὰ χαλκίον τι[5] ἐκπέταλον λεβητῶδες, ἴσως δύο δύο ὦτα ἔχον ἐξ ἀμφοτέρων τῶν
μερῶν. Παρθένιος δ' ὁ τοῦ Διονυσίου ἀμφίθετον
ἀκούει τὴν ἀπύθμενον φιάλην. Ἀπολλόδωρος δ'
ὁ Ἀθηναῖος ἐν τῷ περὶ τοῦ Κρατῆρος ῥησειδίῳ[6]
τὴν κατὰ τὸν πυθμένα μὴ δυναμένην τίθεσθαι καὶ
ἐρείδεσθαι, ἀλλὰ κατὰ τὸ στόμα. τινὲς δέ φασιν,
ὃν τρόπον ἀμφιφορεὺς λέγεται ὁ ἀμφοτέρωθεν
κατὰ τὰ ὦτα δυνάμενος φέρεσθαι, οὕτως καὶ τὴν

---

    [1] ὡς Kock, εἰ Herwerden.   [2] Musurus: εὔνικος A.
    [3] ὑαστικόν C, ὑστιακκός Hesychius.
    [4] σὺ added by Wilamowitz; but the verse is still incomplete.
Sc. διείς?   [5] χάλκεόν τι AC: καὶ after τι in A, om. CE.
    [6] Heyne: ῥησειδίου A.   Kaibel's doubt is not warranted.

---

    [a] Above, 474 e (pp. 94 ff.).
    [b] Hesych. s. γαυλοί· καὶ τὰ Φοινικικὰ πλοῖα γαῦλοι καλοῦνται.
So the κάνθαρος (" schooner ") and the ἄκατος meant both
cup and boat, 474 c (p. 94), 502 a (p. 244).
    [c] 497 b (p. 216); so Antiphanes, p. 237.
    [d] Kaibel 185. Hesychius s. ὑστιακκός says it was in use
among the Greeks of Italy.

goat-stags, *carchesia*,[a] and pails of solid gold. B. Do you mean boats[b]? A. No; for all the pot-bellied gentry call wine-jars pails."

Trireme. That trireme also is a kind of drinking-cup is shown by Epinicus in *Child-foisting Wives.* The testimony has been cited above.[c]

Hystiakon.—A sort of cup, Rhinthon in *Heracles*[d]: " And in a cup (*hystiakon*) you were soaking a white bun,[e] and gobbling up white meal and barley crumbs."

Phialê. When Homer says,[f] " He set as a prize an *amphithetos phialê* untouched by fire," and again,[g] " A golden *phialê* and double-folded fat," he is not speaking of the cup known as *phialê*, but of a flat, basin-like vessel of bronze, probably having two handles extending from both sides.[h] But Parthenius, the disciple of Dionysius, understands by *amphithetos* the vessel that has no stem. Similarly, Apollodorus of Athens in his little speech *On the Mixing-bowl*[i] says that it is the vessel that cannot be set up and supported firmly on its stem, but only on its brim. Some, on the other hand, declare that just as the vessel that can be carried by its handles on both sides is called an *amphiphoreus*,[j] so also the *amphithetos* vessel gets its

---

[e] Aristoph. *Acharn.* 245 ὦ μῆτερ, ἀνάδος δεῦρο τὴν ἐτνήρυσιν (ladle), ἵν' ἔτνος (broth) καταχέω τοὐλατῆρος τουτουί, on which the Scholiast says: " the ἐλατήρ is a broad flat cake." Kaibel thinks the verses from Rhinthon are addressed to Heracles, in reproach for his gluttony.

[f] *Il.* xxiii. 270. The expression here means " two-handled pot," but since *phialê* later meant a flat cup, like a saucer, the word became the subject of much debate, as the text shows; *cf.* 468 d.

[g] *Il.* xxiii. 243 καὶ τὰ μὲν (the ashes of Patroclus) ἐν χρυσέῃ φιάλῃ καὶ δίπλακι δημῷ θείομεν.   [h] *Cf.* above, 475 e, p. 100.

[i] A " bagatelle speech," such as Lysias's *Cruet-stand.* See P.-W. i. 2872.   [j] Later form *amphoreus*, Lat. *amphora.*

239

b ἀμφίθετον φιάλην. Ἀρίσταρχος δὲ τὴν δυναμένην
ἐξ ἀμφοτέρων τῶν μερῶν τίθεσθαι, κατὰ τὸν πυθμένα καὶ κατὰ τὸ στόμα. Διονύσιος δ' ὁ Θρᾶξ
τὴν στρογγύλην, τὴν ἀμφιθέουσαν κυκλοτερεῖ τῷ
σχήματι. Ἀσκληπιάδης δ' ὁ Μυρλεανὸς " ἡ μὲν
φιάλη," φησί, " κατ' ἀντιστοιχίαν ἐστὶ πιάλη, ἡ τὸ
πιεῖν ἅλις¹ παρέχουσα²· μείζων γὰρ τοῦ ποτηρίου.
ἡ δὲ ἀμφίθετος καὶ³ ἀπύρωτος· ἡ ψυχρήλατος ἢ
c ἐπὶ πῦρ οὐκ ἐπιτιθεμένη, καθότι καὶ λέβητα καλεῖ
ὁ ποιητὴς τὸν μὲν ἐμπυριβήτην, τὸν δὲ ἄπυρον⁵·

    κὰδ δὲ λέβητ' ἄπυρον βοὸς ἄξιον ἀνθεμόεντα,

τὸν δεχόμενον ἴσως ὕδωρ ψυχρόν, ὥστε καὶ τὴν
φιάλην εἶναι χαλκίῳ⁶ προσεοικυῖαν ἐκπετάλῳ
δεχομένην ψυχρὸν ὕδωρ. τὴν δ' ἀμφίθετον πότερα
δύο βάσεις ἔχειν δεῖ νομίζειν ἐξ ἑκατέρου μέρους
ἢ τὸ μὲν ἀμφὶ σημαίνει τὸ περί, τοῦτο δ' αὖ τι
περιττόν; ὥστε λέγεσθαι τὴν περιττῶς πεποιημένην ἀμφίθετον, ἐπεὶ τὸ ποιῆσαι θεῖναι πρὸς τῶν
d ἀρχαίων ἐλέγετο. δύναται δὲ καὶ ἡ ἐπὶ τὸν
πυθμένα καὶ τὸ στόμα τιθεμένη· ἡ δὲ τοιαύτη θέσις
τῶν φιαλῶν Ἰωνική ἐστι καὶ ἀρχαία. ἔτι γοῦν
καὶ νῦν οὕτως Μασσαλιῆται⁷ τιθέασι τὰς φιάλας
ἐπὶ πρόσωπον."

---

¹ ἅλις corrected from ἅλες CE: ἅλες A.
² παρέχουσα Kaibel, Etym. Mag. 793. 21: ἔχουσα ACE.
³ Schweighäuser deleted ἀμφίθετος καί; but the colon in A
shows that the colon in A shows that αμφίθετος καὶ ἀπύρωτος constitute the lemma, the
latter epithet being explained first.
⁴ Casaubon (cf. Eustath. 1300. 2): ἡ ACE.
⁵ CE: ἐν πυρὶ βήτην, τὸν δὲ ἀπύρωτον A.
⁶ χαλκείῳ ACE.   ⁷ μασσαλιῶται CE.

ᵃ i.e. it is set in place or lifted by handles on both sides.

name.[a] But Aristarchus explains that it means the vessel which can be set down on both sides, on the base or on the brim. Again, Dionysius of Thrace says that it simply means "round," the vessel that runs round (*amphitheousa*) in a circular shape. Asclepiades of Myrlea derives the word *phialê*, by the substitution of a letter, from *pialê*, *i.e.* the vessel that supplies "drink (*piein*) in plenty (*halis*)"; for it was larger than the cup.[b] Now as to the terms *amphithetos* and *apyrotos*: the latter is equivalent to "cold-forged,"[c] or "never put on the fire," just as the Poet calls a cauldron in one case "made to stand on the fire," in another case "unfired"[d]: "And among them (he set) a cauldron unfired, worth an ox, and embossed with flowers"—meaning perhaps a receptacle for cold water; wherefore the *phialê* also is like a flat vessel of bronze, containing cold water. Then as to the adjective *amphithetos*, are we to imagine that it means "having two bases," one at each end, or does the prefix *amphi* signify the same as *peri*, which in turn means "extraordinary"[e]? On this latter theory any vessel exquisitely made would be said to be *amphithetos*, since the verb *theinai*[f] was used for *poiêsai*[g] by the ancients. But it can also mean "the vessel that is set both on its stem and on its brim"; and this mode of setting the *phialai* is Ionic and ancient. At any rate the people of Massilia to this very day place the *phialai* face down.

---

[b] *i.e.* Homer's *phialê* was larger than the cup so called.
[c] Plutarch 434 A uses ψυχρήλατος of Euboean ironwork.
[d] *Il.* xxiii. 885, of the prize offered by Achilles for javelin-throwing.
[e] "Over" or "beyond the ordinary," "remarkable," "exquisite."   [f] Implied in *-thetos*
[g] "Make," so that *-thetos* equals *-poiêtos*, "made."

Κρατίνου δ' εἰπόντος ἐν Δραπέτισιν·

δέχεσθε φιάλας τάσδε βαλανειομφάλους,[1]

Ἐρατοσθένης ἐν τῷ ἑνδεκάτῳ περὶ Κωμῳδίας τὴν
λέξιν ἀγνοεῖν φησι Λυκόφρονα· τῶν γὰρ φιαλῶν οἱ
ὀμφαλοὶ καὶ τῶν βαλανείων οἱ θόλοι παρόμοιοι·
εἰς δὲ τὸ εἶδος οὐκ ἀρρύθμως παίζονται. Ἀπίων
e δὲ καὶ Διόδωρός φησι· " φιάλαι ποιαί, ὧν ὁ
ὀμφαλὸς παραπλήσιος ἠθμῷ." ὁ δὲ Μυρλεανὸς
Ἀσκληπιάδης ἐν τοῖς περὶ τῆς Νεστορίδος· " αἱ
φιάλαι ὑπὸ[2] Κρατίνου βαλανειόμφαλοι," φησίν,
" λέγονται ὅτι οἱ ὀμφαλοὶ αὐτῶν καὶ τῶν βαλανείων
οἱ θόλοι ὅμοιοί εἰσιν." καὶ Δίδυμος δὲ τὰ αὐτὰ
εἰπὼν παρατίθεται τὰ[3] Λυκόφρονος οὕτως ἔχοντα·
" ἀπὸ τῶν ὀμφαλῶν τῶν ἐν ταῖς γυναικείαις
πυέλοις, ὅθεν τοῖς σκαφίοις ἀρύουσιν.[4]" Τίμαρχος
δ' ἐν τετάρτῳ περὶ τοῦ Ἐρατοσθένους Ἑρμοῦ
" πεπαῖχθαί τις ἂν οἰηθείη," φησί, " τὴν λέξιν, διότι
τὰ πλεῖστα τῶν Ἀθήνησι βαλανείων κυκλοειδῆ
ταῖς κατασκευαῖς ὄντα τοὺς ἐξαγωγοὺς ἔχει κατὰ
μέσον, ἐφ' οὗ[5] χαλκοῦς ὀμφαλὸς ἔπεστιν." Ἴων δ'
ἐν Ὀμφάλῃ·

[1] βαλανιομφάλους (*i.e.* βαλανωτούς) Kaibel.
[2] περὶ τῆς . . . ὑπὸ Kaibel: περὶ κρατίνου A.
[3] τὰ added by Toup.
[4] Casaubon: ἀροῦσιν A.
[5] Musurus: ἀφ' οὗ ACE, ὅθι Eustath. 1261. 24, οὗ "where" Kaibel.

---

[a] Kock i. 27.
[b] "With acorn-bosses" was the meaning intended by
Cratinus (see critical note 1). But the following discussion

Cratinus says in *Runaway Girls* [a] : " Receive these cups (*phialai*) with their acorn-bosses. [b] " On this Eratosthenes in the eleventh book of his work *On Comedy* asserts [c] that Lycophron is ignorant of the meaning of the word ; for the bosses on the *phialai* and the domed chambers [d] of the public baths are much alike ; hence the joke on the shape is not without point. Apion and Diodorus both say : " A certain kind of *phialai*, the boss of which is rather like (the plug of) a drain." And Asclepiades of Myrlea, in his remarks *On Nestor's Cup*, says that the *phialai* are called " bath-bossed " by Cratinus because their bosses and the *tholoi* [e] of public baths are similar. And Didymus, though he also says [f] the same, quotes the comment of Lycophron to the following tenor [g] : " Derived from the plugs used in women's bath-tubs ; it is there that they draw off the water by means of small bowls." Timarchus, too, in the fourth book *On the Hermes of Eratosthenes*,[h] remarks : " One may regard the word as spoken in jest,[i] because most of the baths at Athens are built in rotunda form and have their drain-pipes in the centre, on top of which is set a plug of bronze." Ion in shows that there was a pun connecting βαλανεῖον "bath " with βάλανος " acorn " ; hence the reading in the text, with the explanation of Eratosthenes. The writer now turns from the Homeric *phialé* (basin) to the saucer-shaped drinking-cup with its characteristic boss.

[c] Frag. 25 Strecker.
[d] This meaning is given in L. & S. (ed. 1930). But it also meant a plug or valve in the water-pipes, see below.
[e] Either plugs or domed chambers.
[f] Schmidt, p. 42.   [g] Frag. 25 Strecker.
[h] Strecker thinks the commentary embraced all of Eratosthenes' works.
[i] Glancing, as it does, at βάλανος " acorn " and βαλανεῖον " bath," with ὀμφαλός or θόλος as the key to both.

ἴτ᾽ ἐκφορεῖτε, παρθένοι,
κύπελλα καὶ μεσομφάλους.

οὕτω δ᾽ εἴρηκε τὰς βαλανειομφάλους, ὧν Κρατῖνος
μνημονεύει·

δέχεσθε φιάλας τάσδε βαλανειομφάλους.

καὶ Θεόπομπος δ᾽ ἐν Ἀλθαίᾳ[1] ἔφη·

502 λαβοῦσα πλήρη χρυσέαν[2] μεσόμφαλον
φιάλην. Τελέστης[3] δ᾽ ἄκατον ὠνόμαζέ νιν,[4]

ὡς τοῦ Τελέστου ἄκατον[5] τὴν φιάλην εἰρηκότος.[6]
Φερεκράτης δὲ ἢ ὁ πεποιηκὼς τοὺς εἰς αὐτὸν
ἀναφερομένους Πέρσας φησί·

στεφάνους τε πᾶσι κὠμφαλωτὰς χρυσίδας.

Ἀθηναῖοι δὲ τὰς μὲν ἀργυρᾶς φιάλας ἀργυρίδας
λέγουσι, χρυσίδας δὲ τὰς χρυσᾶς. τῆς δὲ ἀργυρίδος[7] Φερεκράτης μὲν ἐν Πέρσαις οὕτως μνημο-
b νεύει·

οὗτος σύ, ποῖ τὴν ἀργυρίδα τηνδὶ φέρεις;

χρυσίδος δὲ Κρατῖνος ἐν Νόμοις·

χρυσίδι σπένδων γέγωνε[8] τοῖς ὄφεσι πιεῖν διδούς·

καὶ Ἕρμιππος ἐν Κέρκωψι·

χρυσίδ᾽ οἴνου πανσέληνον[9] ἐκπιὼν ὑφείλετο.

---

[1] Schweighäuser: ἀλθαι A.
[2] Pierson: χρυσέων A.   [3] τελεστὴς A.
[4] ἄκατον . . . νιν Porson: ἄκρατον ὠνόμαξεν ἴν᾽ A.
[5] ἄκατον with ρ written above A.
[6] ὡς . . . εἰρηκότος have been suspected, and Schweighäuse[r]
thought that the quotation ended in μεσόμφαλον. Suppl[.]
παίζων, referring to Θεόπομπος.
[7] φιάλης after ἀργυρίδος deleted by Meineke.
[8] Capps: γέγραφε A.
[9] πανσελήνοις Meineke, Πεντελῆσιν Kock.

Omphalê[a] : " Go, ye maidens, carry forth the cups and the bossed centres." By this he meant the acorn-bossed *phialai* which Cratinus mentions [b] : " Receive these cups with their acorn-bosses." And Theopompus also said in *Althaea*[c] : " She took a golden *phialê*, filled, and bossed in the middle. But Telestes called it a pinnace," wherein Theopompus ridicules Telestes for calling the *phialê* a pinnace. And Pherecrates, or whoever has written *The Persians* ascribed to him, says [d] : " Wreaths for all, and bossed *phialai* of gold." Now the Athenians speak of silver *phialai* as *argyrides*, golden *phialai* as *chrysides*.[e] The *argyris* is mentioned by Pherecrates in *The Persians* thus [f] : " Here, you ! Where are you carrying that *argyris* to ? " Whereas the *chrysis* is mentioned by Cratinus in *The Laws*[g] : " Pouring a libation from a *chrysis*, he called out loudly to the snakes as he offered it to them to drink." So Hermippus in *The Cercopes*[h] : ' A *chrysis* of wine shining like the full moon he drank

---

[a] *T.G.F.*[2] 735.   [b] Above, 501 d.
[c] Kock i. 734; on ἄκατος see above, 500 f (p. 238 note *b*), and Bekker, *Anec.* 371. 5 ἄκατος· φιάλη, διὰ τὸ ἐοικέναι στρογγύλῳ πλοίῳ (" round-bottomed boat ")· οὕτω Θεόπομπος. For Telestes of Selinus, lyric poet, see *P.L.G.*[4] iii. 627, Diehl ii. 155, Edmonds iii. 278, Athen. 616 f, 617 b, 625 f, 637 a.
[d] Kock i. 182. Compare the report of the Envoy in Aristoph. *Acharn.* 73 ἐπινόμην ἐξ ὑαλίνων (glass) ἐκπωμάτων καὶ χρυσίδων (Kock). But the scene may also have been like that in Aristoph. *Ran.* 504 ff.
[e] *Cf.* above, 496 e (p. 214).   [f] Kock i. 182.
[g] *Ibid.* 52, cf. Athen. 496 e (p. 214). *Cf.* Aristoph. *Plut.* 732 ὁ θεὸς (Asclepius) ἐπόππυσεν (called with a smacking noise). ἐξῃξάτην οὖν δύο δράκοντ' ἐκ τοῦ νεώ (" two snakes darted out from the shrine "). I owe this interpretation, with the correction of the unmetrical γέγραφε, to Professor Capps On snakes and the art of healing see Brock's Galen (L.C.L.) *Introd.*   [h] Kock i. 234. See critical note 8.

καὶ ὅ γε ἐ . . .¹ ἐκαλεῖτο δέ τις καὶ βαλανωτ
φιάλη, ἧς τῷ πυθμένι χρυσοῖ ὑπέκειντο ἀστρά
γαλοι. Σῆμος δ' ἐν Δήλῳ ἀνακεῖσθαί φησι χαλ
κοῦν φοίνικα, Ναξίων ἀνάθημα, καὶ καρυωτὰ
φιάλας χρυσᾶς. Ἀναξανδρίδης δὲ φιάλας Ἄρεο
καλεῖ τὰ ποτήρια ταῦτα. Αἰολεῖς δὲ τὴν φιάλη
ἀράκην² καλοῦσι.

ΦΘΟΙΣ. πλατεῖαι φιάλαι ὀμφαλωτοί. Εὔπολι
" σὺν φθοῖσι προσπεπτωκώς.³ " ἔδει δὲ ὀξύνεσθα
ὡς Καρσί, παισί, φθειρσί.

ΦΙΛΟΤΗΣΙΑ. κύλιξ τις ἦν κατὰ φιλίαν προὔπινο
ὥς φησι Πάμφιλος. Δημοσθένης δέ φησι· " κα
φιλοτησίας⁴ προὔπινεν." Ἄλεξις·

> φιλοτησίαν σοι τήνδ' ἐγὼ
> ἰδίᾳ τε καὶ κοινῇ κύλικα προπίομαι.⁵

ἐκαλεῖτο δὲ καὶ τὸ ἑταιρικὸν συνευωχούμενο
φιλοτήσιον. Ἀριστοφάνης·

---

¹ These words close the second column of folio 239 vers
in A. An entire leaf is then missing. The text from thi
point to 502 b (see below, p. 248 critical note 3) is that of CE
² ἀρακὶν CE. Cf. Hesych. ἀράη (now read as ἀράκην) anc
ἐξ ἀρακάων· ἐκ φιαλῶν.
³ σὺν φθοῖσι προσπεπτωκώς CE: προπεπωκώς Casaubon
⟨Πόλε⟩σιν (" in *Island-cities* ") φθοῖσι προπεπωκὼς Kock.
⁴ Demosth.: φιλοτησίαν CE.
⁵ προπίομαι Schweighäuser: προπίνομεν C.

ᵃ See critical note 1.
ᵇ Ornamented with acorns, an epithet scarcely accountec
for by the explanation given in the relative clause. Pollu:
vi. 98 shows that the original text was quite different. He
has μεσόμφαλοι δὲ φιάλαι καὶ βαλανειόμφαλοι τὸ σχῆμα προσ
ηγορίαν ἔχουσι (" are so named from their shape "), χρυσόμφαλα

ut and stole." And he at least. . . ."[a] There was
also a *phialê* called *balanotê*,[b] under the bottom of
which were set knobs of gold. And Semus says[c]
that in Delos there is dedicated a bronze palm-tree,
a votive offering of the Naxians, and golden *phialai*
adorned with dates.[d] Anaxandrides calls[e] these
cups " saucers of Ares." The Aeolians call the
phialê an *arakê*.

Phthois. Flat saucers with bosses. Eupolis[f] :
" Lying prostrate, saucers (*phthoîsi*) and all." But
the word ought to have the acute accent on the last
syllable, like *Karsi, paisi, phtheirsi.*[g]

Philotesia.—A kind of cylix which they pledged in
the way of friendship, as Pamphilus explains. And
Demosthenes says[h] : " And he pledged him loving-
cups." Alexis[i] : "This cup of kindness will I
pledge you separately and together." So also any
company feasting together was called a *philotesion*.

ἐ τὴν ὕλην (" from the material of which they were named ")
ς αἱ Σαπφοῦς χρυσαστράγαλοι (" with knobs of gold ").
[c] *F.H.G.* iv. 495.
[d] Or walnuts (L. & S., 1930). But the context here seems
to point to the meaning " date." See *I.G.* 11 (2). 161 B 30.
[e] Kock ii. 164, Athen. 433 d (vol. iv. p. 462). The truth
seems to be that Timotheüs called Nestor's shield (not his
cup) the saucer of Ares.
[f] Kock i. 357. Text and meaning are uncertain; φθοῖς
properly were round cakes, Athen. 489 d (p. 176), with a
bossed top, like some forms of brioches; Polybius vi. 25. 7
τοῖς ὀμφαλωτοῖς ποπάνοις.
[g] Dative plurals signifying " Carians," " children," " lice."
[h] *De falsa Legat.* 128 : the subject is Aeschines, congratu-
lating Philip on his victories. Again we have a name that
is general, like " cup of kindness," *cf.* Athen. 85 b, used
ironically (vol. i. p. 366). With φιλοτησία, an adjective,
understand κύλιξ, " cup."
[i] Kock ii. 402, *cf.* Athen. 431 a (vol. iv. p. 452).

ἐπτάπους γοῦν ἡ σκιά 'στιν
ἡ 'πὶ τὸ δεῖπνον· ὡς ἤδη καλεῖ μ᾿[1]
ὁ χορὸς[2] ὁ φιλοτήσιος.

διὰ δὲ τὴν τοιαύτην πρόποσιν ἐκαλεῖτο καὶ κύλιξ
φιλοτησία, ὡς ἐν Λυσιστράτῃ·

δέσποινα Πειθοῖ καὶ κύλιξ φιλοτησία.

ΧΟΝΝΟΙ. παρὰ Γορτυνίοις ποτηρίου εἶδος, ὅμοιον
Θηρικλείῳ, χάλκεον· ὃ δίδοσθαι τῷ ἁρπασθέντι ὑπὸ
τοῦ ἐραστοῦ φησιν Ἑρμῶναξ.

ΧΑΛΚΙΔΙΚΑ ποτήρια· ἴσως ἀπὸ τῆς Χαλκίδος τῆς
Θρακικῆς εὐδοκιμοῦντα.

ΧΥΤΡΙΔΕΣ. Ἄλεξις ἐν Ὑποβολιμαίῳ[3]·

ἐγὼ Πτολεμαίου τοῦ βασιλέως τέτταρα
χυτρίδι᾿ ἀκράτου[4] τῆς τ᾿ ἀδελφῆς προσλαβὼν
τῆς τοῦ βασιλέως ταῦτ᾿,[5] ἀπνευστί τ᾿[6] ἐκπιὼν
ὡς ἄν τις ἥδιστ᾿ ἴσον ἴσῳ κεκραμένον,
c   καὶ τῆς Ὁμονοίας, διὰ τί[7] νῦν μὴ κωμάσω
ἄνευ λυχνούχου[8] πρὸς τὸ τηλικοῦτο[8] φῶς ;

Ἡρόδοτος δ᾿ ἐν τῇ πέμπτῃ τῶν Ἱστοριῶν νόμον

[1] A corrupt line, here given as written and punctuated
in C.   [2] Casaubon: χρόος C, χρό⁰ E, καιρὸς Nauck.
[3] With βολιμαίῳ fol. 240 recto, col. 1, begins in A. CE have
χυτρίδες· ἄλεξις. ἐν Ὑπο- added by Casaubon (cf. Athen.
431 b).   See critical note 1 on 502 b (p. 246).
[4] C: χυτρίδια ἀκράτου A.
[5] ταῦτ᾿ Kaibel: ταυτ᾿ A (no accent).
[6] 431 b: ἐκπνευστ᾿ A.   [7] διὰ τί AC: δύο, τί Meineke.
[8] Porson: λύχνου and τηλικοῦτον ACE.

[a] Kock i. 557.
[b] An early hour for dinner; when the shadow of the
gnomon (dial) extended six feet, it marked the time for the
bath, ten feet marked the time (usually) for dinner, Aristoph.
Eccles. 652, Athen. 8 c (vol. i. p. 34).

Aristophanes *a* : " The shadow, at any rate, that
bids to the dinner, stands at seven feet *b* ; (I must go,)
or already the band of friendship calls me." And
because of this kind of pledging there was a cylix
called the cup of friendship, as in *Lysistrata c* : " May
our Lady Persuasion and the cup of friendship . . ."

Chonnoi. Among the people of Gortyna a kind of
cup, similar to a *Therikleios*, made of bronze ; this is
given to the boy who has been carried off by his lover,
according to Hermonax.*d*

Chalcidic Cups. Perhaps so called from Chalcis in
Thrace. They are celebrated.*e*

Chytrides. Alexis in *Supposititious f* : " Now that
have drunk in honour of King Ptolemy four pots
(*chytridia*) of neat wine and as many again for the
king's sister, and have drained them without stopping
to take breath—mixed to the sweetest a man can
have, half and half—and another in honour of the
Concord too—why should I not now go revelling
without a lamp in view of a light so brilliant ? "

Herodotus in the fifth book of his *Histories* says *g* that

c Aristoph. *Lys.* 203 ; Lysistrata prays for acceptance of
the women's sacrifice.

d See above, 782 c (p. 42) ; for the *Thericleios*, 470 e
(pp. 74 ff.).

e *Cf.* Cleon in Aristoph. *Eq.* 237, denouncing contraband
wares : τουτὶ τί δρᾷ τὸ Χαλκιδικὸν ποτήριον; οὐκ ἔσθ᾽ ὅπως οὐ
Χαλκιδέας ἀφίσταται.

f Kock ii. 386, Athen. 431 b (vol. iv. p. 454). The words
Ὁμόνοια and φῶς refer to the general harmony which ensued
on the death of Pyrrhus?) 272-270. Ptolemy Philadelphus
and his sister-wife Arsinoë are the royalties mentioned.
Alexis lived to be 106 years old ; see Capps, *Am. J. Phil.*
xxi. (1900) 59.

g Chap. 88. The prohibition against imports from Attica
resulted from a long-standing quarrel, *cf.* Herod. v. 82 ff.

φησὶ θέσθαι Ἀργείους καὶ Αἰγινήτας Ἀττικοι
μηδὲν προσφέρειν πρὸς τὰς θυσίας μηδὲ κέραμον,[1]
ἀλλ' ἐκ χυτρίδων ἐπιχωρίων τὸ λοιπὸν αὐτόθι
εἶναι πίνειν. καὶ Μελέαγρος δ' ὁ κυνικὸς ἐν τῷ
Συμποσίῳ οὑτωσὶ γράφει· " κἂν τοσούτῳ πρόποσιν
αὐτῷ βαρεῖαν διέδωκε, χυτρίδια βαθέα δώδεκα."

d ΨΥΓΕΥΣ ἢ ΨΥΚΤΗΡ. Πλάτων Συμποσίῳ[2]· " ἀλλὰ
φέρε, παῖ, φάναι, τὸν ψυκτῆρα ἐκεῖνον, ἰδόντα
αὐτὸν πλέον ἢ ὀκτὼ κοτύλας χωροῦντα. τοῦτον
οὖν ἐμπλησάμενον πρῶτον μὲν αὐτὸν ἐκπιεῖν
ἔπειτα τῷ Σωκράτει κελεύειν ἐγχεῖν." . .
" παραμηκύνειν ἐγχειροῦντος τοῦ Ἀρχεβούλου
εὐκαιρότατα προχέων ὁ παῖς τοῦ οἰναρίου ἀνα
τρέπει τὸν ψυκτῆρα." Ἄλεξις ἐν Εἰσοικιζομένῳ
φησὶ " τρικότυλον ψυγέα." Διώξιππος Φιλαργύρῳ
          παρ' Ὀλυμπίχου δὲ Θηρικλείους ἔλαβεν ἕξ,
          ἔπειτα τοὺς δύο ψυγέας.[4]

e Μένανδρος δ' ἐν τῷ ἐπιγραφομένῳ δράματι Χαλ
κεῖά φησιν·
          τοῦτο δὴ τὸ νῦν ἔθος
" ἄκρατον " ἐβόων, " τὴν μεγάλην." ψυκτῆρά τις
προύπινεν ἂν τοὺς ἀθλίους ἀπολλύων.[5]

---

[1] μήτε τι ἄλλο προσφέρειν πρὸς τὸ ἱρὸν μήτε κέραμον Herod.
[2] ἐν συμποσίῳ C.
[3] Schweighäuser: οἰκιζομένωι A.
[4] Meineke, ἕξ, | ἔπειτα τοὺς δύο ψυκτῆρας Schweighäuser
unmetrically: ἐξιτάτους β' ψυκτῆρας A.
[5] ἂν τοὺς Dobree, ἀπολλύων Bentley: αὐτοὺς . . . ἀπώλ
λυον A.

---

[a] Meleager of Gadara, quoted at 157 b (vol. ii. p. 214)
on Homer.
[b] 213 e; Alcibiades has elected himself to the position o
toast-master.
[c] Two quarts.

he people of Argos and Aegina passed a law that no
article from Attica should be brought to their sacrifices,
not even a piece of crockery, but in future drinking
should be done there from pots (*chytrides*) of local
manufacture. The Cynic Meleager [a] also quotes the
word, writing as follows in his *Symposium*: "The
crisis being so great, he assigned to him a heavy task
of toast-drinking, twelve deep pots (*chytridia*)."

Psygeus or *Psykter*. Plato in his *Symposium* [b]:
"'Rather,' he said, 'bring us, slave, that cooler'—
having spied one that held more than eight *kotylai*. [c]
So he filled this and drank it out first himself, and
then he commanded that it be filled for Socrates." . . .
"When Archebulus [d] undertook to lengthen out (the
drinking-bout), the slave in the very nick of time
spilled some of the beastly wine and upset the cooler."
Alexis in *The New Tenant* says [e]: "A cooler containing three half-pints." Dioxippus in *The Miser* [f]:
"From Olympichus he got six Theracleian cups
and then the two coolers." Menander in the play
entitled *Tinkers' Holiday* says [g]: "That's the custom
nowadays, as you know; they bawled 'Unmixed
wine!' 'The big cup!' And one would offer a
cooler-full for a toast, simply killing the poor devils

[d] The source of this quotation is unknown. The only
Archebulus mentioned in literature was the poet of Thera,
teacher of Euphorion.
[e] Kock ii. 319. For the title, said of one who moves into
a new house, *cf.* Aristoph. *Peace* 260 ἐχθὲς εἰσῳκίσμεθα
"we moved in yesterday."
[f] Kock iii. 359.
[g] *Ibid.* 146, Allinson 456. The Χαλκεῖα was a festival
celebrated on the last day of the autumn month Pyanopsion
in honour of Hephaestus, Harpocr. *s.v.*, *Etym. Mag.* 805. 43.
For τὴν μεγάλην *sc.* κύλικα *cf.* Alexis in Athen. 254 a (vol. iii.
p. 144, 668 f. (vol. vii. p. 82).

Ἐπιγένης δ' ἐν Ἡρωίνῃ καταλέγων πολλὰ ποτήρια
καὶ τοῦ ψυγέως οὕτως μνημονεύει·

τὴν Θηρίκλειον δεῦρο καὶ τὰ Ῥοδιακὰ
κόμισον λαβὼν τοὺς παῖδας. εἶτ' οἴσεις[1] μόνος
ψυκτῆρα, κύαθον, κυμβία.

Στράττις Ψυχασταῖς·

ὁ δέ τις ψυκτῆρ', ὁ δέ τις κύαθον
χαλκοῦν κλέψας. ἀπορῶν κεῖται,
κοτύλῃ[2] δ' ἀνὰ χοίνικα μάττει.[3]

f Ἄλεξις δ' ἐν Ἱππίσκῳ ψυκτηρίδιον καλεῖ διὰ
τούτων·

ἀπήντων τῷ ξένῳ
εἰς τὴν κατάλυσιν οὗ συνῆν Ἀγωνίδι.[4]
τοῖς παισί τ' εἶπα (δύο γὰρ ἦγον οἴκοθεν)
τἀκπώματ'[5] εἰς τὸ φανερὸν ἐκνενιτρωμένα
θεῖναι· κύαθος δ' ἦν ἀργυροῦς (οὗτος μὲν οὖν[6]
ἦγεν δύο δραχμάς), κυμβίον δὲ τέτταρας
503 ἴσως ἑτέρας,[7] ψυκτηρίδιον δὲ[8] δέκ'[9] ὀβολούς,
Φιλιππίδου λεπτότερον.

Ἡρακλέων δὲ ὁ Ἐφέσιος " ὃν ἡμεῖς," φησί
" ψυγέα καλοῦμεν, ψυκτηρίαν τινὲς ὀνομάζουσιν
τοὺς δ' Ἀττικοὺς καὶ κωμῳδεῖν τὸν ψυγέα ὡς
ξενικὸν ὄνομα." Εὔφρων[10] ἐν Ἀποδιδούσῃ·

ἐπὰν δὲ καλέσῃ ψυγέα τὸν[11] ψυκτηρίαν,

---

[1] εἶτ' οἴσεις Meineke : εἰσοίσεις A.
[2] κοτύλῃ Gulick : κοτύλη A. The full stop after κλέψας,
with the consequent interpretation, is due to Capps.
[3] μετρεῖ Capps.
[4] οὗ . . . Ἀγωνίδι Herwerden : ησουην αἴθων ἀνήρ A.
[5] τ' ἐκπώματ' A.   [6] οὗτος . . . οὖν Kaibel : τἀκπώματα A.
[7] ἴσως ἑτέρας added from 230 c.

off." And Epigenes, when giving a long list of cups in *The Glorified Woman*, mentions also the cooler (*psygeus*) in these words [a] : " Take the slave-boys and fetch the Thericleian and the Rhodian cups here. Then you by yourself shall carry a cooler, a ladle, sauce-boats." Strattis in *Keeping Cool* [b] : " Another steals a cooler, still another a bronze ladle. The victim is left wondering what to do, and has to knead (his dough), quart by quart, with a half-pint cup." Alexis in *The Scarf* calls the cooler a *psykteridion* in these lines [c] : " I started to meet the stranger at the lodging-house where I used to stay with Agonis. And I told my slaves (since I had brought two from home) to place the cups, cleaned with soda, for all to see. And there was a ladle of silver (this, to be sure, weighed two drachms), a gravy-dish weighing perhaps four more, and a small cooler weighing one and two-thirds drachms, of metal thinner than Philippides."

Heracleon of Ephesus asserts that " what we call a *psygeus* (cooler) some writers name *psykterias* ; and the Attic comedians even deride the term *psygeus* as being a foreign word." Euphron in *She gave It back* [d] : " A. And when a man calls the cooler

[a] Kock ii. 417, Athen. 469 c (p. 70).
[b] Kock i. 728. The meaning is more than doubtful; for κοτύλη see above, 479 a (p.120). Reading μετρεῖ: " he measures [his flour]," etc.
[c] Kock ii. 297; Athen. 230 b (vol. iii. p. 34) explains the context. Agonis was the mistress of the young man who speaks. See critical note 4.
[d] Kock iii. 320.

---

8 Schweighäuser: τε ACE.
9 δέκ' 230 c: δύο ACE.
10 Meineke: εὐφορίων ACE.
11 Casaubon: τὴν ACE.

τὸ τευτλίον δὲ σεῦτλα,[1] φακέαν τὴν φακῆν,
τί δεῖ ποιεῖν; σὺ[2] γὰρ εἶπον. Β. ὥσπερ χρυσίου
b   φωνῆς ἀπότεισον,[3] Πυργόθεμι, καταλλαγήν.

'Αντιφάνης Ἱππεῦσι·

πῶς οὖν διαιτώμεσθα; Β. τὸ μὲν ἐφίππιον
στρῶμ' ἐστὶν ἡμῖν, ὁ δὲ καλὸς πῖλος[4] κάδος,[5]
ψυκτήρ—τί βούλει;[6]—πάντ'. 'Αμαλθείας κέρας.

ἐν δὲ τῇ Καρίνῃ[7] σαφῶς δηλοῦται ὅτι τούτῳ
ἐχρῶντο οἰνοχοοῦντες κυάθῳ. εἰπὼν γάρ·

τρίποδα καὶ κάδον
παραθέμενος ψυκτῆρά τ' οἴνου . . .
μεθύσκεται,

ἐν τοῖς ἑξῆς ποιεῖ αὐτὸν λέγοντα·

ἔσται πότος[8]
c   σφοδρότερος. οὐκοῦν μὴ κεράσῃ[9] τις, οὐκ ἔτι
ἔξεστι κυαθίζειν παρ' ἡμῖν.[10] παῖ, τρέχε,[11]
τὸν δὲ κάδον ἔξω καὶ τὸ ποτήριον λαβὼν
ἀπόφερε τἆλλα πάντα.

Διονύσιος δὲ ὁ τοῦ Τρύφωνος ἐν τῷ περὶ 'Ονομάτων " τὸν ψυγέα," φησίν, " ἐκάλουν οἱ ἀρχαῖοι
δῖνον." Νίκανδρος δ' ὁ Θυατειρηνὸς καλεῖσθαί
φησι ψυκτῆρας[12] καὶ τοὺς ἀλσώδεις καὶ συσκίους

---

[1] Schweighäuser: τὸ σευτλίον δὲ τεῦτλα ACE.
[2] Schweighäuser: εὖ A.   [3] ἀπότισον A.
[4] πῖλὸς A.   [5] Dobree: καλὸς A.
[6] A: ὅ τι βούλει, Kock.
[7] Fabricius: καρνηι A.   [8] Dobree: πότος ἔσται A
[9] μὴ κεράσῃ Kock: εἰ φράσαι A.
[10] παρ' ἡμῖν Herwerden: γὰρ A.
[11] παῖ, τρέχε added by Kock.
[12] ψυκτήρας CE: ψυκτῆρα A, ψυκτήρια Casaubon needlessly.

---

[a] Cf. Diphilus in Athen. 371 a (vol. iv. p. 180). The

254

psygeus, the beet *seutlon*,[a] lentil-soup *phakea*, what
are we to do? Suppose you tell me. B. Why, pay
him back, Pyrgothemis, with a word of your own, as
if you were exchanging money."[b] Antiphanes in
The Horsemen[c]: " A. But how, then, are we going
to live? B. The saddle-cloth is our blanket, our nice
helmet is our jug, as for a cooler—what would you?
It's everything! We've got a horn of Plenty." And
in *The Carian Wailing-woman* it is clearly shown
that they used the cooler (*psykter*), pouring in
the wine by means of a ladle. For after saying[d]:
" He causes to be placed beside him a tripod and
a jug, also a cooler of wine . . . and then gets
drunk"; in the next lines he makes the drinker
say[e]: " I'm going to have a stronger drink. Therefore let nobody mix the wines; no longer is it permitted, in our house, to ladle water in. Run, then,
slave, and take the jug and the cup out of the room,
and carry away everything else as well." Dionysius,
the disciple of Tryphon, in his *Onomasticon* says:
" The men of old called the cooler (*psygeus*) a *dinos*."[f]
But Nicander of Thyateira says that all grove-like,
shady places dedicated to the gods, in which one may

first speaker is a woman with the high-sounding name
Pyrgothemis, "lording it from the heights," found only here.
For καταλλαγή "exchange" *cf.* Athen. 225 a (vol. iii. p 12).
[b] *i.e.* keep to your own idiom, whatever the critics say.
[c] Kock ii. 54. For Ἀμάλθεια *cf.* above, 497 c (p. 218),
198 a (vol. ii. p. 396); in a transferred sense 542 a (p. 452).
Cicero, *De Fin.* iii. 4. 15, mentions together *ephippia* and
acratophori (= ψυκτῆρες).
[d] Kock ii. 56. For the title see 175 a (vol. ii. p. 295 note b).
[e] Kock ii. 56. I give doubtfully Kock's supplements and
interpretation.
[f] Pollux vi. 98, *cf.* Aristoph. *Nub.* 828, where it means
" vortex."

τόπους τοὺς τοῖς θεοῖς ἀνειμένους, ἐν οἷς ἔστιν
ἀναψῦξαι. Αἰσχύλος Νεανίσκοις·

σαύρας[1] ὑποσκίοισιν ἐν ψυκτηρίοις.[2]

d Εὐριπίδης Φαέθοντι·

ψυκτήρια
δένδρεα[3] φίλαισιν ὠλέναισι δέξεται.[4]

καὶ ὅ[5] τὸν Αἰγίμιον δὲ ποιήσας εἴθ' Ἡσίοδός ἐστιν
ἢ Κέρκωψ ὁ Μιλήσιος·

ἔνθα ποτ' ἔσται ἐμὸν ψυκτήριον, ὄρχαμε λαῶν.

ΩΙΔΟΣ.[6] Οὕτως ἐκαλεῖτο τὸ ποτήριον, φησὶ Τρύ-
φων ἐν τοῖς Ὀνοματικοῖς, τὸ ἐπὶ τῷ σκολιῷ[7]
διδόμενον, ὡς Ἀντιφάνης παρίστησιν ἐν Διπλα-
σίοις·

τί οὖν ἐνέσται τοῖς θεοῖσιν; Β. οὐδὲ ἕν,
e ἂν[8] μὴ κεράσῃ τις. Α. ἴσχε, τὸν ᾠδὸν λάμβανε.
ἔπειτα μηδὲν τῶν ἀπηρχαιωμένων
τούτων περάνῃς, τὸν Τελαμῶνα μηδὲ τὸν
Παιῶνα μηδ' Ἁρμόδιον.

ΩΙΟΣΚΤΦΙΑ. Περὶ τῆς ἰδέας τῶν ποτηρίων Ἀσκληπιάδης ὁ Μυρλεανὸς ἐν τῷ περὶ τῆς Νεστορίδος
φησὶν ὅτι δύο πυθμένας ἔχει, ἕνα μὲν τὸν κατὰ τὸ
κύτος αὐτῷ συγκεχαλκευμένον, ἕτερον δὲ τὸν πρόσ-
f θετον[9] ἀπ' ὀξέος ἀρχόμενον, καταλήγοντα δὲ εἰς
πλατύτερον, ἐφ'[10] οὗ ἵσταται τὸ ποτήριον.

---

[1] αὔρας " breezes " Valckenaer.
[2] CE : ὑπηκόοισιν ἐν ψυκτηρίοισι A.
[3] δένδρη Valckenaer, δένδρων Dobree.
[4] Casaubon : λέξεται A.
[5] ὁ Casaubon : ὅταν A.
[6] ᾠδὸς C.
[7] Musurus : σκοδίωι A.
[8] ἐὰν A.
[9] πρόσθετον C : πρόσθε τὸν A.
[10] CE : ἀφ' A.

find refreshment,[a] are called *psykteres.* Aeschylus in *The Younger Generation* [b] : " Lizards in the shadowed cooling-places." Euripides in *Phaëthon* [c] : " Cooling trees will welcome thee with loving arms." And again the writer of the poem *Aegimius,* whether it is Hesiod or Cercops of Miletus, says [d] : " There one day my place of refreshment shall be, thou ruler of the people."

Odos. Thus was called the cup, says [e] Tryphon in his *Nouns Substantive,* which was given when the glee was sung, as Antiphanes makes clear in *Twice as Much* [f] : " A. What, then, will be in it for the gods ? B. Not a thing, unless somebody mixes it. A. Stop ! Take the cup (*odos*). But then don't string out any of those old-fashioned glees, the ' Telamon ' or the ' Paeon ' or ' Harmodius.' "

Ooskyphia. Respecting the shape of these cups Asclepiades of Myrlea, in his work *On Nestor's Cup,* says [g] that it has two stems, one fashioned at the rounded body of the cup, and another attached separately, beginning in a slender shaft, but widening out where it ends, to form the base on which the cup stands.[h]

---

[a] The verb ἀναψῦξαι means to revive, to restore by fresh air.

[b] *T.G.F.*[2] 48. This was the third play in the trilogy of Lycurgus, dealing probably with the adoption of the Dionysiac religion by the young men of the Edonians. See critical note 1.

[c] *T.G.F.*[2] 611 ; here, if the text be right, ψυκτήριος is used in its original adjective sense.

[d] Frag. 7 Rzach.   [e] Frag. 115 Velsen.

[f] Kock ii. 45. For the thought *cf.* Aristoph. *Nub.* 1354 ff., 1366, and for the skolion on Harmodius and Aristogeiton, the national Hymn of Athens, Athen. 695 a-b (vol. vii. p. 223).

[g] *Cf.* above, 488 f (p. 174).

[h] The meaning, apparently, is that the second stem, of gradually widening proportions, is in the same axis as the first, which is simply a continuation of the body or bowl.

ΩΙΟΝ. Δίνων ἐν γ΄ Περσικῶν φησιν οὕτως· " ἐστὶ
δὲ ποτίβαζις ἄρτος κρίθινος καὶ πύρινος ὀπτὸς καὶ
κυπαρίσσου στέφανος καὶ οἶνος κεκραμένος ἐν ᾠῷ
χρυσῷ, οὗ αὐτὸς[1] βασιλεὺς πίνει."

Τοσαῦτα εἰπὼν ὁ Πλούταρχος καὶ ὑπὸ πάντων
κροταλισθεὶς ᾔτησε φιάλην, ἀφ᾽ ἧς σπείσας ταῖς
Μούσαις καὶ τῇ τούτων Μνημοσύνῃ[2] μητρὶ προὔπιε
πᾶσι φιλοτησίαν. ἐπειπὼν δέ[3]·

504   φιάλαν ὡς εἴ τις ἀφνεᾶς ἀπὸ χειρὸς ἑλὼν
       ἔνδον ἀμπέλου καχλάζοισαν δρόσῳ[4]
       δωρήσεται,

οὐ μόνον " νεανίᾳ[5] γαμβρῷ προπίνων," ἀλλὰ καὶ
πᾶσι τοῖς φιλτάτοις ἔδωκε τῷ παιδὶ περισοβεῖν
ἐν κύκλῳ[6] κελεύσας, τὸ κύκλῳ πίνειν τοῦτ᾽ εἶναι
λέγων, παρατιθέμενος Μενάνδρου ἐκ Περινθίας·

                   οὐδεμίαν ἡ γραῦς[7] ὅλως
       κύλικα παρῆκεν, ἀλλὰ πίνει τὴν κύκλῳ.

καὶ πάλιν ἐκ Θεοφορουμένης·

                               καὶ ταχὺ
       πάλιν[8] τὸ πρῶτον περισοβεῖ ποτήριον
       αὐτοῖς ἀκράτου.

---

[1] αὐτὸς Casaubon: ὁ αὐτὸς A.
[2] Probably a gloss and deleted by Wilamowitz. Plut.
749 b εὐχώμεθα τῇ μητρὶ τῶν Μουσῶν. μητρὶ Μνημοσύνῃ would
be a more natural order.   [3] δέ added by Kaibel.
[4] δρόσῳ Pindar: om. ACE.   [5] CE: νεανίαν A.
[6] ἐν κύκλῳ deleted by Nauck; yet cf. C: ὅτι τὸ περισοβεῖν
ἐν κύκλῳ τὸ κύκλῳ πίνειν, δῆλον.
[7] ἡ γραῦς Musurus (cf. Terence, Andria 231 aniculae):
ἤγρευσ᾽ A.
[8] πάλι A: deleted by Cobet, who read the imperative
περισόβει (περισοβεῖ ACE).

Oön. Dinon in the third book of his *Persian History* says [a] : " There is also the *potibazis*—barley and wheaten bread baked—and a wreath of cypress, and wine mixed [with water] in a golden egg (*oön*), from which the king himself drinks."

After this long recital by Plutarch,[b] who was applauded by all, he asked for a *phialê*, from which he poured a libation to the Muses and their mother Mnemosynê [c] and proceeded to toast all in a loving-cup. Then he continued [d] : " As when one grasps with a hand that knows not poverty a golden cup (*phialê*) foaming with the dew of the vine, and gives it " not merely " to the young son-in-law whom he welcomes with a toast," but also to all his nearest and dearest friends—he gave it to the slave with the command to " rush [e] it about " explaining that this meant ` drinking in a circle," and citing *The Girl from Perinthus* of Menander [f] : " The old crone never misses a single cup, but drinks from the circling bowl." And again, from *The Inspired Woman* [g] : "And quickly again he rushes the first cup of unmixed wine round among

---

[a] *F.H.G.* ii. 92. The word ποτίβαζις (without accent in A) was traced by Scaliger to a Hebrew base variously rendered by τράπεζα or δεῖπνον in the Septuagint, *e.g.* Daniel i. 5 ἐν τῇ τραπέζῃ τοῦ βασιλέως καὶ ἐν τῷ οἴνῳ ἀπὸ τοῦ ποτου αὐτοῦ.

[b] Beginning at 461 e (p. 13).

[c] *Cf.* Solon frag. 1 Diehl, frag. 13 Edmonds, Μνημοσύνης αἱ Ζηνὸς Ὀλυμπίου ἀγλαὰ τέκνα Μοῦσαι Πιερίδες; Plato, *Critias* 108 c, D.

[d] Pindar, *Ol.* vii. 1.

[e] περισοβεῖν is slang, " to send whizzing round the circle," Athen. 130 c (vol. ii. p. 98); *cf.* ἐπεσόβει, p. 146.

[f] Kock iii. 113, Allinson 422. See Athen. vol. iii. p. 351, note d, and Terence, *Andria* 229 ff.

[g] Kock iii. 64, Allinson 358.

b καὶ Εὐριπίδης δ᾽ ἐν Κρήσσαις·

τὰ δ᾽ ἄλλα χαῖρε κύλικος ἑρπούσης κύκλῳ.

αἰτοῦντος δὲ τοῦ γραμματικοῦ Λεωνίδου μείζον
ποτήριον καὶ εἰπόντος " κρατηρίζωμεν, ἄνδρες
φίλοι . . .[1] οὕτως δὲ τοὺς πότους Λυσανίας[2] φησὶν
ὁ Κυρηναῖος Ἡρόδωρον εἰρηκέναι ἐν τούτοις
' ἐπεὶ[3] δὲ θύσαντες πρὸς δεῖπνον καὶ κρατῆρα[4] καὶ
εὐχὰς καὶ παιῶνας ἐτράποντο.' καὶ ὁ τοὺς Μίμους
δὲ πεποιηκὼς οὓς αἰεὶ διὰ χειρὸς ἔχειν Δοῦρίς
φησι τὸν σοφὸν Πλάτωνα, λέγει που ' κήκρατηρί-
χημες' ἀντὶ τοῦ[5] ' ἐπεπώκειμεν.[6] " " ἀλλὰ μήν, πρὸς
c θεῶν," ὁ Ποντιανὸς ἔφη, " οὐ δεόντως ἐκ μεγάλων
πίνετε ποτηρίων, τὸν ἥδιστον καὶ χαριέστατον
Ξενοφῶντα πρὸ ὀφθαλμῶν ἔχοντες, ὃς ἐν τῷ
Συμποσίῳ φησίν· ' ὁ δ᾽ αὖ Σωκράτης εἶπεν· ἀλλὰ
πίνειν μέν, ὦ ἄνδρες, καὶ ἐμοὶ πάνυ δοκεῖ. τῷ
γὰρ ὄντι ὁ οἶνος ἄρδων τὰς ψυχὰς τὰς μὲν λύπας
ὥσπερ ὁ μανδραγόρας ἀνθρώπους, κοιμίζει, τὰς δὲ
φιλοφροσύνας, ὥσπερ ἔλαιον[7] φλόγας,[8] ἐγείρει
δοκεῖ μέντοι μοι καὶ τὰ τῶν ἀνδρῶν[9] σώματα τὸ
αὐτὰ πάσχειν ἅπερ καὶ τὰ τῶν ἐν γῇ φυομένων

---

[1] Lacuna marked by Kaibel, since a lemma in A has ὅτ
κρατηρίζειν τὸ πίνειν καὶ κρατῆρα τοὺς πότους ἐκάλουν. C reads
κρατηρίζωμεν φησὶν ἀντὶ τοῦ συμπίνωμεν (sc. εἰς μέθην Plato
Minos 320 Α).

[2] Valckenaer: δυσανίας A.   [3] Musurus: ἐπὶ A.

[4] Wilamowitz (see critical note 1): κρατῆρας A.

[5] Words divided by Valckenaer: κηκρατηριχημεσαντιτου A
κήκρατηρίχθημες?   [6] πεπώκειμεν A.

[7] φιλοφροσύνας ὥσπερ ἔλαιον added from Xenophon.

[8] φλόγα Xen.

[9] ἀνδρῶν Xen, A: ἀνῶν with ἀνδρῶν above C, ἀνῶν (abbrev.
for ἀνθρώπων) E.

them." Also Euripides in *The Women of Crete*[a] :
' As for all else, rejoice while the cup goes circling
round ! " Thereupon the grammarian Leonides
demanded a larger cup and cried out, " Let's drink
out of the mixing-bowl, my friends.[b] . . . This is the
way, according to Lysanias of Cyrenê, in which
Herodorus speaks of drinking-bouts, in these words[c] :
When they had offered sacrifice and had betaken
themselves to banqueting and the mixing-bowl,
prayers, and paeans.' And the writer also of those
Mimes which, according to Duris,[d] were always in the
hands of the wise Plato, says, I believe,[e] ' and we
were bowled,' instead of ' we had drunk thoroughly.' "

" Nevertheless," said Pontianus, " the gods are my
witness that you ought not to drink out of large cups
when you have before your very eyes the words of
the delightful and gracious Xenophon, who says in
The Symposium[f] : ' And Socrates on his part replied :
Yes, gentlemen, I too think that we ought by all
means to have a drink. For wine in fact nourishes
souls,[g] lulling to sleep its pains, as mandragora lulls
men to sleep, and on the other hand it stirs feelings of
friendship, as oil stirs flames. I think, however, that
even strong men's bodies experience the same effects
that things growing in the ground undergo. For in

---

[a] *T.G.F.*[2] 504. The line illustrates the use of κύκλῳ, not
περισοβεῖν, despite Phot. *Lex.* περισο(βεῖν)· περιφέρειν. Εὐριπίδης.
[b] To the point of intoxication. See critical note 5 and
Hesychius s. ἐκρατηρίχημες· ἐμεθύσθημεν.
[c] *F.H.G.* ii. 41, J. 1. 227. [d] *F.H.G.* ii. 480, J. 2 A 155.
[e] Sophron, Kaibel 171. [f] Chap. 2. 24.
[g] Aristoph. *Eq.* 96 τὸν νοῦν ἵν' ἄρδω καὶ λέγω τι δεξιόν.

d καὶ γὰρ ἐκεῖνα, ὅταν μὲν ὁ θεὸς αὐτὰ ἄγαν ἀθρόως
ποτίζῃ, οὐ δύναται ὀρθοῦσθαι οὐδὲ ταῖς ὥραις
διαπλοῦσθαι[1]· ὅταν δὲ ὅσῳ ἥδεται τοσοῦτο[2] πίνῃ
καὶ μάλα ὀρθά τε αὔξεται καὶ θάλλοντα ἀφικνεῖται
εἰς τὴν[3] καρπογονίαν. οὕτω δὴ καὶ ἡμεῖς, ἢν μὲν
ἀθρόον τὸ ποτὸν ἐγχεώμεθα, ταχὺ ἡμῶν καὶ τὰ
σώματα καὶ αἱ γνῶμαι σφαλοῦνται, καὶ οὐδ' ἀνα-
πνεῖν μὴ ὅτι λέγειν δυνησόμεθα· ἢν δὲ ἡμῖν οἱ
παῖδες μικραῖς κύλιξι μικρὰ[4] ἐπιψακάζωσιν, ἵνα
e καὶ ἐγὼ Γοργιείοις[5] ῥήμασιν εἴπω, οὕτως οὐ
βιαζόμενοι μεθύειν[6] ὑπὸ τοῦ οἴνου, ἀλλ' ἀναπειθό-
μενοι πρὸς τὸ παιγνιωδέστερον ἀφιξόμεθα.'

"Εἰς ταῦτά τις ἀποβλέπων τὰ τοῦ καλοῦ Ξενοφῶντος ἐπιγινώσκειν δυνήσεται ἣν εἶχε πρὸς αὐτὸν ὁ
λαμπρότατος Πλάτων ζηλοτυπίαν, ἢ τάχα φιλο-
νίκως[7] εἶχον ἀρχῆθεν πρὸς ἑαυτοὺς οἱ ἄνδρες οὗτοι,
αἰσθόμενοι τῆς ἰδίας ἑκάτερος ἀρετῆς, καὶ ἴσως καὶ
περὶ πρωτείων διεφέροντο, οὐ μόνον ἐξ ὧν περὶ
Κύρου εἰρήκασι τεκμαιρομένοις ἡμῖν, ἀλλὰ κἀκ
τῶν αὐτῶν ὑποθέσεων. Συμπόσια μὲν γὰρ γεγρά-

---

[1] ταῖς ὥραις διαπλοῦσθαι ACE: ταῖς αὔραις διαπνεῖσθαι "ex-
hale with the breezes" Xen.
[2] Basle ed.: τοσούτωι Xen., A (τοσούτω CE), τοσοῦτον
Stobaeus: τοσούτου? Plat. *Rep.* 372 B.
[3] τὴν om. C.   [4] πυκνά Xen.
[5] γοργείοισι A, γοργείοις CE.
[6] μεθύειν deleted by Orelli: πρὸς τὸ μεθύειν Richards.
[7] φιλονείκως ACE.

---

[a] Diels, *Vorsokratiker* iii. 1. 47. Among the peculiarities
of Gorgias's style was his use of extraordinary words for
simple ideas (here ἐπιψακάζωσιν for "pour a little"). Xenophon's πυκνά, "frequent drops," in contrast with μικραῖς

their case also, when the god moistens them too
copiously, they cannot remain upright, or even unfold
in blossom at their proper seasons ; but when they
drink only so much as they can take pleasure in, they
grow up very straight and reach the fruiting period in
flourishing condition.   In like manner we also, when
we allow our drink to be poured out copiously for us,
shall quickly lose control of our bodies and minds as
well, and shall not even be able to take breath, to say
nothing of being able to speak.   Yet if our slaves
let small drops drizzle into small cups—if I too
may indulge in Gorgias-like phrases [a]—we are then
not violently forced into drunkenness by the wine,
but are gradually led on and on until we arrive at a
more playful mood.'

"When one regards these words of the noble
Xenophon, he will be able to recognize the jealousy
which the most illustrious Plato felt toward him, or it
may be that both these gentlemen felt envious of
each other from the beginning, when they came to
perceive the peculiar merit each of the other ; and
perhaps they contended also for the chief rank, as we
may infer not merely from what they have said on
the subject of Cyrus, but also from those works of
theirs which deal with the same topic.[b]   For both
have written *Symposia*, and in them one is for banish-

κύλιξι, "little cups," also shows Gorgias's fondness for
antithesis.   On the various Γοργίεια σχήματα see Norden,
Kunstprosa 15.

[b] Explained in the following sentence ; Cyrus is considered
later.   But this fragment of Alexandrian literary gossip is
badly mutilated.   Aul. Gell. xiv. 3 and Diog. Laert. iii. 34
describe the unfriendly relations between the two ; Pauly-
Wissowa viii. 975 ff.   See Athen. 215 c (vol. ii. pp. 494-496),
quoting Herodicus, and Shorey, *What Plato Said*, pp. 35 ff.

φασιν ἀμφότεροι, καὶ ἐν αὐτοῖς ὁ μὲν τὰς αὐλη-
f τρίδας ἐκβάλλει, ὁ δὲ εἰσάγει· καὶ ὁ μέν, ὡς πρόκειται, παραιτεῖται πίνειν μεγάλοις ποτηρίοις, ὁ δὲ
τὸν Σωκράτην παράγει τῷ ψυκτῆρι πίνοντα μέχρι
τῆς ἕω. κἂν τῷ περὶ Ψυχῆς δὲ ὁ Πλάτων κατα-
λεγόμενος ἕκαστον τῶν παρατυχόντων[1] οὐδὲ κατὰ
μικρὸν τοῦ Ξενοφῶντος μέμνηται. καὶ περὶ τοῦ
Κύρου οὖν ὁ μὲν λέγει ὡς ἐκ πρώτης ἡλικίας
ἐπεπαίδευτο πάντα τὰ πάτρια, ὁ δὲ Πλάτων ὥσπερ
505 ἐναντιούμενος ἐν τρίτῳ Νόμων φησί· 'μαντεύομαι
δὲ περὶ Κύρου τὰ μὲν ἄλλα στρατηγὸν αὐτὸν
ἀγαθὸν εἶναι καὶ φιλόπονον,[2] παιδείας δ' ὀρθῆς
οὐδὲ ἧφθαι τὸ παράπαν, οἰκονομία δ' οὐδ' ἡτινιοῦν[3]
προσεσχηκέναι. ἔοικε δ' ἐκ νέου στρατεύεσθαι,
παραδούς τε τοὺς παῖδας ταῖς γυναιξὶ τρέφειν.'
πάλιν ὁ μὲν Ξενοφῶν συναναβὰς Κύρῳ εἰς[4] Πέρσας
μετὰ τῶν μυρίων Ἑλλήνων καὶ ἀκριβῶς εἰδὼς τὴν
προδοσίαν τοῦ Θεσσαλοῦ Μένωνος, ὅτι αὐτὸς
b αἴτιος ἐγένετο τοῖς περὶ Κλέαρχον τῆς ἀπωλείας
τῆς ὑπὸ Τισσαφέρνου[5] γενομένης, καὶ οἷός τις ἦν
τὸν τρόπον, ὡς χαλεπός, ὡς ἀσελγής, διηγήσα-

---

[1] περιτυχόντων C.   [2] ACE: φιλόπολιν Plato.
[3] Dindorf: οὐδητινι οὖν A, οὐδὲν τὸν νοῦν Plato.
[4] ὡς C.   [5] ὑπὸ της σαφέρνου A.

---

[a] Plat. Symp. 176 E, Eryximachus proposes τὴν ἄρτι εἰσ-
ελθοῦσαν αὐλητρίδα χαίρειν ἐᾶν.
[b] As a member of the Syracusan impresario's troupe,
Xen. Symp. 2. 1.   [c] Xenophon ; 504 d above.
[d] Plato, Symp. 213 E, cf. 223 c. Aristodemus reports that
he awoke at cockcrow and saw Agathon, Aristophanes, and
Socrates still awake and drinking in turn ἐκ φιάλης μεγάλης.
[e] Phaedo 59 B; περὶ Ψυχῆς is a sub-title. The critic
264

ng flute-girls,[a] whereas the other brings them in[b];
again, one of them, as set forth above,[c] declines to
drink from large cups, whereas the other represents
Socrates as drinking from the cooler until daylight.[d]
And in the dialogue *On the Soul*, when Plato is giving
a list of all who happened to be present,[e] he does not
make the slightest mention of Xenophon.   And now
coming to the subject of Cyrus, the one says[f] that
from earliest youth he was thoroughly educated in
all the traditional subjects, whereas Plato, as if in
contradiction, declares in the third book of *Laws*[g]:
'Regarding Cyrus, I suspect that although in general
he was a brave and energetic[h] commander of troops,
yet he had never even so much as essayed a genuine
course of training at all, or had even interested himself in any branch of household management whatever.   Further, it is apparent that from his early
youth he was in the army, giving over his sons to the
women to bring up.'   Again, Xenophon accompanied
Cyrus in his march against the Persians[i] with the
10,000 Greeks ; he knew in detail about the treachery
of the Thessalian Menon, and that Menon was himself
responsible for the killing of Clearchus and his staff
at the hands of Tissaphernes,[j] and he plainly describes what sort of man Menon was in character, how

apparently thinks Plato might at least have explained that
Xenophon was in Asia Minor at the time.   Yet he does
mention that Aristippus and Cleombrotus were in Aegina,
and that he himself was ill.

[f] Xen. *Cyrop.* i. 3. 1.

[g] 694 c, of Cyrus the Great.   The Athenian Stranger (*i.e.*
Plato himself) speaks.

[h] Plato said " patriotic."

[i] As narrated in the *Anabasis*; of course the younger
Cyrus is meant here.

[j] *Anab.* ii. 5. 28, *cf.* ii. 6. 21 ff.

265

μενος φαίνεται.¹ ὁ δὲ² καλὸς Πλάτων μονονουχ
εἰπὼν ‘ οὐκ ἔστ’ ἔτυμος λόγος³ οὗτος ’ ἐγκώμι
αὐτοῦ διεξέρχεται, ὁ τοὺς ἄλλους ἁπαξαπλῶ
κακολογήσας, ἐν μὲν τῇ Πολιτείᾳ Ὅμηρο
ἐκβάλλων καὶ τὴν μιμητικὴν ποίησιν, αὐτὸς δ
τοὺς διαλόγους μιμητικῶς γράψας, ὧν τῆς ἰδέα
οὐδ’ αὐτὸς εὑρετής ἐστιν.   πρὸ γὰρ αὐτοῦ τοῦ
εὗρε τὸ εἶδος τῶν λόγων ὁ Τήιος Ἀλεξαμενός,⁴ ὡ
c Νικίας ὁ Νικαεὺς ἱστορεῖ καὶ Σωτίων. Ἀρισ
τοτέλης δ’ ἐν τῷ περὶ Ποιητῶν οὕτως γράφει
‘ οὔκουν⁵ οὐδὲ ἐμμέτρους ὄντας⁶ τοὺς καλουμένου
Σώφρονος Μίμους μὴ φῶμεν εἶναι λόγους, ἢ μ
μιμήσεις τοὺς⁷ Ἀλεξαμενοῦ⁸ τοῦ Τηίου τοὺς πρώ
τους γραφέντας τῶν Σωκρατικῶν λόγων,’⁹ ἄντι
κρυς φάσκων ὁ πολυμαθέστατος Ἀριστοτέλης πρ
Πλάτωνος διαλόγους γεγραφέναι τὸν Ἀλεξαμενόν.
διαβάλλει δὲ ὁ Πλάτων καὶ Θρασύμαχον τὸ

¹ διηγησάμενος φαίνεται CE : διηγησαμένου alone A.
² δὲ CE : om. A.   ³ ὁ λόγος CE
⁴ CE : ἀλεξαμενος A.   ⁵ οὔκουν Jahn : οὐκοῦν A
⁶ ὄντας added by Kaibel.
⁷ ἢ μὴ μιμήσεις τοὺς Jahn : καὶ μιμήσεις ἢ τοὺς A.
⁸ E : ἀλεξαμένου A.
⁹ λόγους Natorp : διαλόγων A, διαλόγοις Bake, λόγω
Susemihl.
¹⁰ E : ἀλεξάμενον A.

ᵃ The opening words of the palinode addressed by Stesi
chorus to Helen, P.L.G.⁴ iii. 217, Diehl frag. 11, Edmond
frag. 18, Athen. vol. ii. p. 479 note d; quoted by Plat
himself, Phaedrus 243 A, in another connexion. See Hor
Epod. xvii. 38 ff.
ᵇ Rep. iii. and x. 595 B.   Plato rejected μίμησις as th
motive and essence of art, and retained διήγησις, or simpl
narration. The question has been often discussed, e.g. b

harsh he was, and how sensual. But the noble **Plato**, all but saying ' That tale is not true,' [a] runs through the gamut of praise in Menon's honour—Plato, who has flatly abused other people, in the *Republic* banishing Homer and imitative poetry (from his city)[b] while he himself wrote imitative dialogues, the pattern of which he did not even invent himself. Before his time, in fact, Alexamenus of Teos had invented this type of literature, as Nicias of Nicaea and Sotion record. And Aristotle in his treatise *On Poets* writes as follows[c] : ' Therefore we shall not deny that even the so-called *Mimes* of Sophron, which are not in verse, are conversations, or that the dialogues of Alexamenus of Teos, which were the first Socratic conversations to be written, are imitations,'[d] and so the most learned Aristotle expressly declares that Alexamenus wrote dialogues before Plato. Plato also reviles Thrasymachus, the sophist of Chalcedon,

[a] V. C. Greene, *Harvard Studies in Classical Philology*, xxix. 1-75.

[c] Frag. 72 Rose. Plato himself ascribes the use of dialogue to Parmenides, *Soph.* 217 c. Diog. Laert. iii. 48 adds another claimant in the Eleatic Zeno, but quotes also Aristotle on the authority of Favorinus. He gives the palm to Plato " for beauty and inventiveness."

[d] *i.e.* artistic representation of life, like the mime. Both Sophron and Alexamenus have one element in common—μίμησις ἐν λόγῳ χωρὶς ἁρμονίας καὶ ῥυθμοῦ. I follow Natorp's interpretation (Pauly-Wissowa i. 1375). In *Poetics* 1447 b Aristotle explains that there is no common name for a mime of Sophron or Xenarchus and a Socratic conversation. See Bywater's note. Bernays (*Zwei Abhandlungen*, 1880, p. 83) keeps the text but changes the sentence to à question. The passage simply means that the unmetrical mimes of Sophron, admittedly works of art (μιμήσεις), come under the head of λόγοι, conversations (which are often not artistic), and *per contra* the prose conversations of Alexamenus are artistic μιμήσεις.

Χαλκηδόνιον σοφιστὴν ὅμοιον εἶναι λέγων τῷ
d ὀνόματι, ἔτι δ᾽ Ἱππίαν καὶ Γοργίαν καὶ Παρ-
μενίδην καὶ ἑνὶ διαλόγῳ τῷ Πρωταγόρᾳ πολλοὺς
ὁ τοιαῦτα ἐν τῇ Πολιτείᾳ εἰπών· ᾽ ὅταν, οἶμαι,
δημοκρατουμένη πόλις ἐλευθερίας διψήσασα κακῶν
οἰνοχόων τύχῃ καὶ ἀκράτου αὐτῆς μεθυσθῇ.᾽
"Λέγεται δὲ ὡς καὶ ὁ Γοργίας αὐτὸς ἀναγνοὺς
τὸν ὁμώνυμον αὐτῷ διάλογον πρὸς τοὺς συνήθεις
ἔφη ᾽ ὡς καλῶς οἶδε Πλάτων ἰαμβίζειν.᾽ Ἕρμιππος δὲ ἐν τῷ περὶ Γοργίου ᾽ ὡς ἐπεδήμησε,᾽ φησί
᾽ ταῖς Ἀθήναις Γοργίας μετὰ τὸ ποιήσασθαι τὴν
ἀνάθεσιν τῆς ἐν Δελφοῖς ἑαυτοῦ χρυσῆς εἰκόνος
e εἰπόντος τοῦ Πλάτωνος, ὅτε εἶδεν αὐτόν, "ἧκε
ἡμῖν ὁ καλός τε καὶ χρυσοῦς Γοργίας," ἔφη ὁ
Γοργίας· " ἦ καλόν γε αἱ Ἀθῆναι καὶ[1] νέον τοῦτο
Ἀρχίλοχον ἐνηνόχασιν." ἄλλοι δέ φασιν ὡς
ἀναγνοὺς ὁ Γοργίας τὸν Πλάτωνος διάλογον πρὸς
τοὺς παρόντας εἶπεν ὅτι οὐδὲν τούτων οὔτ᾽ εἶπεν
οὔτ᾽ ἤκουσε παρὰ Πλάτωνος.[2]᾽ ταῦτά φασι κα

---

[1] καὶ ACE : bracketed by Meineke and Kaibel.
[2] παρὰ Πλάτωνος (ACE) deleted by Rossi.

---

[a] The name Thrasymachus means "bold fighter." His
truculence appears in Plat. *Rep.* 336 c, 341 c, and elsewhere,
but the actual pun on the name is credited to Herodicus
(Prodicus ?) in Aristot. *Rhet.* ii. 23. 29 ἀεὶ θρασύμαχος εἶ.
[b] The unfavourable description in *Protagoras, Hippias
Maior, Hippias Minor,* and *Gorgias* may be exaggerations
but seem to rest on fact, at least so far as they apply to Hippias
and Gorgias. On Parmenides see Plat. *Parm.* 127 в. The
defence of the Sophists against Plato, begun in modern
times by Grote, *Hist. of Greece,* chap. lxvii., has been carried
to extremes by Gomperz and Dupréel.
[c] 562 c, Athen. 433 f, 443 f (vol. iv. p. 465 note *j*). Apparently
ently the author of this diatribe (Herodicus ?) took evil wine

saying that he was like his name,[a] as again he reviles Hippias, Gorgias, and Parmenides, and in a single dialogue, the *Protagoras*, many others,[b] and used such terms as these in the *Republic* [c] : ' Whenever, I fancy, a democratic state, in its thirst for liberty, has the bad luck to get evil wine-pourers as its leaders, and has become intoxicated with strong wine.'

" It is reported that Gorgias, himself reading the dialogue named after him, remarked to his intimates, ' What nice satire Plato knows how to write ! ' [d] And Hermippus in his work *On Gorgias* says [e] : ' When [f] Gorgias arrived in Athens after dedicating the gold statue of himself at Delphi, Plato seeing him said : " Here comes our noble and golden Gorgias " ; to which Gorgias replied : " Noble indeed and new is this Archilochus that Athens has produced." Others, again, say that when Gorgias read Plato's dialogue to his audience he observed that he had neither spoken any of these lines nor had he heard them from Plato.[g] '

pourers to refer to the Sophists, though Plato is speaking of demagogues.

[d] A similar story is told of Socrates, Diog. Laert. iii. 35 : Socrates hearing Plato read his *Lysis* cried out, " Heracles, what a heap of lies this young man tells about me ! " *Cf.* below, 507 d (p. 278) ; ἰαμβίζειν, says Hesychius *s.v.*, is λοιδορεῖν, κακολογεῖν. The early iambographs were the first writers of satire ; hence the mention of Archilochus (" Archilochum proprio rabies armavit iambo," Horace, *A.P.* 79, *cf. Ep.* i. 19. 23). [e] *F.H.G.* iii. 48.

[f] So Socrates greets Hippias at the beginning of *Hipp. Mai.* (281 a) : Ἱππίας ὁ καλός τε καὶ σοφός. Epicurus sarcastically turned the epithet " golden " upon Plato himself, Diog. Laert. x. 8. On the statue see Cicero, *De Orat.* iii. 32. 129, Val. Max. viii. 15, Pliny, *N.H.* xxxiii. 83. But Paus. x. 18. 7 says it was gilded.

[g] Meaning, of course, from Socrates, the protagonist of the piece.

269

Φαίδωνα εἰπεῖν ἀναγνόντα τὸν περὶ Ψυχῆς. διὸ
καλῶς ὁ Τίμων περὶ αὐτοῦ ἔφη·

> ὡς ἀνέπλαττε Πλάτων[1] ὁ πεπλασμένα θαύματα[2]
> εἰδώς.

f Παρμενίδῃ μὲν γὰρ καὶ ἐλθεῖν εἰς λόγους τὸν τοῦ
Πλάτωνος Σωκράτην μόλις ἡ ἡλικία συγχωρεῖ,
οὐχ ὡς καὶ τοιούτους εἰπεῖν ἢ ἀκοῦσαι λόγους.
τὸ δὲ πάντων σχετλιώτατον καὶ τὸ εἰπεῖν οὐδεμιᾶς κατεπειγούσης χρείας ὅτι παιδικὰ γεγόνοι
τοῦ Παρμενίδου Ζήνων ὁ πολίτης αὐτοῦ. ἀδύ-
νατον δὲ καὶ Φαῖδρον οὐ μόνον κατὰ Σωκράτην
εἶναι, ἦ πού γε καὶ ἐρώμενον αὐτοῦ γεγονέναι.
ἀλλὰ μὴν οὐ δύνανται οὐδὲ[3] Πάραλος καὶ Ξάνθ-
506 ιππος οἱ Περικλέους υἱοὶ τελευτήσαντος[4] τῷ λοιμῷ
Πρωταγόρᾳ διαλέγεσθαι ὅτε δεύτερον[5] ἐπεδήμησε
ταῖς ᾿Αθήναις, οἱ ἔτι[6] πρότερον τελευτήσαντες.
πολλὰ δ᾽ ἔστι καὶ ἄλλα λέγειν περὶ αὐτοῦ καὶ
δεικνύναι[7] ὡς ἔπλαττε τοὺς διαλόγους.

" ῞Οτι δὲ καὶ δυσμενὴς ἦν πρὸς ἅπαντας, δῆλον καὶ
ἐκ τῶν ἐν τῷ ῎Ιωνι ἐπιγραφομένῳ,[8] ἐν ᾧ πρῶτον
μὲν κακολογεῖ πάντας τοὺς ποιητάς, ἔπειτα καὶ
τοὺς ὑπὸ τοῦ δήμου προαγομένους, Φανοσθένη τὸν

---

[1] ἀνέπλαττε πλάτων CE: ἀνέπλαττεν ὁ πλάτων A.
[2] Diog. Laert. iii. 26: θύματα A.
[3] οὐδὲ CE: om. A.
[4] τελευτήσαντος Brinkmann: τελευτήσαντες ACE.
[5] τὸ δεύτερον Kaibel (cf. 218 b). But δεύτερον often occurs
alone in later Greek.
[6] πέμπτῳ ἔτει Casaubon, πολλοῖς ἔτεσι Kaibel.
[7] ἐκ πολλῶν δὲ καὶ ἄλλων ἔστι δεῖξαι C.
[8] Casaubon: ἐπιγραφομένων A.

---

[a] Wachsmuth 172, Diels iii. 1. 188. The verb and participle refer to things imagined, moulded, trumped up.

The same observation, they say, was made by Phaedo on reading the dialogue *On the Soul.* Hence Timon well said of him [a] : ' What portentous platitudes Plato plaited purposely ! ' In fact, to make Plato's Socrates converse with Parmenides is scarcely possible on account of Socrates' youth, which would have prevented him from making or listening to such a discourse.[b] But the most outrageous thing of all is also to say, without any compelling need,[c] that Zeno, Parmenides' fellow-citizen, was his darling. And it is also impossible for Phaedrus [d] to have been a contemporary of Socrates, to say nothing of being his lover. But what is more, it is impossible also that Paralus and Xanthippus, the sons of Pericles, who died of the plague,[e] should have conversed with Protagoras when he made his second visit to Athens, since they had died still earlier. Many other things, too, may be said of Plato from which one may show that he trumped up his dialogues.

" That Plato was in fact inimical toward everybody is plain also from what one reads in the dialogue entitled *Ion,* in which he first abuses all the poets, and then also the men promoted to power by the people,[f] Phanosthenes of Andros, Apollodorus of Cyzicus, and

[b] Macrobius i. 1. 5 "huius (Socratis) pueritia vix illius adprehenderit senectutem, et tamen inter illos de rebus arduis disputatur." Plato, *Soph.* 217 c, makes Socrates say: Παρμε-νίδη . . . διεξιόντι λόγους παγκάλους παρεγενόμην ἐγὼ νέος ὤν, ἐκείνου μάλα δὴ τότε ὄντος πρεσβύτου.

[c] Plato, *Parm.* 127 b, reports this as gossip: λέγεσθαι αὐτὸν παιδικὰ τοῦ Παρμενίδου γεγονέναι.

[d] Macrob. i. 1. 5 speaks of Timaeus in the same way.

[e] 429 b.c. See *Prot.* 315 a. On the relations between Plato and Protagoras see Grote's *Plato,* chap. xxiii.; on the second visit of Protagoras, Athen. 218 b (vol. ii. p. 488).

[f] *Ion* 534, 541 d.

271

Ἄνδριον κἀπολλόδωρον τὸν Κυζικηνόν, ἔτι δὲ τὸν
Κλαζομένιον Ἡρακλείδην. ἐν δὲ τῷ Μένωνι καὶ
b τοὺς μεγίστους παρ' Ἀθηναίοις γενομένους Ἀρι-
στείδην καὶ Θεμιστοκλέα, Μένωνα δὲ ἐπαινεῖ τὸν
τοὺς Ἕλληνας προδόντα. ἐν δὲ τῷ Εὐθυδήμῳ
Εὐθύδημον[1] καὶ τὸν ἀδελφὸν αὐτοῦ Διονυσόδωρον[2]
προπηλακίζων καὶ καλῶν ὀψιμαθεῖς ἔτι τε ἐριστὰς
ὀνομάζων[3] ὀνειδίζει αὐτοῖς καὶ τὴν ἐκ Χίου τῆς
πατρίδος φυγήν, ἀφ' ἧς ἐν Θουρίοις κατῳκίσθησαν.
ἐν δὲ τῷ περὶ Ἀνδρείας Μελησίαν τὸν Θουκυδίδου
τοῦ ἀντιπολιτευσαμένου Περικλεῖ καὶ Λυσίμαχον
τὸν Ἀριστείδου τοῦ δικαίου, τῆς τῶν πατέρων
c ἀρετῆς ἀναξίους εἶναι φάσκων. ἃ δὲ περὶ Ἀλκιβιάδου εἴρηκεν ἐν τῷ Συμποσίῳ οὐδ' εἰς φῶς
λέγεσθαί ἐστιν ἄξιον, ἔν τε τῷ προτέρῳ τῶν εἰς
αὐτὸν διαλόγων· ὁ γὰρ δεύτερος ὑπό τινων Ξενοφῶντος εἶναι λέγεται, ὡς καὶ ἡ Ἀλκυὼν Λέοντος
τοῦ Ἀκαδημαϊκοῦ, ὥς φησι Νικίας ὁ Νικαεύς. τὰ
μὲν οὖν κατὰ Ἀλκιβιάδου λεχθέντα σιωπῶ· ὅτι δὲ
τὸν Ἀθηναίων δῆμον εἰκαῖον[4] εἴρηκε κριτὴν ἔτι τε
πρόκοπον,[5] Λακεδαιμονίους δὲ ἐπαινῶν ἐπαινεῖ
d καὶ τοὺς πάντων Ἑλλήνων ἐχθροὺς Πέρσας. καὶ
τὸν ἀδελφὸν δὲ τοῦ Ἀλκιβιάδου Κλεινίαν[6] μαινό-

---

[1] Εὐθύδημον added by Dindorf.   [2] διονυσιόδωρον A.
[3] ὀνομάζων corrected from ὀνειδίζων A.
[4] δῆμον εἰκαῖον Musurus : δημονικαῖον A.
[5] ἔτι τε πρόκοπον deleted by Dindorf, who thought the
words had crept in through εὐπρόσωπον below.
[6] Κλεινίαν Valckenaer : καὶ νικίαν ACE.

---

[a] Cf. Menon 93, 94, and above, 505 a (p. 264).
[b] Plato ironically uses the word πάσσοφοι, not ὀψιμαθεῖς.
[c] Euthyd. 271 c.

also Heracleides of Clazomenae. In the *Menon* he abuses even the men who became greatest among the Athenians, Aristeides and Themistocles, but praises Menon, the betrayer of the Greeks.[a] Again, in the *Euthydemus* he foully abuses Euthydemus and his brother Dionysodorus, calling them pedants [b] and giving them the name of wranglers, and he reproaches them for their flight from their native Chios,[c] from which they went and settled in Thurii. And in the dialogue *On Courage* [d] he asserts that Melesias, son of the Thucydides who opposed Pericles in politics, and Lysimachus, son of Aristeides the Just, were not the equals of their fathers in merit. As to what he has said in the *Symposium* regarding Alcibiades, that is not even worth bringing to light in any discussion, any more than what he says in the first of the two dialogues addressed to him [e] ; the second *Alcibiades*, in fact, is said by some to be the work of Xenophon, just as *The Halcyon* is ascribed to Leon the Academic, according to Nicias of Nicaea. Now, what is said in disparagement of Alcibiades, I pass over in silence ; but note that he speaks of the Athenian populace as a hasty and even rash judge, whereas in praising the Lacedaemonians he praises even the Persians, who were the foes of all the Greeks.[f] And the brother of Alcibiades, Cleinias, he stigmatizes as

[d] *Laches* 179 B-c ; περὶ 'Ανδρείας is a sub-title.
[e] *Symp.* 212 c, etc., *Alcib. I* 103 A, etc. *Alcib. II* is attributed to Plato by Diog. Laert. iii. 59. Shorey pp. 419, 570.
[f] *Alcib. I* 121. For epithets describing the Athenians *cf.* the Corinthian delegation's words in Thuc. i. 70 (νεωτεροποιοὶ καὶ ἐπινοῆσαι ὀξεῖς). They are ταχύβουλοι and μετάβουλοι, rash and fickle, Aristoph. *Acharn.* 630 ff. The epithets quoted above (from Hegesander of Delphi ? see below, 507 a) do not occur in Plato.

273

μενόν τε ἀποκαλεῖ[1] καὶ τοὺς υἱοὺς αὐτοῦ ἠλιθίους
Μειδίαν τε ὀρτυγοκόπον,[2] καὶ τὸν τῶν Ἀθηναίων
δῆμον εὐπρόσωπον μὲν εἶναι, δεῖν δ' αὐτὸν ἀποδύσαντας[3] θεωρεῖν· ὀφθήσεται γάρ, φησί, περίβλεπτον
ἀξίωμα περικείμενος κάλλους οὐκ ἀληθινοῦ.

" ' Ἐν δὲ τῷ Κίμωνι οὐδὲ τῆς Θεμιστοκλέους[4]
φείδεται κατηγορίας οὐδὲ τῆς Ἀλκιβιάδου καὶ
Μυρωνίδου,[5] ἀλλ' οὐδ' αὐτοῦ τοῦ Κίμωνος. καὶ ὁ
Κρίτων δ' αὐτοῦ Κρίτωνος, ἡ δὲ Πολιτεία καὶ[6]
Σοφοκλέους περιέχει καταδρομήν, ὁ δὲ Γοργίας οὐ
μόνον ἀφ' οὗ τὸ ἐπίγραμμα, ἀλλὰ καὶ Ἀρχελάου
e τοῦ Μακεδονίας βασιλέως, ὃν οὐ μόνον ἐπονείδιστον
γένος ἔχειν, ἀλλ' ὅτι καὶ ἀπέκτεινε τὸν δεσπότην.
οὗτος δ' ἐστὶ Πλάτων, ὃν Σπεύσιππός φησι φίλ-
τατον ὄντα[7] Φιλίππῳ τῆς βασιλείας αἴτιον γενέσθαι.
γράφει γοῦν Καρύστιος ὁ Περγαμηνὸς ἐν τοῖς
Ἱστορικοῖς Ὑπομνήμασιν οὕτως· ' Σπεύσιππος
πυνθανόμενος Φίλιππον βλασφημεῖν περὶ Πλάτωνος
εἰς ἐπιστολὴν ἔγραψέ τι τοιοῦτον· '' ὥσπερ ἀγνοοῦν-

---

[1] CE: ἀποφαίνει A.
[2] Olympiodorus, Schol. Plato, ACE: ὀρτυγοτρόφον Plat.
codd. BT.
[3] AE: ἀποδύσαντα Plat. C (altered to ἀποδύσαντας).
[4] περικλέους CE, which Dobree read for Ἀλκιβιάδου below.
[5] Μιλτιάδου Casaubon.
[6] Κρίτωνος . . . καί added by Wilamowitz.
[7] Ἀρχελάῳ (ACE) after ὄντα deleted by Gomperz. See
note h.

---

[a] *Alcib. I* 118 E. The sons of Pericles, not of Alcibiades,
are called ἠλίθιοι by Plato, *ibid.*
[b] Lit. "quail-striker," referring to the game ὀρτυγοκοπία,
analogous to cock-fighting. *Alcib. I* 120 A.
[c] *Ibid.* 132 A.
[d] Plato nowhere says this. Perhaps the author was
Hegesander or Herodicus.

insane,[a] his sons as silly fools, Meidias as a gamester,[b] and says that although the Athenian people have fair countenances, we should observe them when they are stripped[c]; as a matter of fact they will be seen, he says,[d] to be invested with an admired reputation for a beauty which is unreal.

"In the *Cimon*[e] Plato is unsparing in his accusation of Themistocles, as also of Alcibiades and Myronides, and even Cimon himself. The *Crito*, also, contains an invective against Crito himself, the *Republic* against Sophocles,[f] while the *Gorgias* is equally critical not only of the man from whose name the title is taken, but also of Archelaüs, the king of Macedonia, of whom it is said not only that he was of shameful origin, but also that he had murdered his master.[g] So this is Plato, of whom Speusippus said that he was very friendly to Philip[h] and was the cause of his becoming king ! At least Carystius of Pergamum in *Historical Notes* writes as follows[i]: 'Speusippus, learning that Philip was uttering slanders about Plato, wrote in a letter something of this sort: " As if the whole world did not know that

[e] There is not, and apparently never was, a dialogue by Plato so entitled. It is thought that the *Gorgias* is meant (esp. 503 c, 515 D), and the text has been altered accordingly. See critical note 5, also *Theages* 126 A.

[f] *Crito* 45 A-B, *Rep.* 329 B?

[g] *Gorg.* 471. Archelaüs was son of Perdiccas II and a woman who was a slave of his uncle (and therefore his master), Alcetas.

[h] The MSS. read: "was very friendly to Archelaüs and was the cause of Philip's becoming king." But even Herodicus could hardly have claimed a friendship between Plato and Archelaüs in view of *Gorg.* 471 and *Alcib. II* 141 D. Possibly Περδίκκᾳ should be read for Ἀρχελάῳ (Gomperz).

[i] *F.H.G.* iv. 356.

τας τοὺς ἀνθρώπους ὅτι καὶ τὴν ἀρχὴν τῆς βασιλείας Φίλιππος διὰ Πλάτωνος ἔσχεν. Εὐφραῖοι
f γὰρ ἀπέστειλε τὸν Ὠρείτην πρὸς Περδίκκαι
Πλάτων, ὃς ἔπεισεν ἀπομερίσαι τινὰ χώραν
Φιλίππῳ. διατρέφων δ' ἐνταῦθα δύναμιν, ὡς ἀπ-
έθανε Περδίκκας, ἐξ ἑτοίμου δυνάμεως ὑπαρχούσης
ἐπέπεσε τοῖς πράγμασι.'' τοῦτο δ' εἴπερ οὕτως
ἀληθείας ἔχει, θεὸς ἂν εἰδείη. ὁ δὲ καλὸς αὐτοῦ
Πρωταγόρας πρὸς τῷ καταδρομὴν ἔχειν πολλῶν
ποιητῶν καὶ σοφῶν ἀνδρῶν ἐκθεατριζόμενον ἔχει
καὶ τὸν Καλλίου βίον μᾶλλον τῶν Εὐπόλιδος Κολάκων. ἐν δὲ τῷ Μενεξένῳ οὐ μόνον Ἱππίας ὁ
Ἡλεῖος χλευάζεται, ἀλλὰ καὶ ὁ Ῥαμνούσιος Ἀντι-
507 φῶν καὶ ὁ μουσικὸς Λάμπρος. ἐπιλίποι[1] δ' ἄν με
ἡ ἡμέρα εἰ πάντας ἐθελήσαιμι ἐπελθεῖν τοὺς κακῶς
ἀκούσαντας ὑπὸ τοῦ σοφοῦ. ἀλλὰ μὴν οὐδ' Ἀντι-
σθένη ἐπαινῶ· καὶ γὰρ καὶ οὗτος πολλοὺς εἰπὼν
κακῶς οὐδ' αὐτοῦ τοῦ Πλάτωνος ἀπέσχετο, ἀλλὰ
καλέσας αὐτὸν φορτικῶς Σάθωνα τὸν ταύτην
ἔχοντα τὴν ἐπιγραφὴν διάλογον ἐξέδωκεν.

'' Ἡγήσανδρος δὲ ὁ Δελφὸς ἐν τοῖς Ὑπομνήμασι
περὶ τῆς πρὸς πάντας τοῦ Πλάτωνος κακοηθείας
λέγων γράφει καὶ ταῦτα· ' μετὰ τὴν Σωκράτους
τελευτὴν ἐπὶ πλεῖον τῶν συνήθων ἀθυμούντων ἔν
b τινι συνουσίᾳ Πλάτων συμπαρὼν λαβὼν τὸ ποτήριον παρεκάλει μὴ ἀθυμεῖν αὐτούς, ὡς ἱκανὸς αὐτὸς

---

[1] Dindorf: ἐπιλείποι A, ἐπιλίπη C, ἐπιλίπη E.

---

[a] Perdiccas III, brother of Philip, reigned 364–359 B.C.
[b] See Plato's letter, *Ep.* 5, and *cf.* below, 508 d (p. 284)
Euphraeus died a martyr, Demosth. ix. 59-62. Diod. Sic
xvi. 2, in his account of Philip's accession, makes no mention
of Euphraeus.

Philip acquired the beginning of his kingship through Plato's agency. For Plato sent to Perdiccas [a] Euphraeus of Oreus,[b] who persuaded Perdiccas to portion off some territory to Philip. Here Philip kept a force, and when Perdiccas died, since he had this force in readiness, he at once plunged into the control of affairs.'' ' Now whether in fact this is really so God alone can know. But his beautiful *Protagoras*, besides containing invectives against numerous poets and men of wisdom, also exposes the life of Callias more theatrically than *The Flatterers* of Eupolis does.[c] In the *Menexenus* it is not only Hippias of Elis that is held up to mockery, but also Antiphon of Rhamnus and the musician Lamprus.[d] But the day would fail me if I should wish to proceed with all who were abused by the philosopher. Nevertheless I do not commend Antisthenes either; for he, too, abused many persons, not even abstaining from Plato himself, but giving him the vulgar appellation of Satho,[e] he published the dialogue which has that title.

"Hegesander of Delphi, in his *Commentaries* discussing Plato's malice toward everyone, writes also these words [f] : ' After the death of Socrates his intimate friends, gathered together on a certain occasion, were very despondent. Plato joined them, and taking up the cup he exhorted them not to be downcast, because he was competent to lead the

[c] The dramatic opening of the *Protagoras* at the house of the rich Callias is one of the best in Plato's writings. On the play of Eupolis see Athen. 218 b-c (vol. ii. p. 488).

[d] *Menex.* 236 A, Diels 582. Hippias is not mentioned in the dialogue. Read Ἀσπασία ἡ Μιλησία?

[e] Athen. 220 d (vol. ii. p. 498). The word Σάθων (Phot. s.v., Bekk. *An.* 394. 5) alludes to the *membrum virile*.

[f] *F.H.G.* iv. 412; how far the citation extends is uncertain, possibly only through the story of Apollodorus.

εἴη ἡγεῖσθαι τῆς σχολῆς, καὶ προέπιεν ᾿Απολλο-
δώρῳ. καὶ ὃς εἶπεν " ἥδιον ἂν παρὰ Σωκράτους
τὴν τοῦ φαρμάκου κύλικα εἰλήφειν ἢ παρὰ σοί
τὴν τοῦ οἴνου πρόποσιν." ἐδόκει γὰρ Πλάτων
φθονερὸς εἶναι καὶ κατὰ τὸ ἦθος οὐδαμῶς εὐδο-
κιμεῖν. καὶ γὰρ ᾿Αρίστιππον πρὸς Διονύσιον ἀπο-
δημήσαντα ἔσκωπτεν, αὐτὸς τρὶς εἰς Σικελίαν
ἐκπλεύσας· ἅπαξ μὲν τῶν ῥυάκων χάριν, ὅτε καὶ
τῷ πρεσβυτέρῳ Διονυσίῳ συγγενόμενος ἐκινδύ-
c νευσεν, δὶς δὲ πρὸς τὸν νεώτερον Διονύσιον
Αἰσχίνου τε πένητος ὄντος καὶ μαθητὴν ἕνα ἔχοντος
Ξενοκράτην, τοῦτον περιέσπασεν. καὶ Φαίδωνι δὲ
τὴν τῆς δουλείας ἐφιστὰς δίκην ἐφωράθη· καὶ τὸ
καθόλου πᾶσι τοῖς Σωκράτους μαθηταῖς ἐπεφύκει
μητρυιᾶς ἔχων διάθεσιν. διόπερ Σωκράτης οὐκ
ἀηδῶς περὶ αὐτοῦ στοχαζόμενος ἐνύπνιον ἔφησεν
ἑωρακέναι πλειόνων παρόντων. δοκεῖν γὰρ ἔφη
" τὸν Πλάτωνα κορώνην γενόμενον ἐπὶ τὴν κεφαλὴν
μου[1] ἀναπηδήσαντα τὸ φαλακρὸν μου[1] κατασκαρι-
d φᾶν καὶ κρώζειν[2] περιβλέπουσαν. δοκῶ οὖν σε
ὦ Πλάτων, πολλὰ κατὰ τῆς ἐμῆς ψεύσεσθαι[3]
κεφαλῆς." ἦν δὲ ὁ Πλάτων πρὸς τῇ κακοηθείᾳ
καὶ φιλόδοξος, ὅστις ἔφησεν· " ἔσχατον τὸν τῆς

---

[1] μου deleted by Kaibel.   [2] Dobree: κρατεῖν AC.
[3] Schweighäuser: ψεύδεσθαι A, ψεύσασθαι CE.

---

[a] From Aetna. For Plato's own account of the volcano
see *Phaedo* 111 c-e; *cf.* the death of the elder Pliny on
Vesuvius, Plin. *Ep.* vi. 16. 20.
[b] Phaedo, though of good birth, had been taken captive
and as a slave had worked in a brothel at Athens. He was

chool himself, and proposed a toast to Apollodorus.
But he said : " I would rather have taken the cup of
poison from Socrates than this toast of wine from
you." For Plato had the reputation of being jealous
and having by no means a good name so far as his
character was concerned. For he actually mocked at
Aristippus for going to live at the court of Dionysius,
although he himself had voyaged to Sicily three times :
once to see the streams of lava,[a] on which occasion
he, in company with the elder Dionysius, risked
his life, and twice to visit the younger Dionysius.
Again, when Aeschines was poor and had only one
pupil, Xenocrates, Plato enticed him to himself. Also
he was caught in the act of instituting against Phaedo
the lawsuit in which Phaedo was charged with being
a slave [b] ; and in general, he was so constituted by
nature as to have the disposition of a stepmother
toward all the disciples of Socrates. Hence Socrates,
on the occasion when, in the presence of several
persons, he told a dream which he had had, made a
guess about him not unwittily. For he said : " Me-
thought Plato had turned into a crow and had lighted
on my head, where he pecked at my bald spot and
croaked as he looked all round. So I infer, Plato, that
you are going to utter many lies over my head."[c]
But besides being malicious, Plato was eager for fame,
for he said : " The last thing we put off at death itself

ransomed at Socrates' instigation by Cebes (Alcibiades,
uid.), but it is intimated here that Plato, for some private
grievance not explained, caused his status to be called in
question. The whole affair remains very obscure (Meier u.
chömann, *Att. Process* ii. 624 note). Diog. Laert. ii. 31,
ul. Gell. ii. 18, Suid. *s.* Φαίδων, and Macrob. i. 11. 41, do
ot repeat the slander, though they tell of Phaedo's captivity.
   c i.e. lies for which the speaker will be held responsible.
ee above, 505 d (p. 269 note *d*).

δόξης[1] χιτῶνα ἐν τῷ θανάτῳ αὐτῷ ἀποδυόμεθα
ἐν διαθήκαις, ἐν ἐκκομιδαῖς, ἐν τάφοις," ὥς φησι
Διοσκουρίδης ἐν τοῖς Ἀπομνημονεύμασιν. καὶ τ
πόλιν δὲ θελῆσαι κτίσαι καὶ τὸ νομοθετῆσαι τί
οὐ φήσει πάθος εἶναι φιλοδοξίας; δῆλον δ᾽ ἐστ
e τοῦτο ἐξ ὧν ἐν τῷ Τιμαίῳ λέγει· " πέπονθά τ
πάθος πρὸς τὴν πολιτείαν, ὥσπερ ἂν εἰ ζωγράφο
ἐβούλετο τὰ ἑαυτοῦ ἔργα κινούμενα καὶ ἐνεργ
ἰδεῖν· οὕτω κἀγὼ τοὺς πολίτας οὓς διαγράφω."

" Περὶ δὲ τῶν ἐν τοῖς διαλόγοις αὐτοῦ λελεγ
μένων[2] τί ἂν καὶ λέγοι τις; ἡ μὲν γὰρ ψυχὴ
διαπλαττομένη ἀθάνατος ὑπ᾽ αὐτοῦ καὶ κατὰ τὴ
ἀπόλυσιν χωριζομένη τοῦ σώματος παρὰ πρώτ
εἴρηται Ὁμήρῳ. οὗτος γὰρ εἶπεν ὡς ἡ το
Πατρόκλου ψυχὴ

Ἄϊδόσδε κατῆλθεν[3]
ὃν πότμον γοόωσα, λιποῦσ᾽ ἀνδροτῆτα καὶ ἥβη

εἰ δ᾽ οὖν καὶ Πλάτωνος φήσειέν τις εἶναι τὸν λόγον
f οὐχ ὁρῶ τίν᾽ ἐσχήκαμεν ἀπ᾽ αὐτοῦ ὠφέλειαν. ἐὰ
γὰρ καὶ συγχωρήσῃ τις μεθίστασθαι τὰς τῶν τετε
λευτηκότων ψυχὰς εἰς ἄλλας φύσεις καὶ πρὸς τὸ
μετεωρότερον καὶ καθαρώτερον ἀνέρχεσθαι τόπον
ἅτε κουφότητος μετεχούσας, τί πλέον ἡμῖν; ὧ
γὰρ μήτ᾽ ἀνάμνησίς ἐστιν οὗ ποτε ἦμεν μήτ
αἴσθησις εἰ[4] καὶ τὸ σύνολον ἦμεν, τίς χάρις ταύτη

---

[1] δόξης A (over an erasure) CE: φιλοδοξίας Kaibel.
[2] τῶν . . . λελεγμένων A (λελεγμένων om. CE): κεκλεμμένα
Kaibel.
[3] βεβήκει Homer.   [4] αἴσθησις εἰ CE: αἴσθησις ἦι εἰ A.
280

the tunic of fame, in our wills, in our funerals, and our tombs "; so says Dioscurides in his *Memoirs*.[a] When it comes to conceiving the wish to form a state and give it laws, who shall say that that is not a bad case of vanity ? This is plain from what he says in the *Timaeus*[b] : " I have a feeling as regards my *Republic* like that of a painter who wanted to see his creations moving and acting ; just so should I like to see the citizens whom I describe." '

" Now in regard to the statements in his dialogues, what *can* one say, really ? The soul, for example, which he conceives as deathless, and which at the dissolution of the body is separated from it, is so spoken of by Homer first. For Homer has said that the soul of Patroclus ' went down to the house of Hades, bewailing its doom, leaving manhood and youth.'[c] Be that as it may, even if one could affirm that the doctrine is Plato's, I cannot see what help we have got from him. For even though one concedes that the souls of the dead change into other beings, and mount upward to the higher and purer region since they share in the quality of lightness, what good does that do us ? For we have neither remembrance of where we once were, nor consciousness whether we ever existed at all, and so what

[a] *F.H.G.* ii. 196. These words do not occur in Plato's extant writings; even if he wrote them, δόξης, which Dioscurides took to mean "fame," may rather mean "false opinion," *cf. Theaet.* 161 E, and to alter the text as Kaibel does is to disguise the lengths to which this detractor will go in distorting what Plato said. See critical note 1.

[b] 19 B; but the text of Plato is very different. With this paraphrase the citation from Hegesander (above, 507 a and p. 277 note *f*) is thought by some to have ended.

[c] *Il.* xvi. 856. Plato himself quotes these lines (with disapproval) *Rep.* 386 D.

ATHENAEUS

τῆς ἀθανασίας· οἱ δὲ συντεθέντες ὑπ᾽ αὐτοῦ Νόμο
508 καὶ τούτων ἔτι πρότερον ἡ Πολιτεία τί πεποιή
κασιν; καίτοι γε ἔδει καθάπερ τὸν Λυκοῦργο
τοὺς Λακεδαιμονίους καὶ τὸν Σόλωνα τοὺς Ἀθη
ναίους καὶ τὸν Ζάλευκον τοὺς Θουρίους, καὶ αὐτόι
εἴπερ ἦσαν χρήσιμοι, πεῖσαί τινας τῶν Ἑλλήνω
αὐτοῖς χρήσασθαι. ᾽ νόμος γάρ ἐστιν,᾽ ὥς φησι
Ἀριστοτέλης, ᾽ λόγος ὡρισμένος καθ᾽ ὁμολογία
κοινὴν πόλεως, μηνύων πῶς δεῖ πράττειν ἕκαστα
ὁ δὲ Πλάτων πῶς οὐκ ἄτοπος,[1] τριῶν Ἀθηναίω
γενομένων νομοθετῶν τῶν γε δὴ γνωριζομένω
Δράκοντος καὶ αὐτοῦ τοῦ[2] Πλάτωνος καὶ Σόλωνο
b τῶν μὲν τοῖς νόμοις ἐμμένειν τοὺς πολίτας, τῶ
δὲ τοῦ Πλάτωνος καὶ προσκαταγελᾶν; ὁ δ᾽ αὐτὸ
λόγος καὶ περὶ τῆς Πολιτείας· εἰ καὶ πασῶν ἐστι
αὕτη βελτίων, μὴ πείθοι δ᾽ ἡμᾶς, τί πλέον
ἔοικεν οὖν ὁ Πλάτων οὐ τοῖς οὖσιν ἀνθρώποι
γράψαι τοὺς νόμους, ἀλλὰ τοῖς ὑπ᾽ αὐτοῦ διαπλατ
τομένοις, ὥστε καὶ ζητεῖσθαι τοὺς χρησομένους
ἐχρῆν οὖν ἃ πείσει[4] λέγων[5] ταῦτα καὶ γράφειν κα
μὴ ταὐτὰ ποιεῖν τοῖς εὐχομένοις, ἀλλὰ τοῖς τῶ
ἐνδεχομένων ἀντεχομένοις.

" Χωρὶς τοίνυν τούτων εἴ τις διεξίοι τοὺς Τιμαίου
c αὐτοῦ καὶ τοὺς Γοργίας καὶ τοὺς ἄλλους δὲ τοῦ

[1] πῶς οὐκ ἄτοπος ACE: πως; οὐκ ἄτοπον Kaibel. disregard
ing the Greek fondness for the personal construction.
[2] τοῦ om. CE. Meineke interchanged the positions o
αὐτοῦ τοῦ Π. and Σόλωνος.
[3] ἐστιν ACE: εἴη Meineke.
[4] οὖν ἃ πείσει Musurus: οὖ ἄπεισι A, οὖν οὐ εἰσι CE.
[5] λέγων A: λέγειν CE.

[a] Zaleucus, whose existence was denied by Timaeus (Cic
282

gratification is derived from that kind of deathlessness? Again, what results have been produced by the *Laws* compiled by him, or from the *Republic*, which is still earlier than the *Laws*? And yet, surely, he ought, after the model set by Lycurgus for the Lacedaemonians, by Solon for the Athenians, and by Zaleucus for the Thurians,[a] in his own case also, supposing that his laws were of any use, to have induced some of the Greeks to adopt them. 'For a law,' as Aristotle says,[b] 'is a definite statement, based on a common agreement in the community, indicating how things are to be done in each case.' Now as to Plato, is he not in a ludicrous position, seeing that of the three Athenians who became lawgivers and who acquired some fame, at least, Draco, Plato himself, and Solon, their fellow-citizens adopted the laws of two of them, but actually laughed at those of Plato? And the same reasoning applies also to the *Republic*; even supposing that this state *is* better than all others, if he fails to convince us of it, what good is it? It is plain, therefore, that Plato did not write his laws for actually existent men, but for those who are conceived in his imagination, so that one must seek far and wide for people who will adopt them. He ought, therefore, to have written down only those things which would win persuasion if he spoke them, and not do the same thing that people do who make pious wishes, but rather what people do who keep a hold on things which are practicable.

"Apart, then, from these considerations, if one should go through his *Timaeuses* and his *Gorgiases*

De Leg. ii. 6. 15), is more commonly associated with the Western Locrians, Athen. 429 (vol. iv. p. 442). On the origin of the laws of Thurii see Pauly-Wissowa iii. 2181.

[b] *Rhet. ad Alex.* 1. 4.

τοιούτους διαλόγους, ἐν οἷς καὶ περὶ τῶν ἐν τοῖς[1]
μαθήμασι διεξέρχεται καὶ περὶ τῶν κατὰ φύσιν
καὶ περὶ πλειόνων ἄλλων, οὐδὲ[2] διὰ ταῦτα θαυ-
μαστέος ἐστίν. ἔχει γάρ τις καὶ παρ' ἑτέρων
ταῦτα λαβεῖν ἢ βέλτιον λεχθέντα ἢ μὴ χεῖρον.
καὶ γὰρ Θεόπομπος ὁ Χῖος ἐν τῷ κατὰ τῆς
Πλάτωνος διατριβῆς ' τοὺς πολλούς,' φησί, ' τῶν
διαλόγων αὐτοῦ ἀχρείους καὶ ψευδεῖς ἄν τις εὕροι·
ἀλλοτρίους δὲ τοὺς πλείους, ὄντας ἐκ τῶν Ἀριστ-
d ίππου διατριβῶν, ἐνίους δὲ κἀκ τῶν Ἀντισθένους,
πολλοὺς δὲ κἀκ τῶν Βρύσωνος τοῦ Ἡρακλεώτου.'
ἀλλὰ τὰ κατὰ τὸν ἄνθρωπον ἅπερ ἐπαγγέλλεται
καὶ ἡμεῖς ζητοῦμεν ἐκ τῶν ἐκείνου λόγων,[3] οὐχ
εὑρίσκομεν, ἀλλὰ συμπόσια μὲν καὶ λόγους ὑπὲρ
Ἔρωτος εἰρημένους καὶ μάλα ἀπρεπεῖς, οὓς κατα-
φρονῶν τῶν ἀναγνωσομένων συνέθηκεν, ὥσπερ
καὶ οἱ πολλοὶ τῶν μαθητῶν αὐτοῦ τυραννικοί τινες
καὶ διάβολοι γεγόνασιν.[4] Εὐφραῖος[5] μὲν γὰρ παρὰ
e Περδίκκᾳ τῷ βασιλεῖ διατρίβων ἐν Μακεδονίᾳ οὐχ
ἧττον αὐτοῦ ἐβασίλευε[6] φαῦλος ὢν καὶ διάβολος· ὃς[6]
οὕτω ψυχρῶς συνέταξε τὴν ἑταιρίαν[7] τοῦ βασιλέως
ὥστε οὐκ ἐξῆν τοῦ συσσιτίου μετασχεῖν εἰ μή τις
ἐπίσταιτο γεωμετρεῖν ἢ φιλοσοφεῖν. ὅθεν, Φιλίππου τὴν ἀρχὴν παραλαβόντος, Παρμενίων[8] αὐτὸν
ἐν Ὠρεῷ λαβὼν ἀπέκτεινεν, ὥς φησι Καρύστιος
ἐν Ἱστορικοῖς Ὑπομνήμασι. καὶ Κάλλιππος δ' ὁ

---

[1] τοῖς om. C. [2] οὐδὲ CE: οὐδ' ὡς A.
[3] ὅπερ in A after λόγων deleted by Dobree.
[4] CE (obviously to make a complete sentence): γενόμενοι A.
Some words have been lost. [5] Casaubon: εὐφρατος ACE.
[6] ἐβασίλευε and ὃς deleted by Kaibel; but this again
weakens the writer's (Herodicus?) exaggeration and destroys
the point of τυραννικοί.

and all other such dialogues, in which Plato discusses
the sciences and things ' in accord with nature ' and
many other subjects besides, not even for this is he
to be admired.   For even from other authorities one
may get these things said either better or not worse.
Why, even Theopompus of Chios, in his *Attack on
Plato's School*, says [a] : ' One would discover that the
majority of his dialogues are useless and false ; and
the greater number are borrowed, being taken from
the discourses of Aristippus, some even from those
of Antisthenes, and many also from those of Bryson
of Heracleia.' Why, those speculations on mankind
which he advertises and which we search for in his
dialogues we fail to find ; rather dinner-parties, and
words spoken on the subject of Eros—very indecent,
too—all of which he compiled in utter contempt of his
future readers, just as most of his disciples proved to
be men of tyrannical and slanderous disposition.   Euphraeus,[b] for example, when staying at the court of
King Perdiccas in Macedonia, lorded it as regally as
the king himself, though he was of low origin and
given to slander ; he was so pedantic in his selection
of the king's associates that nobody could share in
the common mess if he did not know how to practise
geometry [c] or philosophy.   For this reason, when
Philip succeeded to the throne, Parmenion seized and
killed Euphraeus in Oreus, according to Carystius in
Historical Notes.[d]   So also Callippus of Athens, another

---

[a] *F.H.G.* i. 325, J. 2 B 591, G. and H. 247.
[b] *Cf.* above, 506 e (p. 276).
[c] Alluding to the inscription said to be written on Plato's
door, ἀγεωμέτρητος μηδεὶς εἰσίτω, Elias, *In Aristot. Categ.
Comment.* 118. 18.   [d] *F.H.G.* iv. 357.

---

[7] CF: ἑταίραν A.   [8] παρμενίδης C.

ATHENAEUS

Ἀθηναῖος, μαθητὴς καὶ αὐτὸς Πλάτωνος, ἑταῖρος
f Δίωνος καὶ συμμαθητὴς γενόμενος καὶ συναποδη-
μήσας αὐτῷ εἰς Συρακούσας, ὁρῶν ἤδη τὸν Δίωνα
ἐξιδιοποιούμενον τὴν μοναρχίαν ἀποκτείνας αὐτὸν
καὶ αὐτὸς τυραννεῖν ἐπιχειρήσας ἀπεσφάγη.[1]
Εὐαίων[2] δ' ὁ Λαμψακηνός, ὥς φησιν Εὐρύπυλος
καὶ Δικαιοκλῆς ὁ Κνίδιος ἐνενηκοστῷ[3] καὶ πρώτῳ
Διατριβῶν, ἔτι δὲ Δημοχάρης ὁ ῥήτωρ ἐν τῷ ὑπὲρ
Σοφοκλέους πρὸς Φίλωνα, δανείσας τῇ πατρίδι
ἀργύριον ἐπὶ ἐνεχύρῳ τῇ ἀκροπόλει ἀφυστερήσας[4]
τυραννεῖν ἐβουλεύετο, ἕως συνδραμόντες ἐπ' αὐτὸν
οἱ Λαμψακηνοὶ καὶ τὰ χρήματα ἀποδόντες ἐξ-
509 έβαλον. Τίμαιος δ' ὁ Κυζικηνός, ὡς ὁ αὐτὸς Δημοχάρης φησίν, χρήματα καὶ σῖτον ἐπιδοὺς τοῖς
πολίταις καὶ διὰ ταῦτα πιστευθεὶς εἶναι χρηστὸς
παρὰ τοῖς Κυζικηνοῖς, μικρὸν ἐπισχὼν χρόνον
ἐπέθετο τῇ πολιτείᾳ δι' Ἀριδαίου. κριθεὶς δὲ καὶ
ἁλοὺς καὶ ἀδοξήσας[5] ἐν μὲν τῇ πόλει ἐπέμενε
παλαιὸς καὶ γεγηρακώς,[6] ἀτίμως δὲ διαζῶν.
τοιοῦτοι δ' εἰσὶ καὶ νῦν τῶν Ἀκαδημαϊκῶν τινες,
ἀνοσίως καὶ ἀδόξως βιοῦντες. χρημάτων γὰρ ἐξ
ἀσεβείας καὶ παρὰ φύσιν κυριεύσαντες διὰ γοητείαν

---

[1] ἀπεσφάγη C (confirming Nauck's emendation): ἐπεσφάγη AE.

[2] Εὐαίων Diog. Laert. iii. 46; εὐάγων ACE (" Romaic influence," T. W. Allen).

[3] ἐν ἐνηκοστῷ A, ἐν εἰκοστῷ Musurus.

[4] ἀφυστερήσας C, καὶ ἀφυστερήσας E: καὶ ἀποστερήσας A.

[5] καὶ ἀδοξήσας bracketed by Wilamowitz. But if anything is to be deleted it is καὶ ἀδόξως after ἀτίμως δὲ (A), omitted in C, cf. below, καὶ ἀδόξως βιοῦντες (in a different sense).

[6] καταγεγηρακὼς Kaibel, who thought παλαιὸς (Lumb πλάνος "vagabond") corrupt.

286

disciple of Plato, though he had been a friend and fellow-pupil of Dion, and had travelled in his company to Syracuse,[a] presently observing that Dion was trying to appropriate the monarchy to himself, killed him and attempted to be tyrant himself, but was murdered. Then there was Euaeon of Lampsacus, as recorded by Eurypylus and Dicaeocles of Cnidus in the ninety-first book of his *Discourses*, also by the orator Demochares in his speech as advocate in the case *Sophocles versus Philon*.[b] He lent money to his native city, taking as security the acropolis, which he retained with the design of becoming tyrant, until the people of Lampsacus combined to resist him, and after paying back his money they threw him out. Then Timaeus[c] of Cyzicus, as Demochares again says, after bestowing a largess of money and grain upon his fellow-citizens, thereby winning confidence among the Cyzicenes that he was a good man, a little while afterwards attacked their constitution through the agency of Aridaeus. He was tried, convicted, and disgraced, and although he remained in the city old and worn with age, he passed his life in dishonour. Some of the Academic philosophers of to-day are like that, living as they do wickedly and disgracefully. For after gaining possession of a fortune by sacrilege and by unnatural courses through trickery, they are

[a] When Dion returned from exile in Athens. See Plat. *Epp.* iii. and vii., Plut. *Dio* 28.
[b] A politician named Sophocles proposed a decree (307/6 B.C.) establishing censorship against the philosophers suspected of sympathizing with Macedon. Philon brought a counter-suit (γραφὴ παρανόμων), which Demochares defended unsuccessfully ; Diog. Laert. v. 38, Athen. 610 e, Democh. Frag. in Baiter and Sauppe, p. 341.
[c] Timolaus of Cyzicus, not Timaeus, is mentioned among Plato's disciples, Diog. Laert. iii. 46.

287

νῦν εἰσιν περίβλεπτοι· ὥσπερ καὶ Χαίρων
b Πελληνεύς, ὃς οὐ μόνον Πλάτωνι ἐσχόλακεν, ἀλλ
καὶ Ξενοκράτει. καὶ οὗτος οὖν τῆς πατρίδο
πικρῶς τυραννήσας οὐ μόνον τοὺς ἀρίστους τῶ
πολιτῶν ἐξήλασεν, ἀλλὰ καὶ τοῖς τούτων· δούλοι
τὰ χρήματα τῶν δεσποτῶν χαρισάμενος καὶ τὰ
ἐκείνων γυναῖκας συνῴκισεν πρὸς γάμου κοινωνίαν
ταῦτ' ὠφεληθεὶς ἐκ τῆς καλῆς Πολιτείας καὶ τῶ
παρανόμων Νόμων."

Διὸ καὶ Ἔφιππος ὁ κωμῳδοποιὸς ἐν Ναυάγι
c Πλάτωνά τε αὐτὸν καὶ τῶν γνωρίμων τινὰ
κεκωμῴδηκεν ὡς καὶ ἐπ' ἀργυρίῳ συκοφαν
τοῦντας, ἐμφαίνων ὅτι καὶ πολυτελῶς ἠσκοῦντ
καὶ ὅτι τῆς εὐμορφίας τῶν καθ' ἡμᾶς ἀσελγῶ
πλείονα πρόνοιαν ἐποιοῦντο· λέγει δ' οὕτως·

> ἔπειτ' ἀναστὰς[1] εὔστοχος νεανίας
> τῶν ἐξ Ἀκαδημίας τις ὑποπλατωνικὸς[2]
> Βρυσωνοθρασυμαχειοληψικερμάτων,[3]
> πληγεὶς ἀνάγκῃ ληψιλογομίσθῳ[4] τέχνῃ
> d συνών τις, οὐκ ἄσκεπτα δυνάμενος λέγειν,
> εὖ μὲν μαχαίρᾳ ξύστ' ἔχων τριχώματα,
> εὖ δ' ὑποκαθιεὶς ἄτομα[5] πώγωνος βάθη,

[1] Jacobs: ἐπεὶ καταστὰς A.
[2] Meineke: ὑπὸ πλάτωνα καὶ A.
[3] Meineke: βρύσων ὁ θρασ- etc. A.
[4] ληψιλογομίσθῳ Meineke: λιψεγυμεσθω A, ληψολιγομίσθ
Hemsterhuys.
[5] Scaliger: ὑποκαθιεῖσα τομα A.

---

[a] Kock ii. 257. Meineke cites the εὐπρεπὴς νεανίας ο
Aristoph. Eccles. 427 ff.; a closer parallel is Aristoph
288

now looked up to with admiration; just like Chaeron of Pellenê, who attended the lectures not only of Plato but also of Xenocrates. He too, as I was saying, ruled his native city with bitter tyranny, and not only drove out its best citizens, but also bestowed upon their slaves the property of their masters, and forced the masters' wives into wedlock with the slaves; these were the beneficial results he derived from the noble *Republic* and from the lawless *Laws*!

"Hence, also, the comic poet Ephippus in *Ship-wrecked* has satirized Plato in person, as well as some of his disciples, for acting as venal informers, indicating that they adorned themselves sumptuously, and that they exercised more care to secure an elegant appearance than the rakes of our own day. He says[a]: 'Then up rose a smart[b] young fellow, with a smattering of Plato—one of the small-coin-seizing-Bryson-Thrasymachus[c] gentry from the Academy; smitten by penury, he had joined the school of lucrative words, and had a faculty for considered speech; well trimmed with scissors[d] was his crop of hair, well did he let his beard grow down to uncut depths, well was

Vesp. 474 ὦ μισόδημε καὶ μοναρχίας ἐραστά, | καὶ ξυνὼν Βρασίδᾳ καὶ φορῶν κράσπεδα (tassels) | στεμμάτων τήν θ' ὑπήνην ἄκουρον τρέφων. *Cf.* also the sophistic art as taught by Euripides, Aristoph. *Ran.* 956 ff. and Athen. 544 f (Antiphanes). Ephippus flourished about the middle of the fourth century B.C.
[b] εὔστοχος, "shrewd," lit. "making good guesses," a "sure-fire" young man.
[c] On Bryson *cf.* above, 508 d. Thrasymachus of Chalcedon (505 c), well known from Plato's *Republic* and *Phaedrus*. The comic poets do not bother to distinguish properly the various sophistic schools.
[d] On this see Nicolson, "Greek and Roman Barbers," *H.S.C.P.* ii. 54.

289

εὖ δ᾽ ἐν πεδίλῳ πόδα[1] τιθεὶς ἐπισφύρων[2]
κνήμης ἱμάντων ἰσομέτροις ἑλίγμασιν,
ὄγκῳ τε χλανίδος εὖ τεθωρακισμένος,
σχῆμ᾽ ἀξιόχρεων ἐπικαθεὶς βακτηρίᾳ,
ἀλλότριον, οὐκ οἰκεῖον, ὡς ἐμοὶ δοκεῖ,
ἔλεξεν· ‘ ἄνδρες τῆς ᾽Αθηναίων χθονός.’ ᾽᾽

Μέχρι τούτων ἡμῖν πεπεραιώσθω[3] καὶ ἥδε ἡ
συναγωγή, φίλτατε Τιμόκρατες. ἑξῆς δὲ ἐροῦμεν
περὶ τῶν ἐπὶ τρυφῇ διαβοήτων γενομένων.

Scaliger: πολλὰ A.   [2] Kaibel: ὑπὸ ξυρὸν A.
        [3] Casaubon (cf. 588 a): πεπαιρεώσθω A.

Αθηναίου ĪᾹ—ĪΒ̄ (fol. 244 verso).

his foot set in a sandal with leg-guard straps in nicely measured wrappings, well was he fortified with a mass of cloak as he leaned his imposing figure on his staff and spoke a word that he had borrowed, not his own, I think : ' Ye citizens of the Athenian soil.' " [a]

So let this compilation end for us at this point, my very dear Timocrates. Next we shall talk about people who made themselves notorious for their luxury.

[a] Here end the strictures on Plato begun by Pontianus, 504 b (p. 260).

IB

510   Ἄνθρωπος εἶναί μοι Κυρηναῖος[1] δοκεῖς,
κατὰ τὸν Ἀλέξιδος Τυνδάρεων, ἑταῖρε Τιμό-
κρατες·

    κἀκεῖ γὰρ ἄν τις ἐπὶ τὸ δεῖπνον ἕνα καλῇ,
    πάρεισιν ὀκτωκαίδεκ' ἄλλοι καὶ δέκα
    ἅρματα συνωρίδες τε[2] πεντεκαίδεκα·
    τούτοις δὲ δεῖ σε τἀπιτήδει' ἐμβαλεῖν,
    ὥστ' ἦν κράτιστον μηδὲ καλέσαι μηδένα.

κἀμοὶ δ' ἦν κράτιστον σιωπᾶν καὶ μὴ ἐπὶ τοσούτοις
b προειρημένοις ἕτερα προστιθέναι· ἀλλ' ἐπεὶ πάνυ
λιπαρῶς ἡμᾶς ἀπαιτεῖς καὶ τὸν περὶ τῶν ἐπὶ
τρυφῇ διαβοήτων γενομένων λόγον καὶ τῆς τούτων
ἡδυπαθείας . . .[3]

Ἡ γὰρ ἀπόλαυσις δήπου μετ' ἐπιθυμίας πρῶτον,
ἔπειτα[4] μεθ' ἡδονῆς. καίτοι Σοφοκλῆς γ' ὁ
ποιητής, τῶν ἀπολαυστικῶν[5] εἷς ὤν, ἵνα μὴ κατ-
ηγορῇ τοῦ γήρως, εἰς σωφροσύνην ἔθετο τὴν ἀσθένειαν αὐτοῦ τὴν περὶ τὰς τῶν ἀφροδισίων ἀπο-

---

[1] Κυρηναῖος has ῠ in Alexis (544 e), Aristoph. *Thesm.* 98,
ῠ in Pind. *Pyth.* iv. 2, Call. *Ap.* 73, 94. Hence Ἄνθρωπε,
Κυρηναῖος εἶναί μοι δοκεῖς Herwerden.

[2] Musurus: ἅρματα· συνωρίδες A, ἅρματα καὶ συνωρίδες CE.

[3] ἀποδώσω added by Madvig after ἀπαιτεῖς. ἄκουε δὴ ὅσα
καὶ περὶ τούτων εἶπον οἱ δειπνοσοφισταί suggested by Kaibel.

292

BOOK XII

Alexis in *Tyndareos*, friend Timocrates,[a] says[b] : "I think you must be a man from Cyrene ; for over there, if a host invites one man to dinner, eighteen others turn up, besides ten chariots and fifteen pairs of horses ; you have to pour in food for all these, so that it would have been best not even to invite a soul." And in my own case, too, it would have been best to keep silence, and not heap other subjects upon the great number of things that I have said before ; but since you are very insistent in your demand for the promised discourse on those persons who made themselves notorious for their luxury, and on their way of enjoying life, (I will proceed).[c]

Now the act of enjoyment, of course, is associated first with desire, and then with satisfaction.[d] And yet the poet Sophocles, a man devoted to enjoyment, avoided finding fault with his old age by ascribing to self-control his failing powers in the enjoyment of

---

[a] In this book there appears no reference to the Deipnosophists ; Athenaeus drops the banquet and discourses in his own name, *cf.* 550 f and see vol. i. p. xi.   [b] Kock ii. 384.
[c] Kaibel supplied thus : "hear then what the Deipnosophists said on this subject."
[d] *Cf.* Aristot. *Eth. Nic.* 1173 b 7-13.

---

[4] A : εἶτα CE and lemma in A.
[5] ἀπολαυστικῶν CE : ἀπολαυστικῶν γε A.

293

λαύσεις, φήσας ἀσμένως ἀπηλλάχθαι αὐτῶν ὥσπερ
c τινὸς ἀγρίου[1] δεσπότου. ἐγὼ δέ φημι καὶ τὴν
τοῦ Πάριδος κρίσιν ὑπὸ τῶν παλαιοτέρων πεποιῆσθαι ἡδονῆς πρὸς ἀρετὴν οὖσαν σύγκρισιν· προ-
κριθείσης γοῦν τῆς Ἀφροδίτης, αὕτη δ' ἐστὶν ἡ
ἡδονή, πάντα συνεταράχθη. καί μοι δοκεῖ καὶ
ὁ καλὸς ἡμῶν Ξενοφῶν τὸν περὶ τὸν Ἡρακλέα
καὶ τὴν Ἀρετὴν μῦθον ἐντεῦθεν πεπλακέναι. κατὰ
γὰρ τὸν Ἐμπεδοκλέα·

οὐδέ τις ἦν κείνοισιν Ἄρης θεὸς οὐδὲ Κυδοιμός
d   οὐδὲ Ζεὺς βασιλεὺς οὐδὲ Κρόνος οὐδὲ Ποσειδῶν
ἀλλὰ Κύπρις βασίλεια.
τὴν οἵ γ' εὐσεβέεσσιν ἀγάλμασιν ἱλάσκοντο[3]
γραπτοῖς τε[4] ζώοισι μύροισί τε δαιδαλεόδμοις
σμύρνης τ'[5] ἀκρήτου θυσίαις λιβάνου τε θυώδους
ξανθῶν τε σπονδὰς μελίτων[6] ῥίπτοντες ἐς οὖδας

καὶ Μένανδρος δ' ἐν Κιθαριστῇ περί τινος μουσι
κευομένου, λέγων φησί·

[1] ἀγρίου added from Plato.   [2] ἡ CE, om. A.
[3] Porphyr. De Abst. ii. 21 : ἱλάσκονται A.
[4] Porphyr.: δὲ A.   [5] Porphyr.: σμύρνοις τε A.
[6] ξουθῶν . . μελιττῶν "humming bees " Porphyr. (μελιτᾶ
Sturz).

[a] Plat. Rep. 329 c. The words " and yet " at the beginning
of the sentence introduce the opposite phase of the matter
that freedom from desire may itself be a satisfaction.
[b] An example of the allegorical method of interpreting the
poets, in vogue from the days of Theagenes of Rhegium to
the Renaissance, and later (cf. Plat. Rep. 378 D). A σύγ-
κρισις was a trial or debate, very common in mediaeval

sexual love, declaring that he was glad to be freed at last from it, as from a savage master.[a] And I for one affirm also that the Judgement of Paris, as told in poetry by the writers of an older time, is really a trial of pleasure against virtue.[b] Aphrodite, for example—and she represents pleasure—was given the preference, and so everything was thrown into turmoil. I think, too, that our noble Xenophon invented the story of Heracles and Virtue with the same motive.[c] For according to Empedocles[d]: "Nor had they any War-god, or Battle-din, nor was Zeus their king, nor Cronus, nor Poseidon, but Cypris only was their queen. Her that folk appeased with pious offerings—painted animals[e] and richly-scented salves,[f] with sacrifices of pure myrrh and fragrant frankincense, while they poured upon the ground libations from the yellow honeycomb."[g] Menander, also, speaking in *The Harper* of someone playing a musical instrument

times, in which different qualities are compared, as in the Choice of Heracles, below.

[c] Xen. *Mem.* ii. 1. 21-34, ascribed to Prodicus (below, 544 d, p. 466). The Judgement of Paris appeared first in *The Cyprian Lays*, a poem of the epic cycle (above, p. 113 and note d, Hdt. ii. 117).

[d] Diels, *Vorsokr.*[3] i. 271; the people of the Golden Age are meant.

[e] Of dough, *cf.* Diog. Laert. viii. 53, Athen. 3 c (vol. i. p. 12), Suidas *s. βοῦς ἕβδομος*, Hdt. ii. 47; a pious fraud to avoid shedding the blood of real animals, Porphyr. *De Abst.* ii. 21, Eisler in *Archiv f. Religionswissenschaft* xiii. 625. Cypris in Empedocles was the principle of love or attraction in the universe, and not, as Athenaeus says, the goddess of pleasure.

[f] Salves, like incense, were often used to keep off evil spirits.

[g] See critical note 6. Eur. *I.T.* 165 ξουθᾶν τε πόνημα μελισσᾶν, also in a libation.

511

φιλόμουσον εἶν'[1] αὐτὸν πάνυ
ἀκούσματ' εἰς τρυφήν τε παιδεύεσθ' ἀεί.[2]

Καίτοι τινές φασι κατὰ φύσιν εἶναι τὴν ἡδονὴν
ἐκ τοῦ πάντα ζῷα δεδουλῶσθαι ταύτῃ, ὥσπερ οὐχὶ
καὶ δειλίας καὶ φόβου καὶ τῶν ἄλλων παθημάτων
κοινῶς μὲν ἐν ἅπασιν ὄντων, παρὰ δὲ τοῖς λογισμῷ
χρωμένοις ἀποδοκιμαζομένων. τὸ οὖν ἡδονὰς διώ-
κειν προπετῶς λύπας ἐστὶ θηρεύειν. διόπερ Ὅμηρος ἐπονείδιστον βουλόμενος ποιῆσαι τὴν ἡδονὴν
b καὶ τῶν θεῶν φησι τοὺς μεγίστους οὐδὲν ὑπὸ τῆς
σφετέρας ὠφελεῖσθαι δυνάμεως, ἀλλὰ τὰ μέγιστα
βλάπτεσθαι παρενεχθέντας[3] ὑπ' αὐτῆς. ὅσα μὲν
γὰρ ἀγρυπνῶν ὁ Ζεὺς ἐφρόντιζεν ὑπὲρ τῶν Τρώων,
ταῦτ' ἀπώλεσεν μεθ' ἡμέραν ὑφ' ἡδονῆς κρατηθείς.
καὶ ὁ Ἄρης ἀλκιμώτατος ὢν ὑπὸ τοῦ ἀσθενεστάτου
Ἡφαίστου συνεποδίσθη καὶ ὦφλεν αἰσχύνην καὶ
ζημίαν ἐκδοὺς ἑαυτὸν ἔρωσιν ἀλογίστοις. φησὶ
γοῦν πρὸς τοὺς θεούς, ὅτ' ἦλθον αὐτὸν θεασόμενοι
δεδεμένον·

οὐκ ἀρετᾷ κακὰ ἔργα· κιχάνει τοι βραδὺς ὠκύν,
c ὡς καὶ νῦν Ἥφαιστος ἐὼν βραδὺς εἷλεν Ἄρηα
ὠκύτατόν περ ἐόντα θεῶν οἳ Ὄλυμπον ἔχουσι,
χωλὸς ἐών, τέχνῃσι· τὸ καὶ ζωάγρι'[4] ὀφέλλει.

" οὐδεὶς δὲ λέγει τὸν Ἀριστείδου βίον ἡδύν, ἀλλὰ
τὸν Σμινδυρίδου τοῦ Συβαρίτου καὶ τὸν Σαρδανα-

___

[1] εἶναι A.
[2] αἰεί A.
[3] Meineke: προενεχθέντας A.
[4] μοιχάγρι' Homer.

___

[a] Kock iii. 81, Allinson 380.
[b] Cf. Eth. Nic. 1172 b 9 Εὔδοξος . . . τὴν ἡδονὴν τἀγαθὸν
296

says [a] : " He is very fond of music, and always practising tunes in luxurious ease."

And yet some people say that pleasure is ordained by nature, because all living things are slaves to it,[b] as if cowardice and fear and other feelings as well did not exist in all alike, though *they* are discountenanced by those who follow reason. And so to pursue pleasures recklessly is to hunt pain.[c] This is why Homer, desiring to represent pleasure as reprehensible, declares that even the highest gods are in no wise protected by their own power, but receive the greatest injuries if they are misled by pleasure. For all the plans that Zeus made for the Trojans as he lay awake were upset when day came because he was over-mastered by pleasure.[d] Even Ares, the most doughty of all, was bound hand and foot by Hephaestus, the weakest of all, and was condemned to shame and a fine because he gave himself up to unreasoning amours. One [e] says to the gods, at least, when they come to look at him in his bonds : " Evil deeds thrive not ; the slow catches the swift, since even Hephaestus, slow though he is, hath overtaken Ares, though swiftest of the gods that hold Olympus—he, the lame one, by his arts ; therefore Ares owes him ransom." [f]

" Still, no one speaks of the life of Aristeides [g] as pleasurable, but only the life of Smindyrides the

(the *summum bonum*) ζ̨̃ετ' εἶναι διὰ τὸ πάνθ' ὁρᾶν ἐφιέμενα αὐτῆς, καὶ ἔλλογα καὶ ἄλογα.   [c] Cf. Plat. *Phaedo* 60 B.

[d] Referring to the fascinations of Hera as described in *Il.* xiv. 159 ff.

[e] The subject in Homer, *Od.* viii. 328, is τις (*i.e.* one god speaking to another), which may have dropped out of the text here.

[f] Homer : " owes him the adulterer's fine (μοιχάγρια)."

[g] " The Just."

πάλλου.¹ καίτοι κατά γε² τὴν δόξαν," φησὶν ἐν τῷ
περὶ Ἡδονῆς Θεόφραστος, "οὐχ ὁμοίως λαμπρός
ἐστιν· ἀλλ᾽ οὐκ ἐτρύφησεν ὥσπερ ἐκεῖνοι. οὐδὲ
τὸν Ἀγησιλάου τοῦ Λακεδαιμονίων βασιλέως,
ἀλλὰ μᾶλλον, εἰ ἔτυχεν, τὸν Ἀνάνιος οὕτως ἀορά-
d του κατὰ δόξαν ὄντος, οὐδὲ τὸν τῶν ἡμιθέων τῶν
ἐπὶ Τροίας, ἀλλὰ πολλῷ μᾶλλον τῶν νῦν.³ καὶ
τοῦτ᾽ εἰκότως. ὁ μὲν γὰρ ἀκατάσκευος καὶ καθάπερ ἀνεύρετος ἦν, οὔτ᾽ ἐπιμιξίας οὔσης οὔτε τῶν
τεχνῶν διηκριβωμένων, ὁ δὲ πᾶσιν ἐξηρτυμένος
πρὸς ῥᾳστώνην καὶ πρὸς ἀπόλαυσιν καὶ πρὸς τὰς
ἄλλας διαγωγάς."

Πλάτων δ᾽ ἐν τῷ Φιλήβῳ φησίν· " ἡδονὴ μὲν
γὰρ ἁπάντων ἀλαζονίστατον. ὡς δὲ λόγος, καὶ ἐν
e ταῖς ἡδοναῖς ταῖς περὶ τὰ ἀφροδίσια, αἳ δὴ μέγι-
σται⁴ δοκοῦσιν εἶναι, καὶ τὸ ἐπιορκεῖν συγγνώμην
εἴληφεν παρὰ θεῶν, ὡς⁵ καθάπερ παίδων τῶν
ἡδονῶν νοῦν οὐδὲ τὸν ὀλίγιστον⁶ κεκτημένων." ἐν
δὲ τῷ ὀγδόῳ τῆς Πολιτείας ὁ αὐτὸς Πλάτων
πρότερος ὑπέδειξε τὸ ὑπὸ τῶν Ἐπικουρείων θρυ-

---

¹ σαρδαναπάλου C.   ² γε om. CE.
³ τῶν νῦν A : τὸν τῶν νῦν Meineke.
⁴ αἳ δὴ μέγισται Plato : ἃ δὴ μέγιστα ACE.
⁵ Plato : ὥσπερ ACE.
⁶ ἡδονῶν (ἡδομένων CE) οὐδὲ τὸν λογισμὸν ACE.

ᵃ Athen. 273 b (vol. iii. p. 226), below, 541 b, Herod. vi. 127.
ᵇ Athen. 335 f (vol. iv. p. 25 note a), 528 f (p. 386).
ᶜ Frag. 84 Wimmer.
ᵈ Ananis, or Ananius, the iambograph, is known chiefly
for his description of high living, Athen. 282 b (vol. iii. p. 266).
ᵉ Of these Socrates said that they preferred death to dishonour, Plat. Apol. 28 B-C.
ᶠ Diod. Sic. v. 39 uses the same word (ἀκατάσκευος) of the
uncivilized Celts and Iberians.

Sybarite,ᵃ or of Sardanapalus.ᵇ And yet, judged **at**
least by the repute that Aristeides won,"Theophrastus
says in his treatise *On Pleasure,*ᶜ " he is more distinguished than they ; but he did not go in for luxury
as they did. Nor do they call the life of Agesilaus,
king of Sparta, one of pleasure, but rather, perhaps,
that of Ananis,ᵈ though he remains so obscure so **far as**
reputation goes ; nor that of the demigods who fought
against Troy,ᵉ but much more the life of the men
of to-day. And this with good reason. For life in
earlier times was lacking in equipment,ᶠ and **as it**
were undiscovered,ᵍ since there was no free intercourse, and the arts had not been brought to perfection ; the life of our own day, on the other hand, is
equipped with everything conducive to ease, enjoyment, and amusements in general."

Plato says in the *Philebus* ʰ : " Pleasure is the
greatest humbug in the world. As report goes, in
the indulgence of sexual pleasures, which are regarded
as the keenest, even an act of perjury receives pardon
from the gods, because, like children, our pleasures
possess not the slightest reasoning power. ⁱ " And
in the eighth book of the *Republic* Plato again is the
first to give an example of the celebrated saying of

ᵍ ἀνεύρετος is used by Diod. Sic. v. 20, in speaking **of a**
remote island in the Atlantic beyond Africa.

ʰ 65 c ; *cf. Symp.* 183 в ἀφροδίσιον γὰρ ὅρκον οὔ φασιν εἶναι
(" is not valid "), and Schol. ; Timotheüs *P.L.G.*⁴ iii. 625, Call.
Ep. 27. " Periuria ridet amantum Iuppiter," Tibullus iii. 6.
49 ; " Iuppiter ex alto periuria ridet amantum," Ovid. *A.A.*
i. 633. Hesych. *s. ἀφροδίσιος ὅρκος* says the thought was first
expressed by Hesiod, of Zeus and Io ; see Hes. frag. 4 and
Rzach's note. " At lovers' perjuries, they say, Jove laughs,"
Romeo and Juliet, ii. ii.

ⁱ Therefore they have no responsibility.

λούμενον, ὅτι " τῶν ἐπιθυμιῶν αἱ μέν εἰσι φυσικαὶ
καὶ ἀναγκαῖαι, αἱ δὲ φυσικαὶ[1] μέν, οὐκ ἀναγκαῖαι
δέ, αἱ δὲ οὔτε φυσικαὶ οὔτε ἀναγκαῖαι," γράφων
οὕτως· " ἆρ' οὖν οὐχὶ ἡ τοῦ φαγεῖν μέχρις ὑγιείας
f καὶ εὐεξίας καὶ αὐτοῦ σίτου καὶ ὄψου ἀναγκαῖος ἂν
εἴη; ἡ μέν γέ που τοῦ σίτου κατ' ἀμφότερα ἀναγκαία, ᾗ τε ὠφέλιμος ᾗ τε[2] παῦσαι ζῶντας δυνατή[3]
—ναί.—ἡ δὲ ὄψου, εἴ πή τινα ὠφέλειαν πρὸς
εὐεξίαν παρέχεται;—πάνυ μὲν οὖν.—τί δαί; ἡ
πέρα τούτων καὶ ἀλλοίων ἐδεσμάτων ἢ τοιούτων
512 ἐπιθυμία, δυνατὴ δὲ κολαζομένη ἐκ νέων πολλῶν
ἀπαλλάττεσθαι, καὶ βλαβερὰ μὲν σώματι, βλαβερὰ
δὲ ψυχῇ πρός τε φρόνησιν καὶ πρὸς τὸ σωφρονεῖν
ἆρά γε ὀρθῶς οὐκ[4] ἀναγκαία ἂν καλοῖτο;—ὀρθό-
τατα μὲν οὖν."

Ἡρακλείδης δ' ὁ Ποντικὸς ἐν τῷ περὶ Ἡδονῆς
τάδε λέγει· " οἱ τύραννοι καὶ οἱ βασιλεῖς τῶν
ἀγαθῶν ὄντες κύριοι καὶ πάντων εἰληφότες πεῖραν
τὴν ἡδονὴν προκρίνουσιν, μεγαλοψυχοτέρας ποιούσης τῆς ἡδονῆς τὰς τῶν ἀνθρώπων φύσεις. ἅπαντες γοῦν οἱ τὴν ἡδονὴν τιμῶντες καὶ τρυφὰ
προηρημένοι μεγαλόψυχοι καὶ μεγαλοπρεπεῖς εἰσιν
b ὡς Πέρσαι καὶ Μῆδοι. μάλιστα γὰρ τῶν ἄλλων[6]
ἀνθρώπων τὴν ἡδονὴν οὗτοι καὶ τὴν τρυφὴν[7]

καὶ ἀναγκαῖαι, αἱ δὲ φυσικαὶ added by Kaibel from Diog.
L. x. 149.   [2] ᾗ τε ὠφέλιμος ᾗ τε A.
[3] μὴ παῦσαι ζῶντα δυνατή Cod. Monac. of Plato: the others
have παῦσαι ζῶντα. The mss. of Athenaeus furnish no
warrant for παῦσαι πεινῶντας (contrary to Burnet).
[4] οὐκ Plato: καὶ A.   [5] τῶν ACE: πάντων Kaibel.
[6] τῶν ἄλλων A: πάντων CE.
[7] τὴν τρυφὴν C: τὸ τρυφᾶν A.

[a] Usener 295, Bailey 86.   [b] Rep. 559 A.

the Epicureans,[a] that " of the desires, some are natural and necessary, others, though natural, are not necessary, while still others are neither natural nor necessary " ; he writes as follows [b] : " Must not, then, the desire of eating to the point of health and fit condition, that is, the desire of just food and a relish, be a necessary desire ? The desire of food, of course, is necessary in two ways, in so far as it is good for us, and in so far as it is capable of causing our lives to stop [c] ?—Yes.—But the desire of a relish is necessary in so far as it affords aid to securing a condition of fitness ?—Quite so.—What then ? The desire which goes beyond these things, for other kinds of edibles than these,—the desire which, if strictly controlled from youth up, is capable in many cases of being got rid of,—as harmful to the body and harmful to the soul in its pursuit of wisdom and self-control,—must not that desire rightly be called unnecessary ?—Nay, most rightly."

Heracleides of Pontus in his work *On Pleasure* has this to say [d] : " Tyrants and kings, being in control of the good things of life, and having had experience of them all, put pleasure in the first place, since pleasure makes men's natures more lordly. All persons, at any rate, who pay court to pleasure and choose a life of luxury are lordly and magnificent, like the Persians and the Medes. For more than any other men in the world they court pleasure and luxury,

[c] *i.e.* hunger must be satisfied or we die. See Adam's note on *Rep.* 559 A, and his Appendix III.
[d] Voss 34. In this extract μεγαλόψυχος varies in meaning from " proud " to " high-minded." *Cf.* the munificent (μεγαλοπρεπής) and the great-souled (μεγαλόθυμος) man of Aristot. *Eth. Nic.* 1122 a 18-1125 a 35. So, too, ἡ τρυφή (τὸ τρυφᾶν) ranges in sense from " prosperity " to " luxury."

τιμῶσιν, ἀνδρειότατοι καὶ μεγαλοψυχότατοι[1] τῶν
βαρβάρων[2] ὄντες. ἐστὶ γὰρ τὸ μὲν ἥδεσθαι καὶ τὸ
τρυφᾶν ἐλευθέρων· ἀνίησι γὰρ τὰς ψυχὰς καὶ αὔξει
τὸ δὲ πονεῖν δούλων καὶ ταπεινῶν· διὸ καὶ σὺ
στέλλονται οὗτοι καὶ τὰς φύσεις. καὶ ἡ ᾿Αθηναίων
πόλις, ἕως[3] ἐτρύφα, μεγίστη τε ἦν καὶ μεγαλοψυ-
χοτάτους ἔτρεφεν ἄνδρας. ἁλουργῆ μὲν γὰρ ἠμ-
c πίσχοντο ἱμάτια, ποικίλους δ᾿ ὑπέδυνον[4] χιτῶνας
κορύμβους δ᾿ ἀναδούμενοι τῶν τριχῶν χρυσοῦ
τέττιγας περὶ τὸ μέτωπον καὶ τὰς κόρρας[5] ἐφόρουν
ὀκλαδίας τε αὐτοῖς δίφρους ἔφερον οἱ παῖδες, ἵνα
μὴ καθίζοιεν ὡς ἔτυχεν. καὶ τοιοῦτοι ἦσαν[6] οἱ
τὴν ἐν Μαραθῶνι νικήσαντες μάχην καὶ μόνοι τὴν
τῆς ᾿Ασίας ἁπάσης δύναμιν χειρωσάμενοι. καὶ οἱ
φρονιμώτατοι δέ, φησίν, καὶ μεγίστην δόξαν ἐπὶ
σοφίᾳ ἔχοντες μέγιστον ἀγαθὸν τὴν ἡδονὴν εἶναι
νομίζουσιν, Σιμωνίδης μὲν οὑτωσὶ λέγων·

τίς γὰρ ἁδονᾶς ἄτερ
θνατῶν[7] βίος ποθεινὸς ἢ ποία τυραννίς;
d τᾶσδ᾿ ἄτερ οὐδὲ θεῶν ζαλωτὸς[8] αἰών.

Πίνδαρος δὲ[9] παραινῶν ῾Ιέρωνι τῷ Συρακοσίῳ
ἄρχοντι·

μηδ᾿ ἀμαύρου, φησί, τέρψιν ἐν βίῳ· πολύ τοι
φέριστον ἀνδρὶ τερπνὸς αἰών.

[1] CE: μεγαλοψυχότεροι A. [2] A: ἀνθρώπων CE.
[3] ἕως μὲν CE. [4] ἐνέδυνον Aelian.
[5] Birt: κόμας ACE.
[6] τοιοῦτοι ἦσαν Wilamowitz (cf. Aelian, τοιοῦτοι ὄντες . .
ἐνίκησαν): οὗτοι ἦσαν οἱ τοιοῦτοι ACE.
[7] Stephanus: θνητῶν AC.
[8] Stephanus: ζηλωτὸς AC. [9] δὲ added by Kaibel

yet they are the bravest and most lordly of the barbarians. Indeed, to have pleasure and luxury is a mark of the freeborn; it eases their minds and exalts them; but to live laborious lives is the mark of slaves and of men of low birth; their very natures also become contracted. And so the city of Athens, as long as it enjoyed luxury, was very great and reared men who were very lordly and proud. For they wrapped themselves in cloaks dyed in purple, they put on embroidered tunics, they bound up their hair in topknots and wore golden cicadas on their forehead and temples [a]; their slaves carried folding stools for them so that they should not sit as chance might have it.[b] Such, then, were the men who won the battle of Marathon, the only people who overcame the power of all Asia. Even the wisest men, Heracleides says, they who enjoy the highest reputation for wisdom, recognize pleasure as the highest good, Simonides, for example, saying [c] : ' What life among mortals is desirable without pleasure, or what lordly power? Without this not even the life of the gods is enviable.' And Pindar, admonishing Hieron, the ruler of Syracuse, says [d] : ' Nor let thy joy grow dim while thou hast life; for joyful life, be sure, is best by far for man.' Homer, also, asserts

---

[a] Thuc. i. 6 χρυσῶν τεττίγων ἐνέρσει (by the insertion of) κρωβύλον (=κόρυμβον above) ἀναδούμενοι τῶν ἐν τῇ κεφαλῇ τριχῶν, Aelian, V.H. iv. 22. But these brooches in the form of cicadas were old-fashioned in Aristophanes' day, see Nub. 984 and Schol. 980. See below, 525 f (p. 372).

[b] i.e. uncomfortably.

[c] P.L.G.[4] iii. 419, Diehl frag. 57, Edmonds frag. 71.

[d] P.L.G.[5] i. 440, Sandys (L.C.L.) 586, see Athen. 635 b, d.

ATHENAEUS

καὶ "Ομηρος δὲ τὴν εὐφροσύνην καὶ τὸ εὐφραίνε-
σθαι τέλος φησὶν εἶναι χαριέστερον,[1] ὅταν δαιτυμόνες
μὲν ἀοιδοῦ ἀκουάζωνται, παρὰ δὲ πλήθωσι τράπεζαι. τοὺς δὲ θεούς φησιν εἶναι ῥεῖα ζώοντας (τὸ
δὲ ῥεῖα ἐστιν ἀπόνως), ὥσπερ ἐνδεικνύμενος ὅτι
μέγιστόν ἐστι τῶν κακῶν ἡ περὶ τὸ ζῆν ταλαιπωρία
καὶ ὁ πόνος."

e Διόπερ καὶ Μεγακλείδης ἐπιτιμᾷ τοῖς μεθ'
"Ομηρον καὶ Ἡσίοδον ποιηταῖς ὅσοι περὶ Ἡρακλέους εἰρήκασιν ὡς στρατοπέδων ἡγεῖτο καὶ
πόλεις ᾕρει· " ὃς μεθ' ἡδονῆς πλείστης τὸν μετ'
ἀνθρώπων βίον διετέλεσε, πλείστας μὲν γυναῖκας
γήμας, ἐκ πλείστων δὲ λάθρα παρθένων παιδοποιη-
σάμενος." εἴποι γὰρ ἄν τις πρὸς τοὺς οὐ[2] ταῦτα
παραδεχομένους· " πόθεν, ὦ οὗτοι, τὴν περὶ τὰς
f ἐδωδὰς αὐτῷ σπουδὴν ἀνατίθετε, ἢ πόθεν παρῆλθεν
εἰς τοὺς ἀνθρώπους τὸ τῆς λοιβαίας κύλικος μηδὲν
ὑπολείπεσθαι, εἰ μὴ τὰ περὶ τὰς ἡδονὰς ἐδοκίμαζεν,
ἢ διὰ τί τὰ θερμὰ λουτρὰ τὰ φαινόμενα ἐκ τῆς γῆς
πάντες Ἡρακλέους φασὶν εἶναι ἱερά, ἢ διὰ τί τὰς
μαλακὰς στρωμνὰς Ἡρακλέους κοίτας εἰώθασι
καλεῖν, εἰ κατεφρόνει τῶν ἡδέως ζώντων;" τοῦτον
οὖν, φησίν, οἱ νεώτεροι[3] ποιηταὶ κατασκευάζουσιν
ἐν λῃστοῦ σχήματι μόνον περιπορευόμενον, ξύλον
ἔχοντα καὶ λεοντῆν καὶ τόξα· καὶ ταῦτα πλάσαι

---

[1] χαριέστατον Meineke.
[2] οὐ om. CE.
[3] CE: νέοι A.

[a] Od. ix. 5; Odysseus says: " There is no more gracious
end (i.e. no more perfect delight) than when merriment
pervades all the people," etc. See below, 513 b, c, e; the
writer here erroneously takes τέλος in the Aristotelian sense
of " goal." [b] Il. vi. 138, Od. iv. 805, etc.

304

that joy and merry-making are a more gracious end,[a] " when feasters listen to a bard, and the tables beside them are laden." Of the gods he says that they live at ease [b] (that is, without toil), as if to indicate that the greatest evil is hardship and toil in living."

This is why, also, Megacleides blames [c] the poets later than Homer and Hesiod who say of Heracles that he was the leader of armies and the taker of cities : " For he passed his life among men in the enjoyment of the greatest pleasure, marrying very many women, begetting children from very many maidens clandestinely." One may say in answer to those who refuse to accept these traditions : " How does it come about, sirs, that you ascribe to him his devotion to food,[d] or how did the custom come among men, that not a drop should be left in the libation-cup to him, if he did not approve of sensual pleasures ? or why are all men agreed that the warm baths which appear out of the earth are sacred to Heracles,[e] or why are people in the habit of calling soft bedding ' Heracles's beds ' [f] if he despised those who live in pleasure ? " It is this hero, Megacleides says, whom the more recent poets dress up in the guise of a highwayman wandering about alone, carrying club and lion-skin and bow; the first to

[c] F.H.G. iv. 443. See Schol. Il. v. 640.
[d] Heracles the glutton is a familiar comic type, Eur. Alc. 788 ff., Aristoph. Av. 1574 ff., Athen. 157 f (vol. i. p. 218), 164 d (ibid. 246).
[e] All hot springs ; so Aristoph. Nub. 1050. Just Logic says : ἐγὼ μὲν οὐδέν᾽ Ἡρακλέους βελτίον᾽ ἄνδρα κρίνω. Unjust Logic : ποῦ ψυχρὰ δῆτα πώποτ᾽ εἶδες Ἡράκλεια λουτρά ; See Schol. But Plin. N.H. iii. 85 mentions an island called Heracleia.
[f] This is apparently the only place where they are mentioned. Yet cf. Soph. Trach. 912 ff.

513 πρῶτον Στησίχορον τὸν Ἱμεραῖον. καὶ Ξάνθος δ'
ὁ μελοποιός, πρεσβύτερος ὢν Στησιχόρου, ὡς καὶ
αὐτὸς ὁ Στησίχορος μαρτυρεῖ, ὥς φησιν ὁ Μεγακλείδης, οὐ ταύτην αὐτῷ περιτίθησι τὴν στολήν,
ἀλλὰ τὴν Ὁμηρικήν. πολλὰ δὲ τῶν Ξάνθου παρα-
πεποίηκεν ὁ Στησίχορος, ὥσπερ καὶ τὴν Ὀρέ-
στειαν καλουμένην. Ἀντισθένης δὲ τὴν ἡδονὴν
ἀγαθὸν εἶναι φάσκων προσέθηκεν τὴν ἀμετα-
μέλητον.

Ὁ δὲ παρὰ τῷ Ὁμήρῳ Ὀδυσσεὺς ἡγεμὼν δοκεῖ
γεγενῆσθαι Ἐπικούρῳ τῆς πολυθρυλήτου ἡδονῆς,
ὅσπερ φησίν·

b   οὐ γὰρ ἔγωγέ τι φημὶ τέλος χαριέστερον εἶναι
ἢ ὅταν εὐφροσύνη μὲν ἔχῃ κάτα[1] δῆμον ἅπαντα,
δαιτυμόνες δ' ἀνὰ δώματ' ἀκουάζωνται ἀοιδοῦ
ἥμενοι ἑξείης, παρὰ δὲ πλήθωσι τράπεζαι
σίτου καὶ κρειῶν, μέθυ δ' ἐκ κρητῆρος ἀφύσσων
οἰνοχόος παρέχῃσι[2] καὶ ἐγχείη δεπάεσσιν.
τοῦτό τί μοι κάλλιστον ἐνὶ φρεσὶν εἴδεται εἶναι.

ὁ δὲ Μεγακλείδης φησὶ τὸν Ὀδυσσέα καθομιλοῦντα
τοὺς καιροὺς[3] ὑπὲρ τοῦ δοκεῖν ὁμοήθη[4] τοῖς
Φαίαξιν εἶναι τὸ ἁβροδίαιτον αὐτῶν ἀσπάζεσθαι,

c προπυθόμενον τοῦ Ἀλκίνου·

αἰεὶ δ' ἡμῖν δαίς τε φίλη κίθαρίς τε χοροί τε
εἵματά τ' ἐξημοιβὰ λοετρά τε θερμὰ καὶ εὐναί·

μόνως γὰρ οὕτως ᾠήθη ὧν ἤλπιζεν μὴ διαμαρτεῖν

---

[1] κατὰ A.   [2] φορέῃσι Homer.

[3] τοὺς καιροὺς ACE, as Schol. Ven. *Ran.* 1001, Athen. 535 e
τοῖς καιροῖς (Kaibel) is better Greek, Schol. *Ran.* 47, 546
Suid. *s.* Θηραμένης.   For accus. in somewhat different sense
see Aristot. *Pol.* 1315 b 4, Plut. *Caes.* 15.

[4] ὁμοήθη CE: ὁμοιοήθη, altered to ὁμοήθης A.

onceive this was Stesichorus of Himera. Yet the lyric poet Xanthus, who was older than Stesichorus, as the latter testifies himself,[a] according to Megaleides, does not put this garb on Heracles, but rather that which Homer gives him. Many of Xanthus's poems have been copied by Stesichorus, as, for instance, that called *The Oresteia.* Antisthenes, too, alleged that pleasure is a good, but he added the qualification that it must be such as not to be repented of.[b]

Now Homer's Odysseus seems to have led the way in showing Epicurus his much-talked-of pleasure, for he says[c] : " As for me, I say that there is no more perfect grace than when joy reigns throughout the whole people, and feasters in the halls listen to a bard as they sit in order, and the tables beside them are laden with bread and meats, and a wine-pourer, drawing the wine from the mixing-bowl, offers it and pours it into the cups. This seems to my sense the fairest thing in the world." But Megacleides says that Odysseus was only deferring to the exigencies of the moment, in order to appear to be in sympathy with the manners of the Phaeacians, when he accepted their effeminacy, because he had previously heard Alcinoüs say[d] : " Ever to us is the feast dear, the harp and dances, raiment oft changed, warm baths, and the love-couch." Only in this way did he expect to get what he hoped from them.[e] Of similar

---

[a] *P.L.G.*⁴ iii. 225, Edmonds ii. 12. The existence of the Sicilian ?) poet Xanthus is questioned by Robert, *Bild u. ied* 174.
[b] An expression used once by Plato, *Timaeus* 59 D.
[c] *Od.* ix. 5 ; *cf.* above, 512 d.   [d] *Od.* viii. 248.
[e] Here ends, according to Müller, the citation from Megaleides ; but it would seem to extend to 513 e.

τοιοῦτός ἐστιν καὶ ὁ παραινῶν Ἀμφιλόχῳ τῷ
παιδί·

ὦ τέκνον,
ποντίου θηρὸς πετραίου χρωτὶ μάλιστα νόον
προσφέρων πάσαις πολίεσσιν ὁμίλει·
τῷ παρεόντι[1] δ᾽ ἐπαινήσαις ἑκὼν
d   ἄλλοτ᾽ ἀλλοῖα φρόνει.

ὁμοίως φησὶν καὶ Σοφοκλῆς ἐν Ἰφιγενείᾳ·

νόει[2] πρὸς ἀνδρί, σῶμα[3] πουλύπους[4] ὅπως
πέτρᾳ, τραπέσθαι γνησίου φρονήματος.

καὶ ὁ Θέογνις·

πουλύπου[5] ὀργὴν ἴσχε πολυπλόκου.[6]

εἰσὶ δ᾽ οἵ φασι ταύτης εἶναι τῆς γνώμης τὸν
Ὅμηρον, προτάττοντα τοῦ σπουδαίου βίου πολλάκις τὸν καθ᾽ ἡδονήν, λέγοντα·

οἱ δὲ θεοὶ πὰρ Ζηνὶ καθήμενοι ἠγορόωντο
e   χρυσέῳ ἐν δαπέδῳ, μετὰ δέ σφισι πότνια Ἥβη
νέκταρ ἐῳνοχόει, τοὶ δὲ χρυσέοις δεπάεσσι
δειδέχατ᾽ ἀλλήλους.

καὶ ὁ Μενέλαος δὲ παρ᾽ αὐτῷ φησιν·

οὐδέ κεν ἡμέας
ἄλλο διέκρινεν φιλέοντέ τε[7] τερπομένω τε.

καί·

ἥμεθα δαινύμενοι κρέα τ᾽ ἄσπετα καὶ μέθυ ἡδύ·
διόπερ καὶ Ὀδυσσεὺς τρυφὴν καὶ λαγνείαν τέλο
τοῦ βίου παρὰ τῷ Ἀλκινόῳ τίθεται.

---

[1] A: τὸ παρεὸν CE.   [2] νοει (sic) A: νοῦν δεῖ Porson.
[3] χρῶμα Bergk.   [4] πολύπους A.   [5] πολύπου ACE.
[6] CE: πουλυπλόκου A.   [7] CE: τε om. A.

character is the man who exhorts the boy named Amphilochus [a] : " Ah, my child, make thy mind most like the skin of the creature which lives among the rocks of the sea,[b] in all the cities where thou resortest; give thy willing approval to him who is with thee, changing thy thought with each change· of place." Likewise also Sophocles says in his *Iphigeneia* [c] : " Be minded, as the polyp changes its body to the colour of a rock, so to turn thyself before a man whose thought is true." So Theognis [d] : " Hold fast to the ways of the tangled polyp." And some say that Homer is of this opinion, because he often puts the life of pleasure above the good life, saying [e] : " Now the gods, seated beside Zeus, were holding assembly on the golden floor, and in the midst the lady Hebe poured out to them their nectar, while they with golden cups pledged one another." And Menelaus, again, says in Homer [f] : " And no other thing would have separated us in our love and joy in each other." Again [g] : " We sat feasting on abundant meat and sweet wine." This is why Odysseus at the court of Alcinoüs assumes luxury and lust to be the " end " of life.[h]

[a] Pindar, *P.L.G.*[5] i. 398, Sandys 516 ; *cf.* Athen. 317 a (vol. iii. p. 424), Antig. Caryst. 25, Bethe, *Theb. Heldenlieder* 6 note 16.
[b] The polyp. " As a lover or chameleon Grows like what looks upon," Shelley, *Prometheus Unbound* iv. 1.
[c] *T.G.F.*[2] 197.
[d] vs. 215 ; *P.L.G.*[4] ii. 140, Diehl 128, Edmonds p. 254, Athen. 317 a.   [e] *Il.* iv. 1.
[f] *Od.* iv. 178 ; Menelaus is speaking of his friendship with Odysseus, and the passage refers to the ordinary pleasures of friendly host and guest, the one welcoming, the other welcomed (E. Abbott).
[g] *Od.* ix. 162.   [h] See p. 304 note *a*.

Διαβόητοι δὲ ἐπὶ τρυφῇ ἐγένοντο πρῶτοι πάν-
f των ἀνθρώπων Πέρσαι, ὧν καὶ οἱ βασιλεῖς ἐχεί-
μαζον μὲν ἐν Σούσοις, ἐθέριζον δὲ ἐν Ἐκβατάνοις
(κληθῆναι δὲ τὰ Σοῦσά φησιν Ἀριστόβουλος καὶ
Χάρης διὰ τὴν ὡραιότητα τοῦ τόπου· σοῦσον γὰρ
εἶναι τῇ Ἑλλήνων φωνῇ τὸ κρίνον.) ἐν Περσεπόλει
δὲ διατρίβουσι φθινόπωρον[1] καὶ ἐν Βαβυλῶνι τ-
λεῖπον[2] τοῦ ἐνιαυτοῦ μέρος.[3] καὶ οἱ Πάρθων δ-
βασιλεῖς ἐαρίζουσι μὲν ἐν Ῥάγαις, χειμάζουσι δ-
514 ἐν Βαβυλῶνι, . . .[4] τὸ λεῖπον[2] τοῦ ἐνιαυτοῦ. κα-
τὸ παράσημον δὲ ὃ ἐπετίθεντο τῇ κεφαλῇ οἱ τῶ-
Περσῶν βασιλεῖς οὐδ' αὐτὸ ἡρνεῖτο τὴν τῆ-
ἡδυπαθείας ἀπόλαυσιν. " κατεσκευάζετο γάρ," ἡ
φησι Δίνων, "ἐκ σμύρνης καὶ τοῦ καλουμένο-
λαβύζου. εὐώδης[5] δ' ἐστὶν ἡ λάβυζος καὶ πολυτιμοτέρα[6] τῆς σμύρνης. ὁπότε δὲ καὶ ἀπὸ το-
ἅρματος κατίοι," φησί, "βασιλεύς, οὔτε καθήλλετ-
ὀλίγου ὄντος ἐπὶ τὴν γῆν τοῦ ὕψους οὔτε διὰ χειρῶ-
ἐρειδόμενος, ἀλλ' αἰεὶ αὐτῷ χρυσοῦς δίφρος ἐτίθετ-
b καὶ τούτῳ ἐπιβαίνων κατῄει· καὶ ὁ βασιλέω-
διφροφόρος εἰς τοῦτο εἵπετο." " φυλάσσουσί τ-
αὐτὸν καὶ τριακόσιαι γυναῖκες, ὡς ἱστορεῖ

---

[1] φθινόπωρον A: φθινοπώρου CE, τὸ φθινόπωρον Kaibel, bu
cf. Hdt. iv. 42, ix. 117.
[2] A: λοιπὸν CE.   [3] μέρος om. CE.
[4] διάγουσι δ' ἐν Ἐκατομπύλῳ supplied by Casaubon.
[5] εὐώδης AE and apparently C: εὐῶδες Kaibel.
[6] πολυτιμοτέρα CE: πολυτιμότερον A.

---

[a] Script. Al. M. 99, 116, J. 2 B 775, 663.
[b] Cf. the Hebrew Susanna, "lily," and Athen. 689 d. Sus
is Shushan (in Nehemiah i. 1 "the palace"). It is tempting
to read ἐκείνων for Ἑλλήνων, giving a clearer meaning
"suson in their language is the lily." See the list of roy
residences in How and Wells, Herodotus ii. 20-21.

The first men in history to become notorious for luxurious living were the Persians, whose kings wintered in Susa and summered in Ecbatana. (Now Susa was so called, according to Aristobulus and Chares,[a] because of the beauty of its situation ; for *suson* is what in the Greek language is called *krinon* or lily.[b]) In Persepolis they spend the autumn, and in Babylon the remaining portion of the year. So also the Parthian kings live in springtime at Rhagae, but they winter at Babylon, (and pass) the rest of the year (in Hecatompylus).[c] The very badge of rank which the Persian kings placed on their heads certainly was not calculated to hide their indulgence in luxury. For, as Dinon says[d] : " It was made of myrrh and what is called *labyzos*. The *labyzos* is fragrant, and more costly than myrrh. Whenever the king descended from his chariot, Dinon says, he never leaped down, although the distance to the ground was short, nor did he lean on anyone's arms ; rather, a golden stool was always set in place for him, and he descended by stepping on this ; and the king's stool-bearer attended him for this purpose." " And so three hundred women watch over him,"

---

[c] Strabo xi. 514. In Diodor. xvii. 75 Hecatompylus is described as a rich city offering every opportunity for enjoyment.

[d] *F.H.G.* ii. 92. Hesychius *s. κίδαρις* variously defines the thing here described as a tiara, a skull-cap, a band round the head. The word λάβυξος occurs only here ; what spice is meant is unknown. The inexact κατεσκευάζετο can only be interpreted as meaning that the turban or tiara built up, as it were, on the king's head, was richly scented with the two spices. For similar cases of obscure phrasing where spices are mentioned see above, 464 c-d (p. 24) and 3 e (vol. i. p. 12).

Κυμαῖος Ἡρακλείδης ἐν α′ Περσικῶν. αὗται δ
τὰς μὲν ἡμέρας κοιμῶνται ἵνα νυκτὸς ἐγρηγορῶσι
τῆς δὲ νυκτὸς ᾄδουσαι καὶ ψάλλουσαι διατελοῦσι
λύχνων καιομένων· χρῆται δὲ αὐταῖς καὶ παλ
λακίσιν[1] ὁ βασιλεύς . . .[2] διὰ τῆς τῶν μηλοφόρων
αὐλῆς. ἦσαν δὲ οὗτοι τῶν δορυφόρων, καὶ τῷ
γένει πάντες Πέρσαι, ἐπὶ τῶν στυράκων μῆλα
χρυσᾶ ἔχοντες, χίλιοι τὸν ἀριθμόν, ἀριστίνδην
c ἐκλεγόμενοι ἐκ τῶν μυρίων Περσῶν τῶν Ἀθανά
των[4] καλουμένων. καὶ διῄει διὰ τῆς τούτων αὐλῆ
πεζὸς ὑποτιθεμένων ψιλοταπίδων Σαρδιανῶν, ἐφ
ὧν οὐδεὶς ἄλλος ἐπέβαινεν ἢ βασιλεύς. ὅτε δὲ εἰ
τὴν ἐσχάτην αὐλὴν ἔλθοι, ἀνέβαινεν ἐπὶ τὸ ἅρμα
ἐνίοτε δὲ καὶ ἐφ᾽ ἵππον[5]· πεζὸς δὲ οὐδέποτ
ἑωράθη ἔξω τῶν βασιλείων. εἰ δὲ ἐπὶ θήρα
ἐξίοι, καὶ αἱ παλλακίδες αὐτῷ συνεξῄεσαν.
δὲ θρόνος ἐφ᾽ ᾧ ἐχρημάτιζεν καθήμενος χρυσοῦ
ἦν, ὃν περιειστήκεσαν[6] τέσσαρες κιονίσκοι λιθο
κόλλητοι χρυσοῖ, ἐφ᾽ ὧν διετέτατο ἱμάτιον ποικίλον
πορφυροῦν.''

d   Κλέαρχος δὲ ὁ Σολεὺς ἐν τετάρτῳ Βίων προ
εἰπὼν περὶ τῆς Μήδων τρυφῆς καὶ ὅτι διὰ ταύτη
πολλοὺς εὐνουχίσαιεν τῶν περικτιόνων, ἐπιφέρει
καὶ τὴν παρὰ Μήδων γενέσθαι Πέρσαις μηλοφορίαι
μὴ μόνον[7] ὧν ἔπαθον τιμωρίαν, ἀλλὰ καὶ τῆς τῶν

---

[1] Meineke: πολλάκις ACE.
[2] Lacuna marked by Dobree.   [3] CE: ἀριστήδην A
[4] CE: ἀσιανατῶν (sic) A.   [5] ἐφ᾽ ἵππον C: ἐφ᾽ ἵππου AE
[6] περιεισπτήκεισαν CE, περιιστήκεσαν A.
[7] Musurus: μόνων A.

---

[a] F.H.G. ii. 95, cf. Athen. 145 a (vol. ii. pp. 160 ff.). Athen
557 b, quoting Dicaearchus, says that Darius III. was accom
panied in battle by 360 concubines.

Heracleides of Cumae records [a] in the first book of his *Persian History*. "These sleep throughout the day in order to stay awake at night, but at night they sing and play on harps continually while the lamps burn; and the king takes his pleasure of them as concubines [b] . . . through the court of the Apple-bearers. These formed his bodyguard, and all of them were Persians by birth, having on the butts of their spears golden apples, and numbering a thousand, selected because of their rank from the 10,000 Persians who are called the Immortals.[c] Through their court also the king would go on foot, Sardis carpets, on which no one else but the king ever walked, having been spread on the ground.[d] And when he reached the last court he would mount his chariot, or sometimes his horse; but he was never seen on foot outside the palace. Even when he went hunting his concubines went out with him. The throne on which he sat in transacting business was of gold, and round it stood four short posts of gold studded with jewels, and on them was stretched an embroidered cloth of purple."

Clearchus of Soli, in the fourth book of his *Lives*, after speaking of the luxury of the Medes and saying that because of it they had made eunuchs of many neighbouring tribes, proceeds to add [e] that the practice of "apple-bearing" was taken over by the Persians from the Medes not only in revenge for what they had suffered, but also as a reminder of what depths

---

[b] We may supply "These were admitted to his presence."
[c] *Cf.* Herod. vii. 41. See below, 539 e (p. 440).
[d] Such luxury impressed the frugal Greeks as arrogance, and is a significant motive in the tragedy of Agamemnon, Aesch. *Agam.* 905 ff. On ψιλοτάπιδες see vol. ii. p. 393 note *c*, and 255 e, vol. iii. p. 150.
[e] *F.H.G.* ii. 304.

δορυφορούντων τρυφῆς εἰς ὅσον ἦλθον ἀνανδρίας
ὑπόμνημα. δύναται γάρ, ὡς ἔοικεν, ἡ παράκαιρος
ἅμα καὶ μάταιος αὐτῶν περὶ τὸν βίον τρυφὴ καὶ
τοὺς ταῖς λόγχαις καθωπλισμένους ἀγύρτας ἀπο-
e φαίνειν. καὶ προελθὼν δὲ γράφει· "τοῖς γοῦν
πορίσασί τι αὐτῷ ἡδὺ βρῶμα διδοὺς ἆθλα¹ τοῦ
πορισθέντος οὐχ ἑτέραις ἡδύνων ταῦτα τιμαῖς παρ-
ετίθει, πολὺ δὲ μᾶλλον αὐτὸς ἀπολαύειν αὐτῶν
νοῦν ἔχων· τοῦτο μὲν γάρ ἐστιν ὁ λεγόμενος, οἶμαι
καὶ Διὸς ἅμα καὶ βασιλέως ἐγκέφαλος." Χάρης
δ' ὁ Μιτυληναῖος ἐν τῇ πέμπτῃ τῶν περὶ Ἀλέξανδρον Ἱστοριῶν " εἰς τοῦτο," φησίν, " ἧκον
τρυφῆς οἱ τῶν Περσῶν βασιλεῖς ὥστε ἔχεσθαι τῆς
βασιλικῆς κλίνης ὑπὲρ κεφαλῆς οἴκημά τι πεντά-
κλινον, ἐν ᾧ χρυσίου πεντακισχίλια διὰ παντὸς
f ἔκειτο² τάλαντα, καὶ τοῦτο ἐκαλεῖτο προσκεφά-
λαιον βασιλικόν. καὶ πρὸς ποδῶν ἕτερον οἴκημα
τρίκλινον, οὗ τάλαντα τρισχίλια ἔκειτο³ ἀργυρίου
καὶ προσηγορεύετο βασιλικὸν ὑποπόδιον. ἦν δ' ἐν
τῷ⁴ κοιτῶνι καὶ λιθοκόλλητος ἄμπελος χρυσῆ ὑπὲρ
τῆς κλίνης." τὴν δ' ἄμπελον ταύτην Ἀμύντας
φησὶν ἐν τοῖς Σταθμοῖς καὶ βότρυας ἔχειν ἐκ τῶν
πολυτελεστάτων ψήφων συντεθειμένους. οὐ μα-

¹ ἆθλον CE.   ² Dindorf: ἔκειντο ACE.
³ ἔκειντο C.   ⁴ ἐν τῷ CE: ἐν τι τῶι A.

ᵃ The meaning of this affected phraseology seems to be
the Persian kings caused their bodyguards, composed of
Persian nobles (see above in c), to assume the apple-ornament
in order to remind the subjugated Medes of their former
splendour, and thus punish them for their former oppression
of the Persians. The Medes had through luxury become like
the emasculated priests of Cybele, the mendicant ἀγύρται, cf
Plat. *Rep.* 364 B.   *Cf.* below, 529 d (p. 388)

f degradation the luxury of the bodyguards had
eached. For their immoderate and at the same time
enseless luxury of life, it is plain, can turn even men
rmed with lances into beggars.[a] Going on, Clearchus
rites [b] : " To those, at any rate, who supplied him
vith any delicacy he gave prizes for the invention,
et when he served these dainties he did not sweeten
hem by bestowing special honours, but preferred to
njoy them all alone, showing his sense ! [c] This, I
hink, is in fact the proverbial, ' A morsel for Zeus '
nd at the same time for the king." Chares of Mity-
ene in the fifth book of his *History of Alexander* says :[d]
The Persian kings reached such a pitch of luxury
hat near the royal bed, beyond the head of it, was
    chamber large enough to contain five couches,[e]
vherein were stored 5000 talents of gold coin filling
he whole, and it was called the royal cushion. At
he foot was a second, three-couch chamber, containing
000 talents in silver money, and called the royal
ootstool. And in the bed-chamber a golden vine,
ewel-studded, extended over the bed." Now Amyn-
as in his *Itinerary* says [f] that this vine had clusters
omposed of the costliest jewels. Not far from it was

---

[c] The obscure text should not be changed, for Clearchus
vrote in a tortuous style, *cf.* 157 c-d (vol. ii. p. 214) and
elow, 515 e. " Special honours " would consist in inviting
thers to partake, as Cyrus the Younger did, Xen. *Anab.*
. 9. 25, Athen. 784 d (p. 54). For the meaning of ἑτέραις,
" different," *cf.* Aesch. *Agam.* 151 θυσίαν ἑτέραν, "extraordin-
ry sacrifice " (of Iphigeneia), and below, 515 c, ἑτέρας σκιάδας.
Che last phrase is ironical ; yet see 529 d. The proverb
Διὸς ἐγκέφαλος, "a delicious morsel fit for Zeus," recurs Athen.
42 f. Here it is expanded to include the king.
[d] *Scr. Al. M.* 117, J. 2 B 658.
[e] *Cf.* Athen. 205 d (vol. ii. p. 428).
[f] *Scr. Al. M.* 136, J. 2 B 629.

κράν τε ταύτης ἀνακεῖσθαι κρατῆρα χρυσοῦν Θεο
515 δώρου τοῦ Σαμίου ποίημα. Ἀγαθοκλῆς δ' ἐ
τρίτῳ περὶ Κυζίκου ἐν[1] Πέρσαις φησὶν εἶναι κα
χρυσοῦν καλούμενον ὕδωρ. εἶναι δὲ τοῦτο λιβάδα
ἑβδομήκοντα, καὶ μηδένα πίνειν ἀπ' αὐτοῦ
μόνον βασιλέα καὶ τὸν πρεσβύτατον αὐτοῦ τῶ
παίδων· τῶν δ' ἄλλων ἐάν τις πίῃ, θάνατος
ζημία.

Ξενοφῶν δὲ ἐν ὀγδόῳ Παιδείας " ἐχρῶντο,'
φησίν, " ἔτι τότε τῇ ἐκ Περσῶν παιδείᾳ καὶ τ
Μήδων στολῇ καὶ ἁβρότητι. νῦν δὲ τὴν μὲν ἐ
Περσῶν καρτερίαν περιορῶσιν ἀποσβεννυμένην
τὴν δὲ τῶν Μήδων μαλακίαν διασῴζονται. σαφη
b νίσαι δὲ βούλομαι καὶ τὴν θρύψιν αὐτῶν. ἐκείνοι
γὰρ πρῶτον μὲν οὐκέτι τὰς εὐνὰς μόνον ἀρκε
μαλακῶς ὑποστόρνυσθαι, ἀλλ' ἤδη καὶ τῶν κλινῶ
τοὺς πόδας ἐπὶ ταπίδων τιθέασιν, ὅπως μὴ ἀντ
ερείδῃ τὸ δάπεδον, ἀλλ' ὑπείκωσιν αἱ τάπιδες. κα
μὴν τὰ πεττόμενα ἐπὶ τράπεζαν ὅσα τε πρότερο
εὕρητο οὐδὲν αὐτῶν ἀφήρηται ἄλλα τε καινὰ αἰε
ἐπιμηχανῶνται, καὶ ὄψα γε ὡσαύτως· καὶ γὰ
c καινοποιητὰς ἀμφοτέρων τούτων κέκτηνται. ἀλλ
καὶ ἐν τῷ χειμῶνι οὐ μόνον κεφαλὴν καὶ σῶμα κα
πόδας αὐτοῖς[2] ἀρκεῖ ἐσκεπάσθαι, ἀλλὰ καὶ περ
ἄκραις ταῖς χερσὶν χειρίδας δασείας καὶ δακτυλή
θρας ἔχουσιν. ἔν γε μὴν τῷ θέρει οὐκ ἀρκοῦσι
αὐτοῖς οὔθ' αἱ τῶν δένδρων οὔθ' αἱ τῶν πετρω

[1] ἐν A : παρὰ CE.   [2] αὐτοὺς A.

---

[a] *F.H.G.* iv. 289. The "golden water " is the Choaspes
river, Athen. 45 b (vol. i. p. 194), "regia lympha Choaspes,'
Tibull. iv. 1. 140, so called from its purity. *Cf. Il.* xxi. 130,
ἀργυροδίνης, " with silver eddies."
316

set up a golden mixing-bowl, the work of Theodorus of Samos. Agathocles, in the third book of his work *On Cyzicus*, says [a] that in Persia there is also water called "golden." This water consists of seventy bubbling pools, and none may drink of it save only the king and his eldest son ; if anyone else drinks it, the penalty is death.

Xenophon, in the eighth book of his *Cyropaedeia*, says [b] : " In those days they still retained the discipline derived from the Persians, and the Medes' luxury in dress. But to-day, while they allow the sturdiness derived from the Persians to pass into extinction, they preserve the effeminacy of the Medes. I wish now to explain the extent of their self-indulgence. In the first place, they are no longer content with having their couches merely covered with soft mattresses, but they proceed to set the feet of the beds on carpets in order that the hard floor may not offer resistance, and that the carpets may give a yielding effect. What is more, not only have none of the things cooked for the table which were invented in earlier times been taken from them, but they also constantly devise other novelties besides ; the same is true also of fancy dishes ; for they possess slaves who are inventive in both these branches.[c] Again, in the wintry season they are not satisfied with having heads, bodies, and feet protected,[d] but they also cover the extremities of their hands with thick gloves and finger-sheaths. In summer, too, the shade of trees or rocks does not

[b] Chap. 8. 15.

[c] *i.e.* they discover new edibles and also new ways of preparing them.

[d] *Cf.* Hdt. vii. 61 ; the Persian garb caused fright to the Greek beholder, Hdt. vi. 112.

σκιαί, ἀλλ' ἐν ταύταις ἑτέρας σκιάδας[1] ἄνθρωποι
μηχανώμενοι αὐτοῖς παρεστᾶσι." κἂν τοῖς ἑξῆς
δέ φησι περὶ αὐτῶν οὑτωσί· " νῦν δὲ στρώματα
πλείω ἔχουσιν ἐπὶ τῶν ἵππων ἢ ἐπὶ τῶν εὐνῶν· οὐ
γὰρ τῆς ἱππείας οὕτως ὡς τοῦ μαλακῶς καθῆσθαι
d ἐπιμέλονται. καὶ τοὺς θυρωροὺς δὲ καὶ τοὺς
σιτοποιοὺς καὶ τοὺς ὀψοποιοὺς καὶ οἰνοχόους καὶ
παρατιθέντας καὶ ἀναιροῦντας καὶ κατακοιμίζοντας
καὶ ἀνιστάντας καὶ τοὺς κοσμητὰς οἳ ὑποχρίουσί τε
καὶ ἐντρίβουσιν αὐτοὺς καὶ τἆλλα ῥυθμίζουσιν . . ."
  Λυδοὶ δὲ εἰς τοσοῦτον ἦλθον τρυφῆς ὡς καὶ
πρῶτοι γυναῖκας εὐνουχίσαι, ὡς ἱστορεῖ Ξάνθος ὁ
Λυδὸς ἢ ὁ τὰς εἰς αὐτὸν[2] ἀναφερομένας ἱστορίας
e συγγεγραφώς—Διονύσιος δ' ὁ Σκυτοβραχίων, ὡς
'Αρτέμων φησὶν ὁ Κασανδρεὺς ἐν τῷ περὶ Συνα-
γωγῆς Βιβλίων, ἀγνοῶν ὅτι Ἔφορος ὁ συγγραφεὺς
μνημονεύει αὐτοῦ ὡς παλαιοτέρου ὄντος καὶ Ἡρο-
δότῳ τὰς ἀφορμὰς δεδωκότος—ὁ δ' οὖν Ξάνθος ἐν
τῇ δευτέρᾳ τῶν Λυδιακῶν 'Αδραμύτην[3] φησὶ τὸν
Λυδῶν βασιλέα πρῶτον γυναῖκας εὐνουχίσαντα
χρῆσθαι αὐταῖς ἀντὶ ἀνδρῶν εὐνούχων. Κλέαρχος δ'
ἐν τῇ τετάρτῃ περὶ Βίων " Λυδοί," φησί, " διὰ τρυφὴν παραδείσους κατασκευασάμενοι καὶ κηπαίους
αὐτοὺς ποιήσαντες ἐσκιατροφοῦντο, τρυφερώτεροι
ἡγησάμενοι τὸ μηδ' ὅλως αὐτοῖς ἐπιπίπτειν τὰς

---

[1] A and Xen. mss. DF: σκιὰς other mss. of Xen.
[2] τὰς εἰς αὐτὸν Meineke: εἰς αὐτὸν τὰς A.
[3] Casaubon: ἀνδραμύτην A, ἀνδραμύτου C in a different construction.   [4] τὸν A (not τῶν).

---

[a] Cyrop. viii. 8. 19-20.
[b] Xenophon concludes: " all these have been raised to the
rank of horsemen in order to serve as mercenary troop
and thus bring in revenues to their masters."

suffice them, but even here slaves stood close to
them, thus providing a new kind of sun-shade." In
succeeding paragraphs Xenophon also says of them [a]:
' But to-day they have more coverings on their horses
than on their couches ; for they care not so much for
horsemanship as for having a soft mount. Even the
door-keepers, the bakers, the cooks, the wine-pourers,
the waiters who serve at table and remove the dishes,
the servants who put them to bed and wake them
up, and the beauty-specialists who paint their eyes
for them and rub them with cosmetics and do other
things to put them into proper shape [b] . . .' "
    The Lydians went so far in wanton luxury that
they were the first to sterilize women, as recorded
by Xanthus of Lydia, or whoever is the author of
the histories ascribed to him—it is Dionysius Scyto-
brachion, according to Artemon of Cassandreia in
his work *On the Collecting of Books*,[c] who, however,
ignores the fact that the historian Ephorus [d] mentions
Xanthus as being older and as having supplied sources
for Herodotus—anyhow, Xanthus says [e] in the second
book of his *Lydian History* that Adramytes, the king
of Lydia, was the first to spay women and employ
them in the place of male eunuchs.[f] And Clearchus in
the fourth book of his *Lives* says [g] : " The Lydians in
their luxury laid out parks, making them like gardens,
and so lived in the shade, because they thought it
more luxurious not to have the rays of the sun fall

[c] A bibliographical compilation ; *F.H.G.* iv. 342, J. i. 228 ;
P.-W. v. 929.
[d] *F.H.G.* i. 262, J. 2 A 95.
[e] *F.H.G.* i. 39.
[f] Suidas *s.* Ξάνθος gives a different account : πρῶτος Γύγης
. . γυναῖκας εὐνούχισεν ὅπως αὐταῖς χρῷτο ἀεὶ νεαζούσαις.
[g] *F.H.G.* ii. 305.

f τοῦ ἡλίου αὐγάς. καὶ[1] πόρρω προάγοντες ὕβρεως
τὰς τῶν ἄλλων γυναῖκας καὶ παρθένους εἰς τὸν
τόπον τὸν διὰ τὴν πρᾶξιν 'Αγνεῶνα κληθέντα
συνάγοντες ὕβριζον. καὶ τέλος τὰς ψυχὰς ἀπο-
θηλυνθέντες ἠλλάξαντο τὸν τῶν γυναικῶν βίον·
διόπερ καὶ γυναῖκα τύραννον ὁ βίος εὕρετο αὐτοῖς
μίαν τῶν ὑβρισθεισῶν 'Ομφάλην[2]· ἥτις πρώτη
κατῆρξε[3] τῆς εἰς Λυδοὺς πρεπούσης τιμωρίας. τὸ
γὰρ ὑπὸ γυναικὸς ἄρχεσθαι ὑβριζομένους σημεῖόν
516 ἐστι βίας.[4] οὖσα οὖν καὶ αὐτὴ ἀκόλαστος καὶ
ἀμυνομένη τὰς γενομένας αὐτῇ πρότερον ὕβρεις
τοῖς ἐν τῇ πόλει δούλοις τὰς τῶν δεσποτῶν παρθένους ἐξέδωκεν ἐν ᾧ τόπῳ πρὸς ἐκείνων ὑβρίσθη·
εἰς τοῦτον οὖν συναθροίσασα μετ' ἀνάγκης συγ-
κατέκλινε[5] τοῖς δούλοις τὰς δεσποίνας. ὅθεν οἱ
Λυδοὶ τὸ πικρὸν τῆς πράξεως ὑποκοριζόμενοι τὸν
τόπον καλοῦσιν[6] Γλυκὺν 'Αγκῶνα. οὐ μόνον δὲ
Λυδῶν γυναῖκες ἄφετοι οὖσαι τοῖς ἐντυχοῦσιν, ἀλλὰ
καὶ Λοκρῶν τῶν 'Επιζεφυρίων, ἔτι δὲ τῶν περὶ
Κύπρον καὶ πάντων ἁπλῶς τῶν ἑταιρισμῷ τὰς
b ἑαυτῶν κόρας ἀφοσιούντων, παλαιᾶς τινος ὕβρεως
ἐοίκασιν[7] εἶναι πρὸς ἀλήθειαν ὑπόμνημα καὶ τιμωρίας.[8] πρὸς ἣν εἰς τῶν Λυδῶν εὐγενὴς ἀνήρ

---

[1] τέλος after καὶ deleted by Kaibel.   [2] ὀμφάλος C.
[3] κατῆρξε CE : κατῆρξε μὲν A.   [4] τοιούτου βίου Capps.
[5] Wilamowitz : συγκατέκλεισε ACE.
[6] γυναικῶν ἀγῶνα after καλοῦσιν (ACE) deleted by Schweighäuser.
[7] ἐοίκασιν C : ἔοικεν A.   [8] τιμωρίας C : τιμωρία AE

---

[a] The name was probably derived from the tree ἄγνος,
agnus castus = λύγος (Athen. 671 f), and the enormity of the
offence was increased in that these trees were sacred to Hera
goddess of marriage, and Artemis, the peculiar goddess of
women, Paus. viii. 23. 5.

upon them at all. And proceeding further in their insolence they would gather the wives and maiden daughters of other men into the place called, because of this action, the Place of Chastity,[a] and there outrage them. And finally, after becoming thoroughly effeminate in their souls, they adopted women's ways of living, whence this way of life earned for them a woman tyrant, one of those who had been outraged, named Omphalê; she was the first to begin that punishment of the Lydians which they deserved. For the fact that they were ruled with outrage by a woman is a proof of their own violence.[b] Being, then, herself a woman of unbridled passions, and avenging herself for the outrages previously done to her, she gave in marriage to the slaves of the city the maiden daughters of the slave-masters, in the very place in which she had been outraged by them; into this place, then, she forcibly collected the women, and made the matrons lie with their slaves. Hence the Lydians, glossing over the malignity of the deed by a euphemism, call the place Sweet Embrace.[c] But it is not merely the women of Lydia who were allowed free range among all comers, but also those of the Western Locrians,[d] also those of Cyprus and of all tribes in general which dedicated their daughters to prostitution; these cases seem to be, in point of fact, a reminder of some ancient outrage and revenge. It was to gain revenge that one of the Lydian

[b] Or, reading βίον, "of the kind of life they had led."
[c] Plato, *Phaedrus* 257 D. Two separate etymologies are here offered. *Cf.* above, 515 f.
[d] In south-eastern Italy. On similar Babylonian customs see Herod. i. 199; *cf.* Plat. *Rep.* 589 E.

ὁρμήσας καὶ τῇ παρ' αὐτοῖς Μίδου βασιλείᾳ
βαρυνθείς, τοῦ μὲν Μίδου ὑπ' ἀνανδρίας[1] κα
τρυφῆς ἐν[2] πορφύρᾳ κειμένου καὶ ταῖς γυναιξὶ
ἐν τοῖς ἱστοῖς συνταλασιουργοῦντος, Ὀμφάλης δ
πάντας τοὺς συγκατακλιθέντας αὐτῇ ξενοκτονού
σης, ἀμφοτέρους ἐκόλασε, τὸν μὲν ὑπὸ ἀπαιδευσίας
κεκωφημένον τῶν ὤτων ἐξελκύσας, ὃς διὰ τὴν τοῦ
φρονεῖν ἔνδειαν τοῦ πάντων ἀναισθητοτάτου[3] ζῴο
τὴν ἐπωνυμίαν ἔσχε· τὴν δὲ[4] . . .''

Πρῶτοι δὲ Λυδοὶ καὶ τὴν καρύκην[5] ἐξεῦρον, περ
ἧς τῆς σκευασίας οἱ τὰ Ὀψαρτυτικὰ συνθέντε
εἰρήκασιν, Γλαῦκός τε ὁ Λοκρὸς καὶ Μίθαικος κα
Διονύσιος Ἡρακλεῖδαί τε δύο γένος Συρακόσιοι
καὶ Ἆγις καὶ Ἐπαίνετος καὶ Διονύσιος[7] ἔτι τ
Ἡγήσιππος καὶ Ἐρασίστρατος καὶ Εὐθύδημος κα
Κρίτων, πρὸς τούτοις δὲ Στέφανος, Ἀρχύτας
Ἀκέστιος, Ἀκεσίας, Διοκλῆς, Φιλιστίων.[8] τοσού
τους γὰρ οἶδα γράψαντας Ὀψαρτυτικά. καὶ κάν
δαυλον δέ τινα ἔλεγον οἱ Λυδοί, οὐχ ἕνα ἀλλὰ τρεῖς

---

[1] CE: ἀνδρείας A.   [2] ἐν CE: καὶ ἐν A.
[3] CE: αἰσθητοτάτου A.   [4] τὴν δὲ E, τήνδε C: om. A.
[5] C, in margin E: καρύκκην ΛΕ.
[6] Ἡρακλεῖδαι . . . Συρακόσιοι om. C.
[7] καὶ Διονύσιος om. C, deleted by Kaibel.
[8] ἀρχύτας καὶ ἄλλοι C : Ἀκέστιος deleted by Kaibel.

---

[a] To make them long, like the ears of an ass.
[b] Of the fate of Omphalè in this Lydian myth we lear
nothing ; see Roscher, Lex. d. griech. u. röm. Mythologie,
"Omphalè 881. Art and literature after Alexander knew
of an exchange of garments between Omphalè and Heracl
(not Midas), she assuming the hero's club and lion-skin, h
clad in saffron robe, with plaited hair like a woman's. Not
the curious masculine form Ὀμφάλος in C.
[c] See 160 b, where καρυκῶν should perhaps be read

nobles, who had been oppressed by the rule of Midas over them, attacked him, since Midas in effeminate luxury lay in his purple robes, or helped the women at their looms to work the wool, while Omphalê slew all the strangers who had lain with her ; so the nobleman punished them both ; Midas, who had become deaf through his stupidity, he pulled by the ears,[a] because by his lack of sense he had acquired the name of the most senseless animal in the world ; and as for Omphalê [b] . . ."

The Lydians were also the first to invent the spiced gravy called *karykê*,[c] on the preparation of which the compilers of works entitled *Art of Cookery* have given directions—Glaucus of Locris, Mithaecus, Dionysius,[d] also the two natives of Syracuse named Heracleides, and Agis, Epaenetus, and Dionysius,[e] again Hegesippus, Erasistratus, Euthydemus, and Crito ; in addition to these, Stephanus, Archytas, Acestius,[f] Acesias,[g] Diocles,[h] and Philistion.[i] Such is the number, I know, of those who wrote works called *Art of Cookery*. The Lydians used also to speak of a dish called *kandaulos*,[j] of which there were three varieties, not one merely ; so exquisitely equipped

though Herodian i. 317 preferred the form with -κκ- ; below, 646 e.   [d] Athen. 326 f.

[e] Perhaps the Dionysius who wrote on agriculture, Varro, *De re rust.* i. 9. But see critical note 7.

[f] Quite unknown. See critical note 8.

[g] Perhaps the physician named in the derisive proverb, Ἀκεσίας ἰάσατο, ἐπὶ τῶν ἐπὶ τὸ χεῖρον ἰωμένων, Zenobius i. 52.

[h] Wellmann, p. 174.

[i] *Ibid.* p. 115 ; Maass, *Aratea* 147.

[j] Athen. 9 a (vol. i. p. 38), 132 f (vol. ii. p. 110), 172 b (*ibid.* p. 280), 644 c (κανδύλοις), 664 c. Κανδαύλας, "dog-throttler," was an epithet of the Lydian Hermes ; Hipponax 4 Diehl, Ἑρμῆ κυνάγχα, Μῃονιστὶ κανδαῦλα.

οὕτως ἐξήσκηντο πρὸς τὰς ἡδυπαθείας. γίνεσθαι δ'
αὑτόν φησιν ὁ Ταραντῖνος Ἡγήσιππος ἐξ ἐφθοῦ
κρέως καὶ κνηστοῦ ἄρτου καὶ Φρυγίου τυροῦ
ἀνήθου τε καὶ ζωμοῦ πίονος. μνημονεύει δ' αὐτοῦ
Ἄλεξις ἐν Παννυχίδι ἢ Ἐρίθοις· μάγειρος δ' ἐστὶν
ὁ προσδιαλεγόμενος·

ὅτι[1] δέ σοι παρὰ τοῦτο κάνδαυλόν τινα
παραθήσομεν. Β. κάνδαυλον; οὐκ ἐδήδοκα
κάνδαυλον[2] οὐδ' ἀκήκο' οὐδεπώποτε.[3]
Α. θαυμαστὸν ἐμὸν εὕρημα· πάνυ πολὺν δ' ἐγὼ
e ἐὰν παραθῶ σοι, προσκατέδει[4] τοὺς δακτύλους
αὐτῷ[5] γε χαίρων. χόρια[6] μὲν ποιήσομεν—
Β. ἄνθρωπε, ποίει λευκὰ καὶ βλέπ' εἰς[7] . . .
Α. εἶτ' ἀντακαῖον ἰχθύων τάριχος ἢ[8]
κρεῶν, βατανίων εὐθέως . . .
δίπυρον παραθήσω κῳὸν[9] ἐπιτετμημένον,
πυόν,[10] μέλιτος ὀξύβαφον ἐπὶ ταγηνιῶν,[11]
τυροῦ τροφάλια χλωρὰ Κυθνίου παρατεμών,
βοτρύδιόν τι, χόριον,[12] ἐν ποτηρίῳ

[1] ἔτι Musurus.   [2] κάνδαυλον added by Meineke.
[3] Jacobs: οὐδέποτε A.
[4] Musurus (προσκατέδῃ): προσκατεδεῖ AC (-εδῆ E).
[5] Herwerden: ἔρια A.   [6] Herwerden: ἔρια A.
[7] Dindorf: βλέπεις A.
[8] εἶτ' . . . τάριχος ἢ Jacobs: ἐπὰν ἀπὸ τῶν κοινῶν ταρίχους ἰχθύων A.
[9] παραθήσω κῳὸν Kock: παραθήσεις ῷὸν A.
[10] πῖον A.   [11] ἐπὶ ταγηνιῶν Dobree: ἀποταγηνιῶ A.
[12] χορειον A.

[a] "Grated bread," Athen. 111 d (vol. ii. p. 24), making a kind of pilaf.
[b] Kock ii. 360; the text is very obscure.

were they for luxurious indulgence. Hegesippus of
Tarentum says that it was made of boiled meat, bread
crumbs,[a] Phrygian cheese, anise, and fatty broth. It
is mentioned by Alexis in *The Vigil*, or *Toilers*; a
cook is the speaker in a dialogue [b] : " cook : And be
sure that side by side with this we will serve you with
a pilaf. B. Pilaf? I have never yet eaten that, and
have never yet heard of it. A. It's a marvellous
invention of mine; no matter how much I shall
set before you, you will eat up your fingers too,[c] you
will enjoy it so much. We will make puddings[d]—
B. Fellow, be sure you make them white, and look
to . . . A. And then, for the fish, we'll have some
salt sturgeon, or for the roast, some . . . straight from
the pans. . . . Some twice-baked bread [e] will I set
before you, and an egg sliced upon it, some beest-
ings,[f] a jar of honey to pour on pancakes, some fresh
green cheese of the Cythnian [g] sort, nicely sliced, a
bunch of grapes, a haggis, and a cup of sweet wine;

[c] There being no forks and no napkins, the fingers were
licked after the dish was eaten. So Aristophon, Athen.
161 e-f (vol. ii. p. 234); Plautus, *Pseudolus* 881 :

> ita convivis cenam conditam dabo
> hodie atque ita suavi suavitate condiam :
> ut quisque quidque conditum gustaverit
> ipsus sibi faciam ut digitos praerodat suos.

Alexis speaks also of the guests biting the dishes in their
enjoyment of the food, Athen. 107 d (vol. ii. p. 4), 169 d (*ibid.*
p. 268).

[d] Athen. 646 e. See critical note 6.

[e] Athen. 110 a (vol. ii. p. 16).

[f] The first milk of a cow or she-goat, much esteemed,
according to Aristoph. *Vesp.* 710.

[g] Pollux vi. 63 says that the Cythnian and Sicilian cheeses
were especially liked. Cythnus is one of the Cyclades. *Cf.*
Aristoph. *Vesp.* 838 τροφαλίδα τυροῦ Σικελικὴν κατεδήδοκεν.

γλυκύν· τὸ τοιοῦτον γὰρ ἀεί πως μέρος
f ἐπιπαίζεται, κεφαλὴ δὲ δείπνου γίνεται.
  Β. ἄνθρωπ᾽ ἐπίπαιζε· μόνον[1] ἀπαλλάγηθί μου,
τοὺς σοὺς[2] δὲ κανδαύλους λέγων καὶ χόρια καὶ
βατάνια. πᾶσαν ἀφανιεῖς[2] τὴν ἡδονήν.

μνημονεύει τοῦ κανδαύλου καὶ Φιλήμων ἐν Παρεισ-
ιόντι[3] οὕτως·

                        τοὺς ἐν τῇ πόλει
  μάρτυρας ἔχω γὰρ ὅτι μόνος φύσκην ποιῶ,
  κάνδαυλον, ᾠόθριον[4] ἐν στενῷ.[5] τί γὰρ[6]
  τούτων διάπτωμ᾽ ἐγένετ᾽ ἢ ἁμάρτημα τί;

517 καὶ Νικόστρατος ἐν Μαγείρῳ·
  ὃς μέλανα ποιεῖν ζωμὸν οὐκ ἠπίστατο,
  θρῖον δὲ καὶ κάνδαυλον.

καὶ Μένανδρος Τροφωνίῳ·
  Ἰωνικὸς πλούταξ, ὑποστάσεις[7] ποιῶν
  κάνδαυλον, ὑποβινητιῶντα βρώματα.

καὶ εἰς τοὺς πολέμους δὲ ἐξιόντες οἱ Λυδοὶ παρα-
τάττονται μετὰ συρίγγων καὶ αὐλῶν, ὥς φησιν
Ἡρόδοτος. καὶ Λακεδαιμόνιοι δὲ μετ᾽ αὐλῶν
ἐξορμῶσιν ἐπὶ τοὺς πολέμους,[8] καθάπερ Κρῆτες
μετὰ λύρας.

b Ἡρακλείδης δ᾽ ὁ Κυμαῖος ὁ τὰ Περσικὰ συγ-
γράψας ἐν τοῖς ἐπιγραφομένοις Παρασκευαστικοῖς
εἰπὼν ὡς ὁ ἐν τῇ λιβανοφόρῳ χώρᾳ βασιλεὺς
αὐτόνομός τέ ἐστι καὶ οὐδενὸς ὑπήκοος, γράφει
καὶ ταῦτα· " οὗτος δ᾽ ὑπερβάλλει τῇ τρυφῇ καὶ

---

[1] μόνον Casaubon: μόνον ἀλλ᾽ Α.
[2] τοὺς σοὺς and ἀφανιεῖς added by Dobree.
[3] Schweighäuser: παριόντι Α.
[4] ᾠόθριον Kaibel: ωαθριον Α. [5] ἐν στενω Α: ἐντέχνως Kock.

that is, somehow or other, the part that comes in as an after-play, but it proves to be the chief part of the dinner. B. ' Play afterwards ' all you want, fellow ; only get out of my way, talking of your pilafs and your haggises and your pans ! You will destroy all my appetite." Philemon also mentions the *kandaulos* in *Butting In* thus [a] : " All the people in the town are my witnesses that I am the only one who can make a black pudding, a pilaf, or an omelette at a pinch.[b] What, pray, was the fault in that, what the crime ? " And Nicostratus in *The Cook* [c] : " He was one who didn't know how to make black broth, but he could make an omelette or a pilaf." Also Menander in *Trophonius* [d] : " The Ionian, bloated with wealth, makes his chief dish of pilaf, and foods that provoke desire." Furthermore, when the Lydians march out to war they all fall in line to the accompaniment of whistles and pipes, as Herodotus says.[e] So too the Lacedaemonians set out for war to the tune of pipes, as the Cretans do to the tune of the lyre.[f]

Heracleides of Cumae, the author of the *Persian History*, in the part entitled *Equipment*, says [g] that the king of the country where frankincense is produced is independent and subject to nobody. He writes also as follows : " This chieftain excels in luxury and

---

[a] Kock ii. 493 ; the title refers to a parasite—in modern slang, " gate-crasher." Athen. 170 f gives the only other quotation from this play.

[b] Or " with proper skill." See critical note 5.

[c] Kock ii. 224, Athen. 664 c.

[d] Kock iii. 132, Allinson 440, Athen. 132 e-f (vol. ii. p. 111 note *a*).   [e] i. 17.

[f] Below, 627 d.   [g] *F.H.G.* ii. 97 ; of Arabia.

[6] γὰρ added by Meineke.   [7] 132 f : ὑπόστασις A.

[8] εἰς τὸν πόλεμον C ; with ἐπὶ we should expect τοὺς πολεμίους, " against the enemy."

ῥαθυμία. διατρίβει τε γὰρ αἰεὶ ἐν τοῖς βασιλείοις[1]
ἐν τρυφῇ καὶ δαπάνῃ τὸν βίον διάγων καὶ πράττει
οὐδὲ ἓν πρᾶγμα αὐτὸς[2] οὐδὲ πολλοῖς πλησιάζει,
ἀλλὰ δικαστὰς ἀποδεικνύει· καὶ ἐάν τις αὐτοὺς
ἡγῆται μὴ δικαίως δεδικακέναι,[3] ἔστι θυρὶς ἐν τῷ
ὑψηλοτάτῳ τῶν βασιλείων καὶ αὕτη[4] ἁλύσει δέδεται.
ὁ οὖν ἡγούμενος ἀδίκως δεδικάσθαι ἐπιλαμβάνεται
τῆς ἁλύσεως καὶ ἕλκει τὴν θυρίδα, καὶ ὁ βασιλεὺς
ἐπειδὰν αἴσθηται εἰσκαλεῖ καὶ αὐτὸς δικάζει. καὶ
ἐὰν φαίνωνται οἱ δικασταὶ ἀδίκως δικάσαντες, ἀπο-
θνήσκουσιν· ἐὰν δὲ δικαίως, ὁ κινήσας τὴν θυρίδα
ἀπόλλυται. τὰ δ' ἀναλώματα λέγεται τῆς ἡμέρας
εἰς τὸν βασιλέα καὶ τὰς περὶ αὐτὸν γυναῖκας καὶ
φίλους γίνεσθαι τάλαντα πεντεκαίδεκα Βαβυλώνια."

d   Παρὰ δὲ Τυρρηνοῖς ἐκτόπως τρυφήσασιν ἱστορεῖ
Τίμαιος ἐν τῇ α΄ ὅτι αἱ θεράπαιναι γυμναὶ τοῖς
ἀνδράσι διακονοῦνται. Θεόπομπος δὲ ἐν τῇ τεσσαρακοστῇ τρίτῃ τῶν Ἱστοριῶν καὶ νόμον εἶναι
φησιν παρὰ τοῖς Τυρρηνοῖς κοινὰς ὑπάρχειν τὰς
γυναῖκας· ταύτας δ' ἐπιμελεῖσθαι σφόδρα τῶν
σωμάτων καὶ γυμνάζεσθαι πολλάκις καὶ μετ'
ἀνδρῶν, ἐνίοτε δὲ καὶ πρὸς ἑαυτάς· οὐ γὰρ αἰσχρὸν
εἶναι αὐταῖς φαίνεσθαι γυμναῖς. δειπνεῖν δὲ αὐτὰς
οὐ παρὰ τοῖς ἀνδράσι τοῖς ἑαυτῶν, ἀλλὰ παρ' οἷς
ἂν[5] τύχωσι τῶν παρόντων, καὶ προπίνουσιν οἷς ἂν[5]
e βουληθῶσιν. εἶναι δὲ καὶ πιεῖν δεινὰς καὶ τὰς

---

[1] βασιλείοις A : βαλανείοις CE.
[2] αὐτὸς transferred hither by Wilamowitz from the next
line (after δικαστὰς).   [3] δεδικάσθαι C (om. αὐτούς).
[4] Schweighäuser : αὐτὴ AC.   [5] ἐὰν ACE.

---

[a] Cf. what is said of Ninyas at 528 f (p. 386).

sloth. In fact he lives always in the palace,[a] spending his life in luxury and expensive outlay, and never does even the least thing, in his own person, nor does he consort with many, but delegates men to act as judges ; and if a man thinks that they have given an unjust verdict, there is a window in the highest part of the palace, and this is fastened by a chain. So the man who thinks he has been unjustly convicted seizes the chain and jerks at the window; when the king perceives it he calls the man in and judges the case himself. And if it transpires that the judges have given an unjust verdict, they are put to death ; if the reverse, the man who moved the window is executed. The daily disbursements for the king and his wives and friends are said to reach the sum of fifteen Babylonian talents.[b]"

Among the Etruscans, who had become extravagantly luxurious, Timaeus records[c] in his first book that the slave girls wait on the men naked. And Theopompus in the forty-third book of his *Histories* says[d] that it is customary with the Etruscans to share their women in common ; the women bestow great care on their bodies and often exercise even with men, sometimes also with one another ; for it is no disgrace for women to show themselves naked. Further, they dine, not with their own husbands, but with any men who happen to be present, and they pledge with wine any whom they wish. They are also

---

[b] In silver, about £8350 or $40,000. Of course in purchasing power the sum would be much greater to-day.

[c] *F.H.G.* i. 197 ; Athen. 153 d (vol. ii. p. 198) gives the title *Histories*, and limits the time of such service until the girls become adults. See Athen. 607 f.

[d] *F.H.G.* i. 315, J. 2 B 577, G. and H. 195.

ὄψεις πάνυ καλάς. τρέφειν δὲ τοὺς Τυρρηνοὺς
πάντα τὰ γινόμενα παιδία, οὐκ εἰδότας ὅτου πατρός
ἐστιν ἕκαστον. ζῶσι δὲ καὶ οὗτοι τὸν αὐτὸν
τρόπον τοῖς θρεψαμένοις,[1] πότους τὰ πολλὰ ποιούμενοι καὶ πλησιάζοντες ταῖς γυναιξὶν ἁπάσαις.
οὐδὲν δ' αἰσχρόν ἐστι Τυρρηνοῖς οὐ μόνον αὐτοὺς
ἐν τῷ μέσῳ τι ποιοῦντας, ἀλλ' οὐδὲ πάσχοντας
φαίνεσθαι·[2] ἐπιχώριον γὰρ καὶ τοῦτο παρ' αὐτοῖς
ἐστι. καὶ τοσούτου δέουσιν αἰσχρὸν ὑπολαμβάνειν
ὥστε καὶ λέγουσιν, ὅταν ὁ μὲν δεσπότης τῆς οἰκίας
f ἀφροδισιάζηται, ζητῇ δέ τις αὐτόν, ὅτι πάσχει τὸ
καὶ τό, προσαγορεύσαντες[3] αἰσχρῶς τὸ πρᾶγμα.
ἐπειδὰν δὲ συνουσιάζωσι καθ' ἑταιρίας[4] ἢ κατὰ
συγγενείας, ποιοῦσιν οὕτως· πρῶτον μὲν ὅταν
παύσωνται πίνοντες καὶ μέλλωσι καθεύδειν, εἰσ-
άγουσι παρ' αὐτοὺς οἱ διάκονοι τῶν λύχνων ἔτι
καιομένων ὁτὲ μὲν ἑταίρας, ὁτὲ δὲ παῖδας πάνυ
καλούς, ὁτὲ δὲ καὶ γυναῖκας· ὅταν δὲ τούτων
ἀπολαύσωσιν, αὖθις[5] νεανίσκους ἀκμάζοντας, οἳ
πλησιάζουσιν αὐτοῖ[6] ἐκείνοις. ἀφροδισιάζουσιν δὲ
καὶ ποιοῦνται τὰς συνουσίας ὁτὲ μὲν ὁρῶντες
ἀλλήλους, ὡς δὲ τὰ πολλὰ καλύβας περιβάλλοντες
περὶ τὰς κλίνας, αἳ πεπλεγμέναι εἰσὶν ἐκ ῥάβδων,
518 ἐπιβέβληται δ' ἄνωθεν ἱμάτια. καὶ πλησιάζουσι
μὲν σφόδρα καὶ ταῖς γυναιξί, πολὺ μέντοι γε
μᾶλλον[7] χαίρουσι συνόντες τοῖς παισὶ καὶ τοῖς
μειρακίοις. καὶ γὰρ γίνονται παρ' αὐτοῖς πάνυ
καλοὶ τὰς ὄψεις, ἅτε τρυφερῶς διαιτώμενοι καὶ
λεαινόμενοι τὰ σώματα. πάντες δὲ οἱ πρὸς ἑσπέραν

---

[1] ταῖς θρεψαμέναις CE.
[2] φαίνεσθαι added by Musurus.
[3] προσαγορεύοντες Kaibel.
[4] ἑταιρείας A.

330

terribly bibulous, and are very good-looking. The Etruscans rear all the babies that are born, not knowing who is the father in any single case. These in turn pursue the same mode of life as those who have given them nurture, having drinking parties often and consorting with all the women. It is no disgrace for Etruscans to be seen doing anything in the open, or even having anything done to them; for this also is a custom of their country. And so far are they from regarding it as a disgrace that they actually say, when the master of the house is indulging in a love affair, and someone inquires for him, that he is undergoing so-and-so, openly calling the act by its indecent name. When they get together for companionship or in family parties they do as follows: first of all, after they have stopped drinking and are ready to go to bed, the servants bring in to them, the lamps being still lighted, sometimes female prostitutes, sometimes very beautiful boys, sometimes also their wives; and when they have enjoyed these, the servants then introduce lusty young men, who in their turn consort with them. They indulge in love affairs and carry on these unions sometimes in full view of one another, but in most cases with screens set up round the beds; the screens are made of latticed wands, over which cloths are thrown. Now they consort very eagerly, to be sure, with women; much more, however, do they enjoy consorting with boys and striplings. For in their country these latter are very good-looking, because they live in luxury and keep their bodies smooth. In fact all the bar-

---

⁵ αὐτοῖς after αὖθις deleted by Dindorf.
⁶ Kaibel: αὐτοῖς A.
⁷ μᾶλλον added by Kaibel (πολὺ μᾶλλον Meineke).

οἰκοῦντες βάρβαροι πιττοῦνται καὶ ξυροῦνται τὰ
σώματα· καὶ παρά γε τοῖς Τυρρηνοῖς ἐργαστήρια
κατεσκεύασται πολλὰ καὶ τεχνῖται τούτου τοῦ
πράγματός εἰσιν, ὥσπερ παρ᾽ ἡμῖν οἱ κουρεῖς.
b παρ᾽ οὓς ὅταν εἰσέλθωσιν, παρέχουσιν ἑαυτοὺς
πάντα τρόπον, οὐθὲν αἰσχυνόμενοι τοὺς ὁρῶντας
οὐδὲ τοὺς παριόντας. χρῶνται δὲ τούτῳ τῷ νόμῳ
πολλοὶ καὶ τῶν Ἑλλήνων τῶν[1] τὴν Ἰταλίαν οἰκούν-
των, μαθόντες παρὰ Σαυνιτῶν καὶ Μεσσαπίων.[2]
ὑπὸ δὲ τῆς τρυφῆς οἱ Τυρρηνοί, ὡς Ἄλκιμος
ἱστορεῖ, πρὸς αὐλὸν καὶ μάττουσιν καὶ πυκτεύουσι
καὶ μαστιγοῦσιν.

c   Διαβόητοι δ᾽ εἰσὶν ἐπὶ τρυφῇ καὶ αἱ τῶν Σικε-
λῶν τράπεζαι, οἵτινες καὶ τὴν παρ᾽ αὐτοῖς θάλατταν
λέγουσιν εἶναι γλυκεῖαν, χαίροντες τοῖς ἐξ αὐτῆς
γινομένοις ἐδέσμασιν, ὥς φησι Κλέαρχος ἐν πέμπτῳ
Βίων. περὶ δὲ Συβαριτῶν τί δεῖ καὶ λέγειν; παρ᾽
οἷς πρώτοις εἰσήχθησαν εἰς τὰ βαλανεῖα λουτρο-
χόοι καὶ παραχύται[3] πεπεδημένοι, τοῦ μὴ θᾶττον
ἰέναι καὶ ὅπως μὴ σπεύδοντες κατακαίωσι τοὺς
λουομένους. πρῶτοι δὲ Συβαρῖται καὶ τὰς ποιούσας
ψόφον τέχνας οὐκ ἐῶσιν ἐπιδημεῖν τῇ πόλει,[4] οἷον
d χαλκέων καὶ τεκτόνων καὶ τῶν ὁμοίων, ὅπως
αὐτοῖς πανταχόθεν ἀθόρυβοι ὦσιν οἱ ὕπνοι· οὐκ
ἐξῆν δ᾽ οὐδ᾽ ἀλεκτρυόνα ἐν τῇ πόλει τρέφεσθαι.

---

[1] καί before τῶν deleted by Schweighäuser.
[2] μεσαππίων ACE.
[3] λουτροχόους περιχύτας C (in a different construction).
[4] τὰς ψοφούσας τέχνας ἐξώρισαν τῆς πόλεως CE.

barians who live in the west remove the hair [a] of their bodies by means of pitch-plasters and by shaving with razors. Also, among the Etruscans at least, many shops are set up and artisans arise for this business, corresponding to barbers among us. When they enter these shops, they offer themselves unreservedly, having no modesty whatever before spectators or the passers-by. This custom is also in use even among many of the Greeks who live in Italy; they learned it from the Samnites and Messapians. In their luxury, the Etruscans, as Alcimus records, [b] knead bread, practise boxing, and do their flogging to the accompaniment of the flute.

The tables also of the Sicilians are notorious for luxury; these people say that the very sea on their coasts is sweet, so much do they enjoy the foods that come out of it; so says Clearchus in the fifth book of his *Lives*. [c] Why need one even speak of the Sybarites? Among them, first of all peoples, the water-carriers and attendants who poured water were brought into the baths with shackles on their feet to prevent them from walking too fast and scalding the bathers in their haste. The Sybarites were also the first to forbid noise-producing crafts from being established within the city, such as blacksmiths, carpenters, and the like, their object being to have their sleep undisturbed in any way; it was not permitted even to keep a rooster inside the city. [d]

[a] In Greece, however, this was usually done by singeing; *cf*. Aristoph. *Thesm.* 215 ff., *Eccl.* 13.
[b] *F.H.G.* iv. 296. *Cf.* Athen. 154 a (vol. ii. p. 200).
[c] *F.H.G.* ii. 307.
[d] A marginal note in A adds here: " This is also mentioned by Alciphron in his work *On the Luxury of Old Times*, who mentions practically all the other facts also."

ἱστορεῖ δὲ περὶ αὐτῶν Τίμαιος ὅτι ἀνὴρ Συβαρίτης
εἰς ἀγρόν ποτε πορευόμενος ἔφη ἰδὼν τοὺς ἐργάτας
σκάπτοντας αὐτὸς ῥῆγμα λαβεῖν· πρὸς ὃν ἀπο-
κρίνασθαί τινα τῶν ἀκουσάντων " αὐτὸς δὲ σοῦ
διηγουμένου ἀκούων πεπονεκέναι[1] τὴν πλευράν."
ἐν Κρότωνι δὲ σκάπτοντί τινι τὴν τῶν ἀθλούντων
κόνιν ἐπιστάντες τινὲς Συβαριτῶν ἐθαύμαζον λέγοντες, εἰ τηλικαύτην ἔχοντες πόλιν οἰκέτας μὴ
κέκτηνται τοὺς σκάψοντας ἑαυτοῖς τὴν παλαίστραν.
e ἄλλος δὲ Συβαρίτης παραγενόμενος εἰς Λακεδαί-
μονα καὶ κληθεὶς εἰς φιδίτιον,[2] ἐπὶ τῶν ξύλων[3]
κατακείμενος καὶ δειπνῶν μετ' αὐτῶν, πρότερον
μὲν ἔφη καταπεπλῆχθαι τὴν τῶν Λακεδαιμονίων
πυνθανόμενος ἀνδρείαν, νῦν δὲ θεασάμενος νομίζειν
μηδὲν τῶν ἄλλων αὐτοὺς διαφέρειν. καὶ γὰρ τὸν
ἀνανδρότατον μᾶλλον ἂν ἑλέσθαι ἀποθανεῖν ἢ
τοιοῦτον βίον ζῶντα καρτερεῖν.

Ἔθος δὲ παρ' αὐτοῖς καὶ τοὺς παῖδας μέχρι τῆς
τῶν ἐφήβων ἡλικίας ἁλουργίδας τε φορεῖν καὶ
πλοκαμίδας ἀναδεδεμένους χρυσοφορεῖν. ἐπιχωριά-
ζειν δὲ παρ' αὐτοῖς διὰ τὴν τρυφὴν ἀνθρωπάρια
f μικρὰ καὶ τοὺς σκωπαίους,[4] ὥς φησιν ὁ Τίμαιος,[5]

---

[1] ACE, confusing direct with indirect discourse.
[2] φειδίτιον ACE.   [3] ἐπὶ ξύλου C.
[4] σκωπαίους CE: σκοπαίους A, ταοὺς ἐκτοπίους Diels.
[5] Schweighäuser: τίμων ACE.

---

[a] F.H.G. i. 205.
[b] To soften the ground for the broad jump and the wrest-
ling. This was done with a pick : see the red-figured vase,
perhaps by Duris, in Gulick, Life of the Ancient Greeks,
p. 93.   [c] Athen. 138 d (vol. ii. p. 132).
[d] This word, skopaioi (see critical note 4), and the following
stilpones, occur only here. It has been explained as referring
to dwarfs, the word for which is ordinarily νᾶνος, and which
have been mentioned in the preceding ἀνθρωπάρια μικρά.

Concerning them Timaeus records *a* that once upon a time a man of Sybaris, going into the country, saw the farmers digging, and he told his friends that the sight had given him a rupture ; one of those who heard him answered, " Listening to your story has given me also a pain in my side." In Croton an athlete was digging up the soil *b* on which the games took place when some Sybarites who were standing by expressed their surprise that, possessing a city of such importance, they yet had no slaves to dig up the wrestling-ground for them. And another Sybarite who went to Sparta was invited to their commons, and as he lay on the wooden benches and ate with them he remarked that he had always before been astounded to hear of the Spartans' courage, but now that he had seen them he did not think they were in any respect superior to other peoples. For the most cowardly man in the world would prefer to die rather than endure living that sort of life.*c*

It was customary also among the Sybarites for the boys, until they reached the age of young manhood, to wear purple cloaks and have their hair tied up in braids secured by gold ornaments. Another national custom arising from their luxurious habits was to keep tiny manikins and owlish jesters,*d* as Timaeus says,

But καί shows that a new category is introduced, and σκω-ταῖοι may have reference to their owl-like faces (σκῶπες), Athen. 391 c, or (less likely) to their scurrilous jests (σκώπτω). *Cf.* also the dance called σιώψ and σκώπευμα, Athen. 629 f. Kaibel read σπάδωνας, " eunuchs," for στίλπωνας, comparing 519 b and the well-known riddle of Panarces, Plat. *Rep.* 479 c and Schol., Athen. 452 c (vol. iv. p. 550). But in that case ἀνδράσιν would have been used below, 519 b, not ἀνθρώποις. There is no question of eunuchs here. The word probably refers to a dwarfish buffoon (*cf.* English " buff," now obsolete, " to make faces "). See Diels, *P.P.F.* iii. 1. 202.

τοὺς καλουμένους παρά τισι στίλπωνας[1] καὶ κυ-
νάρια Μελιταῖα, ἅπερ αὐτοῖς καὶ ἕπεσθαι εἰς τὰ
γυμνάσια.   πρὸς οὓς καὶ τοὺς ὁμοίους τούτοις
Μασσανάσσης[2] ὁ τῶν Μαυρουσίων βασιλεὺς ἀπεκρίνατο, ὥς φησι Πτολεμαῖος ἐν ὀγδόῳ Ὑπομνημάτων, ζητοῦσιν συνωνεῖσθαι πιθήκους· " παρ'
ὑμῖν, ὦ οὗτοι, αἱ γυναῖκες οὐ τίκτουσιν παιδία; "
παιδίοις γὰρ ἔχαιρεν ὁ Μασσανάσσης[2] καὶ εἶχε
519 παρ' αὐτῷ τρεφόμενα τῶν υἱῶν (πολλοὶ δὲ ἦσαν)
τὰ τέκνα καὶ τῶν θυγατέρων ὁμοίως. καὶ πάντα
ταῦτα αὐτὸς ἔτρεφεν μέχρι τριῶν ἐτῶν· μεθ' ἃ
ἀπέπεμπε πρὸς τοὺς γεγεννηκότας, παραγινομένων
ἄλλων.   τὰ δ' αὐτὰ ἔφη καὶ Εὔβουλος ὁ κωμικὸς
ἐν Χάρισιν οὕτως·

> καὶ γὰρ πόσῳ κάλλιον, ἱκετεύω, τρέφειν
> ἄνθρωπον ἔστ' ἄνθρωπον, ἂν ἔχῃ βίον,
> ἢ χῆνα πλατυγίζοντα καὶ κεχηνότα
> ἢ στρουθὸν ἢ πίθηκον, ἐπίβουλον κακόν.

b καὶ Ἀθηνόδωρος δὲ ἐν τῷ περὶ Σπουδῆς καὶ
Παιδιᾶς[3] Ἀρχύταν[4] φησὶ τὸν Ταραντῖνον πολιτικὸν
ἅμα καὶ φιλόσοφον γενόμενον πλείστους οἰκέτας
ἔχοντα αἰεὶ τούτοις[5] παρὰ τὴν δίαιταν ἀφιεμένοις
εἰς τὸ συμπόσιον[6] ἥδεσθαι. ἀλλ' οἱ Συβαρῖται
ἔχαιρον τοῖς Μελιταίοις κυνιδίοις καὶ ἀνθρώποις
οὐκ ἀνθρώποις.

---

[1] σπάδωνες (Lat. *spadones*) Kaibel.
[2] A : μασσανάσσης CE.   [3] Musurus: παιδείας A.
[4] ἀρχύτας CE (in a different construction): ἀρχύτην A.
[5] τούτων τοῖς παιδίοις Casaubon (*cf.* Aelian, *V.H.* xii. 15).
[6] ἀφικνουμένοις C (om. εἰς τὸ συμπόσιον).

---

[a] *F.H.G.* iii. 188, J. 2 B 985.   [b] Kock ii. 205.

he men called in some communities *stilpones* ; also Melitê lap-dogs, which accompany them even to the gymnasia. To these and men like them Massinissa, he king of the Mauretanians, made an answer recorded by Ptolemy in the eighth book of his *Commentaries* [a] ; they wanted to buy up a large number of monkeys, but he said to them : " In your country, sirs, don't the women bear babies ? " For Massinissa delighted in babies and kept the children of his sons—he had many—as also those of his daughters, in his own house. And he reared them all himself until they were three years old ; after hat he sent them back to their parents, and others ook their places. The comic poet Eubulus said the ame thing in his *Graces* thus [b] : " For how much better, I ask you, for a human being to bring up a human being provided he have the means, than a plashing, quacking goose, or a sparrow, or a monkey, always plotting mischief ! " And Athenodorus in is book *On Jest and Earnest* says [c] that Archytas of Tarentum, who was at once statesman and philosopher, and who owned many slaves, always delighted in having them [d] let loose in the dining-room when he was at meals. The Sybarites, on the contrary, took delight in Melitê puppies and human beings who were less than human.[e]

[c] See *F.H.G.* iii. 486, col. 2, Diels i. 252, Hense in *Rhein. Mus.* 62. 313 ff.

[d] Rather, their children ; see critical note 5.

[e] See above, p. 334 note *d*. Their dwarfs with owl faces and monkey habits seemed scarcely human ; Sueton. *Augustus* 3 : " ludebat cum pueris minutis quos facie et garrulitate amabilis undique conquirebat, praecipue Mauros et Syros. Iam pumilos (dwarfs) atque distortos et omnis generis eiusdem ut ludibria naturae malique ominis abhorrebat."

Ἐφόρουν δ' οἱ Συβαρῖται καὶ ἱμάτια Μιλησίω
ἐρίων πεποιημένα· ἀφ' ὧν δὴ καὶ αἱ φιλίαι ταῖ
πόλεσιν ἐγένοντο, ὡς ὁ Τίμαιος ἱστορεῖ. ἠγάπω
c γὰρ τῶν μὲν ἐξ Ἰταλίας Τυρρηνούς, τῶν δ' ἔωθεῖ
τοὺς Ἴωνας ὅτι τρυφῇ προσεῖχον. οἱ δ' ἱππεῖς τῶ
Συβαριτῶν ὑπὲρ τοὺς πεντακισχιλίους ὄντες ἐπόμ
πευον ἔχοντες κροκωτοὺς ἐπὶ τοῖς θώραξιν, καὶ το
θέρους οἱ νεώτεροι αὐτῶν εἰς τὰ τῶν Νυμφῶ
ἄντρα[2] τῶν Λουσιάδων ἀποδημοῦντες διετέλου
μετὰ πάσης τρυφῆς. οἱ δ' εὔποροι αὐτῶν ὁπότ
εἰς ἀγρὸν παραβάλλοιεν,[3] καίπερ ἐπὶ ζευγῶ
πορευόμενοι τὴν ἡμερησίαν πορείαν ἐν τρισὶν ἡμέ
ραις διήνυον. ἦσαν δέ τινες αὐτοῖς καὶ τῶν εἰ
d τοὺς ἀγροὺς φερουσῶν ὁδῶν κατάστεγοι. τοῖς δ
πλείστοις αὐτῶν ὑπάρχουσιν οἰνῶνες ἐγγὺς τῆς θα
λάσσης, εἰς οὓς δι' ὀχετῶν τῶν οἴνων ἐκ τῶν ἀγρῶ
ἀφειμένων τὸν μὲν ἔξω τῆς χώρας πιπράσκεσθα
τὸν δὲ εἰς τὴν πόλιν τοῖς πλοίοις διακομίζεσθα
ποιοῦνται δὲ καὶ δημοσίᾳ πολλὰς καὶ πυκνὰ[4]
ἑστιάσεις καὶ τοὺς λαμπρῶς φιλοτιμηθέντας χρυ
σοῖς στεφάνοις τιμῶσι καὶ τούτους ἀνακηρύτ
τουσιν ἐν ταῖς δημοσίαις θυσίαις καὶ τοῖς ἀγῶσιι

---

[1] ἔωθεν E : ἔξωθεν A, ἔξωθεν superscr. ἔωθεν C.
[2] λουτρὰ Kaibel.
[3] A : παραβάλοιεν CE, μεταβάλλοιεν Kaibel unnecessarily.
[4] πολλὰς καὶ πυκνὰς A : πυκνὰς alone CE, πολλὰς καὶ ποικίλ
Kaibel.

---

[a] Accounted the best, Aristoph. Lys. 729 and Scho
Aelian, Nat. Anim. xvii. 34; below, 540 d (p. 444), 553
(p. 512).   [b] F.H.G. i. 205.

The Sybarites, besides, wore clothes made of Milesian wool[a]; and it was from these things that friendships also arose between States, as Timaeus records.[b] For they came to like the Etruscans among the people of Italy, while among the people of the East they liked the Ionians, because both were devoted to luxury. The horsemen of the Sybarites, more than 5000 strong,[c] paraded with saffron-coloured coats[d] over their breastplates, and in summer their young men journeyed to the grottoes of the Nymphs on the Lusias river[e] and there spent the time in every form of luxury. Whenever the wealthy among them went for a vacation[f] to the country they took three days to finish the one-day journey, although they travelled in carriages. Further, some of their roads leading into the country were roofed over. Most of them own wine-cellars near the seashore, into which the wines are sent through pipes from their country-estates; part of it is sold outside the country, part of it, again, is carried over to the city in boats. They also hold many public banquets at frequent intervals, and they reward with golden crowns the men[g] who have striven brilliantly for honours, and publish their names at the State sacrifices and games, proclaiming

[c] The Athenian cavalry numbered only 1000.
[d] Cf. Athen. 198 c (vol. ii. p. 398).
[e] The modern Lucino, the waters of which were very clear, Aelian, Nat. Anim. x. 38.
[f] Cf. Aristot. Eth. Nic. 1153 b 34 παραβάλλειν εἰς αὐτάς (sc. ἡδονάς), "turn for recreation to pleasures."
[g] e.g. the choregi were called upon to furnish the feast as a public service, λῃτουργία. For the common formula used in Athens cf. Aeschin. iii. 49 τὸν κήρυκα ἀναγορεύειν ἐν τῷ θεάτρῳ πρὸς τοὺς Ἕλληνας (at the Greater Dionysia) ὅτι στεφανοῖ αὐτὸν (Demosthenes) ὁ δῆμος ὁ Ἀθηναίων ἀρετῆς ἕνεκα καὶ ἀνδραγαθίας.

339

προσκηρύττοντες οὐκ εὔνοιαν,[1] ἀλλὰ τὴν εἰς τὰ
e δεῖπνα χορηγίαν· ἐν οἷς στεφανοῦσθαι καὶ τῶν
μαγείρων τοὺς ἄριστα τὰ παρατεθέντα διασκευά-
σαντας. παρὰ Συβαρίταις δ᾽ εὑρέθησαν καὶ πύελοι
ἐν αἷς κατακείμενοι ἐπυριῶντο. πρῶτοι δὲ καὶ
ἀμίδας ἐξεῦρον, ἃς εἰσέφερον εἰς τὰ συμπόσια.
καταγελῶντες δὲ τῶν[2] ἀποδημούντων ἐκ τῶν
πατρίδων αὐτοὶ ἐσεμνύνοντο ἐπὶ τῷ γεγηρακέναι
ἐπὶ ταῖς τῶν ποταμῶν γεφύραις.

Δοκεῖ δὲ μέγα[3] τῆς εὐδαιμονίας αἴτιον[4] εἶναι ὅτι
ἐκ τῆς χώρας, ἀλιμένου τῆς θαλάσσης παρηκούσης
f καὶ τῶν καρπῶν σχεδὸν ἁπάντων ὑπὸ τῶν πολιτῶν
καταναλισκομένων, ὅ τε[5] τῆς πόλεως τόπος καὶ ὁ
παρὰ τοῦ θεοῦ χρησμὸς συμπαροξῦναι πάντας
ἐκτρυφῆσαι καὶ ποιῆσαι ζῆσαι ὑπὲρ τὸ μέτρον
ἐκλελυμένως. ἡ δὲ πόλις αὐτῶν ἐν κοίλῳ κειμένη
τοῦ μὲν θέρους ἕωθέν τε καὶ πρὸς ἑσπέραν ψῦχος
ὑπερβάλλον ἔχει, τὸ δὲ μέσον τῆς ἡμέρας καῦμα
ἀνυπόιστον· ὥστε τοὺς πλείστους αὐτῶν ὑπειλη-
520 φέναι πρὸς ὑγίειαν διαφέρειν τοὺς πότους[6]· ὅθεν καὶ
ῥηθῆναι ὅτι τὸν βουλόμενον ἐν Συβάρει μὴ πρὸ
μοίρας ἀποθανεῖν οὔτε δυόμενον οὔτε ἀνίσχοντα τὸν
ἥλιον ὁρᾶν δεῖ. ἔπεμψαν δέ ποτε καὶ εἰς θεοῦ τοὺς

---

[1] Schweighäuser added εἰς τὸν δῆμον, certainly required in
the translation. [2] δὲ τῶν CE : λέγων A.
[3] Musurus : μετὰ A. [4] Kaibel : αὐτῶν A.
[5] ὀλίγα πάνυ ἐξήγετο, ὁ δὲ Kaibel.
[6] Dobree : ποταμοὺς AC.

---

[a] Not so common in the sixth century (Sybaris was
destroyed 510 B.C.) as they were later. With their " tubs "
(πύελοι) the Sybarites anticipated the πυριατήριον, suda-
torium. This may be a parenthetic note, since C begins it
with ὅτι.

ot so much their loyalty to the State as their service
n providing dinners ; on these occasions they crown
ven the cooks who have most skilfully concocted
he dishes served. Among the Sybarites were also
evised tubs in which they lay and enjoyed vapour
baths.[a] They, too, were the first to invent chamber-
pots, which they carried to their drinking-parties.[b]
Ridiculing those who travelled away from their native
ities, they prided themselves in their turn on having
rown to old age at the bridges of their two rivers.[c]

An important reason for their prosperity would
eem to have resulted from the country they lived in,[d]
ince the sea that stretches beside it affords no harbour,
nd so practically all the produce is consumed by the
atives ; and besides the situation of their city, the
oracle which came from the god seems to have aided
n provoking them all to excessive luxury, and to have
aused them to adopt a life of loose indulgence beyond
ll measure. Their city lying, as it does, in a hollow,
n summer enjoys very great coolness in the morning
nd evening, but at noon it has intolerable heat ;
ence most of them thought that drinking-bouts
ontributed greatly to health ; whence also it came
o be said that anyone in Sybaris who did not wish
o die before his allotted time must look neither upon
he rising nor the setting sun.[e] Now they once sent

[b] Athen. 17 e (vol. i. p. 76), Aristoph. *Ran.* 544.
[c] Crathis and Sybaris, Athen. 269 f (vol. iii. p. 212), Diodorus
ii. 9. For pride in the local river *cf.* Psaumis in Pindar, *Ol.*
. 10, Sandys 48.
[d] The sentence as it stands is anacoluthous. See critical
ote 5.
[e] Athen. 273 c (vol. iii. p. 228 and note *a*), *cf.* below,
26 b (p. 372). The Sybarites thought that the drinking
hould begin before sundown and continue until after sunrise.

χρησομένους, ὧν ἦν εἰς Ἄμυρις,[1] πυνθανόμενο
μέχρι τίνος εὐδαιμονήσουσι. καὶ ἡ Πυθία ἔφη·

εὐδαίμων, Συβαρῖτα, πανευδαίμων[2] σὺ μὲν αἰεὶ
ἐν θαλίῃσιν ἔσῃ, τιμῶν γένος αἰὲν ἐόντων.

εὖτ᾽ ἂν δὲ[3] πρότερον θνητὸν θεοῦ ἄνδρα σεβίσσῃς,
b τηνίκα σοι πόλεμός τε καὶ ἔμφυλος[5] στάσις ἥξε

τούτων ἀκούσαντες ἔδοξαν[6] λέγειν αὐτοῖς τὸν θεὸ
ὡς οὐδέποτε παύσοιντο[7] τρυφῶντες· οὐδέποτε γὰ
τιμήσειν ἄνθρωπον μᾶλλον θεοῦ. ἐγένετ᾽ οὖ
αὐτοῖς τῆς τύχης ἡ μεταβολὴ ἐπεί τις τῶν οἰκετῶ
τινα μαστιγῶν[8] τοῦτον καταφυγόντα εἰς τὰ ἱερ
πάλιν ἐμαστίγου· ὡς δὲ τὸ τελευταῖον κατέδραμε
ἐπὶ τὰ τοῦ πατρὸς αὐτοῦ μνήματα, ἀφῆκεν αἰδε
c σθείς. ἐξαναλώθησαν δὲ φιλοτιμούμενοι πρὸς ἑαυ
τοὺς τρυφαῖς, καὶ ἡ πόλις δὲ πρὸς ἁπάσας τὰ
ἄλλας ἡμιλλᾶτο περὶ τρυφῆς. εἶτα μετ᾽ οὐ πολ
γινομένων αὐτοῖς σημείων πολλῶν τῆς[9] ἀπωλείας
περὶ ἧς οὐ κατεπείγει λέγειν, διεφθάρησαν.

Εἰς τηλικοῦτον δ᾽ ἦσαν τρυφῆς ἐληλακότες ὡ
καὶ παρὰ τὰς εὐωχίας τοὺς ἵππους ἐθίσαι πρὸ
αὐλὸν ὀρχεῖσθαι. τοῦτ᾽ οὖν εἰδότες οἱ Κροτωνιᾶτα
ὅτε αὐτοῖς ἐπολέμουν, ὡς καὶ Ἀριστοτέλης ἱστορε

---

[1] εἰς Ἄμυρις Adam: ἰσαμυρισ (sic) A.
[2] Συβαρῖτα, πανευδαίμων added by Casaubon (cf. Steph
Byz. s. Σύβαρις).
[3] Schweighäuser: δὴ A.   [4] σεβίξῃ Steph. B.
[5] Porson: ἐμφύλιος A.   [6] A: ἐδόκουν CE.
[7] Kaibel (παύσεσθαι in a different construction CE): πα
σαιντο A.
[8] καὶ after μαστιγῶν A, om. C.
[9] τῆς Casaubon: καὶ A (καὶ καταφανῶν τῆς Kaibel).

342

men, one of whom was Amyris, to the temple of the
god to consult the oracle, because they wanted to
learn how long they should enjoy prosperity. The
Pythian priestess replied : " Happy, thou Sybarite,
all happy shalt thou ever be in thy abundance, whilst
honouring the race of them that live for ever. But
whensoever thou hold a mortal man in awe rather
than a god, then shall war and civil strife come upon
thee." When they heard this they concluded that
the god meant they would never stop living in luxury ;
for they did not think they would ever honour a
human being more than a god. Well, the change in
their fortunes came about when a man was flogging
one of his slaves, and continued flogging him again
after he had fled for refuge to the sanctuaries ; but
when, finally, he ran to the tomb of his master's
father, the master let him go, out of reverence. And
they were exhausted by an eager rivalry among themselves in self-indulgence, and the whole community
also contended with all other States in luxury. And
so, not long afterward, when many signs of their
impending ruin came to them, concerning which
there is no pressing need to speak now, they were
destroyed.[a]

To such a point had they carried their luxurious
refinement that they had even trained their horses
to dance at their feasts to the accompaniment of
pipes. Now the people of Croton knew this when
they made war on the Sybarites, as Aristotle

[a] The account of the destruction of Sybaris is postponed
to 521 f (p. 350 below).

d διὰ τῆς Πολιτείας αὐτῶν, ἐνέδοσαν τοῖς ἵπποι
τὸ ὀρχηστικὸν μέλος· συμπαρῆσαν γὰρ αὐτοῖς κα
αὐληταὶ ἐν στρατιωτικῇ σκευῇ· καὶ ἅμα αὐλούντα
ἀκούοντες οἱ ἵπποι οὐ μόνον ἐξωρχήσαντο, ἀλλὰ κα
τοὺς ἀναβάτας ἔχοντες ηὐτομόλησαν πρὸς τοι
Κροτωνιάτας. τὰ ὅμοια ἱστόρησε καὶ περὶ Καρ
διανῶν ὁ Λαμψακηνὸς Χάρων ἐν δευτέρῳ Ὥρα
γράφων οὕτως· " Βισάλται εἰς Καρδίην ἐστρατεύ
σαντο καὶ ἐνίκησαν. ἡγεμὼν δὲ τῶν Βισαλτέω
ἦν ὁ Νάρις.¹ οὗτος δὲ παῖς ὢν ἐν τῇ Καρδίη
e ἐπράθη καί τινι Καρδιηνῷ δουλεύσας κορσωτεὺς
ἐγένετο. Καρδιηνοῖς δὲ λόγιον ἦν ὡς Βισάλτα
ἀπίξονται ἐπ᾽ αὐτούς, καὶ πυκνὰ περὶ τούτου δι
ἐλέγοντο ἐν τῷ κορσωτηρίῳ ἱζάνοντες. καὶ ἀποδρα
ἐκ τῆς Καρδίης εἰς τὴν πατρίδα τοὺς Βισάλτα
ἔστειλεν ἐπὶ τοὺς Καρδιηνοὺς ἀποδειχθεὶς ἡγεμὼ
ὑπὸ τῶν Βισαλτέων. οἱ δὲ Καρδιηνοὶ πάντες τοὶ
ἵππους ἐδίδαξαν ἐν τοῖς συμποσίοις ὀρχεῖσθαι ὑπ
τῶν αὐλῶν, καὶ ἐπὶ τῶν ὀπισθίων ποδῶν ἱστάμενο
τοῖς προσθίοις ὥσπερ χειρονομέοντες⁴ ὠρχοῦντ
ἐξεπιστάμενοι τὰ αὐλήματα. ταῦτ᾽ οὖν ἐπιστά
μενος ὁ Νάρις⁵ ἐκτήσατο ἐκ τῆς Καρδίης αὐλη

---

¹ ὁ Νάρις Cobet: ηαρις A, Ὄναρις Musurus, Νάρις (om.
Kaibel.
² καρδίαι A.   ³ κορσωτὴς (or κορσεὺς) Kaibel.
⁴ ὥσπερ χειρονομέοντες added by Kaibel from Jul. Afric.
⁵ Cobet: ὄναρις A.

ᵃ Frag. 583 Rose. Jul. Africanus, *Cest.* p. 293, says tha
a flute-player of the Sybarites, in revenge for an insult, re
vealed the fact and the tune to the Crotoniates. At a sign
in the battle all the Crotoniate pipers played the melody
which the horses were accustomed, whereupon they rose o

ecords [a] in his account of their *Constitution*, and
truck up [b] the dance tune for the horses ; for they
ad with them pipers in military uniform ; and no
ooner did the horses hear the pipers than they danced
way,[c] and not only that, but with their riders on
heir backs they deserted to the people of Croton.
he same story is recorded [d] also of the people of
`ardia by Charon of Lampsacus in the second book
f his *Annals*, writing as follows : " The Bisaltians
ook the field against Cardia and won the victory.
Naris was leader of the Bisaltians. He, when a child,
ad been sold in Cardia, and after serving as a slave
o a Cardian had become a barber. Now the Cardians
ad an oracle that the Bisaltians would come against
hem, and they would often talk about it as they sat
n the barber-shop.[e] So Naris, escaping from Cardia
o his native land, put the Bisaltians in readiness
o attack the Cardians, and was appointed leader by
he Bisaltians. All the Cardians had schooled their
orses to dance at their drinking-parties to the
ccompaniment of the pipes, and rising on their hind
egs and, as it were, gesticulating with their front
eet, they would dance, being thoroughly accustomed
o the pipe-melodies. Knowing these facts, Naris

heir hind legs, throwing off their riders, and so caused an
asy victory for Croton. *Cf.* Aelian, *Nat. Anim.* xvi. 23.
  [b] Sounded off, or gave the keynote, τὸ ἐνδύσιμον 556 a.
  [c] Aelian, *loc. cit.*, says " they danced away the battle," τὸν
όλεμον ἐξωρχήσαντο, *cf.* Hdt. vi. 129, of Hippocleides, suitor
or the daughter of Cleisthenes : ἀπορχήσαό γε μὲν τὸν γάμον,
you've certainly danced away your marriage."
  [d] *F.H.G.* i. 34. On Bisaltia see Athen. 77 e, 401 b (vol. i.
. 334, vol. iv. p. 314).
  [e] Theophrastus, commenting on the gossip of the barbers'
hops, called them wineless symposia, ἄοινα συμπόσια, Plut.
79 A.

f τρίδα, καὶ ἀφικομένη ἡ αὐλητρὶς εἰς τοὺς Βισάλτα
ἐδίδαξε πολλοὺς αὐλητάς· μεθ' ὧν δὴ καὶ στρατεύε
ται ἐπὶ τὴν Καρδίην. καὶ ἐπειδὴ ἡ μάχη συνε
στήκει, ἐκέλευσεν αὐλεῖν τὰ αὐλήματα ὅσα οἱ ἵππ
τῶν Καρδιηνῶν ἐξεπιστέατο.[1] καὶ ἐπεὶ ἤκουσα
οἱ ἵπποι τοῦ αὐλοῦ, ἔστησαν ἐπὶ τῶν ὀπισθίω
ποδῶν καὶ πρὸς ὀρχησμὸν[2] ἐτράποντο· τῶν δ
Καρδιηνῶν ἡ ἰσχὺς ἐν τῇ ἵππῳ ἦν, καὶ οὕτω
ἐνικήθησαν.''

521   Συβαριτῶν δέ τις εἰς Κρότωνά ποτε διαπλεῦσα
βουληθεὶς ἐκ τῆς Συβάρεως ἰδιόστολον ἐναυλώσατ
πλοῖον, ἐφ' ᾧ οὔτε ῥαντισθήσεται οὔτ' ἐμβήσετα
ἕτερος καὶ ἐφ' ᾧ τὸν ἵππον ἀναλήψεται.   τοῦ δ
οὕτως συμφωνήσαντος ἐνεβίβασέν τε τὸν ἵππο
καὶ ὑποστορέσαι τῷ ζῴῳ ἐκέλευσεν. ἔπειτα τινὸ
τῶν προπεμπόντων ἐδεῖτο συμπλεῦσαι αὐτῷ, λέγω
ὅτι προδιεστειλάμην τῷ πορθμεῖ ἵνα παρὰ τὴν γῆ
πλέῃ. ὁ δὲ ἀπεκρίνατο ὅτι μόλις ἄν σου ὑπήκουσ
εἰ παρὰ τὴν θάλασσαν ἔμελλες πεζεύειν καὶ μ
παρὰ τὴν γῆν πλεῖν.

b   Φύλαρχος δ' ἐν τῇ πέμπτῃ καὶ εἰκοστῇ τῶ
Ἱστοριῶν εἰπὼν ὅτι παρὰ Συρακοσίοις νόμος ἦ
τὰς γυναῖκας μὴ κοσμεῖσθαι χρυσῷ μηδ' ἀνθιν
φορεῖν μηδ' ἐσθῆτας ἔχειν πορφυρᾶς ἐχούσας παρυ

---

[1] ἐξεπίσταιντο CE.
[2] C: ὀρχισμὸν A.   C with a change of construction add
τραπομένων συνήθως τοῖς προσθίοις ποσί, καὶ ἀποσεισαμένων τοῦ
ἐπιβάτας.

---

[a] Sybaris was only about 25 miles from Croton, but a tire
some journey for any Sybarite by any conveyance. Th
blasé Sybarite would not take it even on land, much less o

346

urchased a flute-girl from Cardia, and on her arrival
n Bisaltia she taught many pipers; accordingly he
et out with them to attack Cardia. And when the
attle was on, he gave orders to play all the pipe-
nelodies which the Cardian horses knew. And when
he horses heard the piping, they stood on their hind
egs and began to dance; but since the whole strength
f the Cardians lay in their cavalry, they were beaten
n this way."

A Sybarite once desired to sail across to Croton
rom Sybaris and hired a boat for his own special use,
tipulating that he shall not be splashed and that no
ne else shall embark on it, and that he shall take his
orse on board. The skipper agreed to these terms,
o he put his horse aboard and gave orders to spread
edding for the animal. He then requested one of
hose who were seeing him off to sail along with him,
aying that he had previously arranged with the
kipper that he should sail close by the land. But
he man answered: "Not I! I would scarcely have
istened to your invitation if you had been intending
o make a land journey by the sea, instead of a sea
ourney by the land." [a]

Phylarchus, in the twenty-fifth book of his *Histories*,
ays [b] that among the Syracusans there was a law
hat a woman should not put on gold ornaments or
vear gaily-coloured dresses or have garments with

ea, even when keeping close to land; the weak joke turns
n the use of παρά as either "close by" or simply "by."
Kaibel thought the story a Byzantine interpolation. The late
vord ῥαντισθήσεται and the mediaeval and modern use of
va excite suspicion. In C the anecdote is given in curtailed
orm at 522 f (p. 350 crit. note 4).

[b] *F.H.G.* i. 347, J. 2 A 176. The quotation extends to
πώλοντο, 521 e.

φὰς ἐὰν μή τις αὐτῶν συγχωρῇ ἑταίρα εἶναι κοινῇ
καὶ ὅτι ἄλλος ἦν νόμος τὸν ἄνδρα μὴ καλλωπίζεσθα
μηδ' ἐσθῆτι περιέργῳ χρῆσθαι καὶ διαλλαττούσῃ
ἐὰν μὴ ὁμολογῇ μοιχεύειν ἢ κίναιδος εἶναι, κα
τὴν ἐλευθέραν μὴ ἐκπορεύεσθαι ἡλίου δεδυκότος
ἐὰν μὴ μοιχευθησομένην· ἐκωλύετο δὲ καὶ ἡμέρα
c ἐξιέναι ἄνευ τῶν γυναικονόμων ἀκολουθούσης αὐτ
μιᾶς θεραπαινίδος. "Συβαρῖται," φησίν, "ἐξοκεί
λαντες εἰς τρυφὴν ἔγραψαν νόμον τὰς γυναῖκας εἰ
τὰς ἑορτὰς καλεῖν καὶ τοὺς εἰς τὰς θυσίας καλοῦν
τας πρὸ ἐνιαυτοῦ τὴν κλῆσιν[1] ποιεῖσθαι, ἵνα ἀξίω
ποιούμεναι[2] τοῦ χρόνου τὴν παρασκευὴν[3] τῶν τ
ἱματίων καὶ τοῦ λοιποῦ κόσμου προάγωσιν οὕτω
εἰς τὰς κλήσεις. εἰ δέ τις τῶν ὀψοποιῶν ἢ
μαγείρων ἴδιον[4] εὕροι βρῶμα καὶ περιττόν, ἐξου
σίαν[5] μὴ εἶναι χρήσασθαι τούτῳ ἕτερον πρὸ ἐνιαυ
τοῦ ἀλλ' αὐτῷ τῷ εὑρόντι, τὸν χρόνον τοῦτον ὅπω
d ὁ πρῶτος εὑρὼν καὶ τὴν ἐργασίαν ἔχῃ, πρὸς τ
τοὺς ἄλλους φιλοπονοῦντας αὐτοὺς ὑπερβάλλεσθα
τοῖς τοιούτοις. ὡσαύτως δὲ[6] μηδὲ τοὺς τὰς ἐγχέ
λεις πωλοῦντας τέλος ἀποτίνειν μηδὲ τοὺς θηρεύον
τας. τὸν αὐτὸν τρόπον καὶ τοὺς τὴν πορφύρα
τὴν θαλαττίαν βάπτοντας καὶ τοὺς εἰσάγοντα
ἀτελεῖς ἐποίησαν.

---

[1] Casaubon: παρασκευῇ A.
[2] Schweighäuser: ποιούμενοι A.
[3] τὴν παρασκευὴν transferred hither by Casaubon. See
Plutarch, Sept. Sap. Conv. 147 E.
[4] CE: ἥδιον A.   [5] τὴν before ἐξουσίαν om. CE
[6] ὡσαύτως ἐνομοθέτησαν C.

---

[a] The Greek word is more euphemistic; ἑταίρα, " com
panion," " friend," may be used in a good sense, Il. iv. 441
Aristoph. Eccl. 528 γυνὴ . . . ἑταίρα καὶ φίλη.

purple borders unless she admitted that she was a common prostitute [a] ; he also says there was another law that a man might not affect foppish ways or adopt a fancy and conspicuous mode of dress unless he confessed to being an adulterer or a pathic, and the free matron was not to go abroad after the sun had set, otherwise it would be a confession that she meant to commit adultery ; she was even forbidden to go out by day without the permission of the Supervisors of Women,[b] and then only when accompanied by at least one maid. " The Sybarites," Phylarchus says, " after drifting into luxury passed a law that women should be invited to the public celebrations, and that those who issued the call to the sacrifices should do so a year beforehand, in order that the women might prepare their dresses and other adornments in a manner in keeping with the long time provided, before going forth in answer to the invitation. Again, if any caterer or cook invented a dish of his own which was especially choice, it was his privilege that no one else but the inventor himself should adopt the use of it before the lapse of a year, in order that the first man to invent a dish might possess the right of manufacture during that period, so as to encourage others to excel in eager competition with similar inventions.[c] On the same principle the eel-sellers were not required to pay a tax, and neither were those who caught them. In the same way they made the dyers of sea-purple and the importers of it exempt from taxes.

[b] See vol. iii. p. 102 note a.
[c] The earliest patent-law known, Cichorius in *Journ. f. Nationalökon.*, 1922, 46-48.

" Πάνυ οὖν ἐξοκείλαντες εἰς ὕβριν τὸ τελευταῖον
παρὰ Κροτωνιατῶν λ' πρεσβευτῶν ἡκόντων ἅπαν
τας αὐτοὺς ἀπέκτειναν καὶ πρὸ τοῦ τείχους τὰ
σώματα ἐξέρριψαν καὶ ὑπὸ θηρίων εἴασαν δια
φθαρῆναι. αὕτη δ' αὐτοῖς καὶ τῶν κακῶν ἐγένετο
e ἀρχὴ μηνίσαντος τοῦ δαιμονίου. ἔδοξαν γοῦν μετ
ὀλίγας ἡμέρας πάντες αὐτῶν οἱ ἄρχοντες τὴν αὐτὴν
ἰδεῖν ὄψιν ἐν τῇ αὐτῇ νυκτί· τὴν γὰρ Ἥραν ἰδόντες
ἐλθοῦσαν εἰς μέσην τὴν ἀγορὰν καὶ ἐμοῦσαν χολήν·
ἀνέβλυσεν δὲ καὶ αἵματος πηγὴ ἐν τῷ ἱερῷ αὐτῆς[1]
καὶ οὐδὲ οὕτως ἔληξαν τῆς ὑπερηφανίας ἕως πάντες
ὑπὸ Κροτωνιατῶν ἀπώλοντο." Ἡρακλείδης δ'
Ποντικὸς ἐν τῷ περὶ Δικαιοσύνης φησίν· " Συ
βαρῖται τὴν Τήλυος τυραννίδα καταλύσαντες τοὺ
f μετασχόντας τῶν πραγμάτων ἀναιροῦντες καὶ φο
νεύοντες ἐπὶ τῶν βωμῶν ἅπαντες[2] . . . καὶ ἐπ
τοῖς φόνοις τούτοις ἀπεστράφη μὲν τὸ τῆς Ἥρα
ἄγαλμα, τὸ δὲ ἔδαφος ἀνῆκε πηγὴν αἵματος, ὥστ
τὸν σύνεγγυς ἅπαντα τόπον κατεχάλκωσαν θυρίσι
βουλόμενοι στῆσαι τὴν τοῦ αἵματος ἀναφοράν·
διόπερ ἀνάστατοι ἐγένοντο καὶ διεφθάρησαν ἅπαν
522 τες, οἱ καὶ τὸν τῶν Ὀλυμπίων τῶν[3] πάνυ ἀγῶν
ἀμαυρῶσαι ἐθελήσαντες. καθ' ὃν γὰρ ἄγεται και
ρὸν ἐπιτηρήσαντες ἄθλων ὑπερβολῇ ὡς αὑτοὺ
καλεῖν ἐπεχείρουν τοὺς ἀθλητάς."[4]
Καὶ Κροτωνιᾶται δ', ὥς φησι Τίμαιος, μετὰ τὰ

---

[1] ἔν τινι τῶν βωμῶν C.
[2] ἅπαντες A : ἀπήντων older edd., ἠφάνισαν Lumb. Lacun
marked by Kaibel.
[3] τὸν C.   [4] C here gives the anecdote of 521 a.

---

[a] F.H.G. ii. 199, Voss 41.
[b] Called a demagogue by Diodorus Sic. xii. 9, who in
general gives a clearer account of the events here outlined.

" Drifting, then, into every kind of arrogance, it finally happened that when thirty ambassadors arrived from Croton the Sybarites murdered them all, tossed their bodies out in front of the wall, and left them to be torn to pieces by wild beasts. And this in fact proved to be the beginning of their disasters, because the divine wrath was provoked. It appeared, at any rate, that all their magistrates, a few days afterwards, had the same dream the same night ; for they saw the goddess Hera come into the centre of the market-place and vomit bile ; also a fountain of blood gushed forth in her temple ; and yet even so they did not relax their pride until all of them were destroyed by the people of Croton." So Heracleides of Pontus says in his tract *On Justice* [a] : " The Sybarites, after abolishing the autocratic government of Telys,[b] put to death those who had taken sides with his cause and murdered them at the steps of the altars . . . and at these murders the statue of Hera turned away,[c] and the pavement sent forth a fountain of blood, so that they had to block up the entire adjacent space with bronze doors in their desire to stop the rising stream of blood. For this reason they were laid waste and entirely destroyed— these people who had even wished to dim the glory of the festival held in honour of the great Olympians.[d] For they waited for the very time that this is held, and then, by an extravagant offer of prizes, they tried to lure the athletes to their own city."

The people of Croton, however, according to

---

[c] *Cf.* Eur. *I.T.* 1165.
[d] The Olympic Games, held every four years in midsummer. The great athlete of the time was Milo of Croton, who later led his townsmen against Sybaris, Diod. xii. 9.

ἐξελεῖν Συβαρίτας ἐξώκειλαν εἰς τρυφήν· ὥστε καὶ
τὸν ἄρχοντα αὐτῶν περιιέναι κατὰ τὴν πόλιν
ἁλουργίδα ἠμφιεσμένον καὶ ἐστεφανωμένον χρυσῷ
στεφάνῳ, ὑποδεδεμένον λευκὰς κρηπῖδας. οἱ δὲ οὐ
b διὰ τρυφήν φασι τοῦτο γεγονέναι, ἀλλὰ διὰ Δη-
μοκήδη τὸν ἰατρόν· ὃς τὸ μὲν γένος ἦν Κροτωνιά-
της, Πολυκράτει δὲ τῷ Σαμίων τυράννῳ συνὼν
καὶ μετὰ τὸν ἐκείνου θάνατον αἰχμαλωτισθεὶς ὑπὸ
Περσῶν ἀνήχθη ὡς βασιλέα, Ὀροίτου τὸν Πολυ-
κράτη ἀποκτείναντος. θεραπεύσας δ᾽ ὁ Δημοκήδης
Ἄτοσσαν τὴν Δαρείου μὲν γυναῖκα, Κύρου δὲ
θυγατέρα, τὸν μαστὸν ἀλγήσασαν, ἤτησε ταύτην
δωρεὰν καταπεμφθῆναι εἰς τὴν Ἑλλάδα ὡς ἐπαν-
ελευσόμενος· καὶ τυχὼν ἧκεν εἰς Κρότωνα. βου-
λομένου τε αὐτόθι καταμένειν, ἐπιλαβομένου τινὸς
c τῶν Περσῶν καὶ λέγοντος ὅτι βασιλέως εἴη
δοῦλος, ἐκεῖνον μὲν ἀφείλαντο[1] οἱ Κροτωνιᾶται,
ἐκδύσαντες δὲ τὴν στολὴν τοῦ Πέρσου ἐνέδυσαν
τὸν ὑπηρέτην τοῦ πρυτανεύοντος. ἐξ οὗ δὴ Περσικὴν ἔχων στολὴν περιέρχεται ταῖς ἑβδόμαις τοὺς
βωμοὺς μετὰ τοῦ πρυτάνεως· οὐ τρυφῆς χάριν
οὐδὲ ὕβρεως, ἀλλ᾽ ἐπηρείας τῆς εἰς τοὺς Πέρσας
τοῦτο πράττοντες.[2] ὕστερον δὲ καὶ οἱ Κροτωνιᾶται,
φησὶν ὁ Τίμαιος, ἐπεχείρησαν τὴν Ὀλυμπικὴν
πανήγυριν καταλῦσαι, τῷ αὐτῷ χρόνῳ προθέντες

[1] ὑφείλοντο Kaibel, Diels.
[2] The sentence is anacoluthous, and there is no reason
with Wilamowitz to delete τοῦτο πράττοντες, nor with Kaibel
to assume a lacuna after ὕστερον δὲ.

[a] F.H.G. i. 212, Diels ii. 656, Voss 42.
[b] On this famous physician and surgeon see Hdt. iii. 125 ff.
Iamblichus, Vita Pythag. 257 implies that he was a Pyth-
agorean.

Timaeus,[a] also drifted into luxury after the destruction of the Sybarites, and their ruler went about the city dressed in a purple robe, crowned with a golden crown, and shod with white boots. Yet others say that this occurred, not because of luxurious extravagance, but on account of the physician Democedes [b]; he was by birth a citizen of Croton, but he joined Polycrates, the tyrant of Samos, and being taken as a prisoner after his death [c] he was carried by the Persians up to the Great King,[d] Oroetes having killed Polycrates. Democedes cured Atossa, the wife of Darius and daughter of Cyrus, when she had a pain in her breast,[e] and he begged of her as a reward that he might be sent back to Greece, promising to return; he gained his request and went back to Croton. He wanted to settle down there, but a Persian apprehended him and declared that he was the king's slave; but the people of Croton took Democedes away from him, and stripping the Persian of his garments they put them on the servant of the chief magistrate. Ever since that time, therefore, he goes about visiting the altars on the seventh day of each month [f] in company with his chief and wearing Persian garments, both of them doing this not so much because of luxurious extravagance or arrogance as to show spite against the Persians. Later, however, the people of Croton also, Timaeus says, tried to abolish the Olympic festival by setting up at the same

---

[c] In 522 b.c.   [d] Darius I.
[e] Hdt. iii. 133 says it was an abscess (φῦμα, not tumour, as L. & S.).
[f] The seventh day (ἑβδόμη) had much religious importance. In Sparta it was sacred to Apollo, Hdt. vi. 57, perhaps also in Croton, Roscher, *Hebdomadenlehren* 210, *Rhein. Mus.* xii. 313.

d ἀργυρικὸν σφόδρα πλούσιον ἀγῶνα. οἱ δὲ Συβαρίτας τοῦτο ποιῆσαι λέγουσιν.

Ταραντίνους δέ φησι Κλέαρχος ἐν τετάρτῳ Βίων
ἀλκὴν καὶ δύναμιν κτησαμένους εἰς τοσοῦτο τρυφῆς
προελθεῖν ὥστε τὸν ὅλον χρῶτα παραλεαίνεσθαι
καὶ τῆς ψιλώσεως ταύτης τοῖς λοιποῖς κατάρξαι.
ἐφόρουν δέ, φησίν, καὶ παρυφὴν διαφανῆ πάντες,
οἷς νῦν ὁ τῶν γυναικῶν ἁβρύνεται βίος. ὕστερον
δ' ὑπὸ τῆς τρυφῆς εἰς ὕβριν ποδηγηθέντες ἀνάστατον μίαν πόλιν Ἰαπύγων ἐποίησαν Κάρβιναν,[2]
e ἐξ ἧς παῖδας καὶ παρθένους καὶ τὰς ἐν ἀκμῇ
γυναῖκας ἀθροίσαντες εἰς τὰ τῶν Καρβινατῶν[3] ἱερὰ
καὶ[4] σκηνοποιησάμενοι γυμνὰ πᾶσι τῆς ἡμέρας τὰ
σώματα παρεῖχον θεωρεῖν· καὶ ὁ βουλόμενος
καθάπερ εἰς ἀτυχῆ παραπηδῶν ἀγέλην ἐθοινᾶτο
ταῖς ἐπιθυμίαις τὴν τῶν ἀθροισθέντων ὥραν, πάντων μὲν ὁρώντων, μάλιστα δὲ ὧν ἥκιστα ἐκεῖνοι
προσεδόκων θεῶν. οὕτω δὲ τὸ δαιμόνιον ἠγανάκ-
τησεν ὥστε Ταραντίνων τοὺς ἐν Καρβίνῃ παρα-
f νομήσαντας ἐκεραύνωσεν πάντας. καὶ μέχρι καὶ
νῦν ἐν Τάραντι ἑκάστη[5] τῶν οἰκιῶν ὅσους[6] ὑπε-
δέξατο[7] τῶν εἰς Ἰαπυγίαν ἐκπεμφθέντων τοσαύτας
ἔχει στήλας πρὸ τῶν θυρῶν· ἐφ' αἷς καθ' ὃ[1]
ἀπώλοντο χρόνον οὔτ' οἰκτίζονται[8] τοὺς ἀποιχο-

---

[1] CE: δεύτερον A.   [2] καρβιναν A.
[3] Musurus: καρβινιατῶν A.   [4] καὶ CE: om. A.
[5] Musurus: ἑκάστηι A.   [6] ὅσους Musurus: οὓς οὐχ A.
[7] Schweighäuser: ὑπεδέξαντο A.
[8] οὔτ' οἰκτίζονται Musurus: οὗτοι κτίζονται A.

time with it games with very rich silver prizes. But others say it was the Sybarites who did this.

Clearchus in the fourth book of his *Lives* says [a] that after the people of Tarentum had acquired strength and power they progressed to such a point of luxury as to have the skin of their entire bodies made smooth, and so inaugurated this practice of removing the hair for all other peoples. All the men, he says, wore a transparent cloak [b] with purple border — garments which to-day are a refinement of women's fashions. But later, blindly led by luxury into outrage, they uprooted Carbina, a city of the Iapygians,[c] made the boys, girls, and women in their prime gather in the temples of Carbina, and there got up a spectacle, exposing their bodies naked for all to gaze at by day; and anyone who wished, leaping like wolves upon a herd into this wretched group, could feast his lust on the beauty of the victims there gathered ; yet while all were looking on, they little suspected that the gods were looking on most of all. For the divine powers were so angry that they blasted with a thunderbolt all the Tarentines who had committed this outrage in Carbina. And even to this day each of the houses in Tarentum has as many columns outside the front doors as it harboured members of the band dispatched to Iapygia [d] ; at these columns, on the anniversary of their destruction, the people neither make lamentation for the departed nor pour

[a] *F.H.G.* ii. 306.
[b] Hesych. *s.* παρι φή (" woven border ") shows that this word ould be extended in use to include the whole garment.
[c] In Calabria.
[d] That is, there was an expiatory column, or stelê, for each member of the expedition who had lived in that house.

μένους οὔτε τὰς νομίμους χέονται χοάς,[1] ἀλλὰ
θύουσι Διὶ Καταιβάτῃ.[2]

Ἰαπύγων τε αὖ τὸ γένος ἐκ Κρήτης ὄντων κατὰ
Γλαύκου[3] ζήτησιν ἀφικομένων καὶ κατοικησάντων,
523 οἱ μετὰ τούτους λήθην λαβόντες τῆς Κρητῶν περὶ
τὸν βίον εὐκοσμίας εἰς τοῦτο[4] τρυφῆς, εἶθ᾽ ὕστερον
ὕβρεως ἦλθον ὥστε πρῶτοι τὸ πρόσωπον ἐντριψά-
μενοι καὶ προκόμια περίθετα[5] λαβόντες στολὰς μὲν
ἀνθινὰς φορῆσαι, τὸ δὲ ἐργάσασθαι[6] καὶ πονεῖν
αἴσχιον[7] νομίσαι. καὶ τοὺς μὲν πολλοὺς αὐτῶν
καλλίονας τὰς οἰκίας ποιῆσαι τῶν ἱερῶν, τοὺς δ᾽
ἡγεμόνας τῶν Ἰαπύγων ἐφυβρίζοντας τὸ θεῖον
b πορθεῖν ἐκ τῶν ἱερῶν τὰ τῶν θεῶν ἀγάλματα,
προειπόντας μεθίστασθαι τοῖς κρείττοσιν. διόπερ
ἐξ οὐρανοῦ βαλλόμενοι πυρὶ καὶ χαλκῷ ταύτην
διέδοσαν τὴν φήμην. ἐμφανῆ γὰρ ἦν[8] μέχρι πόρρω
κεχαλκευμένα τῶν ἐξ οὐρανοῦ βελῶν· καὶ πάντες οἱ
ἀπ᾽ ἐκείνων μέχρι τήμερον ἐν χρῷ κεκαρμένοι καὶ
πένθιμον στολὴν[9] ἀμπεχόμενοι ζῶσιν, πάντων τῶν
πρὶν ὑπαρξάντων ἀγαθῶν σπανίζοντες.

[1] τὰς . . . χοάς Musurus: τοὺς . . . χόας A.
[2] Musurus: κατηβατη A.
[3] Δαιδάλου Schweighäuser.   [4] AC: τοσοῦτο E.
[5] περίθετα C: περιθετά τε E, περίθε|άτε A.
[6] ἐργάζεσθαι Kaibel.
[7] αἴσχιον ACE: αἰσχρὸν Meineke.
[8] ἐμφανῆ γὰρ ἦν early edd.: ἐφάνη γὰρ ην A.
[9] A: στολὴν πένθιμον C.

---

[a] Lit. " who descends " (in thunder).
[b] No record has survived of this search (see critical note 3)
but the legends of a Glaucus are multifarious, see Athen
296 d (vol. iii. pp. 328 ff.), and he may have been that son of
Minos who went to Italy, Serv. *Aen.* vii. 796 ; see Pauly-
Wissowa vii. 1415, *cf.* 1409. The Glaucus of Athen. 296

the customary libations in their honour, but sacrifice to Zeus the Thunderer.[a]

So, again, the Iapygians. They were natives of Crete who had come to look for Glaucus [b] and settled there; but their successors, forgetting [c] the Cretan discipline of life, went so far in luxury, and then later in arrogance, that they became the first to rub cosmetics on their faces and assume false fronts attached to their hair;[d] and while they wore gaily-coloured robes, they regarded working and toiling at a trade as too disgraceful. Most of them made their houses more beautiful than the temples,[e] and the leaders of the Iapygians, in utter contempt of deity, looted the statues of the gods from the temples, giving notice to their betters[f] to go elsewhere. Wherefore they were struck from the heavens with fire and copper, and handed on to posterity the report of it.[g] For in evidence there were shown for a long time afterward copper specimens of the missiles from the sky[h]; and all the survivors from those times to the present day live with hair close-cropped, clad in mourning garb, and lacking all the good things they had formerly enjoyed.

knew the elixir of life, and the Iapygians may have set out to find it, like the followers of Ponce de Leon who discovered Florida. For Glaucus cf. also the story in Ps.-Apollod. iii. 3. 1.

[c] The affected language of the original says, "assuming forgetfulness." This passage also is probably from Clearchus.

[d] In Aristoph. Thesm. 258 Agathon lends Mnesilochus a κεφαλὴν περίθετον, "wig," to make him look like a woman.

[e] Such a practice would have been scandalous in the Athens of the fifth century, Dem. Olynth. iii. 25, cf. Stob. Fl. xliv. 40, Ps.-Dicaearch. in F.H.G. ii. 254.

[f] i.e. the gods.

[g] Namely, the copper from heaven.

[h] Probably referring to meteoric stones found in Calabria.

Ἴβηρες δὲ καίτοι ἐν τραγικαῖς[1] στολαῖς καὶ ποικίλαις προιόντες καὶ χιτῶσι ποδήρεσι χρώμενοι
οὐδὲν ἐμποδίζονται τῆς πρὸς τοὺς πολέμους ῥώμης.
c Μασσαλιῶται δ᾽ ἐθηλύνθησαν οἱ τὸν αὐτὸν Ἴβηρσι
τῆς ἐσθῆτος φοροῦντες κόσμον. ἀσχημονοῦσι γοῦν
διὰ τὴν ἐν ταῖς ψυχαῖς μαλακίαν, διὰ τρυφὴν
γυναικοπαθοῦντες· ὅθεν καὶ παροιμία παρῆλθε
" πλεύσειας[2] εἰς Μασσαλίαν."

Καὶ οἱ τὴν Σῖριν δὲ κατοικοῦντες, ἣν πρῶτοι
κατέσχον οἱ ἀπὸ Τροίας ἐλθόντες, ὕστερον δὲ Κολοφώνιοι,[3] ὥς φησι Τίμαιος καὶ Ἀριστοτέλης, εἰς
d τρυφὴν ἐξώκειλαν οὐχ ἧσσον Συβαριτῶν. καὶ γὰρ
ἰδίως παρ᾽ αὐτοῖς ἐπεχωρίασεν φορεῖν ἀνθινοὺς
χιτῶνας, οὓς ἐζώννυντο μίτραις πολυτελέσιν, καὶ
ἐκαλοῦντο διὰ τοῦτο ὑπὸ τῶν περιοίκων μιτροχί-
τωνες, ἐπεὶ Ὅμηρος τοὺς ἀζώστους ἀμιτροχίτωνας
καλεῖ. καὶ Ἀρχίλοχος δ᾽ ὁ ποιητὴς ὑπερτεθαύμακε
τὴν χώραν τῶν Σιριτῶν διὰ τὴν εὐδαιμονίαν. περὶ
γοῦν τῆς Θάσου λέγων ὡς ἥσσονός φησιν·

οὐ γάρ τι καλὸς χῶρος οὐδ᾽ ἐφίμερος
οὐδ᾽ ἐρατός, οἷος ἀμφὶ Σίριος ῥοάς.

ὠνομάσθη δ᾽ ἡ Σῖρις, ὡς μὲν Τίμαιός φησιν καὶ
Εὐριπίδης ἐν Δεσμώτιδι Μελανίππῃ,[4] ἀπὸ γυναικός

---

[1] τραγικαῖς Musurus : τρατικαις A, στρατηγικαῖς CE.
[2] πλεύσειεν C, εἰς Μασσαλίαν πλεύσειας Plut.
[3] κολοφώνιοι C, οἱ κολοφώνιοι E : ὑπὸ κολοφωνίων A. The
reading in A is probably right, but something has been lost,
cf. Strabo 264.
[4] Schweighäuser: δεσμώτιδι ἢ μελανίππηι A.

---

[a] Plutarch, *Proverb. Alex.* 60, adds that they wore their
hair long and reeking with perfumery. But Strabo 181
praises the people of Massilia for their culture and simplicity
of life.

As for the Iberians, though they go forth in stately embroidered robes and wear tunics reaching to the feet, they are not at all impeded in the strength they display in war. But the people of Massilia, who wore the same fashion of dress as the Iberians, became effeminate.[a] At any rate their behaviour is indecent on account of the weakness of their souls, and they are effeminate through luxury; whence also a proverb has become current, " May you sail to Massilia ! "

Again, the people who made a settlement in Siris,[b] which was occupied first by the refugees from Troy, and later by Colophonians, as stated by Timaeus[c] and Aristotle,[d] drifted into luxury no less than the Sybarites. It became the peculiar custom in their country to wear gaily-coloured tunics which they belted with very costly sashes, and for this reason they were called by their neighbours " sash-tunics," since Homer calls men without belts " non-sash-tunics.[e] " The poet Archilochus had great admiration for the country of the Sirites on account of its prosperity. Speaking, at any rate, of the island of Thasos as a place quite inferior, he says[f] : " For in no wise is it a fair land, or desirable, or lovely, like that about the streams of Siris." It was called Siris, as Timaeus[g] says, and Euripides[h] also in *Melanippê Bound*, after a woman named Siris ; but according to

---

[b] First the name of the river (now Sinno) in Lucania, then of the town. See Strabo vi. 264.

[c] *F.H.G.* i. 206.   [d] Frag. 584 Rose.

[e] Of the Lycians under Sarpedon, *Il.* xvi. 419. For the epithets, used as nouns, *cf.* " black-shirts " and " the great unwashed."

[f] *P.L.G.*⁴ ii. 389, Diehl frag. 18, Edmonds frag. 21a.

[g] *F.H.G.* i. 206.

[h] *T.G.F.*² 521.

e τινος Σίριδος· ὡς δ' Ἀρχίλοχος, ἀπὸ ποταμοῦ. οὐκ ὀλίγον δὲ πρὸς τὴν τρυφὴν καὶ τὴν εὐδαιμονίαν τοῦ σύμπαντος τούτου κλίματος καὶ τὸ πλῆθος ἐγένετο τῶν ἀνθρώπων. διὸ καὶ Μεγάλη Ἑλλὰς ἐκλήθη πᾶσα σχεδὸν ἡ κατὰ τὴν Ἰταλίαν κατ-οίκησις.

Μιλήσιοι δ' ἕως μὲν οὐκ ἐτρύφων, ἐνίκων Σκύ-θας, ὥς φησιν Ἔφορος, καὶ τάς τε ἐφ' Ἑλλη-σπόντῳ πόλεις ἔκτισαν καὶ τὸν Εὔξεινον Πόντον κατῴκισαν πόλεσι λαμπραῖς, καὶ πάντες ὑπὸ[1] τὴν
f Μίλητον ἔθεον. ὡς δὲ ὑπήχθησαν ἡδονῇ καὶ τρυφῇ, κατερρύη τὸ τῆς πόλεως ἀνδρεῖον, φησὶν ὁ Ἀριστοτέλης, καὶ παροιμία τις ἐγεννήθη ἐπ' αὐτῶι "πάλαι ποτ' ἦσαν ἄλκιμοι Μιλήσιοι." Ἡρα-κλείδης δ' ὁ Ποντικὸς ἐν δευτέρῳ περὶ Δικαιοσύνης φησίν· " ἡ Μιλησίων πόλις περιπέπτωκεν ἀτυχίαις διὰ τρυφὴν βίου καὶ πολιτικὰς ἔχθρας· οἳ τὸ ἐπιει-κὲς οὐκ ἀγαπῶντες ἐκ ῥιζῶν ἀνεῖλον τοὺς ἐχθρούς.
524 στασιαζόντων γὰρ τῶν τὰς οὐσίας ἐχόντων καὶ τῶν δημοτῶν, οὓς ἐκεῖνοι Γέργιθας[2] ἐκάλουν, πρῶτοι μὲν κρατήσας ὁ δῆμος καὶ τοὺς πλουσίους ἐκβαλὼν καὶ τὰ τέκνα τῶν φυγόντων εἰς ἁλωνίας συναγαγών, βουσὶ[3] συνηλοίησαν καὶ παρανομωτάτῳ θανάτῳ διέφθειραν. τοιγάρτοι πάλιν οἱ πλούσιοι κρατή-σαντες ἅπαντας ὧν κύριοι κατέστησαν μετὰ τῶν

[1] ὑπὸ CE: ἐπὶ A. [2] γεργιθας A: γέργηθας CE.
[3] τὰ τέκνα . . συναγαγών, βουσὶ C: συναγαγὼν τὰ τέκνα
. . . βοῦς συναγαγόντες A, βοῦς εἰσαγαγόντες Kaibel, βοῦς τε ἐπαγαγόντες Casaubon.

[a] F.H.G. i. 260, J. 2 A 95. See Dopp, Geog. Studien d Ephorus, iii. (1909), Rostovtseff, Skythien und der Bosporus, 28.

Archilochus, after the name of a river. In proportion to the luxury and prosperity of all that region the size of the population also became great. Hence the name Magna Graecia was given to practically all the Greek settlements in Italy.

The Milesians, so long as they did not enjoy luxury, were able to defeat the Scythians, according to Ephorus,[a] and so they founded the towns on the Hellespont and settled the Euxine Sea with splendid cities, and they all ran races at Miletus. But after they had succumbed to pleasure and luxury, the masculine vigour of the state collapsed, as Aristotle says,[b] and a proverb referring to them came into being, " Once on a time, long ago, the Milesians were mighty men." [c] Heracleides of Pontus in the second book of his work *On Justice* says [d] : " The city of Miletus fell upon disasters through luxury of living and civil animosities ; for, not content with reasonable moderation, they destroyed their enemies root and branch. The men of property were at strife with the populace, whom they called *Gergithes*,[e] and at first the populace got the upper hand, and after they had ejected the rich from the city, they gathered the children of the exiles on the threshing-floors and trod them to death with oxen, destroying them with a most outrageous death. Therefore the rich, again getting the upper hand, tarred and burned to death all whom they could

[b] Frag. 557 Rose.
[c] Aristoph. *Plut.* 1002, 1075, *cf. Vesp.* 1060 and Schol.
[d] Voss 41.
[e] A contemptuous term for manual labourers, *cf.* Gergithius, name of the parasite in Athen. 255 c (vol. iii. p. 150). Hdt. v. 122 says they were the last remnant of the ancient Teucri, *cf.* vii. 43.

τέκνων κατεπίττωσαν. ὧν καιομένων φασὶν ἄλλα
τε πολλὰ γενέσθαι τέρατα καὶ ἐλαίαν ἱερὰν αὐτο-
b μάτην ἀναφθῆναι. διόπερ ὁ θεὸς ἐπὶ πολὺν χρόνον
ἀπήλαυνεν αὐτοὺς τοῦ[1] μαντείου καὶ ἐπερωτώντων
διὰ τίνα αἰτίαν ἀπελαύνονται εἶπεν·

καί μοι Γεργίθων τε φόνος μέλει ἀπτολεμίστων[2]
πισσήρων τε[3] μόρος καὶ δένδρεον αἰεὶ ἀθαλλές.[4]

Κλέαρχος δὲ ἐν τετάρτῳ Βίων ζηλώσαντάς φησι
τοὺς Μιλησίους τὴν Κολοφωνίων τρυφὴν διαδοῦναι
καὶ τοῖς πλησιοχώροις, ἔπειτ' ὀνειδιζομένους λέγειν
ἑαυτοῖς· " οἴκοι τὰ Μιλήσια κἀπιχώρια καὶ μὴ ἐν
c τῷ μέσῳ."

Καὶ περὶ Σκυθῶν δ' ἐξῆς ὁ Κλέαρχος τάδε
ἱστορεῖ· " μόνον δὲ νόμοις κοινοῖς πρῶτον ἔθνος
ἐχρήσατο τὸ Σκυθῶν· εἶτα πάλιν ἐγένοντο πάντων
ἀθλιώτατοι βροτῶν διὰ τὴν ὕβριν. ἐτρύφησαν μὲν

---

[1] αὐτοὺς τοῦ Musurus: αυ|τοῦ A (divided between two
lines).
[2] CE: ἀπτολεμιστω A.
[3] πισσηρός τε CE, perhaps rightly.
[4] αἰεὶ ἀθαλλές Schweighäuser: ἀειθαλές ACE.

---

[a] The olive, associated especially with the worship of Zeus
and of Athena, was one of the most sacred trees throughout
Greece.   The removal even of a stump that had been marked
as consecrated (μορία) was accounted a crime, Lysias, Or.
vii. ; see Pauly-Wissowa iii. 164.
[b] F.H.G. ii. 306.
[c] When Aristagoras of Miletus pleaded for an alliance
with the Spartans against Persia (Hdt. v. 50), he appeared
in rich robes.   An Ephor said to him, " Milesian things
should stay at home and not come here," Eustath. 1358. 11,
Zenob. v. 57, Suid. s. Οἴκοι.   The Milesians in Clearchus's
version turned the proverb on themselves.

get hold of, along with their children. While they were burning, among many other portents that are said to have arisen, a sacred olive-tree burst into flames spontaneously.[a] Hence the god for a long time repelled them from his oracle, and when they asked him for what reason they were repelled he said : ' I too am mindful of the slaughter meted out to the helpless Gergithes, of their doom that were covered with pitch, and the tree that bloometh nevermore.' " Clearchus in the fourth book of his *Lives* says [b] that the Milesians emulated the luxury of the Colophonians and passed it on to their neighbours ; afterwards, being reproached for this, they said to themselves, " Things that are Milesian and native with us must stay at home and are not for everybody." [c]

Clearchus next goes on to record the following facts about the Scythians : [d] " The Scythian nation alone adopted at first impartial laws : afterwards, however, they became the most wretched of all mortals [e] through their insolence. For they lived

---

[d] *F.H.G.* ii. 306, Latyschev, *Scythia et Caucasia*, i. 627 (with Russian translation).

[e] *Cf.* Eurip. *Antigone* frag. 157-158 (*T.G.F.*[2] 405) of Oedipus, quoted in Aristoph. *Ran.* 1182, 1187 : ἦν Οἰδίπους τὸ πρῶτον εὐδαίμων ἀνήρ, εἶτ' ἐγένετ' αὖθις ἀθλιώτατος βροτῶν. "Impartial laws" are here the supposedly simple laws of a primitive people as opposed to the laws of a complex civilization, Aesch. (*T.G.F.*[2] 66) εὔνομοι Σκύθαι. The conception of the Scythians varied at different times and in different authors. Herodotus stresses their cruelty, later writers idealized them as examples either of " the noble savage " or of a civilization superior to the Greek in freedom and enlightenment. See Minns, *Scythians and Greeks*, especially ch. iv., Rostovtseff, *Skythien und der Bosporus* 6 ff., 80 ff., 88 note 2. St. Paul apparently contrasts βάρβαρος and Σκύθης *Coloss.* iii. 11.

γὰρ ὡς οὐδένες ἕτεροι, τῶν πάντων εὐροίας[1] καὶ
πλούτου καὶ τῆς λοιπῆς αὐτοὺς χορηγίας κατα-
σχούσης. τοῦτο δὲ δῆλον ἐκ τῆς ἔτι καὶ νῦν ὑπο-
λειπούσης[2] περὶ τοὺς ἡγεμόνας αὐτῶν ἐσθῆτός τε
d καὶ διαίτης. τρυφήσαντες δὲ καὶ μάλιστα δὴ καὶ
πρῶτοι πάντων τῶν ἀνθρώπων ἐπὶ τὸ τρυφᾶν
ὁρμήσαντες εἰς τοῦτο προῆλθον ὕβρεως ὥστε πάντων τῶν ἀνθρώπων εἰς οὓς ἀφίκοιντο[3] ἠκρωτη-
ρίαζον τὰς ῥῖνας· ὧν[4] οἱ ἀπόγονοι μεταστάντες
ἔτι καὶ νῦν ἀπὸ τοῦ πάθους ἔχουσι τὴν ἐπωνυμίαν.
αἱ δὲ γυναῖκες αὐτῶν τὰς Θρᾳκῶν τῶν πρὸς ἑσπέραν
καὶ ἄρκτον περιοίκων[5] γυναῖκας ἐποίκιλλον τὰ
σώματα, περόναις γραφὴν ἐνεῖσαι.[6] ὅθεν πολλοῖς
ἔτεσιν ὕστερον αἱ ὑβρισθεῖσαι τῶν Θρᾳκῶν γυναῖκες
e ἰδίως ἐξηλείψαντο τὴν συμφορὰν προσαναγραψά-
μεναι τὰ λοιπὰ τοῦ χρωτός, ἵν' ὁ τῆς ὕβρεως καὶ
τῆς αἰσχύνης ἐπ' αὐταῖς χαρακτὴρ εἰς ποικιλίαν
καταριθμηθεὶς κόσμου προσηγορίᾳ τοὔνειδος ἐξ-
αλείψῃ· πάντων δὲ οὕτως ὑπερηφάνως προέστησαν
ὥστε οὐδένων ἄδακρυς ἡ τῆς δουλείας ὑπουργία
γιγνομένη διήγγειλεν εἰς τοὺς ἐπιγινομένους τὴν

---

[1] Musurus: εὐβοίας A.   [2] Musurus: ὑπολιπούσης A.
[3] ἀφίκοντο C.   [4] ὧν Kaibel: ἀφ' ὧν ACE.
[5] τῶν before περιοίκων (A) deleted by Wyttenbach.
[6] ἐνεῖσαι Charitonides.

---

[a] They were called Rhinocorurites (Ρινοκορουρῖται), Dock-
Noses, Steph. Byz. *s.v.* See Josephus, *Bell. Iud.* i. 14. 2,
iv. 11. 5, Strabo 759, Seneca, *De Ira* iii. 20 (who give a
different account). They lived on the borders of Palestine
and Egypt.

[b] They complicated the original designs, and therefore
partially obliterated them, with designs of their own, and
called the whole thing κόσμος, decoration. See *J.H.S.* ix. 146.

[c] This would ordinarily mean "any phrase or compound

in wanton luxury, as no others ever did, since an abundance of all things, wealth and other advantages, had got the mastery over them. This is evident from the mode of dress and manner of living that still survive to-day among their chieftains. But having become luxurious, and having in greatest degree and first of all men rushed eagerly into luxurious living, they proceeded so far in insolence that they cut off the noses of all men into whose lands they penetrated; and the descendants of these men migrated to other places and bear to this very day a name derived from that outrage.[a] And their women tattooed the bodies of the women in the Thracian tribes who lived near them on the west and north, injecting the design with pins. Hence many years later, the Thracian women who had been thus outraged effaced the memory of that calamity in their own way by painting the rest of their skin, that the mark of outrage and shame upon them, being now included in a variety of other designs, might efface the reproach under the name of ornamentation.[b] With such arrogance did the Scythians lord it over everybody that no service rendered them by their slaves was free from tears, but rather caused the meaning of ' the phrase derived from Scythians '[c] to be known only too well among

containing the word *Scythian*," and Clearchus so uses it. But in a larger sense it refers to the rude, blunt mode of speech among the Scythians, like the threatening answer given by their king Idanthyrsus to Darius, Hdt. iv. 127 where, however, the words τοῦτό ἐστι ἡ ἀπὸ Σκυθέων ῥῆσις seem to be interpolated. Diog. L. i. 101 says that the Scythian Anacharsis gave the impulse to the proverb " because he was free in his speech." *Cf.* Aelian. *Ep. Rust.* xiv. That relentless cruelty and not mere bluntness is implied in the proverb seems clear from Lucian, *Dial. Mer.* x. 4.

ἀπὸ Σκυθῶν ῥῆσιν οἷα τις ἦν. διὰ τὸ πλῆθος οὖν
τῶν κατασχουσῶν αὐτοὺς συμφορῶν, ἐπεὶ διὰ τὸ
f πένθος ἅμα τόν τε τῶν βίων ὄλβον καὶ τὰς κόμας
περιεσπάσθησαν, παντὸς ἔθνους οἱ ἔξω τὴν ἐφ'
ὕβρει κουρὰν ἀπεσκυθίσθαι προσηγόρευσαν."

Τοὺς δὲ σύμπαντας Ἴωνας ἐπισκώπτων Καλλίας
ἢ Διοκλῆς ἐν Κύκλωψί φησιν·

τί γὰρ ἡ τρυφερὰ καὶ καλλιτράπεζος Ἰωνία εἴφ'
ὅ τι πράσσει.

καὶ Ἀβυδηνοὶ (Μιλησίων δ' εἰσὶν ἄποικοι) ἀνει-
μένοι τὴν δίαιτάν εἰσιν καὶ κατεαγότες, ὡς παρίστησιν Ἕρμιππος ἐν Στρατιώταις·

χαῖρ', ὦ[1] διαπόντιον
στράτευμα, τί πράττομεν[2];
τὰ μὲν πρὸς ὄψιν μαλακῶς
ἔχειν ἀπὸ σώματος,[3]
525   κόμη τε νεανικῇ
σφρίγει τε βραχιόνων.
Β. ἤσθου τὸν Ἀβυδόθ'[4] ὡς
ἀνὴρ γεγένηται;

καὶ Ἀριστοφάνης Τριφάλητι παρακωμῳδῶν πολλοὺς τῶν Ἰώνων·

ἔπειθ' ὅσοι παρῆσαν ἐπίσημοι[5] ξένοι
ἐπηκολούθουν κἠντιβόλουν προσκείμενοι,

---

[1] Dobree: χαίρω A.   [2] Dobree: πραττομένων A.
[3] τὰ μὲν γὰρ ἀπ' ὀμμάτων | δοκεῖτε καλῶς (?) ἔχειν Kock.
[4] Ἀβυδόθ' Dobree: ἄβυδον A.   [5] ἐπίδημοι Meineke.

---

[a] Or "Scythification." Clearchus here outdoes himself
in obscurity, and the text cannot be right. For the customs

posterity. And so, as a result of the multitude of disasters that got the mastery over the Scythians, and after they had been stripped, in their mourning, of the felicity their lives once knew, as well as of their long hair, other peoples beyond their borders, of every nationality, called the cutting of another's hair to do him outrage by the word *aposcythize*." [a]

All the Ionians without exception are satirized by Callias (or Diocles) in *The Cyclopes* when he says [b]: " Come, tell us ! How is yonder luxurious and richly-tabled Ionia doing these days ? " And the people of Abydus (colonists from Miletus) are quite loose in their ways and wholly enervated, as Hermippus makes clear in *Soldiers* [c] : " A. Hail, battalion from over seas, how are we getting on ? To judge from your looks, soft of body you are, with your long locks of foppish youth, and your plumpness of arm. B. Did you ever notice that a native of Abydus has ever shown himself a man ? " Again, Aristophanes in *Triple-Phales* incidentally satirizes many of the Ionians [d] : " Then all the distinguished foreigners who were there followed close on his heels and besought him with insistence

of the Scythians in time of mourning, often involving great cruelty, see Herod. iv. 71 ff. For their practice of scalping (σκυθίζω, ἀποσκυθίζω, περισκυθίζω), here confused with cutting off the hair in mourning, see Herod. iv. 64, cf. Cic. *In Pison.* viii.   [b] Kock i. 695.

[c] *Ibid.* 241. The third and fourth vss. are corrupt, nor can Kock's emendation be correct.

[d] *Ibid.* 529. The title is derived from Φαλῆς (cf. φαλλός), Aristoph. *Acharn.* 263, 276, companion of Bacchus ; cf. also the gods Τριβαλλοί, Aristoph. *Av.* 1529 ff. (= Τρίφαλλοι, Usener, *Götternamen* 359). The play was aimed at Alcibiades, and is quoted by Athen. only here, at least by name. The poet ridicules the Ionic form ὅκως for ὅπως, in dialect " haow."

ὅκως[1] ἔχων τὸν παῖδα πωλήσει ᾽ς[2] Χίον,
ἕτερος δ᾽ ὅκως[1] ἐς Κλαζομενάς, ἕτερος δ᾽ ὅκως[3]
ἐς Ἔφεσον, ὁ[4] δ᾽ ἐς Ἄβυδον. ἦν δὲ πάνθ᾽
" ὅκως."[5]

περὶ δὲ τῶν Ἀβυδηνῶν Ἀντιφῶν ἐν τῷ κατὰ Ἀλκιβιάδου λοιδορίας γράφει οὕτως· " ἐπειδὴ ἐδο-
κιμάσθης ὑπὸ τῶν ἐπιτρόπων, παραλαβὼν παρ᾽
αὐτῶν τὰ σαυτοῦ[6] χρήματα ᾤχου ἀποπλέων εἰς
Ἄβυδον, οὔτε χρέος ἴδιον σαυτοῦ πραξόμενος
οὐδὲν οὔτε προξενίας οὐδεμιᾶς ἕνεκεν, ἀλλὰ τῇ
σαυτοῦ παρανομίᾳ καὶ ἀκολασίᾳ τῆς γνώμης
ὁμοίους ἔργων τρόπους μαθησόμενος παρὰ τῶν ἐν
Ἀβύδῳ γυναικῶν, ὅπως ἐν τῷ ἐπιλοίπῳ βίῳ[7] ἔχοις
χρῆσθαι αὐτοῖς."

c Ἀπώλοντο δὲ καὶ Μάγνητες οἱ πρὸς τῷ Μαιάν-
δρῳ διὰ τὸ πλέον ἀνεθῆναι, ὥς φησι Καλλῖνος ἐν
τοῖς Ἐλεγείοις καὶ Ἀρχίλοχος· ἑάλωσαν γὰρ ὑπὸ
Ἐφεσίων. καὶ περὶ αὐτῶν δὲ τῶν Ἐφεσίων Δη-
μόκριτος ὁ[8] Ἐφέσιος ἐν τῷ προτέρῳ περὶ τοῦ ἐν
Ἐφέσῳ Ναοῦ διηγούμενος περὶ τῆς χλιδῆς αὐτῶν
καὶ ὧν ἐφόρουν βαπτῶν ἱματίων γράφει καὶ τάδε·
" τὰ δὲ τῶν Ἰώνων ἰοβαφῆ καὶ πορφυρᾶ καὶ
κρόκινα ῥόμβοις ὑφαντά· αἱ δὲ κεφαλαὶ κατ᾽
d ἴσα διειλημμέναι ζῴοις. καὶ σαράπεις μήλινοι καὶ

---

[1] Musurus: ὅπως A.   [2] Casaubon: πωλήσεις A.
[3] ὅκῶς A.   [4] ὁ Meineke: οἱ δ᾽ A.
[5] ἦν δὲ πάνθ᾽ " ὅκως" Kaibel: ἦν δὲ ἐκεῖνα πάνθ᾽ ὁδῷ A.
[6] BP: αὐτοῦ A.
[7] σαυτοῦ after βίῳ deleted by Wilamowitz.
[8] ὁ CE: om. A.

how that, having the lad, he should sell him in Chios,
another, how that he should sell him in Clazomenae,
another, in Ephesus, still another, in Abydus. It was
nothing but ' how that ' ! " Again, with reference
to the people of Abydus Antiphon writes as follows
in the speech *Against Alcibiades*, a libel case[a]: " After
you had reached your majority, and with the approval
of your guardians, you took over from them your
estate and sailed away to Abydus, not with the
intention of calling in any debt owing to you, nor
again to get any consulship,[b] but rather to learn
from the women of Abydus modes of action that would
correspond to your own lawlessness and licentiousness
of mind, in order that you might be able to use them
in your future career."

The Magnesians, also, who live near the Maeander,
perished through their excessive looseness, as Callinus
says in his *Elegies*,[c] also Archilochus[d]; for they
were overcome by the Ephesians. With reference
to the Ephesians themselves Democritus of Ephesus,
in the first of his two books *On the Temple of Ephesus*,
tells the story of their luxury and of the dyed garments
which they wore, writing as follows[e]: " The garments
of the Ionians are violet-dyed, and crimson, and yellow,
woven in a lozenge pattern ; but the top borders are
marked at equal intervals with animal patterns.

[a] Blass[2] frag. 67.
[b] A *proxenus* performed the duties of a modern consul,
but was a citizen of the country in which he resided.
[c] *P.L.G.*[4] ii. 5 with Bergk's note on frag. 3, Edmonds
i. 42, Strabo 647.
[d] *P.L.G.*[4] ii. 388, Diehl frag. 19, Edmonds frag. 20.
Strabo, *loc. cit.*, says they were destroyed by the Treres, a
Cimmerian tribe.
[e] *F.H.G.* iv. 383. On the great temple of Artemis see
Athen. 183 c (vol. ii. p. 308), Strabo 640, *Act. Apost.* xix. 27.

πορφυροῖ καὶ λευκοί, οἱ δὲ ἁλουργεῖς. καὶ καλασίρεις Κορινθιουργεῖς· εἰσὶ δ' αἱ μὲν πορφυραῖ
τούτων, αἱ δὲ ἰοβαφεῖς, αἱ δὲ ὑακίνθιναι· λάβοι δ'
ἄν τις καὶ φλογίνας καὶ θαλασσοειδεῖς. ὑπάρχουσιν δὲ καὶ Περσικαὶ καλασίρεις, αἵπερ εἰσὶ
κάλλισται πασῶν. ἴδοι δ' ἄν τις," φησίν, " καὶ τὰς
καλουμένας ἀκταίας, ὅπερ ἐστὶ καὶ πολυτελέ-
στατον ἐν τοῖς Περσικοῖς περιβλήμασιν. ἐστὶν δὲ
τοῦτο σπαθητὸν ἰσχύος καὶ κουφότητος χάριν·
e καταπέπασται[1] δὲ χρυσοῖς κέγχροις· οἱ δὲ κέγχροι
νήματι πορφυρῷ πάντες εἰς τὴν εἴσω μοῖραν ἅμματ'
ἔχουσιν ἀνὰ μέσον."[2] τούτοις πᾶσι χρῆσθαί φησι
τοὺς Ἐφεσίους ἐπιδόντας εἰς τρυφήν.

Περὶ δὲ τῆς Σαμίων τρυφῆς Δοῦρις ἱστορῶν
παρατίθεται Ἀσίου ποιήματα, ὅτι ἐφόρουν χλιδῶνας
περὶ τοῖς βραχίοσιν καὶ τὴν ἑορτὴν ἄγοντες τῶν
Ἡραίων ἐβάδιζον κατεκτενισμένοι[3] τὰς κόμας ἐπὶ
τὸ μετάφρενον καὶ τοὺς ὤμους. τὸ δὲ νόμιμον
τοῦτο μαρτυρεῖται καὶ ὑπὸ παροιμίας τῆσδε
" βαδίζειν εἰς[4] Ἡραῖον ἐμπεπλεγμένον." ἐστὶ δὲ
τὰ τοῦ Ἀσίου ἔπη οὕτως ἔχοντα·

f   οἱ δ' αὔτως φοίτεσκον ὅπως πλοκάμους κτενί-
          σαιντο[5]
    εἰς Ἥρας τέμενος, πεπυκασμένοι[6] εἵμασι καλοῖς,
    χιονέοισι χιτῶσι πέδον χθονὸς εὐρέος εἶχον·

---

[1] Dalechamp, Schweighäuser : καταπέπλασται ACE.
[2] At this point C has : ἐν δὲ τῷ σχολίῳ τοῦ βιβλίου ὅθεν αἱ
παρεκβολαὶ τάδε ἦσαν περὶ τοῦ ἄνω γεγραμμένου ῥόμβου· ῥόμβος
ἐστὶ τροχίσκος ὃν τύπτοντες ἱμᾶσι καὶ στρέφοντες ποιοῦσι περι-
δινεῖσθαι καὶ ψόφον ἀποτελεῖν· ῥύμβον δὲ αὐτὸν εὔπολις εἶπε·
καλεῖται δὲ καὶ βρυτήρ=Schol. Ap. Rhod. i. 1139. See
Athen. 636 a.

Then there are robes called *sarapeis* dyed with quince-yellow, crimson, and white, others again with sea-purple. And long robes (*kalasireis*) of Corinthian manufacture; some of these are crimson, others violet, others dark red [a]; one might also buy these robes in flame-colour or sea-green. There are also Persian *kalasireis*, which are the finest of all. One might also see, Democritus goes on, the so-called *aktaiai*, and this in fact is the most costly among Persian wraps. It is compactly woven to give solidity and lightness, and is strewn all over with gold beads; all the beads are fastened to the inner side of the robe by a purple cord attached at the centre." All these, he says, are used by the Ephesians in their devotion to luxury.

Discoursing on the luxury of the Samians, Duris quotes [b] verses from Asius to show that they wore bracelets on their arms, and when they celebrated the festival of Hera they marched with their long hair carefully combed down over the breast and shoulders. This custom is attested also by this proverb, " Marching to the Heraeum with braided hair." The hexameter verses of Asius go thus [c]: " And they, even so, whene'er they had combed their locks, would hie them to the precinct of Hera, swathed in beautiful vestments, with snowy tunics that swept the floor

---

[a] It is uncertain what shade is meant in " hyacinthine."
[b] *F.H.G.* ii. 480, J. 2 A 152.   [c] *Frag. ep.* 206.

[3] CE : κατεκνενισμένοι A.   [4] εἰς added by Meineke.
[5] οἱ δ' ὅτε φοίτεσκον ὀπίσω πλοκάμους κτενίσαντες Kaibel.
[6] Musurus : πεποικασμένοι A.

χρύσειαι δὲ κορύμβαι ἐπ' αὐτῶν τέττιγες ὥς·
χαῖται δ' ἠωρεῦντ' ἀνέμῳ χρυσέοις ἐνὶ δεσμοῖς,
δαιδάλεοι δὲ χλιδῶνες ἄρ' ἀμφὶ βραχίοσιν ἦσαν,
. . . τες ὑπασπίδιον πολεμιστήν.[1]

Ἡρακλείδης δ' ὁ Ποντικὸς ἐν τῷ περὶ Ἡδονῆς
526 Σαμίους φησὶ καθ' ὑπερβολὴν τρυφήσαντας διὰ
τὴν πρὸς ἀλλήλους μικρολογίαν ὥσπερ Συβαρίτας
τὴν πόλιν ἀπολέσαι.

Κολοφώνιοι δ', ὥς φησι Φύλαρχος, τὴν ἀρχὴν
ὄντες σκληροὶ ἐν ταῖς ἀγωγαῖς, ἐπεὶ εἰς τρυφὴν
ἐξώκειλαν πρὸς Λυδοὺς φιλίαν καὶ συμμαχίαν
ποιησάμενοι, προῇεσαν διηοκημένοι τὰς κόμας
χρυσῷ κόσμῳ, ὡς καὶ Ξενοφάνης φησίν·

ἁβροσύνας[2] δὲ μαθόντες ἀνωφελέας παρὰ Λυδῶν
    ὄφρα τυραννίης ἦσαν ἄνευ[3] στυγερῆς,
b ἤεσαν εἰς ἀγορὴν παναλουργέα φάρε' ἔχοντες,
    οὐ μείους ὥσπερ χίλιοι εἰς[4] ἐπίπαν,
αὐχαλέοι, χαίτῃσιν[5] ἀγαλλόμεν' εὐπρεπέεσσιν[6]
    ἀσκητοῖς ὀδμὴν χρίμασι[7] δευόμενοι.

οὕτω δ' ἐξελύθησαν διὰ τὴν ἄκαιρον μέθην ὥστε
τινὲς αὐτῶν οὔτε ἀνατέλλοντα τὸν ἥλιον οὔτε δυόμενον ἑωράκασιν. νόμον τε ἔθεντο, ὃς ἔτι καὶ ἐφ'
c ἡμῶν ἦν, τὰς αὐλητρίδας καὶ τὰς ψαλτρίας καὶ
πάντα τὰ τοιαῦτα τῶν ἀκροαμάτων τὰ μισθώματα

---

[1] κοῦφα ποσὶν προβιβάντες, ὑπασπίδιοι πολεμισταί? "Advanc-
ing with light step, warriors protected by their shields," an
ironical reminiscence of Il. xiii. 158.
[2] Schneider: ἀφροσύνας A.   [3] Dindorf: ἠσσα|νευ A
[4] χίλιοι· εἰσ A.   [5] Musurus: χαιτισιν A
[6] ἀγαλμένοι Wilamowitz, εὐχρύσοισι Edmonds.
[7] Musurus: χρήμασι A.

of wide earth; and golden head-pieces [a] surmounted
them, like cicadas; their tresses waved in the breeze
mid their golden bands, and bracelets wrought with
cunning circled their arms . . . [b] a warrior sheltered
beneath his shield." Heracleides of Pontus, in his
work *On Pleasure*, declares [c] that the people of Samos,
after living in excessive luxury, lost their city, like
the Sybarites, because of their meanness toward
one another.

The people of Colophon, according to Phylarchus,[d]
were in the beginning rigid in their discipline, but
after they had drifted into luxury they contracted
friendship and alliance with the Lydians, and went
forth with their long locks decked with golden ornaments, as Xenophanes also says [e] : " Learning useless refinements from the Lydians while they were
still free from loathsome tyranny, they used to walk
to the place of assembly clad in robes all of purple,
no fewer than a thousand in all, with proud mien,
delighting in their beautiful locks, drenched with
the smell of ointments artfully prepared." And so
dissolute did they become in unseasonable carousing
that some of them never saw the sun either rising or
setting.[f] And so they passed a law, which was still
in force in our day,[g] that the flute-girls and harp-girls
and all such entertainers should receive wages from

[a] See above, 512 c (p. 302) and note *a*. Here the word for
top-knot (κόρυμβος, κρωβύλος, κορύμβη) is used for the brooch
which fastened it. Pollux ii. 30 has the form κοσύμβη.
[b] See critical note 1.   [c] Voss 36.
[d] *F.H.G.* i. 353, J. 2 A 184.
[e] *P.L.G.*[4] ii. 113 Diehl, Edmonds frag. 3, Diels, *Vorsokrat.*
46, *Poet. Phil.* iii. 1. 37.   Aristot. *Pol.* 1290 b 16 says that
after the Colophonians had acquired wealth they made war
on the Lydians.   [f] Above, 520 a (p. 340) and note *e*.
[g] Phylarchus lived in the third century B.C.

λαμβάνειν ἀπὸ πρωὶ μέχρι μέσου¹ ἡμέρας καὶ μέχρ[
λύχνων ἀφῶν²· ἀπὸ δὲ τούτου τὴν λοιπὴν νύκτ
ἦσαν πρὸς τῷ μεθύειν. Θεόπομπος δ' ἐν πεντε
καιδεκάτῃ Ἱστοριῶν χιλίους φησὶν ἄνδρας αὐτῶ
ἁλουργεῖς φοροῦντας στολὰς ἀστυπολεῖν· ὃ δὴ³ κ[
βασιλεῦσιν σπάνιον τότ' ἦν καὶ περισπούδαστο[
ἰσοστάσιος γὰρ ἦν ἡ πορφύρα πρὸς ἄργυρον ἐξετα
ζομένη. τοιγαροῦν διὰ τὴν τοιαύτην ἀγωγὴν ε[
τυραννίδι καὶ στάσεσι γενόμενοι αὐτῇ πατρί[
d διεφθάρησαν. ταῦτα⁴ εἴρηκεν περὶ αὐτῶν κ[
Διογένης ὁ Βαβυλώνιος ἐν τῷ πρώτῳ τῶν Νόμω[
κοινῶς δὲ περὶ πάντων⁵ Ἰώνων τρυφῆς Ἀντιφά
νης ἐν Δωδώνῃ⁶ τάδε λέγει·

> πόθεν οἰκήτωρ, ἤ τις⁷ Ἰώνων
> τρυφεραμπεχόνων ἁβρὸς ἡδυπαθὴς
> ὄχλος ὥρμηται;

Θεόφραστος δ' ἐν τῷ περὶ Ἡδονῆς καὶ δὴ καὶ τοι
Ἰωνάς φησι διὰ τὴν ὑπερβολὴν τῆς τρυφῆς . .
ἔτι καὶ νῦν ἡ χρυσῆ παροιμία διαμεμένηκε.

Καὶ τῶν παρωκεανιτῶν δέ τινάς φησι Θεόπομπα

---

¹ μεσούσης Kaibel. ² Musurus: ἀφ' ὧν A.
³ ὃ δὴ Coraes: ὅθεν ACE. ⁴ ταυτα (sic) A.
⁵ πάντων CE, lemma in A: πάντων τῶν A.
⁶ Δωδωνίδι Meineke.
⁷ ἤ τις Meineke: ἢ τίς A, εἰ· τίς CE.
⁸ Lacuna marked by Casaubon. Schweighäuser supplie[
ἀφορμὴν διδόναι τῇ παροιμίᾳ. ἔ.κ.ν. ἡ χρῆσις τῆς παροιμίας δια[

ᵃ One of the earliest laws regulating hours of labou[
The text is obscure, but the original meaning may be inferre[
There were three " shifts " in the day, and wages were pai[
as from dawn until noon, or from noon until after dark, [
from after dark until early dawn ; a fraction of any perio[

early in the morning until midday, and from then until lamplight ; and from this time on they were immersed in drinking for the rest of the night.[a] Theopompus says [b] in the fifteenth book of his *Histories* that a thousand of them thronged the city wearing purple robes ; this, as every one knows, was at that time a colour rare even for princes, and very much desired. For purple [c] was reckoned as equivalent to its weight in silver. Consequently, by reason of this kind of regimen they became involved in tyranny and party quarrels,[d] and were destroyed, fatherland and all. The same account of them is given by Diogenes of Babylon in the first book of his *Laws*. And Antiphanes has these lines on the luxury of all Ionians in general in his *Dodona* [e] : " Whence come they and where do they dwell ? Or is it some crowd of luxuriantly-cloaked Ionians, dainty and on pleasure bent, that here comes forth ? " Theophrastus, too, in his tract *On Pleasure*, says that the Ionians, as well as other peoples, on account of their excess of luxury . . . even to this day the golden proverb has survived.[f]

Some, also, of the peoples living on the coast of the

had to be paid for as a whole period. The pay, of course, went to the owner of the girls, who were slaves.

[b] *F.H.G.* i. 299, J. 2 B 563, G. and H. 114. The quotation obviously is based on Xenophanes, like that of Phylarchus.

[c] Or " the purple-shell." Schweighäuser " purpurea vestis." Aesch. *Ag.* 959 πορφύρας ἰσάργυρον κηκῖδα.

[d] A case of *hysteron proteron* : party quarrels led to tyranny, or dictatorship.

[e] Kock ii. 48 ; the only quotation from this play.

[f] The meaning may be : " On account of their excesses they gave occasion for the expression ' Ionic luxury,' the use of which still survives." See Hesych. *s.* Ἰωνικόν· τρυφερόν, and critical note 8.

ἐν ὀγδόῃ Φιλιππικῶν ἁβροδιαίτους γενέσθαι. περὶ
δὲ Βυζαντίων καὶ Καλχηδονίων ὁ αὐτός φησι
e Θεόπομπος τάδε· " ἦσαν δὲ οἱ Βυζάντιοι καὶ διὰ
τὸ δημοκρατεῖσθαι πολὺν ἤδη χρόνον καὶ τὴν πόλιν
ἐπ᾽ ἐμπορίου κειμένην ἔχειν καὶ τὸν δῆμον ἅπαντα
περὶ τὴν ἀγορὰν καὶ τὸν λιμένα διατρίβειν ἀκόλα-
στοι καὶ συνουσιάζειν καὶ πίνειν εἰθισμένοι ἐπὶ τῶν
καπηλείων. Καλχηδόνιοι δὲ πρὶν μὲν μετασχεῖν
αὐτοῖς τῆς πολιτείας ἅπαντες ἐν ἐπιτηδεύμασι καὶ
βίῳ βελτίονι διετέλουν ὄντες, ἐπεὶ δὲ τῆς δημο-
f κρατίας τῶν Βυζαντίων[1] ἐγεύσαντο, διεφθάρησαν εἰς
τρυφήν, καὶ τὸν καθ᾽ ἡμέραν βίον ἐκ σωφρονε-
στάτων καὶ μετριωτάτων φιλοπόται καὶ πολυτελεῖς
γενόμενοι."[2] κἀν τῇ πρώτῃ δὲ πρὸς ταῖς εἴκοσι
τῶν Φιλιππικῶν τὸ τῶν Ὀμβρικῶν φησὶν ἔθνος
(ἐστὶν δὲ περὶ τὸν Ἀδρίαν) ἐπιεικῶς εἶναι ἁβροδίαιτον παραπλησίως τε βιοτεύειν τοῖς Λυδοῖς χώραν
527 τε ἔχειν ἀγαθήν, ὅθεν προελθεῖν εἰς εὐδαιμονίαν.

Περὶ δὲ Θετταλῶν λέγων ἐν τῇ τετάρτῃ φησὶν
ὅτι " ζῶσιν οἱ μὲν σὺν ταῖς ὀρχηστρίσιν καὶ ταῖς
αὐλητρίσιν διατρίβοντες, οἱ δ᾽ ἐν κύβοις καὶ πότοις
καὶ ταῖς τοιαύταις ἀκολασίαις διημερεύοντες, καὶ
μᾶλλον σπουδάζουσιν ὅπως ὄψων παντοδαπῶν τὰς
τραπέζας παραθήσονται[3] πλήρεις ἢ τὸν αὑτῶν βίον
ὅπως παρασχήσονται[4] κεκοσμημένον. Φαρσάλιοι

---

[1] τῆς βυζαντίων δημοκρατίας C.
[2] The sentence is defective.
[3] Musurus : παραθήσωνται A.
[4] Musurus : παρασχήσωνται A.

---

[a] F.H.G. i. 287, J. 2 B 546, G. and H. 65.
[b] At 329 a the name was spelled Chalcedonians. The same mutation is found in inscriptions.
[c] Not all cities were ἐμπόρια, or market-centres.

Ocean are said [a] by Theopompus in the eighth book of his *History of Philip* to have been effeminate. And again, of the Byzantians and the Calchedonians [b] Theopompus says: "The Byzantians had by this time long had a democratic government; also their city was situated at a trading-post,[c] and the entire populace spent their time in the market-place and by the water-side; hence they had accustomed themselves to dissipation and amours and drinking in the taverns. As for the Calchedonians, before they all came to have a share with the Byzantians in the government, they devoted themselves unceasingly to the better pursuits of life; but after they had once tasted of the democratic liberties of the Byzantians, they sank utterly into corrupt luxury, and in their daily lives, from having been the most sober and restrained, they became wine-bibbers and spend-thrifts." And in the twenty-first book of his *History of Philip* Theopompus says [d] that the Umbrian nation (who live near the Adriatic) are pretty effeminate and live a life comparable to that of the Lydians, possessing good land which caused their advance in prosperity.

Speaking of the Thessalians in the fourth book, he says [e]: "Their lives are spent, in the case of some of them, in the continual company of dancing-girls and flute-girls, while others pass the livelong day in gaming, drinking, and the like forms of dissipation,[f] and they are more interested in having the tables that are served to them laden with all sorts of dainties than in making their own lives decent. But of all

[a] *F.H.G.* i. 302, J. 2 B 567, G. and H. 127.
[e] *F.H.G.* i. 286, J. 2 B 545, G. and H. 51.
[f] A similar expression occurs in Lysias, *Or.* xvi. 11 περὶ κύβους ἢ πότους ἢ τὰς τοιαύτας ἀκολασίας τυγχάνουσι τὰς διατριβὰς ποιούμενοι.

δὲ πάντων," φησίν, "ἀνθρώπων εἰσὶν ἀργότατοι καὶ πολυτελέστατοι." ὡμολόγηνται δ' οἱ Θετταλοί, ὡς b καὶ Κριτίας φησί, πάντων Ἑλλήνων πολυτελέστατοι γεγενῆσθαι περί τε τὴν δίαιταν καὶ τὴν ἐσθῆτα· ὅπερ αὐτοῖς αἴτιον ἐγένετο κατὰ τῆς Ἑλλάδος ἐπαγαγεῖν τοὺς Πέρσας, ζηλώσαντας τὴν τούτων τρυφὴν καὶ πολυτέλειαν. περὶ δὲ Αἰτωλῶν Πολύβιος μὲν ἐν τρισκαιδεκάτῃ Ἱστοριῶν φησιν ὡς διὰ τὴν τῶν πολέμων συνέχειαν καὶ τὴν τῶν βίων πολυτέλειαν κατάχρεοι ἐγένοντο. Ἀγαθαρχίδης δ' ἐν δωδεκάτῃ Ἱστοριῶν "Αἰτωλοί," φησί, "τοσούτῳ c τῶν λοιπῶν ἑτοιμότερον ἔχουσι πρὸς θάνατον ὅσῳπερ καὶ ζῆν πολυτελῶς[1] ἐκτενέστερον ζητοῦσι τῶν ἄλλων."

Διαβόητοι δ' εἰσὶ περὶ τρυφὴν Σικελιῶταί τε καὶ Συρακόσιοι, ὡς καὶ Ἀριστοφάνης φησὶν ἐν Δαιταλεῦσιν·

ἀλλ' οὐ γὰρ ἔμαθε ταῦτ'[2] ἐμοῦ πέμποντος, ἀλλὰ μᾶλλον
πίνειν, ἔπειτ' ᾄδειν κακῶς, Συρακοσίαν τράπεζαν
Συβαρίτιδάς τ' εὐωχίας καὶ Χῖον ἐκ Λακαινᾶν[3] ...

Πλάτων δ' ἐν ταῖς Ἐπιστολαῖς φησιν· "ταύτην δὴ τὴν διάνοιαν ἔχων εἰς Ἰταλίαν τε καὶ Σικελίαν d ἦλθον ὅτε πρῶτον ἀφικόμην. ἐλθόντα δέ με ὁ ταύτῃ βίος[4] οὐδαμῇ οὐδαμῶς ἤρεσεν, δίς τε τῆς

---

[1] καὶ after πολυτελῶς deleted by Meineke.
[2] Elmsley: ἐμάθετε ταῦτα A.   [3] ἐκλάκαιναν A.
[4] Plato adds: ὁ ταύτῃ λεγόμενος αὖ βίος εὐδαίμων, Ἰταλιωτικῶν τε καὶ Συρακοσίων τραπεζῶν πλήρης.

---

men in the world (Theopompus says) the Pharsalians
are the laziest and the most given to spending."
Yet it is generally agreed that the Thessalians, as
Critias also says,[a] are the most extravagant of all
Greeks [b] in their food and clothing ; this was their
reason for bringing the Persians against Greece, since
they emulated Persian luxury and extravagance.
Concerning the Aetolians Polybius, in the thirteenth
book of his *Histories*, says [c] that on account of their
continual wars and extravagant lives they became
overwhelmed with debt. And Agatharchides, in the
twelfth book of his *Histories*, says [d] : " The Aetolians
are so much the more ready than other men to face
death, in proportion as they strive more strenuously
to live in an extravagant way than other people do."

Notorious for luxury also are the Greeks of Sicily,
particularly the Syracusans, as Aristophanes says in
Men of Dinnerville [e] : " But that's not what he
learned when I sent him to school ; rather, he
learned to drink, then to sing dirty songs, to set
a Syracusan table and feasts such as the Sybarites
have, and to take a swig of Chian from Laconian . . .
cups." And Plato in his *Letters* says [f] : " It was with
this intention,[g] accordingly, that I went to Italy and
Sicily on the occasion of my first visit. But when I
arrived, the life there satisfied me in no way or

[b] So Theopompus, Athen. 260 b (vol. iii. p. 170), 663 a ;
Plato, *Crito* 53 d ἐκεῖ γὰρ δὴ πλείστη ἀταξία καὶ ἀκολασία.
[c] Chap. 1. 1 (*init.*).
[d] *F.H.G.* iii. 192, J. 2 A 208, of the Aetolian League and
its members.
[e] Kock i. 446, Athen. 484 f (p. 152) and note *f*.
[f] 326 b : translated by Cicero, *Tusc.* v. 35.
[g] To study governments and interest Dion in his schemes
of reform.   Shorey, *What Plato Said*, pp. 40 ff.

ἡμέρας ἐμπιπλάμενον ζῆν καὶ μηδέποτε κοιμώ
μενον μόνον νύκτωρ καὶ ὅσα τούτῳ[1] ἐπιτηδεύματ
συνέπεται τῷ βίῳ.[2] ἐκ γὰρ τούτων τῶν ἐθῶν οὔτ
ἂν φρόνιμος οὐδείς ποτε γενέσθαι τῶν ὑπὸ τὸ
οὐρανὸν ἀνθρώπων ἐκ νέου ἐπιτηδεύων δύναιτο
σώφρων δ' οὐδ' ἂν μελλήσαι[3] ποτὲ γενέσθαι." κὰ
τρίτῳ δὲ Πολιτείας γράφει οὕτως· " Συρακοσία
δέ, ὦ φίλε, τράπεζαν καὶ Σικελικὴν ποικιλίαν ὄψου
e ὡς ἔοικας, οὐκ αἰνεῖς· ψέγεις δὲ καὶ Κορινθίαν
κόρην φίλην εἶναι ἀνδράσιν μέλλουσιν εὖ σώματο
ἕξειν καὶ Ἀττικῶν πεμμάτων τὰς δοκούσας εἶνα
εὐπαθείας."

Ποσειδώνιος δ' ἑκκαιδεκάτῃ Ἱστοριῶν περὶ τῶ
κατὰ τὴν Συρίαν πόλεων λέγων ὡς ἐτρύφων γράφε
καὶ ταῦτα· " τῶν γοῦν ἐν ταῖς πόλεσιν ἀνθρώπω
διὰ τὴν εὐβοσίαν τῆς χώρας ἀπὸ τῆς περὶ τ
ἀναγκαῖα κακοπαθείας συνόδους νεμόντων πλείονας
ἐν αἷς εὐωχοῦντο συνεχῶς, τοῖς μὲν γυμνασίοις ὡ
f βαλανείοις χρώμενοι, ἀλειφόμενοι[4] ἐλαίῳ πολυτελε
καὶ μύροις, τοῖς δὲ γραμματείοις[5]—οὕτως γὰ
ἐκάλουν τὰ κοινὰ τῶν συνδείπνων—ὡς οἰκητηρίοι
ἐνδιαιτώμενοι,[6] καὶ τὸ πλεῖον τῆς ἡμέρας γαστριζό
μενοι ἐν αὐτοῖς οἴνοις καὶ βρώμασιν, ὥστε κα
προσαποφέρειν πολλὰ καὶ καταυλουμένους πρὸ
χελωνίδος πολυκρότου ψόφον, ὥστε τὰς πόλει

---

[1] Stephanus: τούτων AC and Plat. codd.
[2] τῷ βίῳ AC: τῶν βίων Plat. codd.: "quae comitantur huié
vitae" Cicero.   [3] CE: μελῆσαι A.
[4] δ' after ἀλειφόμενοι deleted by Meineke.
[5] E: γραμματίοις AC.
[6] οἰκ ἐνδιαιτώμενοι 210 f: ἐν οἰκ. διαιτώμενοι AE (διαιτᾶσθα
in a different constr.) C.

manner [a]; think of a life of stuffing twice a day, and never being able to lie alone at night, to say nothing of all the other practices which accompany that mode of living! For with these customs no man under Heaven can ever become wise if he pursues them from boyhood, and no one can even begin to be virtuous." And in the third book of the *Republic* he writes as follows [b]: " A Syracusan table, my friend, and Sicilian variety of dainty food, you apparently do not commend; and you also disapprove of a Corinthian girl's being the mistress of men who want to be strong of body, and you disapprove of the supposed delights of Athenian pastry."

Poseidonius, in the sixteenth book of his *Histories*, tells of the cities in Syria and how luxurious they were, writing as follows [c]: " The people in the cities, at any rate, because of the great plenty which their land afforded, (were relieved) of any distress regarding the necessaries of life; hence they held many gatherings at which they feasted continually, using the gymnasia as if they were baths, anointing themselves with expensive oil and perfumes, and living in the ' bonds ' [d] —for so they called the commons where the diners met—as though they were their private houses, and putting in the greater part of the day there in filling their bellies—there, in the midst of wines and foods so abundant that they even carried a great deal home with them besides—and in delighting their ears with sounds from a loud-twanging tortoise-shell, so that their towns rang from end to end

---

[a] " The life," says Plato, " which is said to be happy, filled with bills of fare Italiot and Syracusan."

[b] 404 D; Socrates addresses Glaucon.

[c] *F.H.G.* iii. 258, J. 2 A 228, Athen. 210 f (vol. ii. p. 452).

[d] Halls designated by letters (γράμματα), vol. ii. p. 453 note d.

ὅλας τοιούτοις κελάδοις συνηχεῖσθαι." Ἀγαθαρχίδης δ' ἐν τῇ τριακοστῇ πέμπτῃ τῶν Εὐρωπιακῶι
528 "'Ἀρυκανδεῖς," φησί, "Λυκίας ὅμοροι ὄντες Λιμυ-
ρεῦσι διὰ τὴν περὶ τὸν βίον ἀσωτίαν καὶ πολυτέλειαν κατάχρεοι γενόμενοι καὶ διὰ τὴν ἀργίαν καὶ
φιληδονίαν ἀδυνατοῦντες ἀποδοῦναι τὰ δάνεια
προσέκλιναν ταῖς Μιθριδάτου ἐλπίσιν, ἆθλον ἕξειν
νομίσαντες χρεῶν ἀποκοπάς." ἐν δὲ τῇ λα΄ Ζα-
κυνθίους φησὶν ἀπείρους εἶναι πολέμου διὰ τὸ ἐν
εὐπορίᾳ καὶ πλούτῳ[1] τρυφῶντας ἐθίζεσθαι.

Πολύβιος δ' ἐν τῇ ἑβδόμῃ Καπυησίους τοὺς ἐν
b Καμπανίᾳ διὰ τὴν ἀρετὴν τῆς γῆς πλοῦτον περι-
βαλομένους[2] ἐξοκεῖλαι εἰς τρυφὴν καὶ πολυτέλειαν,
ὑπερβαλλομένους τὴν[3] περὶ Κρότωνα καὶ Σύβαριν
παραδεδομένην[4] φήμην. "οὐ δυνάμενοι οὖν," φησίν,
"φέρειν τὴν παροῦσαν εὐδαιμονίαν ἐκάλουν τὸν
Ἀννίβαν· διόπερ ὑπὸ Ῥωμαίων ἀνήκεστα[5] ἔπαθον.
Πετηλῖνοι δὲ τηρήσαντες τὴν πρὸς Ῥωμαίους
πίστιν εἰς τοσοῦτον καρτερίας ἦλθον πολιορκού-
c μενοι ὑπ' Ἀννίβα ὥστε μετὰ τὸ πάντα μὲν τὰ κατὰ
τὴν πόλιν δέρματα καταφαγεῖν, ἁπάντων δὲ τῶν
κατὰ τὴν πόλιν δένδρων τοὺς φλοιοὺς καὶ τοὺς

---

[1] πλείω C.
[2] Schweighäuser: περιβαλλομένους A, πλουτήσαντας simply C
[3] CE: τῆι A.   [4] παραδεδομένην om. C.
[5] CE: ἀνήκεστα δεινὰ A.

---

[a] F.H.G. iii. 194, J. 2 A 210.
[b] According to E. Meyer (Königsreich Pontos 53) not a
king of Pontus, but a son of Antiochus III who had command of his father's campaign in Lycia against the
Ptolemies. See Livy xxxiii. 19. 10; Niese, Gesch. d. griech
Staaten, ii. 639.
[c] F.H.G. and J. loc. cit. Philip III, son of Demetrius III

with such noises." And Agatharchides in the thirty-fifth book of his *European History* says[a]: "The Arycandians of Lycia, who live on the borders of the Limyrians, became involved in debt through their prodigality and extravagance of living, and being unable to pay their debts because they were lazy and pleasure-loving, they lent themselves to the ambitious projects of Mithradates,[b] thinking that they would have as reward the abolition of their debts." Again, in the thirty-first book he says[c] that the Zacynthians were unskilled in war because they were accustomed to live luxuriantly in abundant wealth.

Polybius, in his seventh book,[d] says of the Capuans who live in Campania that after they had come into the possession of wealth through the excellence of their soil, they drifted into luxury and extravagance surpassing the traditional fame of Croton and Sybaris. "And so," he says, "being unable to bear the prosperity they had,[e] they sent a call to Hannibal; wherefore they suffered irreparable disasters at the hands of the Romans. But the people of Petelia,[f] keeping faith with the Romans, went so far in endurance when they were besieged by Hannibal that after eating up all the hides in the city and consuming the shoots and

took over the power in Zacynthus 217 B.C., Polybius v. 102. 10.   [d] Chap. 1. 1.
    [e] *i.e.* not content with their lot. Flor. i. 16. 6 says that they stood but little lower than Rome and Carthage in population and wealth. In their arrogance they demanded that one consul should always be a Capuan, Liv. xxiii. 6. 6, Cic. *In Pison.* 24, a demand which Rome rejected.
    [f] In the territory of the Bruttii, north of Croton, 216 B.C. Livy xxiii. 30 says they were besieged by Himilco (or Hanno, ch. 37, so Appian), and after consuming everything else, "postremo coriis herbisque et radicibus et corticibus teneris strictisque foliis vixere."

ἁπαλοὺς[1] πτόρθους ἀναλῶσαι[2] ἕνδεκα μῆνας ὑπο-
μείναντες τὴν πολιορκίαν οὐδενὸς βοηθοῦντος οὐδὲ
συνευδοκοῦντος Ῥωμαίων παρέδοσαν ἑαυτούς.''

Τοὺς δὲ Κουρῆτας Φύλαρχος διὰ τῆς ια' τῶν
Ἱστοριῶν Αἰσχύλον ἱστορεῖν διὰ τὴν τρυφὴν τυχεῖν
τῆς προσηγορίας·

χλιδῶν τε πλόκαμος ὥστε παρθένοις ἀβραῖς[3]·
ὅθεν καλεῖν Κουρῆτα λαὸν[4] ᾔνεσαν.

d Ἀγάθων δ' ἐν τῷ Θυέστῃ τοὺς τὴν Πρώνακτος
θυγατέρα μνηστεύοντας τοῖς τε λοιποῖς πᾶσιν
ἐξησκημένους ἐλθεῖν καὶ κομῶντας τὰς κεφαλάς,
ἐπεὶ δ' ἀπέτυχον τοῦ γάμου,

κόμας ἐκειράμεσθα (φησὶν) μάρτυρας τρυφῆς,
ᾗ που ποθεινὸν χρῆμα παιζούσῃ φρενί.
ἐπώνυμον γοῦν εὐθὺς ἔσχομεν κλέος
Κουρῆτες εἶναι, κουρίμου χάριν τριχός.

καὶ Κυμαῖοι δὲ οἱ ἐν Ἰταλίᾳ, ὥς φησιν Ὑπέροχος
ἢ ὁ ποιήσας τὰ εἰς αὐτὸν ἀναφερόμενα Κυμαϊκά,
e διετέλεσαν χρυσοφοροῦντες καὶ ἀνθιναῖς ἐσθῆσι
χρώμενοι καὶ μετὰ γυναικῶν εἰς τοὺς ἀγροὺς
ἐξιόντες ἐπὶ ζευγῶν ὀχούμενοι.

Περὶ μὲν οὖν ἐθνῶν καὶ πόλεων τρυφῆς τοσαῦτα
μνημονεύω. περὶ δὲ τῶν κατ' ἄνδρα τάδ' ἤκουσα.

---

[1] ἁπαλοὺς CE: ἁπλοῦς A.
[2] CE: ἀναλῶσαι καὶ A.
[3] παρθένου ἁβρᾶς C and Eustath. 1292. 53.
[4] A: λοιπὸν CE.

---

[a] F.H.G. i. 339, J. 2 A 167, T.G.F.[2] 97 ; Aeschylus connects the word with κοῦρος " young man," see Il. ix. 529
For the construction cf. Il. xvii. 51 κόμαι Χαρίτεσσιν ὁμοῖαι,
and " an eye like Mars" (not Mars').
[b] Rather, their luxuriant, youthful locks.

384

tender stalks of all the trees in the city they finally surrendered, having endured the siege for eleven months without the aid or comfort of any Roman."

Of the Curetes Phylarchus, in the eleventh book of his *Histories*, quotes [a] Aeschylus as recording that they received their name because of their luxury [b] : " A ringlet as luxuriant as that of dainty maidens ; whence they approved the calling of that folk ' the Youthful.' " And Agathon in *Thyestes* describes the suitors for the hand of the daughter of Pronax as arriving adorned with all other embellishments and wearing the hair of their heads in long ringlets ; but when they failed to obtain their suit (he says) [c] : " We have shorn our locks, witnesses of our luxury, verily a possession we desired when our hearts were gay. Henceforth, at least, we have won the glory of a new name, Curetes, because of our close-cut hair." Again, the Cumaeans of Italy, according to Hyperochus or whoever wrote the *History of Cumae* which is ascribed to him,[d] continually wore gold ornaments and adopted gaily-coloured clothes, and rode into the country with their wives in two-horse chariots.

So much, then, I recall concerning the luxury of nations and cities. And now concerning that of individuals I have heard the following accounts. Ctesias

[a] *T.G.F.*[2] 763; Agathon connects the name with κουρά, "cropping of the hair" (from κείρω, "shear"), a sign of mourning. Kaibel, however, takes χρῆμα as referring to ἐκειράμεσθα, and παιξούσῃ as said in mockery. He would apparently render 'Verily that was a thing we chose to do with derisive intent." But it is hard to see how the close crop can signify derision when it is self-applied. Slaves and hetaerae were required (by others, of course) to wear short hair. The daughter of Pronax is named Amphithea by Ps.-Apollodorus i. 9. 13. Pronax was the brother of Eriphŷlê, wife of Amphiaraus.

[d] *F.H.G.* iv. 434.

Κτησίας ἐν τρίτῃ Περσικῶν καὶ πάντας μέν φησι
τοὺς βασιλεύσαντας τῆς ᾿Ασίας περὶ τρυφὴν σπου-
δάσαι, μάλιστα δὲ Νινύαν τὸν Νίνου καὶ Σεμιρά-
f μιδος[1] υἱόν. καὶ οὗτος οὖν ἔνδον μένων καὶ τρυ-
φῶν ὑπ᾿ οὐδενὸς ἑωρᾶτο εἰ μὴ ὑπὸ τῶν εὐνούχων
καὶ τῶν ἰδίων γυναικῶν. τοιοῦτος δ᾿ ἦν καὶ
Σαρδανάπαλλος,[2] ὃν οἱ μὲν ᾿Ανακυνδαράξεω λέγουσιν υἱόν, οἱ δὲ ᾿Αναβαραξάρου. ὅτε δὴ οὖν ᾿Αρ-
βάκης,[3] εἷς τῶν ὑπ᾿ αὐτὸν στρατηγῶν Μῆδος γένος,
διεπράξατο διά τινος τῶν εὐνούχων Σπαραμείζου
θεάσασθαι Σαρδανάπαλλον καὶ μόλις αὐτῷ ἐπ-
ετράπη ἐκείνου ἐθελήσαντος, ὡς εἰσελθὼν εἶδεν
αὐτὸν ὁ Μῆδος ἐψιμυθιωμένον καὶ κεκοσμημένον
γυναικιστὶ καὶ μετὰ τῶν παλλακίδων ξαίνοντα
529 πορφύραν ἀναβάδην τε μετ᾿ αὐτῶν καθήμενον, τὰς
ὀφρῦς μεμελασμένον,[4] γυναικείαν δὲ[5] στολὴν ἔχοντα
καὶ κατεξυρημένον τὸν πώγωνα καὶ κατακεκι-
σηρισμένον[6] (ἦν δὲ καὶ γάλακτος λευκότερος καὶ
ὑπεγέγραπτο τοὺς ὀφθαλμούς) ἐπεὶ δὲ καὶ προσ-
εῖδεν[7] τὸν ᾿Αρβάκην τὰ λευκὰ ἐπαναβαλὼν[8] τοῖν
ὀφθαλμοῖν[9]· οἱ μὲν πολλοί, ὧν ἐστι καὶ Δοῦρις,[10]
ἱστοροῦσιν ὑπὸ τούτου ἀγανακτήσαντος εἰ τοιοῦ-

---

[1] CE: σεμειράμιδος A.   [2] A: σαρδανάπαλος CE.
[3] ἀρβάκης superscr. σα CE (=᾿Αρσάκης), ᾿Αρβάκης Diodorus.
Arbactus Justin.
[4] μεμελασμένον added by Gulick, cf. Pollux v. 102: τὰς
ὀφρῦς om. CE, deleted by Dindorf.   [5] τε C.
[6] κατακεκισσησμισμένον C.   [7] Casaubon: προσίδεν A.
[8] Potter, cf. Clem. Al. Paed. iii. 11. 70 (ἐπαναβάλλων)·
ἐπαναλαβὼν A.
[9] Meineke: τοῖς ὀφθαλμοῖς A, τῶν ὀφθαλμῶν Clem. and
Poll. ii. 60.   [10] θοῦρις C.

---

[a] Frag. 20 Müller.

in the third book of his *Persian History* says [a] that all the rulers of Asia devoted themselves to luxury, but Ninyas the son of Ninus and Semiramis especially did so. He too stayed indoors [b] in his self-indulgence and was never seen by anyone except the eunuchs and his own wives. Such a man also was Sardanapalus,[c] whom some call the son of Anacyndaraxes, others, of Ana-baraxares.[d] Well, Arbaces, a Mede by birth, and one of the generals of his realm, entered into an intrigue with a eunuch named Sparameizes [e] to obtain a view of Sardanapalus, and the king reluctantly giving his consent, an audience was permitted him ; when the Mede entered he saw the king with his face covered with white lead and bejewelled like a woman, comb-ing purple wool in the company of his concubines and sitting among them with knees uplifted,[f] his eye-brows blackened,[g] wearing a woman's dress and having his beard shaved close and his face rubbed with pumice (he was even whiter than milk, and his eyelids were painted), and when he looked upon Arbaces he rolled the whites of his eyes; most authorities, including also Duris, record [h] that Arbaces, outraged to think

[b] *Cf.* 517 b (p. 328) and Justin, *Epit. Trog.* i. 2. 11 " Ninus (=Ninyas) . . . veluti sexum cum matre mutasset, raro a viris visus in feminarum turba consenuit."

[c] Ashurbanipal, 668-626 b.c. On these legends see Streck, *Assurbanipal u. die letzten assyrischen Könige,* i. pp. ccclxxxvi-cdv (a reference kindly supplied by Professor R. H. Pfeiffer). Athen. 294 e and note *a* (vol. iii. p. 321), 335 f (vol. iv. p. 24), 511 c, Justin, *op. cit.* i. 3. 2, Strabo p. 672.

[d] Neither was really a proper name, Pauly-Wissowa i. 2052.

[e] This, too, is not a proper name, but means " eunuch "; *cf.* Plut. *Artax.* 15.

[f] The attitude assumed on a couch when one was reading, or carding wool.

[g] See critical note 4. [h] *F.H.G.* ii. 473, J. 2 A 149.

τος αὐτῶν βασιλεύει συγκεντηθέντα ἀποθανεῖν.
b Κτησίας δὲ[1] λέγει εἰς πόλεμον αὐτὸν καταστῆναι[2]
καὶ ἀθροίσαντα πολλὴν στρατιὰν καὶ καταλυθέντα
ὑπὸ τοῦ Ἀρβάκου τελευτῆσαι ἑαυτὸν ἐμπρήσαντα
ἐν τοῖς βασιλείοις, πυρὰν νήσαντα ὕψος τεσσάρων
πλέθρων, ἐφ᾽ ἧς ἐπέθηκεν[3] χρυσᾶς κλίνας ἑκατὸν
καὶ πεντήκοντα καὶ ἴσας τραπέζας καὶ ταύτας
χρυσᾶς. ἐποίησε δὲ ἐν τῇ πυρᾷ καὶ οἴκημα ἑκατόμ-
πεδον[4] ἐκ ξύλων κἀνταῦθα κλίνας ὑπεστόρεσε καὶ
κατεκλίθη[5] αὐτός τε μετὰ καὶ τῆς γυναικὸς[6] καὶ αἱ
παλλακίδες ἐν ταῖς ἄλλαις κλίναις. τοὺς γὰρ τρεῖς
υἱοὺς καὶ δύο θυγατέρας ὁρῶν τὰ πράγματα κακού-
μενα προπεπόμφει[7] εἰς Νίνον πρὸς τὸν ἐκεῖ βασιλέα
c δοὺς αὐτοῖς τρισχίλια χρυσίου τάλαντα· ἐπεστέ-
γασεν δὲ τὸ οἴκημα δοκοῖς μεγάλαις τε καὶ παχεί-
αις, ἔπειτα ἐν κύκλῳ περιέθηκε πολλὰ ξύλα καὶ
παχέα, ὥστε μὴ εἶναι ἔξοδον. ἐνταῦθα ἐπέθηκεν
μὲν[8] χρυσίου μυριάδας χιλίας, ἀργυρίου δὲ μυρίας
μυριάδας ταλάντων καὶ ἱμάτια καὶ πορφύρας καὶ
στολὰς παντοδαπάς. ἔπειτα ὑφάψαι ἐκέλευσε[9] τὴν
πυράν, καὶ ἐκαίετο πεντεκαίδεκα ἡμέρας.[10] οἱ δὲ
ἐθαύμαζον ὁρῶντες τὸν καπνὸν καὶ ἐδόκουν αὐτὸν
d θυσίας ἐπιτελεῖν· ταῦτα δὲ μόνοι ᾔδεσαν οἱ εὐνοῦχοι.
ὁ μὲν οὖν Σαρδανάπαλλος ἐκτόπως ἡδυπαθήσας
ὡς ἐνῆν γενναίως ἐτελεύτησεν.

Κλέαρχος δὲ περὶ τοῦ Περσῶν βασιλέως διηγούμενος ὅτι " τοῖς αὐτῷ πορίσασιν ἡδύ τι βρῶμα

---

[1] δὲ CE: om. A.
[2] καταστῆναι τῶν (τῷ ?) ἀρβάκῃ C.
[3] ἐπέθηκε C.   [4] E: ἑκατόμποδον C, ἑκατόνπεδον A.
[5] κατεκλίθη CE: κατεκλίθη ἐνταῦθα A.
[6] αὐτοῦ after τῆς γυναικὸς (A) om. CE.
[7] πεπόμφει C.   [8] A: ἐπέθηκε (om. μὲν) C.

388

that such a person should be their king, stabbed him to death. But Ctesias says [a] that the king got into a war, and after collecting a large army was defeated by Arbaces and died by setting fire to himself in the palace ; he heaped up a pyre four hundred feet high, on which he placed a hundred and fifty gold couches and an equal number of tables, these also of gold. On the pyre he constructed a chamber of wood one hundred feet long, in which he spread the couches and lay down ; and not only he, but his queen was with him, and the concubines were on the other couches. As for his three sons and two daughters, when he saw that things were going badly, he had sent them previously to Nineveh [b] and its ruler there, giving them three thousand talents in gold ; he then roofed the chamber with huge, thick beams, and piled all round many thick timbers so that there should be no exit. In it he placed ten million talents of gold, one hundred million of silver, and garments, purple cloths, and robes of every description. He then gave orders to light the pyre, and it burned for fifteen days. The people beheld the smoke with astonishment and thought he was offering sacrifices ; only the eunuchs knew the facts. And so Sardanapalus, after he had enjoyed pleasure in strange ways, died as nobly as he could.

Clearchus, in his account of the Persian king, says [c] that "for those who supplied him with any

[a] Frag. 20 Müller. The war was against Arbaces (see critical note 2). On the conflagration, Streck ii. 37, Luckenbill, *Anc. Records of Assyria* ii. pp. 303-304.
[b] A mistake, since Nineveh was his own capital. Diod. ii. 26 says Paphlagonia, where the viceroy Cotta had remained loyal.　　　　[c] *F.H.G.* ii. 305 ; above, 514 e (p. 314).

─────────────────────────────

[9] CE: ἐκέλευε A.　　　[10] ἡμέρας C: ἡμέραις A.

ἆθλα ἐτίθει . . . νοῦν ἔχων[1]· τοῦτο γάρ ἐστιν ὁ
λεγόμενος, οἶμαι, Διὸς ἅμα καὶ βασιλέως ἐγκέ-
φαλος· ὅθεν ὁ πάντων εὐδαιμονέστατος Σαρδανάπαλλος, ὁ παρ' ὅλον τὸν βίον τιμήσας τὰς ἀπολαύσεις, καὶ τελευτήσας δείκνυσιν ἐν τῷ τοῦ
μνήματος τύπῳ τοῖς δακτύλοις ἀποκροτοῦντι[2] οἷου
καταγέλωτός ἐστιν ἄξια τὰ τῶν ἀνθρώπων πράγ-
e ματα, οὐκ ἄξια ὄντα ψόφου δακτύλων ὄν[3] πεποίηται
ποιούμενος δὶς ἐν χορῷ . . .[4] ἡ περὶ τὰ λοιπὰ
σπουδή. φαίνεται γοῦν[5] οὐκ ἄπρακτος γενόμενος
Σαρδανάπαλλος· καὶ γὰρ ἐπιγέγραπται αὐτοῦ τῷ
μνήματι· ' Σαρδανάπαλλος Ἀνακυνδαράξεω Ἀγχιάλην ἔδειμε καὶ Ταρσὸν μιῇ ἡμέρῃ, ἀλλὰ νῦν
τέθνηκεν.' " Ἀμύντας δὲ ἐν τρίτῳ Σταθμῶν ἐν τῇ
Νίνῳ φησὶν εἶναι χῶμα ὑψηλόν, ὅπερ κατασπάσαι
Κῦρον ἐν τῇ πολιορκίᾳ ἀντιχωννύντα τῇ πόλει·
f λέγεσθαι δὲ τὸ χῶμα τοῦτ' εἶναι Σαρδαναπάλλου
τοῦ βασιλεύσαντος Νίνου, ἐφ' οὗ καὶ ἐπιγεγράφθαι
ἐν στήλῃ λιθίνῃ Χαλδαϊκοῖς γράμμασιν ὃ μετ-
ενεγκεῖν Χοιρίλον ἔμμετρον ποιήσαντα. εἶναι δὲ
τοῦτο· " ἐγὼ δὲ ἐβασίλευσα καὶ ἄχρι ἑώρων τοῦ
ἡλίου φῶς, ἔπιον, ἔφαγον, ἠφροδισίασα, εἰδὼς[6]
530 τόν τε χρόνον ὄντα βραχὺν ὃν ζῶσιν οἱ ἄνθρωποι

---

[1] ἔχων Schweighäuser: οὐκ ἔχων ACE.
[2] ἀποκροτοῦντι added by Kaibel (cf. 530 b).
[3] ὃν χορεύων CE (C postpones δείκνυσιν . . . πεποίηται το
530 c, after ἔοικε λέγειν).
[4] Lacuna marked by Gulick.
[5] γοῦν Gulick: οὖν A.   [6] εἰδὼν C.

---

[a] See critical note 1, and the interpretation offered at
514 e. In the epitomized text it is impossible to tell which
reading is correct, but cf. below, 545 b-d.
[b] See critical note 2, and Callisthenes frag. 32 Müller. The
390

delicacy he set prizes . . . showing his sense [a]; this, I think, is in fact the proverbial, 'A morsel for Zeus' and at the same time for the king. Hence Sardanapalus, he who was the most prosperous man in the world, he who prized enjoyment throughout his whole life, shows also in death, by his attitude on his tomb as he snaps his fingers,[b] that human affairs are worth nothing but mockery, not being worth the snap of a finger which he is represented as making twice in the choral procession. . . . [c] Yet his interest in other matters (besides pleasure is evident). At any rate it is plain that Sardanapalus was not wholly inactive, as is proved by the fact that on his tomb is the inscription : 'Sardanapalus the son of Anacyndaraxes built Anchialê and Tarsus in a single day, yet now he is dead.'" Amyntas[d] says in the third book of his *Stages* that in Nineveh is a high mound which Cyrus demolished in raising counter-walls against the city during the siege ; and that this mound is said to be the work of Sardanapalus, who had been king in Nineveh ; surmounting it was a stone column, on which was an inscription in Chaldaean letters, which Choerilus translated and put into verse ; it is this [e] : " I became king, and whilst I looked upon the sun's light I drank, I ate, I loved, for that I knew the time to be short which

common source of Clearchus and Callisthenes was Hellanicus, Niese, Marburg *Progr.* 1880, Jacoby, Hellanicus 63 b.

[c] The text is in desperate condition. That the figure of the king was shown at least twice as in a kind of dance is certain, if δὶς ἐν χορῷ be right. CE have simply ὃν χορεύων πεποίηται.

[d] *Scr. Alex. M.* 136, J. 2 B 628. The siege of Babylon by Cyrus occurred 538 B.C.; Daniel v. (where Darius appears instead of Cyrus), Hdt. i. 188 ff. Nineveh had fallen in 612, long before Cyrus's birth.

[e] *Cf. Frag. ep.* 309, 310, Athen. 336 f (vol. iv. p. 28). It is impossible to restore the verse form.

καὶ τοῦτον πολλὰς ἔχοντα μεταβολὰς καὶ κακοπαθείας, καὶ ὧν ἂν καταλίπω ἀγαθῶν ἄλλοι ἔξουσι
τὰς ἀπολαύσεις. διὸ κἀγὼ ἡμέραν οὐδεμίαν παρ-
έλιπον τοῦτο ποιῶν." Κλείταρχος δ' ἐν τῇ τετάρτῃ
τῶν περὶ Ἀλέξανδρον γήρᾳ τελευτῆσαί φησιν Σαρδανάπαλλον μετὰ τὴν ἀπόπτωσιν τῆς Σύρων ἀρχῆς.
b Ἀριστόβουλος δ' " ἐν Ἀγχιάλῃ, ἣν ἐδείματο," φησί,
" Σαρδανάπαλλος, Ἀλέξανδρος ἀναβαίνων εἰς Πέρσας κατεστρατοπεδεύσατο. καὶ ἦν οὐ πόρρω τὸ
τοῦ Σαρδαναπάλλου μνημεῖον, ἐφ' οὗ ἑστάναι τύπον
λίθινον συμβεβηκότα τῆς δεξιᾶς χειρὸς τοὺς
δακτύλους, ὡς ἂν ἀποκροτοῦντα.[1] ἐπιγεγράφθαι
δ' αὐτῷ Ἀσσυρίοις γράμμασι· 'Σαρδανάπαλλος
Ἀνακυνδαράξεω[2] παῖς Ἀγχιάλην καὶ Ταρσὸν
c ἔδειμεν ἡμέρῃ μιῇ.[3] ἔσθιε, πῖνε, παῖζε· ὡς τἆλλα
τούτου οὐκ ἄξια,' τοῦ ἀποκροτήματος ἔοικε λέγειν."

Οὐ μόνος δὲ ὁ Σαρδανάπαλλος διετέθρυπτο, ἀλλὰ
καὶ Ἀνδρόκοττος[4] ὁ Φρύξ. καὶ γὰρ οὗτος ἐν
ἐδέδυτο[5] ἀνθινὴν ἐσθῆτα καὶ γυναικὸς εὐπρεπέστερον
ἐκοσμεῖτο, ὡς Μνασέας φησὶν ἐν τρίτῳ Εὐρώπης.
Κλέαρχος δ' ἐν πέμπτῳ Βίων Σάγαρίν φησι τὸν
Μαριανδυνὸν ὑπὸ τρυφῆς σιτεῖσθαι μὲν μέχρι
γήρως ἐκ τοῦ τῆς τίτθης στόματος, ἵνα μὴ μασώ-
μενος πονέσειεν,[6] οὐ πώποτε δὲ τὴν χεῖρα κα-
d τωτέρω[7] τοῦ ὀμφαλοῦ προενέγκασθαι. διὸ καὶ

---

[1] Niese: ἐπικροτοῦντα ACE.
[2] ἀνακυνδαράξου ACE. [3] μιῇ E: μιᾶι AC.
[4] ἀνδρόκοτος CE. [5] ἐνεδέδυτο C: ἐνεδύσατο A.
[6] C: πονέσειε A. [7] CE: κατώτερον A.

---

[a] Frag. 2 Müller, J. 2 B 744.
[b] Assyria ; a common confusion, Hdt. vii. 63.
[c] Scr. Al. M. 76, J. 2 B 772.

mortals live, and moreover hath many changes and mishaps, and others will have joy of the goods I leave behind. Wherefore I have let no day go by whilst I pursued this my way." Cleitarchus, however, in the fourth book of his *History of Alexander* says [a] that Sardanapalus died of old age after he was deposed from the throne of Syria.[b] Aristobulus says [c] : " In Anchialê, which Sardanapalus built, Alexander pitched his camp when he was marching inland against the Persians. And not far distant was the tomb of Sardanapalus, on which stood a stone figure with the fingers [d] of the right hand brought closely together, as if snapping them. On it was inscribed, in Assyrian letters : ' Sardanapalus, son of Anacyndaraxes, built Anchialê and Tarsus in a single day. Eat, drink, and play [e] ; for other things are not worth *that* '—meaning, he seems to say, the snap of a finger."

Yet Sardanapalus was not the only one who pampered himself, but there was also Androcottus the Phrygian. For he too put on gaily-coloured clothes and adorned himself more brilliantly than a woman, as Mnaseas says [f] in the third book of his *Europe*. And Clearchus in the fifth book of his *Lives* says [g] that Sagaris the Mariandynian in his luxurious indulgence was fed until he was an old man at the lips of his nurse, not wishing to take the trouble to chew, and that he never carried his hand down lower than his navel. Wherefore Aristotle also used to say jokingly

---

[d] The thumb and middle finger. The figure was carved in relief on a rock.

[e] This meaning of παῖζε accords with that of εὐφραίνου, 'be merry," in *Ev. Luc.* xii. 19 ; but it is more general, and includes erotic adventures.

[f] *F.H.G.* iii. 152. Androcottus is not otherwise known.

[g] *F.H.G.* ii. 307.

Ἀριστοτέλης Ξενοκράτην τὸν Χαλκηδόνιον[1] σκώπτων ὅτι οὐρῶν οὐ προσῆγε τὴν χεῖρα τῷ αἰδοίῳ ἔλεγεν·

χεῖρες μὲν ἁγναί, φρὴν δ᾽ ἔχει μίασμά τι.[2]

Κτησίας δὲ ἱστορεῖ Ἄνναρον τὸν βασιλέως ὕπαρχον καὶ τῆς Βαβυλωνίας δυναστεύσαντα στολῇ χρῆσθαι γυναικείᾳ καὶ κόσμῳ, καὶ ὅτι βασιλέως δούλῳ ὄντι αὐτῷ εἰς τὸ δεῖπνον εἰσῄεσαν πεντήκοντα καὶ ἑκατὸν ψάλλουσαι καὶ ᾄδουσαι[3] γυναῖκες· ἔψαλλον δὲ αὗται καὶ ᾖδον ἐκείνου δειπνοῦντος

e Φοῖνιξ δ᾽ ὁ Κολοφώνιος ποιητὴς περὶ Νίνου λέγων ἐν τῷ πρώτῳ τῶν Ἰάμβων φησίν·

ἀνὴρ Νίνος τις ἐγένετ᾽, ὡς ἐγὼ κλύω,[4]
Ἀσσύριος· ὅστις εἶχε χρυσίου πόντον,
τάλαντα πολλῷ[5] πλέονα Κασπίης ψάμμου·
ὃς οὐκ ἴδ᾽[6] ἀστέρ᾽ οὐδ᾽ ἰδὼν ἐδίζητο,[7]
οὐ παρ᾽ μάγοισι[8] πῦρ ἱερὸν ἀνέστησεν,
ὥσπερ νόμος, ῥάβδοισι τοῦ θεοῦ ψαύων·
οὐ μυθιήτης,[9] οὐ δικασπόλος κεῖνος,
οὐ λεωλογεῖν ἐμάνθαν᾽, οὐκ ἀμιθρῆσαι,

f ἀλλ᾽ ἦν ἄριστος ἐσθίειν τε καὶ πίνειν κῆρᾶν,[10] τὰ δ᾽ ἄλλα πάντα κατὰ πετρῶν ὤθει.

---

[1] καλχηδόνιον C.   [2] CE: μιασματα A.
[3] ψάλλουσαι καὶ ᾄδουσαι deleted by Kaibel.
[4] κλύω A: ᾽κούω Meineke, since υ is elsewhere short (yet cf. κλῦθι).
[5] χρυσίου . . . πολλῷ Haupt: χρυσειου πόντον καὶ ταλλα πολλον A, χρυσίου τάλαντα (om. πόντον) πολλῷ CE.
[6] ὃς οὐκ ἴδ᾽ CE: ὃς οὐκι δ᾽ A.
[7] οὐδ᾽ ἰδὼν ἐδίζητο Naeke: οὐδιζωνεδιζητο A.
[8] παρ᾽ μάγοισι A.
[9] Schweighäuser (μυθιητὴς): μυθηητης A, μυήθη CE.
[10] CE: κηραν A.

394

of Xenocrates of Chalcedon that when he made water he never put his hand to his member, and he would quote [a] : " My hands are pure, it is my mind that has a taint." Ctesias records [b] that Annarus,[c] the viceroy of the Great King and ruler over Babylonia, wore women's garments and ornaments, and that, although he was himself a slave of the king, there always came to him at dinner a hundred and fifty women, playing on harps and singing. And they continued to play and sing while he dined. The poet Phoenix of Colophon, speaking of Ninus in the first book of his *Iambics*, says [d] : " There was a man named Ninus, as I have heard, an Assyrian ; he had an ocean of gold, talents far more numerous than the sands of Caspia ; he never looked at a star, nor, if he did, searched out its meaning,[e] nor with the Magi did he raise the sacred fire as is the custom, reaching for the god with rods [f] ; no orator he, no lawgiver, he understood not how to gather the people together nor how to count them, but he was the best at eating and drinking and loving, whereas all other business he

[a] Eur. *Hipp.* 317 ; Phaedra speaks. Aristotle's remark (not in Rose) was preceded by one on Sardanapalus and his tomb, Cic. *Tusc.* v. 35 " quid aliud in bovis, non in regis sepulcro inscriberes ? "
[b] Frag. 52 Müller.
[c] Not otherwise known ; Nicol. Dam. *F.H.G.* iii. 360 has the form Νάναρος. Xenophon was the first to use the word σατράπης (satrap) instead of ὕπαρχος or ἔπαρχος.
[d] Diehl fr. 3, Powell p. 231 ; Gerhard, *Phoinix v. Kol.* p. 185, calls attention to the confusion of Ninus, who was frugal (Athen. 421 d), with his son Ninyas (above, p. 386). The metre is choliambic (see critical note 4).
[e] As was the custom in the Chaldaean astrology ; *cf.* Hdt. vii. 142 διζημένων τὸ μαντήιον.
[f] For the divining-rod in Lycia see Athen. 333 d-e (vol. iv. p. 14).

395

ὡς δ' ἀπέθαν' ὡνήρ, πᾶσι κατέλιπε ῥῆσιν
ὅκου Νίνος νῦν ἐστι καὶ τὸ σῆμ' ἄδει[1]·
ἄκουσον, εἴτ' Ἀσσύριος εἴτε καὶ Μῆδος
εἶς ἢ Κόραξος ἢ ἀπὸ τῶν ἄνω λιμνῶν
Σινδὸς[2] κομήτης· οὐ γὰρ ἀλλὰ[3] κηρύσσω·
ἐγὼ Νίνος πάλαι ποτ' ἐγενόμην πνεῦμα,
νῦν δ' οὐκ ἔτ' οὐδέν, ἀλλὰ γῆ πεποίημαι.
ἔχω δ' ὁκόσον[4] ἔδαισα[5] χὠκός'[6] ἤεισα
χὠκόσσ' ἐράσθην[7] . . . .
τὰ δ' ὄλβι' ἡμέων[8] δήιοι συνελθόντες
531 φέρουσιν, ὥσπερ ὠμὸν ἔριφον αἱ Βάκχαι.
ἐγὼ δ' ἐς Ἅιδην οὔτε χρυσὸν οὔθ' ἵππον
οὔτ' ἀργυρῆν ἅμαξαν ᾠχόμην ἕλκων·
σποδὸς δὲ πολλή[9] χὠ μιτρηφόρος κεῖμαι.

Θεόπομπος δ' ἐν πεντεκαιδεκάτῃ Φιλιππικῶν
Ἱστοριῶν Στράτωνά φησι τὸν Σιδώνιον βασιλέα
ὑπερβαλεῖν[10] ἡδυπαθείᾳ καὶ τρυφῇ πάντας ἀνθρώπους. οἷα γὰρ τοὺς Φαίακας Ὅμηρος ποιεῖν μεμυ-
θολόγηκεν ἑορτάζοντας καὶ πίνοντας καὶ κιθαρῳδῶν
καὶ ῥαψῳδῶν ἀκροωμένους, τοιαῦτα καὶ ὁ Στράτων
διετέλει ποιῶν πολὺν χρόνον. καὶ τοσούτῳ μᾶλλον
ἐκείνων παρεκεκινήκει[11] πρὸς τὰς ἡδονὰς ὅσον[12] οἱ
μὲν Φαίακες, ὥς φησιν Ὅμηρος, μετὰ τῶν οἰκείων
γυναικῶν καὶ θυγατέρων ἐποιοῦντο τοὺς πότους,

---

[1] Naeke: σῆμα ιδει A.   [2] Schweighäuser: ἰνδὸς A
[3] Meineke: ἀλλα A.   [4] CE: ὁκόσσον A.
[5] A, ἔδεσα CE: ἔπαισα Kaibel.   [6] χὠκόσσ' A (om. CE).
[7] χὠκοσσ' ἐράσθην ΑC. Kaibel, reading ἔπαισα for ἔδαισα
conjectured χὠκόσ' ἔφαγον ἔπιόν τε with Naeke's χὠκόσ
ἠράσθην, Kalinka χὠκόσσ' ἐλουσάμην τε χὠκόσσ' ἠράσθην.
[8] ἡμῶν CE.   [9] πελλὴ "ash-coloured " Meineke.
[10] ὑπερέβαλεν CE (in a different construction), ὑπερβαλέσθαι
σπεῦσαι Aelian: ὑπερβάλλειν A.

thrust over the rocks. When the man died, he left
behind him a saying to tell all men where Ninus now
is, and his tomb sings it : Hear, be thou Assyrian or
Median or Coraxian or long-haired Sindian from the
northern marshes [a] ; for I cannot but proclaim that
I, who once aforetime was a breath called Ninus, am
now no longer anything, but am made into dust.
I have only what I got in feasting,[b] in singing, in
love-making. . . . The foemen have come together
and plundered our wealth even as the Bacchants tear
apart the raw flesh of a kid.[c] I meanwhile have
gone to Hades with neither gold nor steed nor silver
cart in my train ; I, even I that wore the tiara, lie
here, a heap of dust." [d]

Theopompus in the fifteenth book of his *History
of Philip* says [e] that Straton, the king of Sidon, over-
topped all men in pleasure and luxury. For the same
holiday festivities that Homer in his story attributes
to the Phaeacians,[f] drinking and listening to harp-
singers and rhapsodists, occupied Straton's time continually. In fact he so far exceeded them in his mad
pursuit of the pleasures of life that whereas the
Phaeacians, according to Homer, held their drinking-
parties in the company of their own wives and

---

[a] Perhaps the Sea of Azov is meant. The Sindians were
a Scythian tribe, the Coraxians (Κοραξοί) a branch of the
Colchians ; Ap. Rhod. iv. 322, Plin. *N.H.* vi. 5. 15.
[b] Or, reading ἔπαισα, " I got in merry-making." For
a similar thought *cf.* Athen. 337 a (vol. iv. p. 28) and above,
530 c.
[c] *Cf.* Eur. *Bacch.* 1128 ff.   [d] See critical note 9.
[e] *F.H.G.* i. 299, J. 2 B 562, G. and H. 111.
[f] *Od.* viii. 248 ff. *Cf.* Aelian, *V.H.* vii. 2.

---

[11] παρακεκινήκει Λ.
[12] Kaibel : πλὴν ὅσον (in different construction) CE : ὅθεν A.

ὁ δὲ Στράτων μετ' αὐλητρίδων καὶ ψαλτριῶν καὶ
κιθαριστριῶν κατεσκευάζετο[1] τὰς συνουσίας· καὶ
μετεπέμπετο πολλὰς μὲν ἑταίρας ἐκ Πελοποννήσου,
πολλὰς δὲ μουσουργοὺς ἐξ Ἰωνίας, ἑτέρας δὲ
παιδίσκας ἐξ ἁπάσης τῆς Ἑλλάδος, τὰς μὲν ᾠδικάς,
c τὰς δὲ ὀρχηστρικάς, ὧν εἴθιστο μετὰ τῶν φίλων
ἀγῶνας τιθέναι καὶ μεθ' ὧν συνουσιάζων διέτριβεν,
χαίρων μὲν καὶ αὐτὸς[2] τῷ βίῳ τῷ τοιούτῳ, δοῦλος
ὢν φύσει τῶν ἡδονῶν, ἔτι δὲ μᾶλλον πρὸς τὸν
Νικοκλέα φιλοτιμούμενος. ἐτύγχανον γὰρ ὑπερ-
φιλοτίμως ἔχοντες πρὸς ἀλλήλους καὶ σπουδάζων
ἑκάτερος αὐτὸς ἥδιον καὶ ῥαθυμότερον ποιεῖσθαι
τὸν βίον· οἵ γε προῆλθον εἰς τοσαύτην ἅμιλλαν, ὡς
ἡμεῖς ἀκούομεν, ὥστε πυνθανόμενοι παρὰ τῶν
d ἀφικνουμένων τάς τε παρασκευὰς τῶν οἰκιῶν καὶ
τὰς πολυτελείας τῶν θυσιῶν τὰς παρ' ἑκατέρῳ
γινομένας ἐφιλονίκουν ὑπερβάλλεσθαι τοῖς τοιούτοις ἀλλήλους. ἐσπούδαζον δὲ δοκεῖν εὐδαίμονες
εἶναι καὶ μακαριστοί. οὐ μὴν περί γε τὴν τοῦ
βίου τελευτὴν διηυτύχησαν, ἀλλ' ἀμφότεροι βιαίῳ
θανάτῳ διεφθάρησαν. Ἀναξιμένης δ' ἐν τῷ ἐπιγραφομένῳ Βασιλέων Μεταλλαγαί περὶ τοῦ Στρά-
τωνος τὰ αὐτὰ ἱστορήσας διημιλλῆσθαί φησιν αὐτὸν
Νικοκλεῖ τῷ τῆς ἐν Κύπρῳ Σαλαμῖνος βασιλεύσαντι
e ἐσπουδακότι περὶ τρυφὴν καὶ ἀσέλγειαν, ἀποθανεῖν τ' ἀμφοτέρους βιαίως.

Ἐν δὲ τῇ α' τῶν Φιλιππικῶν Θεόπομπος περὶ

---

[1] Kaibel: κατεσκεύαστο A.
[2] αὐτὸς added by Kaibel, deleting καὶ before δοῦλος.

---

[a] Cf. Plato, Rep. 363 c συμπόσιον κατασκευάσαντες.
[b] See Diod. xvi. 42 ff., who gives the name Tennês, not
Straton, to the king of Sidon.

aughters, Straton, on the other hand, used to arrange
is parties *a* in the company of flute-girls, singing-girls,
nd girls who played on the harp ; and he used to
ummon many courtesans from Peloponnesus, many
inging-girls from Ionia, besides girls from every part
f Greece, some of whom were singers, some dancers ;
e was in the habit of getting up contests among them
n the company of his friends, and in their society he
pent all his time, since he himself enjoyed this kind
f life, being by nature a slave to his pleasures, but
till more because be strove to outdo Nicocles.*b* For,
s it happened, they were exceedingly jealous of each
ther, and each was eager to live in greater pleasure
nd ease than the other ; why ! they went so far in
his rivalry, as we have heard, that they would ask
rom all comers about each other's household arrange-
nents and the cost of the sacrifices held there, and
hen did their utmost to outdo each other in these
natters. And they made it a great point to seem
ich and enviable. Nevertheless they did not carry
heir good luck through when it came to ending their
ives, for both of them perished by a violent death.
So Anaximenes, in the work entitled *Vicissitudes of
Kings*, after recounting the same facts about Straton,
ays *c* that he kept up a constant rivalry with Nicocles,
he ruler of Salamis in Cyprus, who had shown great
agerness for luxury and licentiousness, and that both
lied a violent death.*d*

Now, in the first book of his *History of Philip*,

c Scr. Al. Mag. 38, J. 2 A 123. Anaximenes' work, partly
istory and partly rhetoric, dealt with kings whose reign
nded in violence.

d Isocrates (*Nicocles*, see especially 31, 32, 45) gives him
n altogether favourable character.

Φιλίππου λέγων φησίν· " καὶ τριταῖος εἰς Ὀνόκαρσιν ἀφικνεῖται, χωρίον τι τῆς Θρᾴκης ἄλσος ἔχον πολὺ κατεσκευασμένον καλῶς καὶ πρὸς τὸ δι-αιτηθῆναι κεχαρισμένον ἄλλως τε καὶ τὴν θερινὴν ὥραν. ἦν γὰρ καὶ τῶν ὑπὸ Κότυος προκριθέντων ὃς ἀπάντων τῶν βασιλέων τῶν ἐν τῇ Θρᾴκῃ γεγενημένων μάλιστα πρὸς ἡδυπαθείας καὶ τρυφὰς

f ὥρμησε, καὶ περιιὼν τὴν χώραν ὅπου κατίδοι τόπους δένδρεσι συσκίους καὶ καταρρύτους ὕδασι, τούτους κατεσκεύασεν ἑστιατόρια[1]· καὶ φοιτῶν εἰς ἑκάστους ὁπότε τύχοι θυσίας τε τοῖς θεοῖς ἐποιεῖτο καὶ συνῆν μετὰ τῶν ὑπάρχων, εὐδαίμων καὶ μακαριστὸς ὢν ἕως εἰς τὴν Ἀθηνᾶν βλασφημεῖν καὶ πλημμελεῖν ἐπεχείρησεν." διηγεῖταί τε ἑξῆς ὁ συγγραφεὺς ὅτι δεῖπνον κατεσκεύασεν ὁ Κότυς ὡς γαμουμένης αὐτῷ τῆς Ἀθηνᾶς καὶ θάλαμον κατα-σκευάσας ἀνέμενεν μεθύων τὴν θεόν. ἤδη δ᾽

532 ἔκφρων γενόμενος ἔπεμπέ τινα τῶν δορυφόρων ὀψόμενον εἰ παραγέγονεν ἡ θεὸς εἰς τὸν θάλαμον ἀφικομένου δ᾽ ἐκείνου καὶ εἰπόντος μηδένα εἶναι ἐν τῷ θαλάμῳ, τοξεύσας τοῦτον ἀπέκτεινεν καὶ ἄλλον δεύτερον ἐπὶ τοῖς αὐτοῖς, ἕως ὁ τρίτος συνεὶς παραγενομένην[2] ἔφη πάλαι τὴν θεὸν αὐτὸν ἀνα-μένειν. ὁ δὲ βασιλεὺς οὗτός ποτε καὶ ζηλοτυπήσας τὴν αὑτοῦ γυναῖκα ταῖς αὑτοῦ χερσὶν ἀνέτεμε τὴν ἄνθρωπον ἀπὸ τῶν αἰδοίων ἀρξάμενος.

Ἐν δὲ τῇ τρισκαιδεκάτῃ τῶν Φιλιππικῶν περὶ

b Χαβρίου τοῦ Ἀθηναίου[3] ἱστορῶν φησιν· " οἱ

---

[1] CE: ἱστιατόρια A.
[2] Kaibel: παραγενόμενος ACE.
[3] ἀθηναίων A (στρατηγοῦ added by Kaibel): χαβρίας δ ἀθηναῖος CE (in a different construction).

400

Theopompus, speaking of Philip, says [a] : "And two days later he arrived at Onocarsis, an estate in Thrace which included a very beautifully planted grove and one well adapted for a pleasant sojourn, especially during the summer season. In fact it had been one of the favourite resorts of Cotys, who, more than any other king that had arisen in Thrace, directed his career towards the enjoyment of pleasures and luxuries, and as he went about the country, wherever he discovered places shaded with trees and watered with running streams, he turned these into banqueting-places; and visiting them in turn, as chance led him, he would offer sacrifices to the gods and hold court with his lieutenants, remaining prosperous and envied until he undertook to blaspheme and offend Athena." And the historian goes on next to relate that Cotys got up a banquet on the pretence that Athena was to be married to him, and after erecting a bridal chamber he awaited the goddess in a drunken revel. And presently going entirely out of his senses he dispatched one of his bodyguard to see whether the goddess had arrived at the bridal chamber. When the poor fellow returned with the announcement that there was nobody in the chamber, Cotys shot him dead with his bow, and then killed a second messenger for the same reason, until the third man sagaciously said that the goddess had arrived a long while before and was waiting for him. This king once in a fit of jealousy against his own wife cut up the poor woman with his own hands, beginning with the pudenda.[b]

In the thirteenth book of his *History of Philip* Theopompus, relating the story of Chabrias of Athens

[a] *F.H.G.* i. 283, J. 2 B 542, G. and H. 32.
[b] *Cf.* the death of Agrippina, Tacitus, *Ann.* xiv. 8.

δυνάμενος δὲ ζῆν ἐν τῇ πόλει τὰ μὲν διὰ τὴ[
ἀσέλγειαν καὶ διὰ τὴν πολυτέλειαν τὴν αὑτοῦ τὴ[
περὶ τὸν βίον, τὰ δὲ διὰ τοὺς Ἀθηναίους· ἅπα[
γάρ[1] εἰσι χαλεποί· διὸ καὶ εἵλοντο αὐτῶν οἱ ἔνδοξ[
ἔξω τῆς πόλεως καταβιοῦν, Ἰφικράτης μὲν ἐ[
Θράκῃ, Κόνων δ' ἐν Κύπρῳ, Τιμόθεος δ' ἐν Λέσβ[
Χάρης δ' ἐν Σιγείῳ,[2] καὶ αὐτὸς ὁ Χαβρίας ἐ[
Αἰγύπτῳ." καὶ περὶ τοῦ Χάρητος ἐν τῇ πέμπτ[
c καὶ τεσσαρακοστῇ φησιν· " Χάρητός τε νωθροῦ τ[
ὄντος καὶ βραδέος, καίτοι γε καὶ πρὸς τρυφὴν ἤδ[
ζῶντος· ὅς γε περιήγετο στρατευόμενος αὐλητρίδα[
καὶ ψαλτρίας καὶ πεζὰς ἑταίρας, καὶ τῶν χρημάτω[
τῶν εἰσφερομένων εἰς τὸν πόλεμον τὰ μὲν ε[
ταύτην τὴν ὕβριν ἀνήλισκε, τὰ δ' αὑτοῦ κατέλειπε[
Ἀθήνησιν τοῖς τε λέγουσιν καὶ τὰ ψηφίσματ[
γράφουσιν καὶ τῶν ἰδιωτῶν τοῖς δικαζομένοις· ἐ[
οἷς ὁ δῆμος ὁ τῶν Ἀθηναίων οὐδεπώποτε ἠγανα[
κτησεν, ἀλλὰ διὰ ταῦτα καὶ μᾶλλον αὐτὸν ἠγάπ[
οἱ πολῖται,[4] καὶ δικαίως· καὶ γὰρ αὐτοὶ τούτων τ[
d τρόπον ἔζων, ὥστε τοὺς μὲν νέους ἐν τοῖς αὐλη[
τριδίοις καὶ[5] παρὰ ταῖς ἑταίραις διατρίβειν, τοὺς [
μικρὸν ἐκείνων πρεσβυτέρους ἐν πότοις καὶ κύβοι[
καὶ ταῖς τοιαύταις ἀσωτίαις, τὸν δὲ δῆμον ἅπαν[
πλείω καταναλίσκειν εἰς τὰς κοινὰς ἑστιάσεις κ[

---

[1] τοῖς εὐδοκιμοῦσιν added by Meineke, cf. Nepos (note a).
[2] CE: σιγίωι A.
[3] κατέλειπε C: κατέλιπεν AE.
[4] ἠγάπων οἱ πολῖται CE: ἠγάπα τῶν πολιτῶν A.
[5] καὶ om. CE.
[6] καὶ κύβοις Kaibel: ἔν τε τοῖς κύβοις A, ἐν κύβοις CE.

---

[a] F.H.G. i. 297, J. 2 B 559, G. and H. 103.
[b] Corn. Nepos, Chab. ch. 3, adds "quos eminere videa[
altius."
[c] F.H.G. i. 318, J. 2 B 580, G. and H. 205.

says [a] : " But he was unable to live in the city, partly on account of his licentiousness and the lavish expense in his manner of living, partly also on account of the Athenians ; for they are harsh toward everybody [b] ; hence their distinguished men chose to pass their lives outside the city, Iphicrates in Thrace, Conon in Cyprus, Timotheüs in Lesbos, Chares at Sigeium, and Chabrias himself in Egypt." Again, of Chares he says in the forty-fifth book [c] : " Chares was sluggish and slow, although he already pursued, to be sure, a life of luxury ; for he took about with him on his campaigns flute-girls, harp-girls, and common prostitutes, and of the sums of money contributed [d] for the war he would expend a part on this wantonness, and part he would leave right there in Athens for the public speakers and proponents of decrees, as well as for private individuals against whom suits were pending [e] ; for all of which the Athenian people have never yet shown indignation, but rather for these reasons the citizens liked him all the more, and with good reason ; for they themselves lived in that manner, so that the young men spent their time among paltry little flute-girls and in the houses of prostitutes, while those who were a little older than they indulged in drinking-bouts and gambling and the like prodigalities,[f] and the populace as a whole squandered more money on the public banquets and

---

[d] The participle alludes to the εἰσφοραί, contributions, or special war taxes.

[e] Meaning poor citizens who could not pay the fines and other exactions of the court. But Casaubon and the French translators take it to mean " to pay off, or defeat, those private citizens who might bring charges against him in his absence." This would require αὐτῷ with τοῖς δικαζομένοις.

[f] Cf. above, 527 a (p. 376).

κρεανομίας ἥπερ εἰς τὴν τῆς πόλεως διοίκησιν."
ἐν δὲ τῷ ἐπιγραφομένῳ τοῦ Θεοπόμπου συγγράμματι περὶ τῶν ἐκ Δελφῶν συληθέντων Χρημάτων
" Χάρητι," φησί, " τῷ ᾿Αθηναίῳ διὰ Λυσάνδρου[1]
τάλαντα ἑξήκοντα. ἀφ' ὧν ἐδείπνισεν ᾿Αθηναίους
e ἐν τῇ ἀγορᾷ θύσας τὰ ἐπινίκια τῆς γενομένης μάχης
πρὸς τοὺς Φιλίππου ξένους." ὧν ἡγεῖτο μὲν
᾿Αδαῖος ὁ ᾿Αλεκτρυὼν[2] ἐπικαλούμενος· περὶ οὗ καὶ
῾Ηρακλείδης[3] ὁ τῶν κωμῳδιῶν ποιητὴς μέμνηται
οὕτως·

> ᾿Αλεκτρυόνα τὸν τοῦ Φιλίππου παραλαβὼν[4]
> ἀωρὶ κοκκύζοντα καὶ πλανώμενον
> κατέκοψεν· οὐ γὰρ εἶχεν οὐδέπω λόφον.
> ἕνα κατακόψας[5] μάλα συχνοὺς ἐδείπνισεν
> Χάρης ᾿Αθηναίων[6] τόθ'· ὡς γενναῖος ἦν.

f τὰ αὐτὰ ἱστορεῖ καὶ Δοῦρις.

᾿Ιδομενεὺς δέ φησι καὶ τοὺς Πεισιστρατίδας
῾Ιππίαν καὶ ῞Ιππαρχον εὑρεῖν θαλίας καὶ κώμους·
διὸ καὶ ἵππων[7] καὶ ἑτέρων[8] πολλῶν ἐπιπολάσαι
τὸ πλῆθος παρ' αὐτοῖς· ὅθεν βαρεῖαν αὐτῶν γενέσθαι τὴν ἀρχήν. καίτοι ὁ πατὴρ αὐτῶν Πεισίστρατος μετρίως ἐχρῆτο ταῖς ἡδοναῖς· ὥστε[9] οὐδ'
ἐν τοῖς χωρίοις οὐδ' ἐν τοῖς κήποις φύλακας

---

[1] διὰ λυσάνδρου A: διαναλωθῆναι Schweighäuser, διαλυθῆναι Wichers.   [2] ὁ ἀλεκτρυὼν CE: ὁ om. A.
[3] CE: ὁ ἡρακλείδης A.
[4] παραλαβὼν A: λαβὼν C, καταλαβὼν Meineke.
[5] κᾶτα κόψας CE, om. ἕνα.   [6] ἀθηναίους CE.
[7] παρασίτων Sintenis.
[8] ἑταίρων Capps (ἑταιρῶν Casaubon).
[9] ὥστε ACE: ὅς γε Meineke.

[a] F.H.G. i. 309, J. 2 B 589, G. and H. 241. Since this refers
to the Sacred War of 355 B.C., Lysander must be a different
person from the Spartan general.   See critical note 1.

listributions of meat than on the administration of he State." And in Theopompus's treatise entitled *On the Funds plundered from Delphi* he says [a] : " To Chares of Athens, through Lysander's agency, were given sixty talents. With this sum he feasted the Athenians in the market-place, offering sacrifices for his victory in the battle which was fought against Philip's mercenaries." These were commanded by Adaeus, nicknamed the Cock, to whom Heracleides, he writer of comedies, alludes in these lines [b] : " He caught Philip's Cock when he was crowing too early and wandering about, and cut him up ; for he had not yet got a crest.[c] Yes, Chares cut up only one, and yet feasted many Athenians on that occasion ; how generous he was ! " The same facts are recorded also by Duris.[d]

Idomeneus says [e] that the Peisistratidae, Hippias and Hipparchus, devised festivities and revels ; hence the great quantity of horses, besides many other things,[f] that swarmed among them, with the result that their rule became oppressive. And yet their father Peisistratus indulged his pleasures moderately, so much so that he did not post guards on his estates

[b] Kock ii. 435 ; the subject is Chares.
[c] Punning on the other sense of λόφος, " top of a hill," as a military vantage-point.
[d] *F.H.G.* ii. 470, J. 2 A 147. The victory occurred at Cypsela 353 B.C. (above, 469 a, p. 68), and was not connected, as Grote thought (ch. lxxxviii.), with operations against Olynthus. See D. M. Robinson in P.-W. *s. Olynthos.*
[e] *F.H.G.* ii. 491.
[f] Or, reading παρασίτων and ἑταιρῶν, " parasites and courtesans." But ἵππων may mean " loose women," at least in the time of Aelian, *N.A.* iv. 11, and the word may have been chosen with cynical reference to the names Hippias and Hipparchus. See 565 c (vol. vi. p. 53).

533 ἐφίστα,[1] ὡς Θεόπομπος ἱστορεῖ ἐν τῇ πρώτῃ καὶ
εἰκοστῇ, ἀλλ᾽ εἴα τὸν βουλόμενον εἰσιόντα ἀπολαύειν καὶ λαμβάνειν ὧν δεηθείη· ὅπερ ὕστερον
ἐποίησε καὶ Κίμων μιμησάμενος ἐκεῖνον. περὶ οὗ
καὶ αὐτοῦ ἱστορῶν ἐν τῇ δεκάτῃ τῶν Φιλιππικῶν
ὁ Θεόπομπός φησι· "Κίμων ὁ Ἀθηναῖος ἐν τοῖς
ἀγροῖς καὶ τοῖς κήποις οὐδένα τοῦ καρποῦ καθίστα
φύλακα, ὅπως οἱ βουλόμενοι τῶν πολιτῶν εἰσιόντες
ὀπωρίζωνται καὶ λαμβάνωσιν εἴ τινος δέοιντο τῶν
ἐν τοῖς χωρίοις. ἔπειτα τὴν οἰκίαν παρεῖχε κοινὴν
b ἅπασι· καὶ δεῖπνον αἰεὶ εὐτελὲς παρασκευάζεσθαι
πολλοῖς ἀνθρώποις καὶ τοὺς ἀπόρους προσιόντας
τῶν Ἀθηναίων εἰσιόντας[2] δειπνεῖν. ἐθεράπευεν δὲ
καὶ τοὺς καθ᾽ ἑκάστην ἡμέραν αὐτοῦ τι δεομένους
καὶ λέγουσιν ὡς περιήγετο μὲν ἀεὶ νεανίσκους δύο
ἢ τρεῖς ἔχοντας κέρματα τούτοις τε διδόναι προσ
έταττεν, ὁπότε τις προσέλθοι αὐτῷ[3] δεόμενος
καί φασι μὲν αὐτὸν καὶ εἰς ταφὴν εἰσφέρειν
ποιεῖν δὲ καὶ τοῦτο πολλάκις, ὁπότε τῶν πολιτῶν
c τινα ἴδοι κακῶς ἠμφιεσμένον, κελεύειν αὐτῷ μετ
ἀμφιέννυσθαι τῶν νεανίσκων τινὰ τῶν συνακολου
θούντων αὐτῷ. ἐκ δὴ τούτων ἁπάντων ηὐδοκίμε
καὶ πρῶτος ἦν τῶν πολιτῶν." ὁ δὲ Πεισίστρατος
καὶ ἐν πολλοῖς βαρὺς ἐγένετο, ὅπου[4] καὶ τι

---

[1] ἐφίστα AC : καθίστα Meineke.
[2] εἰσιόντας om. BP : Kaibel would delete προσιόντας.
[3] αὐτῷ C : αὐτοῦ A.
[4] ὅπου ACE : ὅτου Kaibel, deleting ἐκείνου. Capps read
καί τι for καὶ τὸ.

in his gardens, according to the account of Theopompus in the twenty-first book,[a] but permitted anyone who wished to enter and take for his enjoyment whatever he desired ; and this is what, at a later time, Cimon also did, following his example. Concerning Cimon in his turn Theopompus, in the account he gives in the tenth book of his *History of Philip*, says [b] : "Cimon of Athens stationed no guard in his fields and gardens to watch the crops and fruit, because he wanted all citizens who wished to enter and gather fruit and take whatever they desired of the products of his estates. Furthermore, he made his house free to all ; and a simple meal was always ready for a large number of persons, and the poor of Athens who came to it could enter and have dinner. He also cared for all who day by day asked him for aid, and they say that he took about with him two or three young fellows who carried small change, and he gave them orders to dole it out to the needy whenever they approached him to ask for aid. They also assert that he likewise contributed to funeral expenses. Here is another thing he often did : whenever he saw one of his fellow-citizens poorly clad he would order one of the young men in his retinue to exchange clothes with the man. As a result of all these kindnesses, therefore, he enjoyed high repute and was foremost among the citizens." But Peisistratus was cruel in many instances, seeing that

---

[a] *F.H.G.* i. 303, J. 2 B 567, G. and H. 131. Peisistratus, however, maintained a guard for his own person, see Hdt. i. 9, Diod. xiii. 95, *cf.* Plat. *Rep.* 566 B.
[b] *F.H.G.* i. 293, J. 2 B 555, G. and H. 89.

Ἀθήνησι τοῦ Διονύσου πρόσωπον ἐκείνου τιν‹
φασιν εἰκόνα.

Περικλέα δὲ τὸν Ὀλύμπιόν φησιν Ἡρακλείδ‹
ὁ Ποντικὸς ἐν τῷ περὶ Ἡδονῆς ὡς ἀπήλλαξεν ‹
τῆς οἰκίας τὴν γυναῖκα καὶ τὸν μεθ᾽ ἡδονῆς βί‹
d προείλετο ᾤκει τε μετ᾽ Ἀσπασίας τῆς ἐκ Μεγάρ‹
ἑταίρας καὶ τὸ πολὺ μέρος¹ τῆς οὐσίας εἰς ταύτ‹
κατανάλωσε.   Θεμιστοκλῆς δὲ οὔπω Ἀθηναί‹
μεθυσκομένων οὐδ᾽ ἑταίραις χρωμένων ἐκφανῶ‹
τέθριππον ζεύξας ἑταιρίδων διὰ τοῦ Κεραμεικ‹
πληθύοντος ἑωθινὸς ἤλασεν.²   ἀμφιβόλως δ᾽ αὐ‹
εἴρηκεν ὁ Ἰδομενεύς, εἴτε ἑταίρας τέτταρας συ‹
ὑπέζευξεν ὡς ἵππους εἴτ᾽ ἀνεβίβασεν αὐτὰς ἐπὶ ‹
τέθριππον.   Πόσσις δ᾽ ἐν τρίτῳ Μαγνητικῶν τ‹
e Θεμιστοκλέα φησὶν ἐν Μαγνησίᾳ τὴν στεφανηφόρ‹
ἀρχὴν ἀναλαβόντα θῦσαι Ἀθηνᾷ καὶ τὴν ἑορτ‹
Παναθήναια ὀνομάσαι καὶ Διονύσῳ Χοοπότῃ θ‹
σιάσαντα καὶ τὴν Χοῶν ἑορτὴν αὐτόθι καταδεῖξα‹
Κλέαρχος δὲ ἐν πρώτῳ περὶ Φιλίας τὸν Θεμι‹
στοκλέα φησὶ τρίκλινον οἰκοδομησάμενον περ‹

---

¹ μέρος om. CE.   ² A: ἤλαυνε E, ἤλαυνον C.

---

[a] This refers to the frightful faces, μορμολυκεῖα, or figur‹
of goblins (like gargoyles) set up to ward off evil.   C‹
Aristoph. frag. 131 (Kock i. 423) and the Roman oscill‹
Here it is implied that the face of Dionysus, and consequentl‹
that of Peisistratus, had the same apotropaic effect, c‹
Pausan. i. 2. 5, Frazer ii. 6.
[b] Voss 36.   The epithet " Olympian " recalls Aristoph‹
Acharn. 530 Περικλέης οὐλύμπιος | ἤστραπτ᾽ ἐβρόντα, cf. Athe‹
436 f (vol. iv. p. 478).
[c] Aspasia came from Miletus, not Megara, a mistak‹

me even say the face of Dionysus at Athens was
likeness of him.[a]

As for the Olympian Pericles, Heracleides of Pontus
his work *On Pleasure* says [b] that he dismissed his
ife from his house and preferred a life of pleasure ;
d so he lived with Aspasia, the courtesan from
egara, and squandered the greater part of his
operty on her.[c] But Themistocles, when as yet the
thenians were not addicted to carousing or resorting
prostitutes, openly yoked four courtesans to a
ariot and drove them in the morning through the
erameicus when it was crowded.[d] Idomeneus[e] in his
count leaves it doubtful whether he put together
ur courtesans to the yoke like horses or whether
: had them get into the chariot.[f] Possis, in the
ird book of his *History of Magnesia*, says[g] that
hemistocles, after assuming the office in Magnesia
hich carries with it the right to wear a crown, made
crifices to Athena, calling the festival Panathenaea,
d again after sacrificing to Dionysus the Pitcher-
rinker he instituted there the festival of Pitchers.[h]
ut Clearchus in the first book of his tract *On Friend-
ip* says[i] that Themistocles, though he caused to
: built a very beautiful triclinium,[j] would have been

ich arose through taking too seriously the joke in *Acharn.*
4 ff. On her true character see Xen. *Oecon.* 3. 14, *cf.*
em. iv. 6. 36, Pauly-Wissowa ii. 1716.
[d] Athen. 576 c. The Cerameicus, or north-western quarter
Athens, contained the market-place.
[e] *F.H.G.* ii. 491.
[f] *Cf.* a similar story of Mark Antony, Cic. *Phil.* ii. 24.
[g] *F.H.G.* iv. 483.
[h] In imitation of the second day of the Anthesteria at
hens.   [i] *F.H.G.* ii. 313.
[j] A dining-room with three couches, capable of receiving
ly nine persons.

καλλέστατον ἀγαπᾶν ἄν[1] (ἔφησεν), εἰ τοῦτον φίλα
πληρώσειεν.

Χαμαιλέων δ᾽ ὁ Ποντικὸς ἐν τῷ περὶ Ἀνα
κρέοντος προθεὶς τὸ

ξανθῇ δ᾽ Εὐρυπύλῃ μέλει
ὁ περιφόρητος Ἀρτέμων,

f τὴν προσηγορίαν ταύτην λαβεῖν τὸν Ἀρτέμων
διὰ τὸ τρυφερῶς βιοῦντα περιφέρεσθαι ἐπὶ κλίνη
καὶ γὰρ Ἀνακρέων αὐτὸν ἐκ πενίας εἰς τρυφῆ
ὁρμῆσαί φησιν ἐν τούτοις·

πρὶν μὲν ἔχων βερβέριον, καλύμματ᾽[2] ἐσφηκω
μένα,

καὶ ξυλίνους ἀστραγάλους ἐν ὠσὶ καὶ ψιλὸν πε
πλευρῇσι δέρριον[3] βοός,

νήπλυτον[4] εἴλυμα κακῆς ἀσπίδος, ἀρτοπώλισιν
534 καθελοπόρνοισιν[5] ὁμιλέων ὁ πονηρὸς Ἀρτέμων
κίβδηλον εὑρίσκων βίον,

πολλὰ μὲν ἐν δουρὶ τιθεὶς[7] αὐχένα, πολλὰ δ᾽
τροχῷ,

πολλὰ δὲ νῶτα σκυτίνῃ[8] μάστιγι θωμιχθεὶ
κόμην

πώγονά τ᾽ ἐκτετιλμένος·
νῦν δ᾽ ἐπιβαίνει σατινέων, χρύσεα φορέω
καθέρματα,

[1] ἄν added by Kaibel.
[2] Κερβερίων καλύμματ᾽ Schweighäuser, Edmonds.
[3] δέρριον added by Bergk[3]: δέρμ᾽ ἔχων Meineke, δέρμ᾽ ?
Bergk[4], Edmonds.
[4] Schoemann: νεόπλυτον CE, νεόπλουτον A.
[5] καὶ ἐθελοπόρνοισιν ACE.
[6] Ἀρτέμων Musurus: ὁ ἀρτέμων A.   [7] δεθεὶς Cobet.
[8] Elmsley: δ᾽ ἐν ὠτω σκυτίνω A.   [9] Casaubon: φαρέων

[a] Frag. 11 Koepke; see Athen. 273 c (vol. iii. p. 22(

glad indeed (so he declared) if he could have filled it with friends.

Chamaeleon of Pontus in his work *On Anacreon*, after quoting the verse,[a] " Yellow-haired Eurypylê was set her heart on that litter-borne Artemon," explains that Artemon got this title because he lived luxuriously and was carried about in a litter. In fact Anacreon does say that he careered from poverty into luxury, in these lines [b] : " In the old days he used to wear a ragged coat,[c] wrappings pinched in at the waist, and wooden knobs in his ears, and a hairless ox-hide strapped to his side, the unwashed covering of a poor shield—that vicious [d] Artemon, associate of bread-selling wenches and all-too-willing pathics, devising a life of fraud ; oft had he had his neck bound to the whipping-stock or else to the wheel, oft had he had his back flogged with a leather scourge, and the hair of his head and beard plucked out. But to-day he, son of Cycê,[e] mounts a chariot and wears necklaces

P.L.G.[4] iii. 261-262, Diehl frag. 16, Edmonds ii. 186. Artemon was a rival of Anacreon. In the fifth century the epithet was wittily applied to another Artemon, an engineer under Pericles, who was lame and had to be carried about in a litter ; Plut. *Per.* 27, Schol. Aristoph. *Acharn.* 850. Pliny, *Nat. Hist.* xxxiv. 56, mentions a statue of him by Polycleitus.

[b] Diehl frag. 54, Edmonds frag. 96. Bergk prints the verses with the preceding, though sharing Blass's belief that they do not belong together.

[c] Or, "of the Cerberians," to be taken with the following καλύμματα. Cerberians was another form for Cimmerians (Hesychius), read also in Aristoph. *Ran.* 187 with the meaning "poor devils." See critical note 2. The word βερβέριον occurs only here.

[d] *Cf.* ὁ περιπόνηρος Ἀρτέμων, " Artemon, that all-round rascal," in allusion to περιφόρητος, Aristoph. *Acharn.* 850.

[e] Obviously a woman of low origin and life. The name means " Mix " or " Mixed." See critical note 1 on p. 412.

ATHENAEUS

b παῖς[1] Κύκης, καὶ σκιαδίσκην ἐλεφαντίνην φορεῖ
γυναιξὶν αὕτως . . .

Περὶ δὲ τοῦ καλοῦ Ἀλκιβιάδου Σάτυρος ἱστορῶν
" λέγεται," φησίν, " ὅτι ἐν Ἰωνίᾳ μὲν ὢν Ἰώνων[2]
ἐφαίνετο τρυφερώτερος, ἐν Θήβαις δὲ σωμασκῶν
καὶ γυμναζόμενος τῶν Θηβαίων αὐτῶν μᾶλλον
Βοιώτιος, ἐν Θετταλίᾳ δὲ ἱπποτροφῶν καὶ ἡνιοχῶν
τῶν Ἀλευαδῶν ἱππικώτερος, ἐν Σπάρτῃ δὲ καρτερίαν καὶ ἀφέλειαν[3] ἐπιτηδεύων ἐνίκα τοὺς Λάκω-
νας, ὑπερῆρεν δὲ καὶ τὴν τῶν Θρακῶν ἀκρατοποσίαν.
c τὴν δὲ αὐτοῦ γυναῖκα πειρῶν ὡς ἕτερος ἔπεμψεν
αὐτῇ χιλίους δαρεικούς. κάλλιστος δὲ ὢν τὴν
μορφὴν κόμην τε ἔτρεφεν ἐπὶ πολὺ τῆς ἡλικίας καὶ
ὑποδήματα παρηλλαγμένα ἐφόρει, ἃ ἀπ' αὐτοῦ
Ἀλκιβιάδες[4] καλεῖται. ὅτε δὲ χορηγοίη πομπεύων
ἐν πορφυρίδι εἰσιὼν εἰς τὸ θέατρον, ἐθαυμάζετο οὐ
μόνον ὑπὸ τῶν ἀνδρῶν ἀλλὰ καὶ ὑπὸ τῶν γυναικῶν.
διὸ καὶ Ἀντισθένης ὁ Σωκρατικὸς ὡς δὴ[5] αὐτὸς
αὐτόπτης γεγονὼς τοῦ Ἀλκιβιάδου ἰσχυρὸν αὐτὸν
καὶ ἀνδρώδη καὶ εὐπαίδευτον[6] καὶ τολμηρὸν καὶ

[1] Dindorf: παῖς A; πασικύκης " a mix-with-all " Edmonds.
[2] Ἰώνων added by Musurus.
[3] Hemsterhuys: ἀσφάλειαν ACE.
[4] ἀλκιβιάδης CE.   [5] δὴ Kaibel: ἂν ACE.
[6] Dalechamp: ἀπαίδευτον ACE.

[a] F.H.G. iii. 160. Cf. Hor. Ep. i. 17. 23 " omnis Aristippum
decuit color et status et res."
[b] Cf. " More Catholic than the Pope," " Plus royaliste
que le Roi."
[c] Cf. the description of " the democratic soul " (thought
by some to refer to Alcibiades) in Plat. Rep. 561 c-D. For
Socrates' bearing in prosperity and adversity see Alcibiades'
description of him in Plat. Symp. 219 D-221 c. On the con-
tradictions in Alcibiades' character see Plut. Alc. 2.

412

of gold, and carries an ivory sunshade just like a woman."

In his account of the handsome Alcibiades Satyrus says [a] : " It is said that when he was in Ionia he was more luxurious than the Ionians ; when in Thebes, he was more Boeotian than the Thebans [b] themselves in his physical exercises and gymnastic training ; when in Thessaly, in his schooling of horses and in his chariot-driving he was more devoted to horseman-ship than the Aleuadae ; in Sparta he could beat the Spartans in the practice of endurance and the simple life ; and on the other hand he outdid the Thracians in their drinking of unmixed wine.[c] Once, to test his wife, he sent her a thousand darics as though they came from someone else. Extremely handsome in appearance, he let his hair grow long during a great part of his life,[d] and he wore shoes of a striking pattern, which from him are called *Alcibiades*.[e] When-ever as choregus [f] he entered the theatre with the procession, robed in purple, he was admired by men and women alike. Hence also Antisthenes, the disciple of Socrates, being one who had seen Alci-biades with his own eyes, affirms that he was strong, manly, cultivated, daring, and beautiful at every

---

[d] Plut. 52 E (*cf. Alc.* 23) says that he cut it close when he went over to the Spartans. Long hair was fashionable among Athenian gallants and especially the Knights (Aristoph. *Eq.* 577 and Schol.); Lysias xvi. 18, Athen. 225 a (vol. iii. p. 14). Schweighäuser preferred to take τῆς ἡλικίας in the sense of " stature," so that the meaning would be " he wore it half way down his back."

[e] Pollux vii. 89 gives a list of similar names ; *cf.* Eng. " Blücher."

[f] The citizen who paid the expenses of the chorus in tragic, comic, and lyric performances. These were preceded by a *proagon*, parade of all participants.

ὡραῖον ἐφ᾽ ἡλικίας πάσης¹ γενέσθαι φησίν. εἰς δὲ
d τὰς ἀποδημίας ὁπότε στέλλοιτο, τέσσαρσι τῶν
συμμαχίδων πόλεων ὥσπερ θεραπαίναις ἐχρῆτο.
σκηνὴν μὲν γὰρ αὐτῷ Περσικὴν ἔπησσον Ἐφέσιοι,
τροφὴν δὲ τοῖς ἵπποις αὐτοῦ Χῖοι² παρεῖχον, ἱερεῖα
δὲ παρίστασαν εἰς τὰς θυσίας καὶ κρεανομίας
Κυζικηνοί, Λέσβιοι δὲ οἶνον παρεῖχον καὶ τὰ ἄλλα
τὰ πρὸς τὴν καθ᾽ ἡμέραν δίαιταν. ἀφικόμενος δ᾽
Ἀθήνησιν ἐξ Ὀλυμπίας δύο πίνακας ἀνέθηκεν,
Ἀγλαοφῶντος γραφήν· ὧν ὁ μὲν εἶχεν Ὀλυμπιάδα
καὶ Πυθιάδα στεφανούσας αὐτόν, ἐν δὲ θατέρῳ
Νεμέα ἦν καθημένη καὶ ἐπὶ τῶν γονάτων αὐτῆς
e Ἀλκιβιάδης, καλλίων φαινόμενος τῶν γυναικείων
προσώπων.   καὶ στρατηγῶν δὲ ἔτι καλὸς εἶναι
ἤθελεν· ἀσπίδα γοῦν εἶχεν ἐκ χρυσοῦ³ καὶ ἐλέφαντος
πεποιημένην, ἐφ᾽ ἧς ἦν ἐπίσημον Ἔρως κεραυνὸν
ἠγκυλημένος.   ἐπικωμάσας δέ ποτε ὡς Ἄνυτον
ἐραστὴν ὄντα καὶ πλούσιον, συνεπικωμαζόντων
αὐτῷ τῶν ἑταίρων ἑνὸς Θρασύλλου (τῶν πενήτων
δ᾽ οὗτος ἦν), προπιὼν τῷ Θρασύλλῳ τὰ ἡμίση τῶν
ποτηρίων τῶν ἐπὶ τῷ κυλικείῳ⁴ προκειμένων
f ἐκέλευσε τοὺς ἀκολούθους ἀποφέρειν πρὸς τὸν
Θράσυλλον· εἶθ᾽ οὕτω φιλοφρονησάμενος τὸν Ἄνυ-
τον⁵ ἀπηλλάσσετο. ὁ δὲ Ἄνυτος πάνυ ἐλευθερίως
καὶ ἐρωτικῶς, λεγόντων τινῶν ὡς ἀγνώμονα εἴη
πεποιηκὼς Ἀλκιβιάδης, " οὐ μὰ Δί᾽," ἔφη, " ἀλλ᾽

¹ πάσης added by Kaibel.
² Casaubon: κῖοι ACE.   ³ CE: χρυσίου A.
⁴ Musurus: κυλικίωι A.   ⁵ Musurus: αὐτὸν A.

ᵃ Cf. Plut. Alc. 12.
ᵇ Plut. Alc. 16 says that this second picture was by
Aristophon, son of Aglaophon and brother of Polygnotus.

period of his life. Whenever he set out on journeys abroad he made use of four of the allied cities as though they were so many maid-servants. That is to say, the Ephesians set up a Persian pavilion for him, the Chians provided fodder for his horses, the Cyzicenes supplied animals for the sacrifices and distribution of the meat, the Lesbians provided wine and everything else for his daily necessities.[a] Returning from Olympia, he dedicated at Athens two tablets painted by Aglaophon; one of these showed figures representing the Olympian and Pythian festivals placing crowns on his head, and on the other was the seated figure of Nemea[b] with Alcibiades on her lap, more beautiful in appearance than the faces of the women. And even when he was a general he wanted to be a dandy still; he carried, for example, a shield made of gold and ivory, on which there was the device of Eros with a thunderbolt poised like a javelin.[c] Once he burst in mad revel into the house of Anytus, who was his lover and rich, in company with one of his boon companions, Thrasyllus (who was poor), and toasting Thrasyllus with half of the cups that stood on the cup-stand he ordered his attendants to carry them off to Thrasyllus's house; he then, after showing in this way his affection for Anytus, took his leave. And when some persons objected that Alcibiades had done what was inconsiderate, Anytus replied like the gentleman and lover that he was, " Not by any means, as Zeus is

t seems unlikely that Aglaophon lived so late in the fifth century, and perhaps the name of Aristophon should be substituted above.

[c] The participle refers to the cord attached to the thrower's wrist and wound round the missile to give it a whirling motion, cf. 782 e note d (p. 45).

εὐγνωμονέστατα· ἔχων γὰρ[1] ἐξουσίαν ἅπαντα λαβεῖ
τὰ ἡμίση κατέλιπεν." Λυσίας δὲ ὁ ῥήτωρ περ
τῆς τρυφῆς αὐτοῦ λέγων φησίν· " ἐκπλεύσαντε
γὰρ κοινῇ Ἀξίοχος καὶ Ἀλκιβιάδης εἰς Ἑλλή
σποντον ἔγημαν ἐν Ἀβύδῳ δύο ὄντε Μεδοντίδα[2] τη

535 Ἀβυδηνὴν καὶ ξυνῳκείτην. ἔπειτα αὐτοῖν γίνετο
θυγάτηρ, ἣν οὐκ ἔφαντο δύνασθαι γνῶναι ὁποτέρο
εἴη. ἐπεὶ δὲ ἦν ἀνδρὸς ὡραία, ξυνεκοιμῶντο κ
ταύτῃ, καὶ εἰ μὲν χρῷτο καὶ ἔχοι Ἀλκιβιάδη
Ἀξιόχου ἔφασκεν εἶναι θυγατέρα· εἰ δὲ Ἀξίοχος
Ἀλκιβιάδου." κεκωμῴδηται δὲ καὶ ὑπὸ Εὐπόλιδο
ὡς[3] ἀκόλαστος πρὸς γυναῖκας ἐν Κόλαξιν οὕτως·

Ἀλκιβιάδης ἐκ τῶν γυναικῶν ἐξίτω. ΑΛΚ.
λήρεῖς;

b οὐκ οἴκαδ᾽ ἐλθὼν τὴν σεαυτοῦ γυμνάσεις δά
μαρτα;

καὶ Φερεκράτης δέ φησιν·

οὐκ ὢν ἀνὴρ γὰρ Ἀλκιβιάδης, ὡς δοκεῖν,[4]
ἀνὴρ ἁπασῶν τῶν γυναικῶν ἐστι νῦν.

ἐν Σπάρτῃ δὲ ὢν ἔφθειρε τὴν Ἄγιδος τοῦ βασιλέα
γυναῖκα Τίμαιαν· ἐπιπληττόντων δ᾽ αὐτῷ τινα
οὐκ ἀκρασίας ἕνεκεν συνελθεῖν ἔφη, ἀλλ᾽ ἵνα
γενόμενος ἐξ αὐτοῦ βασιλεύσῃ τε τῆς Σπάρτης κ

---

[1] εὐγνωμονέστατα· ἔχων γὰρ CE : εὐγνώμονα· ἔχων (om. γὰρ) A
[2] 574 d : μεδοντιάδα ACE.
[3] ὡς Meineke : ὡς καὶ A.   [4] δοκεῖν CE : δοκεῖ A.

---

[a] Cf. Plut. Alc. 4.
[b] Thalheim, p. 346; below, 574 d.
[c] Kock i. 300; the second speaker seems to be Alcibiad
himself, called a woman by the first, who may be his ἐραστή
[d] i.e. cease to be a woman, cf. Diog. Laert. iv. 49 ἔλεγε
(Socrates) ὡς νέος μὲν ὢν τοὺς ἄνδρας ἀπαγάγοι τῶν γυναικῶ

ny witness ; rather, he has acted most considerately, eeing that when he had it in his power to take hem all, he left one half behind."[a] The orator ysias, speaking of his licentiousness, says[b] : " For Axiochus and Alcibiades sailed forth together to the Iellespont and married in Abydus, the two of them, Iedontis of Abydus, with whom they cohabited. Later a daughter was born to them, of whom they Declared they could not tell whose child she was. But when she became marriageable, they cohabited with her also ; whenever Alcibiades enjoyed possession f her, he would say she was the daughter of Axiochus ; but when Axiochus did so, he would say she was the daughter of Alcibiades." He is held up to idicule by Eupolis also in *The Flatterers* as a profligate n his relations with women, in these words[c] : " A. Let Alcibiades depart from the woman-class.[d] ALC. What nonsense ! Why don't you go home and exercise our own wife ? " And Pherecrates also says[e] : " For hough Alcibiades is not a man, as it would seem, et he is to-day the one man[f] of all the women." When he was in Sparta he seduced Timaea, the wife of King Agis ; and when certain persons reproached him or the act, he said that he had not consorted with her rom incontinence, but because he wanted the child hat sprang from him to be king of Sparta and the

εανίσκος δὲ γενόμενος τὰς γυναῖκας τῶν ἀνδρῶν, " when he was a oung boy he lured husbands away from their wives, but vhen he was a young man he lured wives away from their usbands."

[e] Kock i. 194: *cf.* Sueton. *Iul.* 52 "Curio pater quadam um (Caesar) oratione omnium mulierum virum et omnium irorum mulierem appellat "; Cic. *Verr.* ii. 78 (192) " magis ir inter mulieres, impura inter viros muliercula proferri on potest."   [f] *i.e.* husband.

ATHENAEUS

c μηκέτι λέγωνται οἱ βασιλεῖς ἀφ' Ἡρακλέους ἀλ
ἀπ' Ἀλκιβιάδου. στρατηγῶν δὲ συμπεριήγετ
αὐτῷ[1] τήν τε Λαΐδος τῆς Κορινθίας μητέρα Τιμάι
δραν καὶ Θεοδότην τὴν Ἀττικὴν ἑταίραν. μετὰ δ
τὴν φυγὴν κυρίους Ἀθηναίους ποιήσας τοῦ Ἑλλησ
πόντου καὶ πλείους τῶν πεντακισχιλίων Πελοποι
νησίους λαβὼν ἀνέπεμψεν εἰς τὰς Ἀθήνας, κατιώ
τε μετὰ ταῦτα εἰς τὴν πατρίδα ἐστεφάνωσε τὰ
Ἀττικὰς τριήρεις θαλλῷ καὶ μίτραις καὶ ταινίαις
καὶ ἀναψάμενος τὰς αἰχμαλώτους ναῦς ἠκρωτη

d ριασμένας εἰς διακοσίας ἱππαγωγούς τε ἄγω
σκύλων καὶ ὅπλων Λακωνικῶν καὶ Πελοποννησια
κῶν μεστὰς εἰσέπλει. ἡ δὲ τριήρης ἐφ' ἧς αὐτὸ
κατέπλει μέχρι μὲν τῶν κλείθρων τοῦ Πειραιέω
προέτρεχεν[2] ἁλουργοῖς ἱστίοις· ὡς δ' ἐντὸς ἦν κα
τὰς κώπας ἔλαβον οἱ ἐρέται, Χρυσόγονος μὲν ηὔλ
τὸ τριηρικὸν ἐνδεδυκὼς τὴν Πυθικὴν στολήν
Καλλιππίδης δ' ὁ τραγῳδὸς ἐκέλευε τὴν ἐπὶ[3] τῆ
σκηνῆς στολὴν ἠμφιεσμένος. διὸ καὶ χαριέντω
εἶπέν τις· " οὔτ' ἂν δύο Λυσάνδρους ὑπήνεγκεν

---

[1] αὐτῷ om. CE.   [2] CE: προσέτρεχεν A.
[3] ἐπὶ ACE: ἀπὸ Kaibel.

---

[a] The two kings of Sparta were descended from the twin
Eurysthenes and Procles, grandsons of Aristomachus, wh
was the great-grandson of Heracles, Hdt. vi. 52.
[b] Cf. Athen. 574 e.
[c] See Duris ap. Plut. Alc. 32. He escaped at Thur
from the ship sent (415 B.C.) to bring him home to stan
trial for the mutilation of the Hermae and the profanation c
the Mysteries. The ban of exile was lifted in 411, but h
remained with the fleet at Samos. After the victories a

418

kings to be no longer said to have come from Heracles,[a] but from Alcibiades. When in command of the army he took with him everywhere Timandra,[b] mother of the Corinthian Laïs, and Theodotê, the Athenian courtesan. After his flight[c] he made the Athenians masters of the Hellespont and sent to Athens more than five thousand Peloponnesians whom he had captured; and later, starting on his return to his native land, he wreathed the Athenian triremes with green branches, streamers, and ribbons, and made fast to them the captive ships, numbering two hundred, the beaks of which had been cut away; and towing them along with the horse-transports, these also laden with booty and arms taken from Spartans and Peloponnesians, he sailed into the harbour. Now the trireme in which he himself returned coursed ahead under purple sails until it reached the entrance[d] to Peiraeus. And when it was inside and the rowers had grasped their oars,[e] Chrysogonus, dressed in his Delphic robes, began to pipe the trireme-tune,[f] while the tragic actor Callippides[g] beat time for him, dressed in his theatrical costume. Hence somebody has wittily said: "Sparta could not have put up with two Lysanders, and neither

Cynossema, Cyzicus, and Byzantium he returned to Athens in 408 or early in 407.

[d] The narrow mouth of the harbour was closed by a boom or chain (κλεῖθρα).　　　　[e] After taking in sail.

[f] Chrysogonus had won a victory as a flute-player at Delphi. The "trieric" tune gave the time to the rowers; jocosely called τὸ ῥυππαπαῖ, Aristoph. *Vesp.* 909; *cf. Ran.* 1073.

[g] One of the most famous tragedians of the Greek stage, although opinions differed as to his merit. The comic poet Strattis wrote a play about him, Athen. 304 b, 656 b. See J. B. O'Connor, *Actors and Acting in Ancient Greece*, pp. 107-109.

θ Σπάρτη οὔτ' ἂν δύ' Ἀλκιβιάδας Ἀθῆναι." ἐμι-
μεῖτο δὲ Ἀλκιβιάδης τὸν Παυσανίου μηδισμὸν καὶ
καθομιλῶν Φαρνάβαζον τὴν Περσικὴν ἐνεδύετο[1]
στολὴν καὶ τὴν Περσικὴν ἔμαθε φωνήν, καθάπερ
καὶ Θεμιστοκλῆς.

Δοῦρις δ' ἐν τῇ δευτέρᾳ καὶ εἰκοστῇ τῶν Ἱστοριῶν " Παυσανίας μέν," φησίν, " ὁ τῶν Σπαρτιατῶν
βασιλεὺς καταθέμενος τὸν πάτριον τρίβωνα τὴν
Περσικὴν ἐνεδύετο στολήν. ὁ δὲ Σικελίας τύραννος
Διονύσιος ξυστίδα καὶ χρυσοῦν στέφανον, ἔτι δ'
f ἐπιπόρπημα[2] μετελάμβανε τραγικόν. Ἀλέξανδρος
δ' ὡς τῆς Ἀσίας ἐκυρίευσεν Περσικαῖς ἐχρῆτο
στολαῖς. Δημήτριος δὲ πάντας ὑπερέβαλεν[3]· τὴν
μὲν γὰρ ὑπόδεσιν ἣν εἶχεν κατεσκεύαζεν[4] ἐκ πολλοῦ
δαπανήματος· ἦν γὰρ κατὰ μὲν τὸ σχῆμα τῆς
ἐργασίας σχεδὸν ἐμβάτης πίλημα[5] λαμβάνων τῆς
πολυτελεστάτης πορφύρας· τούτῳ δὲ χρυσοῦ πολλὴν ἐνύφαινον ποικιλίαν ὀπίσω καὶ ἔμπροσθεν
ἐνιέντες οἱ τεχνῖται. αἱ δὲ χλαμύδες αὐτοῦ ἦσαν
ὄρφνινον ἔχουσαι τὸ φέγγος τῆς χρόας, τὸ δὲ πᾶν[6]
ἐνύφαντο χρυσοῦς ἀστέρας ἔχον[7] καὶ τὰ δώδεκα
536 ζῴδια. μίτρα δὲ χρυσόπαστος ἦν, ἥ[8] καυσίαν
ἁλουργῆ οὖσαν ἔσφιγγεν, ἐπὶ τὸ νῶτον φέρουσα τὰ
τελευταῖα καταβλήματα τῶν ὑφασμάτων.   γινο-

---

[1] A: ἐνεδύσατο CE.
[2] ἔτι δ' ἐπιπόρπημα Hullemann, Jacoby: ἐπὶ περόνῃ A.
[3] A: ὑπερέβαλλε CE.   [4] ACE: κατεσκευάζετο Kaibel.
[5] Musurus: πίλημμα A.
[6] After τὸ δὲ πᾶν the gloss ὁ πόλος deleted by Vollgraff.
[7] ἔχον Vollgraff: ἔχων A.
[8] ἥν, ἡ Schweighäuser: ἥν A.

ould Athens have put up with two Alcibiadeses." [a]
Alcibiades imitated also the Persian habits of Pausanias, and by way of winning the favour of Pharnabazus he used to dress himself in Persian raiment and learned the Persian language, as Themistocles likewise did.[b]

Duris in the twenty-second book of his *Histories* says [c]: " Pausanias, the king of the Spartans, laid aside the coarse coat of his country and dressed himself in Persian raiment. So, too, Dionysius, the tyrant of Sicily, assumed a long robe [d] and crown of gold, besides a buckled mantle usually worn by tragic actors. And Alexander, as soon as he became master of Asia, began to wear Persian dress. But Demetrius [e] surpassed them all ; for the footwear that he wore was made at great expense ; as to the shape in which it was made, it was practically a half-boot, but it had a felt covering of the costliest purple ; into this the manufacturers had woven, behind and in front, a very intricate pattern of gold. His riding-cloaks had a lustrous dark-grey colour, and the universe with its golden stars and the twelve signs of the Zodiac were woven in it. His headband was spangled with gold, and held tightly in place a hat of purple ; the fringed ends of its woven material extended down to his back. When the festival of

---

[a] Aelian, *V.H.* xi. 7, credits the Spartan Eteocles with the remark about Lysander, the Athenian Archestratus with that about Alcibiades; *cf.* Plut. *Alc.* 16, *Lys.* 19. Lysander rose from poverty (Athen. 271 f) ; on his character see Plut. *Lys.* 8, below, p. 458.
[b] Thuc. i. 138.   [c] *F.H.G.* ii. 477, J. 2 A 142.
[d] The ξυστίς was ordinarily worn by women, or by men on ceremonial occasions : *cf.* Plat. *Rep.* 420 E.
[e] Poliorcetes, son of Antigonus ; *cf.* Plut. *Demetr.* 41.

μένων δὲ τῶν Δημητρίων 'Αθήνησιν ἐγράφετο ἐπὶ τοῦ προσκηνίου ἐπὶ τῆς Οἰκουμένης ὀχούμενος."

Νύμφις δ' ὁ Ἡρακλεώτης ἐν ἕκτῳ τῶν περὶ τῆ πατρίδος " Παυσανίας," φησίν, " ὁ περὶ Πλαταιὰ νικήσας Μαρδόνιον, τὰ τῆς Σπάρτης ἐξελθὼν νόμιμα καὶ εἰς ὑπερηφανίαν ἐπιδοὺς περὶ Βυζάν b τιον διατρίβων τὸν χαλκοῦν κρατῆρα τὸν ἀνακεί μενον[1] τοῖς θεοῖς τοῖς ἐπὶ τοῦ στόματος ἱδρυμένοις ὃν ἔτι καὶ νῦν εἶναι συμβαίνει, ἐτόλμησεν ἐπι γράψαι, ὡς αὐτὸς ἀναθείς,[2] τόδε τὸ ἐπίγραμμα, διὰ τὴν τρυφὴν καὶ ὑπερηφανίαν ἐπιλαθόμενος αὐτοῦ·

μνᾶμ' ἀρετᾶς ἀνέθηκε Ποσειδάωνι ἄνακτι
Παυσανίας, ἄρχων Ἑλλάδος εὐρυχόρου,
πόντου ἐπ' Εὐξείνου, Λακεδαιμόνιος γένος, υἱὸς
Κλεομβρότου, ἀρχαίας Ἡρακλέος γενεᾶς."

'Ετρύφησεν δὲ καὶ Φάραξ ὁ Λακεδαιμόνιος, ὡς c Θεόπομπος ἐν τῇ τεσσαρακοστῇ ἱστορεῖ· καὶ ταῖ ἡδοναῖς οὕτως ἀσελγῶς ἐχρήσατο καὶ χύδην ὥστε πολὺ μᾶλλον διὰ τὴν αἰτίαν ταύτην αὐτὸν ὑπο λαμβάνεσθαι Σικελιώτην ἢ διὰ τὴν πατρίδα Σπαρ τιάτην. ἐν δὲ τῇ νβ' φησὶν ὡς 'Αρχίδαμος ὁ Λάκων ἀποστὰς τῆς πατρίου διαίτης συνηθίσθη ξενικῶς καὶ μαλακῶς· διόπερ οὐκ ἠδύνατο τὸ οἴκοι βίον ὑπομένειν, ἀλλ' ἐσπούδαζεν αἰεὶ διὰ

[1] Kaibel: τὸν χαλκοῦν τὸν ἀνακείμενον κρατῆρα A; τὸ χαλκοῦν Ποσειδῶνος κρατῆρα CE.
[2] ὑποθείς after ἀναθείς (A) deleted by Gulick.
[3] A: συνειθίσθαι C, συνειθίσθη E.

[a] Not in honour of Demeter, but of Demetrius himsel Athen. 253 a (vol. iii. p. 138). See Am. J. Philol. 1928, 142
[b] The title περὶ Ἡρακλείας is given below, 549 a; F.H.G iii. 15.
[c] Cf. the epigram, by Simonides, which Pausanias in

the Demetria[a] was celebrated at Athens, he was represented, in a painting on the front wall of the proscenium, riding on the inhabited world."

Nymphis of Heracleia, in the sixth book of the work dealing with his native city,[b] says : " Pausanias, the victor over Mardonius at Plataeae, departed entirely from Spartan customs, and when he was staying at Byzantium he gave himself over completely to arrogance ; he had the impudence, on the bronze bowl dedicated to the gods whose shrines are at the entrance —which bowl, as it happens, exists even to this day— to inscribe the following epigram as though he alone had made the dedication, entirely forgetting who he was in his wanton arrogance [c] : ' This monument of his prowess is dedicated to lord Poseidon by Pausanias, ruler of Hellas with its wide spaces, at the Euxine sea ; a Lacedaemonian by birth, the son of Cleombrotus, of the ancient race of Heracles.' "

The Spartan Pharax also lived luxuriously, as Theopompus records in his fortieth book[d] ; in fact he indulged in his pleasures so wantonly and lavishly that he was for this reason far more apt to be taken for a Greek of Sicily than, because of the place of his birth, for a Spartan. In the fifty-second book Theopompus says [e] that the Spartan Archidamus deserted the traditional mode of life and adopted customs which were foreign and effeminate ; hence he could not bear to live at home, but did his utmost to stay always abroad in order to satisfy his incontinence.

scribed on the gold tripod at Delphi, Thuc. i. 132, Hdt. ix. 81, Pausan. (the Periegete) iii. 8. It was afterwards erased.

[d] *F.H.G.* i. 314, J. 2 B 576. *Cf.* Diod. xii. 79, Plut. *Timoleon* 11.

[e] *F.H.G.* i. 322, J. 2 B 586, G. and H. 225. Archidamus III is meant.

ἀκρασίαν ἔξω διατρίβειν. καὶ Ταραντίνων πρεσβευσαμένων περὶ συμμαχίας ἔσπευσε συνεξελθεῖν
d αὐτοῖς βοηθός· κἀκεῖ γενόμενος καὶ ἐν τῷ πολέμῳ ἀποθανὼν οὐδὲ ταφῆς κατηξιώθη, καίτοι Ταραντίνων πολλὰ χρήματα ὑποσχομένων τοῖς πολεμίοις ὑπὲρ τοῦ ἀνελέσθαι αὐτοῦ τὸ σῶμα.

Φύλαρχος δὲ ἐν τῇ ι΄ τῶν Ἱστοριῶν Θρακῶν φησι τῶν καλουμένων Κροβύζων βασιλέα γενέσθαι Ἰσάνθην, τρυφῇ πάντας τοὺς καθ᾽ ἑαυτὸν ὑπερβαλλόμενον. ἦν δὲ καὶ πλούσιος καὶ καλός. ἐν
e δὲ τῇ δευτέρᾳ καὶ εἰκοστῇ ὁ αὐτὸς Πτολεμαῖον φησι τὸν δεύτερον Αἰγύπτου βασιλεύσαντα, πάντων σεμνότατον γενόμενον τῶν δυναστῶν καὶ παιδείας εἴ τινα καὶ ἄλλον καὶ αὐτὸν ἐπιμεληθέντα οὕτως ἐξαπατηθῆναι τὴν διάνοιαν καὶ διαφθαρῆναι ὑπὸ τῆς ἀκαίρου τρυφῆς ὥστε τὸν πάντα χρόνον ὑπολαβεῖν βιώσεσθαι καὶ λέγειν ὅτι μόνος εὕροι τὴν ἀθανασίαν. κατατεινόμενον οὖν ὑπὸ ποδάγρας πλείους ἡμέρας, ὥς ποτ᾽ οὖν ἐρράισεν[1] καὶ κατεῖδεν[2] διά τινων ὑπολαμπάδων τοὺς Αἰγυπτίους παρὰ τὸν ποταμὸν ἀριστοποιουμένους καὶ τὰ τυχόντα προσφερομένους ἐπί τε τῆς ἄμμου χύδην ἐρριμμένους, εἶπεν· " ὦ τάλας ἐγώ, τὸ μηδὲ τούτων ἕνα γενέσθαι."
f Περὶ δὲ Καλλίου καὶ τῶν τούτου κολάκων φθάνομεν καὶ πρότερον εἰπόντες· ἀλλ᾽ ἐπεὶ καινῶς

---

[1] ποτ᾽ οὖν ἐράϊσεν A, ποτε ἐρράϊσε C (ἐρράιζε E).
[2] E, κατεῖδε C: κατίδεν A.

---

[a] F.H.G. i. 338, J. 2 A 166.
[b] F.H.G. i. 345, J. 2 A 172.
[c] Some device for admitting light is meant; Ditt. Syll.[2] 588. 219 ἐπισκευάσαντι τὸ κλεῖθρον τῆς ὑπολαμπάδος, " for repairing the bolt of the hypolampas (in a temple)."

So, when the people of Tarentum sent an embassy to treat for an alliance, he hastened to march out with them to their assistance ; and when he reached there and was killed in the war he was not even accorded the honour of burial, although the Tarentines promised large sums of money to the enemy for the recovery of his body.

Phylarchus, in the tenth book of his *Histories*, says [a] that Isanthes, who became king of the Thracian tribe called Crobyzi, surpassed all his contemporaries in luxury. He was rich and handsome. And in the twenty-second book the same author says [b] of Ptolemy, the second of that name who became king of Egypt, that in spite of his being the most august of all princes and devoted, if anyone ever was, to culture and learning, he was nevertheless so utterly distorted in judgement and spoiled by his unmeasured luxury that he thought he was going to live for ever, and boasted that he was the only one who had found exemption from death. And so, tortured by an attack of gout which lasted several days, when he began to feel somewhat easier, and spied through some windows [c] the Egyptians at lunch by the river-side eating plain food as they lay sprawled on the sands, he cried out, " Unlucky devil that I am ! To think that I cannot even be one of those fellows ! " [d]

Concerning Callias and his flatterers we have already spoken in an earlier passage [e] ; but inasmuch

[d] These words form parts of two verses, Kock iii. 492. See Haupt, *Opusc.* iii. 570.

[e] No mention of Callias's flatterers occurs in the present work, though parasites have been discussed at length in 234 ff. (vol. iii. pp. 54-178). The prodigality of Callias is mentioned at 169 a (vol. ii. p. 266).

Ἡρακλείδης ὁ Ποντικὸς ἐν τῷ περὶ Ἡδονῆς ἱστορεῖ περὶ αὐτοῦ, ἄνωθεν ἀναλαβὼν διηγήσομαι. " ὅτε τὸ πρῶτον εἰς Εὔβοιαν ἐστράτευσαν οἱ Πέρσαι, τότε, ὥς φασιν, Ἐρετριεὺς ἀνὴρ Διόμνηστος κύριος ἐγένετο τῶν τοῦ στρατηγοῦ χρημάτων. ἔτυχεν γὰρ ἐν τῷ ἀγρῷ τῷ ἐκείνου σκηνῶν καὶ τὰ χρήματα εἰς οἴκημά τι θέμενος τῆς οἰκίας. 537 τελευτησάντων δὲ πάντων διέλαθεν ἔχων ὁ Διόμνηστος τὸ χρυσίον. ἐπεὶ δὲ πάλιν ὁ τῶν Περσῶν βασιλεὺς ἀπέστειλεν εἰς τὴν Ἐρέτριαν στράτευμα, προστάξας ἀνάστατον[1] ποιῆσαι τὴν πόλιν, εἰκότως ὑπεξετίθεντο ὅσοι χρημάτων ηὐπόρουν. οἱ οὖν καταλελειμμένοι τῆς τοῦ Διομνήστου οἰκίας παρ' Ἱππόνικον τὸν Καλλίου τὸν Ἄμμωνα ἐπικαλούμενον ὑπεξέθεντο τὰ χρήματα εἰς τὰς Ἀθήνας, καὶ ἀνασκευασθέντων ὑπὸ τῶν Περσῶν ἁπάντων τῶν[2] Ἐρετριέων κατέσχον οὗτοι τὰ χρήματα πολλὰ b ὄντα. ὥστε Ἱππόνικος ὁ ἀπ' ἐκείνου γεγονὼς τοῦ τὴν παρακαταθήκην λαβόντος ᾔτησεν Ἀθηναίους ποτὲ ἐν Ἀκροπόλει τόπον ἵν' οἰκοδομήσηται τοῖς χρήμασιν ὅπου κεῖσαι, λέγων ὡς οὐκ ἀσφαλὲς[3] ἐν ἰδιωτικῇ οἰκίᾳ πολλὰ χρήματα εἶναι. καὶ ἔδοσαν Ἀθηναῖοι· νουθετηθεὶς δ' ὑπὸ τῶν

---

[1] γενέσθαι after ἀνάστατον deleted by Dindorf.
[2] τῶν added by Musurus.
[3] ἀσφαλὲς C: ἀσφαλὲς ὂν A (so Meineke, Kaibel, deleting λέγων). It is possible that both λέγων and ὂν are right; Kühner-Gerth ii. 94-95.

---

[a] Voss 37.
[b] This story is accepted as true by Boeckh-Fränkel, *Staatshaushaltung*, i. 566, rejecting the other story, invented to explain the epithet λακκόπλουτος, as told in Suid. *s.v.*, *cf.* Plut. *Arist.* 5 and Aristodemus, J. 2 A 501. The Persian

as Heracleides of Pontus in his tract *On Pleasure* records [a] some strange facts about him, I will take up the relation of them from the beginning. " It was at the time when the Persians made their first expedition into Euboea,[b] they say, that a man of Eretria named Diomnestus came into possession of the commanding officer's money. For the officer,[c] as it happened, had pitched his tent in the field which belonged to Diomnestus and had stored the money in one of the rooms of his house. When they all died, Diomnestus remained in possession of the gold without the knowledge of anyone else. When, however, the Persian king again dispatched his army to Eretria, with orders to destroy the city utterly, of course all who were rich in funds sent these to a place of safety. Accordingly, the survivors of Diomnestus's family sent their money to Athens for safe keeping with Hipponicus, nicknamed Ammon, the son of Callias. On the removal by the Persians of all the Eretrians,[d] bag and baggage, this money was retained by Hipponicus and Callias, being considerable in amount. Hence the Hipponicus who was descended [e] from the recipient of the deposit begged of the Athenians on one occasion a place on the Acropolis where he might cause to be built a storehouse for the funds, saying that it was not safe for so much money to lie in a private house ; and the Athenians granted permission ; but being warned against this by his friends,

---

inroads occurred in 490 and 480 B.C., Hdt. vi. 100 and viii. 4. There is no record of an earlier invasion, and Grote thinks this story of Heracleides a myth, *Hist. of Greece*, chap. xxxvi.; P.-W. viii. 1908.   [c] The Persian Datis?

   [d] From Euboea to Ecbatana. See the fine epigram, attributed to Plato, on the " Babylonian captivity " of the Eretrians, *Anth. Pal.* vii. 256.   [e] He was his grandson.

φίλων μετενόησεν. τούτων οὖν τῶν[1] χρημάτω
Καλλίας κύριος γενόμενος καὶ πρὸς ἡδονὴν βιώσα
(ποῖοι γὰρ οὐ κόλακες ἢ τί πλῆθος οὐχ ἑταίρω

c περὶ αὐτὸν ἦσαν, ποίας δὲ δαπάνας οὐχ ὑπερεώρ
᾿κεῖνος[2];) ἀλλ᾿ ὅμως εἰς τοσοῦτον αὐτὸν περι
έστησεν ὁ περὶ ἡδονὴν βίος ὥστε μετὰ γραδίο
βαρβάρου διατελεῖν ἠναγκάσθη καὶ τῶν ἀναγκαίω
τῶν καθ᾿ ἡμέραν ἐνδεὴς γενόμενος τὸν βίον ἐτε
λεύτησεν. τὸν δὲ Νικίου,᾿᾿ φησί, ᾿᾿ τοῦ Περγασῆθε
πλοῦτον ἢ τὸν Ἰσχομάχου τίνες ἀπώλεσαν; οὐ
Αὐτοκλέης καὶ Ἐπικλέης, οἳ μετ᾿ ἀλλήλων ζῆ
προελόμενοι καὶ πάντ᾿ ἐν ἐλάττονι ποιούμενοι τῆ
ἡδονῆς, ἐπειδὴ πάντα κατανάλωσαν, κώνειο
πιόντες ἅμα τὸν βίον ἐτελεύτησαν[4];᾿᾿

d Περὶ δὲ τῆς Ἀλεξάνδρου τοῦ πάνυ τρυφῆ
Ἔφιππος μὲν ὁ Ὀλύνθιος ἐν τῷ περὶ τῆς Ἡφαι
στίωνος καὶ Ἀλεξάνδρου Τελευτῆς φησιν ὅτι ἐν τ
παραδείσῳ ἔκειτο αὐτῷ χρυσοῦς θρόνος καὶ κλῖνα
ἀργυρόποδες, ἐφ᾿ ὧν καθεζόμενος ἐχρημάτιζε μετε
τῶν ἑταίρων. Νικοβούλη δέ φησιν ὅτι παρὰ τ
δεῖπνον πάντες οἱ ἀγωνισταὶ ἐσπούδαζον τέρπει
τὸν βασιλέα καὶ ὅτι ἐν τῷ τελευταίῳ δείπνῳ αὐτὸ
ὁ Ἀλέξανδρος ἐπεισόδιόν τι μνημονεύσας[5] ἐκ τῆ
Εὐριπίδου Ἀνδρομέδας ἠγωνίσατο καὶ τὸν ἄκρατο

e προθύμως προπίνων καὶ τοὺς ἄλλους ἠνάγκαζε
Ἔφιππος δέ φησιν ὡς Ἀλέξανδρος καὶ τὰς ἱερὰ

---

[1] τῶν CE: ὄντων A.   [2] κεῖνος A.   [3] CE: κώνιον A
[4] ἐτελεύτησαν Schweighäuser: κατανάλωσαν· ἐτελεύτησαν A
ἀπέθανον alone CE.
[5] ἀπομνημονεύσας Kaibel.   But see Bekker, Anecd. 436. 1

---

[a] Third of the name, born ca. 455 B.C. ; his house is th
scene of Plato's Protagoras, above, 506 f (p. 276).

he changed his mind. So Callias[a] became the possessor of this money and lived for pleasure. What flatterers, indeed, what crowds of companions did not gather about him ! What lavish expenses did he not treat with careless disdain ![b] But nevertheless his life of pleasure brought him to such a reversal of circumstances that he was compelled to live alone with a poor old woman of foreign birth, and died at last in need of the commonest necessities.[c] Who was it that lost the fortune of Nicias of Pergasê,[d] or that of Ischomachus[e] ? Was it not Autocles and Epicles, who elected to live in company with each other and regarded everything as of less consequence than pleasure, and who then, after they had squandered all, drank hemlock and died together ? "

Speaking of Alexander the Great's luxury, Ephippus of Olynthus in his book *On the Death of Hephaestion and Alexander* says[f] that in the park there was erected for him a golden throne and couches with silver legs, on which he sat when transacting business in the company of his boon companions. And Nicobulê says[g] that during dinner every sort of contestant exerted their efforts to entertain the king, and that in the course of his last dinner Alexander in person acted from memory a scene from the *Andromeda* of Euripides, and pledging toasts in unmixed wine with zest compelled the others also to do likewise. Ephippus, again, says[h] that Alexander also wore the sacred vest-

---

[b] He is beginning to "moult," being "plucked by the women," in Aristoph. *Av.* 284 (414 b.c.), see Schol. *ad loc.*
[c] *Cf.* Schol. Aristoph. *Eccl.* 805. Ael. *V.H.* iv. 23 speaks of suicide.
[d] Not the famous commander of the Sicilian expedition.
[e] See Lys. *Or.* xix. 46. [f] *Scr. Al. M.* 125, J. 2 B 666.
[g] *Scr. Al. M.* 157, J. 2 B 667. [h] *Scr. Al. M.* 157, J. 2 B 666.

ἐσθῆτας ἐφόρει ἐν τοῖς δείπνοις, ὁτὲ μὲν τὴν τοῦ
Ἄμμωνος πορφυρίδα καὶ περισχιδεῖς[1] καὶ κέρατα
καθάπερ ὁ θεός, ὁτὲ δὲ τὴν τῆς Ἀρτέμιδος, ἣν καὶ
ἐπὶ τοῦ ἅρματος ἐφόρει πολλάκις, ἔχων τὴν Περσικὴν στολήν, ὑποφαίνων ἄνωθεν τῶν ὤμων τό
τε τόξον καὶ τὴν σιβύνην, ἐνίοτε δὲ καὶ τὴν τοῦ
Ἑρμοῦ· τὰ μὲν ἄλλα σχεδὸν καὶ καθ᾿ ἑκάστην
ἡμέραν χλαμύδα τε πορφυρᾶν καὶ χιτῶνα μεσό-
λευκον καὶ τὴν καυσίαν ἔχουσαν τὸ διάδημα τὸ
f βασιλικόν, ἐν δὲ τῇ συνουσίᾳ τά τε πέδιλα καὶ τὸν
πέτασον ἐπὶ τῇ κεφαλῇ καὶ τὸ κηρύκειον ἐν τῇ
χειρί, πολλάκις δὲ καὶ λεοντῆν καὶ ῥόπαλον ὥσπερ
ὁ Ἡρακλῆς. τί οὖν θαυμαστὸν εἰ καὶ καθ᾿ ἡμᾶς
Κόμμοδος ὁ αὐτοκράτωρ ἐπὶ τῶν ὀχημάτων παρα-
κείμενον εἶχεν τὸ Ἡράκλειον ῥόπαλον ὑπεστρωμέ-
νης αὐτῷ λεοντῆς καὶ Ἡρακλῆς καλεῖσθαι ἤθελεν,
Ἀλεξάνδρου τοῦ Ἀριστοτελικοῦ τοσούτοις αὐτὸν
ἀφομοιοῦντος θεοῖς, ἀτὰρ καὶ τῇ Ἀρτέμιδι;
ἔρρανε[2] δὲ ὁ Ἀλέξανδρος καὶ μύρῳ σπουδαίῳ καὶ
538 οἴνῳ εὐώδει τὸ δάπεδον.[3] ἐθυμιᾶτο δὲ αὐτῷ
σμύρνα καὶ τὰ ἄλλα θυμιάματα· εὐφημία τε[4] καὶ
σιγὴ κατεῖχε πάντας ὑπὸ δέους τοὺς παρόντας.
ἀφόρητος γὰρ ἦν καὶ φονικός. ἐδόκει γὰρ εἶναι
μελαγχολικός. ἐν Ἐκβατάνοις δὲ ποιήσας τῷ
Διονύσῳ θυσίαν καὶ πάντων δαψιλῶς ἐν τῇ θοίνῃ

---

[1] περισχιδῆ CE: read λεπτοσχιδεῖς?   [2] CE: ἔρανε A.
[3] δάκρυον C (!).   [4] δὲ CE.

---

[a] Since the περισχιδεῖς are said by Phot. and Hesych. to
have been worn by slaves, perhaps we should read λεπτοσχιδεῖς, described as a handsomely embroidered shoe by the
comic poet Cephisodorus, Kock i. 801.

430

ments at his dinner-parties, at one time putting on the purple robe of Ammon, and thin slippers *a* and horns just like the god's,*b* at another time the costume of Artemis, which he often wore even in his chariot, wearing the Persian garb and showing above the shoulders the bow and hunting-spear of the goddess, while at still other times he was garbed in the costume of Hermes; on other occasions as a rule, and in everyday use, he wore a purple riding-cloak, a purple tunic with white stripes,*c* and the Macedonian hat with the royal fillet; but on social occasions he wore the winged sandals and broad-brimmed hat on his head, and carried the caduceus in his hand *d*; yet often, again, he bore the lion's skin and club in imitation of Heracles. What wonder, then, that the Emperor Commodus of our time *e* also had the club of Hercules lying beside him in his chariot with the lion's skin spread out beneath him, and desired to be called Hercules, seeing that Alexander, Aristotle's pupil, got himself up like so many gods, to say nothing of the goddess Artemis? Alexander sprinkled the very floor with valuable perfumes and scented wine. In his honour myrrh and other kinds of incense went up in smoke; a religious stillness and silence born of fear held fast all who were in his presence. For he was hot-tempered and murderous, reputed, in fact, to be melancholy-mad. At Ecbatana he arranged a festival in honour of Dionysus, everything being supplied at the feast

---

b The ram-horned god of Egyptian Thebes; see the horned head of Alexander on a coin, Roscher, *Lex. Myth.* i. 290.

c Q. Curt. iii. 3. 17 "purpureae tunicae medium album intextum erat," Athen. 215 c (vol. ii. p. 474).

d All these are the attributes of Hermes.

e See vol. i. p. ix, and the long list of his titles in Dio Cass. lxxii. 15. 5, including Ῥωμαῖος Ἡρακλῆς.

ATHENAEUS

παρασκευασθέντων, καὶ Σατραβάτης ὁ σατράπης
τοὺς στρατιώτας εἱστίασε πάντας. ἀθροισθέντων
δὲ πολλῶν ἐπὶ τὴν θέαν, φησὶν ὁ Ἔφιππος, κηρύγ-
ματα ἐγίνετο ὑπερήφανα καὶ τῆς Περσικῆς ὑπερ-
οψίας αὐθαδέστερα. ἄλλων γὰρ ἄλλο τι ἀνακηρυτ-
τόντων καὶ στεφανούντων τὸν Ἀλέξανδρον, εἷς τις
τῶν ὁπλοφυλάκων[1] ὑπερπεπαικὼς πᾶσαν κολακείαν
κοινωσάμενος τῷ Ἀλεξάνδρῳ ἐκέλευσε τὸν κήρυκα
ἀνειπεῖν ὅτι " Γόργος ὁ ὁπλοφύλαξ Ἀλέξανδρον
Ἄμμωνος υἱὸν στεφανοῖ χρυσοῖς τρισχιλίοις, καὶ
ὅταν Ἀθήνας πολιορκῇ, μυρίαις πανοπλίαις καὶ
τοῖς ἴσοις καταπέλταις καὶ πᾶσι τοῖς ἄλλοις βέλεσιν
εἰς τὸν πόλεμον ἱκανοῖς."

Χάρης δ' ἐν τῇ δεκάτῃ τῶν περὶ Ἀλέξανδρον
Ἱστοριῶν " ὅτε," φησίν, " εἷλε Δαρεῖον, γάμους
συνετέλεσεν ἑαυτοῦ τε καὶ τῶν ἄλλων φίλων,
ἐνενήκοντα καὶ δύο[2] θαλάμους κατασκευασάμενος
ἐν τῷ αὐτῷ τόπῳ. ἦν δὲ ὁ οἶκος ἑκατοντάκλινος,
ἐν ᾧ ἑκάστη ἦν κλίνη κεκοσμημένη στολῇ γαμικῇ
εἴκοσι μνῶν ἀργυρᾶ[3]· ἡ δὲ αὐτοῦ χρυσόπους ἦν.
συμπαρέλαβεν δὲ εἰς τὸ συμπόσιον καὶ τοὺς ἰδιοξέ-
νους ἅπαντας καὶ κατέκλινεν ἀντιπροσώπους ἑαυτῷ
τε καὶ τοῖς ἄλλοις νυμφίοις, τὴν δὲ[4] λοιπὴν δύναμιν

---

[1] Schweighäuser: ὀπισθοφυλάκων A.
[2] καὶ δύο om. C and Aelian.
[3] CE: ἀργυρᾶι A, ἀργυρόπους Aelian.
[4] Kaibel: τε ACE.

---

[a] This name of the Median prince whose daughter was
married to Perdiccas occurs only here; the mss. of Arrian
Anab. have Ἀτροβάτης or Ἀτροπάτης (the correct form),
432

with lavish expense, and Satrabates[a] the satrap entertained all the troops. Many gathered to see the sight, says Ephippus[b]; proclamations were made which were exceedingly boastful and more insolent than the usual Persian arrogance. For among the various proclamations made at the crowning of Alexander, one man in particular, a custodian of munitions, overstepped all the bounds of flattery and, in collusion with Alexander, he bade the herald proclaim that " Gorgus, the custodian of munitions, presented Alexander, son of Ammon, with three thousand gold pieces,[c] and promised that whenever he should besiege Athens he would give him ten thousand complete suits of armour, the same number of catapults, and all other missiles besides, enough to prosecute the war."

Chares in the tenth book of his *Histories of Alexander* says[d] : " When he overcame Darius, he concluded marriages of himself and of his friends besides, constructing ninety-two bridal chambers in the same place. The structure was large enough for a hundred couches, and in it every couch was adorned with nuptial coverings, and was made of silver worth twenty minae[e] ; but his own couch had supports of gold. He also included in his invitation to the banquet all his personal friends[f] and placed them on couches opposite himself and the other bridegrooms, while the

Diod. xviii. 3 Ἀτράπης (=Ἀτροπάτης), Justin xiii. 4 Atropatos. The year of this event is 324 B.C.
  [b] *Scr. Al. M.* 125, J. 2 B 666.
  [c] *i.e.* staters, considerably over 3000 guineas in all.
  [d] *Scr. Al. M.* 118, J. 2 B 659, Aelian, *V.H.* viii. 7.
  [e] About £75 in bullion value.
  [f] The word ἰδιόξενοι refers to friends who were not fellow-countrymen, but of foreign birth.

433

πεζήν τε καὶ[1] ναυτικὴν καὶ τὰς πρεσβείας καὶ τοὺς
d παρεπιδημοῦντας ἐν τῇ αὐλῇ. κατεσκεύαστο δὲ ὁ
οἶκος πολυτελῶς καὶ μεγαλοπρεπῶς ἱματίοις τε καὶ
ὀθονίοις πολυτελέσιν, ὑπὸ δὲ ταῦτα πορφυροῖς καὶ
φοινικοῖς χρυσουφέσιν. τοῦ δὲ μένειν τὴν σκηνὴν
ὑπέκειντο κίονες εἰκοσαπήχεις περίχρυσοι καὶ
διάλιθοι καὶ περιάργυροι. περιεβέβληντο δὲ ἐν τῷ
περιβόλῳ πολυτελεῖς αὐλαῖαι ζῳωτοὶ καὶ διάχρυσοι,
κανόνας ἔχουσαι περιχρύσους καὶ περιαργύρους.
τῆς δ' αὐλῆς ἦν τὸ περίμετρον στάδιοι τέσσαρες.
ἐγίνετο δὲ τὰ δεῖπνα πρὸς σάλπιγγα τότε μὲν ἐν
τοῖς γάμοις, καὶ ἄλλως δ' αἰεὶ ὅτε τύχοι σπονδο-
e ποιούμενος,[2] ὥστε πᾶν εἰδέναι τὸ στρατόπεδον.
ἐπὶ πέντε δὲ ἡμέρας ἐπετελέσθησαν οἱ γάμοι,
καὶ ἐλειτούργησαν πάνυ πολλοὶ καὶ βαρβάρων καὶ
Ἑλλήνων, καὶ οἱ ἀπὸ τῆς Ἰνδικῆς θαυματοποιοὶ
ἦσαν διαπρέποντες, ἔτι δὲ[3] Σκύμνος Ταραντῖνος καὶ
Φιλιστίδης Συρακόσιος Ἡράκλειτός τε ὁ Μιτυ-
ληναῖος· μεθ' οὓς ἐπεδείξατο ῥαψῳδὸς Ἄλεξις
Ταραντῖνος. παρῆλθον δὲ καὶ φιλοκιθαρισταὶ
Κρατῖνος Μηθυμναῖος, Ἀριστώνυμος Ἀθηναῖος,
f Ἀθηνόδωρος Τήιος· ἐκιθαρῴδησαν δὲ Ἡράκλειτός
τε ὁ Ταραντῖνος καὶ Ἀριστοκράτης ὁ Θηβαῖος.
αὐλῳδοὶ δὲ παρῆλθον Διονύσιος ὁ Ἡρακλεώτης,
Ὑπέρβολος Κυζικηνός· παρῆλθον δὲ καὶ αὐληταί, οἳ

---

[1] ἱππικὴν καὶ added by Kaibel from Aelian. But it is even
more necessary to add Ἕλληνας with τοὺς παρεπιδημοῦντας
from the same source.
[2] Dindorf: σπενδοποιούμενος A.
[3] ἔτι δὲ added by Gulick.

---

[a] i.e. the Greeks who happened to be visiting the city,
Aelian viii. 7.   [b] About half a mile.

rest of his forces, both land and naval, he entertained in the courtyard with the foreign embassies and tourists.[a] Moreover the structure was decorated sumptuously and magnificently with expensive draperies and fine linens, and underfoot with purple and crimson rugs interwoven with gold. To keep the pavilion firmly in place there were columns thirty feet high, gilded and silvered and studded with jewels. The entire enclosure was surrounded with rich curtains having animal patterns interwoven in gold, their rods being overlaid with gold and silver. The perimeter of the courtyard measured four stadia.[b] The call to dinner was sounded on the trumpet, not only at the time of the nuptial banquets, but always when on other occasions he chanced to be making libation, so that the entire army knew what was going on. The nuptials lasted for five days, and very many persons, foreigners as well as Greeks, contributed their services; for example, the jugglers from India were especially noteworthy; also Scymnus of Tarentum, Philistides of Syracuse, and Heracleitus of Mitylene[c]; after them the rhapsode Alexis of Tarentum gave a recital. There appeared also the harp-virtuosi Cratinus of Methymna,[d] Aristonymus of Athens, Athenodorus of Teos; there were songs with harp-accompaniment by Heracleitus of Tarentum and Aristocrates of Thebes. The singers to flute-accompaniment who appeared were Dionysius of Heracleia and Hyperbolus of Cyzicus; there came on also flute-

[c] See Athen. 20 a (vol. i. p. 86). Aelian *loc. cit.* does not mention them by name, but says that the Indians surpassed the jugglers from all other countries.

[d] A coin of Methymna in the Cabinet des Médailles, Paris, is noteworthy for the handsome hexachord cithara there depicted, *Encycl. de la musique* (Lavignac), i. 416.

πρῶτον τὸ Πυθικὸν ηὔλησαν, εἶθ' ἑξῆς μετὰ τῶν
χορῶν, Τιμόθεος, Φρύνιχος, Καφισίας,[1] Διόφαντος,
ἔτι δὲ Εὔιος ὁ Χαλκιδεύς. καὶ ἔκτοτε οἱ πρότερον καλούμενοι Διονυσοκόλακες Ἀλεξανδροκόλακες
ἐκλήθησαν διὰ τὰς τῶν δώρων ὑπερβολάς, ἐφ' οἷς
καὶ ἥσθη ὁ Ἀλέξανδρος.[2] ὑπεκρίθησαν δὲ τραγῳδοὶ
μὲν Θεσσαλὸς καὶ Ἀθηνόδωρος καὶ Ἀριστόκριτος,
539 κωμῳδοὶ δὲ Λύκων καὶ Φορμίων καὶ Ἀρίστων,
παρῆν δὲ καὶ Φασίμηλος[3] ὁ ψάλτης. οἱ δὲ
πεμφθέντες," φησί, " στέφανοι[4] ὑπὸ τῶν πρεσβευτῶν
καὶ τῶν λοιπῶν ταλάντων ἦσαν μυρίων πεντακισχιλίων."

Πολύκλειτος δ' ὁ Λαρισαῖος ἐν τῇ ὀγδόῃ τῶν
Ἱστοριῶν καὶ ἐπὶ χρυσῆς κλίνης κοιμᾶσθαί φησι
τὸν Ἀλέξανδρον καὶ αὐλητρίδας αὐτῷ καὶ αὐλη-
τὰς αἰεὶ ἕπεσθαι ἐπὶ τὸ στρατόπεδον καὶ πίνειν
b ἄχρι τῆς ἕω. Κλέαρχος δ' ἐν τοῖς περὶ Βίων περὶ
Δαρείου λέγων τοῦ καθαιρεθέντος ὑπὸ τοῦ Ἀλεξάνδρου φησίν· " ὁ Περσῶν βασιλεὺς ἀθλοθετῶν
τοῖς τὰς ἡδονὰς αὐτῷ πορίζουσιν[5] ὑπὸ πάντων τῶν
ἡδέων ἡττωμένην ἀπέδειξε τὴν βασιλείαν καὶ κατα-
γωνιζόμενος ἑαυτὸν οὐκ ἤσθετο πρότερον ἢ τὸ

[1] 629 b: σκαφισίας A.
[2] καὶ ἔκτοτε . . . ὁ Ἀλέξανδρος should have been placed
after 538 b (Kaibel). But this is equally true of the last
sentence in the paragraph (οἱ δὲ . . . πεντακισχιλίων). C, as
usual, has διονυσιοκόλακες.
[3] Φρασίμηλος or Φρασίδαμος (?) Kaibel.
[4] C adds τηνικαῦτα after στέφανοι, perhaps rightly.
[5] Kaibel: γνωρίζουσιν ACE. The citation from Clearchus
is rightly placed by C at the end of 540 a.

[a] In 586 B.C. (Paus. x. 7. 3) or 582 (Sandys, Pindar, L.C.L.
p. xxvii note 2) flute contests were added at Delphi to those
with the lyre, and it was allowable to render the " Pythian

virtuosi, who first played the Pythian melody [a] and after that accompaniments for the bands of singers and dancers; they were Timotheus,[b] Phrynichus, Caphisias,[c] Diophantus, and Evius of Chalcis. And from that day forth the people who had previously been called 'Dionysus-flatterers' were called 'Alexander-flatterers' because of the extravagant presents in which Alexander took such delight.[d] Plays were acted by the tragedians Thessalus, Athenodorus, and Aristocritus, and by the comedians Lycon, Phormion, and Ariston. There was present also the harper Phasimelus.[e] The crowns (Chares says) brought by the ambassadors and others were worth 15,000 talents."

Polycleitus of Larisa, in the eighth book of his *Histories*, says [f] that Alexander slept upon a golden couch, and that flute-players, female and male alike, always accompanied him to camp and drank with him until daybreak. Clearchus, in his volumes *On Lives*, speaking of the Darius who was conquered by Alexander, says [g]: "The Persian king gave prizes to those who catered to his pleasures, but brought his kingdom to defeat through all these indulgences, and did not perceive that he was defeating himself until

nomos," or hymn which celebrated Apollo's victory over the Python, by the flute,—a kind of mimetic "programme-music," *cf.* Strabo p. 421 ἀποδώσοντάς τι μέλος ὃ καλεῖται νόμος Πυθικός.   [b] See Athen. 565 a.   [c] Athen. 629 a.
[d] On the "courtiers of Dionysus" (=actors) see Athen. 249 f (vol. i. p. 124), 254 b, 435 e (vol. iv. p. 472), and Aristot. *Rhet.* iii. 2. 10 with Cope's note. Plato's followers also were called "Dionysus-flatterers" by Epicurus, Diog. Laert. x. 8. See critical note 2.   [e] This name occurs only here.
[f] *Scr. Al. M.* 132, J. 2 B 668.
[g] *F.H.G.* ii. 309, *cf.* above, 514 e, 529 d. The remarks about Darius interrupt the account of Alexander.

σκῆπτρον ἕτεροι λαβόντες ἀνεκηρύχθησαν." Φύλ
αρχος δ' ἐν τῇ τρίτῃ καὶ εἰκοστῇ τῶν Ἱστοριῶν
καὶ Ἀγαθαρχίδης ὁ Κνίδιος ἐν τῷ δεκάτῳ περ
c Ἀσίας καὶ τοὺς ἑταίρους φησὶ τοὺς Ἀλεξάνδρο
ὑπερβαλλούσῃ τρυφῇ χρήσασθαι. ὧν εἷς ὢν κα
Ἄγνων χρυσοῦς ἥλους ἐν ταῖς κρηπῖσι[1] ἐφόρει
Κλεῖτος δ' ὁ Λευκὸς καλούμενος ὅτε χρηματίζει
μέλλοι, ἐπὶ πορφυρῶν ἱματίων διαπεριπατῶν τοῖς
ἐντυγχάνουσιν διελέγετο. Περδίκκᾳ δὲ καὶ Κρα
τερῷ φιλογυμναστοῦσιν ἠκολούθουν διφθέραι στα
διαῖαι τοῖς μεγέθεσιν, ὑφ' αἷς περιλαμβάνοντες[2]
τόπον ἐν ταῖς καταστρατοπεδείαις[3] ἐγυμνάζοντο
ἠκολούθει δὲ αὐτοῖς καὶ ὑποζύγια πολλὰ τὰ τὴ
κόνιν κομίζοντα πρὸς τὴν ἐν τῇ παλαίστρᾳ χρείαν
d Λεοννάτῳ δὲ καὶ Μενελάῳ φιλοκυνήγοις οὖσι
αὐλαῖαι σταδίων ἑκατὸν ἠκολούθουν, αἷς περι
ιστάντες τὰς θήρας ἐκυνήγουν. τὰς δὲ χρυσᾶ
πλατάνους καὶ τὴν χρυσῆν ἄμπελον ὑφ' ἣν ο
Περσῶν βασιλεῖς ἐχρημάτιζον πολλάκις καθήμενοι
σμαραγδίνους βότρυς ἔχουσαν[4] καὶ τῶν Ἰνδικῶ
ἀνθράκων ἄλλων τε παντοδαπῶν λίθων ὑπερβαλ
λόντων ταῖς πολυτελείαις, ἐλάττω[5] φησὶν ὁ Φύλ
αρχος φαίνεσθαι τῆς καθ' ἡμέραν ἑκάστοτε[6] γινο
μένης παρ' Ἀλεξάνδρῳ δαπάνης. ἦν γὰρ αὐτο

[1] The gloss καὶ τοῖς ὑποδήμασιν after κρηπῖσι om. by Plutarcl
and Aelian, bracketed by Kaibel.
[2] καταλαμβάνοντες C.   [3] CE: καταστρατοπεδιαῖς A.
[4] Schweighäuser: ἐχούσας ACE.   The καὶ following is
probably a mistake for ἐκ, but συντεθειμένους is also required
(cf. 514 f).   [5] ἐλάττους C.   [6] ἑκάστοτε om. C

[a] F.H.G. i. 345, J. 2 A 172.
[b] F.H.G. iii. 196, J. 2 A 207, cf. Aelian ix. 3.
[c] Hagnon of Teos, Plut. Alex. 40.

others had seized his sceptre and were proclaimed rulers." Phylarchus in the twenty-third book of his *Histories* [a] and Agatharchides of Cnidus in the tenth book of his work *On Asia* [b] say that Alexander's courtiers also indulged in extravagant luxury. One of these was Agnon,[c] who wore gold studs in his military boots. Whenever Cleitus, who was called the White, had business to transact, he walked about on purple cloths while conversing with those who had audience with him. Likewise Perdiccas and Craterus, who were lovers of gymnastic sports, always had in their train piles of goatskins that would fill a stadium,[d] under cover of which, after appropriating a place in the encampments, they would carry on their exercise; they were also followed by a long train of animals [e] carrying sand to be used in the wrestling-school. Again, Leonnatus and Menelaus, who were fond of hunting, had in their luggage curtains measuring a hundred stadia,[f] with which they surrounded the hunting-grounds and pursued the quarry. Moreover, the famous plane-trees of gold, even the golden vine under which the Persian kings often sat and held court, with its clusters of green crystals [g] and rubies from India and other gems of every description, exceedingly costly though they were, appeared to be of less worth, says Phylarchus, than the expense lavished daily on all occasions at Alexander's court. For his pavilion alone contained

---

[d] *i.e.* there were so many of them that when spread out they covered 600 feet, which compares well with the Big Tent in a modern circus.

[e] Camels, according to Plut. *Alex.* 40.

[f] About 12 miles.

[g] Emeralds? *Cf.* Athen. 94 b (vol. i. p. 405 note *a*), and above, 514 f (p. 314).

ἡ σκηνὴ κλινῶν ρ΄, χρυσοῖ δὲ κίονες ν΄ κατεῖχον
e αὐτήν. οἱ δὲ ὑπερτείνοντες οὐρανίσκοι διάχρυσοι
ποικίλμασιν ἐκπεπονημένοι[1] πολυτελέσιν ἐσκέπαζον
τὸν ἄνω τόπον. καὶ πρῶτοι μὲν Πέρσαι φ΄ μηλο-
φόροι περὶ αὐτὴν ἐντὸς εἱστήκεσαν πορφυραῖς
καὶ μηλίναις ἐσθῆσιν ἐξησκημένοι· μετὰ δὲ τούτους τοξόται τὸν ἀριθμὸν χίλιοι, οἱ μὲν φλόγινα
ἐνδεδυκότες, οἱ δὲ ὑσγινοβαφῆ,[2] πολλοὶ δὲ καὶ
κυάνεα εἶχον περιβόλαια. προειστήκεσαν δὲ τούτων ἀργυράσπιδες Μακεδόνες πεντακόσιοι. κατὰ
δὲ μέσην τὴν σκηνὴν χρυσοῦς ἐτίθετο δίφρος, ἐφ᾽
οὗ καθήμενος ἐχρημάτιζεν ὁ Ἀλέξανδρος τῶν σω-
f ματοφυλάκων πανταχόθεν ἐφεστηκότων. ἔξωθεν
δὲ κύκλῳ τῆς σκηνῆς τὸ τῶν ἐλεφάντων ἄγημα
διεσκευασμένον ἐφειστήκει[3] καὶ Μακεδόνες χίλιοι
Μακεδονικὰς στολὰς ἔχοντες, εἶτα μύριοι Πέρσαι,
τό τε τὴν πορφύραν ἔχον πλῆθος εἰς πεντακοσίους
ἦν, οἷς Ἀλέξανδρος ἔδωκε φορεῖν τὴν στολὴν ταύτην. τοσούτων δὲ ὄντων καὶ τῶν φίλων καὶ τῶν
θεραπευόντων οὐδεὶς ἐτόλμα προσπορεύεσθαι Ἀλεξ-
άνδρῳ· τοιοῦτον ἐγεγόνει τὸ περὶ αὐτὸν ἀξίωμα.
ἔγραψεν δὲ καί ποτε[4] Ἀλέξανδρος ταῖς[5] ἐν Ἰωνίᾳ
πόλεσιν καὶ πρώτοις Χίοις, ὅπως αὐτῷ πορφύραν
540 ἀποστείλωσιν. ἤθελεν γὰρ τοὺς ἑταίρους ἅπαντας
ἁλουργὰς ἐνδῦσαι στολάς. ἀναγνωσθείσης δὲ τῆς
ἐπιστολῆς Χίοις παρὼν Θεόκριτος ὁ σοφιστὴς[6] νῦν
ἐγνωκέναι ἔφη τὸ παρ᾽ Ὁμήρῳ εἰρημένον·

---

[1] Perizonius (cf. Aelian, V.H. ix. 3, Polyaenus iv. 3):
ἐκπεμπόμενοι A. [2] CE: ὑσσινοβαφῆ A.
[3] CE: ἐφεστήκει. [4] καί ποτε Kaibel: καὶ τότε A.
[5] ταῖς Musurus: καὶ ταῖς A.
[6] Valois and lemma in A: σοφὸς ACE.

a hundred couches and was supported by fifty golden uprights. The canopies stretched over the upper part to cover the whole were elaborately worked with gold in sumptuous embroideries. Inside, all round it, stood first of all five hundred Persians, Apple-bearers,[a] with gay uniforms of purple and quince-yellow; after them bowmen to the number of a thousand, some dressed in flame-colour, others in crimson; but many, too, had mantles of dark blue. At the head of these stood five hundred Silver-Shields,[b] Macedonians. In the centre of the pavilion was placed a golden chair, sitting on which Alexander held court with his bodyguard stationed close on all sides. Outside the tent the elephant-division was posted near in a circle with full equipment, also a thousand Macedonians in Macedonian uniform, next ten thousand Persians, and the large body, amounting to five hundred, who wore the purple; for Alexander had granted them the privilege of wearing this garment. And the number of his friends and servitors being so great, no one dared to approach Alexander; such was the majesty associated with his person. On one occasion Alexander actually wrote to the cities in Ionia, and first of all the Chians, directing them to dispatch purple dye to him. For he wanted to dress all his friends in garments dyed with sea-purple. When the letter was read to the Chians in the presence of the sophist Theocritus, he declared that now at last he understood the meaning of the

---

[a] See above, 514 b (p. 312).
[b] A special body of Macedonians, Polyb. v. 79. 4, Diod. xvii. 57, Arrian, *Anab.* vii. 11. 3, Aelian, *V.H.* ix. 3; Bevan, *House of Seleucus* ii. 285.

ἔλαβε πορφύρεος θάνατος καὶ μοῖρα κραταιή.

Ἀντίοχον δὲ τὸν Γρυπὸν ἐπικαλούμενον βασιλέα
φησὶ Ποσειδώνιος ἐν τῇ ὀγδόῃ καὶ εἰκοστῇ τῶν
Ἱστοριῶν τὰς ἐπὶ Δάφνῃ πανηγύρεις ἐπιτελοῦντα
b ὑποδοχὰς λαμπρὰς ἐπιτελεῖν.[1] ἐν αἷς τὸ μὲν πρῶτον ἀναδόσεις ἐγίγνοντο ὁλομελῶν βρωμάτων, εἶτ᾽
ἤδη καὶ ζώντων χηνῶν καὶ λαγωῶν[2] καὶ δορκάδων·
ἀνεδίδοντο δέ, φησίν, καὶ χρυσοῖ στέφανοι τοῖς
δειπνοῦσιν καὶ ἀργυρωμάτων πλῆθος καὶ θεραπόντων καὶ ἵππων καὶ καμήλων. ἔδει τε ἀναβάντα
ἐπὶ τὴν κάμηλον ἔκαστον πιεῖν καὶ λαβεῖν τὴν[3]
κάμηλον καὶ τὰ ἐπὶ τὴν κάμηλον καὶ τὸν παρ-
εστῶτα παῖδα. ἐν δὲ τῇ τεσσαρεσκαιδεκάτῃ περὶ
τοῦ ὁμωνύμου αὐτοῦ Ἀντιόχου λέγων τοῦ ἐπ᾽
c Ἀρσάκην εἰς Μηδίαν στρατεύσαντός φησιν ὅτι
ὑποδοχὰς ἐποιεῖτο καθ᾽ ἡμέραν ὀχλικάς· ἐν αἷς
χωρὶς τῶν ἀναλισκομένων καὶ ἐκφανιζομένων
σωρευμάτων ἔκαστος ἀπέφερε τῶν ἑστιατόρων
ὁλομελῆ κρέα χερσαίων τε καὶ πτηνῶν καὶ θαλαττίων ζώων ἀδιαίρετα ἐσκευασμένα, ἅμαξαν πλη-
ρῶσαι δυνάμενα· καὶ μετὰ ταῦτα μελιπήκτων καὶ
στεφάνων ἐκ σμύρνης καὶ λιβανωτοῦ σὺν[4] ἀνδρο-
μήκεσι λημνίσκων χρυσῶν πιλήμασιν πλήθη.

---

[1] ποιεῖσθαι would be better, cf. below and 210 e.
[2] λαγωιῶν A.
[3] λαβεῖν τὴν 210 e: λαβεῖν τε τὴν AC, λαβεῖν τήν τε Meineke.
[4] σὺν added from 210 d.

---

[a] Il. v. 83, of Hypsenor, whose arm had been cut off by
the sword of Eurypylus. "Purple" here of course means
"dark."

[b] F.H.G. iii. 263, J. 2 A 232, Athen. 210 e (vol. ii. p. 450).
These games at Daphne began soon after 120 B.C. Con-

verse in Homer,[a] " Purple death seized him, and a fate overpowering."

Poseidonius, in the twenty-eighth book of his *Histories*, says[b] that King Antiochus, nicknamed Grypus, held brilliant receptions when he celebrated the games at Daphne. In the course of them, he at the beginning made distributions of uncarved meats; afterwards of live geese, hares, and gazelles. There were also distributed to the diners, he says, gold wreaths and a great quantity of silver vessels, slaves, horses, and camels. And it was the duty of each man, after mounting his camel, to drink a toast and accept the camel and everything upon it as well as the attending slave. Again, in the fourteenth book Poseidonius tells about the ruler who bore the same name, the Antiochus,[c] that is, who conducted the campaign into Media against Arsaces, and says[d] that he held receptions every day to great crowds; on these occasions, not counting the heaps of food that were consumed or thrown out as waste scraps,[e] every one of the feasters would carry home uncarved meat of land-animals, fowls, and creatures of the sea prepared whole, and capable of filling a cart; and after all that, quantities of honey-cakes and wreaths of myrrh and frankincense with matted fillets of gold as long as a man.

cerning the hawk-nose of Antiochus VIII which gave him the nickname Grypus see Bevan, *House of Seleucus*, ii. 303.

[c] Antiochus VII Euergetes (Sidetes), Bevan, *op. cit.* ii. 242 ff.

[d] *F.H.G.* iii. 257, J. 2 A 227, Athen. 210 c-d, 439 e.

[e] *Cf.* Athen. 270 d (vol. iii. p. 214) ἐκφατνίσματα. The method of cooking here described is known in America as a barbecue, from the large iron frame (Spanish *barbacoa*) on which animals are roasted whole (*cf.* ὁλομελῆ, ἀδιαίρετα ἐσκευασμένα above).

Κλύτος δ' ὁ 'Αριστοτελικὸς ἐν τοῖς περὶ Μιλήτου Πολυκράτην φησὶ τὸν Σαμίων[1] τύραννον ὑπὸ
τρυφῆς τὰ πανταχόθεν[2] συνάγειν, κύνας μὲν ἐξ
d 'Ηπείρου, αἶγας δὲ ἐκ Σκύρου, ἐκ δὲ Μιλήτου
πρόβατα, ὗς δ' ἐκ Σικελίας. "Αλεξις δ' ἐν τρίτῳ
Σαμίων "Ωρων[3] ἐκ πολλῶν πόλεων φησιν κοσ-
μηθῆναι τὴν Σάμον ὑπὸ τοῦ Πολυκράτους, κύνας
μὲν Μολοττικὰς καὶ Λακαίνας εἰσαγαγόντος, αἶγας
δ' ἐκ Σκύρου καὶ Νάξου, πρόβατα δ' ἐκ Μιλήτου
καὶ τῆς 'Αττικῆς. μετεστέλλετο δέ, φησί, καὶ
τεχνίτας ἐπὶ μισθοῖς μεγίστοις. πρὸ δὲ τοῦ τυραν-
e νῆσαι κατασκευασάμενος στρωμνὰς πολυτελεῖς καὶ
ποτήρια ἐπέτρεπε χρῆσθαι τοῖς ἢ γάμον ἢ μείζονας[4]
ὑποδοχὰς ποιουμένοις.

'Εκ πάντων οὖν τούτων ἄξιον θαυμάζειν τὸν
τύραννον ὅτι οὐδαμόθεν ἀναγέγραπται γυναῖκας ἢ
παῖδας μεταπεμψάμενος, καίτοι περὶ τὰς τῶν ἀρ-
ρένων ὁμιλίας ἐπτοημένος, ὡς καὶ ἀντερᾶν 'Ανα-
κρέοντι τῷ ποιητῇ· ὅτε καὶ δι' ὀργὴν ἀπέκειρε τὸν
ἐρώμενον. πρῶτος δ' ὁ Πολυκράτης καὶ ναῦς
τινας[5] πήξας ἀπὸ τῆς πατρίδος Σαμαίνας[6] ἐκάλεσεν.
f Κλέαρχος δέ φησιν ὡς Πολυκράτης ὁ τῆς ἁβρᾶς
Σάμου τύραννος διὰ τὴν περὶ τὸν βίον ἀκολασίαν

---

[1] CE : σάμιον A.
[2] τὰ πανταχόθεν A : τὰ πάντα C, πάντα πανταχόθεν (?) Kaibel.
[3] Musurus : ὅρων A.   [4] μείζους CE.
[5] ναῦς τινας C : ναῦς A.
[6] Meineke (cf. Hesych. s. Σαμιακὸς τρόπος) : σαμίας ACE.

---

[a] F.H.G. ii. 333.
[b] On the excellence of Milesian wool see above, p. 338
note a, Verg. G. iii. 306, iv. 334.   [c] F.H.G. iv. 299.
[d] Cf. the case of the Megarian engineer Eupalinus, who
built the great tunnel in Samos, Hdt. iii. 60. So Pericles two
generations later, Lysias xii. 4.

Clytus the Aristotelian, in his work *On Miletus*, says [a] of Polycrates the tyrant of Samos that his instinct for luxury moved him to get together the special products of every country—hounds from Epeirus, goats from Scyros, sheep from Miletus,[b] and swine from Sicily. Alexis, too, in the third book of *Samian Chronicles* says [c] that Samos was enriched by Polycrates with the products of many cities: he imported Molossian and Laconian hounds, goats from Scyros and Naxos, and sheep from Miletus and Attica. He also encouraged, Alexis says, the immigration of artisans at very high wages.[d] Before he acquired supreme power he ordered the manufacture of sumptuous draperies and drinking-cups, and permitted them to be used by persons who were celebrating a wedding or holding unusually large [e] receptions.

In the light of all this, then, one must feel surprise that the tyrant is nowhere recorded as having summoned to his court women or boys, although he was passionately devoted to liaisons with males, so much so as to be a rival of the poet Anacreon; at that time he even cut off his favourite's hair in a burst of temper. Polycrates was the first man to build ships of the kind he called *Samainai*,[f] after the name of his country. Clearchus says [g]: "Polycrates, the tyrant of luxurious Samos, came to ruin on account of his

[e] The Greek has the comparative, "larger." Polycrates' policy seems to have changed later, "for he used to say that he could cause a friend more gratification by restoring what he had taken away from him than if he had never taken it at all," Hdt. iii. 39.

[f] Hesychius says that they had a beak shaped like a swine's snout. See critical notes 5 and 6.

[g] *F.H.G.* ii. 310; *cf.* above, 515 d (p. 318).

ἀπώλετο, ζηλώσας τὰ Λυδῶν μαλακά. ὅθεν τῷ
τ' ἐν Σάρδεσιν[1] Ἀγκῶνι Γλυκεῖ προσαγορευομένῳ
τὴν παρὰ τοῖς Σαμίοις λαύραν ἀντικατεσκεύασεν
ἐν τῇ πόλει καὶ τοῖς[2] Λυδῶν ἄνθεσιν ἀντέπλεξε[3] τὰ
διαγγελθέντα Σαμίων ἄνθεα. τούτων δὲ ἡ μὲν
Σαμίων λαύρα στενωπή[4] τις ἦν γυναικῶν δημιουργῶν πλήθουσα[5] καὶ τῶν πρὸς ἀπόλαυσιν καὶ
ἀκρασίαν πάντων βρωμάτων ὄντως ἐνέπλησε τὴν
541 Ἑλλάδα· τὰ δὲ Σαμίων ἄνθη γυναικῶν καὶ ἀνδρῶν
κάλλη διάφορα.[6] ἔτι δὲ τῆς συμπάσης πόλεως ἐν
ἑορταῖς τε καὶ μέθαις . . . καὶ ταῦτα μὲν ὁ Κλέαρχος. οἶδα δὲ κἀγὼ παρὰ τοῖς ἐμοῖς Ἀλεξανδρεῦσι
λαύραν τινὰ καλουμένην μέχρι καὶ νῦν Εὐδαιμόνων, ἐν ᾗ πάντα τὰ πρὸς ·τρυφὴν ἐπωλεῖτο.

Ἀλκισθένην δὲ τὸν Συβαρίτην φησὶν Ἀριστοτέλης ἐν τοῖς[7] Θαυμασίοις ὑπὸ τρυφῆς ἱμάτιον
τοιοῦτον κατασκευάσασθαι[8] τῇ πολυτελείᾳ ὡς

---

[1] τῷ τ' ἐν Σάρδεσιν Kaibel: τῷ μὲν Σάρδεων A, τῷ Σάρδεων
CE, τῷ τῶν Σάρδεων Eustath.

[2] τοῖς Kaibel (τοῖς τῶν Schweighäuser): τῶν (alone) A.

[3] Meineke: ἄνθεσι πάντ' ἔπλησε A.

[4] Toup: στενή ACE.

[5] πλήθουσα Eustath. and C (in a different construction):
om. A.

[6] εὐωχητήρια ("places of enjoyment") ἦν κάλλει διάφορα
(?) Kaibel.

[7] περὶ τρυφῆς after ἐν τοῖς deleted by Casaubon.

[8] Schweighäuser: κατασκευάσαι A, κατεσκεύασεν C (in a
different construction).

---

[a] A sort of " Midway Plaisance " or " Quartier latin ";
λαύρα is literally an alley.

[b] See the explanations of this name given above, p. 321.
The language of the quotation, with its play on the word
ἄνθεα (note the Ionic form) and its false antithesis, as
Schweighäuser remarks, is a true flosculus of Clearchus
(see above, p. 315 note c).

dissipated mode of life, emulating as he did the effeminate practices of the Lydians. From this motive he constructed in the city the famous ' Quarter ' [a] of Samos to rival the park at Sardis called Sweet Embrace,[b] and in competition with the flowers of Lydia he wove the widely heralded ' Flowers ' of the Samians.[c] Of these two innovations, the Samian Quarter was a lane crowded with professional women,[d] and he literally filled Hellas with all kinds of foods that tempted to sensuality and incontinence ; the flowers of the Samians, on the other hand, are the various charms of women and men.[e] But while the whole city was still engaged in holiday revels and drunken orgies (the Persians attacked and conquered it [f])." So much, then, we have on the authority of Clearchus. But I also know myself of a lane in my own Alexandria still called " Rich Man's Row " to this day, where everything conducive to wanton indulgence used to be sold.

Aristotle in his *Wonders* says[g] of Alcisthenes the Sybarite that his desire for luxury led him to have a cloak made of such expensive magnificence that he

---

[c] By " Flowers " seem to be meant (1) any of the celebrated products of Lydian luxury, *e.g.* their sauces, Athen. 160 b, 516 c ; pottery, 432 e, etc. ; (2) as applied to Samos, the quarter or street where brothels abounded, *cf.* " tenderloin," and Ps.-Plut. *Prov. Alex.* lxi., Eustath. 1082. 36.

[d] " Mulieribus corpore merentibus," Schweighäuser. *Cf.* Hesych. δαμιουργοί· αἱ πόρναι, and Eustath. *l.c.*

[e] This definition departs somewhat from that given in *Prov. Alex.* just cited (which simply calls the Flowers a τόπος), but to alter the text is unwarranted.

[f] Some such supplement (O. Crusius) is necessary, though it differs from the account given by Hdt. iii. 120 ff. But Clearchus was a moralist, not a historian.

[g] Apelt, p. 69, where the name of the Sybarite is Alcimenes.

προτίθεσθαι αὐτὸ ἐπὶ Λακινίου ἐν τῇ πανηγύρει τῆς
Ἥρας, εἰς ἣν συμπορεύονται πάντες Ἰταλιῶται,
b καὶ τῶν δεικνυμένων μάλιστα[1] πάντων ἐκεῖνο θαυ-
μάζεσθαι. οὗ φασι κυριεύσαντα Διονύσιον τὸν πρε-
σβύτερον ἀποδόσθαι Καρχηδονίοις ρ΄ καὶ κ΄ ταλάντων. ἱστορεῖ δὲ καὶ Πολέμων περὶ αὐτοῦ ἐν τῷ
ἐπιγραφομένῳ περὶ τῶν ἐν Καρχηδόνι Πέπλων.
περὶ δὲ Σμινδυρίδου τοῦ Συβαρίτου καὶ τῆς τούτου
τρυφῆς ἱστόρησεν Ἡρόδοτος ἐν τῇ ἕκτῃ ὡς ἀποπλέων ἐπὶ τὴν μνηστείαν τῆς Κλεισθένους τοῦ
Σικυωνίων τυράννου θυγατρὸς Ἀγαρίστης, φησίν,
" ἀπὸ μὲν Ἰταλίης ἦλθε[2] Σμινδυρίδης ὁ Ἱππο-
κράτεος[3] Συβαρίτης, ὃς ἐπὶ πλεῖστον δὴ χλιδῆς εἰς
c ἀνὴρ ἀφίκετο." εἵποντο γοῦν αὐτῷ χίλιοι μάγειροι
καὶ ὀρνιθευταί. ἱστορεῖ περὶ αὐτοῦ καὶ Τίμαιος
διὰ τῆς ἑβδόμης.[4]

Περὶ δὲ τῆς Διονυσίου τοῦ νεωτέρου Σικελίας
τυράννου τρυφῆς Σάτυρος ὁ Περιπατητικὸς ἱστορῶν
ἐν τοῖς Βίοις πληροῦσθαί φησιν παρ' αὐτῷ τρια-
κοντακλίνους οἴκους ὑπὸ τῶν εὐωχουμένων. καὶ
Κλέαρχος δὲ ἐν τῷ τετάρτῳ τῶν Βίων γράφει
οὕτως· " Διονύσιος δ' ὁ Διονυσίου ἁπάσης γενόμενος Σικελίας ἀλάστωρ εἰς τὴν Λοκρῶν πόλιν
d παρελθὼν οὖσαν αὐτῷ μητρόπολιν (Δωρὶς γὰρ ἡ
μήτηρ αὐτοῦ τὸ γένος ἦν Λοκρίς) στρώσας οἶκον
τῶν ἐν τῇ πόλει τὸν μέγιστον ἑρπύλλοις καὶ ῥόδοις

μάλιστα Aristot.: om. A.
[2] ἦλθε added from Hdt.   [3] ἱπποκράτειος A.
[4] διὰ τῆς ἑβδόμης Dindorf: ἐν τῆι τῆς ἑβδόμης A.

---

[a] About $130,000. See Bullock in *Class. Journ.* xxv.
260 ff. Dionysius robbed the temple, Justin xx. 5, Aelian
xii. 61.   [b] Page 132 Preller.
448

set it up for display at Lacinium during the festival of Hera, at which all the Greeks of Italy gather, and that of all the objects exhibited it was admired the most. They say that when Dionysius the Elder came into possession of it he sold it to the Carthaginians for one hundred and twenty talents.[a] Polemon, too, gives an account of it in the work entitled *On the Robes at Carthage*.[b] Respecting the Sybarite Smindyrides and his luxury Herodotus has recorded in the sixth book [c] that when he sailed away to sue for the hand of Agaristê, the daughter of Cleisthenes tyrant of Sicyon, "from Italy (Herodotus says) came Smindyrides, the son of Hippocrates, of Sybaris, who had attained the highest degree of luxury possible for one man." He was followed, for example, by one thousand cooks and fowlers. Timaeus, also, gives an account of him in the course of his seventh book.[d]

In narrating stories concerning the luxury of Dionysius the Younger, tyrant of Sicily, Satyrus the Peripatetic in his *Lives* says [e] that rooms in his palace with a capacity of thirty couches were filled by the banqueters. In the same strain Clearchus, in the fourth book of his *Lives*, writes as follows [f] : "Dionysius, the son of Dionysius, proved to be the evil genius of all Sicily ; once he went over to the city of the Locrians, which was the town of his own origin (for Doris, his mother, was a Locrian by birth), and strewing the largest hall in the city with tufted thyme and roses, he summoned one after the other the

---

[c] Chap. 126 f., Athen. 273 b (vol. iii. p. 226), 511 c, 526 b.

[d] *F.H.G.* i. 204.

[e] *F.H.G.* iii. 160 ; the number of rooms is not given.

[f] *F.H.G.* ii. 307 ; *cf.* Strabo p. 259, Aelian, *V.H.* ix. 8.

μετεπέμπετο μὲν ἐν μέρει τὰς Λοκρῶν παρθένους
καὶ γυμνὸς μετὰ γυμνῶν οὐδὲν αἰσχύνης παρέλιπεν
ἐπὶ τοῦ στρώματος κυλινδούμενος. τοιγαροῦν μετ'
οὐ πολὺν χρόνον οἱ ὑβρισθέντες γυναῖκα καὶ τέκνα
ἐκείνου λαβόντες ὑποχείρια ἐπὶ τῆς ὁδοῦ στήσαντες
μεθ' ὕβρεως ἐνηκολάσταινον αὐτοῖς· καὶ ἐπεὶ τῆς
ὕβρεως πλήρεις ἐγένοντο, κεντοῦντες ὑπὸ τοὺς
e τῶν χειρῶν ὄνυχας βελόναις ἀνεῖλον αὐτούς. καὶ
τελευτησάντων τὰ μὲν ὀστᾶ κατέκοψαν ἐν ὅλμοις,
τὰ δὲ λοιπὰ κρεανομησάμενοι[1] ἐπηράσαντο[2] τοῖς μὴ
γευσαμένοις αὐτῶν· ὅθεν πρὸς τὴν ἀνόσιον ἀρὰν
κατήλεσαν[3] αὐτῶν τὰς σάρκας, ἵν' ἡ τροφὴ σιτο-
ποιουμένων κατεδεσθῇ· τὰ δὲ λείψανα κατεπόντω-
σαν. αὐτὸς δὲ Διονύσιος τέλος μητραγυρτῶν καὶ
τυμπανοφορούμενος[4] οἰκτρῶς τὸν βίον κατέστρεψεν.
εὐλαβητέον οὖν τὴν καλουμένην τρυφὴν οὖσαν τῶν
βίων ἀνατροπὴν ἁπάντων τε ὀλέθριον ἡγεῖσθαι τὴν
ὕβριν."

Διόδωρος δ' ὁ Σικελιώτης ἐν τοῖς περὶ Βιβλιο-

---

[1] Meineke : κρέα, νεμησάμενοι AE (μεμησάμενοι C).
[2] ἐπηράσαντο CE : ἐπηράσαντο πάντες A, πᾶσι Meineke.
[3] CE : κατηλέησαν A. ὅθεν . . . κατεδεσθῇ om. Aelian.
But though obscure, the words complete the description
of the rite.
[4] τυμπανοφορῶν Schweighäuser.

---

[a] The text is corrupt, but it is obvious that it has to do with
a savage rite of an expiatory nature, or at least designed to
prevent the ghosts of the dead victims from rising to take
vengeance ; cf. Frazer, *Golden Bough*[3], ii. 148 ff.   Strabo

young girls of the Locrians ; then naked among the naked girls he omitted no indecency as he rolled with them upon the pavement. Not long afterward, therefore, the outraged fathers got his wife and children into their own power, and standing them up in the street they indulged their lust upon them with brutal violence. And when they had sated themselves with outrage, they thrust needles under their finger-nails and killed them. They then chopped up the bones of the dead victims in mortars ; the rest of the bodies they divided up as meat-portions and pronounced a curse on whosoever refused to taste them ; the reason why they ground up their flesh, in view of the unholy curse, was that the food might be entirely consumed as they ate their bread ; what was left over they sunk in the sea.[a] As for Dionysius himself, he ·finally brought his life to a pitiable close as a mendicant priest of the Mother of the Gods, in whose rites he carried a tambourine.[b] We should, therefore, beware of what men call luxury, since it is a subverter of lives ; and likewise we should regard insolence as certain to bring on the ruin of all concerned."[c]

Diodorus of Sicily in his work called *The Library*

p. 260 says that they burnt the bodies and ground up the bones ; but it seems clear that the flesh was removed from the bones first and then roasted and mingled with bread dough. *Cf.* Plat. *Rep.* 565 D.

[b] This refers to the orgiastic worship of Cybele ($\mu\acute{\eta}\tau\eta\rho$ $\theta\epsilon\hat{\omega}\nu$) : Demosth. *De Cor.* 259 brands with contempt the participation of Aeschines and his mother in these rites ; see J. H. Wright in *H.S.C.P.* vi. 67 note 1.

[c] *i.e.* to those who practise it, as well as to those upon whom it is practised ; the moralist here recalls the ancient epic and tragic sequence of cause and effect : satiety ($\kappa\acute{o}\rho os$) begets insolence, insolence ($\mathring{v}\beta\rho\iota s$) begets ruin ($\mathring{a}\tau\eta$, $\mathring{o}\lambda\epsilon\theta\rho os$).

f θήκης 'Ακραγαντίνους φησὶ κατασκευάσαι Γέλωνι
κολυμβήθραν πολυτελῆ τὸ περίμετρον ἔχουσαν
σταδίων ζ', βάθος δὲ πηχῶν κ', εἰς ἣν ἐπαγομένων
ποταμίων[1] καὶ κρηναίων ὑδάτων ἰχθυοτροφεῖον
εἶναι καὶ πολλοὺς παρέχεσθαι ἰχθῦς εἰς τὴν τρυφὴν
καὶ ἀπόλαυσιν τῷ Γέλωνι· καθίπτασθαι δὲ καὶ
κύκνων πλῆθος εἰς αὐτήν, ὡς γίνεσθαι ἐπιτερπε-
στάτην τὴν θέαν. ὕστερον δὲ αὕτη διεφθάρη
542 καταχωσθεῖσα. Δοῦρις δὲ ἐν τῇ δ'[2] τῶν περὶ
'Αγαθοκλέα καὶ πλησίον 'Ιππωνίου πόλεως ἄλσος τι
δείκνυσθαι κάλλει διάφορον καὶ κατάρρυτον ὕδασιν,
ἐν ᾧ καὶ τόπον τινὰ εἶναι καλούμενον 'Αμαλθείας
Κέρας, ὃ τὸν Γέλωνα κατασκευάσαι. Σιληνὸς δ' ὁ
Καλακτῖνος[3] ἐν τρίτῳ Σικελικῶν περὶ Συρακούσας[4]
φησὶν κῆπον εἶναι πολυτελῶς κατεσκευασμένον ὃν
καλεῖσθαι Μῦθον, ἐν ᾧ χρηματίζειν 'Ιέρωνα τὸν
βασιλέα. ἡ δὲ Πανορμῖτις τῆς Σικελίας πᾶσα
κῆπος προσαγορεύεται διὰ τὸ πᾶσα εἶναι πλήρης
δένδρων ἡμέρων, ὥς φησιν Καλλίας ἐν ὀγδόῃ τῶν
b περὶ 'Αγαθοκλέα 'Ιστοριῶν. Ποσειδώνιος δ' ἐν τῇ
ὀγδόῃ τῶν 'Ιστοριῶν περὶ Δαμοφίλου λέγων τοῦ
Σικελιώτου, δι' ὃν ὁ δουλικὸς ἐκινήθη πόλεμος, ὅτι
τρυφῆς ἦν οἰκεῖος, γράφει καὶ ταῦτα· " τρυφῆς οὖν

---

[1] CE: ποταμῶν A.
[2] Hullemann: δεκάτηι A.
[3] Holsten (from Καλὴ 'Ακτή): καλλατιανὸς A.
[4] CE: συρακούσσας A.

---

[a] Diod. xi. 25, referring to the public works at Agrigentum, Syracuse, and Himera after the victory at Himera, 480
B.C.; the only citation from Diod. Sic. in Athenaeus. The
pool measured nearly a half-mile square. Since the excerpt
is an ungrammatical jotting from Diodorus, the translation is

says [a] that the people of Agrigentum built a swimming-pool for Gelon at great cost ; it had a perimeter of seven stadia and a depth of thirty feet, and into it water was drawn from rivers and springs to make a fish-preserve supplying many fish for the luxurious taste and enjoyment of Gelon ; there lighted on it also a large quantity of swans, so that the spectacle was most delightful to see. At a later time, however, it was filled up with earth and abolished. Duris, in the fourth book of his *Agathocles and his Times*, says [b] also that near the city of Hipponium there is shown a grove exceedingly beautiful and well supplied with flowing streams, in which also there is a place called the Horn of Amaltheia, [c] which Gelon constructed. Silenus of Calacte in the third book of his *History of Sicily*, says [d] that in the neighbourhood of Syracuse there is a garden magnificently constructed which is called the " Word " [e] ; in it Hieron the king held audience. But then the entire region round Panormus in Sicily is called a garden, because it is full of cultivated trees, according to Callias in the eighth book of his *Histories of Agathocles*.[f] Poseidonius, too, in the eighth book of his *Histories* says of the Sicilian Greek Damophilus, who caused the stirring up of the slave war,[g] that he was addicted to luxury, and writes

based largely on his text. The proper title of his history is Βιβλιοθήκη Ἱστορική, " Historical Library."

[b] *F.H.G.* ii. 479, J. 2 A 144, Strabo p. 257.

[c] See above, p. 49 note *f*.

[d] *F.H.G.* iii. 101, J. 2 B 901.

[e] *i.e.* the place of conversation, like Eng. *parlour*. Cf. the names of market-quarters in Athens, ὁ οἶνος, ὁ χλωρὸς τυρός, etc. Pollux ix. 47, x. 19.

[f] *F.H.G.* ii. 382.

[g] His inhumanity toward his slaves occasioned the first uprising of slaves in Sicily *ca.* 139 B.C.

δοῦλος ἦν καὶ κακουργίας, διὰ μὲν τῆς χώρας τετρακύκλους ἀπήνας περιαγόμενος καὶ ἵππους καὶ θεράποντας ὡραίους καὶ παραδρομὴν ἀνάγωγον κολάκων τε καὶ παίδων στρατιωτικῶν. ὕστερον δὲ πανοικίᾳ ἐφυβρίστως κατέστρεψε τὸν βίον ὑπὸ τῶν οἰκετῶν περιυβρισθείς."

Δημήτριος δ' ὁ Φαληρεύς, ὥς φησι Δοῦρις ἐν τῇ c ἑκκαιδεκάτῃ τῶν Ἱστοριῶν, χιλίων καὶ διακοσίων ταλάντων κατ' ἐνιαυτὸν κύριος γενόμενος καὶ ἀπὸ τούτων βραχέα δαπανῶν εἰς τοὺς στρατιώτας καὶ τὴν τῆς πόλεως διοίκησιν τὰ λοιπὰ πάντα διὰ τὴν ἔμφυτον ἀκρασίαν ἠφάνιζεν, θοίνας καθ' ἑκάστην ἡμέραν λαμπρὰς ἐπιτελῶν καὶ πλῆθός τι συνδείπνων ἔχων. καὶ ταῖς μὲν δαπάναις ταῖς εἰς τὰ δεῖπνα τοὺς Μακεδόνας ὑπερέβαλλε,[1] τῇ δὲ καθαρειότητι[2] Κυπρίους καὶ Φοίνικας· ῥάσματά τε μύρων ἔπιπτεν d ἐπὶ τὴν γῆν, ἀνθινά τε[3] πολλὰ τῶν ἐδαφῶν ἐν τοῖς ἀνδρῶσιν κατεσκευάζετο διαπεποικιλμένα ὑπὸ δημιουργῶν. ἦσαν δὲ καὶ πρὸς γυναῖκας ὁμιλίαι[4] σιωπώμεναι καὶ νεανίσκων ἔρωτες νυκτερινοί, καὶ ὁ τοῖς ἄλλοις τιθέμενος θεσμοὺς Δημήτριος καὶ τοὺς βίους τάττων ἀνομοθέτητον ἑαυτῷ τὸν βίον κατεσκεύαζεν. ἐπεμελεῖτο δὲ καὶ τῆς ὄψεως, τήν τε τρίχα τὴν ἐπὶ τῆς κεφαλῆς ξανθιζόμενος καὶ παιδέρωτι τὸ πρόσωπον ὑπαλειφόμενος καὶ τοῖς ἄλλοις ἀλείμμασιν ἐγχρίων ἑαυτόν· ἠβούλετο γὰρ τὴν ὄψιν ἱλαρὸς καὶ τοῖς ἀπαντῶσιν ἡδὺς φαίνεσθαι.

[1] ὑπερβαλών (in different construction) CE.
[2] CE: καθαριότητι A.
[3] Musurus: ἄθινα τε A.
[4] αὐτῷ ὁμιλίαι CE.

[a] F.H.G. iii. 257, J. 2 A 227, cf. Diod. xxxiv. 2.

as follows [a] : " He was, therefore, a slave to luxury and vice, driving round about over the countryside in four-wheeled carts,[b] with horses and handsome grooms and a retinue of parasites and lads dressed as soldiers swarming beside him. But later he, with his whole household, ended his life after an outrageous fashion, having been grievously outraged by the slaves."

Demetrius of Phalerum, as Duris declares in the sixteenth book of his *Histories*,[c] came into the control of twelve hundred talents a year,[d] and of this sum he spent but little on the troops and the administration of the State, but squandered all the remainder in the indulgence of his inborn lusts, celebrating splendid feasts every day and entertaining a multitude of guests. In fact he surpassed the Macedonians in his lavish outlays on banquets, and in his refinement the Cyprians and Phoenicians ; showers of perfume descended upon the ground, and many floors in the dining-halls were decorated in highly-elaborate flower-patterns by artists. Assignations with women were carried on in secret, as well as nocturnal amours with lads, and the Demetrius who made statutes and ordained the conduct of lives for other people constructed his own life with utter freedom from law. He was also careful about his personal appearance, dyeing the hair of his head a blonde colour, rubbing his face with rouge, and smearing himself with salves besides ; for he wanted to have a glad appearance

[b] For this form of luxury *cf.* Aristoph. *Acharn.* 71. Diod. says " grooms dressed as soldiers and a retinue of handsome lads."

[c] *F.H.G.* ii. 475, J. 2 A 140. Aelian, *V.H.* ix. 9, tells this story of Demetrius Poliorcetes.

[d] Nearly £270,000.

ATHENAEUS

e ἐν δὲ τῇ πομπῇ τῶν Διονυσίων ἦν ἔπεμψεν ἄρχων
γενόμενος, ᾖδεν ὁ[1] χορὸς εἰς αὐτὸν[2] ποιήματα
Καστορίωνος[3] τοῦ Σολέως, ἐν οἷς ἡλιόμορφος
προσηγορεύετο·

  ἐξόχως δ᾽[4] εὐγενέτας ἡλιόμορφος[5] ζαθέοισ᾽ ἄρχων
  σε τιμαῖσι[6] γεραίρει.

Καρύστιος δὲ ὁ Περγαμηνὸς ἐν τρίτῳ Ὑπομνημάτων "Δημήτριος," φησίν, "ὁ Φαληρεὺς Ἱμεραίου[7]
τοῦ ἀδελφοῦ ἀναιρεθέντος ὑπ᾽ Ἀντιπάτρου αὐτὸς
μετὰ Νικάνορος διέτριβεν, αἰτίαν ἔχων ὡς τὰ
f ἐπιφάνεια τοῦ ἀδελφοῦ θύων. Κασάνδρῳ δὲ γενόμενος φίλος μέγα ἴσχυσεν. καὶ κατ᾽ ἀρχὰς μὲν ἦν
αὐτοῦ τὸ ἄριστον ὀξύβαφα παντοδαπὰς ἐλαίας
ἔχοντα καὶ τυρὸν νησιωτικόν. ὡς δ᾽ ἐπλούτησε,
Μοσχίωνα τὸν ἄριστον τῶν τότε μαγείρων καὶ
δειπνοποιῶν ἐωνήσατο, καὶ τοσαῦτα ἦν αὐτῷ τὰ
ἐν δείπνοις παρασκευαζόμενα[8] καθ᾽ ἡμέραν ὥστε
χαρισαμένου τῷ Μοσχίωνι τὰ λείψανα Μοσχίων ἐν

---

[1] ὁ CE: om. A.
[2] τὸν θεὸν Meineke, quite unnecessarily.
[3] Leopardi: σείρωνος A.   [4] δὲ A: τε CE.
[5] Kuhn: ἠπιόμοιρος ACE.
[6] Meineke: τιμαῖσ A (originally τιμαῖσι).
[7] Correction in red ink in A: ἱμαιρέου.
[8] ἦν αὐτῷ . . . παρασκευαζόμενοι CE: ἦν τὰ παρασκευαζόμενα A.

---

[a] *P.L.G.*[4] iii. 634, Diehl frag. 2. The verses were a dithy-
ramb in honour of Dionysus. Excessive flattery appears in
the very first words, for Demetrius was the son of a slave;
he became Chief Archon in 309 B.C. The adjective ζαθέοισ
with τιμαῖσι, rendered " divine " above, may also mean
" rich," " fragrant," H. Fränkel, *De Simia Rhod.* 51; but
see below (note *d*), on divine honours.
[b] *F.H.G.* iv. 358, J. 2 B 957.

and seem attractive to all who met him. And in the procession at the Dionysia which he marshalled when he became archon, the chorus sang verses in his honour written by Castorion of Soli, in which he was called " in beauty like the Sun "[a] : " The archon above all others noble, in beauty like the Sun, celebrates thee with divine honours."

Carystius of Pergamum in the third book of his *Notes* says[b] that Demetrius of Phalerum, when his brother Himeraeus was murdered by order of Antipater,[c] went himself to live with Nicanor, having been accused of celebrating the divine appearing of his brother.[d] Becoming a friend of Cassander[e] he acquired great power. In the beginning, to be sure, his luncheon had consisted of bowls of olives, of any and every kind, and some island cheese.[f] But when he became rich he bought Moschion, the best cook and caterer of those days ; and so huge were the dinner menus prepared for him daily that Moschion, who received as gratuities what was left over, was

[c] Antipater had sent his henchman Archias, who had been an actor, to apprehend the orators Hypereides and Demosthenes as well as Himeraeus, Plut. *Demosth.* 28, Luc. *Dem. Enc.* 31, in 322 B.C. ; Ferguson, *Hellenistic Greece*, pp. 20, 38.

[d] Evidently his brother, as he thought, appeared to him as Patroclus had appeared to Achilles. The rites performed by Demetrius, probably in secret, were interpreted by his enemies as a sacrilegious act, implying that he believed his brother to be divine. Their real motive was political animosity, divine honours to the dead and even the living being common enough; see Pauly-Wissowa, Suppl. iv. 304 (*s. Epiphaneia*).

[e] Through Nicanor (then in the Peiraeus), who was a partisan of Cassander, the son of Antipater (who had died 319 B.C.) ; Ferguson, *op. cit.* pp. 31 ff.

[f] Doubtless a poorer sort ; it is not mentioned at 658 a-c. For the various kinds of olives see 56 a-d (vol. i. p. 242).

ἔτεσι δύο τρεῖς συνοικίας ἐωνήσατο παῖδάς τε
ἐλευθέρους ὕβριζεν καὶ γυναῖκας τὰς τῶν ἐπι-
φανεστάτων. ἐζηλοτύπουν δὲ πάντες οἱ παῖδες τὸν
ἐρώμενον αὐτοῦ Δίογνιν[1]· καὶ τοσοῦτον ἦν τῷ
Δημητρίῳ προσελθεῖν ὥστε μετ' ἄριστον αὐτοῦ
543 περιπατήσαντος παρὰ τοὺς Τρίποδας συνῆλθον[2] εἰς
τὸν τόπον παῖδες οἱ κάλλιστοι[3] ταῖς ἑξῆς ἡμέραις,
ἵν' ὀφθεῖεν αὐτῷ."

Νικόλαος δ' ὁ Περιπατητικὸς ἐν τῇ δεκάτῃ καὶ
ἑκατοστῇ[4] τῶν Ἱστοριῶν Λεύκολλόν φησιν ἀφ-
ικόμενον εἰς Ῥώμην καὶ θριαμβεύσαντα λόγον τε
ἀποδόντα τοῦ πρὸς Μιθριδάτην πολέμου ἐξοκείλαι
εἰς πολυτελῆ δίαιταν ἐκ τῆς παλαιᾶς σωφροσύνης
τρυφῆς τε πρῶτον εἰς ἅπαν Ῥωμαίοις ἡγεμόνα
γενέσθαι, καρπωσάμενον δυεῖν βασιλέων πλοῦτον
Μιθριδάτου καὶ Τιγράνου. διαβόητος δ' ἦν παρὰ
b Ῥωμαίοις καὶ Σίττιος ἐπὶ τρυφῇ καὶ μαλακίᾳ
ὥς φησι Ῥουτίλιος. περὶ γὰρ Ἀπικίου προειρήκαμεν. Παυσανίαν δὲ καὶ Λύσανδρον ἐπὶ τρυφῇ
διαβοήτους γενέσθαι σχεδὸν πάντες ἱστοροῦσι.
διόπερ καὶ Ἆγις ἐπὶ Λυσάνδρου ἔφη ὅτι " δεύτερον
τοῦτον ἡ Σπάρτη φέρει Παυσανίαν." Θεόπομπος[5]
δὲ ἐν τῇ δεκάτῃ τῶν Ἑλληνικῶν τἀναντία φησι
περὶ τοῦ Λυσάνδρου, ὅτι " φιλόπονος[6] ἦν καὶ
θεραπεύειν δυνάμενος καὶ ἰδιώτας καὶ βασιλεῖς,
σώφρων ὢν καὶ τῶν ἡδονῶν ἁπασῶν κρείττων.
γενόμενος γοῦν τῆς Ἑλλάδος σχεδὸν ἁπάσης

---

[1] Θέογνιν Musurus.   [2] συνήρχοντο C.
[3] παῖδες οἱ κάλλιστοι Kaibel: παῖδες κάλλιστοι A, οἱ παῖδες alone CE.   [4] Valois: εἰκοστῆι A.
[5] CE: θεόπος A.   [6] φιλύπονός τε CE.

---

[a] F.H.G. iii. 416, J. 2 A 378, Athen. 274 e-f (vol. iii. p. 234).

able in the space of two years to buy three apartment-houses and practise wanton lust on freeborn boys and the wives of the most eminent citizens. But all the boys were jealous of Demetrius's favourite Diognis; and so great was their ambition to come into relations with Demetrius that when he went for a stroll after lunch in Tripod Street the handsomest boys gathered in that place on the succeeding days in the hope of being seen by him.

Nicolas the Peripatetic, in the hundred and tenth book of his *Histories*, says [a] that after Lucullus returned to Rome, celebrated his triumph, and rendered an account of his campaign against Mithradates, he abandoned the old-time sobriety and drifted into an extravagant mode of life, becoming the foremost guide of the Romans in every form of luxury, because he enjoyed the wealth taken from two kings, Mithradates and Tigranes. Notorious also among the Romans for luxury and effeminacy was Sittius, according to Rutilius. [b] Of Apicius we have spoken earlier. [c] Practically all authorities record that Pausanias and Lysander were notorious for luxury. [d] Hence Agis said of Lysander, " Here is a second Pausanias that Sparta has produced." But Theopompus, in the tenth book of his *History of Greece*, says [e] just the opposite about Lysander, namely that " he was fond of hard work, ready and able to help private citizens as well as princes, self-controlled and master over all lures to pleasure. At any rate, although he won supreme power over practically all of Greece,

Plut. *Luc.* 39 ff. The third Mithradatic war is meant, in
74 B.C.   [b] *F.H.G.* iii. 200.
   [c] Vol. i. p. 28, *cf.* vol. ii. p. 264 note *b*.
   [d] Above, pp. 421 and note *a*, 423, and 233 f (vol. iii. p. 52).
   [e] *F.H.G.* i. 281, J. 2 B 538, G. and H. 21, Plut. *Lys.* 30.

c κύριος ἐν οὐδεμιᾷ φανήσεται τῶν πόλεων οὔτε πρὸς
τὰς ἀφροδισίους ἡδονὰς ὁρμήσας οὔτε μέθαις καὶ
πότοις ἀκαίροις χρησάμενος.''

Οὕτω δὲ παρὰ τοῖς ἀρχαίοις τὰ τῆς τρυφῆς καὶ
τῆς πολυτελείας ἠσκεῖτο ὡς καὶ Παρράσιον τὸν
Ἐφέσιον[1] ζωγράφον πορφύραν ἀμπέχεσθαι, χρυσοῦν
στέφανον ἐπὶ τῆς κεφαλῆς ἔχοντα, ὡς ἱστορεῖ
Κλέαρχος ἐν τοῖς Βίοις. οὗτος γὰρ παρὰ μέλος
ὑπὲρ τὴν γραφικὴν τρυφήσας λόγῳ τῆς ἀρετῆς
ἀντελαμβάνετο καὶ ἐπέγραφεν[2] τοῖς ὑπ' αὐτοῦ[3]
ἐπιτελουμένοις ἔργοις·

d   ἁβροδίαιτος ἀνὴρ ἀρετήν τε[4] σέβων τάδ' ἔγραψεν.

καί τις ὑπεραλγήσας ἐπὶ τούτῳ παρέγραψεν
" ῥαβδοδίαιτος ἀνήρ." ἐπέγραψεν δ' ἐπὶ πολλῶν
ἔργων αὐτοῦ καὶ τάδε·

  ἁβροδίαιτος ἀνὴρ ἀρετήν τε σέβων τάδ' ἔγραψεν
  Παρράσιος κλεινῆς πατρίδος ἐξ Ἐφέσου.
  οὐδὲ πατρὸς λαθόμην Εὐήνορος, ὅς ῥά μ' ἔφυσε[5]
  γνήσιον, Ἑλλήνων πρῶτα φέροντα τέχνης.

ηὔχησε[6] δ' ἀνεμεσήτως ἐν τούτοις·

e   εἰ καὶ ἄπιστα κλύουσι, λέγω τάδε· φημὶ γὰρ ἤδη
τέχνης εὑρῆσθαι τέρματα τῆσδε σαφῆ

---

[1] Ἐφέσιον C (ἐφέσιος in a different construction): om. A.
  [2] A : ἐπέγραψε CE.
  [3] τοῖς αὐτοῦ C, τοῖς ὑφ' αὐτοῦ Dindorf.
    [4] AC : δὲ E.
  [5] ῥά μ' ἔφυσε Meineke : ἀνέφυσε A.   [6] ηὔχει CE.

---

[a] F.H.G. ii. 304, Athen. 687 b (where the third book is
mentioned as the source).

there is not a single one of its cities in which it can be proved that he was tempted into sexual indulgences or resorted to carousals and excessive drinking."

To such an extent were the delights of luxury and sumptuous expense cultivated among the ancients that even the Ephesian painter Parrhasius dressed himself in purple and wore a gold crown on his head, as Clearchus records in his *Lives.*[a] For he indulged in luxury in a way offensive to good taste and beyond his station as a painter,[b] and yet in talk claimed the possession of virtue, inscribing on the works of art wrought by him the following verse: "A man who lives *in dainty style* and at the same time honours virtue, hath written these words." Whereupon a certain person who felt great annoyance at this claim wrote by way of correcting him: " A man who lives *by the painter's stile.*" Now Parrhasius inscribed on many of his works the following[c]: "A man who lives in dainty style and at the same time honours virtue, hath written these lines—Parrhasius, from Ephesus, his glorious fatherland. Nor have I left my father forgotten, Evenor who begot me, his own son, to carry off the first honours in Greek art." He also made a boast, without provoking the wrath of the gods, in these lines[d]: " Though I speak to them that hear and believe not, yet I speak thus: I declare that now at last the sure goals of this art have been reached by my hand;

[b] On the low social status of artists in Athens as conceived by Wilamowitz (without documentation) see his *Aristot. u. Athen.* ii. 100 note 36.

[c] *P.L.G.*[4] ii. 320, Diehl i. 95, Edmonds ii. 18.

[d] *P.L.G.*[4] ii. 321, Diehl i. 95, Edmonds ii. 20. The last words explain why the anger of the gods was not aroused. *Cf.* the story of Zeuxis in Ael. Aristeid. ii. 170. On the art of Parrhasius see Plin. *N.H.* xxxv. 67 ff.

χειρὸς ὑφ' ἡμετέρης· ἀνυπέρβλητος δὲ πέπηγεν
οὖρος. ἀμώμητον δ' οὐδὲν ἔγεντο[1] βροτοῖς.

ἀγωνιζόμενος δέ ποτε πρὸς καταδεέστερον[2] ἐν
Σάμῳ τὸν Αἴαντα καὶ ἡττηθείς, συναχθομένων
αὐτῷ τῶν φίλων, ἔφη ὡς αὐτὸς μὲν ὀλίγον φρον-
τίζοι, Αἴαντι δὲ συνάχθοιτο δεύτερον ἡττηθέντι.
f ἐφόρει δὲ ὑπὸ τρυφῆς πορφυρίδα καὶ στρόφιον
λευκὸν ἐπὶ τῆς κεφαλῆς[3] εἶχεν σκίπωνί τε ἐπ-
εστηρίζετο[4] χρυσᾶς ἕλικας ἐμπεπαισμένῳ χρυσοῖς
τε ἀνασπαστοῖς ἐπέσφιγγε τῶν βλαυτῶν τοὺς ἀν-
αγωγέας. ἀλλ' οὐδὲ τὰ κατὰ τὴν τέχνην ἀηδῶς
ἐποιεῖτο ἀλλὰ ῥᾳδίως, ὡς καὶ ᾄδειν γράφοντα, ὡς
ἱστορεῖ Θεόφραστος ἐν τῷ περὶ Εὐδαιμονίας.
τερατευόμενος δὲ ἔλεγεν, ὅτε τὸν ἐν Λίνδῳ Ἡρακλέα ἔγραφεν, ὡς ὄναρ αὐτῷ ἐπιφαινόμενος ὁ θεὸς
σχηματίζοι αὐτὸν πρὸς τὴν τῆς γραφῆς ἐπιτηδειό-
τητα. ὅθεν καὶ ἐπέγραψεν τῷ πίνακι·

544 οἷος δ' ἐννύχιος[5] φαντάζετο πολλάκι φοιτῶν
    Παρρασίῳ δι' ὕπνου, τοῖος ὅδ' ἐστὶν ὁρᾶν.

Καὶ φιλοσόφων δὲ αἱρέσεις ὅλαι τῆς περὶ τὴν
τρυφὴν αἱρέσεως ἀντεποιήσαντο· καὶ ἥ γε Κυρη-
ναϊκὴ καλουμένη ἀπ' Ἀριστίππου τοῦ Σωκρατικοῦ
τὴν ἀρχὴν λαβοῦσα, ὃς ἀποδεξάμενος τὴν ἡδυ-

---

[1] ἐγένετο ACE.
[2] οὐ κατὰ πολὺ ἐνδεεστέρῳ (sc. συνέτυχε) Aelian.
[3] περὶ τὴν κεφαλὴν C.   [4] C: ἐστηρίζετο A.
[5] ἐννύχιος CE (superscr.): ἐννύχιον ACE.

---

[a] Pliny, op. cit. xxxv. 72, giving a clearer narrative of the
facts, says that he was beaten by Timanthes when he painted
Ajax contending with Odysseus for the arms of Achilles.
Cf. Ael. V.H. ix. 11, on the authority of Theophrastus.
[b] Pliny, loc. cit. " quod iterum ab indigno victus esset."

insurmountable is the boundary that I have fixed. Yet nothing that mortals have done is without blame." On one occasion, in Samos, he competed against an inferior artist[a] with a painting of Ajax and was beaten; when his friends condoled with him he replied that he cared little so far as he himself was concerned, but he sympathized with Ajax for being defeated a second time.[b] In his fondness for luxury he wore a purple cloak and had a white band on his head; he also supported himself with a staff embossed with gold spirals, and kept tight the straps of his sandals by means of gold latchets. Yet, on the other hand, he did not work at his art without pleasure; on the contrary, it was easy for him, so much so that he even sang while he painted, as Theophrastus records in his treatise *On Happiness*.[c] In solemn earnest he used to tell how, when he began to paint the Heracles of Lindus, the god appeared to him in a dream, and assumed exactly the pose that was appropriate for the picture. Hence he wrote on the panel[d]: "As he appeared in the watches of the night, oft visiting Parrhasius whilst he slept, even so stands he here to behold."

In fact, whole schools of philosophers, even, have claimed the pursuit of luxury as the guiding principle of life; there is, for example, the so-called Cyrenaic School, which derived its origin from Aristippus the Socratic[e]; he taught that this life of easy-going

---

[c] Frag. 79 Wimmer.

[d] *P.L.G.*[4] ii. 321, Diehl i. 96, Edmonds ii. 20. *Cf.* Plat. *Phaedo* 60 E πολλάκις μοι φοιτῶν τὸ αὐτὸ ἐνύπνιον, " the same dream visiting me often."

[e] In this case the adjective refers to Aristippus's admiration of Socrates, not to any adherence to the latter's doctrine; *cf.* Diog. Laert. ii. 65.

πάθειαν ταύτην τέλος εἶναι ἔφη καὶ ἐν αὐτῇ τὴν
εὐδαιμονίαν βεβλῆσθαι· καὶ μονόχρονον αὐτὴν
εἶναι, παραπλησίως τοῖς ἀσώτοις οὔτε τὴν μνήμην
τῶν γεγονυιῶν ἀπολαύσεων πρὸς αὐτὸν ἡγούμενος
b ὔτε τὴν ἐλπίδα τῶν ἐσομένων, ἀλλ' ἑνὶ μόνῳ τὸ
ἀγαθὸν κρίνων τῷ παρόντι, τὸ δὲ ἀπολελαυκέναι
καὶ ἀπολαύσειν οὐδὲν νομίζων πρὸς αὐτόν, τὸ μὲν
ὡς οὐκέτ' ὄν, τὸ δὲ οὔπω καὶ ἄδηλον· ὁποῖον καὶ
οἱ τρυφῶντες πάσχουσι τὸ παρὸν εὖ ποιεῖν ἀξιοῦντες.
ὡμολόγησεν δ' αὐτοῦ τῷ δόγματι καὶ ὁ βίος, ὃν
ἐβίωσεν ἐν πάσῃ τρυφῇ καὶ πολυτελείᾳ μύρων καὶ
ἐσθήτων καὶ γυναικῶν. Λαΐδα γοῦν ἀναφανδὸν
εἶχε τὴν ἑταίραν καὶ ταῖς Διονυσίου πολυτελείαις
c ἔχαιρεν καίτοι πολλάκις ἐνυβριζόμενος. Ἡγήσανδρος γοῦν φησιν ὡς καὶ ἀδόξου ποτὲ κλισίας
παρ' αὐτῷ τυχὼν ἤνεγκεν ἐρωτήσαντός τε τοῦ
Διονυσίου τί φαίνεται ἡ κατάκλισις πρὸς τὴν χθὲς
ἔφησεν παραπλησίαν εἶναι. "ἐκείνη τε γάρ," ἔφησεν,
"ἀδοξεῖ τήμερον χωρισθεῖσα ἐμοῦ, χθὲς δὲ πασῶν
ἦν ἐνδοξοτάτη δι' ἡμᾶς, αὕτη τε[1] τήμερον καὶ
ἔνδοξος γέγονεν διὰ τὴν ἡμετέραν παρουσίαν, χθὲς
δὲ ἠδόξει μὴ παρόντος ἐμοῦ." καὶ ἐν ἄλλοις δέ
d φησιν ὁ Ἡγήσανδρος· "Ἀρίστιππος ῥαινόμενος
μὲν ὑπὸ τῶν τοῦ Διονυσίου θεραπόντων, σκωπτό-
μενος δ' ἐπὶ τῷ[3] ἀνέχεσθαι ὑπ' Ἀντιφῶντος, ' εἰ δ'

_____

[1] CE: δὲ A.   [2] καὶ om. CE.

[3] Ménage: το (sic) A.

_____

[a] The " end," or *summum bonum.*
[b] As opposed to Plato's view that the Chief Good is per-
manent.   [c] *F.H.G.* iv. 417.

pleasure we have discussed is the goal,[a] and that happiness is based upon it ; further, that it is for the single moment[b] ; like men of profligate life, he regarded the memory of past enjoyments as having no importance for himself, any more than the expectation of pleasures to come ; rather, he judged the Good by the sole criterion of the present, and thought that past and future enjoyment had no relevancy to himself, because the first no longer had being, the second had no being as yet, and was uncertain ; which is exactly what persons who indulge in luxury feel in claiming that only the present can do any good. Moreover, his mode of life was in harmony with his doctrine, for he lived amid every form of luxury and expensive indulgence in perfumes, clothes, and women. At least he made no secret of keeping the courtesan Laïs, and shared the enjoyment of Dionysius's extravagances although often treated with ignominy by him. Hegesander, at any rate, says [c] that once he was assigned a couch at Dionysius's court in an obscure corner, but bore it with equanimity, and when Dionysius asked him what he thought of the place to which he had been assigned as compared with the one he had the day before, he replied that it was about the same. " For the one I had yesterday," he said, " is to-day in dishonour because it is so far from me, though yesterday it was the most honourable place of all on account of my presence ; and so this one that I have to-day has actually become honoured by my presence, though yesterday it was in dishonour because I was not there." In another passage Hegesander says also [c]: " When the slaves of Dionysius spilled some water on him and Antiphon taunted him for putting up with it he replied : ' Suppose I

465

ἁλιευόμενος ἐτύγχανον,' ἔφη, ' καταλιπὼν τὴν ἐργασίαν ἂν ἀπῆλθον;'" διέτριβεν δ' ὁ Ἀρίστιππος τὰ
πολλὰ ἐν Αἰγίνῃ τρυφῶν· διὸ καὶ ὁ Ξενοφῶν ἐν τοῖς
Ἀπομνημονεύμασί φησιν ὅτι πολλάκις ἐνουθέτει
αὐτὸν ὁ Σωκράτης καὶ τὴν ἠθοποιίαν ᾿πλάσας τῆς
Ἀρετῆς καὶ τῆς Ἡδονῆς εἰσῆγεν. ὁ δ' Ἀρίστιππος ἐπὶ τῆς Λαΐδος ἔλεγεν " ἔχω καὶ οὐκ ἔχομαι."
καὶ παρὰ Διονυσίῳ διηνέχθη τισὶ περὶ τῆς ἐκ-
e λογῆς τῶν τριῶν γυναικῶν. καὶ μύροις ἐλούετο
καὶ ἔφασκεν ὅτι·

        κἂν βακχεύμασιν
οὖσ' ἥ γε σώφρων οὐ διαφθαρήσεται.

κωμῳδῶν δὲ αὐτὸν Ἄλεξις ἐν Γαλατείᾳ[1] ποιεῖ τινα
θεράποντα διηγούμενον περί τινος τῶν μαθητῶν
τάδε·

    ὁ δεσπότης οὑμὸς περὶ λόγους γάρ ποτε
    διέτριψε μειρακίσκος ὢν καὶ φιλοσοφεῖν
    ἐπέθετο. Κυρηναῖος ἦν ἐνταῦθά τις,[2]
    ὥς φασ', Ἀρίστιππος, σοφιστὴς εὐφυής,
f   μᾶλλον δὲ πρωτεύων ἁπάντων τῶν[3] τότε
    ἀκολασίᾳ τε τῶν γεγονότων διαφέρων.
    τούτῳ τάλαντον δοὺς μαθητὴς γίνεται

[1] γαλατίαι A.
[2] τις, in A placed after Ἀρίστιππος, transposed by
Schweighäuser.
[3] τῶν added by Casaubon.

---

[a] ii. 1, where the parable of Prodicus is cited, cf. Athen.
510 c (above, p. 294).

had been fishing, should I have left my job and gone home ? ' " Aristippus spent most of his time in Aegina, where he lived in luxury ; hence Xenophon in his *Memorabilia* declares [a] that Socrates would often admonish him and bring in the moralizing parable which he had composed [b] of Virtue and Pleasure. But Aristippus, referring to Laïs, would say, " I possess her and am not possessed by her." [c] And at the court of Dionysius he disagreed with some persons on the choice of the three women.[d] He bathed himself in perfume and declared that [e] " Even in the revels of Bacchus she that is really modest will not be corrupted." And Alexis, satirizing him in *Galateia*, makes a slave say the following concerning one of Aristippus's pupils [f] : " My master once went in for dialectic when he was a lad, and essayed to be a philosopher. There was a man of Cyrene in the town named Aristippus, as the story goes, a wise man of genius, or rather, a man who stood at the forefront of all men at that time, and exceeded all men who had ever lived—in dissipation. To him my master paid a talent and became his pupil,[g]

[b] Prodicus, not Socrates, was the author.

[c] *Cf.* Athen. 350 f (vol. iv. p. 88) and 588 e.

[d] The story here is lost, but is supplied by Diog. Laert. ii. 67 : Dionysius told him to choose one of three courtesans, but he took them all, remarking that Paris had had bad luck in taking only one.

[e] Eur. *Bacch.* 317 ; Teiresias reassures Cadmus.

[f] Kock ii. 311.

[g] The receiving of pay for his teaching and the idea of a commercial relation between teacher and taught were repugnant to Socrates ; see Plato, *Apol.* 19 D (where his avoidance of the word " pupil " is as noteworthy as his refusal to take pay). Aristoph. *Nub.* 98 f. is a gross perversion of the truth.

ὁ δεσπότης, καὶ τὴν τέχνην μὲν οὐ πάνυ
ἐξέμαθε, τὴν δ᾽ ἀρτηρίαν συνήρπασεν.[1]

'Αντιφάνης δ᾽ ἐν 'Ανταίῳ περὶ τῆς τῶν φιλοσόφων
τρυφερότητος διαλεγόμενός φησιν·

A. ὦ τάν, κατανοεῖς τίς ποτ᾽ ἐστὶν οὑτοσὶ
ὁ γέρων; B. ἀπὸ τῆς μὲν ὄψεως Ἑλληνικός·
545 λευκὴ χλανίς, φαιὸς χιτωνίσκος καλός,
πιλίδιον[2] ἁπαλόν, εὔρυθμος βακτηρία,
βαυκὶς τρυφῶσα[3]—τί μακρὰ δεῖ λέγειν; ὅλως
αὐτὴν ὁρᾶν γὰρ τὴν 'Ακαδημίαν δοκῶ.

'Αριστόξενος δ᾽ ὁ μουσικὸς ἐν τῷ 'Αρχύτα[4] Βίῳ
ἀφικέσθαι φησὶ[5] παρὰ Διονυσίου τοῦ νεωτέρου
πρεσβευτὰς πρὸς τὴν Ταραντίνων πόλιν, ἐν οἷς
εἶναι καὶ Πολύαρχον τὸν ἡδυπαθῆ ἐπικαλούμενον,
ἄνδρα περὶ τὰς σωματικὰς ἡδονὰς ἐσπουδακότα
b καὶ οὐ μόνον τῷ ἔργῳ ἀλλὰ καὶ τῷ λόγῳ. ὄντα
δὲ γνώριμον τῷ 'Αρχύτα καὶ φιλοσοφίας οὐ
παντελῶς ἀλλότριον ἀπαντᾶν εἰς τὰ τεμένη καὶ
συμπεριπατεῖν τοῖς περὶ τὸν 'Αρχύταν ἀκροώμε-
νον τῶν λόγων. ἐμπεσούσης δέ ποτε ἀπορίας καὶ
σκέψεως περί τε τῶν ἐπιθυμιῶν καὶ τὸ σύνολον
περὶ τῶν σωματικῶν ἡδονῶν ἔφη ὁ Πολύαρχος·
" ἐμοὶ μέν, ὦ ἄνδρες, πολλάκις ἤδη πέφηνεν ἐπισκο-
ποῦντι κομιδῇ ἄτοπον[6] τὸ τῶν ἀρετῶν τούτων κατα-

---

[1] Suspected and variously emended, but τὴν ἀρτηρίαν should
be kept. The arteries were supposed to contain wind; the
disciple became a mere windbag.
[2] CE, corr. in A : πολίδιον A.
[3] βαυκὶς τρυφῶσα Gulick : βαια τράπεζα ACE (βαια corr. to
βεβαια CE). [4] ἀρχύται A.
[5] ἀφικέσθαι φησὶ Casaubon : ἀφίησι A.
[6] ἄτοπον added by Capps.

---

[a] See critical note 1. For the verb cf. Lucian, De Domo 16.

nd though he did not exactly learn his doctrine to
perfection, he ruined his own windpipe utterly."[a] And
Antiphanes, talking about the softness of philosophers
in *Antaeus*, says [b] : " A. Do you know, my friend, who
hat old man can be ? B. Judging from his looks,
he comes from Greece ; his cloak is white, his grey
tunic is in good condition, his felt cap is soft, his
walking-stick is nicely balanced,[c] his pumps luxuriant [d]
—why need I give a long description ? To put it in
a word, methinks I'm looking at the Academy itself."

Aristoxenus, the writer on music, says [e] in his
Life of Archytas that among the envoys sent by
Dionysius the Younger to the city of Tarentum was
Polyarchus, nicknamed the High-Liver, a man entirely
devoted to physical pleasures, and this not merely in
act, but also by his own confession. He was a
disciple of Archytas and not an utter stranger to
philosophic teachings ; he frequented the temple-en-
closures and would walk about with the other followers
of Archytas, listening to the discussion. On one
occasion a question and debate arose concerning the
appetites and in general the pleasures of the body,
and Polyarchus said [f] : " To me at least, gentlemen, it
has often before this appeared plain, as I considered
the question, that the whole system which sets up these

[b] Kock ii. 23, the only extant fragment of this play ; the
title obviously denotes a contemporary character, in spite of
the mythological allusion in it.
[c] Pope, *Rape of the Lock*, iv. 123, " Sir Plume of amber
snuff-box justly vain, and the nice conduct of a clouded
i.e. malacca) cane."
[d] See critical note 3. The βαυκίς was a fancy shoe worn
by women and effeminate men, *H.S.C.P.* x. 89.
[e] *F.H.G.* ii. 276, Diels *Vorsokr.*[3] i. 324.
[f] *Cf.* the theory of Eudoxus, Aristot. *Eth. Nic.* 1172 b 9,
also 1152 b 8, Cic. *Cato M.* xii. 39.

σκεύασμα καὶ πολὺ τῆς φύσεως ἀφεστηκὸς εἶναι.
ἡ γὰρ φύσις ὅταν φθέγγηται τὴν ἑαυτῆς φωνήν,
ἀκολουθεῖν κελεύει ταῖς ἡδοναῖς καὶ τοῦτό φησιι
c εἶναι νοῦν ἔχοντος· τὸ δὲ ἀντιτείνειν καὶ κατα-
δουλοῦσθαι τὰς ἐπιθυμίας οὔτ' ἔμφρονος οὔτε
εὐτυχοῦς οὔτε ξυνιέντος εἶναι[1] τίς ποτε ἐστὶν ἡ
τῆς ἀνθρωπίνης φύσεως σύστασις. τεκμήριον δ
ἰσχυρὸν εἶναι τὸ πάντας ἀνθρώπους, ὅταν ἐξουσίας
ἐπιλάβωνται μέγεθος ἀξιόχρεων ἐχούσης, ἐπὶ τὰς
σωματικὰς ἡδονὰς καταφέρεσθαι καὶ τοῦτο νομίζειν τέλος εἶναι τῆς ἐξουσίας, τὰ δὲ ἄλλα πάντο
σχεδὸν ἁπλῶς εἰπεῖν ἐν παρέργου[2] τίθεσθαι χώρα,
προφέρειν δ' ἔξεστι νῦν μὲν τοὺς Περσῶν βασιλεῖς
d καὶ[3] εἴ τίς που τυραννίδος ἀξιολόγου κύριος ὢ
τυγχάνει· πρότερον δὲ τούς τε Λυδῶν καὶ τοὺς
Μήδων καὶ ἔτι ἀνώτερον καὶ τοὺς Σύρων· οἱ
οὐδὲν γένος ἡδονῆς ἀζήτητον γενέσθαι, ἀλλὰ κα
δῶρα παρὰ τοῖς Πέρσαις προκεῖσθαι λέγεται[5] τοῖς
δυναμένοις ἐξευρίσκειν καινὴν ἡδονήν· καὶ μάλα
ὀρθῶς. ταχὺ γὰρ ἡ ἀνθρωπίνη φύσις ἐμπίπλατα
τῶν χρονιζουσῶν ἡδονῶν, κἂν ὦσιν σφόδρα δι
ηκριβωμέναι· ὥστε ἐπεὶ μεγάλην ἔχει δύναμιν ἡ
καινότης πρὸς τὸ μεῖζω φανῆναι τὴν ἡδονήν, οὐκ
e ὀλιγωρητέον,[6] ἀλλὰ πολλὴν ἐπιμέλειαν αὐτῆς ποιη
τέον. διὰ ταύτην δὲ τὴν αἰτίαν πολλὰ μὲν ἐξ
εὑρεθῆναι βρωμάτων εἴδη, πολλὰ δὲ πεμμάτων
πολλὰ δὲ θυμιαμάτων καὶ μύρων, πολλὰ δὲ ἱματίω

---

[1] Casaubon: εἰδέναι A.
[2] Kaibel: παρέργωι ACE.
[3] νῦν δὲ before καὶ deleted by Schweighäuser.
[4] Kaibel: τῶν A.   [5] λέγεται A: om. CE.
[6] οὖν after ὀλιγωρητέον deleted by Meineke.

virtues is quite absurd, and far removed from nature's
intent. For when nature speaks in her own voice,
she bids us follow our pleasures, and declares that
this is the right course for a man of sense [a]; but to
resist them, to subjugate the appetites, is the mark
of one who is neither prudent nor happy nor com-
prehends the composite character of human nature.
A strong proof of this is the fact that all men, whenever they attain to a power of sufficient magnitude,
are borne along in the direction of their bodily
pleasures, and regard this course as the end and
aim of power, while they regard practically all other
matters, to put it simply, as occupying a subordinate
station. To-day one may cite the case of the Persian
kings and anyone else who happens to be lord of a
considerable monarchy; in earlier times again, there
were the rulers of Lydia, Media, and still farther
back, Assyria; not a single variety of pleasure was
left untried by them; on the contrary, it is said that
rewards were offered among the Persians for all
who could invent a new pleasure; and with very
good reason. For man's nature is such that it is soon
surfeited with protracted pleasures, no matter how
elaborately they have been perfected; consequently,
since novelty has a mighty power to make pleasure
seem greater, it is not to be ignored,[b] but great
attention should be paid to it. For this reason many
kinds of food have been invented, many kinds of
cakes, many kinds of incense and perfume, many

[a] Above, 514 e, 529 d.
[b] Aristot. op. cit. 1175 a 6 ἔνια δὲ τέρπει καινὰ ὄντα, ὕστερον
δὲ οὐχ ὁμοίως διὰ ταὐτό.

καὶ στρωμάτων καὶ ποτηρίων[1] καὶ τῶν ἄλλων
σκευῶν· πάντα γὰρ δὴ ταῦτα συμβάλλεσθαί τινας
ἡδονάς, ὅταν ᾖ ἡ ὑποκειμένη ὕλη τῶν θαυμαζο-
μένων ὑπὸ τῆς ἀνθρωπίνης φύσεως· ὃ δὴ πε-
πονθέναι δοκεῖ ὅ τε χρυσὸς καὶ ἄργυρος καὶ τὰ
πολλὰ τῶν εὐοφθάλμων τε καὶ σπανίων, ὅσα καὶ
f κατὰ τὰς ἀπεργαζομένας τέχνας διηκριβωμένα
φαίνεται.”

Εἰπὼν δὲ τούτοις ἑξῆς τὰ περὶ τῆς θεραπείας
τῆς τοῦ Περσῶν βασιλέως, οἵους καὶ ὅσους ἔχει
θεραπευτῆρας, καὶ περὶ τῆς τῶν ἀφροδισίων αὐτοῦ
χρήσεως καὶ τῆς περὶ τὸν χρῶτα αὐτοῦ ὀδμῆς
καὶ τῆς εὐμορφίας καὶ τῆς ὁμιλίας καὶ περὶ τῶν
θεωρημάτων καὶ τῶν ἀκροαμάτων, εὐδαιμονέ-
στατον ἔφη κρῖναι[2] τῶν νῦν τὸν τῶν Περσῶν βασιλέα.
“πλεῖσται γάρ εἰσιν αὐτῷ καὶ τελειόταται παρ-
εσκευασμέναι ἡδοναί. δεύτερον δέ,” φησί, “τὸν
ἡμέτερον[3] τύραννον θείη τις ἂν καίπερ πολὺ λειπόμε-
546 νον. ἐκείνῳ μὲν γὰρ ἥ τε Ἀσία ὅλη χορηγεῖ . . .,[4]
τὸ δὲ Διονυσίου χορηγεῖον παντελῶς ἂν εὐτελές
τι φανείη πρὸς ἐκεῖνο συγκρινόμενον. ὅτι μὲν
οὖν περιμάχητός ἐστιν ὁ τοιοῦτος βίος φανερὸν ἐκ
τῶν συμβεβηκότων. Σύρους μὲν γὰρ Μῆδοι μετὰ
τῶν μεγίστων κινδύνων ἀφείλαντο[5] τὴν βασιλείαν
οὐκ ἄλλου τινὸς ἕνεκα ἢ τοῦ κυριεῦσαι τῆς Σύρων
ἐξουσίας, Μήδους δὲ Πέρσαι διὰ τὴν αὐτὴν αἰτίαν·
αὕτη δ᾽ ἐστὶν ἡ τῶν σωματικῶν ἡδονῶν ἀπόλαυσις.

---

[1] ποτηρίων CE: ποτηρίων δὴ A.
[2] ἔφη κρῖναι A: κρίνει (alone) CE.
[3] Musurus: ὑμέτερον A.
[4] Lacuna marked by Casaubon.
[5] ἀφείλαντο A, late form: ἀφείλοντο recent edd.

kinds of garments and rugs, of cups, too, and other utensils; for all these things do, in fact, contribute certain pleasures, whenever the basic material belongs to those things which are admired by human nature; this certainly is what happens in the case of gold and silver and most things that are a delight to the eye as well as rare—all, in fact, that are regarded as perfectly made according to the rules of those arts which work in them."

Following these remarks he described the comforts enjoyed by the king of Persia, the variety and number of purveyors that he had, his indulgence in sexual pleasures, the perfumed odour of his body, his elegance and manners of conversation, the spectacles and the entertainments by artists, and declared that he had decided that the king of Persia was the happiest man of the times.[a] " For he has pleasures secured for him in greatest number and completest form. Next to him (he continued) one might set down our own ruler, though far behind. For in the case of the king, all Asia supplies (his pleasure), as well as . . .,[b] whereas the service rendered to Dionysius must appear as something utterly trifling when compared with the other. That, therefore, such a life is eagerly desired is plain from what happens as the consequence of it. For the Medes hazarded the greatest dangers to deprive the Assyrians of their empire, for no other reason than to become masters of the Assyrians' wealth, and the Persians did the same thing to the Medes from the same motive; and the motive here is the enjoyment of physical pleasures. But lawgivers,

[a] We may have here an allusion to, and contradiction of, Plat. *Rep.* 580 A-B.
[b] The names of Egypt and Europe have dropped out.

ATHENAEUS

οἱ δὲ νομοθέται ὁμαλίζειν βουληθέντες τὸ τῶν
b ἀνθρώπων γένος καὶ μηδένα τῶν πολιτῶν τρυφᾶν,
ἀνακύψαι πεποιήκασι τὸ τῶν ἀρετῶν εἶδος· καὶ
ἔγραψαν νόμους περὶ συναλλαγμάτων καὶ τῶν
ἄλλων ὅσα¹ ἐδόκει πρὸς τὴν πολιτικὴν κοινωνίαν
ἀναγκαῖα εἶναι καὶ δὴ καὶ περὶ ἐσθῆτος καὶ τῆς
λοιπῆς διαίτης, ὅπως ᾖ ὁμαλής. πολεμούντων
οὖν τῶν νομοθετῶν τῷ τῆς πλεονεξίας γένει πρῶτον
μὲν ὁ περὶ τὴν δικαιοσύνην ἔπαινος ηὐξήθη, καί
πού τις καὶ ποιητὴς ἐφθέγξατο·

δικαιοσύνας τὸ χρύσεον πρόσωπον.

καὶ πάλιν·

τὸ χρύσεον ὄμμα τὸ τᾶς² Δίκας.

ἀπεθεώθη δὲ καὶ αὐτὸ τὸ τῆς Δίκης ὄνομα, ὥστε
c παρ' ἐνίοις καὶ βωμοὺς καὶ θυσίας γίνεσθαι Δίκῃ.
μετὰ ταύτην δὲ καὶ Σωφροσύνην καὶ Ἐγκράτειαν
ἐπεισεκόμισαν³ καὶ πλεονεξίαν ἐκάλεσαν τὴν ἐν
ἀπολαύσεσιν ὑπεροχήν· ὥστε τὸν πειθαρχοῦντα⁴
τοῖς νόμοις καὶ τῇ τῶν πολλῶν φήμῃ μετριάζειν
περὶ τὰς σωματικὰς ἡδονάς."

Καὶ Δοῦρις δέ φησιν ἐν τῇ κγ' τῶν Ἱστοριῶν
ὡς ἦν τὸ παλαιὸν τοῖς δυνάσταις ἐπιθυμία τῆς

¹ καὶ before ὅσα deleted by Schweighäuser.
² τὰς A and mss. of Stob. Ecl. p. 59. 2.
³ ἐπεισεκόμισαν Dalechamp: ἐπεισεκώμασαν ACE (not
properly transitive, see Plat. Rep. 500 b, Athen. 231 e).
Possibly we should read ἐνεκωμίασαν, "composed encomia
on," cf. Isocr. Panath. 255 d.
⁴ E: τῶν πειθαρχούντων (abbrev.) C, τὸν πιθαρχοῦντα A.

ᵃ A whimsical allusion to class legislation? If εἶδος here is
to be distinguished from γένος, the class (εἶδος) of the virtues
is made to emerge above the general level of the race (γένος).
474

in their desire to reduce the human race to one level and to bar every citizen from luxury, have caused a class of things called virtues to bob up;[a] and so they have written statutes dealing with contracts and all other matters which they thought were essential in furthering the social partnership, and in particular concerning dress and manner of living in general, in order that it might be of the same nature for all. Since, therefore, the lawgivers were carrying on their fight against all forms of greed, the praise of justice began to be extended, and some poet, I believe, uttered the phrase, 'The golden countenance of Justice.'[b] And again[c]: 'The golden eye of Justice.' And the very name of Justice came to be deified, so that among some peoples there arose altars and sacrifices to Justice.[d] Next to her they brought in Sobriety and Self-control besides, and gave the name ' greed '[e] to superior advantages in pleasure; thus it came about that the man who obeyed the laws and the voice of the common herd was moderate in his bodily pleasures."[f]

Duris, in the twenty-third book of his *Histories*, adds his testimony that in ancient times all monarchs had a consuming desire for drink.[g] Hence, he says,

[b] Euripides, *Melanippê*, T.G.F.² 512, Aristot. *Eth. Nic.* 1129 b 28 and Schol.
[c] Sophocles, *Locrian Ajax*, T.G.F.² 133.
[d] Hesiod, *Theog.* 901, Pindar, *Ol.* xiii. 6, make her daughter of Zeus and Themis; often in tragedy, *e.g.* Aesch. *Ag.* 773, *Cho.* 639.
[e] Lit. "unfair advantage." *Cf.* Plat. *Rep.* 430 E, 560 D-E.
[f] An awkward way of stating the Sophistic proposition that the moderate man was moderate merely through forced obedience to convention. *Cf.* Plat. *Rep.* 358 E-360 D.
[g] *F.H.G.* ii. 477, J. 2 A 143.

μέθης. διὸ ποιεῖν τὸν Ὅμηρον τῷ Ἀγαμέμνον[ι]
λοιδορούμενον τὸν Ἀχιλλέα καὶ λέγοντα·

οἰνοβαρές, κυνὸς ὄμματ᾽ ἔχων.

d καὶ τὸν θάνατον δ᾽ ἀποσημαίνων τοῦ βασιλέω[ς]
φησίν·

ὡς ἀμφὶ κρητῆρα τραπέζας τε πληθούσας
κείμεθα,

δεικνύων καὶ τὸν θάνατον αὐτοῦ παρ᾽ αὐταῖς ταῖ[ς]
ἐπιθυμίαις τῆς μέθης γενόμενον.

Φιλήδονος ἦν καὶ Σπεύσιππος ὁ Πλάτωνος συγ[-]
γενὴς καὶ διάδοχος τῆς σχολῆς. Διονύσιος γοῦν [ὁ]
τῆς Σικελίας τύραννος ἐν τῇ πρὸς αὐτὸν Ἐπιστολ[ῇ]
κατὰ τῆς φιληδονίας αὐτοῦ εἰπὼν καὶ φιλαργυρία[ν]
αὐτῷ ὀνειδίζει καὶ τὸν Λασθενείας τῆς Ἀρκαδικῆ[ς]
ἔρωτα, ἥτις καὶ Πλάτωνος ἠκηκόει.

e Οὐ μόνος δ᾽ Ἀρίστιππος καὶ οἱ ἀπ᾽ αὐτοῦ τὴ[ν]
κατὰ κίνησιν ἡδονὴν ἠσπάζοντο, ἀλλὰ καὶ Ἐπί[-]
κουρος καὶ οἱ ἀπὸ τούτου. καὶ ἵνα μὴ τοὺς κατα[ι-]
γισμοὺς λέγω καὶ τὰ ἐπεντρώματα,[1] ἅπερ πολλάκι[ς]
προφέρεται ὁ Ἐπίκουρος, καὶ τοὺς γαργαλισμοὺ[ς]
καὶ τὰ νύγματα ἃ ἐν τῷ περὶ Τέλους εἴρηκεν
τούτων μνησθήσομαι. φησὶν γάρ· "οὐ γὰρ ἔγωγ[ε]
δύναμαι νοῆσαι τἀγαθὸν ἀφαιρῶν μὲν τὰς διὰ
χυλῶν ἡδονάς, ἀφαιρῶν δὲ τὰς δι᾽ ἀφροδισίων[,]

[1] So Philo i. 115: ἐπικεντρώματα Meineke.

---

[a] Il. i. 225.
[b] Od. xi. 419; the shade of Agamemnon in Hades re[-]
counts his own death with that of his men, at the hands o[f]
Aegisthus, to Odysseus, saying that the latter would have
been most grieved at the sight of the bowl, etc.

Homer represents Achilles as reviling Agamemnon and saying [a]: " Thou, heavy with wine, and with the eyes of a dog." And when he describes the manner of the king's death he says [b]: " How we lay round the mixing-bowl and the tables laden," thereby showing that even his death occurred at the very time when he was indulging his appetite for drink.

Another devotee of pleasure was Speusippus, Plato's kinsman [c] and successor as head of the school. Dionysius, at any rate, the tyrant of Sicily, in his *Letter* to Speusippus, after denouncing his fondness for pleasure, reproaches him also for his avarice as well as for his love of Lastheneia, the Arcadian woman, who had also been Plato's pupil.

Yet Aristippus and his followers were not alone in welcoming the pleasure which is the result of motion,[d] but Epicurus and his followers did the same. And, not to enter into an account of his " gusts [e] " and his " titillations," all of which Epicurus quotes many times, also the " ticklings " and " solicitations " which he speaks of in his treatise *On the End*, I will mention the following. He says, namely [f]: " As for myself, I cannot conceive the Good if I exclude the pleasures derived from taste, or those derived from sexual intercourse, or those derived from enter-

[c] Nephew. On his reputation as a profligate see Athen. 279 e (vol. iii. p. 256).

[d] On pleasure, regarded as motion, κίνησις, see Aristot. *Eth. Nic.* 1173 a 30. Diog. Laert. ii. 86 says that the Cyrenaics distinguished two kinds of πάθη, feelings, one rough = πόνος, suffering, the other smooth = pleasure. On Aristippus *cf.* above, 544 a (p. 462).

[e] *i.e.* of passion; Usener, *Epicurea*, frag. 413, pp. 280, 293. The terms here quoted refer to various sense-stimuli.

[f] Athen. 280 a (vol. iii. p. 258), Bailey 122, 390.

ATHENAEUS

ἀφαιρῶν δὲ τὰς δι' ἀκροαμάτων, ἀφαιρῶν δὲ καὶ τὰς διὰ μορφῆς κατ' ὄψιν ἡδείας κινήσεις." καὶ

f Μητρόδωρος ἐν ταῖς Ἐπιστολαῖς φησιν· " περὶ γαστέρα, ὦ φυσιολόγε Τιμόκρατες, περὶ γαστέρα ὁ κατὰ φύσιν βαδίζων λόγος τὴν ἅπασαν ἔχει σπουδήν." καὶ ὁ Ἐπίκουρος δέ φησιν· " ἀρχὴ καὶ ῥίζα παντὸς ἀγαθοῦ ἡ τῆς γαστρὸς ἡδονή· καὶ τὰ σοφὰ καὶ¹ τὰ περισσὰ ἐπὶ ταύτην ἔχει τὴν ἀναφοράν." κἂν τῷ περὶ Τέλους δὲ πάλιν φησίν· " τιμητέον τὸ καλὸν καὶ τὰς ἀρετὰς καὶ τὰ τοιουτότροπα, ἐὰν ἡδονὴν παρασκευάζῃ· ἐὰν δὲ μὴ παρασκευάζῃ, χαίρειν ἐατέον," σαφῶς ὑπουργὸν ἐν τούτοις ποιῶν τὴν ἀρετὴν

547 τῆς ἡδονῆς καὶ θεραπαίνης τάξιν ἐπέχουσαν. κἂν ἄλλοις δέ φησιν· " προσπτύω τῷ καλῷ καὶ τοῖς κενῶς αὐτὸ θαυμάζουσιν, ὅταν μηδεμίαν ἡδονὴν ποιῇ."

Καλῶς ἄρα ποιοῦντες Ῥωμαῖοι οἱ πάντα ἄριστοι Ἀλκαῖον² καὶ Φιλίσκον τοὺς Ἐπικουρείους³ ἐξέβαλον τῆς πόλεως, Λευκίου τοῦ Ποστουμίου ὑπατεύοντος, δι' ἃς εἰσηγοῦντο ἡδονάς. ὁμοίως δὲ καὶ Μεσσήνιοι κατὰ ψήφισμα ἐξέωσαν τοὺς Ἐπικουρείους, Ἀντίοχος δὲ ὁ βασιλεὺς καὶ πάντας τοὺς φιλοσόφους τῆς αὑτοῦ βασιλείας, γράψας τάδε·

b " βασιλεὺς Ἀντίοχος Φανίᾳ. ἐγράψαμεν ὑμῖν καὶ πρότερον ὅπως μηδεὶς ᾖ φιλόσοφος ἐν τῇ πόλει μηδ'

---

¹ καὶ added from 280 a (τὰ περιττά).
² Ἀλκαῖον Aelian, V.H. ix. 12: ἄλιον A, ἅλιον CE.
³ CE: ἐπικουρίους A.

ᵃ Athen. 280 a (vol. iii. p. 256).
ᵇ Frag. 409, Usener, pp. 278, 120.
ᶜ Usener 123, Athen. 280 b (vol. iii. p. 258).
ᵈ Usener 315. Metrodorus had used the same words of physical pleasure, Plut. 1088 в.
ᵉ Either in 173 or 155 в.c.

478

tainments to which we listen, or those derived from the motions of a figure delightful to the eye." So Metrodorus says in his *Letters* [a] : " Yes, Timocrates, devoted to the study of nature as you are, it is indeed the belly, the belly and nothing else, which any philosophy that proceeds according to nature makes its whole concern." And Epicurus, again, says [b] : " The beginning and root of all good is the satisfaction of the belly, and all wise and exquisite things have in this their standard of reference." And in the treatise *On the End* he says again [c] : " We should prize the Good and the virtues and such things as that, provided they give us pleasure ; but if they do not give pleasure, we should renounce them " ; by these statements clearly making virtue the minister of pleasure, and occupying the station of a handmaid. In another passage he says [d] : " I spit upon the Good and those who fruitlessly admire it, whensoever it causes no pleasure."

The Romans, therefore, the most virtuous of men in all things, did a good job when they banished the Epicureans Alcaeus and Philiscus from the city, in the consulship of Lucius Postumius,[e] because of the pleasures which they introduced. Similarly the people of Messenia thrust out the Epicureans by public decree, as King Antiochus also ejected from his kingdom all philosophers, writing the following order[f] : " King Antiochus to Phanias : We have written to you before now that there shall be no philosopher

---

[f] Radermacher, *Rhein. Mus.* lvi. 202 ff., thinks the rescript a Jewish forgery ; he is certainly right in keeping the eccentric syntax. Which king of this name is meant is unknown. In any case it was a later Antiochus : Bevan, *House of Seleucus*, ii. 277, thinks of Antiochus XIII, nicknamed the Asiatic.

ἐν τῇ χώρᾳ. πυνθανόμεθα δὲ οὐκ ὀλίγους εἶναι καὶ
τοὺς νέους λυμαίνεσθαι διὰ τὸ μηθὲν πεποιηκέναι
ὑμᾶς ὧν ἐγράψαμεν περὶ τούτων. ὡς ἂν οὖν λάβῃς
τὴν ἐπιστολήν, σύνταξον κήρυγμα ποιήσασθαι ὅπως
οἱ μὲν φιλόσοφοι πάντες ἀπαλλάσσωνται[1] ἐκ τῶν
τόπων ἤδη, τῶν δὲ νεανίσκων ὅσοι ἐὰν[2] ἁλίσκωνται
πρὸς τούτοις γινόμενοι διότι κρεμήσονται, καὶ οἱ
πατέρες αὐτῶν ἐν αἰτίαις ἔσονται ταῖς μεγίσταις·
καὶ μὴ ἄλλως γίνηται.[3]''

c   Τῆς δ' ἡδονῆς πρὸ 'Επικούρου εἰσηγητὴς ἐγένετο Σοφοκλῆς ὁ ποιητὴς ἐν 'Αντιγόνῃ τοιαῦτα
εἰπών·

τὰς γὰρ ἡδονὰς
ὅταν προδῶσιν ἄνδρες, οὐ τίθημ' ἐγὼ
ζῆν τοῦτον, ἀλλ' ἔμψυχον ἡγοῦμαι νεκρόν.
πλούτει τε γὰρ κατ' οἶκον, εἰ βούλει, μέγα
καὶ ζῇ τύραννον σχῆμ' ἔχων· ἐὰν δ' ἀπῇ
τούτων τὸ χαίρειν, τἄλλ' ἐγὼ καπνοῦ σκιᾶς
οὐκ ἂν πριαίμην ἀνδρὶ πρὸς τὴν ἡδονήν.

d   Καὶ Λύκων δὲ ὁ Περιπατητικός, ὥς φησιν
'Αντίγονος ὁ Καρύστιος, κατ' ἀρχὰς ἐπιδημήσας
παιδείας ἕνεκα ταῖς 'Αθήναις περὶ συμβολικοῦ
κώθωνος καὶ πόσον ἑκάστη τῶν ἑταιρουσῶν ἐπράτ-
τετο μίσθωμα ἀκριβῶς ἠπίστατο. ὕστερον δὲ καὶ
τοῦ Περιπάτου προστὰς ἐδείπνιζε τοὺς φίλους
ἀλαζονείᾳ καὶ πολυτελείᾳ πολλῇ χρώμενος. χωρὶς

---

[1] ACE: ἀπαλλάξονται Meineke, Kaibel.   But see G.M.T.
§ 339.
[2] ἐὰν ACE, as often in late Greek.
[3] γίνηται ACE: γένηται Casaubon.

in the capital or even in the country. Yet we learn that there are not a few, and that our young men are being corrupted because of your failure to do any of the things which we have prescribed concerning them. So soon, then, as you receive this letter, draw up a proclamation to effect the immediate departure of all philosophers from our territories, and as for all the young men who shall be found in their company, they shall be strung up,[a] and their fathers shall be held to answer for the gravest charges ; and let it not be otherwise."

Before Epicurus, however, the poet Sophocles proved to be an exponent of pleasure when he uttered such language as the following in *Antigone* [b] : " For when men abandon pleasurable deeds I reckon such a one not alive, but I regard him as a living corpse. Ay, heap up mighty wealth in your house, if you so desire, and live in sovereign state ; if, however, joy be absent from these things, I would not purchase all the rest from a man at the price of the shadow of smoke, in comparison with pleasure."

Lycon, too, the Peripatetic, according to Antigonus of Carystus,[c] when he began his residence at Athens in order to carry on his studies, acquired an accurate knowledge of drinking-bouts in which all stood treat, and of how big a price every one of the ladies of easy virtue exacted. And even later, when he became head of the Peripatetic school,[d] he used to entertain his friends at dinner with much ostentatious expense.

---

[a] Before a culprit was flogged it was customary to tie him up on a pillar by his hands ; see Pollux iii. 79, Athen. 459 a (vol. iv. p. 583 note c), and *cf.* Herodas iii. 59-61.

[b] 1165 ff. ; *cf.* Athen. 280 b (vol. iii. p. 258).

[c] Wilamowitz p. 84, *cf.* p. 264.

[d] The Lyceum, founded by Aristotle.

γὰρ τῶν παραλαμβανομένων εἰς αὐτὰ ἀκροαμάτων
καὶ ἀργυρωμάτων καὶ στρωμνῆς ἡ λοιπὴ παρα-
σκευὴ καὶ ἡ τῶν δείπνων περιεργία καὶ ὁ τῶν
τραπεζοποιῶν[1] καὶ μαγείρων ὄχλος τοσοῦτος ἦν
e ὥστε πολλοὺς ὀρρωδεῖν καὶ βουλομένους προσιέναι
πρὸς τὴν διατριβὴν ἀνακόπτεσθαι, καθάπερ[2] εἰς
πολίτευμα πονηρὸν καὶ χορηγιῶν[3] καὶ λειτουργιῶν
πλῆρες εὐλαβουμένους προσάγειν. ἔδει γὰρ ἄρξαι
τε τὴν νομιζομένην ἐν τῷ περιπάτῳ ἀρχὴν (αὕτη
δ' ἦν ἐπὶ τῆς εὐκοσμίας τῶν ἐπιχειρούντων)
τριάκονθ' ἡμέρας, εἶτα τῇ ἔνῃ καὶ νέᾳ λαβόντα
ἀφ' ἑκάστου τῶν ἐπιχειρούντων ἐννέα ὀβολοὺς ὑπο-
δέξασθαι μὴ μόνον αὐτοὺς τοὺς τὴν συμβολὴν εἰσ-
ενεγκόντας, ἀλλὰ καὶ οὓς παρακαλέσειεν ὁ Λύκων,
ἔτι δὲ καὶ τοὺς ἐπιμελῶς συναντῶντας τῶν πρεσβυ-
f τέρων εἰς τὴν σχολήν, ὥστε γίνεσθαι μηδὲ εἰς τὸν
μυρισμὸν καὶ τοὺς στεφάνους ἱκανὸν τὸ ἐκλεγό-
μενον ἀργύριον· ἱεροποιῆσαί τε καὶ τῶν Μουσείων[4]
ἐπιμελητὴν γενέσθαι. ἃ δὴ πάντα ἐφαίνετο λόγου
μὲν ἀλλότρια καὶ φιλοσοφίας εἶναι, τρυφῆς δὲ καὶ
περιστάσεως οἰκειότερα. καὶ γὰρ εἰ παρίεντό
τινες τῶν μὴ δυναμένων εἰς ταῦτα ἀναλίσκειν ἀπὸ
βραχείας καὶ τῆς τυχούσης ὁρμώμενοι χορηγίας, ὅ
γ' ἐθισμὸς[5] ἱκανῶς ἦν ἄτοπος. οὐ γὰρ ἵνα συρ-

---

[1] Meineke: τραπεζῶν A.
[2] καθάπερ Schweighäuser, following Casaubon: καὶ κσθάπερ Λ.
[3] Musurus: χορηγίαν A.
[4] U. Koehler: μουσῶν A.
[5] Wilamowitz: ὅ γε μισθὸς A.

For besides all the artists called in to furnish entertainments, and all the silver-ware and couch-coverings, the other arrangements, the elaborate fare at the dinners, and the mob of servers and cooks, were such that many persons were afraid, and although they wanted to join the school they were brought up short, like persons who fear to enter a city the government of which is vicious and burdened with expensive taxes.[a] For they were obliged to assume the regular administration of the school for a period of thirty days, which meant that they were in charge of the good behaviour of the new students ; then on the last day of the month they received ninepence from each of the new students, and on that sum they had to entertain at dinner not only those who had paid the fee, but any others whom Lycon invited, besides all those among the older men who made a business of visiting the school ; consequently the money collected was not enough even to pay for the perfumery and the wreaths ; he also had charge of the sacrifices, and was administrator of the rites in honour of the Muses. Now all this plainly had nothing to do with dialectic and philosophy, but was more appropriate to the pomp and circumstance of luxurious living. For even supposing that some who were unable to spend money on these things were excused from the duty because the resources at their disposal were too meagre and trifling, yet the practice was very harmful, to say the least. For surely the followers

---

[a] Lit. " filled with the duty of equipping choruses and of rendering public services." On the expenses laid upon the choregus see Haigh, *Att. Theatre*[3] 37 ff. ; on the various services rendered in lieu of taxes in cash, Gulick, *Life of the Ancient Greeks*, pp. 62, 199.

ρυέντες ἐπὶ τὸ αὐτὸ τῆς ἕως τοῦ ὀρθρίου[1] γενομένης
τραπέζης ἀπολαύσωσιν ἢ χάριν ἑξοινίας ἐποιή-
σαντο τὰς συνόδους ταύτας οἱ περὶ Πλάτωνα καὶ
548 Σπεύσιππον, ἀλλ' ἵνα φαίνωνται καὶ τὸ θεῖον τιμῶντες καὶ μουσικῶς[2] ἀλλήλοις συμπεριφερόμενοι,
καὶ τὸ πλεῖστον, ἕνεκεν ἀνέσεως καὶ φιλολογίας. ἃ
δὴ πάντα γέγονεν δεύτερα παρὰ τοῖς[3] ὕστερον τῶν τε
χλανίδων καὶ τῆς πολυτελείας τῆς εἰρημένης· οὐ
γὰρ ἔγωγε τοὺς λοιποὺς ὑπεξαιροῦμαι. ὁ δὲ Λύκων
ὑπ' ἀλαζονείας καὶ ἐν τῷ ἐπιφανεστάτῳ τῆς πόλεως
b τόπῳ ἐν τῇ Κόνωνος οἰκίᾳ εἶχεν εἰκοσίκλινον οἶκον,
ὃς ἦν ἐπιτήδειος αὐτῷ πρὸς τὰς ὑποδοχάς. ἦν δὲ
ὁ Λύκων καὶ σφαιριστὴς ἀγαθὸς καὶ ἐπιδέξιος.

Περὶ δὲ Ἀναξάρχου Κλέαρχος ὁ Σολεὺς ἐν
πέμπτῳ Βίων οὕτω γράφει· " τῷ εὐδαιμονικῷ καλου-
μένῳ[4] 'Αναξάρχῳ διὰ τὴν τῶν χορηγησάντων ἄγνοιαν
περιπεσούσης ἐξουσίας γυμνὴ μὲν ᾠνοχόει παι-
δίσκη πρόσηβος ἡ προκριθεῖσα διαφέρειν ὥρᾳ τῶν
ἄλλων, ἀνασύρουσα πρὸς ἀλήθειαν τὴν τῶν οὕτως
αὐτῇ χρωμένων ἀκρασίαν. ὁ δὲ σιτοποιὸς χειρίδας
c ἔχων καὶ περὶ τῷ στόματι κημὸν ἔτριβε τὸ σταῖς, ἵνα
μήτε[5] ἱδρὼς ἐπιρρέοι[6] μήτε τοῖς φυράμασιν ὁ τρίβων
ἐμπνέοι." διὸ πρεπόντως ἄν τις εἴποι τῷ σοφῷ
τούτῳ φιλοσόφῳ τὰ ἐκ τοῦ Ἀναξίλα Λυροποιοῦ[7]·

---

[1] ὀρθρίου Musurus: θρίου A.
[2] μουσικῶς Bergk: φυσικῶς ACE.
[3] Schweighäuser: παρ' αὐτοῖς A.
[4] Schweighäuser: τῶν εὐδαιμονικῶν καλουμένων A.
[5] E: μή τι C, μηδὲ A.   [6] CE: ἐπιρρέῃι A.
[7] Casaubon: ἀναξιλαυροποιου (sic) A.

---

[a] Plato himself recommended the use of the early morning,
but for different purposes, Prot. 313 B, Laws 961 B.
[b] F.H.G. ii. 308, Diels i. 456, Athen. 250 f (vol. iii. p. 130).
[c] Another example of Clearchus's obscure style. He

of Plato and Speusippus did not rush in throngs to the same place and form their gatherings merely to enjoy a dinner that lasted until the morning hours [a] or to get drunk, but rather to show that they revered the gods and consorted with one another as cultivated persons should ; and, chief of all, to gain relaxation and take part in learned discussions. But all these aims, as we have seen, became in the eyes of their successors secondary to their love of soft cloaks and the lavish expense just described ; nor do I except any of the others. But Lycon was so vulgar in his ostentation that he took a twenty-couch room in Conon's house, in the most conspicuous part of the city, which suited him for holding his receptions. Lycon, moreover, was a good and skilful ball-player.

Concerning Anaxarchus, Clearchus of Soli, in the fifth book of his *Lives*, writes as follows [b] : " After great wealth had fallen to the lot of Anaxarchus (who was called the philosopher of eudaemonism) through the folly of those who rendered him benefits,[c] his wine was poured out for him by a naked young girl who had been selected because she surpassed in beauty all others, although, to tell the truth, she laid bare not so much her own nakedness as the lustfulness of those who treated her in this way. His bread-maker wore gloves, and had a mask to cover his mouth when he kneaded the dough, to prevent sweat from streaming upon it and the kneader from breathing upon the mixture." Hence one might appropriately quote for this wise philosopher the verses from *The Harp-maker* of Anaxilas [d] : " Oiling his skin with

means that many persons supported Anaxarchus in luxury through mistaken notions of his worth. On his heroic death see Diog. L. ix. 59.

[d] Kock ii. 268 ; the verses are anapaests.

ξανθοῖς τε μύροις χρῶτα λιπαίνων,
χλανίδας θ' ἕλκων, βλαύτας σύρων,
βολβοὺς τρώγων, τυροὺς κάπτων,
ᾠὰ κολάπτων,[1] κήρυκας ἔδων,[2]
Χῖον πίνων, καὶ πρὸς τούτοις
ἐν σκυταρίοις ῥαπτοῖσι φορῶν
Ἐφεσήια γράμματα καλά.

Πόσῳ γὰρ τούτων βελτίων Γοργίας ὁ Λεοντῖνος,
d περὶ οὗ φησιν ὁ αὐτὸς Κλέαρχος ἐν τῷ ὀγδόῳ τῶν
Βίων ὅτι διὰ τὸ σωφρόνως ζῆν σχεδὸν ρι'[3] ἔτη τῷ
φρονεῖν συνεβίωσεν. καὶ ἐπεί τις αὐτὸν ἤρετο τίνι
διαίτῃ χρώμενος οὕτως ἐμμελῶς καὶ μετὰ αἰσθή-
σεως τοσοῦτον χρόνον ζήσειεν, "οὐδὲν πώποτε,"
εἶπεν, "ἡδονῆς ἕνεκεν πράξας." Δημήτριος δὲ ὁ
Βυζάντιος ἐν τετάρτῳ περὶ Ποιημάτων "Γοργίας,"
φησίν, "ὁ Λεοντῖνος ἐρωτηθεὶς τί αὐτῷ γέγονεν
αἴτιον τοῦ βιῶσαι πλείω[4] τῶν ρ' ἐτῶν, ἔφη ' τὸ
μηθὲν πώποτε ἑτέρου[5] ἕνεκεν πεποιηκέναι.' "
e Ὦχος δὲ πολλῷ χρόνῳ τὴν βασιλείαν καὶ τὴν
λοιπὴν περὶ τὸν βίον χορηγίαν διαρκῆ κτησάμενος,

---

[1] ACE: ᾧ' ἐκλάπτων Kock, Kaibel.
[2] Toup: ἔχων ACE.
[3] ρι' Diels: π̄ (= ὀγδοήκοντα) ACE. The correction is
certain; cf. ἑκατόν below.　　　　　[4] A: πλεῖον CE.
[5] ἐντέρου Meineke, ἤτρου, "stomach," Tucker.

---

[c] This is the earliest occurrence in literature of this famous
phrase, originally applied to six magical words cited by
Hesychius and Clement of Alexandria (*Strom.* v. 242, *cf.*
Plut. 706 E), useful in warding off evil spirits. Pauly-
Wissowa, v. 2771; Wolfgang Schultz, *Rätsel*, i. 82 ff. The
ā in κᾱλά is curious, if not incredible (as Kock thinks) in
a writer of Attic comedy; but Anaxilas was not an
Athenian by birth. If κᾱλά be rejected, we might read βαιά,

yellow unguents, flaunting soft cloaks, shuffling fine slippers, munching bulbs,[a] bolting pieces of cheese, pecking at eggs, eating periwinkles,[b] drinking Chian, and what is more, carrying about, on little bits of stitched leather, lovely Ephesian letters.[c]"

How much nobler than these persons was Gorgias of Leontini! Of him Clearchus, whom we just quoted, says[d] in the eighth book of his *Lives* that because of his sobriety of life he lived in the full possession of his senses for nearly one hundred and ten years.[e] And when somebody asked him what his mode of life was, seeing that he had lived so long a time so comfortably and with senses intact, he replied, " I have never done anything for the sake of pleasure." But Demetrius of Byzantium in the fourth book of his work *On Poetry* says[f] : " When Gorgias of Leontini was asked what was the cause of his living more than a hundred years he answered, ' The fact that I have never yet done anything for the sake of anybody else.' "[g]

Ochus,[h] again, held the throne much later, and acquired, in general, resources for living in a style that

"little." A small phylactery, with a cylindrical case which was hung on a gold necklace, is in the British Museum, No. 3155. See Conway, *From Orpheus to Cicero*, p. 9.

[d] *F.H.G.* ii. 308, Diels i. 547.

[e] Plat. *Phaedr.* 261 c calls him Nestor. Apollodorus says he lived to be 109, Diog. Laert. viii. 58, and no other authority gives so low a figure as Athen. MSS. See critical note 3.

[f] *F.H.G.* ii. 624 note.

[g] This agrees well with the self-centred character ascribed to him by his own pupil, Isocrates, *Or.* xv. 156 (83). Yet see critical note 5.

[h] Surname of Artaxerxes III, praised for frugality, Athen. 150 b (vol. ii. p. 184). But Plut. *Artax.* 30 says he was cruel and bloodthirsty.

ὡς τελευτῶντος[1] ἠρώτησεν ὁ πρεσβύτατος τῶν
υἱῶν τί πράσσων τοσαῦτ' ἔτη διαφυλάξειεν τὴν
βασιλείαν, ἵνα καὶ αὐτὸς τοῦτο μιμοῖτο, "τὰ
δίκαια πράττων," εἶπε, "πρὸς ἅπαντας ἀνθρώπους
καὶ θεούς." Καρύστιος δ' ὁ Περγαμηνὸς ἐν
Ἱστορικοῖς Ὑπομνήμασιν " Κηφισόδωρος," φησίν,
" ὁ Θηβαῖος Πολύδωρον τὸν Τήιον ἰατρὸν Ἀντι-
πάτρῳ συσσιτεῖν ψιλοτάπιδα ἔχοντι[2] κρικωτὴν
f καθάπερ τοὺς στρωματεῖς εὐτελῆ, ἐφ' ἧς κατα-
κεῖσθαι, κάδους δὲ χαλκοῦς καὶ ποτήρια ὀλίγα·
γεγονέναι γὰρ ὀλιγοδίαιτον καὶ τρυφῆς ἀλλότριον."

Τιθωνὸν δ' ἀπὸ τῆς ἔω μέχρι δυσμῶν κοιμώ-
μενον μόλις αἱ[3] ἐπιθυμίαι πρὸς ἑσπέραν ἐπήγειρον·
ὅθεν Ἠοῖ συγκοιμᾶσθαι λεχθείς, διὰ τὸ ταῖς ἐπιθυμίαις ἐμπεπλέχθαι ἐπὶ γήρως ἐν ταλάρῳ[4] καθ-
549 εἴρκται, κρεμαστὸς ὢν πρὸς ἀλήθειαν ἐκ τούτων.
καὶ Μελάνθιος δὲ τὸν αὑτοῦ τράχηλον κατατείνων
ἀπήγχετο ἐκ τῶν ἀπολαύσεων, κνισότερος ὢν τοῦ
Ὀδυσσέως Μελανθίου. πολλοὶ δὲ καὶ ἄλλοι πᾶν
τὸ σῶμα διεστράφησαν διὰ τὰς ἀκαίρους ἡδονάς,
οἱ δὲ καὶ εἰς πάχος σώματος ἐπέδωκαν, ἄλλοι δὲ
καὶ εἰς ἀναισθησίαν διὰ πολλὴν τρυφήν. Νύμφις
γοῦν ὁ Ἡρακλεώτης ἐν τῷ ιβ'[5] περὶ Ἡρακλείας

---

[1] τελευτῶντα CE.   [2] Dutheil: ἔχοντα A.
[3] αἱ added by Kaibel.
[4] ἐπὶ γήρως ἐν ταλάρῳ Kaibel, cf. Adam at Athen. 6 c: ἐπὶ
τῶι γήραι alone ACE.
[5] ιβ' Müller: β' A.

---

[a] F.H.G. ii. 85, iv. 357, J. 2 B 524.
[b] Cf. Athen. 435 d (vol. iv. p. 472). Antipater's economy
led him to spread on his dinner-couch an ordinary curtain
or rug-container, which had rings for suspending the curtain

would suffice for anyone. When he was dying his eldest son asked him what he had done in order to preserve his kingdom so many years (since he desired to imitate him in this), and he answered, " I have practised justice before all men and gods." Carystius of Pergamum in *Historical Notes* quotes Cephisodorus of Thebes as saying [a] that Polydorus, the physician of Teos, ate at the same mess with Antipater ; the latter had a cheap curtain to which the rings were still attached as in the case of the bales used for carrying rugs ; on this he would recline at dinner, with a few bronze jars and cups for service ; for he lived on a small scale and was entirely alien to a life of luxury.[b]

As for Tithonus,[c] lying as he did in bed from morning until sunset, his desires could hardly excite him when evening drew on ; hence he is said to have lain with Dawn, but because he was so wrapped up in his lusts, in his old age he is shut up in a birdcage, being literally " suspended " as a result. And Melanthius,[d] too, stretched his neck so far that he choked himself to death with his indulgence, being greedier than Odysseus's Melanthius.[e] And many other persons have become completely deformed in body through their unmeasured indulgence in pleasure, others have grown to bodily fatness, while still others through great luxury have actually reached the point of insensibility to pain. For example Nymphis of Heracleia in the twelfth book of his work *On Heracleia*

on a pole, or for drawing a thong through them when rugs were transported in it.
[c] The difficult and allegorical language, as well as the content, points to Clearchus as the author of this note, *cf.* Athen. 6 c (vol. i. p. 26). For the story of Tithonus, changed in undying old age into a chirping cicada, see Schol. *Il.* xi. 1.
[d] Vol. i. p. 25 note *c*.　　　　[e] *Od.* xvii. 247 *et passim.*

"Διονύσιος," φησίν, "ὁ Κλεάρχου τοῦ πρώτου τυραν-
νήσαντος ἐν Ἡρακλείᾳ υἱὸς καὶ αὐτὸς τῆς πατρίδος
τυραννήσας ὑπὸ τρυφῆς καὶ τῆς καθ' ἡμέραν
b ἀδηφαγίας ἔλαθεν ὑπερσαρκήσας, ὥστε διὰ τὸ
πάχος ἐν δυσπνοίᾳ αὐτὸν συσχεθῆναι καὶ πνιγμῷ.
διὸ συνέταξαν οἱ ἰατροὶ κατασκευάσαι βελόνας
λεπτὰς τῷ μήκει διαφερούσας, ἃς[1] διὰ τῶν πλευ-
ρῶν καὶ τῆς κοιλίας διωθεῖν ὅταν εἰς ὕπνον τύχῃ
βαθύτερον ἐμπεσών. μέχρι μὲν οὖν τινος ὑπὸ τῆς
πεπωρωμένης ἐκ τοῦ στέατος σαρκὸς οὐκ ἐνεποίει
τὴν αἴσθησιν· εἰ δὲ πρὸς τὸν καθαρὸν τόπον ἡ
c βελόνη διελθοῦσα ἔθιγεν, τότε διηγείρετο. τοὺς δὲ
χρηματισμοὺς ἐποιεῖτο τοῖς βουλομένοις προτιθέ-
μενος κιβωτὸν τοῦ σώματος ἵνα τὰ μὲν λοιπὰ μέρη
κρύπτοι,[2] τὸ δὲ πρόσωπον μόνον ὑπερέχων δια-
λέγοιτο τοῖς ἀπαντῶσιν. μνημονεύει δ' αὐτοῦ
Μένανδρος ἥκιστά γ'[3] ὢν λοίδορος ἐν τοῖς Ἁλιεῦσιν,
τὸν μῦθον ὑποστησάμενος ὑπέρ τινων φυγάδων ἐξ
Ἡρακλείας·

παχὺς γὰρ ὗς ἔκειτ' ἐπὶ στόμα.

καὶ πάλιν·

ἐτρύφησεν, ὥστε μὴ πολὺν τρυφᾶν χρόνον.

καὶ ἔτι·

ἴδιον ἐπιθυμῶν, μόνος μοι θάνατος οὗτος φαίνεται
εὐθάνατος, ἔχοντα πολλὰς χολλάδας κεῖσθαι
παχὺν

---

[1] Schweighäuser: αἷς ACE.
[2] κρύπτοι Meineke (ἀποκρύπτοιτο Aelian): κρύπτῃι ACE.
[3] γ' Musurus: τ' A.

says [a] that Dionysius, the son of Clearchus, first tyrant
of Heracleia, who also became tyrant of his native
land, gradually became overloaded with flesh by
reason of the luxury and gluttony in which he lived
daily ; hence, because of his obesity, he was afflicted
with shortness of breath and fits of choking. So the
physicians prescribed that he should get some fine
needles, exceedingly long, which they thrust through
his ribs and belly whenever he happened to fall into
a very deep sleep. Now up to a certain point under
the flesh, completely calloused as it was by fat, the
needle caused no sensation ; but if the needle went
through so far as to touch the region which was free
of fat, then he would be thoroughly aroused. When
he held audiences with people who desired to see him
he placed a box in front of his body in order that while
hiding the other parts of his person, his face alone
might project above them as he conversed with his
interviewers. Menander, by no means given to
malicious description, mentions him in *The Fishermen*,
after first telling the story of some refugees from
Heracleia. They say [b] : " Indeed he was a fat hog
lying upon his snout " ; and again : " He enjoyed
luxury—but in such wise that he won't enjoy it long."
And farther on [c] : " One thing for my own self I
desire—and this seems to me the only death that is
a happy dying—to lie on my back with its many rolls

[a] *F.H.G.* iii. 15, Aelian *V.H.* ix. 13; *cf.* Memnon *ap.*
Phot. *Bibl.* 224 b 13 (Bekker), Diod. xvi. 88.
[b] Kock iii. 10, Allinson (L.C.L.) 316. The citations from
Menander were apparently not in Nymphis ; Müller omits
them.
[c] Here Dionysius himself is supposed to be speaking : the
metre is the trochaic tetrameter.

d ὕπτιον, μόλις λαλοῦντα καὶ τὸ πνεῦμ᾽ ἔχοντ᾽
ἄνω,
ἐσθίοντα καὶ λέγοντα ' σήπομ᾽ ὑπὸ τῆς ἡδονῆς.'

ἀπέθανεν δὲ βιώσας ἔτη πέντε πρὸς τοῖς πεντήκοντα, ὧν ἐτυράννησεν τρία καὶ τριάκοντα, ἁπάντων τῶν πρὸ αὐτοῦ τυράννων πραότητι καὶ ἐπι-
εικείᾳ διενηνοχώς."

Τοιοῦτος ἐγεγόνει καὶ Πτολεμαῖος ὁ ἕβδομος
Αἰγύπτου βασιλεύσας, ὁ αὑτὸν μὲν Εὐεργέτην
ἀνακηρύττων, ὑπὸ δὲ Ἀλεξανδρέων Κακεργέτης
ὀνομαζόμενος. Ποσειδώνιος γοῦν ὁ στωϊκός, συν-
e αποδημήσας Σκιπίωνι τῷ Ἀφρικανῷ κληθέντι
εἰς Ἀλεξάνδρειαν καὶ θεασάμενος αὐτόν, γράφει
ἐν ἑβδόμῃ τῶν Ἱστοριῶν οὕτως· " διὰ δὲ τρυφὴν
διέφθαρτο τὸ σῶμα ὑπὸ παχύτητος καὶ γαστρὸς
μεγέθους, ἣν δυσπερίληπτον εἶναι συνέβαινεν· ἐφ᾽
ἧς χιτωνίσκον ἐνδεδυκὼς ποδήρη μέχρι τῶν καρπῶν χειρίδας ἔχοντα[1]· προήει δὲ οὐδέποτε πεζὸς
εἰ μὴ διὰ Σκιπίωνα." ὅτι δὲ τρυφῆς οὐκ ἦν
ἀλλότριος ὁ βασιλεὺς οὗτος, αὐτὸς περὶ ἑαυτοῦ
μαρτυρεῖ ἐν τῷ ὀγδόῳ τῶν Ὑπομνημάτων διηγούμενος ὅπως τε ἱερεὺς ἐγένετο τοῦ ἐν Κυρήνῃ
f Ἀπόλλωνος καὶ ὅπως δεῖπνον παρεσκεύασε τοῖς
πρὸ αὐτοῦ γενομένοις ἱερεῦσι, γράφων οὕτως·

[1] The verb is lost; Kaibel added περιήει.

---

[a] For this meaning of χολλάδες (not in L. & S.) see Bekk.
Anecd. 72. 19.

[b] In gluttony, whence his nickname Physcon (Fat-Belly).
See vol. ii. pp. 312 and 529.

[c] F.H.G. iii. 255, J. 2 A 223, 226. Scipio (son of Aemilius

of fat,[a] scarce uttering a word, gasping for breath, while I eat and say, 'I'm rotting away in pleasure.'" Yet he did not die until he had lived fifty-five years, during thirty-three of which he had been tyrant, and had excelled all tyrants before him in mild temper and decent conduct.

Like him [b] also was the seventh Ptolemy who ruled over Egypt, the king who proclaimed himself Benefactor, to be sure, but who received from the Alexandrians the name of Malefactor. The Stoic Poseidonius, at least, who travelled with Scipio Africanus when he was invited to Alexandria, and saw Ptolemy, writes in the seventh book of his *Histories*[c]: "Through indulgence in luxury his body had become utterly corrupted with fat and with a belly of such size that it would have been hard to measure it with one's arms; to cover it he wore a tunic which reached to his feet and which had sleeves reaching to his wrists; but he never went abroad on foot except on Scipio's account."[d] And that this king was not a stranger to luxury is attested by himself in the eighth book of his *Commentaries*, when he relates of himself how he became priest of Apollo in Cyrene, and got up a banquet for those who had been priests before him; he writes as follows[e]: "The Artemitia is a very

Paulus, adopted son of the elder Africanus, conqueror of Carthage 146 B.C.) made this journey *ca.* 136 B.C., a year or so before Poseidonius was born. His Stoic friend and companion was Panaetius, the teacher of Poseidonius. The same confusion (Poseidonius for Panaetius) recurs at 657 f. Scipio himself exemplified and preached all the virtues, Plut. 318 E, 199 F, Athen. 273 a (vol. iii. pp. 226, 228), Aul. Gell. iv. 20.

[d] Note the pun on his name, since σκίπων means a staff; hence διὰ Σκιπίωνα also means "with the aid of a staff."

[e] *F.H.G.* iii. 187, J. 2 B 985.

" Ἀρτεμίτια μεγίστη ἑορτὴ ἐν Κυρήνη,[1] ἐν ᾗ ὁ
ἱερεὺς τοῦ Ἀπόλλωνος (ἐνιαύσιος δ' ἐστί) δειπνίζει
τοὺς πρὸ αὐτοῦ ἱερευσαμένους καὶ παρατίθησιν
ἑκάστῳ τρύβλιον[2]· τοῦτο δ' ἐστὶ κεραμεοῦν ἄγγος
ἐπιδεχόμενον ὡς εἴκοσι ἀρτάβας, ἐν ᾧ πολλὰ μὲν
τῶν ἀγριμαίων[3] ἔγκειται πεπονημένα, πολλὰ δ' ἐσθ'
ὅτε[4] καὶ τῶν ἡμέρων ὀρνίθων, ἔτι δὲ θαλαττίων
550 ἰχθύων ταρίχου τε ξενικοῦ πλείονα γένη· πολλάκις
δέ τινες καὶ καθάριον[5] ἀκολουθίσκον προσδιδόασιν.
ἡμεῖς δὲ περιειλόμεθα τὰ τοιαῦτα,[6] φιάλας δ'
ὁλαργύρους κατασκευάσαντες, τὸ τίμημα ἔχουσαν
ἑκάστην ἧς προειρήκαμεν δαπάνης, ἵππον τε κατεσκευασμένον σὺν ἱπποκόμῳ καὶ φαλάροις δια-
χρύσοις ἐδώκαμεν καὶ παρεκαλέσαμεν ἕκαστον ἐπὶ
αὐτοῦ καθεσθέντα οἴκαδ' ἀπιέναι." εἰς πάχος δ'
ἐπεδεδώκει[7] καὶ ὁ υἱὸς αὐτοῦ Ἀλέξανδρος, ὁ τὴν
ἑαυτοῦ μητέρα ἀποκτείνας συμβασιλεύουσαν αὐτῷ.
b φησὶ γοῦν περὶ αὐτοῦ Ποσειδώνιος ἐν τῇ ἑβδόμῃ
καὶ τεσσαρακοστῇ τῶν Ἱστοριῶν οὕτως· " ὁ δὲ
τῆς Αἰγύπτου δυνάστης μισούμενος μὲν ὑπὸ τῶν
ὄχλων, κολακευόμενος δ' ὑπὸ τῶν περὶ αὐτόν, ἐν
πολλῇ δὲ τρυφῇ ζῶν, οὐδὲ ἀποπατεῖν[8] οἷός τε ἦν,
εἰ μὴ δυσὶν ἐπαπερειδόμενος ἐπορεύετο. εἰς δὲ

---

[1] μεγίστη ἑορτὴ ἐν κυρήνη C: μ. ἑορτὴ ἐν κυρήνηι ἑορτὴ A.
[2] Meineke: τρύβλια (sic) A.   [3] CE: ἀγριμέων A.
[4] ἐσθ' ὅτε Capps: δὲ σῖτα ACE.
[5] καθάριον Casaubon: κιθάριον A.
[6] CE: περιειλομενα (sic) τοιαῦτα A.
[7] Schweighäuser: δὲ ἐδεδώκει A, δ' ἐκδεδώκει CE.
[8] ἀποπατεῖν Capps: πατεῖν ACE.

---

[a] Somewhat over thirty bushels.
[b] The word ἀκολουθίσκος, " little attendant," occurs only
here; cf. Antiphanes καθαρὸς δοῦλος Kock ii. 15 (Bekk. Anec.
105. 5). Kaibel retained κιθάριον (occurring only here), ex-

494

important festival in Cyrene, at which the priest of
Apollo (who is chosen annually) gives a dinner to
those who have preceded him in that office, and places
before each guest a bowl; this is an earthenware
vessel capable of holding about twenty *artabae*,[a] in
which are placed many pieces of wild game, nicely
cooked, sometimes also many from domestic fowls,
and several kinds of sea-fish and imported smoked
fish; some persons often add the gift of a neat little
foot-boy.[b] But we abolished all that sort of thing,
and procured *phialai* of solid silver, each alone having
as great value as the entire outlay for the things we
have mentioned; moreover we added a horse, all
caparisoned, along with a groom and bridle-orna-
ments inlaid with gold, and invited every guest on
leaving for home to mount the horse and ride."
Ptolemy's son Alexander also grew fatter and fatter
—the one who killed his own mother when she was
joint ruler with him. At any rate Poseidonius says
of him, in the forty-seventh book of his *Histories*[c]:
" The master of Egypt, a man who was hated by
the masses, though flattered by his courtiers, lived
in great luxury; but he could not even go out to
ease himself unless he had two men to lean upon as
he walked. And yet when it came to the rounds of

plaining it as diminutive of κίθαρος, a fish sacred to Apollo
(Athen. 287 a, 306 a, 325 b, vol. iii. p. 460). But it is hard
to see why another fish should be added, and a gift answering
to the horse and groom mentioned later is required here.

[c] *F.H.G.* iii. 265, J. 2 A 233. Ptolemy Alexander was
a younger son of Ptolemy Physcon. The assassination of
his mother (named Cleopatra) occurred in 90 B.C. His life
was spent in quarrels with his elder brother Ptolemy Lathyrus
and alternate exchanges of rule in Cyprus and in Egypt, in
which Lathyrus was finally victorious, Alexander dying in
89 B.C.

τὰς ἐν τοῖς συμποσίοις ὀρχήσεις ἀπὸ μετεώρων
κλινῶν καθαλλόμενος ἀνυπόδητος συντονωτέρας
αὐτὰς τῶν ἠσκηκότων ἐποιεῖτο."

Ἀγαθαρχίδης δ' ἐν τῇ ἑκκαιδεκάτῃ Εὐρωπιακῶν
Μάγαν φησὶ τὸν Κυρήνης βασιλεύσαντα ἔτη πεντή-
c κοντα ἀπολέμητον γενόμενον καὶ τρυφῶντα κατά-
σαρκον γενέσθαι ἐκτόπως τοῖς ὄγκοις κατὰ τὸν
ἔσχατον καιρὸν καὶ ὑπὸ τοῦ πάχους ἀποπνιγῆναι δι'
ἀργίαν σώματος καὶ τῷ[1] προσφέρεσθαι πλῆθος
τροφῆς. παρὰ δὲ Λακεδαιμονίοις ὁ αὐτὸς ἱστορεῖ
διὰ τῆς ἑβδόμης καὶ εἰκοστῆς οὐ τῆς τυχούσης
ἀδοξίας νομίζεσθαι, εἴ τις ἢ[2] τὸ σχῆμα ἀνανδρό-
τερον ἔχων ἢ τὸν ὄγκον τοῦ σώματος προπετῆ[3]
ἐφαίνετο, γυμνῶν κατὰ δέκα ἡμέρας παρισταμένων
τοῖς ἐφόροις τῶν νέων. καθεώρων[4] δ' οἱ ἔφοροι καὶ
d καθ' ἑκάστην ἡμέραν καὶ τὰ περὶ τὴν ἔνδυσιν καὶ
τὴν στρωμνὴν τῶν νέων· εἰκότως. καὶ γὰρ ὀψο-
ποιοὶ ἦσαν παρὰ Λακεδαιμονίοις κρέως σκευασίας,
ἄλλου δ' οὐδενός. κἂν τῇ δὲ ἑβδόμῃ καὶ εἰκοστῇ[5]
ὁ Ἀγαθαρχίδης[6] ἔφη ὡς Λακεδαιμόνιοι Ναυκλεί-
δην τὸν Πολυβιάδου παντελῶς ὑπερσαρκοῦντα τῷ
σώματι καὶ παχὺν διὰ τρυφὴν γενόμενον καταβι-
βάσαντες εἰς μέσην τὴν ἐκκλησίαν καὶ Λυσάνδρου

---

[1] τὸ later hand in A.
[2] ἦν before ἢ deleted by Schweighäuser.
[3] CE: προπετὴς A.
[4] καθεώρων ACE: κάφεώρων Kaibel, which would require
the bracketing of καὶ following.
[5] τῇ δὲ ὀγδόῃ καὶ εἰκοστῇ Müller: τῇ αὐτῇ δὲ Jacoby.
[6] ἀγαθαρχίδας A.

---

[a] F.H.G. iii. 192, J. 2 A 208. Magas died some time after
259 B.C.; he made war on his half-brother Ptolemy Philadelphus when he so desired.
[b] F.H.G. iii. 193, J. 2 A 209.

dancing at a drinking-party he would jump from a high couch barefoot as he was, and perform the figures in a livelier fashion than those who had practised them."

Agatharchides in the sixteenth book of his *European History* says [a] that Magas, who reigned over Cyrene for fifty years, was so undisturbed by wars that he abandoned himself to luxury, and was weighted down with monstrous masses of flesh in his last days ; in fact he choked himself to death because he was so fat, never taking any exercise and always eating quantities of food. The same authority, on the other hand, records [b] in the twenty-seventh book that among the Lacedaemonians it was accounted no ordinary disgrace to a man if he was seen to have either a figure somewhat lacking in virility or a corpulence that made his belly prominent ; hence, every ten days, the young warriors were made to stand naked before the ephors. The ephors also closely observed every day both the clothing worn by the young men and also the bedding they used ; [c] and with good reason. There were, it is true, cooks in Sparta who were skilled in the preparation of meat, but of nothing else whatever. Again, in the twenty-seventh book Agatharchides has said [d] that the Lacedaemonians summoned Naucleides the son of Polybiades, whose body was overlaid with excessive flesh, having become obese through luxurious indulgence, to come before the assembly ; there Lysander

[c] The piling on of bed-clothes for warmth was condemned in Athens as a weakening influence, *cf.* Aristoph. *Nub.* 10.

[d] *F.H.G.* iii. 193, J. 2 A 209, *cf.* Aelian xiv. 7. The citation seems to have come rather from the twenty-eighth book, in which the efforts of Agis and Cleomenes to restore the Lycurgan discipline were described (Müller).

πολλὰ ὀνειδίσαντος ἐν τῷ κοινῷ ὡς τρυφῶντι παρ'
ὀλίγον ἐξέβαλον ἐκ τῆς πόλεως, ἀπειλήσαντες τοῦτο
e ποιήσειν εἰ μὴ τὸν βίον ἐπανορθώσοιτο,[1] εἰπόντος
τοῦ Λυσάνδρου ὅτι καὶ Ἀγησίλαος, ὅτε διέτριβεν
περὶ τὸν Ἑλλήσποντον πολεμῶν τοῖς βαρβάροις,
ὁρῶν τοὺς Ἀσιαγενεῖς ταῖς μὲν στολαῖς[2] πολυτελῶς
ἠσκημένους, τοῖς σώμασιν δ' οὕτως ἀχρείους
ὄντας, γυμνοὺς πάντας ἐκέλευσε τοὺς ἁλισκομένους
ἐπὶ τὸν κήρυκα ἄγειν καὶ χωρὶς πωλεῖν τὸν τούτων
ἱματισμόν, ὅπως οἱ σύμμαχοι γιγνώσκοντες διότι
πρὸς μὲν ἆθλα μεγάλα, πρὸς δ' ἄνδρας εὐτελεῖς ὁ
ἀγὼν συνέστηκε, προθυμότερον ταῖς ψυχαῖς ὁρμῶ-
f σιν ἐπὶ τοὺς ἐναντίους. καὶ Πύθων δ' ὁ Βυζάντιος
ῥήτωρ, ὡς Λέων ἱστορεῖ ὁ πολίτης αὐτοῦ, πάνυ ἦν
παχὺς τὸ σῶμα· καὶ τοῖς πολίταις ποτὲ στασιά-
ζουσι πρὸς ἀλλήλους[3] παρακαλῶν εἰς φιλίαν ἔλεγεν·
" ὁρᾶτέ με, ἄνδρες πολῖται, οἷός εἰμι τὸ σῶμα·
ἀλλὰ καὶ γυναῖκα ἔχω πολλῷ ἐμοῦ παχυτέραν.
ὅταν οὖν ὁμονοῶμεν, καὶ τὸ τυχὸν ἡμᾶς σκιμπόδιον
δέχεται· ἐὰν δὲ στασιάσωμεν, οὐδὲ ἡ σύμπασα
οἰκία."

Πόσῳ οὖν κάλλιόν ἐστιν, ἀγαθὲ Τιμόκρατες,
551 πενόμενον εἶναι λεπτότερον[4] ὧν καταλέγει Ἑρμ-

---

[1] Wilamowitz: ἐπανορθώσαιτο ACE.

[2] ταῖς μὲν στολαῖς Schweighäuser: τοὺς μὲν στολαῖς A,
στολαῖς μὲν CE.

[3] καὶ τοῖς π. ποτὲ . . . ἀλλήλους C: καὶ Βυζαντίοις ποτὲ . . .
ἀλλήλους τοῖς πολίταις A.

[4] πενομένους . . . λεπτοτέρους CE.

---

[a] In 397 B.C., undertaken at the instance of Lysander,
Xen. *Hellen.* iii. 4. 2 ff. On the quarrel between him and
Agesilaus, and later reconciliation, *ibid.* §§ 8, 9, Plut. *Ages.* 8.

in open meeting reviled him so bitterly as a wanton profligate that the Lacedaemonians almost ejected him from the city, and warned him that they would certainly do so if he did not reform his manner of life; Lysander also remarked that when Agesilaus was quartered near the Hellespont in his war against the barbarians,[a] observing that the Asiatics, while in the matter of clothing they were expensively dressed, yet as regards their bodies were for that very reason useless, he gave orders that those who were captured should be taken to the auctioneer stripped of their clothes, which should be sold separately, for he wanted his allies to understand that the contest ahead of them was for large stakes, but against worthless men, and so hurl themselves with more alacrity of spirit against their opponents. Again, Python the orator of Byzantium, was very corpulent, as Leon, his fellow-citizen, records[b]; and on one occasion, he said to his fellow-citizens, when their factions were quarrelling with one another, by way of exhorting them to a reconciliation : " You, fellow-citizens, can see what my person is like ; but I have a wife who is much fatter even than I. When, then, we are of one mind, even an ordinary narrow bed can hold us; but if we quarrel, the whole house isn't big enough."

How much better it is, therefore, my good Timocrates, for us to be poor and rather thin as compared

[b] *F.H.G.* ii. 329, J. 2 B 677. For Python, a pupil of Isocrates, see Dem. *De Cor.* 136, and Goodwin p. 270, Philostr. *Vit. Apollon.* vii. 37. He spoke in the interest of Philip, the sedition in Byzantium having been stirred up by the Athenians. But the same story is told of Leon, here cited as the authority for it ; see Suidas *s.* Λέων Λέοντος. Python and Leon seem to be confused with each other in Philostr. *Vit. Soph.* 514 (L.C.L. p. 70).

ιππος ἐν Κέρκωψιν ἢ ὑπερπλουτοῦντας¹ τῷ Ταναγραίῳ κήτει ἐοικέναι, καθάπερ οἱ προειρημένοι ἄνδρες. φησὶ δ' οὕτως ὁ Ἕρμιππος πρὸς τὸν Διόνυσον τὸν λόγον ποιούμενος·

οἱ γὰρ² πενόμενοι
ἀνάπηρά σοι θύουσιν ἤδη βούδια,³
Λεωτροφίδου⁴ λεπτότερα καὶ Θουμάντιδος.

καὶ Ἀριστοφάνης δ' ἐν Γηρυτάδῃ λεπτοὺς τούσδε καταλέγει, οὓς καὶ πρέσβεις ὑπὸ τῶν ποιητῶν b φησιν εἰς Ἅιδου πέμπεσθαι πρὸς τοὺς ἐκεῖ ποιητὰς λέγων οὑτωσί·

καὶ τίς νεκρῶν κευθμῶνα καὶ σκότου πύλας
ἔτλη κατελθεῖν; Β. ἕνα γὰρ⁵ ἀφ' ἑκάστης τέχνης
εἱλόμεθα κοινῇ γενομένης ἐκκλησίας,
οὓς ᾖσμεν ὄντας⁶ ἀδοφοίτας καὶ θαμὰ
ἐκεῖσε φιλοχωροῦντας. Α. εἰσὶ γάρ τινες
ἄνδρες παρ' ὑμῖν ἀδοφοῖται; Β. νὴ Δία
μάλιστά γ', ὥσπερ Θρᾳκοφοῖται. πάντ' ἔχεις.
Α. καὶ τίνες ἂν εἶεν; Β. πρῶτα μὲν Σαννυρίων

---

¹ ὑπερπλουτοῦντα CE.   ² οἱ γὰρ CE: νῦν οἱ γὰρ A.
³ Dindorf (cf. Bekk. Anecd. 85. 29): βοΐδια ACE.
⁴ CE: λεωτρεφίδου A.   ⁵ γὰρ Hermann: δ' A.
⁶ Tyrwhitt: οὐ σημαίνοντας A.

ᵃ That this was a fat fish and not a fat man, as Meineke thought, is certain. Pausanias ix. 20. 4 tells of a marvellous Triton which he had seen in Tanagra ; according to Aelian, A.N. xiii. 21 it was mummified (τάριχον Τρίτωνα). See Frazer, Pausanias v. 83 ff.; Wernicke, J. Arch. Inst. ii. 114 ff.

with the persons enumerated by Hermippus in
The Cercopes, in preference to being excessively rich
and look like the sea-monster of Tanagra,[a] as the
aforesaid worthies did ! For Hermippus, addressing
Dionysus, says[b] : "The poor, indeed, are already
sacrificing to thee small maimed cattle, skinnier than
Leotrophides or Thumantis." Aristophanes also, in
Gerytades, gives the following list of skinny people—
men, he says, dispatched by the poets as envoys to
Hades to visit the poets down there. He says[c] : "A.
And who to ' the hiding-place of the dead, unto the
gates of darkness ' has dared to descend ? B. Why,
we have chosen, in general convocation assembled,
one representative of every art, men who, we know,
are Hades-visitants and who love often to go down
there. A. What, are there really men among you
who are Hades-visitants ? B. Certainly, just as there
are people who are Thrace-visitants. Heaven is my
witness. You've got it exactly. A. And who may
they be ? B. Well, first of all there's Sannyrion—he's

---

[b] Kock i. 233 ; Leotrophides was a byword for leanness
(Aristoph. *Av.* 1406 and Schol.), the memory of whom lasted
until the time of Lucian (*Hist. Conscr.* 34) : "It would be
worth a good deal to be able to turn lead into gold or . . .
Leotrophides into Milo." Thumantis is a "homeless"
wanderer in Aristoph. *Eq.* 1266.

[c] Kock i. 428 ; the first verse is adapted from Eurip. *Hec.* 1.
Of Meletus, ridiculed again by Sannyrion below, very little
is known, except that he was "a rather frigid poet" (Suidas
s.v.). He wrote tragedies, drinking-songs (Aristoph. *Ran.*
1302), and erotic verse (Athen. 605 e). He was the father
of the Meletus who accused Socrates in 399 B.C., for whom
see Plato, *Euthyph.* 2 B and *Apol. passim.* Aristophanes did
not approve the imperialistic designs of Athens in Thrace.
Hesychius defines "Hades-visitants" as the lean and thin,
with one foot in the grave (ἐγγὺς θανάτου ὄντες).

c ἀπὸ τῶν τρυγῳδῶν,[1] ἀπὸ δὲ τῶν τραγικῶν χορῶν
Μέλητος, ἀπὸ δὲ τῶν κυκλίων[1] Κινησίας.

εἶθ' ἑξῆς φησιν·

ὡς σφόδρ' ἐπὶ λεπτῶν ἐλπίδων ὠχεῖσθ'[2] ἄρα·
τούτους γάρ, ἦν πολλῷ[3] ξυνέλθῃ,[4] ξυλλαβὼν
ὁ τῆς διαροίας[5] ποταμὸς ἐξοιχήσεται.

περὶ δὲ τοῦ Σαννυρίωνος καὶ Στράττις ἐν Ψυχα-
σταῖς φησιν·

Σαννυρίωνος σκυτίνην ἐπικουρίαν.

περὶ δὲ Μελήτου αὐτὸς ὁ Σαννυρίων ἐν Γέλωτι
λέγει οὕτως·

Μέλητον τὸν ἀπὸ Ληναίου νεκρόν.

d ἦν δ' ὄντως λεπτότατος καὶ μακρότατος ὁ Κινησίας, εἰς ὃν καὶ ὅλον δρᾶμα γέγραφεν Στράττις,
Φθιώτην Ἀχιλλέα αὐτὸν καλῶν διὰ τὸ ἐν τῇ αὑτοῦ
ποιήσει συνεχῶς τὸ Φθιῶτα λέγειν· παίζων οὖν εἰς
τὴν ἰδέαν αὐτοῦ ἔφη " Φθιῶτ' Ἀχιλλεῦ." ἄλλοι
δ' αὐτόν, ὡς καὶ Ἀριστοφάνης, πολλάκις εἰρήκασι
φιλύρινον Κινησίαν διὰ τὸ φιλύρας[6] λαμβάνοντα[7]

---

[1] Bentley: τραγῳδῶν ACE, κυλίκων A.
[2] Casaubon: ὤχεσθ A.
[3] πολὺς Bergk.   [4] κατέλθῃ Blaydes.
[5] Schweighäuser (cf. εὐροίας 524 c): διαρροίας A; so Dawes,
reading οἰχήσεται.
[6] The gloss τοῦ ξύλου after φιλύρας deleted by Kaibel.
[7] CE: λαμβάνοντας A.

---

[a] Dithyrambic and other lyric choruses sung in a ring
round the altar of Dionysus.
[b] Cf. Aristoph. Ran. 146: "sinners in Hades wallow in
mire and dung."
[c] Kock i. 727. Dalechamp interprets "the leather help"
as padding of some sort worn by Sannyrion under his clothes
502

from the ranks of comedy, while from the tragic choruses there's Meletus, and from the cyclic choruses[a] Cinesias." F ther on he says : " How very *thin* are the hopes you were riding on, after all ! For these poor devils, if the river[b] of diarrhoea come on all at once too vehemently, will be caught up by it and carried away." Regarding Sannyrion, Strattis, also, says in *Keeping Cool*[c] : " Sannyrion's leathern reinforcement." And of Meletus Sannyrion himself says in *Laughter*[d] : " Meletus, that corpse from the Lenaeum.[e]" As for Cinesias, he really was very thin and very tall, and Strattis has written a whole play on him, in which he calls him[f] " Phthian Achilles," because he constantly used the word Phthian in his poetry ; so, with jesting reference to his figure, he says " Phthian Achilles." Others, again, like Aristophanes,[g] often speak of him as " linden Cinesias," because he got a board of linden-wood and

to hide his leanness. The futility of such a device is further hinted at by the pun on the phrase συκίνη ἐπικουρία, " weak help "—fig-wood being proverbially useless, *cf.* Athen. 98 f (vol. i. p. 426) ; σκυτίνη ἐπικουρία is also used of the ὄλισβος, Aristoph. *Lys.* 110.

[d] Kock i. 793.

[e] The precinct sacred to Dionysus Lenaeus, god of the wine-press ; see Dörpfeld u. Reisch, *Griech. Theater* 7 ff. Meletus appears to have come off badly in a contest of tragedy at the Lenaea. In Lenaeum there is an allusion also to the deme to which Meletus belonged, Πίθος, which means "cask," and which the audience would associate with Dionysus, the god of the festival.

[f] Kock i. 716.

[g] *Av.* 1377. The scholiast cites Callistratus as explaining φιλύρινον, " having the colour of linden-wood," *i.e.* with a greenish-yellow complexion ; but Euphronius, he says, referred the epithet to the lightness of the wood : Cinesias's poetry was thin in quality. See Plat. *Gorg.* 501 E.

σανίδα συμπεριζώννυσθαι ἵνα μὴ κάμπτηται διά τε
τὸ μῆκος καὶ τὴν ἰσχνότητα. ὅτι δὲ ἦν ὁ Κινησίας
νοσώδης καὶ δεινὸς τἆλλα Λυσίας ὁ ῥήτωρ ἐν
e τῷ ὑπὲρ Φανίου παρανόμων ἐπιγραφομένῳ λόγῳ
εἴρηκεν, φάσκων αὐτὸν ἀφέμενον τῆς τέχνης
συκοφαντεῖν καὶ ἀπὸ τούτου πλουτεῖν. ὅτι δὲ ὁ
ποιητής ἐστι καὶ οὐχ ἕτερος, σαφῶς αὐτὸς[1] ὢν
σημαίνεται ἐκ τοῦ καὶ ἐπὶ ἀθεότητι κωμῳδούμενον
ἐμφανίζεσθαι καὶ διὰ τοῦ λόγου τοιοῦτον δείκνυσθαι. λέγει δ᾽ οὕτως ὁ ῥήτωρ· " θαυμάζω δὲ εἰ μὴ
βαρέως φέρετε ὅτι Κινησίας ἐστὶν ὁ τοῖς νόμοις
βοηθός, ὃν ὑμεῖς πάντες ἐπίστασθε ἀσεβέστατον
ἁπάντων καὶ παρανομώτατον ἀνθρώπων γεγονέναι.
f οὐχ οὗτός ἐστιν ὁ τοιαῦτα περὶ θεοὺς ἐξαμαρτάνων
ἃ τοῖς μὲν ἄλλοις αἰσχρόν ἐστι καὶ λέγειν, τῶν
κωμῳδοδιδασκάλων[2] δ᾽ ἀκούετε καθ᾽ ἕκαστον
ἐνιαυτόν; οὐ μετὰ τούτου ποτὲ Ἀπολλοφάνης
καὶ Μυσταλίδης καὶ Λυσίθεος συνειστιῶντο,[3] μίαν
ἡμέραν ταξάμενοι τῶν ἀποφράδων, ἀντὶ δὲ νου-
μηνιαστῶν κακοδαιμονιστὰς σφίσιν αὐτοῖς τοὔνομα
θέμενοι, πρέπον μὲν ταῖς αὐτῶν τύχαις· οὐ μὴν ὡς
τοῦτο διαπραττόμενοι τὴν διάνοιαν ἔσχον, ἀλλ᾽ ὡς
καταγελῶντες τῶν θεῶν καὶ τῶν νόμων τῶν
552 ὑμετέρων. ἐκείνων μὲν οὖν ἕκαστος ἀπώλετο

---

[1] Meineke: αὐτὸς A.
[2] Musurus (adding δ᾽): κωμῳδιδασκάλων A.
[3] συνεστιῶντο A.

---

[a] Frag. 53 Thalheim. Harpocration s. Κινησίας
says that Lysias prosecuted two cases against Cinesias.
[b] Here the " teachers " of comedies (" stage-managers ")
are still identified with the playwrights; see Flickinger,
Greek Theater, chap. ix.

fastened it by straps around him in order not to be bent in two by his height and leanness. Further, the orator Lysias in the speech entitled *In Defence of Phanias*—the case involved an accusation of proposing an unconstitutional law—alleges that Cinesias was sickly and also in general clever, asserting that he gave up his profession, became a blackmailer, and got rich as a result. Note that he means the poet and not another Cinesias; he is clearly the same, as indicated not only from the emphatic way in which he (as poet) is ridiculed in comedy for godlessness, but also from the speech of Lysias, in which he is pointed to as a godless man. The orator speaks as follows [a] : " I am astonished that you feel no indignation because Cinesias poses as the defender of our laws, when you all know that he is the most impious and lawless man in the world. Is he not the man who commits crimes of such enormity against the gods that it is a scandal even to mention them to others, though you hear about them from the producers of comedy [b] every year? Was it not in his company that Apollophanes, Mystalides, and Lysitheus once dined together, appointing a day that religion forbids, and adopting the name for themselves of Evil-Spirit-Votaries instead of New-Mooners [c]—appropriately enough, considering their evil fate; not, to be sure, that they had got the notion that they were actually bringing this upon themselves, but simply because they mocked the gods and your laws. Now every one of those miscreants died as you might have expected such men

[c] *i.e.* celebrators of the new moon, or first day of the month, a legitimate feast-day, *cf.* Lucian, *Lexiph.* 6; Athen. 397 d (vol. iv. p. 298).

ὥσπερ εἰκὸς τοὺς τοιούτους. τοῦτον δὲ τὸν ὑπὸ πλείστων γιγνωσκόμενον οἱ θεοὶ οὕτως διέθεσαν ὥστε τοὺς ἐχθροὺς βούλεσθαι αὐτὸν ζῆν μᾶλλον ἢ τεθνάναι παράδειγμα τοῖς ἄλλοις, ἵν' εἰδῶσιν[1] ὅτι τοῖς λίαν ὑβριστικῶς πρὸς τὰ θεῖα διακειμένοις οὐκ ἀεὶ[2] εἰς τοὺς παῖδας ἀποτίθενται τὰς τιμωρίας, ἀλλ' αὐτοὺς κακῶς ἀπολλύουσι, μείζους καὶ b χαλεπωτέρας καὶ τὰς συμφορὰς καὶ τὰς νόσους ἢ τοῖς ἄλλοις ἀνθρώποις προσβάλλοντες. τὸ μὲν γὰρ ἀποθανεῖν ἢ καμεῖν νομίμως κοινὸν ἡμῖν ἅπασίν ἐστι, τὸ δ' οὕτως ἔχοντα τοσοῦτον χρόνον διατελεῖν καὶ καθ' ἑκάστην ἡμέραν ἀποθνῄσκοντα μὴ δύνασθαι τελευτῆσαι τὸν βίον τούτοις μόνοις προσήκει τοῖς τὰ τοιαῦτα ἅπερ οὗτος ἐξημαρτηκόσιν." περὶ μὲν οὖν Κινησίου ταῦτα ὁ ῥήτωρ εἴρηκεν.

Λεπτότερος δ' ἦν καὶ Φιλίτας[3] ὁ Κῷος ποιητής, ὃς καὶ διὰ τὴν τοῦ σώματος ἰσχνότητα σφαίρας ἐκ μολύβου πεποιημένας εἶχε[4] περὶ τὼ πόδε ὡς μὴ ὑπὸ ἀνέμου ἀνατραπείη. Πολέμων δ' ὁ περι-
c ηγητὴς ἐν τῷ περὶ Θαυμασίων Ἀρχέστρατόν φησι τὸν μάντιν ἁλόντα ὑπὸ πολεμίων καὶ ἐπὶ ζυγὸν ἀναβληθέντα ὀβολοῦ ὁλκὴν εὑρεθῆναι ἔχοντα· οὕτως ἦν ἰσχνός. ὁ δ' αὐτὸς ἱστορεῖ ὡς[5] καὶ Πανάρετος ἰατρῷ μὲν οὐδενὶ[6] ὡμίλησεν, Ἀρκεσιλάου δὲ ἠκροᾶτο τοῦ φιλοσόφου, καὶ ὅτι συνεγένετο Πτολεμαίῳ τῷ Εὐεργέτῃ τάλαντα δώδεκα τὸν ἐνιαυτὸν λαμβάνων· ἦν δὲ ἰσχνότατος, ἄνοσος διατελέσας·[7]

---

[1] Musurus : ἴδωσιν ΑΕ, ἴδω C.   [2] ἀεὶ added by Gulick.
[3] A : φιλήτας CE.   [4] CE : ἔχει A.
[5] ὡς A : καὶ ὅτι C.   [6] CE : οὐδὲν A.
[7] ἦν . . . διατελέσας placed before Ἀρκεσιλάου . . . λαμβάνων in C.

would; but in the case of Cinesias, the one known to the largest number of persons, the gods reduced him to such a condition that his enemies, rather than have him die, preferred to have him live as an example to others, so that they might know that for those who adopt an outrageously insolent attitude to religion the gods do not always put off vengeance upon the children,[a] but miserably destroy the culprits themselves, laying upon them larger and severer punishments, in the shape of disaster and disease, than those which they visit upon other men. For to die or to fall ill in a normal way is the common lot of us all, but to continue for so long a time in such a condition as his, dying every day without being able to end his life, is the proper reward for those only who have committed such crimes as he has." This, then, is what the orator has to say about Cinesias.

Philitas, the poet of Cos, was also rather thin; why, his leanness of body was such that he had to wear on his feet balls made of lead to keep him from being upset by the wind. And Polemon the Periegete, in his book *On Wonders*, says [b] that Archestratus the soothsayer, when captured by the enemy, was placed on the scales and found to have the weight of a penny; he was so lean! The same writer records also that Panaretus never resorted to a physician (he was a student of the philosopher Arcesilaus, and Polemon says he lived at the court of Ptolemy Euergetes, from whom he received twelve talents a year).[c] But he was very thin, though

---

[a] Perhaps an allusion to Solon i. (xiii.) 31 ἀναίτιοι ἔργα τίνουσιν, ἢ παῖδες τούτων ἢ γένος ἐξοπίσω; *cf.* Exodus xx. 5.

[b] Frag. 84 Preller. See Aelian, *V.H.* x. 6.

[c] For pensioners of Ptolemy Philadelphus see 493 e.

Μητρόδωρος δ' ὁ Σκήψιος ἐν δευτέρῳ περὶ Ἀλειd πτικῆς Ἱππώνακτα τὸν ποιητὴν οὐ μόνον μικρὸν
γενέσθαι τὸ σῶμα ἀλλὰ καὶ λεπτόν, ἀκρότονον δ'
οὕτως ὡς πρὸς τοῖς ἄλλοις καὶ κενὴν λήκυθον
βάλλειν μέγιστόν τι διάστημα, τῶν ἐλαφρῶν
σωμάτων διὰ τὸ μὴ δύνασθαι τὸν ἀέρα τέμνειν οὐκ
ἐχόντων βιαίαν τὴν φοράν. λεπτὸς δ' ἦν καὶ
Φιλιππίδης, καθ' οὗ λόγος ἐστὶν Ὑπερείδῃ τῷ
ῥήτορι, λέγων αὐτὸν ἕνα τῶν πολιτευομένων εἶναι.
ἦν δ' εὐτελὴς τὸ σῶμα διὰ λεπτότητα, ὡς ὁ Ὑπερείδης ἔφη. Ἄλεξίς τ' ἐν Θεσπρωτοῖς φησιν·

Ἑρμῆ νεκρῶν[1] προπομπὲ καὶ Φιλιππίδου
e κληροῦχε, Νυκτός τ' ὄμμα τῆς μελαμπέπλου.

καὶ Ἀριστοφῶν Πλάτωνι·

ἐν ἡμέραις τρισὶν
ἰσχνότερον αὐτὸν[2] ἀποφανῶ Φιλιππίδου.

Β. οὕτως ἐν ἡμέραις ὀλίγαις νεκροὺς ποιεῖς;

Μένανδρος δὲ Ὀργῇ·

ὁ λιμὸς ὑμῶν[3] τὸν καλὸν τοῦτον δακὼν
Φιλιππίδου λεπτότερον ἀποδείξει νεκρόν.[4]

ὅτι δὲ καὶ πεφιλιππιδῶσθαι[5] ἔλεγον τὸ λελεπτύνθαι
Ἄλεξις ἐν Μανδραγοριζομένῃ φησίν·

κακῶς ἔχεις,[6] στρουθὶς ἀκαρὴς νὴ Δί' ἐγένου·[7]

---

[1] Casaubon: θεῶν A.
[2] Jacobs: ἐν ἡμέραις αὐτὸν τρισὶν ἰσχνότερον ACE.
[3] ὑμῖν Bentley.   [4] νεκρόν deleted by Meineke.
[5] Casaubon: πεφιλιππῶσθαι ACE.
[6] Casaubon: ἔχει A.   [7] Kaibel: εἶ A.

---

always free from illness. Metrodorus of Scepsis in the second book of his treatise *On Training* says [a] that the poet Hipponax was not only small of body, but also thin; and yet he was so muscular that, besides other feats, he could throw even an empty jug a very great distance; (a notable feat,) since unweighted substances, being unable to cleave the air, cannot have as a rule a forcible momentum. Another thin man was Philippides, against whom there is a speech by the orator Hypereides, who says that he was one of the politicians. His thinness made him insignificant in bodily appearance, as Hypereides says.[b] And so Alexis says in *The Thesprotians*[c]: "Thou, Hermes, escorter of the dead,[d] thou to whom Philippides is allotted, and thou, eye of Night in sables robed." And Aristophon in *Plato* [e]: "A. Within three days I'll make him skinnier than Philippides. B. What, you can make men corpses in so few days?" And Menander in *Temperament*[f]: "If the famine in your country ever bites that fine fellow, it will make of him a skinnier corpse than Philippides." It is clear that "to be philippidized" was said for "to be very thin," from what Alexis says in *The Woman who drank Belladonna*[g]: "A. You're in a bad way, you've turned into a plucked chicken, Zeus is my witness! You've been philip-

---

[b] Perhaps this is why he could " dance a jig and play the buffoon," Hyper. *Or.* ii. 7 Kenyon.
[c] Kock ii. 325 ; *cf.* Athen. 230 c (vol. iii. p. 36) = 503 a (p. 252), 238 c (vol. iii. p. 72).
[d] See critical note 1. Hermes guided souls to the underworld.   [e] Kock ii. 279.   [f] Kock iii. 106.
[g] Kock ii. 349 ; the same curious verb, with the same mistake in spelling (see critical note 5 and p. 510 note 1), is quoted by Aelian, *V.H.* x. 6.

f πεφιλιππίδωσαι.¹ Β. μὴ σὺ καινῶς μοι λάλει·
ὅσον οὐ² τέθνηκα. Α. τοῦ ταλαιπώρου πάθους.

Πολλῷ οὖν κάλλιόν ἐστι τοιοῦτόν τινα εἶναι τὴν
ἰδέαν ἢ ὥς φησιν Ἀντιφάνης ἐν Αἰόλῳ·

τοῦτον οὖν
δι᾿ οἰνοφλυγίαν καὶ πάχος τοῦ σώματος
ἀσκὸν καλοῦσι πάντες οὑπιχώριοι.³

Ἡρακλείδης δὲ ὁ Ποντικὸς ἐν τῷ περὶ Ἡδονῆς
Δεινίαν φησὶ τὸν μυροπώλην διὰ τρυφὴν εἰς ἔρωτα⁴
ἐμπεσόντα καὶ πολλὰ χρήματα ἀναλώσαντα, ὡς ἔξω
τῶν ἐπιθυμιῶν ἐγένετο, ὑπὸ λύπης ἐκταραχθέντα
553 ἐκτεμεῖν⁵ αὑτοῦ τὰ αἰδοῖα· ταῦτα πάντα ποιούσης
τῆς ἀκολάστου τρυφῆς.

Ἔθος δ᾿ ἦν Ἀθήνησι καὶ τοὺς πόδας τῶν τρυ-
φώντων ἐναλείφειν μύροις, ὡς Κηφισόδωρος μὲν ἐν
Τροφωνίῳ φησίν·

ἔπειτ᾿ ἀλείφεσθαι τὸ σῶμά μοι· πρίω⁶
μύρον ἴρινον καὶ ῥόδινον, ἄγε μοι,⁷ Ξανθία·
καὶ τοῖς ποσὶν χωρὶς πρίω μοι βάκκαριν.

Εὔβουλος δ᾿ ἐν Σφιγγοκαρίωνι·

ἐν θαλάμῳ μαλακῶς κατακείμενον· ἐν δὲ κύκλῳ
νιν

---

¹ Casaubon: πεφιλιππῶσθαι A.
² Toup: οσομου A.   ³ οἱ ἐπιχώριοι ACE.
⁴ ACE: ἔρωτας Wilamowitz. But the name of some exacting
courtesan may have been lost here.
⁵ ἐξέτεμεν (orat. rect.) CE: ἐκτέμνειν A.
⁶ πρίω A.   ⁷ ἄγε μοι Kock: ἄγαμαι A.

ᵃ Kock ii. 17. In spite of the horrible example given in

pidized. B. Stop using new-fangled words on me;
I'm as good as dead already. A. What a miserable
deal you have had!"

Now it is much better to be like that in appearance
than like the man of whom Antiphanes says in
Aeolus [a] : "This fellow, then, because of his drunken
habits and his fat body, is called 'Wineskin'[b] by all
the natives." And Heracleides of Pontus in the
tract *On Pleasure* says[c] that Deinias the perfume-
seller after plunging into a love-affair through self-
indulgence and squandering large sums, when he
had lost the power to satisfy his desires, became so
crazed by grief that he castrated himself; all these
cases[d] are the result of unbridled indulgence.

There was a custom at Athens, among persons who
lived in luxury, of anointing even the feet with perfumes; so Cephisodorus says in *Trophonius* [e] : "Then
you must anoint my body; buy me some scent of
orris and of rose, hurry, Xanthias, and for my feet
besides, buy me some asarabacca."[f] Eubulus in
Sphinx-Cario [g] : "(You should have seen me) lying at

---

the last quotation, the writer returns to his assertion made at
551 a (p. 498).

   [b] *Cf.* the slang word "tank."   [c] Voss 37.

   [d] Implying that others have been given in a passage not
quoted (Kaibel).

   [e] Kock i. 800, Athen. 689 f.

   [f] On this see 690 a-d. It seems to have been applied,
at least to the feet, in the form of a powder made from the
root of ἄσαρον, Hesych. *s.* βάκκαρις. In that case Athenaeus
has either confused it with an unguent, or else used ἀλείφειν
in the wider sense of "spread on." Athen. 690 c himself
doubts whether it is a μύρον, "unguent."

   [g] Kock ii. 203. The text is uncertain, the unmetrical
words, τὸν ἐμόν, at the end remaining unintelligible. The
verses may have contained a riddle, like those cited from
Eubulus at 449 e (vol. iv. p. 536).

παρθενικαὶ τρυφεραί,[1] χλιδαναὶ μάλα καὶ[2] κατά-
    θρυπτοι,
τὸν πόδ' ἀμαρακίνοισι μύροις[3] τρίψουσι τὸν
    ἐμόν.

b ἐν δὲ Προκρίδι[4] λέγει τις πῶς δεῖ ἐπιμελεῖσθαι τοῦ
τῆς Προκρίδος κυνὸς ὡς περὶ ἀνθρώπου τοῦ κυνὸς
τὸν λόγον ποιούμενος·

οὐκοῦν ὑποστορεῖτε μαλακῶς τῷ κυνί·
κάτω μὲν ὑποβαλεῖτε τῶν Μιλησίων
ἐρίων, ἄνωθεν δ' ἐπιβαλεῖτε ξυστίδα.
Β. Ἄπολλον. Α. εἶτα χόνδρον αὐτῷ δεύσετε
γάλακτι χηνός. Β. Ἡράκλεις. Α. καὶ τοὺς πόδας
ἀλείψετ'[5] αὐτοῦ τῷ Μεγαλλείῳ[6] μύρῳ.

Ἀντιφάνης δὲ ἐν μὲν Ἀλκήστιδι ἐλαίῳ τινὰ ποιεῖ
c χριόμενον τοὺς πόδας. ἐν δὲ Μητραγύρτῃ φησί·

        τήν τε παῖδ' ἀλείμματα
παρὰ τῆς θεοῦ λαβοῦσαν εἶτα τοὺς πόδας
ἐκέλευ' ἀλείφειν πρῶτον, εἶτα τὰ γόνατα.
ὡς θᾶττον ἡ παῖς δ' ἥψατ'[7] αὐτοῦ τῶν ποδῶν
ἔτριψέ τ', ἀνεπήδησεν.

καὶ ἐν Ζακυνθίῳ[8]·

εἶτ' οὐ δικαίως εἰμὶ φιλογύνης ἐγὼ
καὶ τὰς ἑταίρας ἡδέως πάσας ἔχω;
τουτὶ γὰρ αὐτὸ πρῶτον ὃ σὺ ποεῖς παθεῖν,
μαλακαῖς καλαῖς τε χερσὶ τριφθῆναι πόδας,
d   πῶς οὐχὶ σεμνόν ἐστιν;

---

[1] Jacobs: παρθενικὰ τρυφερὰ A.
[2] Meineke: χλανιδανα μαλακὰ A.
[3] Jacobs: μύροισι A.   [4] Musurus: προκρίδα A.
[5] Cobet: ἀλείψατ' A.

512

ease in the bed-chamber! and all about me luxuriant demoiselles, very voluptuous and mincing, will rub my foot with unguents of amaracus.[a]" And in *Procris* someone tells how Procris's hound is to be cared for, always speaking of it as if it were a human being[b]: "A. So then, you shall spread a nice soft bed for the hound; underneath you will lay cloths of Milesian wool, while over him you will spread a soft robe. B. Apollo defend us! A. Then you will soak for him some wheat groats in goose milk. B. Heavens above! A. And smear his feet with Megallus scent.[c]" And Antiphanes in *Alcestis* represents[d] a man as anointing his feet with olive-oil. So in *The Begging Priest* he says[e]: "He then told the girl to buy some ointment from the goddess and smear first his feet with them, after that his knees. And no sooner had the girl touched his feet and rubbed them than he jumped up." And in *The Man from Zante*[f]: "Well, then, haven't I a right to be a philanderer and take delight in keeping all these mistresses? Why, just to enjoy the very thing you are doing now, and have my feet rubbed with fair, soft hands, isn't it magnificent?"

[a] Possibly sweet marjoram.
[b] Kock ii. 195. On this Molossian hound Laelaps, to which Zeus gave a soul, see Pollux v. 39, Ovid, *Met.* vii. 754.
[c] Named after a Sicilian Greek.
[d] Kock ii. 23.
[e] *Ibid.* 74. *Cf.* the title Μηναγύρτης (p. 83 note *e*). These mendicant friars of Cybele sold quack medicines as well as indulgences (Plato, *Rep.* 364 B). *Cf.* Eng. *charlatan* from Ital. *ciarlatano*, a quack doctor. [f] Kock ii. 51.

---

[6] Μεγαλλείῳ, cf. 690 f: μεγαλλιωι AC.
[7] δ' ἤψατ' Koppiers: διήψατο A.
[8] Koppiers: ξακύνθωι A.

καὶ ἐν Θορικίοις[1]·

λοῦται δ' ἀληθῶς; ἀλλὰ τί;

B. ἐκ χρυσοκολλήτου γε[2] κάλπιδος μύρῳ
Αἰγυπτίῳ μὲν τοὺς πόδας καὶ τὰ σκέλη,[3]
φοινικίνῳ δὲ τὰς γνάθους καὶ τιτθία,
σισυμβρίνῳ δὲ τὸν ἕτερον βραχίονα,[4]
ἀμαρακίνῳ δὲ τὰς ὀφρῦς καὶ τὴν κόμην,
ἑρπυλλίνῳ[5] δὲ τὸ γόνυ καὶ τὸν αὐχένα . . .

Ἀναξανδρίδης δὲ ἐν Πρωτεσιλάῳ·

μύρον τε[6] παρὰ Πέρωνος, οὗπερ ἀπέδοτο
ἐχθὲς Μελανώπῳ, πολυτελοῦς Αἰγυπτίου,
ᾧ[7] νῦν ἀλείφει[8] τοὺς πόδας Καλλιστράτου.

καὶ τὸν ἐπὶ Θεμιστοκλέους δὲ βίον Τηλεκλείδης ἐν
Πρυτάνεσιν ἁβρὸν ὄντα παραδίδωσι. Κρατῖνός τ'
ἐν Χείρωσι τὴν τρυφὴν ἐμφανίζων τὴν τῶν παλαι-
τέρων φησίν·

ἁπαλὸν δὲ σισύμβριον ἢ[9] ῥόδον ἢ κρίνον παρ'
οὖς ἐθάκει,
μετά[10] χερσὶ δὲ μῆλον ἕκαστος ἔχων σκίπωνά
τ' ἠγόραζον.

Κλέαρχος δ' ὁ Σολεὺς ἐν τοῖς Ἐρωτικοῖς " διὰ τί,"
φησί, " μετὰ χεῖρας ἄνθη καὶ μῆλα καὶ τὰ τοιαῦτα
φέρομεν; πότερον ὅτι καὶ διὰ τῆς τούτων ἀγα-
πήσεως ἡ φύσις μηνύει τοὺς τῆς ὥρας ἔχοντας

---

[1] θορυκιοις A. [2] Musurus: τε A (δὲ 689 e).
[3] 689 e: τὰς χεῖρας A. [4] τὸν βραχίον' ἑκάτερον Kock.
[5] ἑρπυλενωι δὲ τὸ γόνυ A. [6] μύρον τε 689 f: μύρῳ δὲ A.
[7] πολυτελοῦς ἐν αιπτιωιαι A. [8] συναλείφει A.
[9] ἢ added by Hermann. [10] Meineke: παρὰ A.

[a] Kock ii. 53, Athen. 689 e.
[b] Why not the other as well?

514

Again, in *The Villagers of Thoricus* [a] : " A. So she's really bathing ? Well then, what ? B. Yes, she has a box inlaid with gold, and from it she anoints her feet and legs with Egyptian scent, her cheeks and nipples with palm-oil, one of her arms [b] with mint, her eyebrows and hair with sweet marjoram, her knee and neck with tufted thyme. . . ." Anaxandrides, too, says in *Protesilaus* [c] : " Perfume bought at Peron's shop, some of which he sold yesterday to Melanopus, and expensive Egyptian it is too ; with it Melanopus anoints the feet of Callistratus." But even in the time of Themistocles [d] the manners of life were luxurious, as Telecleides testifies in *The Prytanes.* [e] And so Cratinus in *The Cheirons* brings out distinctly the luxury of the earlier times when he says [f] : " Every man sat in the assembly with a sprig of soft mint, or a rose, or a lily at his ear, or lounged about the market-place with an apple and a staff in his hands."

Now Clearchus of Soli in his *Amatoria* says [g] : " Why is it that we carry in our hands flowers and apples and such things as that ? Is it because Nature tries to reveal through our love for these things those who have a desire for beauty [h] ? Is

[c] Kock ii. 151 ; Athen. 689 f mentions again the perfume-seller Peron. The demagogue Callistratus was notoriously self-indulgent, Athen. 44 a, 166 a, 449 f. His opponent Melanopus could be bought off with bribes, Plut. *Demosth.* 13.

[d] In the new prosperity after the Persian Wars, in the second quarter of the fifth century.

[e] Kock i. 215 ; the quotation is lost.

[f] Kock i. 86. Cratinus is describing a period earlier than his own ; *cf.* frag. 238 (Kock i. 85) μακάριος ἦν ὁ πρὸ τοῦ βίος βροτοῖσι πρὸς τὰ νῦν.   [g] *F.H.G.* ii. 315.

[h] From the word ὥρα, " season," " ripe season," " beauty," came ὡραῖα, " fruits," " flowers."

τὴν ἐπιθυμίαν; διὰ τοῦτ' οὖν οἰονεὶ δεῖγμα τῆς
φύσεως[1] τὰ ὡραῖα μετὰ χεῖρας ἔχουσιν καὶ χαίρουσιν αὐτοῖς· ἢ δυοῖν χάριν ταῦτα περιφέρουσιν·
ἀρχή τε γὰρ ἐντυχίας[2] καὶ παράδειγμα τῆς βου-
λήσεως αὐτοῖς γίνεται διὰ τούτων, αἰτηθεῖσι μὲν[3]
τὸ προσαγορευθῆναι, δοῦσι δὲ τὸ[4] προυπογράφειν
554 ὅτι δεῖ καὶ αὐτοὺς μεταδιδόναι τῆς ὥρας. ἡ γὰρ
τῶν ὡραίων ἀνθῶν καὶ καρπῶν αἴτησις εἰς ἀντίδοσιν
τῆς τοῦ σώματος ὥρας προκαλεῖται τοὺς λαβόντας.
ἢ τὴν τούτων ὥραν παραψυχὴν καὶ παραμυθίαν
τῆς ἐπὶ τῶν ἐρωμένων ὥρας ταῖς ἐπιθυμίαις χαίροντες ἔχουσιν αὐτοῖς.[5] ἐκκρούεται γὰρ ὑπὸ τῆς
τούτων παρουσίας ὁ τῶν ἐρωμένων πόθος. εἰ μὴ
ἄρα τοῦ περὶ αὐτοὺς κόσμου χάριν, καθάπερ ἄλλο
τι τῶν πρὸς καλλωπισμὸν συντεινόντων, ἔχουσί
τε ταῦτα καὶ χαίρουσιν αὐτοῖς. οὐ γὰρ μόνον
στεφανουμένων τοῖς ὡραίοις ἄνθεσιν, ἀλλὰ καὶ
μετὰ χεῖρας ἐχόντων τὸ πᾶν εἶδος ἐπικοσμεῖται.
b τάχα δ' ἴσως διὰ τὸ φιλοκάλους εἶναι· δηλοῖ δὲ τὸ
τῶν καλῶν ἐρᾶν καὶ πρὸς τὰ ὡραῖα φιλικῶς ἔχειν.
καλὸν γὰρ τὸ τῆς[6] ὀπώρας καὶ τὸ τῆς ὥρας ὄντως
πρόσωπον ἔν τε καρποῖσι καὶ ἄνθεσι θεωρούμενον.
ἢ πάντες οἱ ἐρῶντες οἷον ἐκτρυφῶντες ὑπὸ τοῦ

---

[1] Dalechamp: ὄψεως A.
[2] Meineke: εὐτυχίας A, συντυχίας Casaubon (cf. ἐρωτικὴν
ξυντυχίαν Thuc. vi. 54).   [3] Musurus: δὲ A.
[4] τὸ added by Kaibel (τῷ Meineke).
[5] Gulick: αὐτοῖς A.
[6] τὸ τῆς Kaibel (following Casaubon): ὅτι τὰς A.

---

[a] On the relation between incontinence and the senses of
sight and smell, more marked in man than in the lower
animals, see Aristot. Eth. Nic. 1118 a 9 ff.
[b] Or, " of autumn and spring." The sentence, omitting

this, then, the reason—as a kind of revelation provided by Nature, why certain persons carry fruits and flowers in their hands and enjoy them ? Or are there, rather, two reasons for their carrying them about ? For in fact they do use these means as a first step towards a meeting, and also as a sign of their desire therefor ;—for those from whom favours are desired, that they permit being accosted, while for those who have given the flower it is the public notice that they themselves have a right to share in the other's beauty. For the solicitation, made in the form of beautiful flowers and fruits, invites those who accept them to give in exchange the flower of their own bodies. Or perhaps they keep for themselves the beauty of the flowers as a comfort and consolation for the beauty possessed by the beloved, thus gratifying their desires.[a] The yearning, that is, for the loved one is diverted by the possession of the flowers. Unless, to be sure, it is for the mere sake of personal adornment, just as they wear any other thing that tends to enhance their beauty, that people carry these things and enjoy them. For it is not only those who put wreaths of beautiful flowers on their heads, but also those who carry them in their hands, whose entire appearance is thereby further adorned. And so it may possibly be on account of their love of beauty ; and there is thus revealed the passion for beautiful things and a fond disposition toward loveliness. Lovely indeed is the aspect of fruitage and prime [b] when one beholds it in fruit and flowers. Or may we say that all lovers are made over-luxurious, as it were, by their passion

ὄντως, is a reminiscence of some poet (so Wilamowitz). Note the poetic form καρποῖσι.

πάθους καὶ ὡραινόμενοι τοῖς ὡραίοις ἁβρύνονται;
φυσικὸν γὰρ δή τι τὸ τοὺς οἰομένους εἶναι καλοὺς
καὶ ὡραίους ἀνθολογεῖν. ὅθεν αἵ τε περὶ τὴν
Περσεφόνην ἀνθολογεῖν λέγονται, καὶ Σαπφώ
φησιν ἰδεῖν ' ἄνθε᾽ ἀμέργουσαν παῖδ᾽ ἄγαν[1]
ἀπαλάν.' ''

c Οὕτω δ᾽ ἐξήρτηντο τῶν ἡδυπαθειῶν οἱ τότε ὡς
καὶ Καλλιπύγου Ἀφροδίτης ἱερὸν ἱδρύσασθαι ἀπὸ
τοιαύτης αἰτίας. ἀνδρὶ ἀγροίκῳ ἐγένοντο δύο
καλαὶ θυγατέρες· αὗται φιλονικήσασαί[2] ποτε πρὸς
ἑαυτὰς προελθοῦσαι ἐπὶ τὴν λεωφόρον διεκρίνοντο
ποτέρα εἴη καλλιπυγοτέρα. καί ποτε παριόντος
νεανίσκου πατέρα πρεσβύτην καὶ πλούσιον[3] ἔχοντος
ἐπέδειξαν ἑαυτὰς καὶ τούτῳ· καὶ ὃς θεασάμενος
ἔκρινε τὴν πρεσβυτέραν· ἧς καὶ εἰς ἔρωτα ἐμπεσὼν
d ἐλθὼν εἰς ἄστυ κλινήρης γίνεται καὶ διηγεῖται τὰ
γεγενημένα τῷ ἀδελφῷ ἑαυτοῦ ὄντι νεωτέρῳ. ὁ
δὲ καὶ αὐτὸς ἐλθὼν εἰς τοὺς ἀγροὺς καὶ θεασάμενος
τὰς παῖδας ἐρᾷ καὶ αὐτὸς τῆς ἑτέρας. ὁ γοῦν
πατὴρ ἐπεὶ παρακαλῶν αὐτοὺς ἐνδοξοτέρους λαβεῖν
γάμους οὐκ ἔπειθεν, ἄγεται ἐκ τοῦ ἀγροῦ τὰς
παῖδας αὐτοῖς, πείσας ἐκείνων τὸν πατέρα, καὶ
ζεύγνυσι[4] τοῖς υἱοῖς. αὗται οὖν ὑπὸ τῶν πολιτῶν
καλλίπυγοι ἐκαλοῦντο, ὡς καὶ ὁ Μεγαλοπολίτης
Κερκιδᾶς ἐν τοῖς Ἰάμβοις ἱστορεῖ λέγων·

---

[1] παῖδ᾽ ἀγνὰν Hermann.
[2] φιλονεικήσασαι AC (-νεικίσασαι C).
[3] καὶ πλούσιον added by Kaibel (πλουσίου τινὸς C).
[4] συζευχθεῖσαι (construction altered) C. The simple form
ζεύγνυσι points to the poetic source of the story.

---

[a] P.L.G.⁴ iii. 129, Diehl frag. 111, Edmonds, frag. 107.

[b] P.L.G.⁴ ii. 513, Diehl frag. 10, Powell 213 ; cf. Alciphron
iv. 11 Schepers, Clem. Al. Protr. ii. 39. 1 p. 29. No extant

and thus inclined to beautify themselves, and so take a wanton pleasure in beautiful things ? It is, indeed, only natural that those who think themselves beautiful and ripe should gather flowers. Hence also the girls in the train of Persephone are said to be gathering flowers, and Sappho says [a] she saw ' A very tender maiden plucking flowers.' "

So dependent on their sensual pleasures were the men of those days that they actually dedicated a temple to Aphrodite of the Beautiful Buttocks, from the following circumstance. A farmer had two beautiful daughters who once fell into a dispute with each other and even went out upon the highway to settle the question as to which of them had the more beautiful curves. One day a lad passed by whose father was a rich old man, and to him they displayed themselves ; and he, after gazing at them, decided in favour of the older girl ; in fact he fell in love with her so passionately that when he returned to town he went to bed ill, and related what had happened to his brother, who was younger than he. So the latter also went into the country to gaze at the girls, and he too fell in love, but with the other girl. Now the father, at least, begged them to contract a more respectable marriage, but since he failed to persuade them, he brought the girls from their country home to his sons, having got the consent of the girls' father, and joined them in marriage to them. The girls, therefore, were called " the fair-buttocked " by the townspeople, as Cercidas of Megalopolis relates in his *Iambic Verses*. He says [b] : " There was a pair

statue can with certainty be styled an Aphrodite Kallipygos ; see Furtwängler in Rosch. *Lex.* i. 418, and especially Heydemann, *J. Arch. Inst.* ii. 125 ; Gerhard, *Wien. Stud.* xxxvii. 1.

ἦν καλλιπύγων ζεῦγος ἐν Συρακούσαις.

αὗται οὖν ἐπιλαβόμεναι οὐσίας λαμπρᾶς ἱδρύσαντο
e Ἀφροδίτης ἱερὸν καλέσασαι Καλλίπυγον τὴν θεόν,
ὡς ἱστορεῖ καὶ Ἀρχέλαος ἐν τοῖς Ἰάμβοις.

Ἐν μανίᾳ δὲ τρυφὴν ἡδίστην γενομένην οὐκ
ἀηδῶς ὁ Ποντικὸς Ἡρακλείδης διηγεῖται ἐν τῷ
περὶ Ἡδονῆς οὕτως γράφων· " ὁ Αἰξωνεὺς Θρά-
συλλος[1] ὁ Πυθοδώρου διετέθη ποτὲ ὑπὸ μανίας
τοιαύτης ὡς πάντα τὰ πλοῖα τὰ εἰς τὸν Πειραιᾶ
καταγόμενα ὑπολαμβάνειν ἑαυτοῦ εἶναι, καὶ ἀπ-
εγράφετο αὐτὰ καὶ ἀπέστελλε[2] καὶ διώκει καὶ κατα-
πλέοντα ἀπεδέχετο μετὰ χαρᾶς τοσαύτης ὅσηςπερ
f ἄν τις ἡσθείη τοσούτων χρημάτων κύριος ὤν.
καὶ τῶν μὲν ἀπολομένων οὐδὲν ἐπεζήτει,[3] τοῖς δὲ
σωζομένοις ἔχαιρεν καὶ διῆγεν μετὰ πλείστης
ἡδονῆς. ἐπεὶ δὲ ὁ ἀδελφὸς αὐτοῦ Κρίτων ἐκ
Σικελίας ἐπιδημήσας συλλαβὼν αὐτὸν παρέδωκεν
ἰατρῷ καὶ τῆς μανίας ἐπαύσατο, διηγεῖτο πολλάκις περὶ τῆς ἐν μανίᾳ διατριβῆς,[4] οὐδεπώποτε
φάσκων κατὰ τὸν βίον ἡσθῆναι πλείονα· λύπην μὲν
γὰρ οὐδ᾽ ἡντινοῦν αὐτῷ παραγίνεσθαι, τὸ δὲ τῶν
ἡδονῶν πλῆθος ὑπερβάλλειν."

---

[1] Aelian: ἀξωνεὺς θρασύλαος A (θρασύλαος also CE).
[2] Meineke: ἀπέστειλε A.
[3] οὐδὲν ἐπεζήτει CE: οὔτε ἐπεζήτησε A.
[4] πολλάκις . . . διατριβῆς added by Kaibel (cf. Aelian, ἐμέμνητο δὲ πολλάκις τῆς κτλ.).

of fair-buttocked sisters in Syracuse." It was they, therefore, who, having come into possession of splendid wealth, founded the temple of Aphrodite, calling the goddess the Fair-buttocked, as recorded also by Archelaus in his *Iambic Verses*.

Not without interest is the story of a very delightful life of luxury resulting from insanity, narrated by Heracleides of Pontus in his work *On Pleasure*. He writes as follows [a] : " Thrasyllus the son of Pythodorus, of the deme Aexonê, was once so afflicted by madness resulting from luxurious living that he imagined all the ships putting in at Peiraeus to be his own, and registered them as such in his accounts ; he would dispatch them forth and transact all business for them, and when they returned from a voyage he would receive them with as exuberant joy as one would feel were he the sole owner of all the goods. To be sure, if they were lost he made no further search for them, but if they came back safe he showed his delight and lived in the greatest satisfaction. On the arrival in Athens of his brother Crito from Sicily, he was apprehended and placed in charge of a physician, who cured him of his insanity. But he often told the story of the way he had lived when mad, alleging that never before in his whole life had he enjoyed himself more ; for no pain of any sort assailed him, and on the other hand the sum of his pleasures was enormous."

[a] Voss 36. See Aelian, *V.H.* iv. 25, and *cf.* Hor. *Epist.* ii. 2. 125.

Additional Note

P. 219 note *c*. Mr. W. W. Tarn, in *J.H.S.* liii. (1933), p. 60, believes, if I understand him aright, that the Saviour Gods are Ptolemy II and Arsinoë, and not Ptolemy I and Berenice. He adds: "probably as yet there were no θεοὶ σωτῆρες in the official sense."

INDEX OF PROPER NAMES

INDEX OF PROPER NAMES

INDEX OF PROPER NAMES

INDEX OF PROPER NAMES

INDEX OF PROPER NAMES

INDEX OF PROPER NAMES

INDEX OF PROPER NAMES

INDEX OF PROPER NAMES

Conon, Athenian general, 532 b, 548 a

Conon, reputed manufacturer of a special kind of cylix and phialê, 486 c and note h, *cf.* 478 b

Coptos, a city in the Egyptian Thebaid, on the Nile, 464 b

Coraxians, 532 f and note a (p. 397)

Corinth, Corinthian, 782 e (p. 44), 470 f (p. 76), 474 a note a, 484 f note d, 488 c, d, 495 c, 506 d note f, 525 d, 527 e, 535 c

Cos, 552 b

Cotta, 529 b note b

Cotys, 482 d and note f, 531 e-f

Cotyto, a Thracian divinity, celebrated with licentious revelry, 479 b and note b

Craterus, Macedonian officer, victor at Crannon (322 B.C.), killed in battle against Eumenes (321 B.C.), 539 c

Crates, comic poet, fr. 25, 478 f

Crates of Mallos, grammarian, 490 e and note c, 495 a, 497 e

Crates, toreutic artist, 782 b (p. 40)

Crathis river, 519 e and note c

Cratinus the Elder, comic poet, commentary on, 495 a; fr. 38, 475 a; fr. 50, 501 d-f; fr. 124, 496, 502 b; fr. 187, 494 b; fr. 239, 553 e; fr. 273, 782 d (p. 42)

Cratinus the Younger, comic poet, fr. 9, 460 f; fr. 14, 469 c

Cratinus of Methymna, harp-player, 538 e

Creon, king of Corinth, in Strattis's *Medea*, 467 e

Cretans, Crete, 782 c (p. 40), 783 f (p. 50), 483 a (p. 142), 491 b, 517 a, 522 f

Critias, poet and historian, one of the Thirty Tyrants, 463 e, 483 b, 486 e and note e, 496 b, 527 b

Crito, friend of Socrates, 506 d

Crito, son of Pythodorus, 554 f

Crito, writer on cookery, 516 c

Crobyzi, a tribe related to the Getae, living on the borders of Thrace and Moesia, near the modern Odessa, 536 d

Cronus, Kronos, father of Zeus, 491 b, 510 d

Croton, 518 d, 520 c-522 c, 528 b and note f

Ctesias, 464 a, 529 b, 530 d

Ctesibius, engineer, 497 d, e

Cumae, 514 b (Kyme in Asia Minor ; 528 d (the Italian Cumae)

Curetes, a mythical people associated with Acarnania, Chalcis, and Crete, 528 c and notes

Curtius, Quintus, 537 e note c

Cybelê, 472 b note e, 514 d note a, 541 e note b, 553 c note e

Cycê (?), in Anacreon, 534 a and note e

Cyclic poems, 465 e

Cyclops, 461 d, 465 c note e, 477 c, e, 481 e

Cyinda, a fortress in Cilicia, west of Tarsus, and used as a storehouse for treasure, 484 c and note a

Cylices (Cups), a place in Illyria, 462 b

Cylicranes, 461 e, 462 a

Cylix, a Lydian, 461 f

Cynossema, Athenian victory at, 535 c note c

Cyprian Lays, 510 c note c

Cypris, Aphrodite, 463 e, 510 d and note e

Cyprus, 783 a (p. 46), 472 a, 480 f, 483 a, 495 c, 516 a, 531 d, 532 b, 542 c, 550 b note c

Cypsela, in southern Thrace, 469 a

Cyrene, 467 f, 480 a, 510 a, 544 a, e, 549 e, f, 550 b

Cyrus the Great, 504 e, f, 505 a, 522 b, 529 e, 530 d note b

Cyrus the Younger, 784 d (p. 54), 514 e note c (p. 315)

Cythera, 476 e

Cythnus, 516 e and note g

Cyzicus, 476 a, 506 a, 509 a, 534 d, 535 c note c, 538 f

Daedalus, 522 f note 3

Damocrates, maker of Rhodian skyphoi, 500 b

Damophilus of Enna, in Sicily (killed in the slave rebellion *ca.* 139 B.C.), 542 b and note g

Damoxenus, comic poet, fr. 1, 468 f

Daniel, 530 d note b

INDEX OF PROPER NAMES

INDEX OF PROPER NAMES

INDEX OF PROPER NAMES

or was cited in Didymus's work thereon, 468 c

Epigenes, comic poet, fr. 3, 498 e; fr. 4, 474 a; fr. 5, 469 c, 502 e; fr. 6, 472 e, 480 a, 486 b

Epinicus, comic poet, fr. 2, 469 a, 497 a, 500 f

Erasistratus, famous physician, 516 c

Eratosthenes, 482 a, 499 e, 501 d, e notes b, h

Eretria, in Euboea, 480 f, 536 f and note d

Eriphylê, betrayed her husband Amphiaraus, 528 d note c

Eros, in Anacreon, 782 a (p. 33); in Plato, 508 d (p. 284); on the shield of Alcibiades, 534 e

Erxion, in Anacreon, 498 c

Erytheia, mythical land of the west, 469 d, 470 d; also one of the Hesperides, 469 f

Erythrae, 475 c

Eteocles, Spartan Ephor? (fourth century B.C), 535 d note a (p. 421)

Etruscans, 517 d-518 b, 519 b

Etymologicum Magnum, 782 a note 10 (p. 39), 783 b note k (p. 47), 783 d note 2 (p. 48), 475 f note d (p. 103), 477 d note 6, 479 c note c, 480 d notes 3, 5, 481 f note 1, 482 f notes 6, g, 496 c note e, 501 b note 2, 502 e note g

Euaeon of Lampsacus, pupil of Plato, 508 f

Εὐανθής, Flowery, epithet of Dionysus, 465 a

Euboea, Euboeans, 462 a, 481 e, 501 b note c, 536 f

Eubulus, comic poet, fr. 31, 471 c; fr. 43, 471 e; fr. 48, 500 e; fr. 56, 471 d; fr. 62, 460 e; fr. 65, 494 e; fr. 69, 467 b (p. 58); fr. 71, 478 c; fr. 80, 81, 473 e; fr. 82, 473 f; fr. 90, 553 b; fr. 108, 553 a; fr. 115, 519 a

Εὐδαιμόνων λαύρα, 541 a

Eudoxus, 511 a note b, 545 b note f

Euegorus, a priest in Eubulus, 478 c (?)

Euergetes. See Ptolemy

Eumaeus, the swineherd in the *Odyssey*, 477 c and note d, 498 f

Eumenes of Cardia, one of the chief secretaries under Alexander the Great, later commander of forces against Antigonus, 484 c note a

Eumolpus, Alexandrian grammarian (period unknown), 477 a, 483 a

Eupalinus of Megara, celebrated engineer (*ca.* 525 B.C.), 540 d note d

Euphorion, epic poet, 475 f, 477 e, 502 c note d

Euphraeus of Oreus, 506 e-f and note b, 508 d

Euphranor of Thurii, a pilot mentioned by Menander, 474 c

Euphron, comic poet, 499 d note g; fr. 3, 503 a

Euphronius, poet and grammarian, 495 c, 551 d note g

Eupolidean verse, 485 d note e

Eupolis, comic poet, 506 f and note c; fr. 158, 535 a; fr. 326, 494 e note e; fr. 373, 502 b

Euripides, 782 e note a (p. 45), 479 b note i (p. 121), 509 c note a, 537 d; *Alc.* 788, 512 e note d; *Bacch.* 317, 544 e; 647, 474 a note b; 1128, 531 a note c; *Hec.* 1, 551 b note c; *Hipp.* 317, 530 d; 525, 486 b note d; *I.A.* 700, 474 d note c; 955, 463 b note b; *I.T.* 165, 510 d note g; 1095, 491 a note c; 1165, 521 f note c; *Med.* 679, 782 f note a (p. 46); *Or.* 136, 474 a note b; *Tro.* 1, 474 b note g; *Frag.* 146, 476 f; 157, 524 c note e; 379, 498 d; 468, 504 b; 486, 546 b; 496, 523 d; 592, 496 b; 782, 503 d; 896, 465 b

Euripides, a character in Ephippus satirized as a turbulent dinnerguest, 482 c, d

Europe, 546 a note b

Eurycleia, in the *Odyssey*, 460 a

Eurypylê, in Anacreon, 523 e

Eurypylus, historian, critic of Plato (third century B.C. ?), 508 f

Eurysthenes, ancestor of Spartan kings, 535 c note a

Eurytus, 461 f, 495 b note a

Eustathius, 460 f note 2, 784 b note 6 (p. 52), 468 e note 4 (p. 66), 477 d note c (p. 113), 480 b note f 485 a note 1, 486 e notes 3, 6, 49

534

INDEX OF PROPER NAMES

537

INDEX OF PROPER NAMES

INDEX OF PROPER NAMES

INDEX OF PROPER NAMES

INDEX OF PROPER NAMES

INDEX OF PROPER NAMES

545

INDEX OF PROPER NAMES

INDEX OF PROPER NAMES

INDEX OF PROPER NAMES

549

INDEX OF PROPER NAMES

Printed in Great Britain by CLARK CONSTABLE LIMITED, *Edinburgh*

THE LOEB CLASSICAL LIBRARY

VOLUMES ALREADY PUBLISHED

LATIN AUTHORS

AMMIANUS MARCELLINUS. J. C. Rolfe. 3 Vols.

APULEIUS : THE GOLDEN ASS (METAMORPHOSES). W. Adlington (1566). Revised by S. Gaselee.

ST. AUGUSTINE : CITY OF GOD. 7 Vols. Vol. I. G. E. McCracken. Vol. II. W. M. Green. Vol. III. D. Wiesen. Vol. IV. P. Levine. Vol. V. E. M. Sanford and W. M. Green. Vol. VI. W. C. Greene. Vol. VII. W. M. Green.

ST. AUGUSTINE, CONFESSIONS OF. W. Watts (1631). 2 Vols.

ST. AUGUSTINE : SELECT LETTERS. J. H. Baxter.

AUSONIUS. H. G. Evelyn White. 2 Vols.

BEDE. J. E. King. 2 Vols.

BOETHIUS : TRACTS AND DE CONSOLATIONE PHILOSOPHIAE. Rev. H. F. Stewart and E. K. Rand. Revised by S. J. Tester.

CAESAR : ALEXANDRIAN, AFRICAN AND SPANISH WARS. A. G. Way.

CAESAR : CIVIL WARS. A. G. Peskett.

CAESAR : GALLIC WAR. H. J. Edwards.

CATO AND VARRO : DE RE RUSTICA. H. B. Ash and W. D. Hooper.

CATULLUS. F. W. Cornish ; TIBULLUS. J. B. Postgate ; and PERVIGILIUM VENERIS. J. W. Mackail.

CELSUS : DE MEDICINA. W. G. Spencer. 3 Vols.

CICERO : BRUTUS AND ORATOR. G. L. Hendrickson and H. M. Hubbell.

CICERO : DE FINIBUS. H. Rackham.

CICERO : DE INVENTIONE, etc. H. M. Hubbell.

CICERO : DE NATURA DEORUM AND ACADEMICA. H. Rackham.

CICERO : DE OFFICIIS. Walter Miller.

CICERO : DE ORATORE, etc. 2 Vols. Vol. I: DE ORATORE, Books I and II. E. W. Sutton and H. Rackham. Vol. II: DE ORATORE, Book III ; DE FATO ; PARADOXA STOICORUM ; DE PARTITIONE ORATORIA. H. Rackham.

CICERO : DE REPUBLICA, DE LEGIBUS. Clinton W. Keyes.

1

THE LOEB CLASSICAL LIBRARY

Cicero: De Senectute, De Amicitia, De Divinatione. W. A. Falconer.

Cicero: In Catilinam, Pro Murena, Pro Sulla, Pro Flacco. New version by C. Macdonald.

Cicero: Letters to Atticus. E. O. Winstedt. 3 Vols.

Cicero: Letters to his Friends. W. Glynn Williams, M. Cary, M. Henderson. 4 Vols.

Cicero: Philippics. W. C. A. Ker.

Cicero: Pro Archia, Post Reditum, De Domo, De Haruspicum Responsis, Pro Plancio. N. H. Watts.

Cicero: Pro Caecina, Pro Lege Manilia, Pro Cluentio, Pro Rabirio. H. Grose Hodge.

Cicero: Pro Caelio, De Provinciis Consularibus, Pro Balbo. R. Gardner.

Cicero: Pro Milone, In Pisonem, Pro Scauro, Pro Fonteio, Pro Rabirio Postumo, Pro Marcello, Pro Ligario, Pro Rege Deiotaro. N. H. Watts.

Cicero: Pro Quinctio, Pro Roscio Amerino, Pro Roscio Comoedo, Contra Rullum. J. H. Freese.

Cicero: Pro Sestio, In Vatinium. R. Gardner.

[Cicero]: Rhetorica ad Herennium. H. Caplan.

Cicero: Tusculan Disputations. J. E. King.

Cicero: Verrine Orations. L. H. G. Greenwood. 2 Vols.

Claudian. M. Platnauer. 2 Vols.

Columella: De Re Rustica, De Arboribus. H. B. Ash, E. S. Forster, E. Heffner. 3 Vols.

Curtius, Q.: History of Alexander. J. C. Rolfe. 2 Vols.

Florus. E. S. Forster; and Cornelius Nepos. J. C. Rolfe.

Frontinus: Stratagems and Aqueducts. C. E. Bennett and M. B. McElwain.

Fronto: Correspondence. C. R. Haines. 2 Vols.

Gellius. J. C. Rolfe. 3 Vols.

Horace: Odes and Epodes. C. E. Bennett.

Horace: Satires, Epistles, Ars Poetica. H. R. Fairclough.

Jerome: Select Letters. F. A. Wright.

Juvenal and Persius. G. G. Ramsay.

Livy. B. O. Foster, F. G. Moore, Evan T. Sage, A. C. Schlesinger and R. M. Geer (General Index). 14 Vols.

Lucan. J. D. Duff.

Lucretius. W. H. D. Rouse. Revised by M. F. Smith.

Manilius. G. P. Goold.

Martial. W. C. A. Ker. 2 Vols. Revised by E. H. Warmington.

Minor Latin Poets: from Publilius Syrus to Rutilius Namatianus, including Grattius, Calpurnius Siculus,

THE LOEB CLASSICAL LIBRARY

Nemesianus, Avianus, with "Aetna," "Phoenix" and other poems. J. Wight Duff and Arnold M. Duff.

Ovid : The Art of Love and other Poems. J. H. Mozley. Revised by G. P. Goold.

Ovid : Fasti. Sir James G. Frazer.   [by G. P. Goold.

Ovid : Heroides and Amores. Grant Showerman. Revised

Ovid : Metamorphoses. F. J. Miller. 2 Vols. Vol. I revised by G. P. Goold.

Ovid : Tristia and Ex Ponto. A. L. Wheeler.

Petronius. M. Heseltine ; Seneca : Apocolocyntosis. W. H. D. Rouse. Revised by E. H. Warmington.

Phaedrus and Babrius (Greek). B. E. Perry.

Plautus. Paul Nixon. 5 Vols.

Pliny : Letters, Panegyricus. B. Radice. 2 Vols.

Pliny : Natural History. 10 Vols. Vols. I-V. H. Rackham. Vols. VI-VIII. W. H. S. Jones. Vol. IX. H. Rackham. Vol. X. D. E. Eichholz.

Propertius. H. E. Butler.

Prudentius. H. J. Thomson. 2 Vols.

Quintilian. H. E. Butler. 4 Vols.

Remains of Old Latin. E. H. Warmington. 4 Vols. Vol. I (Ennius and Caecilius). Vol. II (Livius, Naevius, Pacuvius, Accius). Vol. III (Lucilius, Laws of the XII Tables). Vol. IV (Archaic Inscriptions).

Sallust. J. C. Rolfe.

Scriptores Historiae Augustae. D. Magie. 3 Vols.

Seneca : Apocolocyntosis. *Cf.* Petronius.

Seneca : Epistulae Morales. R. M. Gummere. 3 Vols.

Seneca : Moral Essays. J. W. Basore. 3 Vols.

Seneca : Naturales Quaestiones. T. H. Corcoran. 2 Vols.

Seneca : Tragedies. F. J. Miller. 2 Vols.

Seneca the Elder. M. Winterbottom. 2 Vols.

Sidonius : Poems and Letters. W. B. Anderson. 2 Vols.

Silius Italicus. J. D. Duff. 2 Vols.

Statius. J. H. Mozley. 2 Vols.

Suetonius. J. C. Rolfe. 2 Vols.

Tacitus : Agricola and Germania. M. Hutton ; Dialogus. Sir Wm. Peterson. Revised by R. M. Ogilvie, E. H. Warmington, M. Winterbottom.

Tacitus : Histories and Annals. C. H. Moore and J. Jackson. 4 Vols.

Terence. John Sargeaunt. 2 Vols.

Tertullian : Apologia and De Spectaculis. T. R. Glover; Minucius Felix. G. H. Rendall.

Valerius Flaccus. J. H. Mozley.

3

THE LOEB CLASSICAL LIBRARY

Varro: De Lingua Latina. R. G. Kent. 2 Vols.
Velleius Paterculus and Res Gestae Divi Augusti.
  F. W. Shipley.
Virgil. H. R. Fairclough. 2 Vols.
Vitruvius: De Architectura. F. Granger. 2 Vols.

GREEK AUTHORS

Achilles Tatius. S. Gaselee.
Aelian: On the Nature of Animals. A. F. Scholfield.
  3 Vols.
Aeneas Tacticus, Asclepiodotus and Onasander. The
  Illinois Greek Club.
Aeschines. C. D. Adams.
Aeschylus. H. Weir Smyth. 2 Vols.
Alciphron, Aelian and Philostratus: Letters. A. R.
  Benner and F. H. Fobes.
Apollodorus. Sir James G. Frazer. 2 Vols.
Apollonius Rhodius. R. C. Seaton.
The Apostolic Fathers. Kirsopp Lake. 2 Vols.
Appian: Roman History. Horace White. 4 Vols.
Aratus. Cf. Callimachus: Hymns and Epigrams.
Aristides. C. A. Behr. Vol. I.
Aristophanes. Benjamin Bickley Rogers. 3 Vols. Verse
  trans.
Aristotle: Art of Rhetoric. J. H. Freese.
Aristotle: Athenian Constitution, Eudemian Ethics.
  Virtues and Vices. H. Rackham.
Aristotle: The Categories. On Interpretation. H. P.
  Cooke; Prior Analytics. H. Tredennick.
Aristotle: Generation of Animals. A. L. Peck.
Aristotle: Historia Animalium. A. L. Peck. 3 Vols.
  Vols. I and II.
Aristotle: Metaphysics. H. Tredennick. 2 Vols.
Aristotle: Meteorologica. H. D. P. Lee.
Aristotle: Minor Works. W. S. Hett. " On Colours,"
  " On Things Heard," " Physiognomics," " On Plants,"
  " On Marvellous Things Heard," " Mechanical Prob-
  lems," " On Invisible Lines," " Situations and Names of
  Winds," " On Melissus, Xenophanes, and Gorgias."
Aristotle: Nicomachean Ethics. H. Rackham.
Aristotle: Oeconomica and Magna Moralia. G. C.
  Armstrong. (With Metaphysics, Vol. II.)
Aristotle: On the Heavens. W. K. C. Guthrie.

4

THE LOEB CLASSICAL LIBRARY

ARISTOTLE: ON THE SOUL, PARVA NATURALIA, ON BREATH. W. S. Hett.

ARISTOTLE: PARTS OF ANIMALS. A. L. Peck; MOVEMENT AND PROGRESSION OF ANIMALS. E. S. Forster.

ARISTOTLE: PHYSICS. Rev. P. Wicksteed and F. M. Cornford. 2 Vols.

ARISTOTLE: POETICS; LONGINUS ON THE SUBLIME. W. Hamilton Fyfe; DEMETRIUS ON STYLE. W. Rhys Roberts.

ARISTOTLE: POLITICS. H. Rackham.

ARISTOTLE: POSTERIOR ANALYTICS. H. Tredennick; TOPICS. E. S. Forster.

ARISTOTLE: PROBLEMS. W. S. Hett. 2 Vols.

ARISTOTLE: RHETORICA AD ALEXANDRUM. H. Rackham. (With PROBLEMS, Vol. II.)

ARISTOTLE: SOPHISTICAL REFUTATIONS. COMING-TO-BE AND PASSING-AWAY. E. S. Forster; ON THE COSMOS. D. J. Furley.

ARRIAN: HISTORY OF ALEXANDER AND INDICA. 2 Vols. Vol. I. P. Brunt. Vol. II. Rev. E. Iliffe Robson.

ATHENAEUS: DEIPNOSOPHISTAE. C. B. Gulick. 7 Vols.

BABRIUS AND PHAEDRUS (Latin). B. E. Perry.

ST. BASIL: LETTERS. R. J. Deferrari. 4 Vols.

CALLIMACHUS: FRAGMENTS. C. A. Trypanis; MUSAEUS: HERO AND LEANDER. T. Gelzer and C. Whitman.

CALLIMACHUS: HYMNS AND EPIGRAMS, AND LYCOPHRON. A. W. Mair; ARATUS. G. R. Mair.

CLEMENT OF ALEXANDRIA. Rev. G. W. Butterworth.

COLLUTHUS. *Cf.* OPPIAN.

DAPHNIS AND CHLOE. *Cf.* LONGUS.

DEMOSTHENES I: OLYNTHIACS, PHILIPPICS AND MINOR ORATIONS: I-XVII AND XX. J. H. Vince.

DEMOSTHENES II: DE CORONA AND DE FALSA LEGATIONE. C. A. and J. H. Vince.

DEMOSTHENES III: MEIDIAS, ANDROTION, ARISTOCRATES, TIMOCRATES, ARISTOGEITON. J. H. Vince.

DEMOSTHENES IV-VI: PRIVATE ORATIONS AND IN NEAERAM. A. T. Murray.

DEMOSTHENES VII: FUNERAL SPEECH, EROTIC ESSAY, EXORDIA AND LETTERS. N. W. and N. J. DeWitt.

DIO CASSIUS: ROMAN HISTORY. E. Cary. 9 Vols.

DIO CHRYSOSTOM. 5 Vols. Vols. I and II. J. W. Cohoon. Vol. III. J. W. Cohoon and H. Lamar Crosby. Vols. IV and V. H. Lamar Crosby.

DIODORUS SICULUS. 12 Vols. Vols. I-VI. C. H. Oldfather. Vol. VII. C. L. Sherman. Vol. VIII. C. B. Welles. Vols.

THE LOEB CLASSICAL LIBRARY

IX and X. Russel M. Geer. Vols. XI and XII. F. R.
Walton. General Index. Russel M. Geer.

DIOGENES LAERTIUS. R. D. Hicks. 2 Vols. New Introduction by H. S. Long.

DIONYSIUS OF HALICARNASSUS : CRITICAL ESSAYS. S. Usher.
2 Vols.

DIONYSIUS OF HALICARNASSUS : ROMAN ANTIQUITIES. Spel-
man's translation revised by E. Cary. 7 Vols.

EPICTETUS. W. A. Oldfather. 2 Vols.

EURIPIDES. A. S. Way. 4 Vols. Verse trans.

EUSEBIUS : ECCLESIASTICAL HISTORY. Kirsopp Lake and
J. E. L. Oulton. 2 Vols.

GALEN : ON THE NATURAL FACULTIES. A. J. Brock.

THE GREEK ANTHOLOGY. W. R. Paton. 5 Vols.

THE GREEK BUCOLIC POETS (THEOCRITUS, BION, MOSCHUS).
J. M. Edmonds.

GREEK ELEGY AND IAMBUS WITH THE ANACREONTEA. J. M.
Edmonds. 2 Vols.

GREEK MATHEMATICAL WORKS. Ivor Thomas. 2 Vols.

HERODES. *Cf.* THEOPHRASTUS : CHARACTERS.

HERODIAN. C. R. Whittaker. 2 Vols.

HERODOTUS. A. D. Godley. 4 Vols.

HESIOD AND THE HOMERIC HYMNS. H. G. Evelyn White.

HIPPOCRATES AND THE FRAGMENTS OF HERACLEITUS. W. H. S.
Jones and E. T. Withington. 4 Vols.

HOMER : ILIAD. A. T. Murray. 2 Vols.

HOMER : ODYSSEY. A. T. Murray. 2 Vols.

ISAEUS. E. S. Forster.

ISOCRATES. George Norlin and LaRue Van Hook. 3 Vols.

[ST. JOHN DAMASCENE]: BARLAAM AND IOASAPH. Rev. G. R.
Woodward, Harold Mattingly and D. M. Lang.

JOSEPHUS. 9 Vols. Vols. I-IV. H. St. J. Thackeray. Vol.
V. H. St. J. Thackeray and Ralph Marcus. Vols. VI
and VII. Ralph Marcus. Vol. VIII. Ralph Marcus and
Allen Wikgren. Vol. IX. L. H. Feldman.

JULIAN. Wilmer Cave Wright. 3 Vols.

LIBANIUS : SELECTED WORKS. A. F. Norman. 3 Vols. Vols.
I and II.

LONGUS : DAPHNIS AND CHLOE. Thornley's translation revised by J. M. Edmonds ; and PARTHENIUS. S. Gaselee.

LUCIAN. 8 Vols. Vols. I-V. A. M. Harmon. Vol. VI. K.
Kilburn. Vols. VII and VIII. M. D. Macleod.

LYCOPHRON. *Cf.* CALLIMACHUS : HYMNS AND EPIGRAMS.

LYRA GRAECA. J. M. Edmonds. 3 Vols.

LYSIAS. W. R. M. Lamb.

THE LOEB CLASSICAL LIBRARY

MANETHO. W. G. Waddell; PTOLEMY: TETRABIBLOS. F. E. Robbins.

MARCUS AURELIUS. C. R. Haines.

MENANDER I. New edition by W. G. Arnott.

MINOR ATTIC ORATORS. 2 Vols. K. J. Maidment and J. O. Burtt.

MUSAEUS: HERO AND LEANDER. *Cf.* CALLIMACHUS: FRAGMENTS.

NONNOS: DIONYSIACA. W. H. D. Rouse. 3 Vols.

OPPIAN, COLLUTHUS, TRYPHIODORUS. A. W. Mair.

PAPYRI. NON-LITERARY SELECTIONS. A. S. Hunt and C. C. Edgar. 2 Vols. LITERARY SELECTIONS (Poetry). D. L. Page.

PARTHENIUS. *Cf.* LONGUS.

PAUSANIAS: DESCRIPTION OF GREECE. W. H. S. Jones. 4 Vols. and Companion Vol. arranged by R. E. Wycherley.

PHILO. 10 Vols. Vols. I-V. F. H. Colson and Rev. G. H. Whitaker. Vols. VI-X. F. H. Colson. General Index. Rev. J. W. Earp.
Two Supplementary Vols. Translation only from an Armenian Text. Ralph Marcus.

PHILOSTRATUS: THE LIFE OF APOLLONIUS OF TYANA. F. C. Conybeare. 2 Vols.

PHILOSTRATUS: IMAGINES; CALLISTRATUS: DESCRIPTIONS. A. Fairbanks.

PHILOSTRATUS AND EUNAPIUS: LIVES OF THE SOPHISTS. Wilmer Cave Wright.

PINDAR. Sir J. E. Sandys.

PLATO: CHARMIDES, ALCIBIADES, HIPPARCHUS, THE LOVERS, THEAGES, MINOS AND EPINOMIS. W. R. M. Lamb.

PLATO: CRATYLUS, PARMENIDES, GREATER HIPPIAS, LESSER HIPPIAS. H. N. Fowler.

PLATO: EUTHYPHRO, APOLOGY, CRITO, PHAEDO, PHAEDRUS. H. N. Fowler.

PLATO: LACHES, PROTAGORAS, MENO, EUTHYDEMUS. W. R. M. Lamb.

PLATO: LAWS. Rev. R. G. Bury. 2 Vols.

PLATO: LYSIS, SYMPOSIUM, GORGIAS. W. R. M. Lamb.

PLATO: REPUBLIC. Paul Shorey. 2 Vols.

PLATO: STATESMAN, PHILEBUS. H. N. Fowler; ION. W. R. M. Lamb.

PLATO: THEAETETUS AND SOPHIST. H. N. Fowler.

PLATO: TIMAEUS, CRITIAS, CLITOPHO, MENEXENUS, EPISTULAE. Rev. R. G. Bury.

PLOTINUS. A. H. Armstrong. 6 Vols. Vols. I-III.

THE LOEB CLASSICAL LIBRARY

PLUTARCH : MORALIA. 16 Vols. Vols. I-V. F. C. Babbitt.
   Vol. VI. W. C. Helmbold. Vol. VII. P. H. De Lacy and
   B. Einarson. Vol. VIII. P. A. Clement, H. B. Hoffleit.
   Vol. IX. E. L. Minar, Jr., F. H. Sandbach, W. C.
   Helmbold. Vol. X. H. N. Fowler. Vol. XI. L. Pearson,
   F. H. Sandbach. Vol. XII. H. Cherniss, W. C. Helmbold.
   Vol. XIII, Parts 1 and 2. H. Cherniss. Vol. XIV. P. H.
   De Lacy and B. Einarson. Vol. XV. F. H. Sandbach.
PLUTARCH : THE PARALLEL LIVES. B. Perrin. 11 Vols.
POLYBIUS. W. R. Paton. 6 Vols.
PROCOPIUS : HISTORY OF THE WARS. H. B. Dewing. 7 Vols.
PTOLEMY : TETRABIBLOS. Cf. MANETHO.
QUINTUS SMYRNAEUS. A. S. Way. Verse trans.
SEXTUS EMPIRICUS. Rev. R. G. Bury. 4 Vols.
SOPHOCLES. F. Storr. 2 Vols. Verse trans.
STRABO : GEOGRAPHY. Horace L. Jones. 8 Vols.
THEOPHRASTUS : CHARACTERS. J. M. Edmonds ; HERODES,
   etc. A. D. Knox.
THEOPHRASTUS : DE CAUSIS PLANTARUM. G. K. K. Link and
   B. Einarson. 3 Vols. Vol. I.
THEOPHRASTUS : ENQUIRY INTO PLANTS. Sir Arthur Hort.
   2 Vols.
THUCYDIDES. C. F. Smith. 4 Vols.
TRYPHIODORUS. Cf. OPPIAN.
XENOPHON : ANABASIS. C. L. Brownson.
XENOPHON : CYROPAEDIA. Walter Miller. 2 Vols.
XENOPHON : HELLENICA. C. L. Brownson.
XENOPHON : MEMORABILIA AND OECONOMICUS. E. C. Mar-
   chant ; SYMPOSIUM AND APOLOGY. O. J. Todd.
XENOPHON : SCRIPTA MINORA. E. C. Marchant and G. W.
   Bowersock.

DESCRIPTIVE PROSPECTUS ON APPLICATION

CAMBRIDGE, MASS.   LONDON
HARVARD UNIV. PRESS   WILLIAM HEINEMANN LTD

HYDRIA

Museum of Fine Arts, Boston

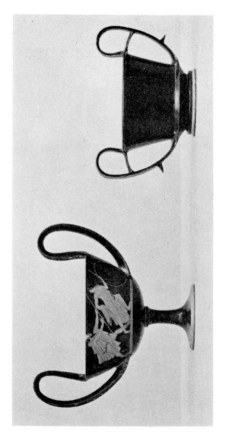

KANTHAROS   KARCHESION (?)

Museum of Fine Arts. Boston

KOTHON

Fogg Art Museum, Harvard University

KRATER

Museum of Fine Arts, Boston

KYLIX
Museum of Fine Arts, Boston

KYLIX

KYLIX WITHOUT STEM
Museum of Fine Arts, Boston

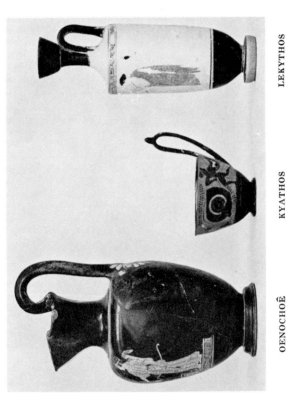

OENOCHOÊ   KYATHOS   LEKYTHOS

Museum of Fine Arts, Boston

OENOCHOÊ WITH BEAKED SPOUT
Metropolitan Museum, New York

OLPÊ (?)

Metropolitan Museum, New York

PSYKTER
British Museum

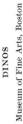

DINOS
Museum of Fine Arts, Boston

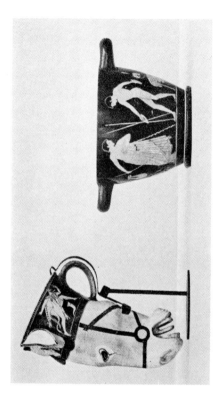

RHYTON   SKYPHOS

Museum of Fine Arts, Boston